AdvancED DOM Scripting
Dynamic Web Design Techniques

Jeffrey Sambells
with Aaron Gustafson

friendsof

DESIGNER TO DESIGNER™

an Apress® company

AdvancED DOM Scripting:
Dynamic Web Design Techniques

Credits

Lead Editor Chris Mills	**Senior Production Editor** Laura Cheu
Technical Reviewers Cameron Turner, Victor Sumner	**Compositor** Dina Quan
Editorial Board Steve Anglin, Ewan Buckingham, Gary Cornell, Jonathan Gennick, Jason Gilmore, Jonathan Hassell, Chris Mills, Matthew Moodie, Jeffrey Pepper, Ben Renow-Clarke, Dominic Shakeshaft, Matt Wade, Tom Welsh	**Artist** Kinetic Publishing Services, LLC **Proofreader** Liz Welch
Senior Project Manager Kylie Johnston	**Indexer** Broccoli Information Management
Copy Edit Manager Nicole Flores	**Cover Image Designer** Bruce Tang
Copy Editor Heather Lang	**Interior and Cover Designer** Kurt Krames
Assistant Production Director Kari Brooks-Copony	**Manufacturing Director** Tom Debolski

For Stephanie and Addison, thanks for smiling.
—Jeffrey Sambells

To my soul mate, Kelly.
—Aaron Gustafson

CONTENTS AT A GLANCE

About the Authors . . . . **xv**

About the Technical Reviewers . . . . **xvi**

About the Cover Image Designer . . . . **xvii**

Acknowledgments . . . . **xviii**

Introduction . . . . **xix**

PART ONE **DOM SCRIPTING IN DETAIL**

Chapter 1 **Do It Right with Best Practices** **3**

Chapter 2 **Creating Your Own Reusable Objects** **51**

Chapter 3 **Understanding the DOM2 Core and DOM2 HTML** **89**

Chapter 4 **Responding to User Actions and Events** **149**

Chapter 5 **Dynamically Modifying Style and Cascading
Style Sheets** **203**

Chapter 6 **Case Study: A Photo Cropping and Resizing Tool** **249**

PART TWO **COMMUNICATING OUTSIDE THE BROWSER**

Chapter 7 **Adding Ajax to the Mix** **285**

Chapter 8 **Case Study: Enabling Asynchronous File Uploads
with Progress Indicators** **345**

PART THREE SOME GREAT SOURCE

Chapter 9 **Using Libraries to Increase Productivity** 375

Chapter 10 **Adding Effects to Enhance User Experience** 405

Chapter 11 **Mashups Galore! Using APIs to Add Maps, Searching, and Much More** 455

Chapter 12 **Case Study: Style Your select with the DOM** 507

Index 555

CONTENTS

About the Authors . . . . **xv**

About the Technical Reviewers . . . . **xvi**

About the Cover Image Designer . . . . **xvii**

Acknowledgments . . . . **xviii**

Introduction . . . . **xix**

PART ONE **DOM SCRIPTING IN DETAIL**

Chapter 1 **Do It Right with Best Practices** **3**

Unobtrusive and progressive enhancement 4
Putting JavaScript to work 5
    Separating your behavior from your structure. 6
        How to include JavaScript the right way 6
        That javascript: prefix 8
    Don't version check! 14
        Use capability detection 14
        When browser version sniffing is OK 16
    Degrade gracefully for guaranteed accessibility 16
        Don't require JavaScript for content—period. 16
    Plan for reuse with namespaces 17
    Simplify things with reusable objects 19
        Beginning the ADS library 20
        The ADS.isCompatible() method 21
        The ADS.$() method 22
        The ADS.addEvent() and ADS.removeEvent() methods 24
        The ADS.getElementsByClassName() method 26
        The ADS.toggleDisplay() method 28
        The ADS.insertAfter() method 28
        The ADS.removeChildren() and ADS.prependChild() methods 29
    Get your hands dirty 30

Common gotchas in the JavaScript syntax 30
Case sensitivity. 30
Single vs. double quotes 31
Breaking lines 31
Optional semicolons and parentheses 32
Overloading (not really) 33
Anonymous functions. 33
Scope resolution and closures 34
Iterating over objects 39
Referencing vs. calling a function (missing parentheses) 40
A practical example: WYSIWYG JavaScript rollover redux 40
Summary 48

Chapter 2 **Creating Your Own Reusable Objects** **51**
What's in an object?. 52
Inheritance 53
Understanding object members 53
Everything's in the window object. 56
Making it all possible with scope and closure 60
Creating your own objects 60
One becomes many: creating the constructor 61
Adding static methods 63
Adding public methods to the prototype. 64
Controlling access with private and privileged members 65
Do public, private, privileged, and static really matter? 67
The object literal 68
What is this? 71
Redefining your context with call() and apply() 73
try { }, catch { }, and exceptions 76
A practical example: your own debugging log 78
Why use a JavaScript logging object? 78
The myLogger() object 78
The myLogger.createWindow() method 80
The myLogger.writeRaw() method. 82
The myLogger.write() and myLogger.header() methods. 85
Summary 87

Chapter 3 **Understanding the DOM2 Core and DOM2 HTML** **89**
The DOM, not JavaScript, is your document 90
Objects and interfaces 90
Levels of the DOM 91
DOM Level 0. 91
DOM Level 1. 91
Level 2 91
Level 3 92
Which level is correct for you?. 93

Creating a sample document. 96
   Creating the DOM file 96
   Choosing a browser. 98
The DOM Core 100
   The importance of inheritance in the DOM. 102
   The Core Node object. 103
      Node names, values, and types. 103
      Node parents, children, and siblings. 108
      Node attributes 111
      The node ownerDocument property 113
      Checking for children and attributes 114
      Manipulating your DOM node tree 115
      Duplicating and moving a node 117
   The Core Element object 119
      Manipulating Element attributes 119
      Locating Element objects within Element objects 120
   The Core Document object. 120
      The document.documentElement property. 121
      Creating nodes with document methods 121
      Locating Elements with Document methods 122
   Traversing and iterating the DOM tree 122
DOM HTML. 125
   The DOM2 HTML HTMLDocument object. 126
   The HTML HTMLElement object 127
A practical example: converting hand-coded HTML to DOM code 127
   The DOM generation tool HTML file. 128
   Testing with an example HTML fragment 130
   Adding to the ADS library. 131
   The generateDOM object framework 133
      The encode() method. 133
      The checkForVariable() method 134
      The generate() method 134
      The processNode() and processAttribute() methods. 136
Summary 146

Chapter 4 Responding to User Actions and Events **149**

DOM2 Events. 150
Types of events. 151
   Object events. 151
      The load and unload events 151
      The abort and error events. 152
      The resize event 153
      The scroll event 153
   Mouse movement events 153
   Mouse click events. 156
   Keyboard events 159

Form-related events. 159
   Form submit and reset events 159
   Blur and focus events. 161
   The change event 163
W3C DOM-specific events 165
Custom events 166
Controlling event flow and registering event listeners 166
   Event flow 167
      Order of events 171
      Two phases and three models 173
      Popping the bubble 175
      Cancelling the default action 176
   Registering events 178
      Inline registration model 178
      The ADS.addEvent() method revisited 178
      The traditional event model 179
      Microsoft-specific event model 181
      W3C DOM2 Events model 181
      The problem with the load event 183
   Accessing the event object from the event listener 186
      Syntactical shortcuts 187
      The ADS.getEventObject() method 187
   Cross-browser event properties and methods 188
      The DOM2 Events object 189
      The DOM2 MouseEvent object. 190
      Browser incompatibilities galore. 192
      Accessing keyboard commands 197
Summary 201

Chapter 5 **Dynamically Modifying Style and Cascading Style Sheets**

Chapter 5 Dynamically Modifying Style and Cascading
         Style Sheets 203
The W3C DOM2 Style specification 203
   CSSStyleSheet objects. 204
   CSSStyleRule objects. 204
   CSSStyleDeclaration 205
   A lack of support 206
When DOM scripting and style collide. 206
   Modifying markup for style. 207
      Removing the extra markup 210
Keeping style out of your DOM script 213
   The style property 213
   Switching styles based on a className 217
      Using common classes with className switching 217
      Drawbacks of using className switching 220
      Why not use setAttribute for class names? 220

Switching the style sheet 220
    Using alternative style sheets 221
    Switching the body className 225
    Dynamically loading and removing style sheets 228
Modifying CSS rules 229
    AdvancED image replacement revisited 234
Accessing the computed style 237
The Microsoft filter property 239
Practical example: a simple transition effect 244
Summary 247

Chapter 6 Case Study: A Photo Cropping and Resizing Tool **249**

The test files 250
The editor objects 254
    Invoking the imageEditor tool 259
    The imageEditor load event 260
    Creating the editor markup and objects 262
    Adding the event listeners to the editor objects 270
    Resizing the image 272
    Cropping the Image 276
    The incomplete image editor 280
Summary 281

PART TWO COMMUNICATING OUTSIDE THE BROWSER

Chapter 7 Adding Ajax to the Mix **285**

Merging technology 286
    Semantic XHTML and the DOM 286
    JavaScript and the XMLHttpRequest object 286
        Making a new request 287
        Acting on the response 288
        Identifying Ajax requests on the server 291
        Beyond GET and POST 294
    XML 295
        Plain text 296
        HTML 296
        JavaScript code 297
        JSON 298
    A reusable object 299
    Is Ajax right for you? 304
Why Ajax may break your site and how to fix it 305
    JavaScript required for content 305
    Bypassing cross-site restrictions with <script> tags 306

Back buttons and bookmarks. 313
 A not so simple fix. 315
 Browser sniffing for product features 316
 Tracking location changes 316
A race to finish the request. 324
 Latency picks the winner 327
 Dealing with asynchronous requests. 329
Increased resources 334
Problems solved? 334
Practical example: an Ajax-enhanced photo album. 334
 Ajaxify the photo browser 338
Summary 343

Chapter 8 Case Study: Enabling Asynchronous File Uploads
      with Progress Indicators **345**

A little life in the loading message 347
 Processing uploads on the server 349
 The magic word 351
The starting point 351
Putting it all together: an upload progress indicator 352
 The addProgressBar() framework 355
 The load event. 357
 The addProgressBar() object 358
  Modifying the file inputs 358
  Redirecting the form 361
  And the magic word is 362
  The progress bar. 363
  Tracking progress 365
Summary 372

PART THREE **SOME GREAT SOURCE**

Chapter 9 Using Libraries to Increase Productivity. **375**

Choosing the library that's right for you. 376
 The libraries 377
  DOMAssistant 378
  jQuery 378
  Mochikit 378
  Prototype. 379
  Yahoo User Interface library 379

Enhancing the DOM 380
    Chaining syntax 380
        Advanced selection with expressions 382
        jQuery with XPath 385
    Filtering with a callback 387
    Manipulating the DOM document 389
        Using DOMAssistant to create elements 389
        Using jQuery to move nodes 389
        Using MochiKit to create elements 390
        Using Prototype to clean up your document 390
        Using YUI to check for intersecting elements. 390
        Iterating over results 391
Handling events 391
    Registering events 392
        The DOMAssistant way 392
        The jQuery way 393
    Custom events 395
Accessing and manipulating style. 396
Communication 397
    Prototype Ajax object 397
    jQuery keeps Ajax simple 400
Summary 402

Chapter 10 **Adding Effects to Enhance User Experience**. **405**

Do it yourself. 406
    Show me the content!. 407
    Providing feedback 411
        The Yellow Fade Technique. 411
        Avoiding shifting content. 412
A few visual effects libraries 414
    Moo.fx 414
    Script.aculo.us 414
Some visual bling. 415
    Mootastic CSS property modification 415
        One property at a time 416
        A mix of properties all at once. 417
        Reusing the effect 417
        Multiple effects on multiple objects. 418
        Sliding with Moo.fx 418
        Form feedback made pretty 420
    Visual effects with Script.aculo.us 427
        Parallel effects 429
    Realistic motion using Moo.fx 430
        Customer form revisited 434
    Rounding corners 435
    The rest of the libraries 437

Behavioral enhancements 437
   Drag and drop with Script.aculo.us 438
     Drag anywhere 438
     Dropping on a target: the droppable 439
     Building a drag-and-drop shopping cart with Script.aculo.us 440
     Interacting with draggables through an observer 448
     More drag and drop fun 451
   Summary 452

Chapter 11 Mashups Galore! Using APIs to Add Maps, Searching, and Much More 455

API keys 457
Client-side APIs: some JavaScript required 457
   Maps put mashups on the map 458
     Retrieving latitude and longitude 464
     Maintaining accessibility using microformats 465
   Ajax search requests 470
     Search results for your site only 476
     Related links 477
   Mashing Search with Maps 481
Server-side APIs: some proxy required 484
   An integrated to-do list with Basecamp 488
     Your Basecamp account information 489
     Building the Basecamp proxy 491
     The Basecamp DOM script 495
   Buddy icons with Flickr 498
     The Flickr API key 499
     Building the Flickr proxy 499
     The DOM script 502
   Summary 504

Chapter 12 Case Study: Style Your select with the DOM 507

That classic feeling 508
Building a better select 509
Strategy? We don't need no stinkin' strategy 510
   The files 511
   The FauxSelect objects 512
   Getting the faux select going 514
   Locating the select elements 515
     A little housekeeping 517
   Building the DOM elements 518
     Creating a faux value 520
     Creating faux options 521
Generating life and other memorable events 522
   Opening, closing, and clicking the select 522
     Selecting a faux option 525

Bling-bling for da form t'ing 527
Behavioral modifications 538
    Closing the faux select 538
    Z index to the rescue! 542
    Keyboard controls and other niceties 543
        Selecting options 543
        Maintaining focus 544
        Closing the faux select 546
    Is select too big for its britches? 549
Knock, knock . . . housekeeping! 551
Further adventures in select replacement 552
Summary 553

Index **555**

ABOUT THE AUTHORS

 **Jeffrey Sambells** is a graphic designer and self-taught web application developer best known for his unique ability to merge the visual world of graphics with the mental realm of code. After obtaining his bachelor of technology degree in graphic communications management with a minor in multimedia, Jeffrey originally enjoyed the paper and ink printing industry, but he soon realized the world of pixels and code was where his ideas would prosper.

In late 1999, he cofounded We-Create Inc., an Internet software company based in Waterloo, Ontario, which began many long nights of challenging and creative endeavors. Currently, as director of research and development for We-Create, Jeffrey is responsible for investigating new and emerging technologies and integrating them into existing products using web-standards-compliant methods. His peers describe him as both a natural programmer and an innovative thinker.

Jeffrey has previously published articles related to print design and has contributed to award winning graphical and Internet software designs. His previous book, *Beginning Google Maps Application Development with PHP and Ajax* (Apress, ISBN-13: 978-1-59059-707-1), was an instant success and has since been rewritten for Rails (Apress, ISBN-13: 978-1-59059-787-3). In late 2005, Jeffrey also became a PHP4 Zend Certified Engineer; he updated the certification to PHP5 in September 2006 to become one of the first PHP5 Zend Certified Engineers! Jeffrey also maintains a blog at http://jeffreysambells.com where he discusses his thoughts and ideas about everything from web development to photography.

He currently lives and plays in Ontario, Canada with his wife Stephanie, his daughter Addison, and their little dog Milo.

 After getting hooked on the web in 1996 and spending several years pushing pixels and bits for the likes of IBM and Konica Minolta, **Aaron Gustafson** founded his own web consultancy—Easy! Designs LLC. Aaron is a member of the Web Standards Project (WaSP) and the Guild of Accessible Web Designers (GAWDS). He also serves as a technical editor for *A List Apart*, is a contributing writer for *Digital Web Magazine* and MSDN, and has built a small library of writing and editing credits in the print world. Aaron has graced the stage at numerous conferences including An Event Apart, COMDEX, SXSW, The Ajax Experience, and Web Directions, and he is frequently called on to provide web standards training in both the public and private sectors.

He blogs at http://easy-reader.net.

ABOUT THE TECHNICAL REVIEWERS

 **Cameron Turner** has been programming computers since age seven and has been developing interactive websites since 1994. In 1999, he and Jeffrey Sambells cofounded We-Create Inc., which specializes in Internet software development and social networking systems. Cameron is the company's chief technology officer.

Based on their experience together at We-Create, Cameron and Jeff also teamed up to write a pair of books about using the Google Maps API in a professional setting. *Beginning Google Maps Applications: From Novice to Professional* has two language editions: PHP (Apress, ISBN-13: 978-1-59059-707-1) and Rails (Apress, ISBN-13: 978-1-59059-787-3). More about these books can be found at http://GoogleMapsBook.com.

Cameron obtained his bachelor's degree in computer science (with honors) from the University of Waterloo with specializations in applied cryptography, database design, and computer security. He lives in Canada's technology capital of Waterloo, Ontario with his wife Tanya, his son Owen, and their dog Katie. His hobbies include geocaching, reading science fiction, biking, hiking, water skiing, and painting.

Victor Sumner is an Internet graphic designer and a self-taught web developer. Introduced early to video design, Victor has spent many late nights working in all aspects of multimedia development, leading to an honors diploma in Internet graphic design. Currently employed at We-Create Inc. as a lead architect, Victor develops and maintains products and applications.

Victor lives in Waterloo, Ontario with his wife Alicia. Victor enjoys hockey, football, photography, camping, and aquariums.

ABOUT THE COVER IMAGE DESIGNER

Bruce Tang is a freelance web designer, visual programmer, and author from Hong Kong. His main creative interest is generating stunning visual effects using Flash or Processing.

Bruce has been an avid Flash user since Flash 4, when he began using Flash to create games, websites, and other multimedia content. After several years of ActionScript, he found himself increasingly drawn toward visual programming and computational art. He likes to integrate math and physics into his work, simulating 3D and other real-life experiences onscreen. His first Flash book was published in October 2005. Bruce's portfolio, featuring Flash and Processing pieces, can be found at www.betaruce.com and his blog at www.betaruce.com/blog.

The cover image uses a high-resolution Henon phase diagram generated by Bruce with Processing, which he feels is an ideal tool for such experiments. Henon is a strange attractor created by iterating through some equations to calculate the coordinates of millions of points. The points are then plotted with an assigned color.

$$x_{n+1} = x_n \cos(a) - (y_n - x_n^P) \sin(a)$$

$$y_{n+1} = x_n \sin(a) + (y_n - x_n^P) \cos(a)$$

ACKNOWLEDGMENTS

Over the years, I've crossed paths with many influential people—family, friends, acquaintances, and strangers—all of whom have helped make this book possible. There are too many to name, so thanks to those not mentioned here.

Thanks to Chris Mills for giving me the chance to dive headfirst into a topic I'm passionate about. Without your guidance, I would never have been able to organize the chaos of ideas in my head. And, to the team at friends of ED and Apress including Kylie Johnston, Heather Lang, Laura Cheu, and everyone else behind the scenes, your feedback has only made this book better, and it was another wonderful experience.

Thanks to Aaron Gustafson for contributing a great case study. It's always a pleasure to be inspired to go beyond the basics.

Thanks to Cameron Turner and Victor Sumner for testing all my late-night, blurry eyed coding. I'm sure there were more than a few frustrations, but the comments and encouragement were always helpful.

Thanks to everyone who openly shares their knowledge and ideas. The advancement of DOM scripting, web standards, and creative innovation wouldn't be possible without your excellent comments, blogs, books, talks, and discussions. Thanks to you all.

A super big thanks to Stephanie, my wife and the love of my life, for your patience and understanding while raising both a newborn and an author—at the same time. I couldn't have done either without you.

Finally, thanks to you for taking the time to read this book. I can only hope you take away as much as I put in.

Jeffrey Sambells

There are so many folks I'd like to thank, but I'm just a contributor here, so I'll keep it brief. Brothercake, your accessibility expertise really helped improve this script; thank you. Jeremy Keith, you drove me to better my bluffing; thank you. Shaun Inman, This is Cereal was an inspiration; thank you. Jeffrey Zeldman, you make me want to be a better writer; thank you. Molly Holzschlag, I owe so much of my success to you. I can never thank you enough for that (but I will keep trying). And last but not least, Kelly, you've put up with the many late nights and weekends I've spent writing code and then writing about it. Thank you, and I love you.

Aaron Gustafson

INTRODUCTION

Document Object Model (DOM) scripting is often misrepresented as any sort of scripting on the Web, but *pure* DOM scripting includes only those features and methods incorporated into a W3C DOM specification—that means no proprietary browser features. In a perfect world, we could follow the standards, ignore proprietary features, and finish with an agnostic script that just works on any device. But it's not a perfect world—yet. As we all know, not all devices or browsers are W3C standards compliant, so where does that leave developers like us when we need to accommodate everyone, and how do we stay true to the W3C DOM?

When trying to answer those questions and deal with multiple browsers while maintaining proper DOM compliance, the idea for this book was born. This book answers those questions and tackles a number of other topics as well:

- Dive deeper into the W3C DOM specifications and fish out the little bits that are often misunderstood, while still providing equivalent options for nonstandard browsers.
- Go further with new methodologies, such as Ajax client-server communication, and push the limits of Ajax to provide a more interactive experience.
- Experiment with some great third-party source that can take away some of the mundane day-to-day tasks.
- Understand and create your very own library of DOM methods that you can use every day.

With these newfound abilities come many temptations. Too often our DOM scripting adventures are focused on the new glittery features and stray from the basics of good, clean web application design. As a result, I've emphasized best practices throughout the book and provided solutions that focus on usability and accessibility for both the end user and you, the developer or designer.

You can keep this book next to your computer as a reference or read it cover to cover—it's up to you. Either way, after working through the mix of theory, code, examples, and case studies you'll find inside, you'll be well on your way to understanding exactly how and why these advanced concepts work—not just what they do to your document.

Who this book is for

AdvancED DOM Scripting: Dynamic Web Design Techniques is for any web developer or designer who's dabbled with the DOM and wants to jump to the next level. With this book's straightforward explanations, you can pick up the advanced concepts with ease, but you'll get much more out of this book if you've already had a little experience with DOM scripting and web standards concepts.

How this book is structured

This book is structured into three main parts, and throughout, you'll be assembling your own library of useful DOM methods. Each chapter will build on the concepts learned in the previous chapters, so each part of the book will act as one cohesive subject, rather than each chapter standing completely on its own.

Part One, "DOM Scripting in Detail," deals with the ins and outs of various W3C DOM specifications, including what is and isn't supported in noncompliant browsers. Beginning with best practices right from the start, you'll be introduced to the DOM2 HTML and DOM2 Core specifications as well as the DOM2 Events and DOM2 style. Each chapter will include a number of browser-agnostic examples. You'll also start to build up your personal scripting library, adding various methods for accessing and manipulating the DOM, styles, and events. These methods will be browser agnostic and will allow you to easily develop your applications using a common set of methods—which you'll create yourself—so you know what's going on in them. Part One will culminate a case study in Chapter 6, where you'll build an interactive image cropping and resizing tool.

After covering everything you'll need to know to manipulate and access the various aspects of your document, Part Two, "Communicating Outside the Browser," focuses on Ajax and client-server communications. I go beyond just a simple how-to and explain the whys, as well as the pitfalls you'll encounter when integrating Ajax interfaces. Part Two finishes by putting your skills to the test, while combining traditional and recent communication methodologies, to create a file uploader with a real progress bar.

Finally, in Part Three, "Some Great Source," I'll focus on third-party source, including libraries and application programming interfaces (APIs). You'll learn how to take advantage of great DOM scripting libraries to speed up your development, including the use of a number of effects to give your web application a little more flare. Also, you'll see how you can integrate things like interactive maps and project management tools using freely available APIs. These sources can offer a lot of advanced programming with minimal effort on your part—but it's important that you understand the hows and whys from Parts One and Two, so that you'll better understand and appreciate the great source in Part Three. This book concludes with a case study by Aaron Gustafson that takes select elements to a whole new level.

Rather than providing an appendix, I'll point you to http://advanceddomscripting.com, where you'll find all the source for the book along with additional examples and references. I'll also be posting the latest and greatest from the DOM scripting world there, so you can check back frequently to keep up to date.

Conventions

To keep this book as clear and easy to follow as possible, the following text conventions are used throughout.

Code is presented in fixed-width font.

New or changed code is normally presented in **bold fixed-width font**.

Pseudocode and variable input are written in *italic fixed-width font*.

Where I want to draw your attention to something, I've highlighted it like this:

> *Ahem, don't say I didn't warn you.*

Sometimes code won't fit on a single line in a book. Where this happens, I use an arrow like this: ➥.

```
This is a very, very long section of code that should be written all on ➥
the same line without a break.
```

To save a bit of space, many of the examples include a . . . cut . . . line. This indicates that a portion of the code has been removed so that the example focuses on the topic at hand. In many instances, a few lines may be included around the . . . cut . . . to better place the code in context. For example, the following code

```
(function(){
window['ADS'] = {};

... cut ...

function helloWorld(message) {
    alert(message);
}
... cut ...

})();
```

indicates that the helloWorld() function is somewhere within the code that begins with (function(){ and ends with })();. If the position in the file is important, that will also be indicated.

In cases where you'll be asked to follow along and build an example with me, I will start with a framework of comments such as this:

```
// Define a variable

// Alert it using the helloWorld() function
```

Then, you'll fill in bits of code after each comment as the example progresses:

```
// Define a variable
var example = 'DOM Scripting is great!';

// Alert it using the helloWorld() function
helloWorld(example);
```

This will make it easy for you to follow along with each example and will help you understand what's going on.

If you check out the online source code, you may also find additional comments that don't appear in the text of this book. Some comments were removed from the printed source so that the code wasn't redundant to the text.

Prerequisites

Creativity, interest, and the desire to learn are about all you need to have before you pick up this book—though a little familiarity with the DOM, JavaScript, web standards, and CSS won't hurt. Where possible, I've tried to explain advanced topics in a manner that a novice web developer will still understand.

The code samples in this book have been tested to work with the following browsers, and I'll explain the various caveats for each as the book progresses:

- Firefox 1.5+
- Microsoft Internet Explorer 6+
- Safari 2+
- Opera 9+

The code should work with other standards-compliant browsers as well, but older browsers will simply degrade to a DOM-script-free version.

Downloading the code

If your fingers are cramping from typing out all the code in this book, I suggest you head over to the friends of ED site (http://friendsofed.com) and just download the source from there. While you're at it, you may also want to peruse some of the other great titles you'll find on topics from web standards, DOM, and CSS to Flash.

If you're still hungry, the source code—along with a lot more information and DOM scripting solutions—can be found in this book's website at http://advanceddomscripting.com.

Contacting the authors

Have questions, comments, or concerns? Feel free to contact me at jeff@advanceddomscripting.com. Also, be sure to check out this book's site at http://advanceddomscripting.com, where I'll post updates and errata as well as new material to help you along the way.

Aaron Gustafson can be contacted at ads-book@easy-designs.net.

Part One

DOM SCRIPTING IN DETAIL

CHAPTER 1

DO IT RIGHT WITH BEST PRACTICES

You're excited; your client is excited. All is well. You've just launched the client's latest website, and it's fantastic. You've put in hours of sweat and tears, tweaking every little detail of the design—expanding menus, interactive Ajax, all the latest bells and whistles. It looks good, works perfectly, and everyone's partying. But a week later disaster begins. The client phones in a panic; it seems they've been getting calls from some customers who can't get past the home page, and others are having problems with some aspects of the feedback form—but it works fine for you and the client. Other people have been calling and complaining that the site is taking too long to download each page, even though it doesn't look like there's much on the page, and you barely notice the load time. To top it off, the client has found that its search engine ranking has plummeted from number one to nowhere. Things are not good after all. But where could you have gone wrong? Let's find out.

Best practices are accepted and tested models for the way you should go about doing things. They're not necessarily the only way or even the best way, but they're the way the majority agrees things should be done. Most of the time, best practices are mentioned near the end of a book, more as a reminder that once you've learned everything and you're on your way, there's actually a proper way to do it. I'm putting best practices up front, because I want to guide you in the right direction before you learn anything new. There's no point in going down dark roads of frustration when there's already a well-lit road ahead.

Unobtrusive and progressive enhancement

Extensible HyperText Markup Language (XHTML), Cascading Style Sheets (CSS), and Document Object Model (DOM) scripting using JavaScript are the big three of web design. XHTML provides the semantic meaning in your document structure; CSS provides the positioning and style for your document layout; and DOM Scripting enhances your document's behavior and interaction. Did you catch that? I said DOM scripting *enhances,* not *provides,* your document's behavior and interaction. The difference between "enhances" and "provides" is an important distinction. We've all learned about XHTML, semantics, and validating our documents so they conform to the W3C specifications, and we all use CSS to properly style our semantically marked up XHTML strict documents (you do, don't you?), but DOM scripting, the third piece, the one that makes things extra slick and gives your web applications extra flare, can be an obtrusive beast.

DOM scripting relies on JavaScript. If you search for "Unobtrusive JavaScript" on the Web, you'll find a flood of different descriptions, but that's only because unobtrusiveness needs to be considered everywhere. It's not a Band-Aid you can just throw onto your code to make it all good. There's no unobtrusive object in JavaScript (Hmm . . . maybe there could be?), and you can't download some "unobtrusive" library to fix your code. Unobtrusiveness is only possible with proper planning and preparation in your web application. It must be considered when interacting with both the user *and* the web developer. Your scripts must be unobtrusive to the user and avoid unnecessary flashy and annoying features (something that gave JavaScript a bad rap in the past). Scripts must also be unobtrusive to allow the page and markup to continue to work, though maybe not as elegantly, without JavaScript. Finally, they must be unobtrusive and easy to implement within your markup, using ID and class hooks to attach behavior and provide a separation of the script from the markup. To better understand unobtrusiveness, and the integration of DOM scripting, XHTML, and CSS, you need to consider the outcomes in the situation we looked at previously and understand the basic principles and their application to your code.

Two methodologies you often hear about with unobtrusiveness are "progressive enhancement" and "graceful degradation." Browsers that lack certain features should receive an equally informational, yet altered, view of the same document by using techniques that either enhance the document as technologies are available (progressive enhancement) or degrade the document when they are missing (graceful degradation). These two concepts are often used interchangeably, but each embraces the idea that not all browsers are created equal—and not all browsers should be treated equally. Also, you shouldn't force a low quality service on everyone just to be able to cater to the lowest common denominator.

One of my favorite quotes about the necessity of progressive enhancement comes from Nate Koechley of Yahoo, who sums it up when describing browser support (http://developer.yahoo.com/yui/articles/gbs/gbs.html):

"Support does not mean that everybody gets the same thing. Expecting two users using different browser software to have the identical experience fails to embrace or acknowledge the heterogeneous essence of the Web. In fact, requiring the same experience for all users creates a barrier to participation. Availability and accessibility of content should be our key priority."

If you're using JavaScript in a way that inhibits the "availability and accessibility of content," you're doing something wrong.

At the same time, progressive enhancement doesn't necessarily mean an all-or-nothing approach to JavaScript. The problem is that, unlike most programming or scripting languages that you would run on your own dedicated servers or computers, JavaScript is an interpreted language that runs within a web browser, so you won't have any control over the wide variety and mix of software, hardware, and operating systems your script will need to handle. To deal with the infinite combinations, you have to be careful and create behavioral enhancements based on the capabilities of the browser and the available technologies, which could mean providing a degraded solution that still relies on lesser parts of JavaScript or a solution that falls back on traditional, JavaScript-free methods.

I'll be stressing these ideas of unobtrusiveness, degradability, and progressive enhancement throughout the book, but I'll also say that I am by no means a zealot. I do realize that your sites do need to support browsers without standards-compliant features. In many cases, proprietary methods will also be required, but the trick is to go for the standards-compliant way and only fall back on the proprietary way if necessary.

When working with DOM scripts and integrating them into your site, you should always write scripts that are

- **Standards compliant**: Future-proof your application and ensure that your web application will continue to support newer and better browsers.
- **Maintainable**: Incorporate reusable and easily understood methods so that you and others can focus on the business task at hand, rather than rewriting the same things over and over.
- **Accessible**: Ensure that everyone can easily and efficiently access your information, even those without the script or JavaScript enabled.
- **Usable**: Something that works great in one situation but is hard to implement or replicate isn't going to be much fun the second or third time around. Usability applies to both the interaction with the end user and the interaction with developers.

These guiding principles overlap in practice, and they all go hand in hand; keeping them in the front of your mind will go a long way to reducing headaches now *and* down the road. In fact, I suggest posting them on a big, bold sign next to your computer, so you can drill them into your head. I'll even provide you with a printable sign at http://advanceddomscripting.com/remember.pdf. Just remember, if the goal of XHTML and CSS is to be universally standard, your JavaScript scripts should be too!

In the rest of this chapter, you'll look at several methods that will help you achieve these goals and keep your clients, coworkers, and yourself as happy as possible. Also, you'll start building up your own library of common methods that you'll use throughout the book while looking at some common JavaScript gotchas.

Putting JavaScript to work

So where do you start? What will make your hard work fit the guiding principles?

Odds are if you were to look at the failed hypothetical site at the beginning of the chapter, you'd probably see some common pitfalls like these:

- `<script>` tags inline within the body of the document
- A reliance on browser sniffing rather than capability detection to test for JavaScript feature compatibility
- Hard-coded `javascript:` prefixes in the `href` attributes of anchor elements
- Redundant, repetitive, highly customized JavaScript

You might wonder what the problem is with these. After all, we've all used at least one quick-and-dirty hack at one time or another. The problem is really in their usefulness and inability to accommodate all situations. If you step back and look at each item critically, you'll realize it doesn't take much more effort to do it the right way—and you'll get additional benefits. To help you avoid these and many other mistakes, let's look at the general ideas behind the problems and what you should remember when implementing your next site.

Separating your behavior from your structure

The number one thing you can do to improve any project involving JavaScript is to separate your behavior from your markup. This key technique is often overlooked or not given enough attention. Following the same design rule of separating CSS from the XHTML documents using external style sheets, your JavaScript should also separate itself into external files. With CSS, you *could* use the `style` attribute on tags to apply CSS to your DOM objects, but that's not any more maintainable than an old-school mess of `<font>` tags. Why, then, does it happen so often that a beautifully designed site will mark up the XHTML with `id` and `class` selectors, nicely separate out all the CSS into an external file, but then throw a whole mess of inline JavaScript into the document? This must be stopped now! JavaScript should follow the same separation rules as CSS.

How to include JavaScript the right way

There are several different ways you can add JavaScript to your web applications. You've probably seen or used all of them, but not all of them are good. I hesitate to show you these methods as I don't want to corrupt you right from the start, but just so we're on the same page, I'll go through each method and point out a few problems.

First, you could add your script embedded between the body tags mixed in with your other markup:

```
<!DOCTYPE html PUBLIC "-//W3C//DTD XHTML 1.0 Strict//EN"
    "http://www.w3.org/TR/xhtml1/DTD/xhtml1-strict.dtd">
<html xmlns="http://www.w3.org/1999/xhtml">
<head>
    <title>Inline JavaScript</title>
</head>
<body>
    <h1>Inline Example</h1>
    <script type="text/javascript">
        //JavaScript Code
    </script>
</body>
</html>
```

But that doesn't provide any sort of separation between your behavioral enhancements and your structured markup. It opens up your code to repetitive and often unnecessary code replication as well.

> *Savvy readers may notice I didn't add any of the typical commenting tags—<!-- and //--> or <!--//--><![CDATA[//><!-- and //--><!]]>—within the script tags to hide the JavaScript from very old browsers or XML parsers. If you've been using JavaScript inline in the <body> of the document, you can join the comment versus no-comments debate, or you can take my advice and ignore inline scripts altogether. Therefore, I'm not going to overcomplicate this information by explaining the comment tags.*

The only time inline JavaScript may be useful is if you want to use the document.write() method to directly modify the page at that point. However, there are better solutions to accomplish the same task, as you'll see later.

Next, you could add your script embedded in the <head> of the document:

```
<!DOCTYPE html PUBLIC "-//W3C//DTD XHTML 1.0 Strict//EN"
      "http://www.w3.org/TR/xhtml1/DTD/xhtml1-strict.dtd">
<html xmlns="http://www.w3.org/1999/xhtml">
<head>
    <title>Head JavaScript</title>
    <script type="text/javascript">
        //JavaScript Code
    </script>
</head>
<body>
    <h1>Head Example</h1>
</body>
</html>
```

This is arguably better. At least it assembles all the code into an appropriate location within the markup, but it's still mixing the structure and behavior, just on a lesser scale.

Finally, you could include it from an external source file:

```
<!DOCTYPE html PUBLIC "-//W3C//DTD XHTML 1.0 Strict//EN"
      "http://www.w3.org/TR/xhtml1/DTD/xhtml1-strict.dtd">
<html xmlns="http://www.w3.org/1999/xhtml">
<head>
    <title>External File JavaScript</title>
    <script type="text/javascript" src="source.js"></script>
</head>
<body>
    <h1>External File Example</h1>
</body>
</html>
```

This is always the correct and best method. As a general rule, most people say that any script that doesn't directly write out to the document (using the document.write() method) should be placed in the <head> of the markup. While this is true, I say take it one step further. No matter what—yes, that's right; no matter what—use an external source file to include *all* your scripts. Pretend you never saw the first two methods. In fact, pretend they don't exist. If there's any JavaScript in your markup, you should go back and remove it to create a clean separation of behavior and structure. There's no situation where you can't put all your code in a source file, and doing so offers a lot of advantages. You'll be forced to rethink how you go about creating your functions and objects: are you keeping things simple and maintainable by creating reusable, generic code, or are you overcomplicating things by creating custom copies of the same logic? External files also offer the advantage of reducing the overall page size. They'll usually be cached by the client's web browser and only downloaded once, reducing the load time of each following page.

The only real difference you may have to overcome is that your beloved document.write() method may not work as expected. However, since this is a DOM scripting book, and we want to use the generic, browser-agnostic DOM methods, you'd be better off using the createElement() and appendChild() DOM methods or the unofficial innerHTML property—but we'll discuss that later.

That javascript: prefix

You may notice I missed a few additional places where JavaScript may crop up in your document, specifically in the attributes of elements. Consider the case of opening a new pop-up window. If you're using a strict DOCTYPE specification, the target attribute of the anchor tag is not valid:

```
<a href="http://advanceddomscripting.com" target="_blank">➡
AdvancED DOM Scripting</a>
```

so the only valid way to open another window is with JavaScript. In these cases, you've probably used, or at least come across, JavaScript in the <a> tags href attribute using the special javascript: prefix:

```
<a href="javascript:window.open('http://advanceddomscripting.com');">➡
AdvancED DOM Scripting</a>
```

But in this case, you won't get the results you're looking for.

> To test these inline examples yourself, see the example page included in the source for this book at chapter1/popup/examples.html or on this book's website at http://advanceddomscripting.com.

One problem with the javascript: prefix is that it can handle only one function, nothing more. And if that function returns a value, the initial page may be overwritten with the result. For example, clicking the previous anchor with javascript:window.open(...) in Firefox opens the new window as expected, but the original window is overwritten with the result of the window.open() method, [object Window], as shown in Figure 1-1.

Figure 1-1. Using the javascript: prefix in the href attribute of an anchor with a method that returns a value sometimes overwrites your page with the value.

This problem, however, can be overcome by including an additional function in a script:

```
function popup(url) {
    window.open(url);
    //do not return anything!
}
```

and referencing it rather than directly referencing window.open:

```
<a href="javascript:popup('http://advanceddomscripting.com');">➡
AdvancED DOM Scripting</a>
```

That's still using the inline javascript: prefix. To avoid the need for the wrapper function, you may have tried to be a little less obtrusive by attaching your JavaScript to elements using the onclick event attribute to directly open the URL and simply placing a # in the href attribute:

```
<a href="#" onclick="window.open('http://advanceddomscripting.com');">➡
AdvancED DOM Scripting</a>
```

The onclick event attribute is a little better, but neither of these methods, when coded directly into your document, offers any separation of behavior and structure nor are they unobtrusive: Using the special javascript: prefix in href attributes is problematic, as it's not part of the official ECMAScript standard (http://www.ecma-international.org/publications/standards/Ecma-262.htm), but it's generally implemented by all browsers supporting ECMAScript. Using the prefix, or the previous onclick attribute, creates a direct reliance on JavaScript to navigate or activate the anchor.

Since neither option is perfect, the best solution is to at *least* use the inline event attribute to alter or use the existing attributes, such as the URL in the href. The previous two anchor examples could be rewritten to alter the existing href value, so when JavaScript is disabled, the anchor would still work as expected:

```
<a href="http://advanceddomscripting.com" onclick="this.href=➡
'javascript:popup(\'http://advanceddomscripting.com\');'">➡
AdvancED DOM Scripting</a>
```

An even better solution would be to retrieve the value of the `href` attribute from within the `onclick` event attribute:

```
<a href="http://advanceddomscripting.com" onclick="popup(this.href);
return false;">AdvancED DOM Scripting</a>
```

When a regular `<a>` link is clicked, the browser normally executes the default action of the anchor, which is to follow the `href` to wherever the path goes. However, when dealing with interactions such as clicks, the `onclick` event attribute must execute first; otherwise, the browsers would have already navigated to its new location before `onclick` had a chance to do its thing and that action would be lost.

Let's look at the first rewritten case where you use the `javascript:` prefix and the `popup()` function in the `onclick` attribute:

```
<a href="http://advanceddomscripting.com" onclick="this.href=
'javascript:popup(\'http://advanceddomscripting.com\');'">
AdvancED DOM Scripting</a>
```

Running this script results in the following actions:

1. Your onclick event occurs, changing the `href` attribute value of the link to

   `href="javascript:popup('http://advanceddomscripting.com');"`

   which uses the `javascript:` prefix to execute the earlier `popup()` function included elsewhere in the document.

2. The anchor's default action, following the `href`, is executed using the new value, which, in turn, executes the pop-up function and opens the desired URL.

By using the `onclick` attribute in this way, you're achieving the same result you would have by simply using the `javascript:` prefix, but the anchor will still function when JavaScript is disabled.

Now let's look at the second rewritten case where you use the `popup()` function by referencing the `href` value of the anchor in the `onclick` attribute:

```
<a href="http://advanceddomscripting.com" onclick="popup(this.href);
return false;">AdvancED DOM Scripting</a>
```

Here's what happens in this case:

1. Your onclick event occurs, executing the same `popup()` function (or `window.open()` directly):

   `popup('http://advanceddomscripting.com');`

2. But you must also return `false` to prevent the default action.

When you return `false` from the inline `onclick` event attribute, you're telling the browser to stop and ignore the rest of the events in the chain, including the default action. In this case, the browser stops execution of the default action and doesn't follow the link in the `href` attribute.

> *You may have noticed the use of* this *to refer to the <a> tag from within the* onclick *event attribute. In JavaScript,* this *is used to control the context of the function and refers to the owner of the object, so in this case, the <a> tag owns the* onclick *event attribute. We'll discuss* this *in more detail later in this book.*

Now that you understand the different ways of writing inline event listeners—by avoiding the use of javascript: coded directly into href attributes and using the appropriate functions assigned to event attributes—*forget that I ever told you about inline event attributes.* Showing you the evolution of the different methods from javascript: to the onclick event attribute is necessary so that you can see the benefits of the next solution. Remember you want to separate your behavior from your markup structure and inline event handlers don't achieve that. The best solution is to use unobtrusive techniques to add the event handlers when the window loads. You can apply the same logic from the inline script by including a script such as popupLoadEvent.js, which contains the following code:

```
// Add a load event to alter the page
ADS.addEvent(window,'load',function(W3CEvent) {

    // Locate all the anchor tags with the popup class in the document
    var popups = ADS.getElementsByClassName('popup', 'a');
    for(var i=0 ; i<popups.length ; i++ ) {

        // Add a click event listener to each anchor
        ADS.addEvent(popups[i],'click',function(W3CEvent) {

            // Open the window using the href attribute
            window.open(this.href);

            // Cancel the default event
            ADS.eventPreventDefault(W3CEvent);
        });
    }
});
```

and then marking up your anchors using a popup class in the class attribute:

```
<a href="http://advanceddomscripting.com" class="popup">➥
AdvancED DOM Scripting</a>
```

> *This example may look a little confusing as it uses a number of methods from an* ADS *object. This is the library of common elements you'll be creating throughout the book, but you haven't started it yet so this example won't work. You'll be starting the* ADS *library later in this chapter.*

In this case, there's a clean separation of behavior and structure, because there's no JavaScript inline in the document at all, with the exception of the <script> tag used to include a JavaScript source file in the head of the document. The document will gracefully degrade if JavaScript isn't available, as the anchor still links to http://advanceddomscripting.com. If JavaScript is available, it will enhance the behavior by adding a click event listener on all the anchors with the popup class. This idea is similar to the Hijax methods that Jeremy Keith describes with reference to Ajax (http://domscripting.com/blog/display/41), but here I've applied it to any event listeners.

An added advantage of using the class (or id) attributes to identify the elements is that you can use the same class name to stylize the anchors uniquely using a .popup CSS selector:

```
.popup {
    padding-right: 25px;
    background: transparent url(images/popup.png) ➥
no-repeat right center;
}
```

which indicate that the anchor's link will open in a pop-up window, as shown in Figure 1-2.

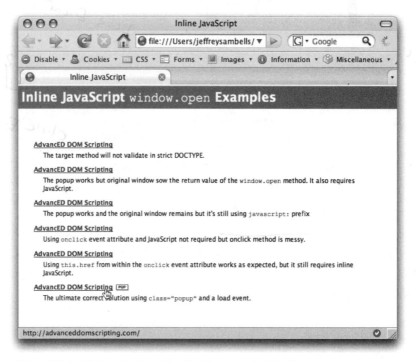

Figure 1-2. A styled anchor indicating that the anchor's link will pop up

> *I've used a simplistic example here with* window.open()*. This same methodology of using load event listeners to enhance the behavior of the page will come up often throughout the book in almost every example where the document is modified.*

This is just a quick introduction to events, event listeners, and proper implementation. We'll be discussing events in much more detail in Chapter 4, so we'll leave the discussion of events for now.

To demonstrate unobtrusiveness in practice—and to give it a bit more of a "wow" factor—I'll mention Lightbox JS written by Lokesh Dhakar of http://www.huddletogether.com. The Lightbox image viewing solution is a perfect example of separation of this behavior and structure. If you haven't heard of or used the Lightbox JS script, you can see it in action at http://www.huddletogether.com/projects/lightbox2 as shown in Figure 1-3.

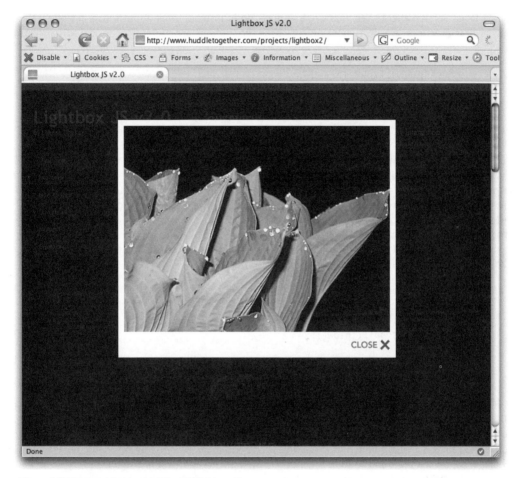

Figure 1-3. The unobtrusive Lightbox JS 2.0 in action

Lightbox is an unobtrusive script that takes your generic links to image files and creates an interactive slide show directly in the browser. To invoke it, you only need to add the appropriate JavaScript and CSS links to the <head> of your document and add rel="lightbox" to each surrounding anchor in the markup that you want to view in the light box:

```
<a href="myphoto.jpg" rel="lightbox">
    <img src="myphoto_thumb.jpg" alt="My Photo"/>
</a>
```

That's it; no inline scripting required. It provides a dramatic enhancement to your site's behavior and interaction while at the same time maintaining accessibility, usability, and unobtrusiveness to both your site's users and web developers.

Don't version check!

What? Don't version check? Yes, that's right—don't do it; instead, think about future-proofing. When talking best practices, "version checking" or "browser sniffing" are generally considered bad words. For the majority of us, we're probably testing against and expecting one of the following browsers:

- Microsoft Internet Explorer 6 and 7
- Firefox 1.5 and 2.0
- Safari 2.0
- Opera 9

However, that doesn't mean those are the only browsers that will ever see the page. If someone is trying to browse your site using an archaic browser, you shouldn't allow the page to explode with errors. At the same time, maybe some new and unknown browser will jump onto the market and blow everyone else away. To write agnostic code, you need to cater to all types and versions of browsers, but you also shouldn't spend hours accounting for each obscure browser on the market. Doing different things based on which browser signature you detect (if it's even the correct signature) is like trying to decide which baseball pitchers should throw a screwball versus a fastball based solely on their given names. Using the baseball analogy, your code may look something like this:

```
if ( pitcher.name == 'Addison' ) {
    pitcher.screwball.throw();
} elseif ( pitcher.name == 'Stephanie' ) {
    pitcher.fastball.throw();
} else {
    alert( 'Sorry, you can't throw the ball.' );
}
```

This restricts your script to work for only Addison or Stephanie, which isn't very useful if any other players join your team. What will happen when a new pitcher named Bobby tries to throw? Your code will simply assume Bobby can't throw at all. To make the code work for Bobby *and* any other pitchers, you'll need to add a whole bunch of if/else logic to account for every name on the team, and players who may be on the team in the future. Do you really want to add new if/else logic every time a new pitcher is added to the team? Probably not, and even if you wanted to, you may have no idea what each person can or can't do. Adding checks can only be done once a problem is found, with no provisions for the future. The best solution is capability detection.

Use capability detection

Capability detection, often call object detection, refers to checking the existence of a script object or method before executing code, rather than relying on your knowledge of which browsers have which features. If the required object or method exists, the browser is *capable* of using it and will execute as expected regardless of the version or signature of the browser. Again, using the baseball analogy, you could rewrite using capability detection as follows:

```
if ( pitcher.screwball ) {
    pitcher.screwball.throw();
} elseif ( pitcher.fastball ) {
    pitcher.fastball.throw();
} else {
    alert( 'Sorry, you can't throw the ball.' );
}
```

Now, when Bobby (who can throw a fastball) comes along, the code will still work, because you're not checking for his name; you're just checking if he can actually throw a fastball. The same applies to browsers. If your code requires document.body, you should use the following:

```
if (document.body) {
    // code that relies on document.body
}
```

If your code runs in a browser that doesn't support document.body (such as Netscape 4 or Internet Explorer 3), the offending portion will be ignored, and if you've written code that degrades gracefully (as we'll discuss next), the browser will still be able to access the information but with less flare. In all other browsers, even newer or future browsers that will eventually support document.body, the code would run without incident or alterations.

You can even use a comparison operator if you need to check multiple objects. To check for document.body.getElementsByTagName, you could use this:

```
if ( document.body && document.body.getElementsByTagName) {
    //  Code that uses document.body.getElementsByTagName
}
```

However, if you only checked the following

```
if (document.body.getElementsByTagName) {
    // Code that uses document.body.getElementsByTagName
}
```

your browser will return an error on the nonexistent document.body.

You also shouldn't check every function and method you're going to use, or you will go insane. Simply do a quick check at the top of your script for all the objects and methods you intend to use, and exit in cases that require the specific set of functionality if it's not going to work out.

```
var W3CDOM = document.createElement && ➡
document.getElementsByTagName;

function exampleFunctionThatRequiresW3CMethods() {
    if(!W3CDOM) return;
    // Code using document.createElement()
    // and document.getElementsById()
}
```

An important thing to remember with capability detection is that the JavaScript object you use in your detection should be related to the object and methods in the code you're about to execute. Don't use an unrelated method in your detection, as that will create a false comparison against what you're actually trying to accomplish.

When browser version sniffing is OK

You should use object-based capability detection whenever possible, but there is one instance where you'll be forced into browser signature detection—when dealing with product-specific features. If each browser implements the same object but interacts with the object, method, or property differently, it's not possible to modify your script based on the existence of a specific object or method. In those instances, you'll be forced to use browser sniffing, as it's the only way to detect product-specific differences with the same object. How you go about detecting which browser is which will depend on the product feature you're testing for. We'll look at this more in Chapter 7, where browser product features will begin to conflict and you'll have to come up with some creative solutions to get around them.

Degrade gracefully for guaranteed accessibility

The first rule when writing DOM scripts is that you can't rely on the availability of JavaScript. The second rule when writing JavaScript is that you can't rely on the availability of JavaScript. Do you know what the third rule is? You guessed it. In the previous two sections, I discussed the best ways to include JavaScript and detect for the appropriate compatibility. Proper inclusion and capability detection will go a long way to help your site handle the widest possible assortment of browsers and versions, but what if there is no JavaScript at all?

Earlier, I stated that your scripts should enhance, not provide, behavior and interaction. This is important to remember as you have to account for those people or programs that will be accessing your site and don't have JavaScript or have only limited or partial JavaScript. Yes, it's true; there are people who don't have JavaScript. According to the W3C (http://www.w3schools.com/browsers/browsers_stats.asp), as of January of 2007, 6 percent of us are using browsers that either don't support JavaScript or have it turned off (down from 10% in January 2006). In reality, however, as the W3C points out, these worldwide statistics shouldn't be taken as a hard, fast rule. If you're developing for a local market, that market's demographics may be wildly different from the worldwide average. Also, unless your target market is web-savvy users, the majority probably won't even know they have JavaScript, let alone how to disable it.

If your scripts are well written using unobtrusive techniques, browsers without JavaScript will be able to access the information as easily as those with JavaScript enabled. Also, for devices with limited or nonstandard JavaScript capabilities, it would be much nicer to say, "Welcome, turn JavaScript off for a more consistent experience." rather than "You need JavaScript to access this site. Go Away."

Don't require JavaScript for content—period.

Regardless of who does or doesn't have JavaScript, there is one group that you can rely on *not* having it at all—search engine bots and spiders. The bots that crawl the web looking at all your pages and content don't execute JavaScript, so if you want to be found, you'd better not rely on JavaScript for your navigation or content; I can't stress this enough.

> If you've been keeping up to date with the latest news on search engine bots, you may
> have heard rumors that Google's bot seems to be downloading CSS and JavaScript
> files along with pages. This could indicate they're attempting to integrate JavaScript
> navigation into their bots, or they could simply be searching your source code for
> http://google.com/codesearch. Either way, if Google's bot figures out a way to
> understand and navigate a JavaScript interface, that bot will be an exception to the
> rule, so don't depend on it.

When it comes to generating the important content of your public pages, you can't rely solely on
JavaScript to add the meat, the stuff you want everyone to see. If a search engine comes along, you
need to be sure it's going to get the right information. It's always a good idea to go through your site
with JavaScript disabled before calling it finished. If you can't get all the content you thought you
could, you still have work to do.

> Try a little experiment: Turn your JavaScript off, and surf the Net for a day. You'll prob-
> ably be very surprised at the number of brick walls you run into when trying to access,
> read, and navigate your favorite sites.

Plan for reuse with namespaces

Have you ever had a friend with the same name as you? If you have, you'll quickly realize the value of
namespaces in your scripts. You can imagine the situation where you need to ask someone a question
and just calling out a name will either get several responses or no response. This can be avoided in
your code by using namespaces, one of the most often overlooked yet easily implemented things
in JavaScript. Now, let me qualify that statement; until JavaScript 2.0 comes into wide use, I'm not talking about *real* namespaces but rather a little trick that can give you your own little world within the
script.

As you'll learn later, JavaScript doesn't complain when you declare a function multiple times; it simply
uses the last declared version. When you have a few different libraries, each doing their thing, you
need to make sure they don't conflict with the code you're writing yourself. You can avoid a lot of
frustration by keeping two simple things in mind: be unique and don't share.

To be unique, you need to pick a name for your space that's not going to be used elsewhere. The
Yahoo Libraries, for example, use YAHOO, whereas Google Maps uses a G prefix for everything. As you'll
see shortly, I'm going to use ADS for Advanced DOM Scripting in all the examples for this book, but
feel free to change that to something more unique for you. If you use your own, you can load the
book's source along with your source and run them side-by-side if you like.

The "not sharing" part is where all the magic happens. By "not sharing," I mean don't share everything,
just what you want to. When writing your scripts, you may often find a need for internal, specialized
functions that aren't necessarily part of the overall script or site, but they would make it much easier
to write or maintain. Let's say you want to create a function in your site called alertNodeName() that
will be accessible to everyone. This function will simply alert the nodeName property of an HTML element. You may also create a function called $() to grab elements by id and use it within
alertNodeName() and other functions in your library:

```
function $(id) {
    return document.getElementById(id);
}
function alertNodeName(id) {
    alert($(id).nodeName);
}
```

That's great, but your $() function isn't the same as the well-known Prototype $() function from the Prototype library (http://prototypejs.org), so now some other public libraries or scripts that are expecting different functionality may stop working. To keep your $() function to yourself, you can employ some JavaScript trickery. The trick in question is a self-executing anonymous function, which looks like this:

```
(function(){
    //your code
})();
```

You may have seen this before and wondered what was going on; really, it's quite elegant. The first enclosing parentheses around the function (function() {}) returns the unnamed function to the script, and the empty set of parentheses executes the returned unnamed function right away. It may be a little easier to understand if I throw in an argument as well:

```
(function(arg){
    alert(arg);
})('This will show in the alert box');
```

> This same idea of fake namespaces can also be accomplished through slightly different objects' syntaxes, but they are all trying to accomplish the same task of keeping your code contained in its own little space.

This doesn't really do anything special in itself, but if you write all your code within this special function wrapper, none of your custom functions or objects will be accessible to anyone else outside the special wrapper—unless you allow access. To avoid conflicts, you place your $() and your alertNodeName() functions inside this fake namespace as follows:

```
(function(){

    function $(id) {
        return document.getElementById(id);
    }

    function alertNodeName(id) {
        alert($(id).nodeName);
    }

    window['myNamespace'] = {};
    window['myNamespace']['showNodeName'] = alertNodeName;

})();
```

Using this fake namespace encapsulates and protects all your functions, objects, and variables. They will still have access to each other—because they're within the same function—but no other parts of the script are able to use your functions. Your $() function is now your own, along with anything else inside the encapsulation.

To globalize part of your protected script, the trailing set of parentheses tells the browser to execute the anonymous function right away, and during this execution, the last few lines assign the alertNodeName() to a window method:

```
window['myNamespace']['showNodeName']
```

This method can then be referenced from other scripts outside the namespace. You'll notice I've renamed alertNodeName() to showNodeName() in the window method to illustrate the point. Outside of the encapsulation there's no way to execute alertNodeName() directly. By assigning your alertNodeName() function to window['myNamespace']['showNodeName'], you're effectively creating a general method with the following nice myNamespace namespace, which will execute as if it were the protected alertNodeName() function:

```
myNamespace.showNodeName('example');
```

This is all possible because of scope and closure, which we'll discuss later in the chapter. When you call myNamespace.showNodeName(), it will execute in the space of your anonymous function namespace, so it will still have access to your special $() function and anything else you have in the namespace, along with anything outside of the encapsulation in the scope chain.

> *If you're a little confused by all this don't be. The remainder of this chapter and Chapter 2 should clear up a lot of the questions you may have regarding objects in JavaScript so bear with me until I introduce you to some of the more advanced features of the JavaScript object structure.*

The added advantage of the anonymous function encapsulation is that you don't need to append your namespace prefix to dozens of functions and objects. The only place where you need to add the namespace and possibly worry about inadvertently overriding something is in the assignment to the window object. Of course, within your fake namespace, any function you override, like $, will act differently, but you'll be aware of the change, so it won't be a problem.

Simplify things with reusable objects

Knowing how to integrate your code using best practices is the first step, but if you pore over many of the great and wonderful JavaScript libraries available on the Internet (see Chapter 9), you'll notice some commonalities among many of them. Over the years, the people who've been using JavaScript have written some handy little functions that we've all come to enjoy. Though not part of the official JavaScript language, using these tried and tested functions will make your code cleaner, more readable, and easier to understand when others need to debug or pick up where you left off. If you search the web for "Top 10 JavaScript", you'll get a list of commonly used functions that most developers can't live without.

Libraries are also another hot topic of debate. Some say they're wonderful tools that no developer should be without, while others say that a dependence on a library without understanding its inner workings encourages laziness and creates bad developers. Personally, I believe it depends on the situation and the library. However, everyone seems to agree that writing *your own* library and incorporating the elements *you* use on a daily basis are very good things. So, along that line, you're going to start a personal library that you'll use and add to throughout the rest of this book.

Beginning the ADS library

First, you'll need a unique namespace. Throughout the rest of this book, I'm going to use ADS for Advanced DOM Scripting, so for now, use that so you can easily follow along with the code in this book. Also, most of the examples will refer to the ADS-final-verbose.js file in the root folder of the source code for this book. This is the completed library and includes all the bits of code you'll be adding, but it also includes comments for each method describing what they do. I recommend you take the time to create this file on your own so that you understand what's in it—which is the whole point—instead of just copying the supplied version. At the same time, if you're stuck and need a working version, you can look at the supplied one for comparison.

Next, create a new JavaScript file called ADS.js to start your own library with the following namespace and method framework (this starting file can be found in chapter1/ADS-start.js in the source for the book):

```
(function(){

//The ADS namespace
if(!window.ADS) { window['ADS'] = {} }

function isCompatible(other) { };
window['ADS']['isCompatible'] = isCompatible;

function $() { };
window['ADS']['$'] = $;

function addEvent(node, type, listener) { };
window['ADS']['addEvent'] = addEvent;

function removeEvent(node, type, listener) { };
window['ADS']['removeEvent'] = removeEvent;

function getElementsByClassName(className, tag, parent){ };
window['ADS']['getElementsByClassName'] = getElementsByClassName;

function toggleDisplay(node,value) { };
window['ADS']['toggleDisplay'] = toggleDisplay;

function insertAfter(node, referenceNode) { };
window['ADS']['insertAfter'] = insertAfter;

function removeChildren(parent) { };
window['ADS']['removeChildren'] = removeChildren;
```

```
    function prependChild(parent, newChild) { };
    window['ADS']['prependChild'] = prependChild;

})();
```

This will be the starting point for your common library and includes the function signatures for a few of the favorite reusable JavaScript methods you'll find on the Web—which we'll discuss as you add the guts of each of these methods. The initial namespace object has also been wrapped in an if statement to allow you to use the same namespace across multiple files:

```
if(!window.ADS) { window['ADS'] = {} }
```

The methods in different files won't be able to access each other the same way, but using different files allows you to separate out less-often-used elements to make your library more modular. The only trick is that you may need to include the ADS object prefix when referencing ADS methods from another file.

> These are only the first of many methods you'll be adding to the ADS.js file through-out the course of this book. The intention is for you to build up your own library as you read, so that at the end, you'll have some great tools as well as a strong under-standing of everything in your library and in this book.

The ADS.isCompatible() method

The ADS.isCompatible() method determines if the current browser is compatible with the entire library. You can start by filling it in as follows, but you may need to add further alterations:

```
function isCompatible(other) {
    // Use capability detection to check requirements
    if( other===false
        || !Array.prototype.push
        || !Object.hasOwnProperty
        || !document.createElement
        || !document.getElementsByTagName
        ) {
        return false;
    }
    return true;
}
window['ADS']['isCompatible'] = isCompatible;
```

This method will give you a quick and easy way of determining if the browser can use all the elements of your library by wrapping code in a simple if statement:

```
if(ADS.isCompatible()) {
    // A bunch of code that uses the ADS library
}
```

This isn't absolutely necessary for every script, as you'll be using capability detection throughout the methods in the ADS library, but some of the code you'll be using in this book relies on JavaScript 1.5, which isn't supported in very old browsers. Rather than throw JavaScript errors or use excessive capability detection for every little line of code, this check will allow quick and graceful degradation of the page by looking for some common objects.

I won't be including this wrapper in all the code examples in this book, because all the examples will be using load events to modify the page. The ADS.addEvent() you'll add later in this chapter and the ADS.addLoadEvent() method you'll be adding in Chapter 4 will include the isCompatible() check within the method, so the load event won't run if it's not compatible.

If you add your own methods that use other, more recent additions to JavaScript to the library, you should edit your ADS.isCompatible() method as necessary.

The ADS.$() method

My favorite popular function is $(). Popularized by the Prototype JavaScript Framework (http://prototypejs.org), it will save your fingers a lot of typing. In essence, it's just a replacement for document.getElementById(). Add the following to your new ADS namespace:

```
function $() {
    var elements = new Array();

    // Find all the elements supplied as arguments
    for (var i = 0; i < arguments.length; i++) {
        var element = arguments[i];

        // If the argument is a string assume it's an id
        if (typeof element == 'string') {
            element = document.getElementById(element);
        }

        // If only one argument was supplied, return the
        // element immediately
        if (arguments.length == 1) {
            return element;
        }

        // Otherwise add it to the array
        elements.push(element);
    }

    // Return the array of multiple requested elements
    return elements;
};
window['ADS']['$'] = $;
```

With this, you can retrieve DOM elements by id in all your scripts simply by including the following reference:

```
var element = ADS.$('example');
```

which is equivalent to

```
var element = document.getElementById('example');
```

> Prototype 1.5 added a much more advanced $() method that adds a number of new methods to the element. This ADS.$() method only retrieves a regular DOM element.

From within your ADS namespace, you can simply use $() without the prefix. It's a fairly simple idea, but in a large complicated library, the savings will be obvious. Additionally, the ADS.$() function you've implemented allows you to request more than one element and retrieve an array containing those elements. You could easily loop over the resulting array and do whatever you need:

```
var elements = ADS.$( 'a' , 'b' , 'c' , 'd' );
for ( e in elements ) {
    // Do something`
}
```

It's also a great addition to your library methods where you need to pass in a reference to a DOM element. If you add a line such as this:

```
if(!(obj = $(obj))) return false;
```

to methods in your ADS library:

```
function exampleLibraryMethod(obj) {
    if(!(obj = $(obj))) return false;
    // Do something with obj
}
window['ADS']['exampleLibraryMethod'] = exampleLibraryMethod;
```

you can optionally specify the argument using a string with an object id:

```
var element = ADS.exampleLibraryMethod('id');
```

or an object reference:

```
var element = ADS.exampleLibraryMethod(ADS.$('id'));
```

Just remember that, if you're writing code within the namespace, you don't need to include the ADS prefix, but any other code you write outside the namespace will need to include the prefix.

The Prototype version also applies several methods to the element, which allows you to use dot notation to stack methods like this:

```
// Prototype adds methods such as getElementsByClassName()
var elements = $('element-id').getElementsByClassName('className');
```

To simplify the examples, your library won't be following this pattern, but you could do so later if you like. Prototype also has a number of other useful functions and objects. I won't go through each one here, but if you want to see more, skip ahead to Chapter 9, where I'll discuss more about the Prototype library, as well as other libraries.

The ADS.addEvent() and ADS.removeEvent() methods

We've already discussed using JavaScript source files and unobtrusive methods to attach events to objects in your markup structure. Doing this, however, can become a tedious task in itself and can occupy the bulk of your code. To keep this simple and much more readable, you can use an addEvent method as you saw earlier in the pop-up window example. Finish the following addEvent() and removeEvent() methods in your ADS namespace:

```
function addEvent( node, type, listener ) {
    // Check compatibility using the earlier method
    // to ensure graceful degradation
    if(!isCompatible()) { return false }

    if(!(node = $(node))) { return false; }

    if (node.addEventListener) {
        // W3C method
        node.addEventListener( type, listener, false );
        return true;
    } else if(node.attachEvent) {
        // MSIE method
        node['e'+type+listener] = listener;
        node[type+listener] = function(){
            node['e'+type+listener](window.event);
        }
        node.attachEvent( 'on'+type, node[type+listener] );
        return true;
    }

    // Didn't have either so return false
    return false;
};
window['ADS']['addEvent'] = addEvent;

function removeEvent(node, type, listener ) {
    if(!(node = $(node))) { return false; }

    if (node.removeEventListener) {
        node.removeEventListener( type, listener, false );
        return true;
    } else if (node.detachEvent) {
        // MSIE method
        node.detachEvent( 'on'+type, node[type+listener] );
        node[type+listener] = null;
        return true;
    }
```

```
      // Didn't have either so return false
      return false;
  };
  window['ADS']['removeEvent'] = removeEvent;
```

There are a variety of different addEvent() flavors scattered about the Web, such as the one written by Dean Edwards (http://dean.edwards.name/weblog/2005/10/add-event). Here, I've included a slightly modified and more verbose version of John Resig's addEvent() and removeEvent() methods (http://ejohn.org/projects/flexible-javascript-events). Each accomplishes the same goal—registering an event listener on an element—but I've included John Resig's version because it's simple, doesn't degrade the various features of the different event methods, and fixes a few inconsistencies between the W3C and Microsoft event registration models.

> *You'll be looking at events in much more detail later in Chapter 4.*

To use your ADS.addEvent() method, you simply specify the element, event type, and listener function you want to combine as you saw earlier when working with the pop-up anchors:

```
ADS.addEvent(window,'load',function(W3CEvent) {
    // Locate all the anchor tags with the popup class in the document
    var popups = ADS.getElementsByClassName('popup', 'a');
    for(var i=0 ; i<popups.length ; i++ ) {

        // Add a click event listener to each anchor
        ADS.addEvent(popups[i],'click',function(W3CEvent) {

            // Open the window using the href attribute
            window.open(this.href);

            // Cancel the default event
            ADS.eventPreventDefault(W3CEvent);
        });
    }
});
```

> *You'll be adding the ADS.eventPreventDefault() method in this example in Chapter 4. It's used to prevent the anchor from following the link in the href attribute.*

You can even use this to add multiple load events for a single window:

```
function sayHello() {
    alert('Hello');
}
ADS.addEvent(window,'load',sayHello);
```

```
function sayGoodbye() {
    alert('Goodbye');
}
ADS.addEvent(window,'load',sayGoodbye);
```

When the window loads, you'll get two alert boxes: the one alerting Hello and another alerting Goodbye, but not necessarily in that order. Having multiple load event listeners can be very useful when you're writing multiple libraries where each requires its own load event. Rather than writing a new, combined, window.onload function that includes the events from each of your objects, each library can add its own load events with ADS.addEvent(window,'load',...).

> Remember that the second parameter doesn't include the on prefix that you would find in the event attributes on a DOM element. Attributes such as onload refer to a specific property of the object while the plain term load is required by the W3C addEventListener() method to identify the event. Always use ADS.addEvent(window,'load',initPage); not ADS.addEvent(window,'onload',initPage);.

The ADS.getElementsByClassName() method

When writing extensive DOM manipulation code, you'll run into the getElementById() method, or now the ADS.$() method, quite often. The problem with using getElementById() is that it retrieves everything based on id and all the ids in a document must be unique. So what do you do when you want to retrieve a group of common items? You can get a list of like tags using getElementsByTagName(), but that won't work for unlike tags. As an alternative, you can assign the same class attribute to all your elements and use this ADS.getElementsByClassName() method after you add it to your ADS namespace:

```
function getElementsByClassName(className, tag, parent){
    parent = parent || document;
    if(!(parent = $(parent))) { return false; }

    // Locate all the matching tags
    var allTags = (tag == "*" && parent.all) ? parent.all : ➥
parent.getElementsByTagName(tag);
    var matchingElements = new Array();

    // Create a regular expression to
    // determine if the className is correct
    className = className.replace(/\-/g, "\\-");
    var regex = new RegExp("(^|\\s)" + className + "(\\s|$)");

    var element;
    // Check each element
    for(var i=0; i<allTags.length; i++){
        element = allTags[i];
        if(regex.test(element.className)){
            matchingElements.push(element);
```

```
        }
    }

    // Return any matching elements
    return matchingElements;
};
window['ADS']['getElementsByClassName'] = getElementsByClassName;
```

The bulk of this version was written by Jonathan Snook (http://www.snook.ca/jonathan) and Robert Nyman (http://www.robertnyman.com) and is one of many variations on the same idea. I've reworked their code to be more verbose, so you can understand what's going on. I've also added the ADS.$() lookup mentioned earlier for the DOM object reference and reversed the order of their arguments so that the class name is first rather than last, because Firefox 3 will be introducing a core getElementsByClassName() method that takes the class as the first argument (matching that will mean fewer code changes if you want to switch to the internal method in the future).

Basically, the method works by walking the DOM document tree looking for a specific className and an optional node and tag filter; it retrieves all the DOM elements associated with the specified class, node, and tag. Take the following document for example:

```
<!DOCTYPE HTML PUBLIC "-//W3C//DTD HTML 4.01//EN"
        "http://www.w3.org/TR/html4/strict.dtd">
<html>
<head>
    <title>ADS.getElementsByClassName() Example</title>
</head>
<body>
    <h1 class="findme">ADS.getElementsByClassName() Example</h1>
    <p class="findme">This is just an <em class="a">example</em>.</p>
    <div id="theList">
        <h2 class="findme">A list!</h2>
        <ol>
            <li class="findme">Foo</li>
            <li class="findme">Bar</li>
        </ol>
    </div>
</body>
</html>
```

If you try the following method:

```
var found = ADS.getElementsByClassName('findme','*',document);
```

you'll end up with an array consisting of the following elements:

- The <h1> element
- The <p> element
- The <em> element
- The <h2> element

- The first `<li>` element in the list
- The second `<li>` element in the list

Likewise, if you do this:

```
var found = ADS.getElementsByClassName(
    'findme', 'li', ADS.$('theList')
);
```

you'll end up with an array of elements consisting only of the two `<li>` elements within the b div.

The ADS.toggleDisplay() method

Another action you'll be often implementing is toggling the display of elements in the DOM tree. It's a fairly simple bit of code, but extracting it out into a common function will reduce unnecessary repetition. Add the rest of this method in your ADS namespace:

```
function toggleDisplay(node, value) {
    if(!(node = $(node))) { return false; }

    if ( node.style.display != 'none' ) {
        node.style.display = 'none';
    } else {
        node.style.display = value || '';
    }
    return true;
}
window['ADS']['toggleDisplay'] = toggleDisplay;
```

Then, when you call the following:

```
ADS.toggleDisplay(ADS.$('example'));
```

the elements display property will be toggled between none and empty (which is the default). If you want to reuse the function for various display types, you can include an optional second parameter to define the desired default display property, for example:

```
ADS.toggleDisplay(ADS.$('example'),'block');
```

or

```
ADS.toggleDisplay(ADS.$('example'),'inline');
```

Reusing a small bit of code like this may seem silly, but doing so will greatly increase the readability of your code—it's obvious where you'll be toggling simply by referencing the name of the method.

The ADS.insertAfter() method

Your browser's implementation of the W3C DOM specifications provides a number of objects that you can use to manipulate your document structure, as you'll see in Chapter 3. But a method that seems to be missing from the DOM core is the `element.insertAfter()` method. The functionality can be replicated by combining a few existing DOM methods, but your code will read much better if you implement this simple wrapper function in your ADS namespace:

```
function insertAfter(node, referenceNode) {
    if(!(node = $(node))) return false;
    if(!(referenceNode = $(referenceNode))) return false;
    return referenceNode.parentNode.insertBefore(
        node, referenceNode.nextSibling
    );
};
window['ADS']['insertAfter'] = insertAfter;
```

This makes things much nicer, as the following line:

```
ADS.insertAfter(ADS.$('example'),domNode);
```

is easier to understand than this one:

```
ADS.$('example').parentNode.insertBefore(ADS.$('example'),domNode);
```

The ADS.removeChildren() and ADS.prependChild() methods

The last two additions to your ADS namespace are the ADS.removeChildren() method:

```
function removeChildren(parent) {
    if(!(parent = $(parent))) { return false; }

    // While there is a child remove it
    while (parent.firstChild) {
        parent.firstChild.parentNode.removeChild(parent.firstChild);
    }

    // Return the parent again so you can chain the methods
    return parent;
};
window['ADS']['removeChildren'] = removeChildren;
```

and ADS.prependChild() method:

```
function prependChild(parent,newChild) {
    if(!(parent = $(parent))) { return false; }
    if(!(newChild = $(newChild))) { return false; }


    if(parent.firstChild) {
        // There is already a child so insert before the first one
        parent.insertBefore(newChild,parent.firstChild);
    } else {
        // No children so just append
        parent.appendChild(newChild);
    }
```

```
        // Return the parent again so you can chain the methods
        return parent;
    }
    window['ADS']['prependChild'] = prependChild;
```

Like the `ADS.insertAfter()` method, these are just wrappers to existing DOM methods that encapsulate some common actions you'll be doing repeatedly in your web applications.

Get your hands dirty

Many developers who come from a design background, or even new developers, often start off in a "what you see is what you get" (WYSIWYG) editor. There are several different ones, but unless you're using their proprietary, built-in, source management methodologies, you're never going to get the result you want when integrating JavaScript. I strongly encourage you to step away from your WYSIWYG editor and not rely on it to create your final behavioral integration. WYSIWYG is good for initial concept and brainstorming, but when it comes down to actually creating the code for a site, the WYSIWYG editors just can't hack it as well as you can yourself. If you want a truly accessible, semantic, and unobtrusive experience, human intervention in the code is necessary.

Writing your own code can only teach you more, and as you become more experienced, you'll only further appreciate what JavaScript has to offer. But that doesn't mean you have to reinvent the wheel. There is an abundance of JavaScript libraries out there, many excellent ones and many very bad ones. I'll be discussing a handful of them in Chapter 9, but until then, here's a short refresher on some of the JavaScript gotchas that you may encounter in your code.

Common gotchas in the JavaScript syntax

Even if you're a seasoned web developer who's been scripting away for a decade, you're going to come across some situation where you've been staring at a problem for hours and just can't figure out what's up. Most of the time, the problem is a simple error that you're just overlooking, so I thought it would be good to point out some of the common ones you may come across as you go through the examples in this book. If you run into a problem while using the methods in this book, check this book's website at http://advanceddomscripting.com to see if others may have had a similar problem, and if not, check back to this section and see if you might have one of these problems.

Case sensitivity

All the functions and variables you create are case sensitive, so

```
function myFunction() { }
```

is not the same as

```
function MyFunction() { }
```

This also includes the JavaScript core objects like `Array` and `Object`.

Single vs. double quotes

There is no special difference between single quotes ('string') and double quotes ("string") in JavaScript, and you can use either to create a string. But as a general rule, most web developers prefer single quotes over double quotes, since the XHTML specification (http://www.w3.org/TR/xhtml1) calls for all XHTML attributes to be quoted with double quotes. Keeping single quotes for JavaScript and double quotes for (X)HTML attributes makes it much easier and nicer to mix the two.

For example, reading and writing the following:

```
var html = '<h2 class="a">A list!</h2>'
    + '<ol>'
    + '<li class="a">Foo</li>'
    + '<li class="a">Bar</li>'
    + '</ol>';
```

is easier than remembering to escape all the double quotes in this example:

```
var html = "<h2 class=\"a\">A list!</h2>"
    + "<ol>"
    + "<li class=\"a\">Foo</li>"
    + "<li class=\"a\">Bar</li>"
    + "</ol>";
```

But you'll still have to escape any inline single quotes:

```
var html = '<p class="a">Don\'t forget to escape single quotes!</p>';
```

Breaking lines

Regardless of the type of quotes you use to create your string, you still can't have a hard line break in the middle of the string:

```
var html = '<h2 class="a">A list!</h2>
    <ol>
        <li class="a">Foo</li>
        <li class="a">Bar</li>
    </ol>';
```

If you do, it will cause a parse error, as the line breaks will be interpreted as a semicolon (;). If you want to split up the string on various lines, you'll need to tell the browser that the line continues by escaping the new line with a backslash:

```
var html = '<h2 class="a">A list!</h2>\
    <ol>\
        <li class="a">Foo</li>\
        <li class="a">Bar</li>\
    </ol>';
```

Just remember that this will preserve the white space and indention in the string, and it could have adverse effects if you are trying to compress your code with a third-party compression tool.

Alternatively, you can use the string concatenation operator (+) and enclose each line in its own set of quotes:

```
var html = '<h2 class="a">A list!</h2>'
    + '<ol>'
    + '<li class="a">Foo</li>'
    + '<li class="a">Bar</li>'
    + '</ol>';
```

By using quotes and concatenation, the resulting string has no white space between the tags.

Optional semicolons and parentheses

It's not necessary for you to include a semicolon (;) to conclude a statement or a line. A line break is generally assumed to be a semicolon unless it's part of a control structure so this snippet

```
alert('hello')
alert('world')
alert('!')
```

is interpreted as follows:

```
alert('hello');
alert('world');
alert('!');
```

However, this snippet

```
if(a==b)
alert('true!')
alert('false?')
```

is *not* interpreted like this:

```
if(a==b);
alert('true!');
alert('false?');
```

Instead, the if control structure makes the interpretation:

```
if(a==b) {
    alert('true!');
}
alert('false?');
```

and will alert 'true!' only in the event that a is equal to b but will always alert 'false? ' regardless of the conditional operator. These interpretations can sometimes become confusing to read for both beginning and experienced developers, especially if they're intermingled with different markup such as HTML. To avoid this confusion, I highly suggest you always use semicolons and parentheses no matter what:

```
if(a==b) {
    alert('true!');
}
alert('false?');
```

Writing your code clearly makes what you're trying to do obvious when you come back later, or, if someone else takes over the project, it will be much easy to follow and understand.

Overloading (not really)

JavaScript doesn't support overloading; it's really more like replacement. Overloading refers to the ability of a programming language to distinguish different functions and methods based on the data types of their arguments. For example, overloading would allow you to declare two functions of the same name as follows:

```
function myFunction(a,b) { alert(a+b); }
function myFunction(a) { alert(a); }
```

and treat them as two separate functions based on the fact that they have different arguments (also including a data type for each argument, which isn't available in JavaScript). Therefore, in a language that supports true overloading, the following function:

```
myFunction(1);
```

would alert '1', while this one

```
myFunction(1,2);
```

would alert '3'. However, if you try that in JavaScript, the second declaration of myFunction() will *replace* the first, so both calls will execute the same function and alert '1'.

When executing, the script will use whichever function was defined *last* in the scope chain, regardless of its arguments. There can only ever be one instance of a function using the same name, so when creating your own functions and methods, be sure not to overwrite an existing JavaScript core element— unless you're trying to. You can overwrite any JavaScript object without a complaint by defining your own object with the same name. If you wrote the following function:

```
function alert(message) {
    ADS.$('messageBox').appendChild(document.createTextNode(message));
}
```

the browser will no longer alert messages as expected but will instead use your new alert function to do whatever you specified; in this case, it's appending to the specified <div>. In some cases, this may be desired but remember, if you're combining libraries and various code sources, they're going to expect the core functions to act the way they should, so you may get unexpected results.

Anonymous functions

A nice feature of JavaScript that you'll often see but may find confusing is the anonymous function. This is a function you define without a name, and they've already appeared a few times in this chapter. They're especially useful when registering event listeners on DOM objects or passing functions around as arguments to other methods. Take the following example, in which you register a click event on an anchor using a named function and the previous ADS.addEvent() method:

```
function clicked() {
    alert('Linked to: ' + this.href);
}
var anchor = ADS.$('someId');
ADS.addEvent(anchor, 'click', clicked);
```

Your clicked() function is defined first and assigned as the anchor's click event listener. Fair enough; this will work perfectly well and makes sense if you're going to be reusing the clicked() function over and over.

Now take a look at an alternative method where you achieve the same goal, but in this instance, you pass an anonymous function directly:

```
var anchor = ADS.$('someId');
addEvent(anchor, 'click', function () {
    alert('Linked to: 'this.href);
});
```

In this case, the function is passed directly into the ADS.addEvent() method without a name, so the function is anonymous. Using an anonymous function would make sense in the cases of either very simple or specific code that applies only to that element, but that's not the only use, as you'll see throughout the book.

> For a lot more on JavaScript objects, see Chapter 2.

Scope resolution and closures

We'll be discussing the JavaScript object model in detail in the next chapters, so I'll just quickly mention scope and closure problems here.

First, let's look at scope. Scope refers to the space of code that has access to a certain property (variable) or method (function). In JavaScript, scope is maintained within functions, so in a function such as this

```
function myFunction() {
    var myVariable = 'inside';
}
```

the myVarialbe scope is restricted to myFunction(). If you try to access the myVariable from outside the function, it won't work:

```
function myFunction() {
    var myVariable = 'inside';
}
myFunction();
alert(myVariable);
```

Likewise, executing the function in this case doesn't affect the external scope:

```
function myFunction() {
    var myVariable = 'inside';
}
// Define the variable
var myVariable = 'outside';
// Execute the function
myFunction();
alert(myVariable); // Will alert "outside"
```

In this example, myFunction() has no effect on myVariable in the function's external scope, because the var keyword was used to keep the scope chain within the function. If you had left the var keyword off the myVariable assignment within myFunction(), the scope of myVariable would resolve to the external scope of myFunction(), and the external variable would be modified:

```
function myFunction() {
    //no var
    myVariable = 'inside';
}
//define the variable
var myVariable = 'outside';
//execute the function
myFunction();
alert(myVariable); //will alert "inside"
```

The scope chain is the term used to describe the path along which a variable's value is determined (or which method to use when a function is called). When myVariable is assigned the value of 'inside', the var keyword is missing in the myFunction() scope, so the assignment looks up the scope chain to where the myFunction() method was executed—in this case within the window object—and modifies that instance of myVariable. In essence the var keyword determines which function is the end of the scope chain of a particular variable. The same logic applies when you retrieving the value of the variable.

> In addition to the var *keyword, including the variable in the function signature, as in the following line, is the same as including* var—*the variable is contained within the scope of the function:* functionmyFunction(**myVariable**) { ... }

Closure is related to scope and refers to how an internal function has access to the properties of its external function, even *after* the external function has finished executing and terminated. When you reference a variable or method, JavaScript tries to resolve the scope by following the scope chain through the object's execution path looking for the most recent value of the variable. Once found, that value is used.

The implications of scope resolution and closures aren't obvious at first and are usually the root of most of the questions I receive about "broken" scripts. To illustrate the point, take a look at the following example:

```
ADS.addEvent(window, 'load', function(W3CEvent) {
    for (var i=1 ; i<=3 ; i++ ) {

        var anchor = document.getElementById('anchor' + i);

        ADS.addEvent(anchor,'click',function() {
            alert('My id is anchor' + i);
        });
    }
});
```

An anonymous function is told to run once the window is finished loading. Now, if we assume our document does have anchors using the IDs anchor1 through anchor3, what would be the expected result? To see for yourself, open the chapter1/scopechain/example1.html file in the source for this book, and try clicking a few of the anchors.

The syntax of the code is correct, but there's a flaw in the logic. Most beginners, and even some experienced programmers, will assume that each anchor, when clicked, would alert My id is anchorX where "X" corresponds to the value of i when the click event listener was assigned. If that is true, the first anchor will alert My id is anchor1, and the third will alert My id is anchor3. This is wrong. When clicked, each anchor will alert the same thing, as shown in Figure 1-4.

Figure 1-4. An alert window showing the actual result of the click

But why is this? Each alert() produces the same message because the value of i isn't actually retrieved from the scope chain until the click event occurs. When the click occurs, initAnchors() has already finished executing, so i will be equal to 4, because it has been incremented to a number greater than 3 to stop the loop.

When the click event listener is invoked and checks its internal scope for the value of i, it doesn't have it, so it looks to its external scope, in this case the initAnchors() function. The value in initAnchors() is 4 so it retrieves it from there. This is illustrated in Figure 1-5.

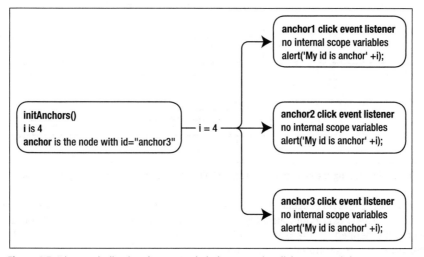

Figure 1-5. Diagram indicating the scope chain between the click event and the initAnchors() method

To achieve the correct result, you need to move the registration of the event listener to its own function and pass in the appropriate values through the function arguments:

```
function registerListener(anchor, i) {
    ADS.addEvent(anchor, 'click', function() {
        alert('My id is anchor' + i);
    });
}
function initAnchors(W3CEvent) {
    for ( i=1 ; i<=5 ; i++ ) {
        var anchor = document.getElementById('anchor'+i);
        registerListener(anchor,i);
    }
}
ADS.addEvent(window, 'load', initAnchors);
```

With the additional function and variable definitions in the scope chain, as you can see by trying chapter1/scopechain/example2.html, the correct value is maintained in the alert, because the external scope of the onclick event is now the registerListener() function, which maintains an internal scope with the unique value for i in each instance, as illustrated in Figure 1-6.

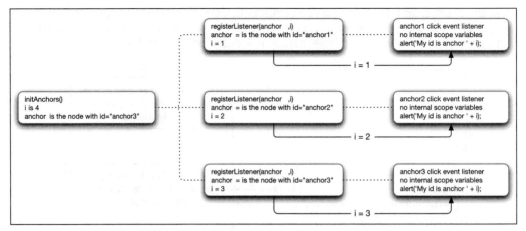

Figure 1-6. Diagram indicating the change in the scope chain with the addition of the registerListener() function

Likewise, replacing registerListener() with the following function, as you can see in chapter1/ scopechain/example3.html, would alert My id is anchorX and initAnchors i is 6. That's because, again, the i value isn't defined in the registerListener() event listener, so it retrieves it from the initAnchors() scope as illustrated in Figure 1-7.

```
function registerListener(anchor,myNum) {
    ADS.addEvent(anchor, 'click', function() {
        alert('My id is anchor' + myNum
            + ' and initAnchors i is ' + i);
    });
}
```

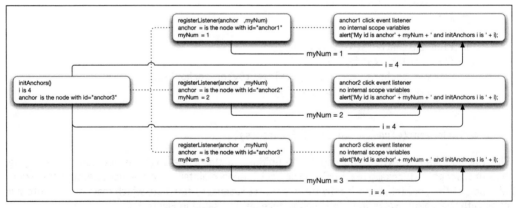

Figure 1-7. Diagram indicating the change in the scope chain with the addition of the registerListener() function and the modification of its input variables

This sort of situation will pop up throughout the book; additional functions will be required so that the proper variable scope can be maintained when dynamically assigning methods to objects.

Iterating over objects

You've probably already used iteration in your script to loop over all the elements in an array using a for loop:

```
var list = [1,2,3,4];
for( i=0 ; i<list.length ; i++ ) {
    alert(list[i]);
}
```

And using the incremental approach probably worked fine. An alternative method of iteration uses the for loop for every property in the list:

```
var list = [1,2,3,4];
for( i in list ) {
    alert(list[i]);
}
```

In this case, it will give you exactly the same results, because list is an Array object.

Exercise caution when you use the for(i in item) approach on objects that act as arrays but aren't Arrays. For instance, the NamedNodeMap object returned from getElementByTagName() acts as an array and has a length property, so you can iterate over it just like you would with a regular array:

```
var all = document.body.getElementsByTagName('*');
for( i=0 ; i<all.length ; i++ ) {
    // Do something with all[i] element
}
```

However, if you try to use the following iteration, the loop will *also* include additional methods of the NamedNodeMap object:

```
var all = document.body.getElementsByTagName('*');
for( i in all) {
    // Do something with all[i] element
}
```

You'll have an iteration where the value of i is equal to length, item, and namedItem, which may cause unexpected errors in your code. In some cases, you may be able to use the object's hasOwnProperty() method to avoid this problem.

The hasOwnProperty() method returns true if the object has the property or method specified, but the check doesn't include any properties or methods inherited from other objects. It only checks properties that were created directly on that particular object itself, such as the elements assigned to the array. If you used this check in the for loop, the loop would skip properties such as length, because length isn't a direct property of the all array but is inherited from the NamedNodeMap object that all is based on:

```
var all = document.body.getElementsByTagName('*');
for( i in all) {
    if(!all.hasOwnProperty(i)) { continue; }
    // Do something with all[i] element
}
```

> *You'll be learning more about inheritance in Chapter 3 as you examine how the two specifications relate to one another.*

Referencing vs. calling a function (missing parentheses)

The last JavaScript gotcha is one you'll come across often throughout this book, and it involves referencing versus calling a function. Functions in JavaScript have some unique properties that I won't go into here, but you need to be aware of the difference between calling a function and assigning the result to a value:

```
var foo = exampleFunction();
```

and assigning a reference of the function to a value:

```
var foo = exampleFunction;
```

See the difference? The difference is the trailing parentheses to execute the function—which has a big impact on the result. Without the parentheses, the function itself is assigned to the variable, not the result. This is important when you need to assign functions or pass functions as arguments to other methods such as the window load event listener:

```
function loadPage() {
    // Load script
}
// No parentheses
ADS.addEvent(window, 'load', loadPage);
```

If you had appended the parentheses on the end of the function, as in the following line, the results of the loadPage() function would be assigned to window's load event listener, not the loadPage() function itself:

```
// With parentheses this won't work as expected
ADS.addEvent(window, 'load', loadPage());
```

A practical example: WYSIWYG JavaScript rollover redux

Before we dive into the JavaScript Object Model in Chapter 2 and the DOM in Chapter 3, I'll leave you with a practical example of how following best practices and the advice in this chapter can reduce the time you spend on your projects.

> *Before you go and send me tons of e-mail complaining about the following JavaScript rollover example—saying that CSS should be used for rollovers—I completely agree. I've only chosen this example as most, if not all, web developers will be familiar with it, and it nicely illustrates many of the points of the chapter.*

Unless this is your first foray into web design and development, you are probably familiar with the mess of mouse events required to achieve a multistate button using JavaScript in a WYSIWYG editor. Generally, your code would contain something similar to the following:

```
<a href="http://example.com"
    onmouseover="swapImage(...)"
    onmouseout="swapImage(...)"
    onmousedown="swapImage(...)"
    onmouseup="swapImage(...)">
<img src="images/button.gif" width="10" height="40" ➥
border="0" alt="Click Me!"></a>
```

The problem is that in a large document with lots of anchors the majority of the markup ends up being inline JavaScript code, and it overpowers the structured markup.

As an example, take a look at the page in Figure 1-8.

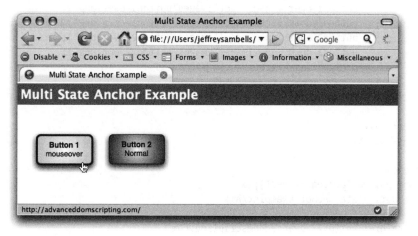

Figure 1-8. A very simple web page with two rollover buttons

Using Adobe ImageReady, the source of the page in Figure 1-8 would resemble the following:

```
<html>
<head>
<title>ImageReady Example</title>
    <link rel="stylesheet" href="style.css"➥
type="text/css" media="screen" />

    <script type="text/javascript">
    <!--

    function newImage(arg) {
        if (document.images) {
            rslt = new Image();
            rslt.src = arg;
```

```
                return rslt;
            }
        }

    function changeImages() {
        if (document.images && (preloadFlag == true)) {
            for (var i=0; i<changeImages.arguments.length; i+=2) {
                document[changeImages.arguments[i]].src =
                    changeImages.arguments[i+1];
            }
        }
    }

    var preloadFlag = false;
    function preloadImages() {
        if (document.images) {
            button1_over = newImage("images/button1-over.png");
            button1_down = newImage("images/button1-down.png");
            button2_over = newImage("images/button2-over.png");
            button2_down = newImage("images/button2-down.png");
            preloadFlag = true;
        }
    }

    // -->
    </script>

</head>
<body onload="preloadImages();">
<h1>Multi State Anchor Example</h1>
    <div>
    <a href="http://advanceddomscripting.com"
        onmouseover="changeImages('button1', ➥
'images/button1-over.png'); return true;"
        onmouseout="changeImages('button1', ➥
'images/button1.png'); return true;"
        onmousedown="changeImages('button1', ➥
'images/button1-down.png'); return true;"
        onmouseup="changeImages('button1', ➥
'images/button1-over.png'); return true;">
        <img name="button1" src="images/button1.png"
            width="113" height="67" alt="button1"></a>
    <a href="http://advanceddomscripting.com"
        onmouseover="changeImages('button2', ➥
'images/button2-over.png'); return true;"
        onmouseout="changeImages('button2', ➥
'images/button2.png'); return true;"
        onmousedown="changeImages('button2', ➥
'images/button2-down.png'); return true;"
```

```
        onmouseup="changeImages('button2', ➡
'images/button2-over.png'); return true;">
        <img name="button2" src="images/button2.png" ➡
width="113" height="67" alt="button2"></a>
    </div>
</body>
</html>
```

Similarly, the source generated using Adobe (formerly Macromedia) Dreamweaver would resemble this:

```
<html>
<head>
<title>Dreamweaver Example</title>
    <link rel="stylesheet" href="style.css" ➡
type="text/css" media="screen" />

    <script type="text/JavaScript">
    <!--

    function MM_preloadImages() { //v3.0
      var d=document; if(d.images){ if(!d.MM_p) d.MM_p=new Array();
        var i,j=d.MM_p.length,a=MM_preloadImages.arguments;
        for(i=0; i<a.length; i++)
        if (a[i].indexOf("#")!=0){ d.MM_p[j]=new Image;
        d.MM_p[j++].src=a[i];}}
    }

    function MM_swapImgRestore() { //v3.0
      var i,x,a=document.MM_sr;
      for(i=0;a&&i<a.length&&(x=a[i])&&x.oSrc;i++) x.src=x.oSrc;
    }

    function MM_findObj(n, d) { //v4.01
      var p,i,x;  if(!d) d=document;
      if((p=n.indexOf("?"))>0&&parent.frames.length) {
        d=parent.frames[n.substring(p+1)].document;
        n=n.substring(0,p);
      }
      if(!(x=d[n])&&d.all) x=d.all[n];
      for (i=0;!x&&i<d.forms.length;i++) x=d.forms[i][n];
      for(i=0;!x&&d.layers&&i<d.layers.length;i++)
          x=MM_findObj(n,d.layers[i].document);
      if(!x && d.getElementById) x=d.getElementById(n); return x;
    }

    function MM_swapImage() { //v3.0
      var i,j=0,x,a=MM_swapImage.arguments; document.MM_sr=new Array;
      for(i=0;i<(a.length-2);i+=3)
```

43

```
            if ((x=MM_findObj(a[i]))!=null){document.MM_sr[j++]=x;
            if(!x.oSrc) x.oSrc=x.src; x.src=a[i+2];}
        }


        //-->
        </script>

    </head>
    <body onload="MM_preloadImages('images/button1-over.png')">
    <h1>Multi State Anchor Example</h1>
    <div>
        <a href="http://advanceddomscripting.com"
            onmouseover="MM_swapImage('button1','', ➥
    'images/button1-over.png',1)"
            onmouseout="MM_swapImgRestore()"
            onmousedown="MM_swapImage('button1','', ➥
    'images/button1-down.png',1)"
            onmouseup="MM_swapImgRestore()">
            <img id="button1" src="images/button1.png"
                width="113" height="67" alt="Button1"></a>
        <a href="http://advanceddomscripting.com"
            onmouseover="MM_swapImage('button2','', ➥
    'images/button2-over.png',1)"
            onmouseout="MM_swapImgRestore()"
            onmousedown="MM_swapImage('button2','', ➥
    'images/button2-down.png',1)"
            onmouseup="MM_swapImgRestore()">
            <img id="button2" src="images/button2.png" ➥
    width="113" height="67" alt="Button2"></a>
    </div>
    </body>
    </html>
```

The site contains two linked images (check the source in chapter1/rollovers/), but as you can see, the JavaScript code overpowers any markup. Arguably, each uses a few reusable functions that could be simply extracted out to an external source file, but in the case of the ImageReady example, some variables are hard-coded in to the preload() function, so you can't extract that from the page without the JavaScript source relying on that specific page. This isn't a very friendly situation for users or developers. It would be much better to mark up the page without any inline script at all and include the necessary JavaScript files in the head of the document. The JavaScript file could then be responsible for enhancing the document structure as needed, using a load event:

```
<!DOCTYPE html PUBLIC "-//W3C//DTD XHTML 1.0 Strict//EN"
        "http://www.w3.org/TR/xhtml1/DTD/xhtml1-strict.dtd">
<html xmlns="http://www.w3.org/1999/xhtml">
<head>
    <title>Multi State Anchor Example</title>
    <link rel="stylesheet" href="style.css" type="text/css" media="screen" />
```

```
<script src="../../ADS-final-verbose.js" type="text/javascript"></script>
<script src="unobtrusiveRollovers.js"
    type="text/javascript"></script>
</head>
<body>
<h1>Multi State Anchor Example</h1>
<div>
    <a href="http://advanceddomscripting.com" ➥
class="multiStateAnchor">
        <img src="images/button1.png" width="113" ➥
height="67" alt="Button 1" />
    </a>
    <a href="http://advanceddomscripting.com" ➥
class="multiStateAnchor">
        <img src="images/button2.png" width="113" ➥
height="67" alt="Button 2" />
    </a>
</div>
</body>
</html>
```

This creates a much smaller and easier to read document. It can also function in the exact same manner as the two WYSIWYG versions if you follow a few rules:

1. Append -over and -down to the image file names to indicate the mouseover and mousedown states.

2. Add class="multiStateAnchor" to each anchor enclosing the single image you wish to modify.

If you follow these rules, you can use the following unobtrusive and reusable unobtrusiveRollovers.js script file, along with your ADS library, to modify as many anchors on the page so that they act the same way the WYSIWYG versions do:

```
function registerMultiStateAnchorListeners➥
(anchor,anchorImage,path,extension) {
    // Load the over state image
    // the loading will occur asynchronously
    // to the rest of the script
    var imageMouseOver = new Image()
    imageMouseOver.src = path + '-over' + extension;

    // Change the image source to the over image on mouseover
    ADS.addEvent(anchor, 'mouseover', function (W3CEvent) {
        anchorImage.src = imageMouseOver.src;
    });

    // Change the image source to the original on mouseout
    ADS.addEvent(anchor, 'mouseout', function (W3CEvent) {
        anchorImage.src = path + extension;
    });
```

```javascript
    // Load the down state image
    var imageMouseDown = new Image()
    imageMouseDown.src = path + '-down' + extension;

    // Change the image source to the down state on mousedown
    ADS.addEvent(anchor, 'mousedown', function (W3CEvent) {
        anchorImage.src = imageMouseDown.src;
    });

    // Change the image source to the original state on mouseup
    ADS.addEvent(anchor, 'mouseup', function (W3CEvent) {
        anchorImage.src = path + extension;
    });
}

function initMultiStateAnchors(W3CEvent) {

    // Locate all the anchors on the page
    var anchors = ADS.getElementsByClassName('multiStateAnchor', ➥
 'a', document);

    // Loop through the list
    for (var i=0; i<anchors.length ; i++) {

        // Find the first child image within the anchor
        var anchorImage = anchors[i].getElementsByTagName('img')[0];

        if(anchorImage) {

            // If there is an image, parse the source
            var extensionIndex = anchorImage.src.lastIndexOf('.');
            var path= anchorImage.src.substr(0, extensionIndex);
            var extension= anchorImage.src.substring(
                extensionIndex,
                anchorImage.src.length
            );

            // Add the various mouse handlers
            // and pre-load the images.
            registerMultiStateAnchorListeners(
                anchors[i],
                anchorImage,
                path,
                extension
            );
        }
    }
}
```

```
// Modified the tagged anchors when the document loads
ADS.addEvent(window,'load',initMultiStateAnchors);
```

Reading from bottom up, this file does several things. First, the script registers a window load event listener using the initMultiStateAnchors() function and the ADS.addEvent() function discussed earlier in the chapter:

```
ADS.addEvent(window,'load',initMultiStateAnchors);
```

The initMultiStateAnchors() function is responsible for locating all the links with the initMultiStateAnchors() class and registering the appropriate mouse event listener on each. To do so, initMultiStateAnchors() uses the ADS.getElementByClassName() function, discussed earlier in the chapter, to retrieve a list of all the <a> anchor tags relative to the document that have the required initMultiStateAnchors() class somewhere in the class property of the tag:

```
var anchors = ADS.getElementsByClassName('multiStateAnchor', ➥
'a', document);
```

After that, it's just a simple matter of looping through the list and parsing the src property of the first <img> tag within each anchor:

```
// Loop through the list
for (var i=0; i<anchors.length ; i++) {

    // Find the first child image within the anchor
    var anchorImage = anchors[i].getElementsByTagName('img')[0];

    if(anchorImage) {

        // If there is an image, parse the source
        var extensionIndex = anchorImage.src.lastIndexOf('.');
        var path= anchorImage.src.substr(0, extensionIndex);
        var extension= anchorImage.src.substring(
            extensionIndex,
            anchorImage.src.length
        );

        // Add the various mouse handlers and pre-load the images.
        registerMultiStateAnchorListeners(
            anchors[i],
            anchorImage,
            path,
            extension
        );
    }
}
```

Here, we're using the first element in the array returned from ADS.getElementsByTagName('img'), which contains the image elements within the anchor element. You could easily modify this source to affect multiple images within the anchor or some other set of associated tags; that's up to you.

Finally, the mousedown and mouseover images are preloaded, and the events for each anchor are registered using a third function, registerMultiStateAnchorListeners(), to maintain the proper scope and values for each anchor:

```
function registerMultiStateAnchorListeners➡
(anchor,anchorImage,path,extension) {

    var imageMouseOver = new Image()
    imageMouseOver.src = path + '-over' + extension;

    ADS.addEvent(anchor, 'mouseover', function (W3CEvent) {
        anchorImage.src = imageMouseOver.src;
    });

    ... cut ...
}
```

Running the assembled script results in the same behavior as the WYSIWYG editor, only your hand-coded one is much easier to maintain and is 100 percent reusable as long as you follow the naming conventions you set for yourself at the start. If you want to add more links with rollovers, you just add a link as normal with the appropriate class and make sure your images are available on the server.

Summary

While integrating your DOM scripts and behavior enhancements into your web applications, you'll save the most time, money, and effort by following the accepted best practices in all your code. Best practices will also help you avoid common pitfalls, such as inaccessible and dysfunctional sites and overloaded source code. Others have come before you and encountered similar problems, so learn from their example, and focus your attention on creativity instead of frustration.

This chapter also revealed that in testing and developing your sites, WYSIWYG editors, inline JavaScript, browser version checking, and script-based content may seem like the obvious, simple, and easy ways to go, but you shouldn't be tempted to do things the quick-and-dirty way over the correct way. Sometimes, following best practices and standards requires you to put in a little more effort in the short term. In the long run, though, you'll save yourself grief, as the right way will always work, but the wrong way will always fail you at some point—it's just a matter of when.

Using common functions like addEvent() and getElementByClass() will make your code easier to understand, but don't let yourself get carried away with using libraries just for the sake of using libraries. Understanding why you should use each function is just as important as understanding how it works. See Chapter 9 more on using and abusing JavaScript libraries.

This chapter also covered a lot of the common gotchas you may encounter in the JavaScript language. You've probably already discovered that JavaScript is wonderfully powerful and wonderfully frustrating all at the same time. Anonymous functions and scope chains aside, the majority of what you'll be doing is pretty straightforward once you get the hang of it.

Throughout the rest of this book, I'll be continually referring back to the ideas in this chapter, so you'll come to understand them well, and you'll be adding even more methods to the ADS library you created here. Now, let's dive deeper into JavaScript in Chapter 2 and see how you can go about creating your own objects.

Chapter 2

CREATING YOUR OWN REUSABLE OBJECTS

JavaScript is all about objects. Objects are the foundation of everything, so if you're unfamiliar with objects, you're going to learn quickly. The goal of this book is not to be a JavaScript or DOM code reference, but in order to make sure you understand a lot of the examples and ideas I'll be presenting, we'll spend a little time discussing objects. A strong understanding of how objects work, specifically in JavaScript, and how fundamental they are will also go a long way in allowing you to create generic, reusable code that saves you time and money.

I need to introduce you to a few key things to remember when working with objects:

- What objects are and how they're constructed
- The difference between static, public, private, and privileged members
- What this refers to
- A bit more about the scope chain
- A bit about object context

At the end of this chapter, we'll build a custom debugging log object to put all this to good use and show how proper definition of members creates a clean, public application programming interface (API) for your objects.

What's in an object?

You've already used objects even though you may not know it. An object, in simplistic terms, is an instance of a contained set of variables, known as properties, combined with functions, known as methods. Objects are usually based on a description called as a class that defines what properties and methods the object will have. Your script can be considered object oriented (OO), as it is constructed using the interaction of various objects. In particular, JavaScript is a prototype-style OO language where there are no classes, and everything is based on a copy of an existing object. Everything from a function to a string is actually an object, and that's what makes JavaScript powerful and frustrating at the same time. Most objects can be grouped into two types:

- Function objects, such as the alert() function, allow you to use arguments to alter the functionality of the object:

  alert('argument');

- Object objects, such as the obj represented in the following snippet, can't be called like functions and have a fixed functionality unless they contain additional Function objects, which you'll see in the "Understanding object members" section:

  var obj = new Object();
  obj('argument'); //will error as obj is not a Function

Function objects can also be divided into two subgroups:

- Function instances, such as alert(), are invoked using arguments.
- Functions that are constructors must be instantiated with the new operator.

To help you out, JavaScript also comes with several built-in objects such as the following:

- Object is the generic base object you can use to create simple static objects.
- Function is the object cloned by all objects that use arguments and is the object you create when defining all the functions in your scripts.
- Array is a special grouping of properties and methods, such as length, that give you iterative access to the object and allow you to access the properties using square bracket notation.
- String, Boolean, and Number are the objects representing all your string, Boolean, and number values respectively.
- Math, Date, RegExp, and several others are included; each has its own unique uses, but we won't get into them all here.

All these built-in objects are instantiated with the new keyword or some other special syntax, such as the function keyword for the Function object, curly brace short form ({}) for Object, and bracket short form ([]) for Array. What's important is that each of these objects provides a set of properties and methods that allow you to manipulate the object in a different way, depending on the object's intended use.

> We'll discuss the new operator and instantiation when you create your own object later in the chapter.

Inheritance

Object inheritance is an important part of object-oriented programming. When creating your own objects, you can extend or inherit properties and methods from existing objects. This inheritance provides a convenient way to reuse the functionality of existing objects, so you can be free to focus on the new and improved code.

Unlike traditional class-based object-oriented languages, there is no underlying class structure to extend one class from another. In JavaScript, inheritance is simply done by copying the methods from one object prototype to another, but the resulting concept is the same:

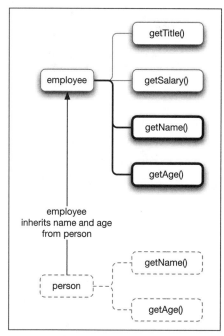

```
// Create a person object instance
var person = {};
person.getName = function() { ... };
person.getAge = function() { ... };

// Create an employee object instance
var employee = {};
employee.getTitle = function() { ... };
employee.getSalary = function() { ... };

// Inherit methods from person
employee.getName = person.getName;
employee.getAge = person.getAge;
```

Each higher object inherits all of the properties and methods of the lower objects, as shown in Figure 2-1.

Figure 2-1.
The general idea of inheritance

> *For more on the specifics of inheritance and some fancy methods that allow you to achieve a close approximation to the classical method, I suggest you check out Douglas Crockford's explanation of "Classical Inheritance in JavaScript" at* http://www.crockford.com/javascript/inheritance.html.

Understanding object members

You're already familiar with plain old functions such as alert(). Functions are just the simple reusable containers that allow you to avoid redundancy in your code. Likewise, you're already familiar with objects, properties, and methods, but you may not know it. When you use something like the body property of a document:

```
document.body
```

or the getElementById() method of a document:

```
document.getElementById('example');
```

you're accessing a member of the document object. Properties and methods are collectively referred to as the members of the object, because they belong to that parent object, in this case document. The body member is a property, because it simply references a single value, whereas the getElementById() member is a method, because it accepts arguments and can manipulate the internal state of the object.

Properties themselves are really just instances of the Object object or another object that extends from Object, such as String or Number. Likewise, methods also extend from the Object object, but because they accept arguments, they're instances of the Function object, so they can also return a value.

You can see the type of object for both body and getElementById by trying the following in the load event in the test document in chapter2/types/types.html:

```
ADS.addEvent(window,'load', function() {
    alert('document.body is a: ' + document.body);
});
```

This event will show that document.body is an [object HTMLBodyElement] object in Firefox and Opera as shown in Figure 2-2.

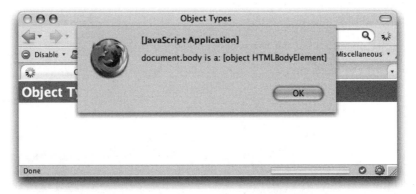
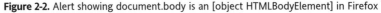

Figure 2-2. Alert showing document.body is an [object HTMLBodyElement] in Firefox

The event will show an [object BODY] in Safari, as illustrated in Figure 2-3.

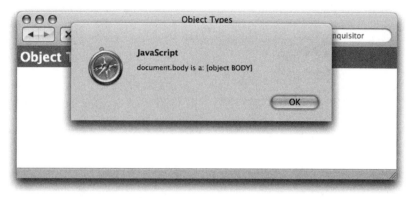

Figure 2-3. Alert showing document.body is an [object BODY] in Safari

It will display [object] in Microsoft Internet Explorer, as shown in Figure 2-4.

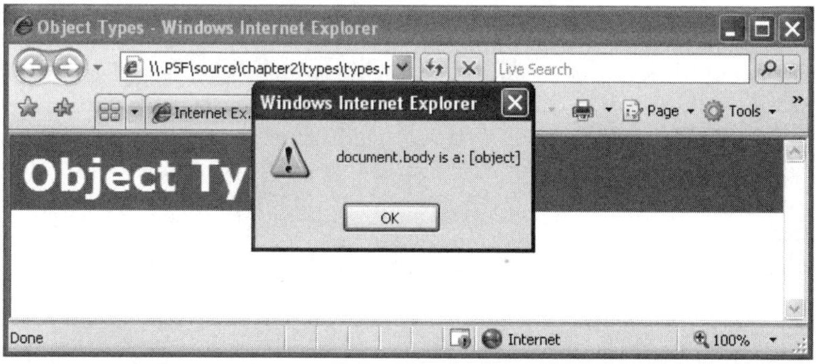

Figure 2-4. Alert showing document.body is an [object] in Microsoft Internet Explorer

These differences among the browsers result from the way DOM objects are handled. If the browser is following the W3C DOM Core and DOM HTML naming conventions, the document.body should be an instance of the DOM HTMLBodyElement object. In Safari, the BODY object represents document.body, and in Internet Explorer, it's simply an object. In both Safari and Internet Explorer, the respective objects still contain many of the HTMLBodyElement methods, but the object's not officially exposed as an HTMLBodyElement object.

If you try alerting the document.getElementById method—without the parentheses that would otherwise execute the method, you'll see that document.getElementById is a function in all browsers; see Figure 2-5:

```
ADS.addEvent(window,'load',function() {
    alert('document.getElementById is a: ' + document.getElementById);
});
```

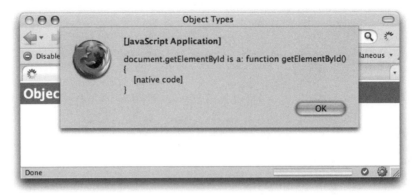

Figure 2-5. Alert showing document.getElementById is a native code function

> *You may be curious why those last two examples reported the object's type when simply alerting the object itself. When an object is passed to a process that is expecting a string value, such as the* alert() *function, the* Object's toString() *method is called to retrieve the a string representation of the object. The* toString() *method originates in the base* Object *and converts the object to a string representation, which is often just the name of the type of object. In the case of* document.body, *the string representation is simply the phrase* [HTMLBodyElement] *(or an alternative), because that's what the* document.body.toString() *method specifies. The* toString() *method on other objects, such as* String *or* HTMLAnchorElement, *returns a different value, such as the value of the string or the content of the* href *on an anchor.*

We'll discuss the various DOM methods and objects later in Chapter 3. All you need to know now is that, like everything else, they're made up of Object objects and Function objects.

Everything's in the window object

If you haven't realized it yet, many of the functions you've been writing are actually methods of the window object. If your script only contains a single function such as the following, it and the built-in functions, such as alert(), are actually methods of a global window object:

```
function myFunction(message) { alert(message); }
```

When you write code in the root of the JavaScript file without another object surrounding it, as you'll find in the chapter2/window/with-without.html file, executing it using the following line:

```
myFunction('Without window object');
```

is exactly the same as executing:

```
window.myFunction('With window object');
```

However, if you create the function within another object, the scope chain applies, and things start to get a little more complicated. To demonstrate, try the following exercise.

Overriding an object in the scope chain

In this simple exercise, you'll see how you can override JavaScript's alert() method and, in some cases, still access the original by referencing the window object directly.

1. Create a simple HTML document called override.html, and include an override.js file in the head:

```
<!DOCTYPE html PUBLIC "-//W3C//DTD XHTML 1.0 Strict//EN"
        "http://www.w3.org/TR/xhtml1/DTD/xhtml1-strict.dtd">
<html xmlns="http://www.w3.org/1999/xhtml">
<head>
<title>Override the alert() method</title>
    <link rel="stylesheet" href="style.css"
        type="text/css" media="screen" />
    <script type="text/javascript" src="override.js"></script>
</head>
<body>
    <h1>Override the alert() method</h1>
    <p>Interesting isn't it?</p>
</body>
</html>
```

2. Create the override.js file, and include the following override() function:

```
function override() {
    // Override the alert function
    var alert = function(message) {
        window.alert('overridden:' + message);
    };
    alert('alert');

    // Call the original alert from the override() scope
    window.alert('window.alert');
}
override();

// Call the alert in the window scope
alert('alert from outside');
```

3. Load the page in your web browser.

> If you're running Internet Explorer 7 with tighter security settings, you may notice some warnings about overriding the alert(). The browser is warning you that you're about to override a JavaScript function, but since that's the whole point of this example, just click Accept, and ignore it.

After loading the page, you'll get three alert boxes. The first alert, shown in Figure 2-6, indicates that the alert() method has been overridden.

Figure 2-6. Alert showing the result of an overridden alert box

The second alert, shown in Figure 2-7, shows that you can still access the regular method through window.alert().

Figure 2-7. Alert indicating access to the original alert method after it has been overridden

And the third alert, shown in Figure 2-8, shows that the regular alert() method is still available as usual from outside the override() function.

As you can see, you've overridden the window's alert() method by declaring a new alert() method, but it only applies within the scope of the override() function:

```
var alert = function(message) {
    window.alert('overridden:' + message);
};
```

Figure 2-8. Alert indicating access to the original alert method outside the override function

The var keyword maintains the scope of your new custom alert method to within the override() function as you saw in Figure 2-6. By referencing window.alert() from within your new alert() method, you can still access the original, unmodified version of the alert() in the global window object, as illustrated in Figure 2-9.

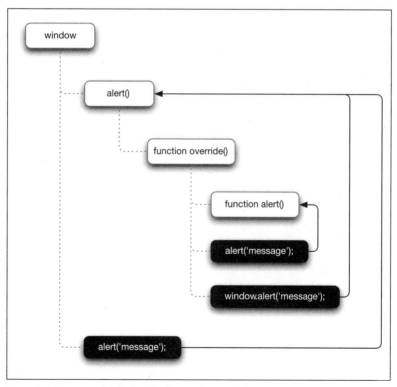

Figure 2-9. The override() function's structure and alert access

Of course, this structure only works as shown in Figure 2-9 because you're overriding and calling alert() from within the override() method. If you had done the following in your override.js file without any surrounding functions:

```
//override the alert function in the window scope
var alert = function(message) {
    window.alert('overridden:' + message);
};

alert('test1');
```

your script would fail because of too much recursion. Overriding the alert() method in the root of your script replaces the window.alert() method with your method, so calling window.alert() from within your alert() method, which is really window.alert(), creates an infinite recursive loop.

Making it all possible with scope and closure

Overriding methods and calling methods from within functions depends on the scope chain within your application and object structure. I already introduced scope chain and closure in Chapter 1 when discussing best practices and JavaScript gotchas. If you haven't read Chapter 1 yet, I suggest you flip back and read the sections on scope resolution and closure before proceeding any further, as I'm going to skip the scope and closure explanations and dive right into objects.

Creating your own objects

To create your own object, let's start off with the simplest object of all: we'll instantiate a new instance of the Object object and assign it to a variable:

```
var myObject = new Object();
```

You can also use the shorthand curly brace syntax:

```
var myObject = {};
```

In either of these cases, your resulting myObject variable is an instance of an Object object, which does nothing special beyond existing as an object. If you're unfamiliar with the concept of instantiation, this may seem a little strange. The new keyword tells JavaScript to create a brand new object based on given object, in this case the Object object. Your new instance is then assigned to a variable, so you can reference that variable to access the new instance of the object. However, for this to work, the object you're instantiating must be a constructor, which is a special kind of method that we'll discuss later in the chapter.

Each of the core objects, such as Object, Function, Array, and String, all have constructors. For example, to create a new Array, you would use the following syntax:

```
var myArray = new Array();
```

The Array object is just like the Object object. However, Array is extended from Object and adds additional properties and methods, such as length.

Once an object has been instantiated, you can't use the new operator on the new instance to create another instance. If you try to use the following script, you will get an error as shown in Figure 2-10:

```
var anotherObject = new myObject();
```

Figure 2-10. An error indicating that myObect() is not a constructor

Your myObject is *already* an instance, so using new on the instance to create another instance is invalid. You can, however, create as many new instances of the original Object as you like.

Unless you're adding your own properties or methods to your new object, the default Object isn't very useful all by itself. To make your own objects serve some purpose beyond an empty container, you need to add properties or methods to them. Also, if you want to be able to replicate your object several times, you'll need to create it as a constructor with varying degrees of access to its internal properties and methods, which you'll do next.

One becomes many: creating the constructor

The Function object serves as the starting point for creating your own constructors. Take the following myConstructor function created using the function keyword:

```
function myConstructor(a) {
    // Some code
}
```

This probably looks familiar, since you've already used functions many times, and you may also have see it defined using an alternative syntax:

```
var myConstructor = function(a) {
    // Some code
}
```

Both syntaxes are functionally equivalent to writing

```
var myConstructor = new Function('a','/* Some code */');
```

but creating functions with the new keyword in this way has performance implications, so stick with the function keyword.

Function objects are special in that the instance of the function can also act as a constructor method, which allows you to create new instances of the function. It's perfectly valid to take any of the preceding myConstructor Function objects and instantiate it with the new operator:

```
var myObject = new myConstructor();
```

In this instance, the myConstructor function acts as the constructor method you would find in class-based OO languages. When the object is instantiated, the constructor will immediately execute any code you've included, as follows:

```
function myConstructor(message) {
    alert(message);
    this.myMessage = message;
}
var myObject = new myConstructor('Instantiating myObject!');
```

Upon instantiation of myObject, the browser will immediately alert, as shown in Figure 2-11.

Figure 2-11. Alert during page load showing that the object constructor was executed immediately upon instantiation

In this case, your message argument is also assigned as the myMessage property of myObject using the this keyword. For now, I'll just say that this refers to the myObject instance, but I'll explain the this keyword in more detail later in the chapter.

Now, with the assignment of the message argument to this.myMessage, myObject has a property called myMessage that's accessible at any time. To retrieve message from the instance, you simply access the myMessage property directly:

```
var message = myObject.myMessage;
```

The key thing for you to remember here is that the myMessage property is only available on the *instantiated* instance of myConstructor, not the myConstructor function itself.

Adding static methods

Before we discuss adding public methods with the prototype property, I'd like to point out an area where people often get confused. In reading about and looking at other JavaScript examples, you may have seen something like this:

```
// Create an Object object instance
var myObject = new Object(); //or var example = {};

// Add a property
myObject.name = 'Jeff';

// Add a method
myObject.alertName = function() {
    alert(this.name);
}

// Execute the method
myObject.alertName();
```

In this case, a property name and method alertName() have been added as static members to the example object by simply using the dot notation directly on the myObject object instance. And that's where the confusion lies. Static members exist only on a specific *instance* of an object, not the constructor. It's valid code and will work just as expected for that instance, but it will only work for that single myObject instance of Object.

The same applies if you use the Function object as the starting point, which makes the object act as a constructor:

```
// Create a Function object instance
var myConstructor = function() {
    //some code
}

// Add a static property
myConstructor.name = 'Jeff';

// Add a method
myConstructor.alertName = function() {
    alert(this.name);
}

// Execute the method
myConstructor.alertName();
```

Again, this works fine, as myConstructor acts as both an instance and a constructor, but the name and alertName members don't apply to any new instances of myConstructor. Creating another instance of myConstructor and trying to access those members, as follows

```
var anotherExample = new myConstructor();
anotherExample.alertName();
```

will result in an error:

```
TypeError: anotherExample.alertName is not a function
```

Understanding the difference between instances and constructors will help clear up many questions you may have had.

Adding public methods to the prototype

You need to modify the constructor's prototype if you want to include public methods when you instantiate new objects. When I say "prototype," I'm not referring to the Prototype JavaScript Framework (http://prototypejs.org), I'm referring to the prototype property of the object. The prototype property is a special member that defines the internal structure of the object itself. It acts sort of like a traditional class would in other object-oriented languages but not exactly. If you're unfamiliar with object-oriented programming and/or prototype frameworks, you can think of the prototype member as a blueprint for the object, but a blueprint that, if altered, instantly alters all the objects and instances based on it.

When you alter the prototype of an object, any object that inherits that object and all instances of that object that already exist will immediately inherit the identical changes. This is both powerful and problematic depending on how you use it, so be cautious when you're altering the prototype of an existing object that isn't your own.

To include public methods in new instances of myConstructor, you simply add a method to its prototype using dot notation:

```
// Create the constructor
function myConstructor(message) {
    alert(message);
    this.myMessage = message;
}

// Add a public method
myConstructor.prototype.clearMessage = function(string) {
    this.myMessage += ' ' + string;
}
```

Unlike the example earlier in the chapter where dot notation was used to add members to an existing instance of an object, adding to the prototype member adds this new method to the myConstructor's underlying definition but not to the myConstructor instance itself!

Calling the clearMessage() method on a new instance will work as planned:

```
var myObject = new myConstructor('Hello World!');
myObject.clearMessage();
```

But you can't call it on myConstructor directly, as the myConstructor instance is an instance of the Function object, not the myConstructor object:

```
myConstructor.clearMessage();
// TypeError: myConstructor.clearMessage is not a function
```

Public methods are perfect for most of the functionality you'll be adding to your objects, but in some cases, you'll want to add a method or property that will only be used internally within the object and isn't intended to be publicly accessible to everyone. In these cases, you want a private or privileged member, which we'll discuss next.

Controlling access with private and privileged members

So far, you've seen how to add public members for your object instances. Providing properties and methods that are all public is fine in most cases, where all the members and methods are required to interact with your object. What if you want to include a member for internal use only you need to use private or privileged members? These can be especially useful in libraries to prevent people from using internal methods in ways you didn't anticipate.

You may be surprised to know that you're already quite familiar with creating private members and have probably used them before. Private members are simply variables and functions defined within another function. To add a private alertMessage() method and private separator property to your previous myConstructor function, you would simply define them using the common var and function keywords within the constructor function:

```
function myConstructor(message) {
    this.myMessage = message;

    // Private properties
    var separator = ' -';
    var myOwner = this;

    // Private method
    function alertMessage() {
        alert(myOwner.message);
    }
    // Show the message on instantiation
    alertMessage();
}
```

You may notice the example also includes an additional private property called myOwner, which refers to this. Assigning this to myOwner will allow your private methods to access the instance of myConstructor by referencing myOwner. Private methods are self-contained objects that exist within the scope of the constructor. They're not real methods on the prototype, so this within the private method will refer to the private method instance, not the myConstructor instance. In the scope chain, myOwner within the private member will resolve to the parent myConstructor instance, as shown in Figure 2-12. I'll discuss the this keyword in more detail later in the chapter in the "What is this?" section.

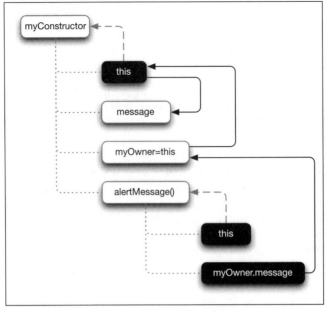

Figure 2-12. Using a myOwner variable to represent the this keyword from the outer scope

You also can't access these private members from outside the object, because they are confined to the scope of the constructor method. Trying to access them in the myObject instance using myObject. alertMessage() or myObject.separator will fail, but at the same time, because they're confined *strictly* to the scope of your constructor, they also can't be accessed from your object's own public methods. If you try to access separator from a public method on the prototype as follows:

```
myConstructor.prototype.appendToMessage = function(string) {
    this.myMessage += separator + string; // will error
}
```

you'll get an error indicating separator is not defined, because the private separator property only exists in your object's constructor. To overcome this limitation, you'll need to use a privileged member instead.

Unlike private methods, privileged methods can be accessed publicly while still maintaining access to private members. Privileged methods are defined within the scope of the constructor using the this keyword:

```
function myConstructor(message) {
    this.myMessage = message;
    var separator = ' -';
    var myOwner = this;

    function alertMessage() {
        alert(myOwner.myMessage);
```

```
    }
    alertMessage();

    // A privileged method
    this.appendToMessage = function(string) {
        this.myMessage += separator + string;
        alertMessage();
    }
}
```

By creating the method this way, your myConstructor has the same appendToMessage() method as the previous prototype example, but now your appendToMessage() method falls within the scope of the constructor and has access to the private separator member through the scope chain. To verify this, instantiate the object, and try it out using the example in chapter2/myConstructor/privleged. html:

```
var myObject = new myConstructor('Hello World!');
myObject.appendToMessage('Jeff');
```

You'll get an alert with Hello World! during instantiation and another with Hello World! -Jeff, because your private separator and alertMessage() members are accessible by your appendToMessage() method. But at the same time, you can't directly access the private alertMessage() using the following line:

```
myObject.alertMessage();
// Error: myObject.alertMessage is not a function
```

At this point, myConstructor is rather simplistic. Later in the chapter, you'll see this sort of thing in action while creating a useful JavaScript debugging object.

Do public, private, privileged, and static really matter?

You may be asking, "Who cares? Why should I be worrying about all this public, private, privileged, and static stuff, and how will it affect my DOM scripting?" If your code is for you alone and no one else will ever see it, then it probably doesn't really matter if your methods are all public. The problem arises when you start sharing your code with multiple developers. Only you know how you *should* use it and what you should and shouldn't do—no one else knows. By defining everything as public, there's no distinction between the public parts of the object and the internal workings. It's confusing to others which members they should be using and which members are just there for use by the object itself. It becomes especially difficult if you don't provide proper documentation. There are lots of libraries on the web, but sometimes it's almost impossible to decipher what's part of the public API and what's part of the private API.

Assembled, your myConstructor() object clearly indicates which members are public and private, so there's no confusion:

```
// Constructor
function myConstructor(message) {
    this.myMessage = message;
```

```
        // Private properties
        var separator = ' -';
        var myOwner = this;

        // Private method
        function alertMessage() {
            alert(myOwner.myMessage);
        }
        alertMessage();

        // Privileged method (still public)
        this.appendToMessage = function(string) {
            this.myMessage += separator + string;
            alertMessage();
        }
    }

    // Public method
    myConstructor.prototype.clearMessage = function(string) {
        this.myMessage = '';
    }

    // Static property
    myConstructor.name = 'Jeff';

    // Static method
    myConstructor.alertName = function() {
        alert(this.name);
    }
```

Understanding the proper way to create objects will make it easier for you and others to use your objects. Also, keeping the following rules in mind will ensure you define things properly:

- Private and privileged members are inside the function, so they go along with every instance of the function.
- Public prototype members are part of the object's blueprint and apply to every instantiated instance of that object, created by the new keyword.
- Static members apply only to a particular instance of an object.

The object literal

So far, the examples in this chapter have all been using dot notation to create objects, members, and the like. I chose this syntax intentionally to initially describe the object model, because you're probably already familiar with dot notation. For a familiar example, you've probably accessed elements using dot notation such as:

```
var h1Elements = document.getElementById('example').➡
getElementsByTagName('h1');
```

Likewise, you've probably assigned values using dot notation:

```
document.getElementById('example).style.color = 'green';
```

When it comes to objects, you've also already used this same dot notation to define a method in the prototype of your myConstructor:

```
myConstructor.prototype.clearMessage = function() { }
```

The object literal, however, is an alternative syntax that is much cleaner and easier to read, especially when adding multiple members. With this syntax, the curly braces represent the object structure:

```
var myObject = {
    propertyA:'value',
    propertyB:'value',
    methodA:function() { },
    methodB:function() { },
    methodC:function() { },
    methodD:function() { }
}
```

which works in exactly same way as the following copy-and-paste method but is much nicer:

```
var myObject = new Object();
myObject.propertyA = 'value';
myObject.propertyB = 'value';
myObject.methodA = function() { };
myObject.methodB = function() { };
myObject.methodC = function() { };
myObject.methodD = function() { };
```

When using the following short form:

```
var myObject = {};
```

you are doing this:

```
var myObject = new Object();
```

The key/value pairs in the syntax {key:value,key:value} become static members of the object. If you specify the value using an anonymous function, it becomes a method; otherwise, it's a property. This is the same notation you'll find in JavaScript Object Notation (JSON), which we'll discuss in Chapter 7. Just remember that the object literal syntax automatically creates an instance of an Object object, so you can't reinstantiate it using the new keyword.

To build a constructor with public methods using the same object literal syntax, you still need to start with a Function object as the constructor:

```
function myConstructor() {
    // Private and privileged members
};
```

or you can use this alternative syntax:

```
var myConstructor = fuction() {
    // Private and privileged members
};
```

> A note of caution with the second syntax in the previous example. When the browser parses your script and comes across a function defined using the first syntax, function example() { . . . }, the example() function will be declared immediately before the script begins to execute. This means you can make calls to example() from anywhere in the script—even if the call to the function occurs before the definition.
>
> With the second alternative syntax, var example2 = function() { . . . }, the example2() function doesn't exist until the script's execution reaches that point in the script. If you try to call example2() before the definition has occurred, it will fail.

You can then use the object literal to populate the prototype property with all your public members:

```
function myConstructor() {
    // Private and privileged members
};

// Public members
myConstructor.prototype = {
    propertyA:'value',
    propertyB:'value',
    methodA:function() { },
    methodB:function() { },
    methodC:function() { },
    methodD:function() { }
}
```

Again, it works exactly same way as the dot syntax, and the only difference is the presentation. Which method you decide to use is up to you. Personally, I prefer the object literal syntax, as it's less redundant and easier to read, so many of my examples throughout the book will use the object literal syntax.

If you're using the object literal, beware of trailing commas. If you define your object and leave a comma on the end of the last item as follows, you're implying a null last item:

```
var badObjectLiteral = {
    a:1,
    b:2, // Extra comma
}
```

Firefox and Mozilla browsers will ignore the null entry, but Internet Explorer will complain with an error when it tries to parse the object. I believe here that Internet Explorer is actually doing the right thing and not trying to fix your ambiguous or broken code, but when copying and pasting large sections of code, on more than one occasion, I've been caught with a working script in Firefox and a broken one in Internet Explorer.

What is this?

this is an ornery beast. Most programmers would consider this to be an identifier, something that refers to a common element within the current scope of the script or object. With JavaScript, however, that's not always the case; this is considered a keyword, and it's resolved depending on the execution context in which it's used. Follow that? Here's an example to clarify:

```
var sound = 'Roar!';
function myOrneryBeast() {
    this.style.color='green';
    alert(sound);
}
```

The this keyword refers to the object of which the containing function is a method when called. So what does that mean for the myOrneryBeast() function? Well, as we discussed earlier, your entire script, every bit of code, is contained within a global object called window. The myOrneryBeast() function is a method of window, the same way the appendToMessage() and clearMessage() functions were methods of your earlier myConstructor. In the root of the script, this refers to the window object. You can see for yourself by running the following line without any wrapping methods or objects, which will reveal the alert in Figure 2-13.

```
alert('Does window === this? ' + (window === this));
```

Figure 2-13. Alert indicating that the window object is equal to this in the context of the root of the script

The alert confirms that this is, indeed, the same as the window object. But how does that apply to this used within the context of the myOrneryBeast() function?

As it stands right now, the myOrneryBeast() function resides as a method of the window object. If you were to just run the function as is

```
myOrneryBeast();
```

the this keyword within the function would resolve to the object of which the containing function is a method when called, so this.style.color would refer to window.style.color, because myOrneryBeast() is called in the context of window, as illustrated in Figure 2-14.

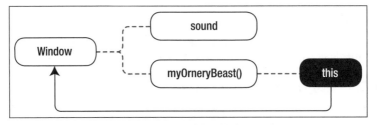

Figure 2-14. The scope chain evaluation of the this keyword

In this case, the myOrneryBeast() method won't be very happy, because style isn't a valid property of the window object. The context of this can change as the method is assigned to different objects, such as an attribute event listener, or by using your ADS.addEvent() method from Chapter 1:

```
var sound = 'Roar!';
function myOrneryBeast() {
    this.style.color='green';
    alert(sound);
}

function initPage() {
    var example = ADS.$('example');

    // Using the event attribute method
    example.onclick = myOrneryBeast;

    // or using the ADS.addEvent method
    ADS.addEvent(example,'mouseover', myOrneryBeast);

}
ADS.addEvent(window,'load',initPage);
```

> *Like good little developers, we're testing here using an included script file and an unobtrusive* load *event listener. The only requirement of the test page in this instance is that it contain an element with* id="example" *and that the* ADS.addEvent() *function is also available. For playing, you could just add this code in the* <head> *inline using* <script> *tags. But I always say that practice makes perfect, so why not set up your sandbox environment the same way you would your production environment? If you're always doing it the correct way, you won't be as tempted to fall back on bad habits!*

Using either event registration model, the element will turn green when clicked, and we'll see 'Roar!' Correct? Are you sure? Yes! You're correct. But the real question is *why*?

Recall that in Chapter 1 we discussed scope and closure, and the id of each link was improperly set because the id referred to the closure of the outer functions scope. If the sound variable is still evaluating to 'Roar!', shouldn't this still be referencing the window object? Well, everything is acting as it should, just maybe not as you expected. Remember, JavaScript resolves this as a keyword in context when the event listener is invoked. In the case of the example, both the onclick attribute and click event are methods of example, so this resolves to the object of which this function is a method or rather, the HTML element of which the event is a method, which is the HTML element.

As for your sound variable, sound still poses the same scope and closure issues discussed earlier in Chapter 1, but because sound is always the same and thus doesn't change in the scope of the initPage() function, it will always resolve to 'Roar!' within the scope chain, as shown in Figure 2-15.

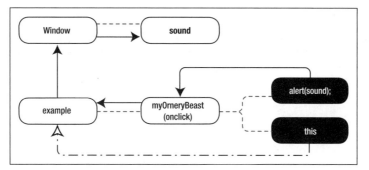

Figure 2-15. How the sound variable is resolved through the scope chain

If you assign something else to sound within the myOrneryBeast() method or elsewhere in the script, the scope chain would reflect those changes. Try experimenting with different values at different locations to see what happens.

Redefining your context with call() and apply()

So far, you've seen how to define your own objects, and you've experimented with this to refer to the object from within methods and the object constructor. Also, you've seen this in the context of a plain old function where it refers to the global window object. That's no big deal; you've got it all down pat. You've also seen how the context of this changes as the function is attached to other objects, such as HTML elements. If you've got all of that sorted out, you're off to a very good start, but there's a problem in that last example, where the context changes. What if that's not the desired effect?

Take the following example, found in chapter2/doubleCheck/without-context.html:

```
function doubleCheck() {
    this.message = 'Are you sure you want to leave?';
}
doubleCheck.prototype.sayGoodbye = function() {
    return confirm(this.message);
}
initPage() {
    var clickedLink = new doubleCheck();
    var links = document.getElementsByTagName('a');
```

```
        for (var i=0 ; i<links.length ; i++) {
            ADS.addEvent(links[i], 'click', clickedLink.sayGoodbye);
        }
    }
    ADS.addEvent(window,'load',initPage);
```

The desired effect of this load event is to loop through all the links on your page and assign the clickedLink.sayGoodbye() method as the click event listener. It seems simple enough, but if you think back to what you just learned about this, you can see the problem. You know from the previous example that when the sayGoodbye() method executes in the context of the <a> HTML element, this will now refer to the HTML element, rather than the clickedLink object you were expecting. Hmm . . . so how do you get around the context problem? You use the call() or apply() method of the Function object.

These two methods, which are available on any instance of a Function object, allow you to specify the context within which the function will execute. If you want the method to run with this referring to the window object, you can use either this script

```
    clickedLink.sayGoodbye.call(window);
```

or this one

```
    clickedLink.sayGoodbye.apply(window);
```

In our case, the clickedLink.sayGoodbye() method has no arguments, but if it did, you would pass them as additional arguments to call() or apply(). For call(), each argument should be included after the object, in the following format:

```
    functionReference.call(object, argument1, argument2, ...)
```

With apply(), the additional arguments are passed as a single array in the second argument:

```
    functionReference.apply(object, arguments)
```

This is the only difference between call() and apply().

The apply() method is especially useful when generating an anonymous function wrapper that will adjust the context for you. The function returned from the following bindFunction() method takes the function in the func argument and applies it to the object in the obj argument:

```
    function bindFunction(obj, func) {
        return function() {
            func.apply(obj,arguments);
        };
    }
```

The tricky part is that the anonymous function returned from bindFunction() uses the special internally scoped arguments parameter as the apply() arguments for the externally scoped obj and func. This basically creates a new context around the original function that takes the identical arguments but applies a different context, as shown in Figure 2-16.

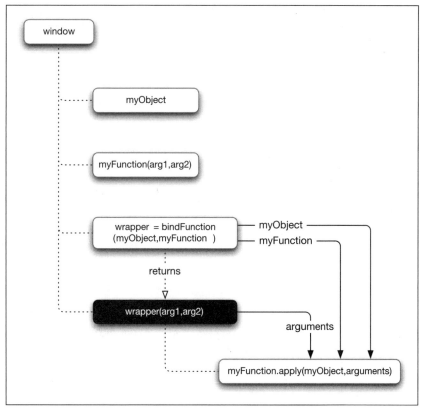

Figure 2-16. Wrapping a function in another function to change context using the apply() method

Take a moment to add the bindFunction() method to your ADS library, as it will come in handy in later chapters:

```
(function(){
if(!window.ADS) { window['ADS'] = {} }
```

... Above here is your existing library ...

```
function bindFunction(obj, func) {
    return function() {
        func.apply(obj,arguments);
    };
};
window['ADS']['bindFunction'] = bindFunction;
```

... Below here is your existing library ...

```
})();
```

With this, you can modify the context of any method simply by using the returned anonymous function as if it were the original function. Applied to the doubleCheck() example, it would now look like this, as found in chapter2/doubleCheck/with-context.html:

```
function doubleCheck() {
    this.message = 'Are you sure you want to leave?';
}
doubleCheck.prototype.sayGoodbye = function() {
    return confirm(this.message);
}

initPage() {
    var clickedLink = new doubleCheck();
    var links = document.getElementsByTagName('a');

    for (var i=0 ; i<links.length ; i++) {
        // remember not to include the () on clickedLink.sayGoodbye
        // as you don't want to execute it.
        ADS.addEvent(
            links[i],
            'click',
            ADS.bindFunction(clickedLink, clickedLink.sayGoodbye)
        );
    }
}
addEvent(window,'load',initPage);
```

With these modifications, the ADS.bindFunction() method returns an anonymous function wrapper where the sayGoodbye() method is called in the context of the clickedLink object as desired, while the anonymous function is assigned as the anchor's event listener. Perfect!

try { }, catch { }, and exceptions

The last things I'll quickly mention about objects are exceptions and how they're used in the try and catch control structures. Dealing with proper use and explaining exceptions could fill an entire chapter in a JavaScript reference book, but since we want to get on to some fun DOM scripting, I'll just give you the one-page condensed version. In many instances, an object will throw an exception to report an error rather than failing silently or returning false. If you try to run the following myOrneryBeast() method within the context of the window object as found in chapter2/myOrneryBeast/exception. html, it will throw the exception TypeError: this.style has no properties, because the style property doesn't exist in the window object:

```
var sound = 'Roar!';
function myOrneryBeast() {
    this.style.color='green';
    alert(sound);
}
myOrneryBeast();
```

This exception will be sent back through scope chain and will cause the method to immediately stop executing. If you haven't done any additional error checking, the error will be logged in the JavaScript error log window or the Firebug console window if you have Firefox and Firebug installed. Alternatively, however, you can catch the exception error in the try/catch control structure and handle it yourself as shown in chapter2/myOrneryBeast/exception-catch.html:

```
var sound = 'Roar!';
function myOrneryBeast() {
    this.style.color='green';
    alert(sound);
}

try {
    myOrneryBeast();
} catch(theException) {
    alert('Oops, we caught an exception! Name: '
        + theException.name
        + ', message: '
        + theException.message
    );
}
```

Running this script will reveal the alert message shown in Figure 2-17.

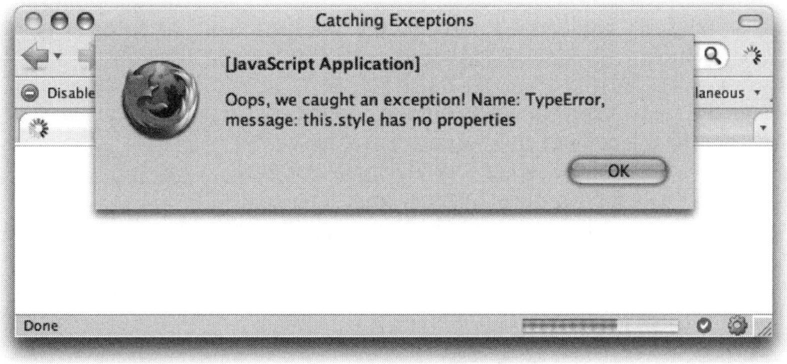

Figure 2-17. Alert showing the result of a captured exception upon page load

With the try/catch control structure in place, you can deal with the error yourself and continue with the appropriate action if desired.

The importance of exceptions will become more apparent as we discuss events in Chapter 4 and Ajax in Chapter 7, but I wanted to mention it here, as some objects (including yours) may also incorporate exceptions, so you should account for them as well.

A practical example: your own debugging log

So far in this chapter, you've learned a lot about objects. To put some of the knowledge to good use, we'll create a quick and simple debugging log object that you can use to replace your alert() debugging techniques. You can use this object in the remainder of this book when experimenting and debugging elements of the DOM.

Why use a JavaScript logging object?

Alert logging is a good starting point to debugging your applications. However, if you've tried to do any sort of DOM scripting, you've probably encountered alert's restrictions. If you try to debug a value of a variable in a large loop, you'll be sitting at your computer clicking OK on the browser alert box for an hour—unless you forcibly quit your browser and restart it. Or maybe you're exploring the DOM and want to see all the methods and properties of the document object:

```
for (i in document) { alert(i); }
```

Using the preceding loop in Firefox will produce about 140 alert boxes for you to examine, but that will be very annoying. What you'll create here is a better solution using a floating debug log where you can record log messages as you please. Rather than alert(), you can then use the following object:

```
for (i in document) { ADS.log.write(i); }
```

With this object, you can easily scroll through the list of 140 entries—no force-quitting required—as illustrated in Figure 2-18.

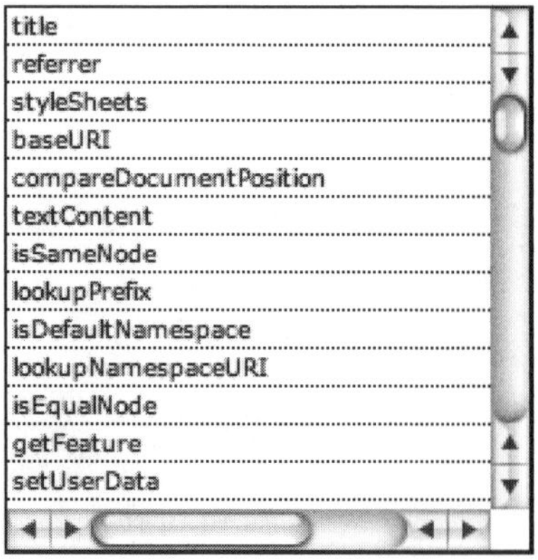

The log window we'll create here will simply be a <div> element of fixed size appended to the body of the document and positioned so that it floats in the center of the window. In later chapters, you'll learn about event and stylization features that you could later apply to your log window to make it draggable, resizable, and a little sexier than the minimalist black-bordered box shown in Figure 2-18.

Figure 2-18.
A representation of the ADS.log() window

> *If you're using Firefox and the Firebug plug-in, you can do a lot of wonderful debugging simply by using* console.log()*. The problem with the Firebug extension is that it's for Firefox only; you can't use it in Microsoft Internet Explorer, Safari, Opera, or any other browser. There is a Firebug Lite library (*http://www.getfirebug.com/lite.html*) that works across browsers and does similar logging, but creating your own object will teach you the ins and outs of objects and allow you to customize the log any way you want.*

The myLogger() object

To begin your own log object, create a quick HTML page and include your ADS library along with a new JavaScript file called myLogger.js. This test file doesn't have to be anything fancy. Next, populate the myLogger.js file with the following structure. The source for this book includes a starting point for you in chpater2/myLogger-start/ if you want to use it. I also suggest assigning a new instance of the myLogger object to the ADS.log member as shown in the following code. Usually, you'll be adding all the logs to the same object, so instantiating the ADS.log member right away will allow you to quickly log messages using ADS.log.write('log message'). You could simply define the ADS.log object using static methods as I described earlier, but we'll use a constructor method here so that you can see how all the object stuff works. In the future, you can also create multiple instances of the log window if you want to separate logs for different things.

```
function myLogger(id) {
    id = id || 'ADSLogWindow';
    var logWindow = null;
    var createWindow = function () { };
    this.writeRaw = function (message) { };
}

myLogger.prototype = {
    write: function (message) {        },
    header: function (message) { }
};

if(!window.ADS) { window['ADS'] = {}; }
window['ADS']['log'] = new myLogger();
```

Your myLogger object takes on several characteristics. First, myLogger is an object with protected, privileged, and public properties and methods. The myLogger object is also a constructor, so you'll need to instantiate it with the new keyword when assigning it to the ADS.log member.

Each member of the myLogger object has a specific, planned purpose:

- logWindow is a protected property that will be used internally by the object to reference the DOM node of the log window.

- createWindow() is a protected method that you'll use to create the logWindow node in the DOM tree.

- writeRaw() is a privileged method that appends a new entry to the log window. It's privileged, because it will also need to execute the protected createWindow() method if logWindow hasn't been defined yet.

- write() is the public method you'll use to do most of your logging. It encodes angle brackets in the message to allow HTML source to show in the log window. It will also apply the object toString() method if the message is an object (and toString() exists). This method will then pass the encoded message string to writeRaw().

- header() is another public method that you can use to add a bold, red entry to use as a header if you're debugging multiple parts of a script as you'll do in Chapter 3.

In the structure you just created, the public prototype methods were also defined using the object literal syntax:

```
myLogger.prototype = {
    write: function(message) {},
    header: function(message) {}
};
```

You could have just as easily used the following syntax:

```
myLogger.prototype.write = function(message) {};
header.prototype.write = function(message) {};
```

But using the object literal makes the code a little less redundant if you decide to add more public methods to your logging object such as link:

```
// Without the object literal
myLogger.prototype.write = function (message) {};
myLogger.prototype.header = function (message) {};
myLogger.prototype.link = function (link) {};

// Using the object literal
myLogger.prototype = {
    write: function (message) {},
    header: function (message) {},
    link: function (link) {}
};
```

Either way will work, so it's up to you.

Your setup of protected, privileged, and public members may not seem necessary at first, but as I said earlier, it should always be considered when creating reusable objects. You may assume that everyone using your log object is always going to use ADS.log.write() to log all their messages. That may well be true, but they could also use ADS.log.writeRaw() to log raw HTML into the window. Since these two methods are public, that should be expected and is planned for in the API. If you also left the createWindow() method as a public method, it wouldn't necessarily cause a problem, but if developers stumble upon the public createWindow() method, they may start calling it for whatever reason they see fit; after all, it is a *public* method that you made available. If you later dramatically change the way the object works internally, any code referencing the new or missing createWindow() method may break unexpectedly. You could argue that whoever used your object inappropriately should expect it to break, but remember, you want to write code that's maintainable and easy to use, so you shouldn't leave any doors open unnecessarily. Now, let's take a look at each of the methods.

The myLogger.createWindow() method

Your private createWindow() method will be responsible for creating the DOM element to hold the list of entries and appending it to the document body. Since the log is a list of items, it makes semantic sense for you to use an unordered list (or an ordered list, if you prefer) so you can simply append each entry as a list item. Within your myLogger constructor, your createWindow() method should resemble this one:

```
// Protected method to create the window
createWindow = function () {

    // Get the left and top position for the new window
    // so it's centered in the browser
    var browserWindowSize = ADS.getBrowserWindowSize();
    var top = ((browserWindowSize.height - 200) / 2) || 0;
    var left = ((browserWindowSize.width - 200) / 2) || 0;
```

```
        // Create the DOM node for the log window using the
        // protected logWindow property to maintain a reference
        logWindow = document.createElement('UL');

        // Assign an ID so you can identify it in the DOM tree if necessary
        logWindow.setAttribute('id', id);

        // Position it centered on the screen
        logWindow.style.position = 'absolute';
        logWindow.style.top = top + 'px';
        logWindow.style.left = left + 'px';

        // Give it a fixed size and allow scrolling
        logWindow.style.width = '200px';
        logWindow.style.height = '200px';
        logWindow.style.overflow = 'scroll';

        // Add some style to make it look a little nicer
        logWindow.style.padding= '0';
        logWindow.style.margin= '0';
        logWindow.style.border= '1px solid black';
        logWindow.style.backgroundColor= 'white';
        logWindow.style.listStyle= 'none';
        logWindow.style.font= '10px/10px Verdana, Tahoma, Sans';

        // Append it to the body
        document.body.appendChild(logWindow);

    };
```

The two key parts of the createWindow() method are highlighted in bold.

First, you're using the DOM createElement() method to create and assign an unordered list element to the private logWindow property. The assignment to logWindow works, because the internal scope of the createWindow() method has no defined instance of logWindow. When the assignment occurs, it looks to the external scope and voilà—there's the private logWindow.

The second part is when you're appending the logWindow to the document.body, which will make it visible in the browser. The private logWindow property will be maintained as a reference to the DOM node so you can refer to logWindow from within the myLogger object to reference the unordered list element in the body of the document.

The createWindow() method also assigns an ID to the logWindow using the optional id argument passed into the constructor. This is only there for convenience, in case you need some other script to identify the log window in the DOM tree.

How you style your log window is up to you. I've chosen to make the example 200×200 pixels, and I've positioned it in the center of the current window. You may have noticed that I've included a reference to an ADS.getBrowserWindowSize() method, which should be placed in your ADS.js namespace wrapper defined as follows:

```
(function(){
if(!window.ADS) { window['ADS'] = {} }

... Above here is your existing library ...

function getBrowserWindowSize() {
    var de = document.documentElement;
    return {
        'width':(
            window.innerWidth
            || (de && de.clientWidth )
            || document.body.clientWidth),
        'height':(
            window.innerHeight
            || (de && de.clientHeight )
            || document.body.clientHeight)
    }
};
window['ADS']['getBrowserWindowSize'] = getBrowserWindowSize;

... Below here is your existing library ...

})();
```

Including a method to retrieve the browser window size doesn't really make sense specifically for a logging object. Also, the method is really only required because of the differences among browsers, so it makes sense that you may want to reuse the same one again in a different object. Putting it in your ADS library namespace makes it available but prevents it from conflicting with anyone else if they defined their own getBrowserWindowSize() function that acts differently.

The myLogger.writeRaw() method

Next is your privileged writeRaw() method that will actually append new entries to the logWindow. Following the same pattern as the createWindow() method, your writeRaw() method should create a DOM list item element, style it, populate it with the log entry, and append it to the logWindow object similar to the following method:

```
this.writeRaw = function (message) {

    // If the initial window doesn't exist, create it.
    if(!logWindow) createWindow();

    // Create the list item and style it appropriately
    var li = document.createElement('LI');
    li.style.padding= '2px';
    li.style.border= '0';
    li.style.borderBottom = '1px dotted black';
    li.style.margin= '0';
    li.style.color= '#000';
    li.style.font = '9px/9px Verdana, Tahoma, Sans';
```

```
        //add the message to the log node
        if(typeof message == 'undefined') {
            li.appendChild(document.createTextNode(➥
    'Message was undefined'));
        } else if(typeof li.innerHTML != undefined) {
            li.innerHTML = message;
        } else {
            li.appendChild(document.createTextNode(message));
        }

        //append this entry to the log window
        logWindow.appendChild(li);

        return true;
    };
```

> You'll notice that the writeRaw() method as well as other methods are using the style attribute to include inline style modifications. As a general rule, you should use other techniques to keep the style separate from the behavior and markup, as you'll see in Chapter 5. Here, however, the log window is a development tool and doesn't relate to the overall style and theme of the site. If you used class names and an external CSS file to define the style, you would also need to include the CSS files along with the myLogger.js, which is an unnecessary step for debugging purposes.

Before you create and append the entry, you'll need to check to see if the log window has been created and, if not, call the private createWindow() method. You could use a window load event listener or other mechanism to initially create the log window, but in the case of a log, it doesn't really make sense to show the empty log window if there aren't any entries. By creating it when an entry is added, you're creating a pseudo-onWhenAnEntryIsAdded event.

It isn't necessary to prefix this on to the private createWindow() method. In fact, if you try to prefix this, it won't work. Using createWindow() follows the same logic as the private logWindow member. When called, the inner scope of the function is examined followed by outer scope, which in this case is the constructor of the myLogger object where the private createWindow() method resides. Using this.createWindow() is the same as calling createWindow() on the instance of the object, and since it's private, that won't work.

Depending on who you talk to, there's one other element of this method that may be considered "bad," but it works well for our purposes: innerHTML. There are two sides of the fence in this debate. One side says that innerHTML is evil, not part of the W3C DOM specification, and a heavy-handed attempt by proprietary browsers to push nonstandard features that throws us back to the days of DHTML. The other side simply says, "Hey, it works. All the browsers have it, and DOM code is longer and more complicated. So why not take advantage of it?" I consider myself to be standing on the fence. There are a lot of advantages to innerHTML, such as the following:

- It's much less code and a lot simpler than the equivalent DOM code.
- It creates cleaner and more legible code, because you can use HTML strings.
- It's faster and easier to implement, so it requires less effort.

There are also a lot of disadvantages, such as these:

- It may lack future support, since it's not part of the W3C specification.
- It's unable to maintain a reference to the newly created DOM nodes.
- It's an HTML-browser-specific feature and won't work in many XML-specific instances.
- Just because it's easier and faster doesn't mean you're going to produce a better product; it may just be simple laziness.

By creating each node individually using the appropriate DOM methods, you have greater control and a clearer understanding of what's happening in your application, so my preference is to use DOM. But I'll use innerHTML sparingly if it makes sense, which it does here.

> Just to whet your appetite a little, in the practical example at the end of Chapter 3, you'll be building a tool to convert HTML into the necessary DOM code. Though it won't work for this particular situation, where the HTML is unknown, you can use the conversion tool to quickly create the necessary DOM code from your WYSIWYG compositions for other projects.

Using innerHTML in this situation offers you some big advantages. When logging, you may want to log raw HTML and have it parse as HTML in the log window. The HTML would become part of the logWindow's DOM structure (and you'd have to be aware of that when debugging), but *what* HTML you might log is unknown at this point, so there's no easy way for you to use DOM methods to create the structure. But just to be on the safe side, you should check to see if the innerHTML property exists on the node, and if not, use the createTextNode() DOM method:

```
if(typeof li.innerHTML != undefined) {
    li.innerHTML = message;
} else {
    li.appendchild(document.createTextNode(message));
}
```

Using createTextNode() won't allow the browser to render raw HTML into DOM, but it will still show the message as a text string in the log window.

At this point, you have a fully working myLogger, and you could start debugging your code using the writeRaw() method:

```
ADS.log.writeRaw('This is raw.');
```

But if you include markup in the log entry as follows, it will be incorporated into the log window's markup as illustrated with the bold entry in Figure 2-19:

```
ADS.log.writeRaw('<strong>This is bold!</strong>');
```

Figure 2-19.
A representation of the ADS.log window with raw entries of plain and strong HTML

Unfortunately, you can't use your newly created log to debug the log itself while you add the rest of the methods. If you want, you could make a copy under a different name and use it to debug the rest of the object as necessary or continue using alert() or the JavaScript console.

To show the log entry source and do a few other fancy things with objects, we'll add a few more methods including write() and header().

The myLogger.write() and myLogger.header() methods

Your write() method is simply a wrapper to your writeRaw() method that performs a few additional checks in case you're trying to log an instance of an object and conversion to transform angle brackets (< and >) to < and >. This way, any HTML fed into the ADS.log.write() method will show as source in the log window rather than the rendered HTML you get with the writeRaw() method. Likewise, using your header() method, you can add a fancy stylized entry as shown in Figure 2-20.

To create the public write() and header() methods, add the following code as the myLogger object's prototype:

Figure 2-20.
A representation of the ADS.log window with the header and escaped HTML

```
myLogger.prototype = {

    write: function (message) {
        // Warn about null messages
        if(typeof message == 'string' && message.length==0) {
            return this.writeRaw('ADS.log: null message');
        }

        // If the message isn't a string try to call the toString()
        // method, if it doesn't exist simply log the type of object
        if (typeof message != 'string') {
            if(message.toString) return this.writeRaw(message.toString());
```

```
                else return this.writeRaw(typeof message);
        }

        // Transform < and > so that .innerHTML doesn't parse
        // the message as HTML
        message = message.replace(/</g,"&lt;").replace(/>/g,"&gt;");

        return this.writeRaw(message);
    },

    //write a header to the log window.
    header: function (message) {
        message = '<span style="color:white;background-color:black;➡
font-weight:bold;padding:0px 5px;">' + message + '</span>';
        return this.writeRaw(message);
    }

};
```

This will now allow you to log a number of different messages to the log window as shown in Figure 2-20.

And that's it! Your log is now complete. Just include a reference to ADS.js in the head of your HTML file and debug until your heart's content.

> *Savvy readers may realize that the functionality provided by the* write() *method could have easily been incorporated into the* writeRaw() *method. I chose to split this functionality into a different method to show you the differences among private, privileged, and public methods and to give you a clean* writeRaw() *method that didn't perform any magic tricks with the input beyond adding the entry to the log. This way, you can add additional methods at your leisure that perform all sorts of tricks.*

The only caution with this logging object is that it does requires the page to be loaded prior to calling any logging actions, because the window is appended to the document's body. If the page hasn't loaded and there's no body, there's no way to show the log window. You could alternatively check to see if the body has loaded yet, and if not, fall back on alerting the log entries, but I'll leave that to you. If you're following the best practices outlined in Chapter 1 (and you are, right?), you'll be using unobtrusive page loading modifications to the document, so you probably won't run into many issues unless there's a complete JavaScript failure (if that's the case, alert() wouldn't work either, so you'll need to debug some other way).

Summary

JavaScript is all about the object, but objects are tricky little things. This chapter introduced you to various ways you can go about creating objects with public, private, privileged, and static methods. Though they may not seem important at first, you clearly saw how controlling access to your functions can benefit the end user by providing a clean API, and it can benefit you by allowing you to control the public API and keep additional helper methods and properties internal. You'll be utilizing much of what you learned here in later chapters as you build on your ADS library and integrate a number of public and private objects.

Now that we've sufficiently covered everything you're going to need to know about JavaScript, let's take an in-depth look at some W3C specifications and learn a little bit more about the DOM2 Core and DOM2 HTML.

Chapter 3

UNDERSTANDING THE DOM2 CORE
AND DOM2 HTML

In our day-to-day activities we take too much for granted. Do you really know how your car's engine works or how it's able to get from one place to the other? Do you know what's involved when you call your friend on the phone or how your voice can travel around the globe in mere seconds? Do you know how your DOM scripts use JavaScript to identify and interact with each part of your HTML document? Odds are you probably take most of these things for granted; well, I'm going to help you with the last one.

If you're a designer at heart, it's time to put on your programmer hat and use the other half of your brain. In this chapter, I'm going to go through the W3C DOM2 Core and DOM2 HTML specifications, which provide the foundation for the DOM representation of your documents. If you dread specifications or if you're cringing at the idea, don't worry; I'm not going to go through every little detail, as that would be boring. You probably already know a lot of what's in the specifications, but understanding how the specifications work and not just how you can use them will give you a much better understanding of things like the differences between Node and Element and how all those methods such as document.getElementById() interact with your document. You may also uncover a few things you didn't know.

The DOM, not JavaScript, is your document

As you know, your web page is a structured document, marked up using a set of predefined XML or HTML tags. When the browser receives the document, it's parsed and displayed visually on the screen according to the doctype and associated style sheets. In a W3C standards-compliant browser, the document can also be referenced using JavaScript objects by following the guidelines in the Document Object Model (DOM) specification (http://www.w3.org/DOM). These objects are made available to your scripts, and they give you a standard, browser-agnostic way of interacting with your document.

The DOM is a set of web standards that describes how your script can interact with and access the structured document. DOM defines the objects, methods, and properties that are required to access, manipulate, and create the content, structure, style, and behavior in your documents.

Before we dive into the specifications, I should remind you of two things:

- The DOM is not JavaScript.
- The DOM is not DHTML.

Despite what you may have heard, read, or thought, the DOM is not the same as JavaScript. As I said, DOM is a set of specifications developed by the W3C. The specifications outline the objects, methods, and properties that languages such as JavaScript need to implement to conform to the standard. By creating a standard and conforming to it, you can write JavaScript code that will behave identically and have the same expected result in different operating environments such as different browsers.

Remember the term DHTML? DHTML isn't the same as DOM either—despite what you read on the Internet. The term DHTML, referring to Dynamic HTML, is simply an ambiguous marketing term created by browser manufacturers for browser manufacturers. It was used to describe a host of new features incorporated into early 4.x browsers that allowed manipulation of the document, style, and behavior much in the same way the DOM does now. According to the W3C, "Dynamic HTML is a term used by some vendors to describe the combination of HTML, style sheets, and scripts that allows documents to be animated" (http://www.w3.org/DOM/#why).

The ideas behind DOM do incorporate DHTML concepts, but DHTML includes nonstandard objects, such as document.all, that vary from browser to browser. Yes, that's right; document.all as well as many other collections are not actually part of W3C standards or recommendations. Using DOM, the document.all collection should be retrieved using something like document.getElementsByTagName('*'). In this book, all the code will shy away from using any nonstandard collections as much as possible and will stick strictly to W3C DOM methods unless otherwise noted.

Objects and interfaces

The W3C specifications define their properties in interfaces, which are implemented by the various JavaScript objects you began to explore in Chapter 2. Each object can incorporate multiple different interfaces, and they can also build on each other through the object inheritance you learned about in Chapter 2. Any language that parses XML-based markup using objects, not just JavaScript, can implement these interfaces.

As you also learned in Chapter 2, JavaScript is all about objects, but it's a prototype-based object-oriented language—there are no classes or interfaces that you can access directly. JavaScript implements the interfaces defined in the specifications automatically within the objects, so throughout this chapter, I'm going to refer to the interfaces defined in the specifications as "objects," because that's what they are in JavaScript. I just want to make this clear, in case you're also looking at the specifications and are confused as to why the specification refers to interfaces but I'm calling them objects.

Levels of the DOM

The W3C DOM is not one all-encompassing specification. It's divided into various levels, each with various subspecifications and modules. Each level implements new features improving on the features of the previous level, but in some cases, one level may become incompatible with the previous level.

DOM Level 0

There is no DOM Level 0, so don't go looking for Level 0 specifications. If someone is referring to "Level 0," they're most likely referring to a set of proprietary DHTML methods, objects, and collections. These were implemented in different ways across the various browsers before there was a standard specification.

DOM Level 1

The Level 1 DOM (http://www.w3.org/DOM/DOMTR#dom1) is the first version of the DOM standard published as a recommendation way back in October of 1998. It's a single specification comprised of two main parts:

- **DOM Core**: Gives you the inner workings of the generic tree node structure for XML documents along with the properties and methods required to create, edit, and manipulate the tree.

- **DOM HTML**: Gives you the objects, properties, and methods for the specific elements associated with HTML documents, collections of tags, and each of the individual HTML tags

The Level 1 specification includes object definitions such as Document, Node, Attr, Element, Text, HTMLDocument, HTMLElement, and HTMLCollection—all of which you'll see in this chapter.

Level 2

The Level 2 DOM (http://www.w3.org/DOM/DOMTR#dom2), published in November of 2000, updates the Core (DOM2 Core) and adds several other specifications. The DOM2 HTML specification was published in January of 2003 and added additional objects, properties, and methods specific to HTML 4.01 and XHTML 1.0. The DOM 2 recommendations are split into six different specifications:

- **DOM2 Core**: Like DOM Core, this gives you control of the structure of the DOM document but adds additional features, such as namespace-specific methods that you can see in the changes Appendix at http://www.w3.org/TR/2000/REC-DOM-Level-2-Core-20001113/changes.html.

- **DOM2 HTML**: Like DOM HTML, this gives you control of HTML-specific DOM documents but includes a few additional properties as noted in the changes Appendix at http://www.w3.org/TR/2003/REC-DOM-Level-2-HTML-20030109/changes.html.

- **DOM2 Events**: This gives you control of mouse-related events including targeting, capturing, bubbling, and canceling but doesn't contain handles for keyboard-related events.

- **DOM2 Style**: Alternatively known as DOM2 CSS, this gives you the ability to access and manipulate all your CSS-related styling and rules.

- **DOM2 Traversal and Range**: These give you iterative access to the DOM, so you can walk and manipulate the document as needed.

- **DOM2 Views**: This gives you the ability to access and update a representation of a document.

Many of these specifications provide standardization for aspects of the document beyond the actual markup structure, such as events and iteration, and many have dependencies on other parts of the specifications as shown in Figure 3-1.

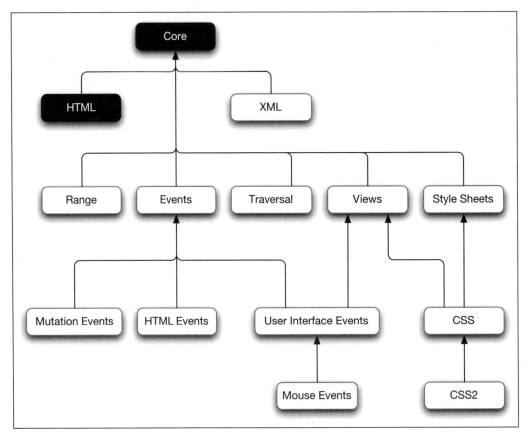

Figure 3-1. The DOM Level 2 specification dependencies

I won't be covering all the DOM2 specifications, but in Chapter 4, we will dabble in DOM2 events, and Chapter 5 will touch on DOM2 style.

Level 3

The Level 3 DOM (http://www.w3.org/DOM/DOMTR#dom3) includes updates to the Core (DOM3 Core) specification and includes three recommended specifications:

- **DOM3 Core**: Adds more new methods and properties to the Core as well as changing a few existing methods as outlined in the changes Appendix at http://www.w3.org/TR/2004/REC-DOM-Level-3-Core-20040407/changes.html
- **DOM3 Load and Save**: Gives you the ability to load the content of an XML document into your DOM document and serialize your DOM document into an XML document
- **DOM3 Validation**: Allows you to ensure your dynamic document is valid and conforms to the doctype

Additionally, there are several other specifications that are still in early stages and haven't yet been finalized as recommendations:

- **DOM3 Events**: Will give access to keyboard- and mouse-related events
- **DOM3 XPath**: Will give access to the DOM document's tree structure using XPath 1.0 queries (http://www.w3.org/TR/xpath)
- **DOM3 Views and Formatting and DOM3 Abstract Schemas**: Will allow you to dynamically access and update the content, structure, and style of documents

Surprisingly, however, many modern browsers support a lot of the DOM 3 specifications, as you can see in Table 3-1. Deciding where to limit your adoption of standards depends on what browsers you plan to support, what your target markets are willing to accept, and how much future-proofing you want to account for.

Which level is correct for you?

To find out what features of the W3C DOM your selected browsers support, you can use the DOMImplementation object, which is part of the Core specification. In your web browser, the DOMImplementation object is instantiated as document.implementation. If a browser officially claims to support a feature, it will report so through the document.implementation.hasFeature() method, which takes two parameters. The first argument is one of the following:

- Core: DOM Levels 1 and 2, basic methods as well as the XML Namespace in DOM Level 2
- XML: DOM Levels 1, 2 and 3, for XML 1.0
- HTML: DOM Levels 1, 2 and 3, for HTML 4.0 and XHTML 1.0 support in DOM Level 2
- Views: DOM Level 2, used with CSS and UIEvents modules
- StyleSheets: DOM Level 2, for associating a style sheet and a document
- CSS: DOM Level 2, extensions for Cascading Style Sheets
- CSS2: DOM Level 2, extensions for Cascading Style Sheets Level 2
- Events: DOM Level 2, for generic events
- UIEvents: DOM Level 2, for generic user interface events
- MouseEvents: DOM Level 2, for mouse events
- MutationEvents: DOM Level 2, for DOM tree event mutation
- HTMLEvents: DOM Level 2, for HTML 4.01 specific events
- Range: DOM Level 2, for DOM tree range manipulation

- Traversal: DOM Level 2, iteration and traversal methods for DOM trees
- LS: DOM Level 3, dynamic loading of a document into a DOM tree
- LS-Async: DOM Level 3, dynamic asynchronous loading of a document into a DOM tree
- Validation: DOM Level 3, schema support

The second parameter is the DOM level number, that is, 1.0, 2.0, or 3.0.

To test for a specific module, such as the Level 2 Core, you would do something like this:

```
if(document.implementation) {
    if(document.implementation.hasFeature('Core','2.0')) {
        alert('DOM2 Core Supported');
    } else {
        alert('DOM2 Core Not Supported')
    }
} else {
    alert('No DOMImplementation Support');
}
```

If document.implementation doesn't exist in your browser, you can be pretty sure that there's probably no DOM support at all, but there could be partial support. For example, Microsoft Internet Explorer 6 reports that HTML is supported but not Core. For HTML to be supported, parts of the DOM Core *must* be supported in some way, because HTML requires Core methods.

To quickly see what modules your browser reports as supported, you can try the test page provided by the W3C at http://www.w3.org/2003/02/06-dom-support.html, which tests all the reported features in the browser you're using to view the page. I've compiled the results of this page in Table 3-1 for the popular modern browsers.

Table 3-1. DOM implementation level compatibility of modules for various browsers, as reported by the W3C

Module	Firefox 1.5	Firefox 2.0	Internet Explorer 6	Internet Explorer 7	Opera 9	Safari 2.0
Core	2	2			2	2
XML	2	1 and 2			1 and 2	1 and 2
HTML	2	1 and 2	1	1	1 and 2	1 and 2
Views	2	2			2	2
StyleSheets	2	2			2	2
CSS	2	2			2	2
CSS2	2	2			2	2
Events	2	2			2	2

Module	Firefox 1.5	Firefox 2.0	Internet Explorer 6	Internet Explorer 7	Opera 9	Safari 2.0
UIEvents	2	2			2	2
MouseEvents	2	2			2	2
MutationEvents					2	2
HTMLEvents	2	2			2	2
Range	2	2			2	2
Traversal					2	2
LS					3	
LS-Async					3	
Validation						

As you can see by looking at the results in Table 3-1, our good friend Microsoft Internet Explorer will be at the root of much grief when working with standards-compliant DOM scripting. This isn't to say that Internet Explorer is limited or has no support; it just goes about things in its own way, so you have to account for the standard way and Internet Explorer's way (note the order on that—the standard way and then the proprietary way, not the other way around).

You can also test more specifically for individual parts of each module using one of the test suites at http://www.w3.org/DOM/Test. They take a little while to run, but they test each individual method of each object, so you can check which methods conform to specifications.

The Core and HTML modules contain the majority of the objects you'll be using in your DOM scripts. The DOM2 Core and DOM2 HTML modules aren't fully supported in all current browsers, as indicated in Table 3-1. To accommodate multiple browsers, you'll have to be cautious and use the appropriate object detection to account for unsupported features.

As I mentioned in the Introduction, the code in this book will focus on the following browsers:

- Microsoft Internet Explorer 6+
- Firefox 1.5+
- Safari 2.0+
- Opera 9+

along with any other browser that implement the W3C specifications. For this reason, this book will also focus on DOM Level 2 recommendations, but there will be a few instances where you'll see element of DOM 3 or other proprietary methods.

Creating a sample document

For the rest of this chapter, we'll be examining the various aspects of DOM2 Core and DOM2 HTML. You may already be familiar with the basics, such as document.getElementById(), but there are a number of other methods that are easy to overlook.

> You'll be making use of the myLogger.js file with the ADS.log object you created at the end of Chapter 2. If you haven't created ADS.log yet, you can find the completed source code accompanying this book.

Creating the DOM file

To test and explore the DOM, create a new DOM script file called domTesting.js, and include it along with your ADS.js file and your myLogger.js file in the head of this sample.html file, as found in the chapter3/testing/sample.html source:

```
<!DOCTYPE html PUBLIC "-//W3C//DTD XHTML 1.0 Strict//EN"
    "http://www.w3.org/TR/xhtml1/DTD/xhtml1-strict.dtd">
<html xmlns="http://www.w3.org/1999/xhtml">
<head>
    <title>AdvancED DOM Scripting Sample Document</title>
    <!-- Include some CSS style sheet to make
        everything look a little nicer -->
    <link rel="stylesheet" type="text/css"
        href="../../shared/source.css" />
    <link rel="stylesheet" type="text/css" href="../chapter.css" />

    <!-- Your ADS library with the common JavaScript objects -->
    <script type="text/javascript" src="ADS.js"></script>
    <!-- Log object from Chapter 2 -->
    <script type="text/javascript" src="myLogger.js"></script>
    <!-- Your testing file -->
    <script type="text/javascript" src="domTesting.js"></script>

</head>
<body>
    <h1>AdvancED DOM Scripting</h1>
    <div id="content">
        <p>Examining the DOM2 Core and DOM2 HTML Recommendations</p>
        <h2>Browsers</h2>
        <p>Typically, you'll be expecting the following browsers:</p>
        <!-- Other browsers could be added but we'll keep the list
        short for the example. -->
        <ul id="browserList">
            <li id="firefoxListItem">
                <a href="http://www.getfirefox.com/"
                    title="Get Firefox"
```

```
                    id="firefox">Firefox 2.0</a>
            </li>
            <li>
                <a href="http://microsoft.com/windows/ie/downloads/"
                    title="Get Microsoft Internet Explorer"
                    id="msie">Microsoft Internet Explorer 7</a>
            </li>
            <li>
                <a href="http://www.apple.com/macosx/features/safari/"
                    title="Check out Safari"
                    id="safari">Safari</a>
            </li>
            <li>
                <a href="http://www.opera.com/download/"
                    title="Get Opera"
                    id="opera">Opera 9</a>
            </li>
        </ul>
    </div>
  </body>
</html>
```

The links to the JavaScript files in this sample HTML file are using relative URLs pointing to the appropriate files as they appear in the source/ folder for the source code of this book. Source examples for all chapters use a common ADS library. Here, the `myLogger.js` file has been referenced from the Chapter 2 folder as well. You can rearrange the files and relink them as necessary if you want to use your own versions. Also, the sample file includes some common CSS files to make the examples look a little nicer.

If you have everything set up right, you should see a plain, simple page similar to the one shown in Figure 3-2.

Figure 3-2. The sample.html document as displayed in Firefox on Mac OS X

97

Choosing a browser

Which browser you choose to develop in is up to you. Personally, I use Firefox for developing, as I have yet to find as wide a variety of developer extensions for any other browser. If you're using Firefox, I suggest you download and install the following extensions:

- **Firebug**: http://getfirebug.com
- **Tamperdata**: http://tamperdata.mozdev.org
- **Web Developer toolbar**: http://chrispederick.com/work/webdeveloper

Firefox, including these extensions, is a developer's dream and just can't be beat!

But, if you're using Internet Explorer, you can at least install the Internet Explorer Developer Toolbar (http://www.microsoft.com/downloads/details.aspx?familyid=e59c3964-672d-4511-bb3e-2d5e1db91038&displaylang=en). Safari users, try out all the developer goodies at http://webkit.org.

The sample.html document consists of a semantic XHTML-compliant document including some regular things like headers, paragraphs, comments, a list, and anchor links. There's nothing too fancy here, as it's just going to be a simple test document for you to experiment with. The markup tree structure is fairly simple and can be generally represented by the diagram in Figure 3-3.

The tree in Figure 3-3 looks simple enough, but when your browser converts your markup to a JavaScript object, it faces a few challenges:

- How should it represent all the different types of tags and their varying attributes?
- How should the object relate nodes to one another to maintain the parent/child relationships?
- What should it do with all the pretty white space formatting between tags?
- What if there's some text mixed in with that white space?

These questions and many more are answered by a combination of the Core and HTML recommendations, as we'll discuss next.

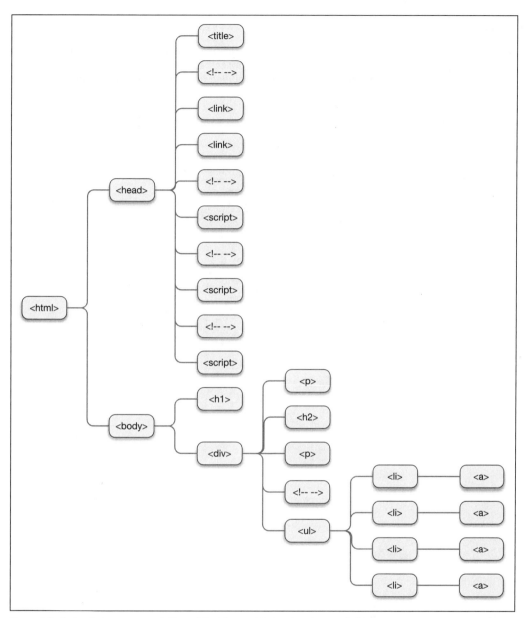

Figure 3-3. A simple tree representation of the document structure in sample.html

The DOM Core

When your web browser parses the markup in sample.html, it converts the markup into an object based on the W3C DOM modules supported by the browser. Each tag in the document can be represented by a Core object, as shown in Figure 3-4 (I've excluded the <head> to make the diagram a little smaller).

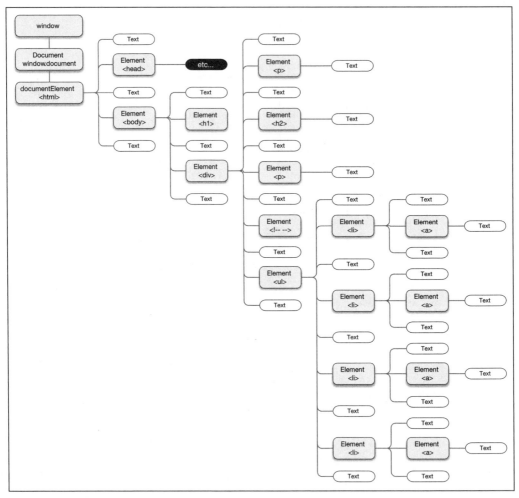

Figure 3-4. How the W3C standard DOM Core sees the document in sample.html

Figure 3-4 shows how the DOM2 Core applies to the markup in sample.html, but other HTML documents will follow a similar pattern. As you can see in the figure, the majority of the items in the tree are Element nodes. The only special cases are the Document, which is the object that represents the entire document, and the DocumentElement, which is the root <html> element in your markup.

You'll also notice in Figure 3-4 that all the white space between each of the tags in your markup has been converted into Text nodes. This is how the DOM specification dictates the white space and new lines should be handled. It makes sense to maintain the white space this way, because ideally, you want your DOM tree to represent all the information associated with your markup. In the case of Internet Explorer, however, the text nodes are only there if they contain additional text besides white space, as shown in Figure 3-5.

Likewise, if you output your HTML as a single line with the tags right against each other as follows, the W3C DOM2 Code representation wouldn't have the additional Text nodes, since there are none (see Figure 3-5):

```
<!DOCTYPE html PUBLIC "-//W3C//DTD XHTML 1.0➡
Strict//EN""http://www.w3.org/TR/xhtml1/DTD/xhtml1-strict.dtd">➡
<html xmlns="http://www.w3.org/1999/xhtml"><head><title>AdvancED➡
DOM Scripting Sample Document</title><!-- include some CSS style➡
sheet to make everything look a little nicer --><link➡
rel="stylesheet" type="text/css" href="../../shared/source.css"➡
/><link rel="stylesheet" type="text/css" href="../chapter.css"➡
<!-- ADS Library (full version from source linked here) --><script➡
type="text/javascript" src="../../ADS-final-verbose.js"></script>➡
<!-- Log object from Chapter 2 --><script type="text/javascript"➡
src="../../chapter2/myLogger-final/myLogger.js"></script><!-- Your➡
testing file --><script type="text/javascript" src="domTesting.js">➡
</script></head><body><h1>AdvancED DOM Scripting</h1><div➡
id="content"><p>Examining the DOM2 Core and DOM2 HTML➡
Recommendations</p><h2>Browsers</h2><p>Typically, you'll be➡
expecting the following browsers:</p><!-- Other browsers could➡
be added but we'll keep the list short for the example. --><ul➡
id="browserList"><li id="firefoxListItem"><a➡
href="http://www.getfirefox.com/"title="Get Firefox"➡
id="firefox">Firefox 2.0</a></li><li><a➡
href="http://www.microsoft.com/windows/ie/downloads/" title="Get➡
Microsoft Internet Explorer" id="msie">Microsoft Internet Explorer➡
7</a></li> <li><a href="http://www.apple.com/macosx/features/safari/"➡
title="Check out Safari" id="safari">Safari</a></li><li><a➡
href="http://www.opera.com/download/" title="Get Opera" id="opera"➡
>Opera 9</a></li> </ul></div></body></html>
```

This is important to remember when you're iterating over the childNodes of each node. W3C DOM2 Core–compliant browsers such as Firefox will have the text nodes mixed in with the other child nodes, whereas Internet Explorer won't have the additional text node and will always resemble Figure 3-5.

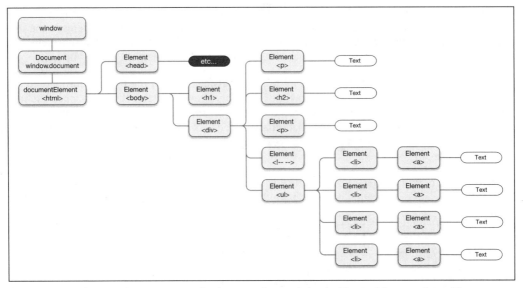

Figure 3-5. How the DOM Core represents the document in sample.html without white space formatting

The importance of inheritance in the DOM

What's not clear in Figure 3-4 or Figure 3-5 is how the different objects in the Core (and DOM2 HTML) build on one another to provide all the features you enjoy taking for granted. You know every element of your document has various features such as id attributes and the ability to append children, but have you ever been frustrated when a property or method you use on one element isn't available on another? These frustrations can be avoided by understanding the inheritance of the objects and which base object is providing which bit of functionality.

After the web browser parses your sample.html document, each node isn't simply an instance of the Element object but rather an extension of the Element object based on a number of things.

Depending on the document's markup, the nodeName, and the DOM HTML specification for that particular tag (which you'll learn about later in this chapter), each item will inherit a specific set of properties and methods. In fact, the Element object itself inherits all the properties and methods of Node, and in the case of an <a> anchor, the tag is instantiated as a DOM HTML HTMLAnchorElement object, which extends from several other objects, as shown in Figure 3-6.

By extending from several objects, the anchor in your markup will have all the properties and methods associated with everything from the base Node object, all the way to the HTMLAnchorElement object itself. As I discussed in Chapter 2, this inheritance is an important part of object-oriented languages and allows you to maintain common functionality among various objects. It also explains why both the paragraph (<p>) and anchor (<a>) objects are Element objects, but they also have some different properties as specified by the DOM HTML HTMLParagraphElement object and HTMLAnchorElement object in the final document DOM object.

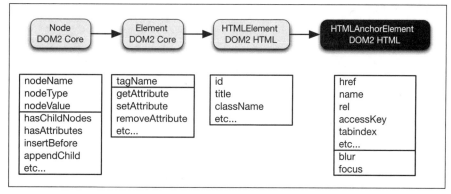

Figure 3-6. Extension of objects from Node to HTMLAnchorElement

The base of almost every object in DOM2 Core and DOM2 HTML is the Node object, so let's take a look at the properties and methods of Node next.

The Core Node object

Each Element in Figure 3-5 extends from the Node object. Even document and documentElement are extended from Node, but they have their own unique properties and members as well. The Node object's properties include identifying characteristics such as nodeName, nodeValue, nodeType, parentNode, childNodes, firstChild, lastChild, previousSibling, nextSibling, attributes, and ownerDocument. These properties are available to all the DOM objects extended from the Node object.

Node names, values, and types

In the case of the Element objects in your document, you'll be using the nodeName property to retrieve the name of the tag you used to specify the node. The nodeName is transformed to uppercase for consistency. For example, if you add the following load event to the domTesting.js file:

```
ADS.addEvent(window, 'load', function() {
    ADS.log.header('testNodeName');
    ADS.log.write('nodeName is: '
        + document.getElementById('firefox').nodeName);
});
```

you'll get the following output in the log window, because the sample.html node with id="firefox" is an anchor node:

```
nodeName is: A
```

For other objects that aren't based on your markup tags, such as the Document object, the value of nodeName depends on the type of object you're referring to. Table 3-2 shows what will be returned for each Core object's nodeType.

Table 3-2. Expected nodeName values for each nodeType in the DOM2 Core specification

Object	Returns
Element.nodeName	The element name, in uppercase
Attr.nodeName	The attribute name, in lowercase
Text.nodeName	#text
CDATASection.nodeName	#cdata-section
EntityReference.nodeName	The entity reference name
Entity.nodeName	The entity name
ProcessingInstruction.nodeName	The target name
Comment.nodeName	#comment
Document.nodeName	#document
DocumentType.nodeName	The doctype name, for example HTML
DocumentFragment.nodeName	#document fragment
Notation.nodeName	The notation name

To retrieve the value associated with a Node, you can use the nodeValue property. This may seem like the obvious choice, but the nodeValue property probably isn't what you think it is. The nodeValue property only applies to a few DOM objects, specifically Attr, ProcessingInstructions, Comments, Text, and CDATASection; all other objects return null. For example, try to retrieve the nodeValue of an anchor tag using this load event:

```
ADS.addEvent(window,'load',function () {
    ADS.log.header('The node value of the anchor');
    ADS.log.write('nodeValue is: '
        + document.getElementById('firefox').nodeValue);
});
```

You'll get the following, because an anchor tag is based on Element, which has no nodeValue associated with it:

```
nodeValue is: null
```

If you have several different load events in your test document, such as this one and the previous one, you may notice that the events don't execute in the order you expect. We'll discuss this more in Chapter 4, but for now, I've included a header in the log so that you can distinguish the results of each event.

To retrieve the string value Firefox 2.0 within the anchor tag, you'll have to look to the childNodes of the anchor, as the string resides in a child Text node, for example:

```
var text = document.getElementById('firefox').childNodes[0].nodeValue;
```

Be aware that this line assumes that the element returned from getElementById() has child nodes. If it didn't, you would get an error, as index 0 doesn't exist in the childNodes.

Like nodeName, the nodeValue property represents different things depending on the type of object you're querying. Table 3-3 shows what will be returned from each Core object type.

Table 3-3. Expected nodeValue values for each nodeType in the DOM2 Core specification

Object	Returns
Element.nodeValue	null
Attr.nodeValue	The value of the attribute as a string
Text.nodeValue	The content of node as a string
CDATASection.nodeValue	The content of node as a string
EntityReference.nodeValue	null
Entity.nodeValue	null
ProcessingInstruction.nodeValue	The content of node as a string
Comment.nodeValue	The comment text string
Document.nodeValue	null
DocumentType.nodeValue	null
DocumentFragment.nodeValue	null
Notation.nodeValue	null

The nodeType, which you've probably guessed is the type of node, contains an integer associated with one of the named constants in Table 3-4. These constants refer to a DOM Core object, so you can determine the type of DOM Core object your given node object has been extended from.

Table 3-4. nodeType constants for DOM Core objects

nodeType Value	Equivalent Named Constant
1	Node.ELEMENT_NODE
2	Node.ATTRIBUTE_NODE

Continued

Table 3-4. nodeType constants for DOM Core objects *(continued)*

nodeType Value	Equivalent Named Constant
3	Node.TEXT_NODE
4	Node.CDATA_SECTION_NODE
5	Node.ENTITY_REFERENCE_NODE
6	Node.ENTITY_NODE
7	Node.PROCESSING_INSTRUCTION_NODE
8	Node.COMMENT_NODE
9	Node.DOCUMENT_NODE
10	Node.DOCUMENT_TYPE_NODE
11	Node.DOCUMENT_FRAGMENT_NODE
12	Node.NOTATION_NODE

If you add another load event to your domTesting.js script:

```
ADS.addEvent(window,'load', function () {
    ADS.log.header('Testing nodeType');
    ADS.log.write('nodeType is: '
        + document.getElementById('firefox').nodeType);
});
```

you can see the nodeType of one of the nodes for yourself:

```
nodeType is: 1
```

As I mentioned earlier, an anchor tag is an instance of the HTMLAnchorElement, but that object is based on an Element, as indicated by the nodeType of 1.

If your code involves checking the nodeType, which it often will, it would be wonderful to use the DOM constants in the comparison, such as:

```
if(node.nodeType == Node.COMMENT_NODE) {
    // Code for a comment node
}
```

rather than this:

```
if(node.nodeType == 8) {
    // Code for... what does 8 mean again?
}
```

I said, "It would be wonderful," because not all browsers support it. Browsers such as Firefox, Safari, and Opera allow you to use the DOM constants without a problem, but in Internet Explorer, the Node object doesn't exist. As I mentioned earlier in this chapter, Internet Explorer doesn't report that it supports DOM2 Core, but it does support parts of it. The appropriate methods and properties such as nodeValue are present in your objects, and they return the appropriate information. However, Internet Explorer doesn't expose any of the Core objects directly, so an error results.

To work around this error, you can define your own constants. Take a moment to add this to your personal ADS library:

```
(function(){
if(!window.ADS) { window['ADS'] = {} }

... Above here is your existing library ...

window['ADS']['node'] = {
    ELEMENT_NODE                   : 1,
    ATTRIBUTE_NODE                 : 2,
    TEXT_NODE                      : 3,
    CDATA_SECTION_NODE             : 4,
    ENTITY_REFERENCE_NODE          : 5,
    ENTITY_NODE                    : 6,
    PROCESSING_INSTRUCTION_NODE    : 7,
    COMMENT_NODE                   : 8,
    DOCUMENT_NODE                  : 9,
    DOCUMENT_TYPE_NODE             : 10,
    DOCUMENT_FRAGMENT_NODE         : 11,
    NOTATION_NODE                  : 12
};

... Below here is your existing library ...

})();
```

> I've used a lowercase node in window['ADS']['node'] so that your ADS library will still have access to the window's Node object using just Node if later versions of Internet Explorer decided to support the Node object directly.

With this addition, you can use the same logic across all browsers:

```
if(node.nodeType == ADS.node.COMMENT_NODE) {
    // Code for a comment node in any browser
}
```

Using a constant offers a number of advantages. Rather than forcing yourself to memorize Table 3-4, you simply need to remember which DOM object you're testing for. Also, your code will be much easier to read, maintain, and debug. The same logic applies if you're planning on sharing your code with others—reading a comparison to `ADS.node.COMMENT_NODE` makes a lot more semantic sense than just a plain number 8, especially when others may not even realize that node type numbers exist.

Node parents, children, and siblings

Most of the properties and methods in the Core deal with building and referencing the items in the tree structure. To make it easy for you to navigate the tree, each Node object has a number of prede-fined properties that reference various other parts of the tree. Each of these properties references an actual DOM object, with the exception of `childNodes`, which references a NodeList of DOM objects that acts like an array.

The `parentNode` property references the single direct parent of the specified node, as illustrated by the arrows in Figure 3-7.

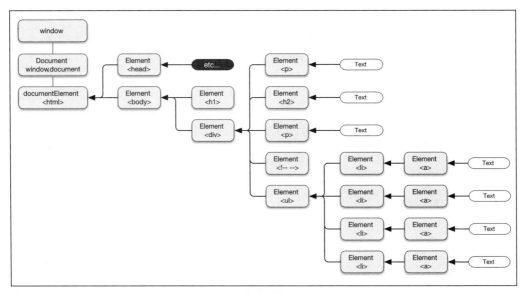

Figure 3-7. How DOM core represents parentNode relationships

The `childNodes` property references all the child elements of the node, as illustrated by the arrows in Figure 3-8.

The `childNodes` property is a NodeList with children represented using numerical indexes in an array. The first child is index 0:

```
var first = document.getElementById('browserList').childNodes[0];
```

And the last child is index `childNodes.length-1`:

```
var list = document.getElementById('browserList');
var last = list.childNodes[list.childNodes.length-1];
```

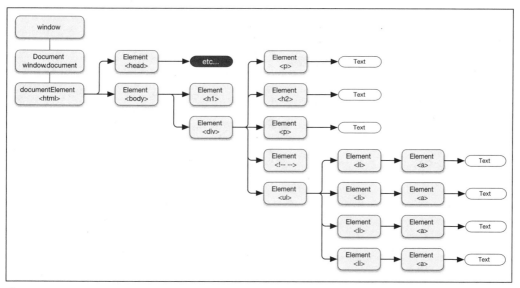

Figure 3-8. How DOM Core defined childNode relationships

To list all the nodes that are children of the body element, you can use the following load event:

```
ADS.addEvent(window, 'load', function() {
    ADS.log.header('List child nodes of the document body');
    for( var i = 0 ; i < document.body.childNodes.length ; i++ ) {
        ADS.log.write(document.body.childNodes.item(i).nodeName);
    }
});
```

Using that event, you would see that the body includes an <h1> and a <div> as well as Text nodes, depending on your browser, as explained earlier.

Note that the NodeList object represents a list of DOM nodes that acts similar to an array. You can iterate over a node list using the item() method to retrieve the indexed items:

```
for( i = 0 ; i < example.childNodes.length ; i++ ) {
    ADS.log.write(example.childNodes.item(i).nodeName);
}
```

Or you can use the same square-bracket notation you use for arrays:

```
for( i = 0 ; i < example.childNodes.length ; i++ ) {
    ADS.log.write(example.childNodes[i].nodeName);
}
```

The Node object also includes firstChild and lastChild properties to reference only the first and last child respectively, as illustrated in Figure 3-9. In cases where there is only one child, firstChild and lastChild will reference the same node. Also, don't forget about the Text nodes. In Firefox, the first and last child nodes for the sample.html file will almost always reference a text node with indenting white space.

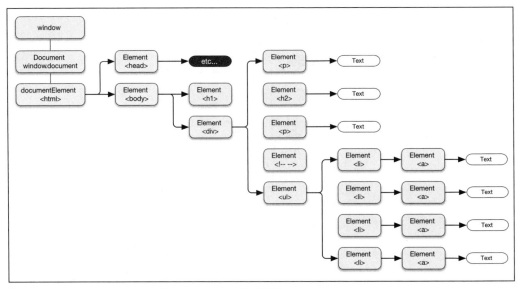

Figure 3-9. How the DOM Core defines firstChild and lastChild relationships

Likewise, the previousSibling and nextSibling properties each reference the sibling node immediately before and after the selected node, as shown in Figure 3-10. When the node you're referencing is the first node at that level, previousSibling will be null. Likewise, if the selected node is the last child, nextSibling will be null.

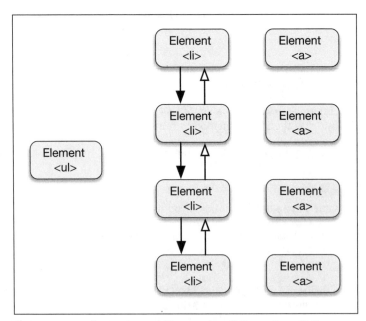

Figure 3-10. How the DOM core defines previousSibling and nextSibling relationships

Feel free to play around with the various properties in your domTesting.js script to see what you find. A lot of your time will be spent navigating through the tree structure and manipulating the children and siblings of your document's nodes, so knowing how to access and reference each part is important.

You can also use the common JavaScript chaining syntax to append multiple methods. For example, the following line would reference the fourth sibling in the body, as shown in Figure 3-11, where I've included the text nodes:

```
document.body.firstChild.nextSibling.nextSibling.nextSibling
```

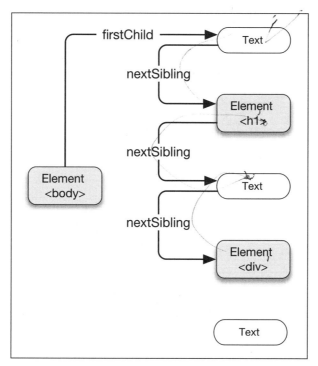

Figure 3-11. Referencing nodes by using multiple nextSibling methods in sequence

If you try this in Internet Explorer, where there are no Text nodes, your DOM script will throw an exception on the second nextSibling in the chain, because there is no third child of the body element.

Node attributes

Just like the rest of the DOM document, attributes are also based on the Node object, but they're not part of the general parent/child relationship tree. Attributes, which are instances of the Core Attr object, are contained in a NamedNodeMap in the node's attributes property. For example, the attributes of the Firefox anchor tag are represented in Figure 3-12.

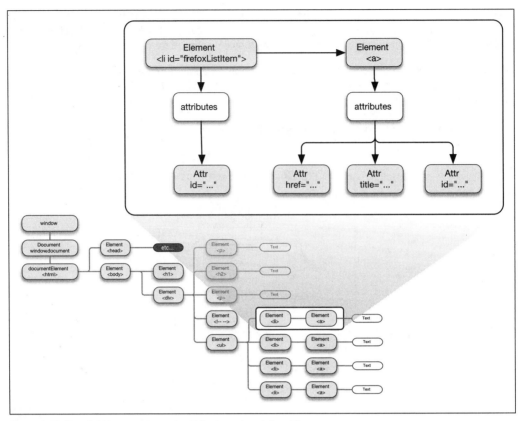

Figure 3-12. How DOM core represents attribute node relationships

The attributes shown in Figure 3-12 can be accessed using the anchor's `attributes` property with the following load event:

```
ADS.addEvent(window, 'load', function() {
    ADS.log.header('Attributes');
    var firefoxAnchor = document.getElementById('firefox');
    for(var i=0 ; i < firefoxAnchor.attributes.length ; i++) {
        ADS.log.write(
            firefoxAnchor.attributes.item(i).nodeName
                + ' = '
                + firefoxAnchor.attributes.item(i).nodeValue
        );
    }
});
```

The resulting log will contain the attributes of the Firefox anchor among many other attributes depending on the browser you're using:

- id = firefox
- title = Get Firefox
- href = http://www.getfirefox.com/

In many browsers, the attributes property will also contain a number of proprietary or DHTML properties.

Like Comment, the value of an Attr node can be retrieved using the nodeValue property, as you did here. The attribute, however, also has a child Text node that contains the same value as nodeValue.

Like NodeList, the items in NamedNodeMap can be accessed using the square bracket notation, so the following line would give you that same result as the previous load event:

```
firefoxAnchor.attributes[i].nodeName
```

Unlike a NodeList object, however, a NodeNameMap object has a few additional methods that can be handy. For example, if you want to retrieve a specific attribute from the attribute's NamedNodeMap, you can use the getNamedItem() method to retrieve reference to the specific attribute node:

```
var link = firefoxAnchor.attributes.getNamedItem('href').nodeValue;
```

This is similar to the getAttribute() method of Element, which you're probably more familiar with, but attributes.getNamedItem() will always work on any node, even ones that aren't instances of the Element object.

The node ownerDocument property

The ownerDocument property of a node is simply a reference to the root document to which that node belongs. In most cases, you can refer to document, in the scope chain, or window.document, as the browser will only have one instance of the document. If, however, the internals of your custom objects override document and use it to reference something else as in the following example:

```
function example(node) {

    // Override document in the scope chain so
    // it refers to something else.
    var document = 'something else';

    // Use the ownerDocument to reference the original DOM document.
    var anotherNode = node.ownerDocument.getElementById('id');

    // This will eror as document is now a string, not the DOM document
    // so the getElementById method doesn't exist.
    var anotherNode = document.getElementById('id');

}
```

you can still access the original document using the ownerDocument property of a DOM Node passed into your object.

Checking for children and attributes

If you need to quickly check if a node has children or attributes, you can use the hasChildNodes()
and hasAttributes() methods as shown in the following load event:

```
ADS.addEvent(window, 'load', function() {
    ADS.log.header('Attributes And ChildNodes');

    var h2 = document.getElementsByTagName('H2')[0];

    ADS.log.write(h2.nodeName);
    ADS.log.write(h2.nodeName + ' hasChildNodes: '
        + h2.hasChildNodes());
    ADS.log.write(h2.nodeName + ' childNodes: ' + h2.childNodes);
    ADS.log.write(h2.nodeName + ' number of childNodes: '
        + h2.childNodes.length);

    ADS.log.write(h2.nodeName + ' attributes: ' + h2.attributes);
    ADS.log.write(h2.nodeName + ' number of attributes: '
        + h2.attributes.length);

    // This line will error in MSIE
    ADS.log.write(h2.nodeName + ' hasAttributes: '
        + h2.hasAttributes());
});
```

Your test log would reveal the following results:

- H2
- H2 hasChildNodes: true
- H2 childNodes: [object NodeList]
- H2 number of childNodes: 1
- H2 attributes: [object NamedNodeMap]
- H2 number of attributes: 0
- H2 hasAttributes: false

You'll notice in Firefox, Opera, and Safari that, even though the node has no defined attributes, the
attributes property is still valid and has a length of 0. The same applies for the childNodes property.
Using the hasChildNodes() and hasAttributes() is good when you simply need to know if a node
has something or not, but if you want to know how many it has (including zero), you can still use the
property. In Internet Explorer, however, the hasAttributes() method isn't valid, so the preceding
example will produce an error on the last log entry:

```
Object doesn't support this property or method
```

Also, attributes is reported to be an Object as discussed earlier, and there are roughly 83 attributes
associated with this particular node, most of which are proprietary to Internet Explorer.

Manipulating your DOM node tree

The primary job of most of your DOM scripts will be to insert, remove, and move nodes in your DOM document. The manipulation members that you've come to adore, such as appendChild() and childNodes, are all members of the Node object that you've been playing with throughout this chapter. Appending new child nodes to Node objects is relatively simple, and you've probably already used the appendChild(newChild) method several times:

```
ADS.addEvent(window, 'load', function() {
    ADS.log.header('Append Child');
    var newChild = document.createElement('LI')
    newChild.appendChild(document.createTextNode('A new list item!'));
    var list = document.getElementById('browserList');
    list.appendChild(newChild);
});
```

By definition, appending always adds the new node to the end of the list, but what if you want to add it to the beginning or maybe even somewhere in the middle? That's where you use the insertBefore(newChild, refChild) method to insert a new child node into the associated node in the location directly before the referenced child node. To insert a new node into the list in sample.html as the second to last item, you could simply add the following load event:

```
ADS.addEvent(window, 'load', function() {
    ADS.log.header('Insert Before');
    var newChild = document.createElement('LI')
    newChild.appendChild(document.createTextNode('A new list item!'));
    var list = document.getElementById('browserList');
    list.insertBefore(newChild,list.lastChild);
});
```

You would have a new list item, as shown in Figure 3-13.

Figure 3-13. The new node as inserted in Firefox

But wait—if you take a closer look at Figure 3-13, you'll notice something wrong. My description of the previous load event said that it would "insert a new node as the second to last item." If you look at Figure 3-14, where the script was run in Microsoft Internet Explorer, you'll see that this is, indeed, true, and the second to last item is your new item.

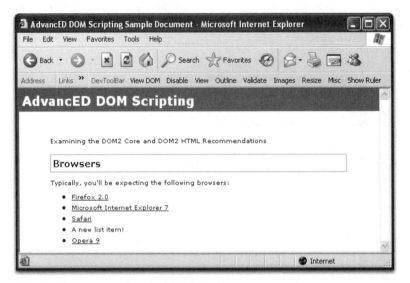

Figure 3-14. The new node as inserted in Firefox

The truth is that Firefox, Opera, Safari, and Figure 3-13 are perfectly correct, and the new node was inserted as the second to last item, but the script failed to account for the white space Text nodes. As I mentioned earlier, Internet Explorer ignores the white space, so lastChild referenced the last <li> list item, whereas the other browsers all referenced the last Text node. When writing your manipulation scripts, be careful to account for the white space nodes as necessary.

For whatever reason, the W3C decided not to include a prependChild() method or insertAfter() method in the Core specification, but you can easily use the existing methods to accomplish the same task as you saw with the methods you added to your ADS library in Chapter 1.

You may think that another option would be to add to the prototype of the Node object, as you did with your objects in Chapter 2, by doing something similar to this:

```
if(!Node.prependChild)
    Node.prototype.prependChild = function (newChild) {
        if(this.firstChild) {
            this.insertBefore(newChild,this.firstChild);
        } else {
            this.appendChild(newChild);
        }
        return this;
    }
}
if(!Node.insertAfter) {
```

```
Node.prototype.insertAfter = function(newChild,refChild) {
    if (refChild.nextSibling) {
        this.insertBefore(newChild, refChild.nextSibling);
    } else {
        this.appendChild(newChild);
    }
    return this;
}
}
```

This seems like a good idea, but there are a few problems.

- As I explained earlier, Internet Explorer doesn't have a native Node object, so this won't work. You could consider modifying the Object.prototype in Internet Explorer, but then all objects would inherit these methods, and they don't apply to all objects.

- In Safari, there is a native Node object, but Safari doesn't allow you to modify its prototype—again, this won't work.

- When you modify prototype, you will override any future additions to the DOM specification with the same method name, so it's best to simply create them as private methods within the namespace of your object, as described in Chapters 1 and 2.

Replacing and removing a node is relatively easy using the replaceChild(newChild,oldChild) and removeChild(oldChild) methods. Replacing your Firefox list item in sample.html with a new node is as easy as creating the node and appending it using something like this load event:

```
ADS.addEvent(window, 'load', function() {
    ADS.log.header('Replace a node');
    var newChild = document.createElement('LI')
    newChild.appendChild(document.createTextNode('A new list item!'));
    var firefoxLi = document.getElementById('firefoxListItem');
    firefoxLi.parentNode.replaceChild(newChild,firefoxLi);
});
```

Or to remove it, just call removeChild() on the node's parent:

```
ADS.addEvent(window, 'load', function() {
    ADS.log.header('Remove a node');
    var firefoxLi = document.getElementById('firefoxListItem');
    firefoxLi.parentNode.removeChild(firefoxLi);
});
```

The important thing to notice is that both the replaceChild() and removeChild() methods are for children of a node and aren't called directly on the node you're trying to replace or remove.

Duplicating and moving a node

The root of another common mistake made by DOM scripting rookies is in the fact that methods such as document.getElementById() return a *reference* to the Node object, not a copy of the object. If you were to add the following load event, how many Firefox list items will there be after it runs?

```
ADS.addEvent(window, 'load', function() {
    ADS.log.header('Clone and Move a Node');
    var firefoxLi = document.getElementById('firefoxListItem');
    var firefoxLiClone = firefoxLi.cloneNode(true);
    var unorderedList = firefoxLi.parentNode;

    // Apped to the list
    unorderedList.appendChild(firefoxLi);
    // Append to the list
    unorderedList.appendChild(firefoxLiClone);
});
```

You may be thinking that there will be three: the original one and the two that are appended. The correct answer is two. When loaded, the page will resemble Figure 3-15, where there are two Firefox entries at the bottom of the list and none at the top.

Figure 3-15. Browser view of sample.html after the Firefox list item node has been cloned as well as appended in a different location

When you retrieve the node using the document.getElementById() method and assign it to the firefoxLi variable as follows, you're retrieving a reference to the node—not a copy:

```
var firefoxLi = document.getElementById('firefoxListItem');
```

Later, when you append the reference to the list, the appendChild() method takes the given firefoxLi node and appends that node to the end of the unorderedlist:

```
unorderedList.appendChild(firefoxLi);
```

In this case, you're asking it to append a reference of a node that already exists in the document, so that node is moved, not copied, to the new location.

The Core Element object

Beyond the Node object, there's the Element object. The Element object and its methods will be the most common things you'll be dealing with in day-to-day DOM scripting. As you saw in Figure 3-4, the majority of the DOM document tree structure consisted of Element nodes but a specific DOM2 HTML object will extend each Element further. All Element objects have the properties and methods of the Node object as well as a few others that facilitate manipulating the attributes of the node and locating child Element objects, as you'll see in the following sections.

Manipulating Element attributes

To simplify handling of attributes, the Element object includes a variety of methods for manipulating the attributes property of the base Node:

- getAttribute(name) allows you to retrieve an attribute based on the name of the attribute as a string, for example:

```
ADS.addEvent(window,'load',function() {
    ADS.log.header('Get Safari href attribute');
    var safariAnchor = document.getElementById('safari');
    var href = safariAnchor.getAttribute('href');
    ADS.log.write(href);
});
```

- setAttribute(name,value) allows you to set the value of an attribute based on the name of the attribute as a string, for example:

```
ADS.addEvent(window,'load',function() {
    ADS.log.header('Set Safari title attribute');
    var safariAnchor = document.getElementById('safari');
    safariAnchor.setAttribute('title','Safari is for Mac OS X');
});
```

- removeAttribute(name) allows you to remove the value of an attribute based on the name of the attribute as a string, for example:

```
ADS.addEvent(window,'load',function() {
    ADS.log.header('Remove Firefox title attribute');
    var firefox = document.getElementById('firefoxListItem');
    firefox.removeAttribute('title');
});
```

Similarly, there are methods for manipulating the attributes based on the actual DOM Attr node object, rather than the name and value strings:

- getAttributeNode(name) allows you to retrieve the Attr node for the specified attribute.
- setAttributeNode(newAttr) allows you to set attributes based on new instances of the Attr object.
- removeAttributeNode(oldAttr) allows you to remove the attribute node the same way you can remove a child node using the removeChild() method.

119

> *Like the* Node *object,* Element *also has methods that are namespace specific. I won't go over them here, as they aren't implemented across all modern browsers.*

Locating Element objects within Element objects

Within the limits of the Element object, the only method available for locating other nodes is the getElementsByTagName() method. The getElementsByTagName() method returns a NodeList object referencing all ancestors with the given tag name. The resulting NodeList is a list of all the elements in the order they appear in the DOM Document if read left to right and top to bottom like this book. The getElementsByTagName() method also allows you to use an asterisk (*) as a wildcard tag name to find all elements. Try this load event:

```
ADS.addEvent(window,'load',function() {
    ADS.log.header('Get all browserList elements by tag name');
    var list = document.getElementById('browserList');
    var ancestors = list.getElementsByTagName('*');
    for(i = 0 ; i < ancestors.length ; i++ ) {
        ADS.log.write(ancestors.item(i).nodeName);
    }
});
```

You'll get the following list of the four list elements and their children, in the order that they appear in sample.html (provided the document hasn't been altered by any other load events):

- LI
- A
- LI
- A
- LI
- A
- LI
- A

Looking at the results, you'll also notice that the * wildcard doesn't include things like the text nodes within the anchor tags. The getElementsByTagName() method only includes Element nodes, no others, as indicated by the "Elements" part in the method name.

The Element object has no methods for creating new Element objects. Creation is handled entirely by the Document object, as you'll discover next.

The Core Document object

As you saw in Chapter 2, JavaScript's global object is the window object. When we're referring to the DOM, we're talking about the window's document property, or window.document. The Document object itself is based on the Node object, so all the Node properties and methods you saw earlier also apply to the Document object.

The window.document property was around in DHTML before the W3C DOM specification came about, so along with the W3C DOM methods, there may be some other browser-specific members such as document.all. Whenever possible, you should avoid using a proprietary, nonstandard member and opt instead for a standards-based one.

If a browser doesn't support a standard method, but it may do so in the future, you can fake the standard way. For example, if your site needs to support archaic browsers like Internet Explorer 4, which supports the nonstandard document.all but not the standard document.getElementById(), just use some simple object detection to add a document.getElementById() method at the start of your script that queries the all method:

```
if(document.all && !document.getElementById) {
    document.getElementById = function(id) {
        return document.all[id];
    }
}
```

With this addition, if document.all exists and document.getElementById() doesn't, a getElmentById() method will be created that returns the same thing as the standard method. Now you can code using the standard method, safe in the knowledge that the rare occurrences of Internet Explorer 4 will still work.

> *You'll have to do this for every method you need to support, so you'll need to decide which browsers you need to support fully and which browsers will get your gracefully degraded version instead.*

The document.documentElement property

The document.documentElement property is a shortcut to the root element of the document. In the case of an HTML document in your web browser, your root element is the <html> tag.

Creating nodes with document methods

The document object has a variety of methods that allow you to create new instances of all the various types of nodes in the DOM core. The types of nodes include Element, as we already discussed, as well as several others:

- createAttribute(name): Creates Attr nodes of type Node.ATTRIBUTE_NODE
- createCDATASection(data): Creates CDATASection nodes of type Node.CDATA_SECTION_NODE
- createComment(data): Creates Comment nodes of type Node.COMMENT_NODE
- createDocumentFragment(): Creates DocumentFragment nodes of type Node.DOCUMENT_FRAGMENT_NODE
- createElement(tagName): Creates Element nodes of type Node.ELEMENT_NODE
- createEntityReference(name): Creates EntityReference nodes of type Node.ENTITY_REFERENCE_NODE

- createProcessingInstruction(target,data): Creates ProcessingInstruction nodes of type Node.PROCESSING_INSTRUCTION_NODE
- createTextNode(data): Creates Text nodes of type Node.TEXT_NODE

There are a few other types of nodes that also deal with namespaces, but they're not compatible with all browsers, so I won't get into those here.

You'll be using these create* methods a lot in your code—whenever you need to create new branches and nodes in the tree. The majority of the time, you'll probably be using createElement() and createAttribute(), but the others will also come in handy.

Locating Elements with Document methods

The other two important methods you'll find in the Core Document object are the getElementsByTagName() method and the getElementById() method.

As you probably know, the getElementById() method returns one element corresponding to the ID you requested. Calling this method

```
document.getElementById('outer-wrapper');
```

would return the Element with the id="outer-wrapper" attribute. It's important to note that the getElementById() method is singular and only returns one element. Although web browsers often allow it, a valid HTML document shouldn't contain more than one instance of the same ID. IDs *must always* be unique throughout the entire document to prevent confusion when using getElementById().

The getElementsByTagName() method functions the same way it does in the Element object, but it's technically not the same function. The Document object doesn't inherit from the Element object, but includes the same getElementsByTagName() method, so you can query the entire document.

At this point you may be wondering why there's no native getElementByClassName() method. Well, it's not part of DOM core because classes don't generally apply to all types of XML documents. This distinction is one of the reasons why understanding the specification can help you understand what's really going on. The getElementsByClassName() method really only consistently applies to HTML documents, not XML documents. Sure, XML documents can have a class attribute, but it's not part of the XML specification. On the other hand, the HTMLElement object in an HTML document does have a className property by specification, so the method getElementsByClassName() would make sense in the DOM2 HTML specification. But the W3C decided not to include one, so you're forced to create your own as you did in Chapter 1.

Traversing and iterating the DOM tree

In many of your scripts, you'll need to examine DOM elements in some fashion. Most times, this will involve examining each node and its children recursively in the document tree. In an ideal world, you'd want to use the DOM2 Traversal and Range specification objects to iterate over your tree, as doing so would provide a cross-browser, standards-compliant method and ensure you always get the right answers (think missing text nodes in Internet Explorer). But Traversal and Range specification objects are only sparsely implemented across the various browsers, so you'll have to come up with your own solution if you want it to work everywhere.

The easiest way to create your own recursive tree-walking method is to create a generic function that does the traversing and executes an anonymous function call on each node as we discussed in Chapter 2. To keep these methods handy while you go through the rest of the book, add them to your ADS library as you go.

If you don't care about the depth of the node in the DOM tree, you can use the document. getElementsByTagName('*') method to retrieve all the Element nodes in the specified node and loop through it:

```
(function(){
if(!window.ADS) { window['ADS'] = {} }

... Above here is your existing library ...

function walkElementsLinear(func,node) {
    var root = node || window.document;
    var nodes = root.getElementsByTagName("*");
    for(var i = 0 ; i < nodes.length ; i++) {
        func.call(nodes[i]);
    }
}

... Below here is your existing library ...

})();
```

I've called this function walkElementsLinear() because it's not recursive and only includes Element objects in the list created with the getElementsByTagName() method.

Alternately, if you need to keep track of the depth of the node or build a path, you could walk the tree recursively:

```
(function(){
if(!window.ADS) { window['ADS'] = {} }

... Above here is your existing library ...

function walkTheDOMRecursive(func,node,depth,returnedFromParent) {
    var root = node || window.document;
    var returnedFromParent = func.call(root,depth++,returnedFromParent);
    var node = root.firstChild;
    while(node) {
        walkTheDOMRecursive(func,root.childNodes[i],
            depth,returnedFromParent);
        node = node.nextSibling;
    }
};

... Below here is your existing library ...

})();
```

You may even want to include the attributes of your node as you go:

```
(function(){
if(!window.ADS) { window['ADS'] = {} }
```

... Above here is your existing library ...

```
function walkTheDOMWithAttributes(node,func,depth,returnedFromParent) {
    var root = node || window.document;
    var returnedFromParent = func(root,depth++,prefix);
    if (root.attributes) {
        for(var i=0; i < root.attributes.length; i++) {
            walkTheDOMWithAttributes(root.attributes[i],
                func,depth-1,returnedFromParent);
        }
    }
    if(root.nodeType != Node.ATTRIBUTE_NODE) {
        var node = root.firstChild;
        while(node) {
            walkTheDOMWithAttributes(node,func,
                depth,returnedFromParent);
            node = node.nextSibling;
        }
    }
}
```

... Below here is your existing library ...

```
})();
```

These aren't the only methods you can use, as there are dozens of possible ways. You could also use the original walkTheDom() function by Douglas Crockford (http://javascript.crockford.com):

```
function walkTheDOM(node, func) {
    func(node);
    node = node.firstChild;
    while (node) {
        walkTheDOM(node, func);
        node = node.nextSibling;
    }
}
```

But I prefer the earlier version (called walkTheDOMRecursive() so it doesn't conflict) as it defaults to the root document object and calls the function in the content of the node. Therefore, you can use this to refer to the node rather than an argument to the function. Using call() also prevents you from doing strange things with the scope of the recursive function.

DOM HTML

Of all the sections in this chapter, the DOM2 HTML section should be the largest—if I were going to cover the entire specification. The DOM2 HTML specification is rather lengthy, as it contains a specific object for every HTML element. I'm going to briefly discuss the general objects and how they work along with the DOM Core, but I'm not going to go through them all, as they're fairly self-explanatory—you would probably get bored and skip the chapter.

Earlier, in Figure 3-4, I indicated how the DOM2 Core represents the document in your sample.html file. Figure 3-16 shows the same representation according to the DOM2 HTML specification.

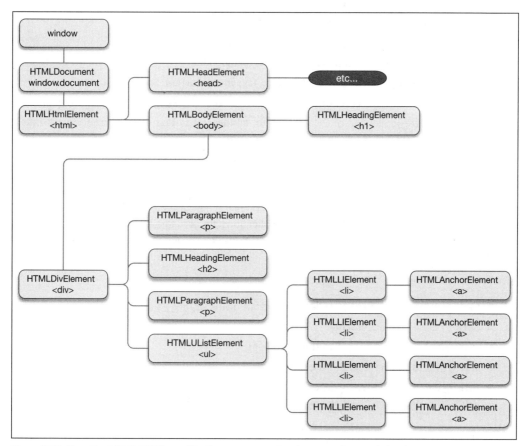

Figure 3-16. How the DOM2 HTML specification represents the document in sample.html

Remember that the original DOM2 Core objects still apply, as each of the DOM2 HTML objects extends from the Core object.

The DOM2 HTML HTMLDocument object

In the case of your HTML document rendered in a web browser, the DOM document object in window.document is actually an instance of the HTMLDocument object, as shown in Figure 3-16. The HTMLDocument object inherits all the members of the Document object from the Core, but adds a few additional properties and methods you're probably already familiar with. The properties, some of which are also known as collections, are as follows:

- title contains the string in the head's <title> tag, AdvancED DOM Scripting in the case of the sample.html file.
- referrer contains the URL of the previous page that linked to the current page.
- domain contains the domain name of the current site.
- URL contains the URL in the address bar of the current page.
- body references the DOM tree starting at the <body> node.
- images is an array collection of all the <img> tags in the current document.
- applets is an array collection of DOM nodes for all the <img> tags in the current document.
- links is an array collection of DOM nodes for all the <link> tags in the current document.
- forms is an array collection of DOM nodes for all the <form> tags in the current document.
- anchors is an array collection of DOM nodes for all the <a> tags in the current document.
- cookie is a string containing all the cookie information for the current page.

If you take a closer look at the list, you'll notice that a few things are missing from it, such as frames, plugins, scripts, stylesheets, and all. These collections are available in many browsers but aren't part of the official DOM2 HTML specification, and therefore, you should use other standards-based means to access the same information, as we discussed earlier with document.all.

HTMLDocument also includes a few methods:

- open() opens a document to collect the output of the write() and writeln() methods.
- close() closes the document.
- write(data) writes the input to the document.
- writeln(data) writes a line to the document.
- getElementsByName(elementName) works the same way as getElementsByTagName() except that it uses the name="example" attribute instead of the tag name.

As you can see, document.write() is actually part of the DOM2 HTML specification, so it doesn't go against standards to use it. You can create a document as follows:

```
var newDocument = document.open("text/html");
var markup = '<html>'
    + '<head><title>Write Example</title></head>'
    + '<body>This isn't really AdvancED!</body></html>';
newDocument.write(markup);
newDocument.close();
```

But it still replaces the content of the existing document and causes other browser quirks that I won't get into here. As you saw in Chapter 1, document.write() can lead to other bad practices, so we'll avoid using it.

The HTML HTMLElement object

Atop the Element from DOM2 Core, the HTMLElement object also adds a few properties that you should already be familiar with:

- id contains all your id="inner-wrapper" attributes that will be used by the document.getElementById('inner-wrapper') method.
- title is used for further semantic description and tooltip rollovers.
- lang is the language code defined in RFC 1766 for the language of the node.
- dir is the direction of the text in the node (by default ltr for "left to right").
- className contains all of your class="button" attributes for CSS hooks.

Each specific tag is further extended with additional properties and methods by one of the many tag-specific DOM HTML objects.

A practical example: converting hand-coded HTML to DOM code

As a web developer, one thing I loathe is repetitive tasks. Do any of us really want to do the same thing over and over and over? One way to cut through the boredom and remove the mundane repetitiveness is to employ reusable objects or libraries like the ADS library you're building now and the reusable objects in Part 3. But that still leaves you with the task of manually coding your DOM document fragments, so let's make that a little easier.

Another way to make things interesting and speed up your development process is to write code that creates code for you. To apply what you've learned in this chapter, we'll create a simple tool that will generate the necessary DOM code from an existing document fragment, as shown in Figure 3-17.

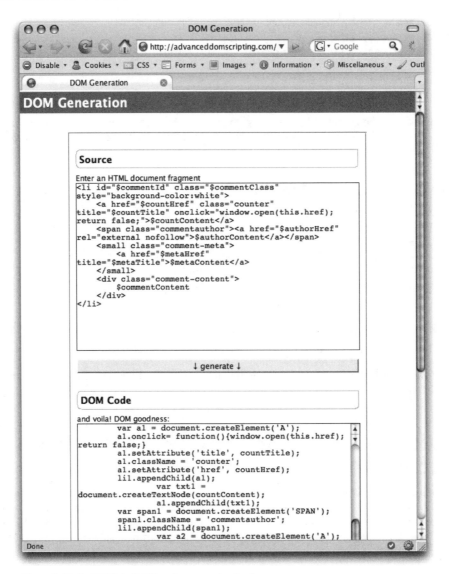

Figure 3-17. An HTML-to-DOM code conversion tool

This will come in handy later when you want to quickly create all the DOM code necessary to replace the use of innerHTML strings.

The DOM generation tool HTML file

Your DOM generation tool will need an HTML form where you can paste in your HTML fragments and convert them as necessary. You can set up this page however you want, but it will need two <textarea> elements and a <button> element, as shown in the chapter3/generateDOM/generate. html source:

```
<!DOCTYPE html PUBLIC "-//W3C//DTD XHTML 1.0 Strict//EN"
    "http://www.w3.org/TR/xhtml1/DTD/xhtml1-strict.dtd">
<html xmlns="http://www.w3.org/1999/xhtml">
<head>
<title>Generate DOM</title>
    <link rel="stylesheet" type="text/css"
        href="../../shared/source.css" />
    <link rel="stylesheet" type="text/css" href="style.css" />
    <!-- ADS Library (full version from source linked here) -->
    <script type="text/javascript"
        src="../../ADS-final-verbose.js"></script>
    <script type="text/javascript" src="generateDom.js"></script>
    <script type="text/javascript" src="load.js"></script>
</head>
<body>
<h1>DOM Generation</h1>
<div id="content">
<form id="generator" action="">
    <fieldset>
        <h2>Source</h2>
        <label for="source">Enter an HTML document fragment</label>
        <textarea id="source" cols="30" rows="15"></textarea>
        <input id="generate" type="button" value="&#8595;
            generate &#8595;" />
        <h2>DOM Code</h2>
        <label for="result">and voila! DOM goodness:</label>
        <textarea id="result" cols="30" rows="15"></textarea>
    </fieldset>
</form>
</div>
</body>
</html>
```

This page will rely on JavaScript and has no alternative method. You'll notice the page includes a generateDOM.js file as well as a very simple load.js script that calls a generateDOM() method to convert the HTML:

```
// Add a load event to the page to register event listeners
ADS.addEvent(window, 'load', function() {

    // Register a click event listener on the button
    ADS.addEvent('generate','click', function(W3CEvent) {

        // Retrieve the HTML source
        var source = ADS.$('source').value;

        // Convert the HTML to DOM and put it in the #result textarea
        ADS.$('result').value = generateDOM(source);
```

```
    });

  });
```

Building the generateDOM() method in the generateDOM.js will be the focus of the rest of this chapter.

Testing with an example HTML fragment

To test your tool, use the following fragment of a typical HTML document. This fragment is actually the comment markup from the K2 WordPress theme (http://binarybonsai.com/wordpress/k2/):

```html
<li id="comment-1" class="comment c1 c-y2007 c-m01 c-d01 c-h05 alt">
    <a href="#comment-1" class="counter"
        title="Permanent Link to this Comment">1</a>
    <span class="commentauthor">
        <a href="http://wordpress.org/" rel="external
            nofollow">Mr WordPress</a>
    </span>
    <small class="comment-meta">
        <a href="#comment-1" title="Permanent Link to this ➥
Comment">Aug 22nd, 2006 at 5:09 pm</a>
    </small>
    <div class="comment-content">
        <p>Hi, this is a comment.<br>To delete a comment, just log ➥
in, and view the posts' comments, there you will have the option ➥
to edit or delete them.</p>
    </div>
</li>
```

If you want to write your own degradable Ajax-based comment system for a K2-themed WordPress site (or any other site), your JavaScript API will need to append a new comment to the current list after submitting the comment. We'll discuss Ajax and proper degradation in Chapter 7, so here, we'll just concentrate on making it easier for you to quickly create the necessary DOM code. Though I'm using the default K2 comment block, you can use any HTML you want.

The overall goal of the tool is to take an HTML fragment such as the following anchor

```html
<a href="http://wordpress.org/" rel="external ➥
nofollow">Mr WordPress</a>
```

and convert it to the equivalent DOM code:

```javascript
var a = document.createElement('A');
a.setAttribute('href','http://wordpress.org');
a.setAttribute('rel','external nofollow');
```

This would be fine if you always want the anchor to point to http://wordpress.org, but in most cases, you'll want the href attribute to use a variable from your DOM script. To identify these variables, modify your HTML, and use a dollar-sign prefix as the value for each of the attributes, for example, $var where var is the variable name you would like the attribute to use:

```
<li id="$commentId" class="$commentClass" style="background-color:white">
    <a href="$countHref" class="counter" title="$countTitle"➥
onclick="window.open(this.href); return false;">$countContent</a>
    <span class="commentauthor"><a href="$authorHref" rel="external➥
nofollow">$authorContent</a></span>
    <small class="comment-meta">
        <a href="$metaHref" title="$metaTitle">$metaContent</a>
    </small>
    <div class="comment-content">
        $commentContent
    </div>
</li>
```

When you examine the node in the generateDOM() method, you can convert any HTML instances of $varName like this one:

```
<a href="$metaHref" rel="external nofollow">Mr WordPress</a>
```

into DOM code that also incorporates variables:

```
var a = document.createElement('A');
a.setAttribute('href',metaHref);
a.setAttribute('rel','external nofollow');
// etc.
```

The anchor now uses the metaHref elsewhere in your script to dynamically define the content of the attribute. You'll also notice that I've added an onclick event to one of the links as well as an inline style attribute to the <li>. These additions will allow you to test out all of the features of the generateDOM object.

> *You may wonder why I chose to use the dollar-sign-prefixed $var as the format. You can use another format if you want, but $ is a common symbol used to define variables in server-side languages such as PHP. Using $ here allows you to quickly copy and paste your server-side HTML templates directly into the tool, and at the same time, it will maintain the same variable names in your DOM script files, keeping everything nicely semantic.*

Adding to the ADS library

Before you start the generateDOM object framework, you'll need to add a few more methods to your ADS.js library.

First, outside your existing ADS namespace, add two new methods to the prototype of the JavaScript String object that will allow you to repeat and trim a string:

```
// Repeat a string
if (!String.repeat) {
    String.prototype.repeat = function(l){
        return new Array(l+1).join(this);
```

```
        }
    }

    // Remove trailing and leading whitespace
    if (!String.trim) {
        String.prototype.trim = function() {
            return this.replace(/^\s+|\s+$/g,'');
        }
    }
```

The `repeat()` method will allow you to repeat the string a given number of times, which is useful when creating indents and other repetitive strings:

```
var example = 'a'.repeat(5);
//example is now: aaaaa
```

For all the text nodes in the HTML fragment, you're going to use the `trim()` method to see if they contain anything other than white space. The trim function is common to many other languages and trims off the white space on either end of a string, reducing it to nothing if it doesn't contain any word characters.

> *The prototype modification is placed outside the ADS namespace to remind you that the modification of the* prototype *of the built-in* String *object affects every string within the entire script, not just those within the* ADS.generateDOM *object. Just like the* prototype *of your custom objects, you can modify the* prototype *of an existing JavaScript object, such as* String, *to add features or override existing features. Also, the methods are only added if they don't already exist so that native methods can be used if available.*

Next, camelize method to the ADS namespace (if you're not using the one I provided with the example):

```
(function(){
if(!window.ADS) { window['ADS'] = {} }

... Above here is your existing library ...

/* convert word-word to wordWord */
function camelize(s) {
    return s.replace(/-(\w)/g, function (strMatch, p1){
        return p1.toUpperCase();
    });
}
window['ADS']['camelize'] = camelize;

... Below here is your existing library ...

})();
```

The ADS.camelize() method will help deal with inline style attributes. Though the example doesn't yet include any, because it was well written using classes and IDs, it's inevitable that at some point you're going to come across some HTML with inline styles. In those cases, your generateDOM object should at least know how to properly handle the style attribute. Because of incompatibility in the CSS and ECMAScript specification, CSS properties use hyphens; hyphens aren't well suited to JavaScript member names, since a hyphen isn't a valid character. In those cases, such as font-size, the style property in JavaScript becomes camel cased, so font-size becomes fontSize, which is handled by the camelize() method.

The generateDOM object framework

The only thing left now is to create the generateDOM object in the generateDOM.js file. Start with the framework that includes a new namespace, a few helper methods, properties, and a final window method assignment:

```
/* A new namespace for the generator */
(function(){

function encode(str) { }

function checkForVariable(v) { }

var domCode = '';
var nodeNameCounters = [];
var requiredVariables = '';
var newVariables = '';

function generate(strHTML,strRoot) { }

function processAttribute(tabCount,refParent) { }

function processNode(tabCount,refParent) { }

window['generateDOM'] = generate;

})();
```

The encode() method

The first method in the generateDOM.js file is encode(). JavaScript already has an escape() method built in, but replaces all non-ASCII characters, including spaces and punctuation, with the hexadecimal encoding %xx, where xx is the ASCII-safe hexadecimal number representing the character. When you escape a space using escape(' '), the space will be converted to %20.

Within the DOM generation methods, the encode() method will be used to make a string safe to use as a JavaScript string, so you only want to change backslashes, single quotes, and new lines, because the strings you'll be generating will be enclosed in single quotes:

```
var example = 'a string';
```

The string 'a string' can't contain plain backslashes, single quotes, or new lines, so you can use your encode() method to properly escape only these characters using a backslash:

```
function encode(str) {
    if (!str) return null;
    str = str.replace(/\\/g,'\\\\');
    str = str.replace(/';/g, "\\'");
    str = str.replace(/\s+^/mg, "\\n");
    return str;
}
```

The checkForVariable() method

The second method in the generateDOM.js file is checkForVariable(). You'll be using this method to look for those special $var strings in all the node values and deal with them as necessary. The method will simply check to see if a dollar sign is contained somewhere in the string, and if so, return either a quoted string or a variable name. Also, the variable declaration will be appended to the requiredVariables string, so they can be reported in the result:

```
function checkForVariable(v) {
    if(v.indexOf('$') == -1) {
        v = '\'' + v + '\'';
    } else {
        // MSIE adds full anchor paths so you need to
        // take the substring from $ to the end of the string
        v = v.substring(v.indexOf('$')+1)
        requiredVariables += 'var ' + v + ';\n';
    }
    return v;
}
```

The generate() method

Now you're ready to test and get to the guts of the object: the generate() method. Start by filling in the generate() method and you'll see how it works:

```
function generate(strHTML,strRoot) {

    //add the HTML to the body so we can walk the tree
    var domRoot = document.createElement('DIV');
    domRoot.innerHTML = strHTML;

    // reset the variables
    domCode = '';
    nodeNameCounters = [];
    requiredVariables = '';
    newVariables = '';

    // process all the child nodes in domRoot using processNode()
    var node = domRoot.firstChild;
```

```
        while(node) {
            ADS.walkTheDOMRecursive(processNode,node,0,strRoot);
            node = node.nextSibling;
        }

        // Output the generated code
        domCode =
            '/* requiredVariables in this code\n' + requiredVariables
            + '*/\n\n'
            + domCode + '\n\n'
            + '/* new objects in this code\n' + newVariables
            + '*/\n\n';

        return domCode;
    }
```

> The walkTheDOMRecursive() method doesn't handle the attribute nodes associated with our HTML nodes. We'll handle those separately in the generate() method, as it will be easier to deal with the special cases required by class and style attributes.

The easiest way to generate the necessary DOM code will be able to walk an existing DOM tree and examine all its parts, re-creating them as necessary. To do that, you cheat a little and use innerHTML to initially create the DOM tree from the HTML string:

```
//add the HTML to the body so we can walk the tree
var domRoot = document.createElement('DIV');
domRoot.innerHTML = HTML;
```

This little trick will force the browser to parse the HTML string into a DOM structure within domRoot. Since the intent of this object is to be a development tool, you can be happy using the innerHTML property, as you'll control which browser you'll run the tool in and under what circumstances.

Next, you finish off the generate() method by looping through the children of domRoot and invoking the walkTheDOMRecursive() method. This uses the processNode() method to deal with each node:

```
var node = domRoot.firstChild;
while(node) {
    walkTheDOMRecursive(processNode,node,0,strRoot);
    node = node.nextSibling;
}
// Output the generated code
domCode =
    '/* requiredVariables in this code\n' + requiredVariables + '*/\n\n'
    + domCode + '\n\n'
    + '/* new objects in this code\n' + newVariables + '*/\n\n';

return domCode;
```

The processNode() and processAttribute() methods

When you loop through the child node of domRoot, you'll use processNode() to analyze each of the nodes in the tree to determine the type, value, and attributes so that you can re-create the appropriate DOM code. Fill in the processNode() method as follows, and then we'll discuss how it works:

```javascript
function processNode(tabCount,refParent) {
    // Repeat a tab character to indent the line
    // to match the depth in the tree
    var tabs = (tabCount ? '\t'.repeat(parseInt(tabCount)) : '');

    // Determine the node type and deal with element and text nodes
    switch(this.nodeType) {
        case ADS.node.ELEMENT_NODE:
            // Increase a counter and create a new variable
            // reference using the tag and the counter, eg: a1,a2,a3
            if(nodeNameCounters[this.nodeName]) {
                ++nodeNameCounters[this.nodeName];
            } else {
                nodeNameCounters[this.nodeName] = 1;
            }

            var ref = this.nodeName.toLowerCase()
                + nodeNameCounters[this.nodeName];

            // Append the line of DOM code that creates this element
            domCode += tabs
                + 'var '
                + ref
                + ' = document.createElement(\''
                + this.nodeName +'\');\n';

            // Append to the list of new variable to report
            // them all in the result
            newVariables += '' + ref + ';\n';

            // Check if there are any attributes and if so, loop through
            // them and walk their DOM tree using processAttribute
            if (this.attributes) {
                for(var i=0; i < this.attributes.length; i++) {
                    ADS.walkTheDOMRecursive(
                        processAttribute,
                        this.attributes[i],
                        tabCount,
                        ref
                    );
                }
            }

            break;
```

```
            case ADS.node.TEXT_NODE:

                // Check for a value in the text node
                // that isn't just whitespace
                var value = (this.nodeValue ? encode( ➥
this.nodeValue.trim()) : '' );
                if(value) {

                    // Increase a counter and create a new txt reference
                    // using the counter, eg: txt1,txt2,txt3
                    if(nodeNameCounters['txt']) {
                        ++nodeNameCounters['txt'];
                    } else {
                        nodeNameCounters['txt'] = 1;
                    }
                    var ref = 'txt' + nodeNameCounters['txt'];

                    // Check if the $var is the value
                    value = checkForVariable(value);

                    // Append the DOM code that creates this element
                    domCode += tabs
                        + 'var '
                        + ref
                        + ' = document.createTextNode('+ value +');\n';
                    // Append to the list of new variable to report
                    // them all in the result
                    newVariables += '' + ref + ';\n';

                } else {
                    // If there is no value (or just whitespace) return so
                    // that this node isn't appended to the parent
                    return;
                }
                break;

        default:
            // Ignore everything else
            break;
    }

    // Append the code that appends this node to its parent
    if(refParent) {
        domCode += tabs + refParent + '.appendChild('+ ref + ');\n';
    }
    return ref;

}
```

Reading through the code, you can see it does several things.

First you determine the indention level in the tree based on the recursion depth and repeat a tab character as necessary:

```
var tabs = (tabCount ? '\t'.repeat(parseInt(tabCount)) : '');
```

The indenting isn't really necessary, but it helps make your code more legible and easier to understand.

Next, you need to do special things depending on what type of node you're processing. For this example, you're only going to deal with two types of nodes: the ADS.node.ELEMENT_NODE (type number 1) and ADS.node.TEXT_NODE (type number 3). You'll also deal with attribute nodes using the processAttribute() method. For the moment, any other node types will be ignored. If you have other code you want to include, feel free to extend this example to include whatever nodes you'd like by adding more cases to the switch statement:

```
switch(node.nodeType) {
    case ADS.node.ELEMENT_NODE:
        //process element nodes
        break;
    case ADS.node.TEXT_NODE:
        //process text nodes
        break;
    default:
        //ignore everything else
        break;
}
```

You'll notice the switch statement uses the ADS.node constants for the comparison, not the numeric value. Again, this makes the code much easier to understand, as you can see.

If the node in the fragment is an ELEMENT_NODE, you create a new variable name using the concatenation of the nodeName and a numeric counter so that you can reference multiple instances of the same nodeType. Additionally, you'll append to the newVariables string so that you can output a nice list of all the new nodes you created:

```
// Increase a counter and create a new variable reference using
// the tag and the counter, eg: a1,a2,a3
if(nodeNameCounters[this.nodeName]) {
    ++nodeNameCounters[this.nodeName];
} else {
    nodeNameCounters[this.nodeName] = 1;
}

var ref = this.nodeName.toLowerCase()
    + nodeNameCounters[this.nodeName];

// Append the line of DOM code that creates this element
domCode += tabs
    + 'var '
    + ref
    + ' = document.createElement(\'' + this.nodeName +'\');\n';
```

```
// Append to the list of new variable to report
// them all in the result
newVariables += '' + ref + ';\n';
```

All ELEMENT_NODE nodes can also have attributes. We discussed earlier how attributes are themselves Nodes but they're not included in the childNodes or sibling iteration. Attribute nodes are contained in the node.attributes array, so you'll have to walk through them separately:

```
if (node.attributes) {
    for(var i=0; i < node.attributes.length; i++) {
        myWalkTheDOM(processAttribute,
            node.attributes[i], tabCount, ref);
    }
}
```

This is the identical process you used to walk through the DOM nodes in domRoot, but here, we're using the processAttribute() method rather than processNode(). You'll create processAttribute() right after we finish with processNode().

The other elements you're processing are TEXT_NODE nodes. As we discussed earlier, text nodes are the nodes containing all the white space and text outside tags. You'll need to capture any text within the tags, but when using DOM methods to create your HTML, you don't need to worry about all the tabbing and new lines you may have included to make your hard-coded HTML look nice. It would be really annoying if your DOM code was littered with hundreds of new line nodes:

```
document.createTextNode('\n');
```

To make cleaner code, you apply the trim() method to each line as we discussed earlier, removing white space from the beginning and end of the content. If the line is empty, you'll just return null and move on to the next node. Also, you'll need to apply your encode() method to convert any characters that aren't allowed into their proper escaped format:

```
var value = (this.nodeValue ? encode(this.nodeValue.trim()) : '' );
```

Like you did for the ELEMENT_NODE, you also create a new variable for the new text node and add it to the newVariables list, but first you use the protected checkForVariable() method to check if the value contains a special $var:

```
// Check if the $var is the value
value = checkForVariable(value);

// Append the line of DOM code that creates this element
domCode += tabs
    + 'var '
    + ref
    + ' = document.createTextNode('+ value +');\n';
// Append to the list of new variable to report
// them all in the result
newVariables += '' + ref + ';\n';
```

Once the node is processed, the only thing left for you to do is add it to the parent node:

```
// Append the code that appends this node to its parent
domCode += tabs + refParent + '.appendChild('+ ref + ');\n';
```

If you try out the tool with the sample HTML fragment, before finishing the processAttribute() method, you'll get a nicely formatted DOM code representation of the HTML fragment:

```
/* requiredVariables in this code
var countContent;
var authorContent;
var metaContent;
var commentContent;
*/

var li1 = document.createElement('li');
document.body.appendChild(li1);
    var a1 = document.createElement('a');
    li1.appendChild(a1);
        var txt1 = document.createTextNode(countContent);
        a1.appendChild(txt1);
    var span1 = document.createElement('span');
    li1.appendChild(span1);
        var a2 = document.createElement('a');
        span1.appendChild(a2);
            var txt2 = document.createTextNode(authorContent);
            a2.appendChild(txt2);
    var small1 = document.createElement('small');
    li1.appendChild(small1);
        var a3 = document.createElement('a');
        small1.appendChild(a3);
            var txt3 = document.createTextNode(metaContent);
            a3.appendChild(txt3);
    var div1 = document.createElement('div');
    li1.appendChild(div1);
        var txt4 = document.createTextNode(commentContent);
        div1.appendChild(txt4);


/* new objects in this code
li1;
a1;
txt1;
span1;
a2;
txt2;
small1;
a3;
txt3;
```

```
div1;
txt4;
*/
```

The result includes all the ELEMENT_NODES and TEXT_NODES nodes along with the integrated variable names, but it's missing all the attributes associated with each node, which is where the processAttribute() method comes in. Fill in your processAttribute() method with the following code:

```
function processAttribute(tabCount,refParent) {

    // Skip text nodes
    if(this.nodeType != ADS.node.ATTRIBUTE_NODE) return;

    // Retrieve the attribute value
    var attrValue = (this.nodeValue ? encode( ➥
this.nodeValue.trim()) : '');
    if(this.nodeName == 'cssText') alert('true');
    // If there is no value then return
    if(!attrValue) return;

    // Determine the indent level
    var tabs = (tabCount ? '\t'.repeat(parseInt(tabCount)) : '');

    // Switch on the nodeName. All types will be processed but
    // style and class need special care.
    switch(this.nodeName){
        default:
            if (this.nodeName.substring(0,2) == 'on') {
                // If the attribute begins with 'on' then
                // it's an inline event and needs to be re-created
                // using a function assigned to the attribute
                domCode += tabs
                    + refParent
                    + '.'
                    + this.nodeName
                    + '= function(){' + attrValue +'}\n';
            } else{

                // Use setAttribute for the rest
                domCode += tabs
                    + refParent
                    + '.setAttribute(\''
                    + this.nodeName
                    + '\', '
                    + checkForVariable(attrValue)
                    +');\n';
            }
        break;
```

```
case 'class':
    // The class is assigned using the className attribute
    domCode += tabs
        + refParent
        + '.className = '
        + checkForVariable(attrValue)
        + ';\n';
    break;
case 'style':
    // Split the style attribute on ; using a regular expression
    // to include adjoining spaces
    var style = attrValue.split(/\s*;\s*/);

    if(style){
        for(pair in style){

            if(!style[pair]) continue;

            // Split each pair on : using a regular expression
            // to include adjoining spaces
            var prop = style[pair].split(/\s*:\s*/);
            if(!prop[1]) continue;

            // convert css-property to cssProperty
            prop[0] = ADS.camelize(prop[0]);

            var propValue = checkForVariable(prop[1]);
            if (prop[0] == 'float') {
                // float is a reserved word so it's special
                // - cssFloat is standard
                // - styleFloat is IE
                domCode += tabs
                    + refParent
                    + '.style.cssFloat = '
                    + propValue
                    + ';\n';
                domCode += tabs
                    + refParent
                    + '.style.styleFloat = '
                    + propValue
                    + ';\n';
            } else {
                domCode += tabs
                    + refParent
                    + '.style.'
                    + prop[0]
                    + ' = '
                    + propValue + ';\n';
            }
```

```
                }
            }
        break;
        }
    }
```

The processAttribute() method follows roughly the same pattern as processNode(), but the attributes act a little differently. The first difference with attributes is the way you access their values. As you saw earlier, attributes have a nodeValue property, so we can retrieve the value of the node that way. The problem, however, is that the DOM walking function you created earlier will still iterate over the TEXT_NODE in the ATTRIBUTE_NODE, so you'll have to stick to using nodeValue and just skip the processing if it's not an ATTRIBUTE_NODE:

```
// Skip text nodes
if(this.nodeType != ADS.node.ATTRIBUTE_NODE) return;

// Retrieve the attribute value
var attrValue = (this.nodeValue ? encode(this.nodeValue.trim()) : '');
if(this.nodeName == 'cssText') alert('true');
// If there is no value then return
if(!attrValue) return;
```

Next, you check each attribute and do a few special things in the case of a class or style attribute. If it's not a class or style attribute, you create some code to use the setAttribute() method on the parent reference, but you also check for inline events and create the necessary function:

```
default:
    if (this.nodeName.substring(0,2) == 'on') {
        // if the attribute begins with 'on' then
        // it's an inline event and needs to be re-created
        // using a function assigned to the attribute
        domCode += tabs
            + refParent
            + '.'
            + this.nodeName
            + '= function(){' + attrValue +'}\n';
    } else{

        // Use setAttribute for the rest
        domCode += tabs
            + refParent
            + '.setAttribute(\''
            + this.nodeName
            + '\', '
            + checkForVariable(attrValue)
            +');\n';
    }
    break;
```

As you saw in Chapter 1, inline events are a big no-no, but if your DOM generator still checks for them, you can use it when upgrading a lot of your legacy code. If the attribute is a class, you assign the class node value to the className property of the node:

```
case 'class':
    // The class is assigned using the className attribute
    domCode += tabs
        + refParent
        + '.className = '
        + checkForVariable(attrValue)
        + ';\n';
    break;
```

However, if it's an inline style attribute (also a no-no), you do a bit of extra processing to split up the different selectors and properties:

```
case 'style':
    // Split the style attribute on ; using a regular expression
    // to include adjoining spaces
    var style = attrValue.split(/\s*;\s*/);

    if(style){
        for(pair in style){

            if(!style[pair]) continue;

            // Split each pair on : using a regular expression
            // to include adjoining spaces
            var prop = style[pair].split(/\s*:\s*/);
            if(!prop[1]) continue;

            // convert css-property to cssProperty
            prop[0] = ADS.camelize(prop[0]);

            var propValue = checkForVariable(prop[1]);
            if (prop[0] == 'float') {
                // float is a reserved word so it's special
                // - cssFloat is standard
                // - styleFloat is IE
                domCode += tabs
                    + refParent
                    + '.style.cssFloat = '
                    + propValue
                    + ';\n';
                domCode += tabs
                    + refParent
                    + '.style.styleFloat = '
                    + propValue
                    + ';\n';
            } else {
```

```
                domCode += tabs
                    + refParent
                    + '.style.'
                    + prop[0]
                    + ' = '
                    + propValue + ';\n';
            }
        }
    }
    break;
```

Now if you run the test page, you'll have a fully functional DOM code that represents the sample HTML comment block:

```
/* requiredVariables in this code
var commentClass;
var commentId;
var countTitle;
var countHref;
var countContent;
var authorHref;
var authorContent;
var metaTitle;
var metaHref;
var metaContent;
var commentContent;
*/

var li1 = document.createElement('li');
li1.style.backgroundColor = 'white';
li1.className = commentClass;
li1.setAttribute('id', commentId);
document.body.appendChild(li1);
    var a1 = document.createElement('a');
    a1.onclick= function(){window.open(this.href); return false;}
    a1.setAttribute('title', countTitle);
    a1.className = 'counter';
    a1.setAttribute('href', countHref);
    li1.appendChild(a1);
        var txt1 = document.createTextNode(countContent);
        a1.appendChild(txt1);
    var span1 = document.createElement('span');
    span1.className = 'commentauthor';
    li1.appendChild(span1);
        var a2 = document.createElement('a');
        a2.setAttribute('rel', 'external nofollow');
        a2.setAttribute('href', authorHref);
        span1.appendChild(a2);
            var txt2 = document.createTextNode(authorContent);
```

```
        a2.appendChild(txt2);
var small1 = document.createElement('small');
small1.className = 'comment-meta';
li1.appendChild(small1);
    var a3 = document.createElement('a');
    a3.setAttribute('title', metaTitle);
    a3.setAttribute('href', metaHref);
    small1.appendChild(a3);
        var txt3 = document.createTextNode(metaContent);
        a3.appendChild(txt3);
var div1 = document.createElement('div');
div1.className = 'comment-content';
li1.appendChild(div1);
    var txt4 = document.createTextNode(commentContent);
    div1.appendChild(txt4);


/* new objects in this code
li1;
a1;
txt1;
span1;
a2;
txt2;
small1;
a3;
txt3;
div1;
txt4;
*/
```

Now, when creating the interactive comment object, you can simply copy and paste this result into your code editor and keep working, saving a lot of mundane DOM scripting.

Summary

Learning all the appropriate DOM methods and properties is fundamental to DOM scripting, but understanding where all those methods and properties come from and how each specification works with the others is going to give you a much better grasp of how far you can go and where you'll have to limit yourself. This chapter covered the basics of the DOM2 Core and DOM2 HTML, only two standards of many, but it allowed you to understand how Core objects such as Element are built on-top of the Core Node object, and that Element is extended even further by the HTML specification into objects such as HTMLElement and specific tag objects. Your understanding of where each property and method originates and how the objects build on one another will help you understand many of the examples in later chapters.

This chapter also introduced the fact that the browser is not a perfect development environment, and the differences among them can often create headaches for developers, such as you, who want to follow standards but also have to account for nonstandard browsers. The best solution to this problem is to develop for standards first and then use the appropriate capability detection to enable nonstandard features. By implementing standards first, all browsers will eventually begin to work as expected, and you can slowly stop supporting nonstandard features, rather than rewriting your code for standardization later.

In this chapter, you've also built on your ADS library and now have a couple of great tools to help in development of the rest of the chapters. To build on what you've learned so far and add to the library, let's take a closer look at events and how you go about responding to use actions in Chapter 4.

CHAPTER 4

RESPONDING TO USER ACTIONS AND EVENTS

Events are the stuff of magic in web applications. Plain old HTML and forms just don't cut it when you're trying to create an advanced user interface. It's archaic to fill out a form, click save, and then wait for the entire document (and all its overhead) to reload just to reveal a tiny little change hidden somewhere in the overall page. When you use your web application it should react in a fluid and unobtrusive way, just like your desktop applications have always done. Giving your web application a more desktop-application-like feel isn't revolutionary, but it does require looking at things differently. With a little ingenuity and forethought, you can provide a desktop-application-like experience with minimal effort, minimal cost, and minimal extra time—but you need to understand a few things about how your browser interacts with you.

Without events, your web page could be compared to an analog television signal. It looks pretty and provides useful information, but you can't interact with it. When I talk about events in the browser or in your DOM scripts, I'm referring to the little things that your browser does when it detects that a certain action has taken place. The *action* could be the browser loading the page or you clicking and scrolling with the mouse.

An event is the detection of actions combined with an execution of a script or invoking event listeners on an object based on the type of action that was detected. In this book, you've already encountered events such as the load event of the window object and the click event of an anchor element. If this book were intelligent and aware of you reading this paragraph, it would have invoked the beginReading event on the paragraph when you began to read it. Likewise, it may be detecting that you're still reading this paragraph, so it will be continually invoking the reading event on the paragraph as you start reading each new word. At the end of this sentence, when the paragraph ends, it will detect that you have finished reading and invoke the finishedReading event on the paragraph.

JavaScript isn't really smart enough to know when you're reading a paragraph (at least not yet), so there are no paragraph reading events, but there are several events based on browser and user actions. You can use these events to create an event listener—some bit of code that you want to run when the event is invoked. How you specify the listeners depends on the type of event and, unfortunately, the type of browser.

In this chapter, you'll be exploring the W3C DOM Level 2 Events and how they apply to the various browsers. You'll also see how browsers vary in the way they register events, invoke events, access events, and do just about everything else with events. Throughout this chapter, you'll be creating many more methods in your ADS library to deal with cross-browser event handling.

Before we get started, I should clarify a few terms, so we're all on the same page. If you've encountered browser events before, or if you've read about them, you may have heard a variety of terms to describe various aspects of events. To be clear, I'll be using the following terms in this chapter:

- **Event**: I want to clarify that events don't start with the word "on." For example, onclick is not an event—click is. As you'll see later in this chapter, onclick refers to the property of an object that you could use to assign a click event to a DOM element. This is an important distinction, because your script won't work if you include the on prefix in the methods of the DOM Level 2 Events specification.

- **Event listeners**: These are the JavaScript functions or methods that will be executed when the specified event occurs. Listeners are sometimes referred to as "event handlers," but I'll use "event listeners" to follow the terminology in the DOM Level 2 Events specification.

- **Event registration**: This is the process of assigning the event listener for a specific event to a DOM element. Registration can be done several different ways, which we'll discuss in this chapter. Event registration is sometimes referred to as event binding.

- **Invoking**: I'll be using the verb "invoke" to describe the instances where your web browser detects an action that, in turn, executes an event listener. In other words, when you click the mouse in the document, the browser will invoke the events associated with a mouse click. You may have also heard this referred to as being called, fired, executed, or triggered.

With these terms in mind, let's take a look at the W3C DOM Level 2 Events specification and the many browser inconsistencies.

DOM2 Events

The DOM Level 2 Events specification (DOM2 Events) defines the methods and properties for a generic event system in the same way that the DOM2 HTML and DOM2 Core specificaitons from Chapter 3 defined the document structure. Unfortunately, the DOM2 Events specification hasn't yet been as widely adopted by browsers so in many cases, mostly dealing with Microsoft Internet Explorer, you'll be forced to do the same thing more than one way. Throughout this chapter, you'll be creating and adding a number of generic event functions to your growing ADS library that will enable agnostic event registration and access across multiple browsers.

Take a quick look at the events listed for each of the different browsers:

- **Firefox**: http://advanceddomscripting.com/links/events/firefox
- **Opera**: http://advanceddomscripting.com/links/events/opera
- **Microsoft Internet Explorer**: http://advanceddomscripting.com/links/events/msie
- **Safari**: http://advanceddomscripting.com/links/events/safari

You'll notice that each has a plethora of events for a variety of different objects, many of which differ from one browser to the other.

The specification incorporates many of the traditional events that existed before standardization, but it also adds several other DOM-specific events that are invoked when you mutate or interact with the DOM document structure. Unfortunately, as I said, the majority of the market is using a browser that doesn't officially support the DOM event model, so I'll focus on the common events and only briefly describe the DOM-specific events that you'll eventually be able to use in your day-to-day coding.

We'll begin the exploration of events with a quick refresher of the various events that are available, and then we'll get into the specifics of registering, invoking, and controlling. In the Chapter 6 case study, you'll put all this knowledge to good use when building an interactive web-based image resizing and cropping tool.

Types of events

Events can be grouped into several categories: object, mouse, keyboard, form, W3C, and browser specific. The last category, browser specific, I'll be avoiding completely unless it's required as an alternative to the DOM solution.

Object events

Object events apply to both JavaScript objects, such as the window object, and DOM objects, such as HTMLImageElement objects.

The load and unload events

Throughout the book you've been using the window's load event to invoke your behavioral enhancements when the page loads:

```
function yourLoadEvent() {
    //do something to the document
}
ADS.addEvent(window, 'load', yourLoadEvent);
```

When applied to the window object, the load and unload events are browser specific and are executed outside the realm of the DOM2 Events specification. The browser invokes the window's load event when it has finished loading the page. By relying on the load event, the unobtrusive behavioral enhancements will only be applied if JavaScript is available.

The one drawback of the window's load *event is that it's not invoked until after all the inline images in the markup have loaded as well. If you've appropriately used CSS style sheets to style your markup, you'll be fine. However, if you have a lot of inline images, your load event listeners won't run until all the images have downloaded, so you may notice a lengthy pause before things get going.*

Later in the chapter, we'll revisit the ADS.addEvent() *method and create an* ADS.addLoadEvent() *method to get around the image loading problems.*

Likewise, the windows unload event is invoked when the user navigates away from the page by either clicking a link or closing the window, so you can use an unload event listener to capture last-minute information before the page closes.

It's not possible to prevent the window from unloading. Regardless of what you try, the browser will still leave the current page and load the next page.

The load event also applies to other DOM objects that load external content such as framesets and images.

The abort and error events

Like load and unload, the error event applies to both the window object and image objects. The error event is very useful for identifying image loading errors when you dynamically load and add images to your document. If you create a new img DOM element, you can use a load event listener to add the DOM element to the document if and only if the image loads successfully. Likewise, you can use an error event listener to indicate if there was an error loading the image and take the appropriate action:

```
ADS.addEvent(window,'load',function() {

    // Create an image
    var image = document.createElement('IMG');

    // Append it to the document body when it loads
    ADS.addEvent(image, 'load', function() {
        document.body.appendChild(image);
    });

    // Append a message if it errors
    ADS.addEvent(image, 'error' ,function() {
        var message = document.createTextNode(➥
'The image failed to load');
        document.body.appendChild(message);
    });

    // Set the src attribute so the browser can retrieve the image
    image.setAttribute(
        'src',
```

```
                'http://advanceddomscripting.com/images/working.jpg'
        );

        // The same as above except this image doesn't exist and will error
        var imageMissing = document.createElement('img');
        ADS.addEvent(imageMissing, 'load', function() {
            document.body.appendChild(imageMissing);
        });
        ADS.addEvent(imageMissing, 'error' ,function() {
            var message = document.createTextNode(➥
    'imageMissing failed to load');
            document.body.appendChild(message);
        });
        imageMissing.setAttribute(
            'src',
            'http://advanceddomscripting.com/images/missing.jpg'
        );


    });
```

When your image loads successfully, it will be added to the unordered list identified by id="galleryList", but if it fails, you'll be alerted there was an error.

The abort event has very little use, and you'll probably never need it. It's invoked for images that fail to load because the browser stopped loading the page before an image had completely loaded. This is usually because you click the Stop button in the browser.

The resize event

The resize event occurs when the browser window is resized and the document's view has changed. The resize event is always invoked when the window has finished resizing, but in some instances, it may be called multiple times throughout the resize action.

The scroll event

The scroll event applies to elements that have a style of overflow:auto and is continually invoked while the element is scrolled. The scrolling action can be invoked by dragging the scroll bar, using a click wheel on the mouse, pressing an arrow key, or other scrolling methods.

Mouse movement events

Most often, you'll want to capture and react to your user's actions by listening for mouse events. When you move the mouse pointer around the page without clicking anything, several events take place:

- The mousemove event is invoked continually on the object below the pointer while the mouse is in motion.
- mouseover events will fire as the pointer moves into new objects.
- mouseout events fire as the pointer moves out of objects.

> *The* mousemove *event has no specified period or distance in which it fires. When the pointer is in motion, it will fire repeatedly, and when the pointer isn't in motion, it won't fire.*

If you go to the source code for this book and open chapter4/move/move.html in your browser, you can see the mouse movement events appear in the ADS.log window you created in Chapter 2. This test file simply consists of a very simple HTML document and appropriate CSS files:

```
<!DOCTYPE html PUBLIC "-//W3C//DTD XHTML 1.0 Strict//EN"
    "http://www.w3.org/TR/xhtml1/DTD/xhtml1-strict.dtd">
<html xmlns="http://www.w3.org/1999/xhtml">
<head>
<title>Mouse Move Events</title>
    <!-- include some CSS style sheet to make
        everything look a little nicer -->
    <link rel="stylesheet" type="text/css"
        href="../../shared/source.css" />
    <link rel="stylesheet" type="text/css" href="../chapter.css" />
    <link rel="stylesheet" type="text/css" href="style.css" />

    <!-- ADS Library (full version from source linked here) -->
    <script type="text/javascript"
        src="../../ADS-final-verbose.js"></script>

    <!-- Log object from Chapter 2
        (full version from source linked here) -->
    <script type="text/javascript"
        src="../../chapter2/myLogger-final/myLogger.js"></script>

    <!-- A quick testing file -->
    <script type="text/javascript" src="move.js"></script>
</head>
<body>
<h1>Mouse Move Events</h1>
<div id="content">
    <div id="box"> Test Box </div>
</div>
</body>
</html>
```

The load event listener in chapter4/move/move.js registers all the mouse movement events on the document and the box elements:

```
ADS.addEvent(window,'load',function(W3CEvent) {

    // A simple logging method to log the type
    // of event and object to the log window
    function logit(W3CEvent) {
        switch(this.nodeType) {
```

```
        case ADS.node.DOCUMENT_NODE:
            ADS.log.write(W3CEvent.type + ' on document');
        break;
        case ADS.node.ELEMENT_NODE:
            ADS.log.write(W3CEvent.type + ' on box');
        break;
    }
}

//add the mouse move events
ADS.addEvent(document,'mousemove',logit);
ADS.addEvent(document,'mouseover',logit);
ADS.addEvent(document,'mouseout',logit);

var box = document.getElementById('box');
ADS.addEvent(box,'mousemove',logit);
ADS.addEvent(box,'mouseover',logit);
ADS.addEvent(box,'mouseout',logit);

});
```

Figure 4-1 shows the events that occur as you move the mouse pointer from the left side of the browser window to the right side of the browser window in the chapter4/move/move.html file.

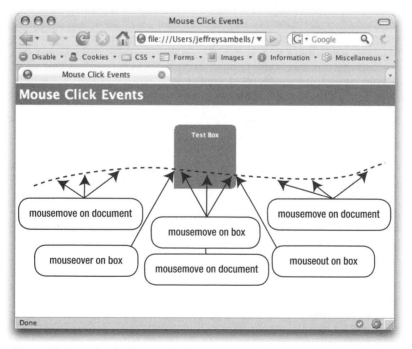

Figure 4-1. Events invoked by moving the mouse pointer from left to right on a sample document

155

Your browser will invoke the mousemove event while the mouse buttons are pressed—as well as invoking click-related events—which is useful for creating draggable objects, as you'll see in Chapter 6.

Mouse click events

When you click your mouse on the page, another chain of events takes place in combination with the mouse movement events. If the mouse pointer remains stationary as you click and release the left mouse button, the browser will invoke the following events:

- A mousedown event when the mouse button is pressed over the object
- A mouseup event when the mouse button is released
- A click event only if the mouse remained stationary
- A dblclick event after the click event, if a quick double-click was performed

Note that the pointer must remain stationary for this order to hold true and that it can be affected by the event flow, which you'll see later in this chapter.

If you try clicking the mouse button and moving the pointer before releasing it, things start to get more interesting. Again, you can experiment using the provided chapter4/click/click.html file that is almost identical to the previous move example, except for its load event listener in chapter4/click/click.js:

```
ADS.addEvent(window,'load',function(W3CEvent) {

    // A simple logging method to log the type
    // of event and object to the log window
    function logit(W3CEvent) {
        switch(this.nodeType) {
            case ADS.node.DOCUMENT_NODE:
                ADS.log.write(W3CEvent.type + ' on the document');
            break;
            case ADS.node.ELEMENT_NODE:
                ADS.log.write(W3CEvent.type + ' on the box');
            break;
        }
    }

    //add the mouse click events
    ADS.addEvent(document,'mousedown',logit);
    ADS.addEvent(document,'mouseup',logit);
    ADS.addEvent(document,'click',logit);
    ADS.addEvent(document,'dblclick',logit);

    var box = document.getElementById('box');
    ADS.addEvent(box,'mousedown',logit);
    ADS.addEvent(box,'mouseup',logit);
```

```
        ADS.addEvent(box,'click',logit);
        ADS.addEvent(box,'dblclick',logit);

    });
```

The test page in chapter4/click/click.html looks the same as the one shown in Figure 4-1, but it assigns click, dblclick, mousedown, and mouseup events to document itself as well as the box element. Depending on where you click and release the mouse, you'll see several different events taking place. First try the locations in Figure 4-2.

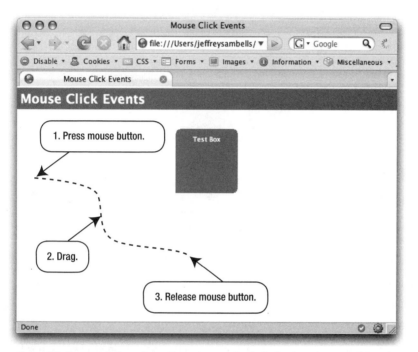

Figure 4-2. Representation of a path on the sample file indicating where to click and release the mouse pointer so that no click event will occur

The path shown in Figure 4-2 will reveal two events in the ADS.log window:

1. A mousedown event on the document object followed by
2. A mouseup event on the document object

Between clicking and releasing, you moved the pointer, so no click event occurred.

Next, try the path shown in Figure 4-3.

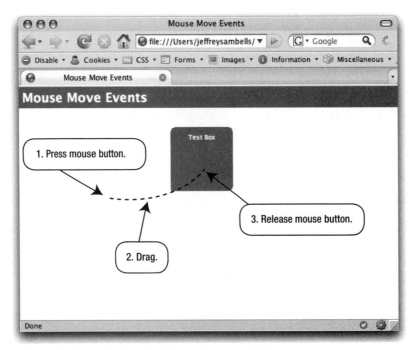

Figure 4-3. Representation of a path on the sample file indicating where to click and release the mouse pointer partially over the box

The path in Figure 4-3 will reveal the following events related to the document and the box:

1. A mousedown event on the document object

2. A mouseup event on the box object

3. A mouseup event on the document object

A mouseup event was invoked on the box, because you moved the pointer over the box before releasing it. The mouseup and mousedown events are related, but they do not always occur together. If you try the reverse path, starting in the grey box and releasing outside of it, you'll get two mousedown events and one mouseup event.

> *The order of the mouseup events can vary depending on which event registration method and event phase is used. It also depends on the way the document is marked up and how objects are positioned on the page. We'll discuss event phases, including the capturing phase and the bubbling phase, and how the visual layout of the page influences the events later in the chapter in the "Controlling Event Flow and Registering Event Listeners" section.*

The important thing to remember here is that many events can be invoked in one action. If you combine the mouse movement and mouse click event listeners, the log window will quickly fill with move events as you navigate around the page between and during click-related events.

You can also determine which mouse button invoked the event by accessing the event object, which we'll discuss later in this chapter.

Keyboard events

Like mouse clicks, pressing a key on the keyboard causes the browser to invoke key-related events, but they only apply to the document object. When a key is pressed, the browser will invoke events along the same line as a click except the events are key related:

1. keydown is invoked when a key is pressed down.
2. keyup is invoked when the key is released.
3. keypress follows keyup and indicates that a key was pressed.

You can also determine which key was pressed by accessing the event object, which we'll discuss shortly when we look at accessing the event object.

Form-related events

Without any additional behavioral enhancements, forms provide a variety of interactive features such as drop-down lists, text boxes, check boxes, radio elements, and the like. These special interactive elements also have their own unique events that occur as you interact with the form elements and the form itself.

Form submit and reset events

The first and most basic events associated with forms are submit and reset. As you can probably guess, the form's submit event invokes when you submit the form to the server by either clicking a submit button or by pressing a key on the keyboard. Likewise the reset event is invoked when a form is reset in a similar manner.

You can use the submit and reset events for a number of things including client-side form validation, or serializing the form content for Ajax actions. Take a look at the chapter4/address/address.html source where I've included a simple address form common to many web sites:

```
<form action="/path/to/server/script"➡
method="post" id="canadianAddress">
    <div>
        <label for="name">Name</label>
        <input type="text" id="name" name="name"/>
    </div>
    <div>
        <label for="postalCode">Postal Code (required)</label>
        <input type="text" id="postalCode"➡
name="postalCode" class="required"/>
        <p>In the format A#A #A#</p>
```

```
        </div>
        <div>
            <label for="street">Street</label>
            <input type="text" id="street" name="street"/>
        </div>
        <div>
            <label for="city">City</label>
            <input type="text" id="city" name="city"/>
        </div>
        <div>
            <label for="province">Province</label>
            <input type="text" id="province" name="province"/>
        </div>
        <div class="buttons">
            <input type="submit" value="submit" />
        </div>
    </form>
```

To verify the information is in the correct format, the example includes a submit event listener. In this case, the form is for a Canadian address, and Canadian postal codes are in the format A#A #A#, where # is a number and A is a letter. The load event in chapter4/address/address.js includes a function to verify the postal code format before the form submits:

```
function isPostalCode(s) {
    return s.toUpperCase().match(➡
/[A-Z][0-9][A-Z]\s*[0-9][A-Z][0-9]/i);
}

ADS.addEvent(window,'load',function() {

    ADS.addEvent(
        document.getElementById('canadianAddress'),
        'submit',
        function(W3CEvent) {

            var postalCode = document.getElementById(➡
'postalCode').value;

            // check if it's valid using a regular expression
            if (!isPostalCode(postalCode)) {
                alert('That\'s not a valid Canadian postal code!');

                // This will also cancel the submit action using the
                // ADS.preventDefault() method discussed later in
                // the chapter
                ADS.preventDefault(W3CEvent);
            }
        }
    );
});
```

When you try and submit the form with bad information, the submit event will indicate the error, as shown in Figure 4-4.

Figure 4-4. An error is displayed when the user attempts to submit the form with an invalid Canadian postal code.

This progressive enhancement allows the form to operate as normal without JavaScript, but when it's available, you're given more immediate feedback. In the event of an error, preventing the form submit action depends on which event registration model you use, as we'll discuss shortly.

> When implementing client-side verification, make sure you don't ignore the server side. The form submission still needs to be verified on the server, because there's nothing preventing a savvy web user from bypassing the JavaScript (or simply disabling it) and submitting bad information.

Blur and focus events

The blur and focus events apply to the <label>, <input>, <select>, <textarea>, and <button> form elements. The focus event is invoked when you give the element focus by clicking it or tabbing to it. Clicking elsewhere or tabbing out of the element invokes the blur event on the element that previously had focus.

Your DOM scripts can use these events to modify the document based on which element is in focus. Looking again at the chapter4/address/address.html postal code example, the background of the postal code field uses a different graphic to visually indicate that it's required, as shown in Figure 4-5.

Figure 4-5. Address form as seen in Firefox indicating that the postal code field is required

The chapter4/address/address.js also includes this load event listener for adding a blur and focus listener to the postal code field:

```
ADS.addEvent(window,'load',function() {
    // Initially style it
    var postalCode = document.getElementById('postalCode');
    postalCode.className = 'inputMissing';

    // When in focus change the class to editing
    ADS.addEvent(postalCode,'focus',function(W3CEvent) {
        //change the class to indicate the user is editing the field
        this.className = 'inputEditing';
    });

    // When blurred verify and restyle depending on the value
    ADS.addEvent(postalCode,'blur',function(W3CEvent) {
```

```
        if(this.value == '') {
            // Change the class to indicate the content is missing
            this.className = 'inputMissing';
        } else if(!isPostalCode(this.value)) {
            // Change the class to indicate the content is invalid
            this.className = 'inputInvalid';
        } else {
            // Change the class to indicate the content is complete
            this.className = 'inputComplete';
        }
    });
});
```

These event listeners modify the input's className property allowing the input's style to change as it gains focus and blurs. When you try to edit the field, the browser will invoke the focus event, changing the class and associated styles as shown in Figure 4-6.

When you exit the field and the browser invokes the blur event, the listener checks if the field contains valid information and reapplies the appropriate class as shown in Figure 4-7.

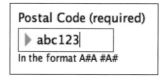

Figure 4-6. Address form postal code field in the focus state

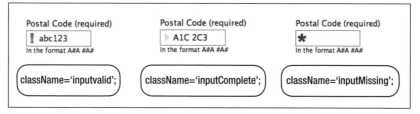

Figure 4-7. The address form postal code field in the blur state after various checks

Ideally, you would use both the submit *and the* blur *events to verify the input as you've seen here. Verifying on* blur *provides immediate feedback as you fill out the form while the* submit *verification checks if you've forgotten anything or ignored earlier warnings.*

The change event

The change event applies to <input>, <select>, and <textarea> form elements and invokes following the blur event when the value of the element changes between the focus and blur events.

You'll find the change event useful when you want to modify your document when the value of a field changes. Again, looking at the chapter4/address/address.html postal code example, when you finish typing a postal code, the change event invokes an XMLHttpRequest to a server-side script. The request could use a server-side service to validate not only the format but also the authenticity of the postal code to verify that it is a real one. At the same time, the server-side scripts could look up the street, city, and Canadian province and pre-populate the rest of the form automatically:

```
ADS.addEvent(window,'load',function() {
    var postalCode = ADS.$('postalCode');

    ADS.addEvent(postalCode,'change',function(W3CEvent) {

        var newPostalCode = this.value

        if(!isPostalCode(newPostalCode)) return;

        var req = new XMLHttpRequest();
        req.open('POST','server.js?postalCode=' + newPostalCode,true);
        req.onreadystatechange = function() {
            if (req.readyState == 4) {
                eval(req.responseText);

                if(ADS.$('street').value == '') {
                    ADS.$('street').value = street;
                }
                if(ADS.$('city').value == '') {
                    ADS.$('city').value = city;
                }
                if(ADS.$('province').value == '') {
                    ADS.$('province').value = province;
                }
            }
        }
        req.send();

    });
});
```

This example uses the XMLHttpRequest object directly, which will prevent it from working in Internet Explorer 6. For an Internet Explorer equivalent version, see Chapter 7. Also, the server.js script referenced here is simply an example JavaScript file containing the street, city, and province test information:

```
var street = '123 Somewhere';
var city = 'Ottawa';
var province = 'Ontario';
```

> In Chapter 7, you'll see a number of different server-side options for real Ajax requests.

The result is a form that both verifies the accuracy of the postal code and retrieves the street, city, and province, as shown in Figure 4-8.

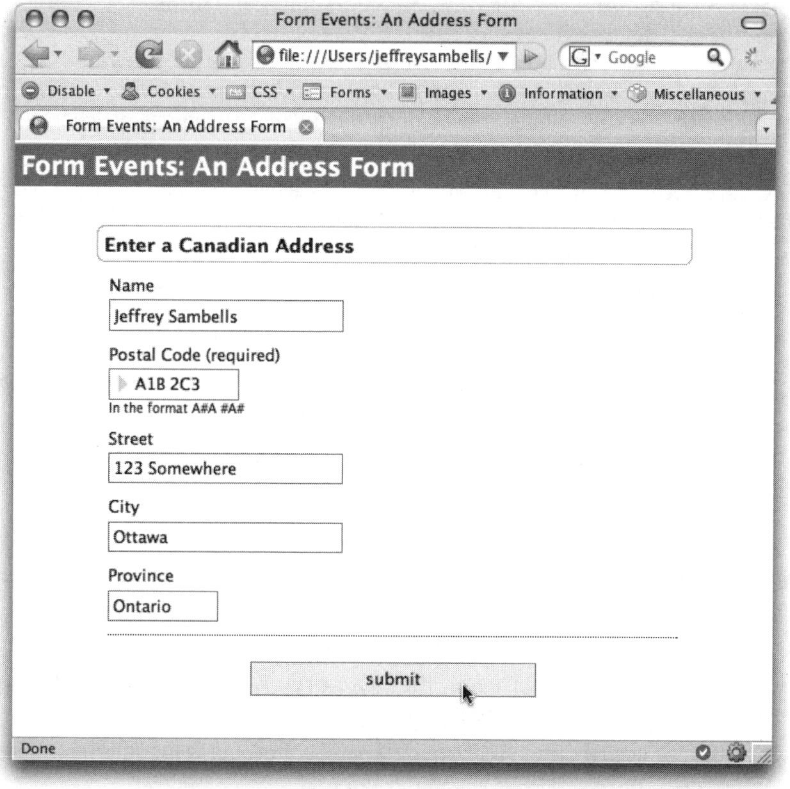

Figure 4-8. The address form automatically populated with a (fake) address after entering a valid postal code

This same method could be used to look up other information, such as a telephone number. A subtle interface enhancement like this will impress users and save them a lot of effort when filling out the form.

> *There are also a number of possible problems with Ajax uses such as this. You'll be looking at Ajax in depth in Chapter 7, so don't worry if you're not familiar with Ajax or can't spot the possible problem yet.*

W3C DOM-specific events

For browsers that support much of the W3C DOM2 Events specification, such as Firefox 2.0, Opera 9, and Safari 2.0, there are a handful of very useful DOM-related events. Currently, they're not supported by Microsoft Internet Explorer, and there is no built-in equivalent functionality. I'll just briefly cover them here so that one day, when they are supported, you can refer to this section to see what they're all about.

Within the DOM2 Events specification, there are three user interface events:

- DOMFocusIn and DomFocusOut act the same as focus and blur. However DOMFocusIn and DomFocusOut apply to *any* DOM element, not just form elements. The browser will invoke these events when the mouse pointer moves onto or out of an element or when the element is tabbed to using the keyboard.

- DOMActivate occurs when a DOM element becomes active by either clicking it with the mouse pointer or by a key press on the keyboard. In addition to the event object, the event listener will receive a numerical argument to indicate the type of activation:

    - 1 indicates a simple activation through a mouse click or the Enter key.

    - 2 indicates a hyperactivation, such as a double-clicking or pressing Shift+Enter.

Additionally, seven mutation events can be invoked when you make changes to the DOM document structure:

- DOMSubtreeModified is a general event that occurs on the DOM node after the rest of the mutation events have occurred.

- DOMNodeInserted occurs on the DOM node when it's added as a child to another node.

- DOMNodeRemoved occurs on the DOM node when it's removed from its parent node.

- DOMNodeRemovedFromDocument occurs on the DOM node when it's removed from the document either directly or as part of a subtree.

- NodeInsertedIntoDocument occurs on the DOM node when it's inserted into the document either directly or as part of a subtree.

- DOMAttrModified occurs on the DOM node when an attribute is modified.

- DOMCharacterDataModified occurs on the DOM node when the CharacterData within the node changes and the node remains in the document.

This is just a brief overview of a few of the DOM-specific methods that you'll eventually be able to use. For more information and updates about these and other DOM-specific features, see this book's web site at http://advanceddomscripting.com.

Custom events

There may be occasions where you will want to provide your own custom events for the objects within your web application. For example, if your web application has a save feature, you may want to provide a save event that other developers could then use to invoke additional events the same way you did earlier using the submit event.

Providing a cross-browser solution for custom events can be a daunting task and is beyond the scope of this book. However, in Chapter 9, we'll look at some tried and tested JavaScript libraries that already have advanced event systems, some of which include custom events.

Controlling event flow and registering event listeners

Let me tell you right up front that there's no pretty solution for advanced cross-browser event handling. Each browser differs in the way it orders events, registers event listeners, and accesses event properties. In this section, I'll discuss the basics of event flow, and you'll create a few more methods for your ADS library that will help you get a better handle on W3C-compliant and cross-browser event handling.

Event flow

Before you start adding and invoking event listeners, you need to familiarize yourself with a few basic ideas about event flow. Quite possibly, up until now, you've ignored or not even been aware of things like the bubbling and capturing phases of an event. These concepts will be important to understand when you start to deal with multiple events on multiple objects that may be nested within one another. It's also important to understand how the flow differs drastically between the Internet Explorer and W3C models.

To help explain the concepts, let's look at another document from this book's source. When you open chapter4/flow/flow.html in your web browser, it should resemble Figure 4-9.

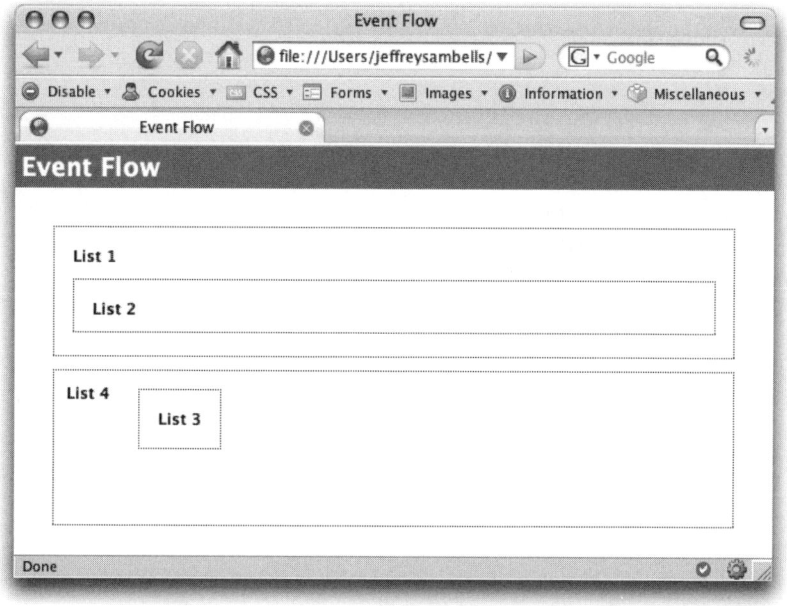

Figure 4-9. The event flow sample page rendered in Firefox

The event flow index.html page markup includes a few nested lists along with links to the appropriate JavaScript and CSS files:

```
<!DOCTYPE html PUBLIC "-//W3C//DTD XHTML 1.0 Strict//EN"
    "http://www.w3.org/TR/xhtml1/DTD/xhtml1-strict.dtd">
<html xmlns="http://www.w3.org/1999/xhtml">
<head>
    <title>Event Flow</title>
    <!-- include some CSS style sheet to make
        everything look a little nicer -->
```

```html
        <link rel="stylesheet" type="text/css"
            href="../../shared/source.css" />
        <link rel="stylesheet" type="text/css" href="../chapter.css" />
        <link rel="stylesheet" type="text/css" href="style.css" />

        <!-- ADS Library (full version from source linked here) -->
        <script type="text/javascript"
            src="../../ADS-final-verbose.js"></script>
        <!-- Log object from Chapter 2
            (full version from source linked here) -->
        <script type="text/javascript"
            src="../../chapter2/myLogger-final/myLogger.js"></script>
        <!-- A quick testing file -->
        <script type="text/javascript" src="flow.js"></script>
    </head>
    <body>
    <h1>Event Flow</h1>
    <div id="content">
        <ul id="list1">
            <li>
                <p>List 1 </p>
                <ul id="list2">
                    <li>
                        <p>List 2 </p>
                        <ul id="list3">
                            <li>
                                <p>List 3 </p>
                            </li>
                        </ul>
                    </li>
                </ul>
            </li>
        </ul>

        <ul id="list4">
            <p>List 4 </p>
        </ul>
    </div>
    </body>
    </html>
```

The supplied CSS has been set up to position the third nested list so that it appears visually outside its ancestors but on top of the fourth list:

```css
#list1 {
    height:80px;
}
#list2 {
    height:20px;
}
```

```
#list3 {
    position:absolute;
    top:190px;
    left:100px;
}

#list4 {
    margin-top:10px;
    height:100px;
}
```

The *visual* aspect versus the markup is the important thing to notice, because even though List 3 appears to be floating on its own above List 4, it's still nested within its ancestor lists.

Next, take a look at the chapter4/flow/flow.js file, and you'll see that I've attached a click event listener to each of the unordered lists. The main job of the listener is to modify the class of the clicked elements:

```
ADS.addEvent(window,'load',function() {

    // Use a modified addEvent method to illustrate
    // a problem. See the text for an explanation.
    function modifiedAddEvent( obj, type, fn ) {
        if(obj.addEventListener) {
            // The W3C Way

            // This method has been modified from the original
            // add event in Chapter 1 to enable capturing rather than
            // bubbling.
            obj.addEventListener( type, fn, true );

        } else if ( obj.attachEvent ) {
            //The Microsoft Way
            obj['e'+type+fn] = fn;
            obj[type+fn] = function(){obj['e'+type+fn](window.event);}
            obj.attachEvent( 'on'+type, obj[type+fn] );
        } else {
            return false;
        }
    }

    var counter = 0;

    // Grab all the unordered lists
    var lists = document.getElementsByTagName('ul');
    for(var i = 0 ; i < lists.length ; i++ ) {

        // Register an event listener for the click event
        modifiedAddEvent(lists[i],'click',function() {
            // Append the click order to the paragraph
```

```
        var append = document.createTextNode(':' + counter++);
        this.getElementsByTagName('p')[0].appendChild(append) ;

        // Change the class name to reveal the clicked elements
        this.className = 'clicked';
    });
}

});
```

If you click List 3 in your browser, you may be surprised to see that List 1 and List 2 also change color, as shown in Figure 4-10, even though you only clicked List 3 which isn't anywhere near those lists.

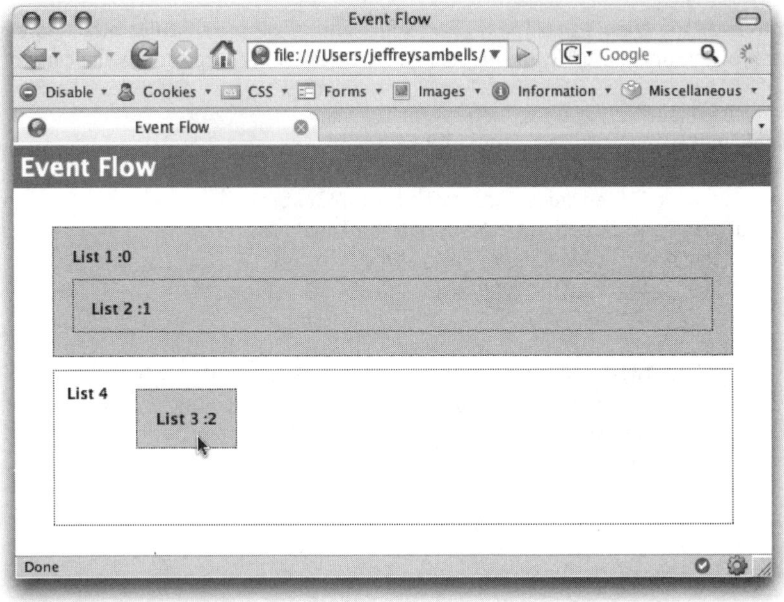

Figure 4-10. The eventFlow index page in Firefox after List 3 was clicked

If you're using Internet Explorer, you may also notice that the numbers after the list name are in reverse order. This is because of the event flow, which I'll explain in a moment.

In these click event listeners, I didn't do anything to prevent or stop the event flow from continuing on through the ancestor tree. This is a little easier to understand if you ignore the *visual* layout and consider only the *markup*, where each child list is nested in a parent. When you click on List 3, as shown in Figure 4-11, you are, in fact, clicking within the ancestors as well.

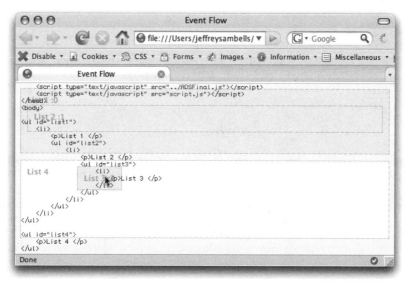

Figure 4-11. The flow.html page as if you were clicking the markup for List 3

You may also be curious why the fourth list didn't change color when you clicked List 3. The visual layout and layering of the object does have an effect on events. The topmost layer is the one that receives the initial event. The event is invoked around the target element and its ancestral markup, but it doesn't pass through the visual layers of the styling. Again, think of it like it appears in Figure 4-11. Looking at the markup, it's impossible to click two distinct elements at the same time, unless they're nested within one another, so you can't have the click event invoke two unrelated elements such as List 3 and List 4 at the same time. You may think this isn't true, since the click event on List 2 also affects List 1, but again, this is because of the ancestral relationship in the markup, not the visual positioning.

Order of events

If you take a closer look at Figure 4-10, you'll notice the numbers after the list name that appeared after the event listeners were invoked. These numbers represent the order in which the events were processed, 0 being the first. If your browser doesn't exactly match Figure 4-10 and the numbers are in the reverse order, it's because you're not using a DOM2 Events–compliant browser. This isn't a flaw in the browsers, as I purposefully used a modified addEvent function to register the click event listeners differently in W3C-compliant browsers:

```
function modifiedAddEvent( obj, type, fn ) {
    if(obj.addEventListener) {
        // The W3C Way

        // This method has been modified from the original
        // add event in Chapter 1 to enable capturing rather than
        // bubbling.
        obj.addEventListener( type, fn, true );
```

```
        } else if ( obj.attachEvent ) {
            // The Microsoft Way
            obj['e'+type+fn] = fn;
            obj[type+fn] = function(){obj['e'+type+fn]( window.event );}
            obj.attachEvent( 'on'+type, obj[type+fn] );
        } else {
            return false;
        }
    }
```

The modified function switches the last parameter of the DOM2 Events addEventListener() method to true, enabling the capturing phase of the event flow, rather than the bubbling phase. This will only affect W3C DOM2 Event–compliant browsers such as Firefox. When the event is registered in the capturing phase, the browser invokes the click event on the outermost ancestor first, working inward toward the target element. Internet Explorer, however, doesn't support capturing, and the attachEvent() method only bubbles events from the target out through the ancestors. I'll explain this in a little more detail next, but first look at the differences between Figures 4-12, which was captured in Firefox, and Figure 4-13, captured in Microsoft Internet Explorer.

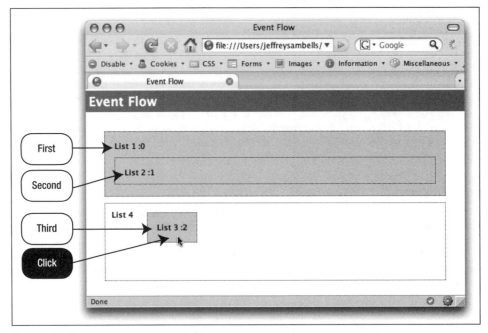

Figure 4-12. The event flow as seen in Firefox

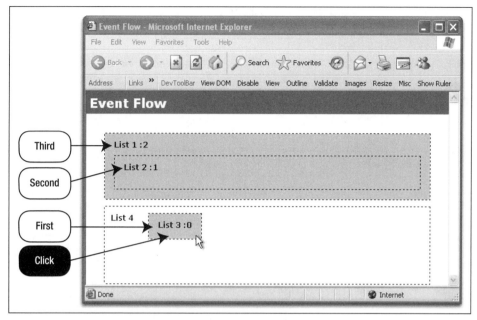

Figure 4-13. The event flow as seen in Microsoft Internet Explorer 6

Two phases and three models

Event bubbling and event capturing are polar opposites, and each was initially introduced by competing browser vendors. With event bubbling, introduced by Microsoft in Internet Explorer, the target's event method takes precedence and is executed first. The event is then propagated through each ancestor until it reaches the document object. Consider the following very simple document:

```
<!DOCTYPE HTML PUBLIC "-//W3C//DTD HTML 4.01//EN"
        "http://www.w3.org/TR/html4/strict.dtd">
<html>
<head>
    <title>Sample Markup</title>
</head>
<body>
    <ul>
        <li>
            <a href="http://example.com">Link 1</a>
        </li>
        <li>
            <a href="http://example.com">Link 2</a>
        </li>
    </ul>
</body>
</html>
```

The bubbling event flow of a click on Link 1 is illustrated by Figure 4-14.

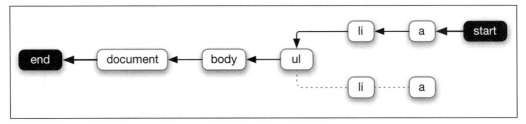

Figure 4-14. The bubbling event flow after clicking one of the anchors

In contrast, event capturing, introduced by Netscape, gives the outermost ancestor precedence, and the event is propagated inward until it reaches the target element, as represented in Figure 4-15.

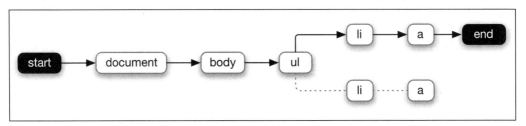

Figure 4-15. The capturing event flow after clicking one of the anchors

In all modern browsers that have support for the W3C DOM, bubbling is the default flow for traditional event registration, so you're probably most familiar with the bubbling method, though you may not have realized it.

> *In the case of Microsoft Internet Explorer version 7 or lower, event bubbling is the only option. Hopefully, Internet Explorer 8 may include more DOM-compliant features, but Microsoft hasn't made any promises.*

The W3C Events specification doesn't introduce a different flow but has approached the problem from each side by including both the capturing and bubbling phases. This allows you to choose which one you want to use for each event listener. In the earlier example, I chose capturing for the W3C method to illustrate how it can differ from Internet Explorer.

When the target is clicked in the W3C DOM2 Events model, all event listeners registered in the capturing phase are invoked until the target element is reached. The event flow then reverses direction, and event listeners registered in the bubbling phase are invoked, as represented in Figure 4-16.

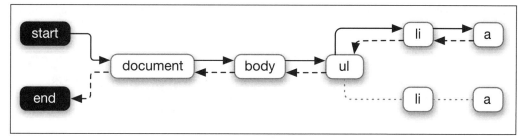

Figure 4-16. The W3C event capturing and bubbling flow after clicking one of the anchors

By combining the two phases into one model, the DOM2 Events method provides the best solution.

Popping the bubble

Just because events bubble doesn't mean they can't be stopped. In most cases, you probably want events to stay put in the specific element you clicked, not propagate to the surrounding elements. It these cases, you can pop the bubble before it leaves the object and cancel any other bubbling events that may occur further along the path.

To cancel the bubbling phase in the W3C DOM2 Events method, you simply call the stopPropagation() method on the event object. Likewise, with Microsoft Internet Explorer, you need to set the cancelBubble property of the event to true.

Take a moment to add the following ADS.stopPropagation() method to your ADS library. Using a bit of capability detection, you can create a nice cross-browser function that will stop the propagation of an event passed into it:

```
(function(){
if(!window.ADS) { window['ADS'] = {} }

... Above here is your existing library ...

function stopPropagation(eventObject) {
    eventObject = eventObject || getEventObject(eventObject);
    if(eventObject.stopPropagation) {
        eventObject.stopPropagation();
    } else {
        eventObject.cancelBubble = true;
    }
}
window['ADS']['stopPropagation'] = stopPropagation;

... Below here is your existing library ...

})();
```

This ADS.stopPropagation() method relies on the event object passed into the method's arguments. We haven't discussed accessing events yet, so the getEventObject() method within this method doesn't exist at this point but will be added to the library later in this chapter.

> *The same DOM* stopPropagation() *method applies to the event capturing phase as well, but remember that, as of Version 7, Microsoft Internet Explorer doesn't support capturing, so there's no Microsoft equivalent to reproduce capturing.*

Cancelling the default action

The last part of the event flow is the default action. I briefly touched on this in Chapter 1, where I discussed using a false return value from a click event listener to prevent the browser from redirecting to the page in the href attribute value. Though this works in some cases, the correct way is to use the appropriate event members.

The default actions of specific elements are not controlled or defined by the DOM2 Events specification. The only influence introduced by DOM2 Events is a way to cancel the default action by using the event's preventDefault() method. Likewise, Internet Explorer will also allow you to cancel the default event by setting the returnValue property of the Internet Explorer event object to false.

Again, take a moment to add the following cross-browser ADS.eventPreventDefault() function to your ADS library, which also relies on the event object passed into the arguments:

```
(function(){
if(!window.ADS) { window['ADS'] = {} }

... Above here is your existing library ...

function preventDefault(eventObject) {
    eventObject = eventObject || getEventObject(eventObject);
    if(eventObject.preventDefault) {
        eventObject.preventDefault();
    } else {
        eventObject.returnValue = false;
    }
}
window['ADS']['preventDefault'] = preventDefault;

... Below here is your existing library ...

})();
```

One caution, however, is that some events associated with a default action can't be cancelled. Table 4-1 lists the various DOM events and their cancelable property.

Table 4-1. Which events can be cancelled in the DOM event flow?

Event	Cancelable
click	Yes
mousedown	Yes
mouseup	Yes
mouseover	Yes
mousemove	No
mouseout	Yes
load	No
unload	No
abort	No
error	No
select	No
change	No
submit	Yes
reset	No
focus	No
blur	No
resize	No
scroll	No
DOMFocusIn	No
DOMFocusOut	No
DOMActivate	Yes
DOMSubtreeModified	No
DOMNodeInserted	No
DOMNodeRemoved	No

Continued

Table 4-1. Which events can be cancelled in the DOM event flow?
(Continued)

Event	Cancelable
DOMNodeRemovedFromDocument	No
DOMNodeInsertedIntoDocument	No
DOMAttrModified	No
DOMCharacterDataModified	No

Registering events

Once you figure out what order your event listeners need to follow, you need to register them as event listeners on the object. Like everything so far, working with different browsers is a nightmare. Not only do browsers differ in what events they have and the way they handle the flow, they also differ in the way they register event listeners.

Inline registration model

In Chapter 1, you explored the various ways of including scripts in your document: using inline <script> elements in the body, inline <script> in the head, and external files. You also saw how inline event listeners such as this:

```
<a href="http://example.com"➥
    onclick="window.open(this.href); return false;"➥
>http://example.com</a>
```

can be done in much better ways using progressive enhancement and unobtrusive DOM scripting techniques. Way back when events were first introduced, inline registration was the *only* method available, and it required you to hard-code each event as an HTML attribute inline in the markup. As the only method, it forced you to replicate the same bit of code for each element, cluttering the markup and drastically increasing file size. Even before the W3C came along with a friendlier event registration solution, browser developers realized the problems with inline registration and incorporated solutions, some of which are incorporated into your earlier ADS.addEvent() method.

The ADS.addEvent() method revisited

All the examples you've seen so far where event listeners have been added to DOM elements have used the custom ADS.addEvent() method introduced in Chapter 1. The addEvent() method was originally developed and popularized by Scott Andrew LePera (http://www.scottandrew.com/weblog/articles/cbs-events) and is a simple wrapper that combines the different W3C and Microsoft models into one function:

```
function addEvent(obj, evType, fn, useCapture){
  if (obj.addEventListener){
    obj.addEventListener(evType, fn, useCapture);
    return true;
```

```
    } else if (obj.attachEvent){
        var r = obj.attachEvent("on"+evType, fn);
        return r;
    } else {
        alert("Handler could not be attached");
    }
}
```

As you'll find out in a moment, the Microsoft and W3C methods differ drastically—and shouldn't be considered the same—so many people believe that using a method such as addEvent() is actually more harmful than good. Applied to this original addEvent() function, I would tend to agree. The Microsoft model doesn't allow capturing, so the useCapture argument is ambiguous. Also, as you'll see next, the this keyword in the context of the listener differs between Internet Explorer and the W3C.

The addEvent() version I've included in Chapter 1 is a slightly modified version of an alternative addEvent() written by John Resig (http://ejohn.org/projects/flexible-javascript-events/):

```
function addEvent( obj, type, fn ) {
    if ( obj.attachEvent ) {
        obj['e'+type+fn] = fn;
        obj[type+fn] = function(){obj['e'+type+fn]( window.event );}
        obj.attachEvent( 'on'+type, obj[type+fn] );
    } else
        obj.addEventListener( type, fn, false );
}
```

This version removes the useCapture argument, defaulting the DOM method to bubbling only, just like Internet Explorer, and it uses an anonymous function trick to give the Microsoft and W3C the same context for the this keyword—where this refers to the object that was assigned to the listener.

I feel that this addEvent() method (and our slightly modified version from Chapter 1) treats the two events models in the same way, so you can safely use it without hesitation.

So that you understand the different models and why things are done the way they are, let's take a quick look at each registration method to reveal the advantages and disadvantages of each.

The traditional event model

To register an event listener on a specific object in any web browser using the traditional method, all you need to do is define the JavaScript method you want to execute when the event occurs and assign that method to the appropriate event listener property on the object. This traditional method is the one you saw in Chapter 1 when using the onclick attribute of an anchor tag similar to this:

```
// Traditional event registration
window.onload = function() {
    var anchor = document.getElementById('example');
    anchor.onclick = function(){
        // Your click event code
    }
}
```

The basic concept of the traditional method is that the event listener is a JavaScript function assigned to a method associated with an event. The object's method for a specific event is the event name, prefixed with on, such as the onclick method for the click event.

To remove the event listener on the anchor, you simply set the method to null, so no listener is defined:

```
anchor.onclick = null;
```

In this traditional method, each event listener acts just like a regular JavaScript method, so you can manually invoke the event by calling the method directly:

```
anchor.onclick();
```

Notice the addition of the parentheses on the end of the method call when manually invoking the event. This is important when you want to actually call the method, as the parentheses tell JavaScript to execute the function. Without them, JavaScript would simply reference the instance of the function as it did when you assigned the eventListener method as the onclick listener. Ideally, you would want to incorporate capability detection to ensure there actually is an onclick method first, so you would do this:

```
if(anchor.onclick ) {
    anchor.onclick();
}
```

By checking first, you'll ensure no accidental errors when JavaScript tries to execute a method that isn't there. Also, manually invoking the event doesn't provide access to the event object, since there isn't one.

The traditional method is the most straightforward and browser-agnostic way to register your event listeners, but it does create a variety of interesting circumstances and isn't ideal.

First, if you recall the discussion of the this keyword in Chapter 2, you'll see that the traditional event registration method has the this keyword referencing the target object. Having this refer to the object to which the event listener is attached is probably exactly what you want, but it's something you need to be aware of.

Second, the event listener can only be a single function. You'll have to wrap multiple listeners into one encompassing function when you want to call more than one listener for a specific event on the same object. That's easy enough to do:

```
link.onclick = function() {
    eventListenerA();
    eventListenerB();
}
```

But preventing one listener involves additional logic to combine event listeners as necessary, and it gets really annoying. It also doesn't allow you to easily remove individual event listeners.

Finally, the traditional method is subject to the browser's default event flow. There's no way to specify whether the event is in a capturing phase or a bubbling phase.

Microsoft-specific event model

Microsoft has taken the traditional method a step further by defining its own event-related methods that you can use to register your event listeners—but these only work in Internet Explorer. With Microsoft, you use the attachEvent() and detachEvent() methods to register and remove event listeners respectively.

To register an event listener on a specific object, you first define the listener as a JavaScript function and then use the object's attachEvent(object,listener) method to assign the listener in the second argument to a specific event defined in the first argument. The event name is defined using the same on prefix used in the traditional method:

```
// Microsoft event registration
function eventListener() {
    // Your click event code
}
window.attachEvent('onload', function() {
    var link = document.getElementById('example');
    link.attachEvent('onclick',eventListener);
});
```

Likewise, you can later remove the event listener using the detachEvent() method with the identical arguments:

```
link.detachEvent('onclick',eventListener);
```

Using the Microsoft methods, you can also specify multiple events for the same object:

```
link.attachEvent('onclick', eventListenerA);
link.attachEvent('onclick', eventListenerB);
link.attachEvent('onclick', eventListenerC);
```

And you can invoke the event manually using the fireEvent() method:

```
link.fireEvent("onclick");
```

Microsoft's model is cleaner than the traditional one, but it still poses a few problems.

First, this model only works with Internet Explorer; it's pretty much useless anywhere else.

Second, unlike the traditional model, the event listener is referenced rather than copied, so if you use the this keyword, this will refer to the context of the original JavaScript function, which is usually within the window object, not the object to which the listener is attached.

Finally, Internet Explorer doesn't support event capturing, so there's no way to specify the capturing phase of the event flow, and events will always bubble unless stopped by the returnValue as you saw earlier. There's no nice solution to this until Internet Explorer implements a capturing phase as well.

W3C DOM2 Events model

To overcome the limitations of the traditional model and further improve the Microsoft model, the W3C has taken the middle ground and included both phases of the event flow along with similar methods.

181

The DOM2 Events specification includes the addEventListener() and removeEventListener() methods, which each take an event and an event listener, like the Microsoft methods, but they also allow you to specify the event phase through a third parameter. As well, the W3C opted to remove the on prefix, so events are identified using just the event name, not the traditional method name:

```
// W3C Event Registration
function eventListener() {
    // Your click event code
}
window.addEventListener('load', function(W3CEvent) {
    var link = document.getElementById('example');
    link.addEventListener('click',eventListener,false);
}, false);
```

If the third parameter is true, the event listener will execute in the capturing phase, and likewise, if false, it will occur in the bubbling phase, as you saw earlier in this chapter.

You can also remove the event using the removeEventListener() method:

```
link.removeEventListener('click',eventListener,false);
```

And again you can add as many events as you like:

```
link.addEventListener('click',eventListenerA,false);
link.addEventListener('click',eventListenerB,false);
link.addEventListener('click',eventListenerC,false);
```

> When specifying multiple event listeners on an object in the same phase of an event, the W3C DOM2 Events specification fails to specify in what order the events will occur. Just because you add eventListenerA first doesn't mean it will necessarily be the first or the last to execute when the event occurs. The only way to ensure that events occur in a specific order is to revert to using a single event listener on each object and calling multiple functions from within the one listener.

With the W3C model, you can also invoke events manually with a combination of the document.createEvent() method and the object's dispatchEvent() method. To simulate a click, you would create a MouseEvent and initiate its properties before dispatching it to the anchor DOM element referenced in anchor:

```
// Manually invokeing events using W3C methods
var event = document.createEvent("MouseEvents");
event.initMouseEvent(
'click', // event type
true, // can bubble
true, // is cancelable
window, // type of view
0, // mouse click count
0, // screen x coordinate
```

```
0, // screen y coordinate
0, // client x coordinate
0, // client y coordinate
false, // was the control key was pressed
false, // was the alt key was pressed
false, // was the shift key was pressed
false, // was the meta key was pressed
0, // the number of the mouse button pressed
null // a related target object
);
anchor.dispatchEvent(evt);
```

We'll discuss the W3C DOM2 Events specification's MouseEvent and its properties in more detail in the next section, where you'll see how to access the event object from within the event listener.

The problem with the load event

Regardless of which event registration method is used, there's an inherent problem with using the window's load event to initiate your DOM scripts. When the page contains a number of large files, such as inline <img> elements in the markup, the load event waits and executes only after all the images have loaded as well. If you haven't used inline images, that may not be a concern. But if you're creating an application that uses inline images, such as a photo management tool, you may want your load event to run before all the inline images finish loading. To account for those cases, add the following ADS.addLoadEvent method to your ADS library:

```
(function(){
if(!window.ADS) { window['ADS'] = {} }

... Above here is your existing library ...

function addLoadEvent(loadEvent,waitForImages) {
    if(!isCompatible()) return false;

    // If the wait flag is true use the regular add event method
    if(waitForImages) {
        return addEvent(window, 'load', loadEvent);
    }

    // Otherwise use a number of different methods

    // Wrap the loadEvent method to assign the correct content for the
    // this keyword and ensure that the event doesn't execute twice
    var init = function() {

        // Return if this function has already been called
        if (arguments.callee.done) return;

        // Mark this function so you can verify if it was already run
        arguments.callee.done = true;
```

```
        // Run the load event in the context of the document
        loadEvent.apply(document,arguments);
    };

    // Register the event using the DOMContentLoaded event
    if (document.addEventListener) {
        document.addEventListener("DOMContentLoaded", init, false);
    }

    // For Safari, use a setInterval() to see if the
    // document has loaded
    if (/WebKit/i.test(navigator.userAgent)) {
        var _timer = setInterval(function() {
            if (/loaded|complete/.test(document.readyState)) {
                clearInterval(_timer);
                init();
            }
        },10);
    }

    // For Internet Explorer (using conditional comments)
    // attach a script that is deferred to the end of the
    // load process and then check to see
    // if it has loaded
    /*@cc_on @*/
    /*@if (@_win32)
    document.write("<script id=__ie_onload defer➥
src=javascript:void(0)><\/script>");
    var script = document.getElementById("__ie_onload");
    script.onreadystatechange = function() {
        if (this.readyState == "complete") {
            init();
        }
    };
    /*@end @*/
    return true;
}
window['ADS']['addLoadEvent'] = addLoadEvent;

... Below here is your existing library ...

})();
```

This load event is based on the solution discussed by Dean Edwards (http://dean.edwards.name/weblog/2005/09/busted) and uses a combination of different methods to invoke your DOM script before the images finish loading:

- If the browser has the addEventListener() method, it uses the DOMContentLoaded event, which invokes when the markup of the document has loaded.

- For Safari, the document's readyState is periodically checked using setInterval() to see if the document has finished loading.

- For Internet Explorer, it gets a little trickier. A new script tag is written to the document, but its loading is deferred until the end of the file. Then, using the onreadystatechange method of the script object, a similar readyState check is done to invoke the load event as necessary.

Setting the second parameter to true invokes a wrapper to the original ADS.addEvent(window, 'load' . . .) method, so that you can easily switch between the two.

You can see the different load events in action by looking at the chapter4/load/load.html file. The example includes a link to a 580KB JPEG Blue Marble photo of the earth on NASA's Visible Earth web site (http://visibleearth.nasa.gov/) and three load events in the chapter4/load/load.js file:

```
// Regular addEvent for the window's load event
ADS.addEvent(window,'load',function(W3CEvent) {
    ADS.log.write('ADS.addEvent(window,load,...) invoked');
});

// The alternate addLoadMethod
ADS.addLoadEvent(function(W3CEvent) {
    ADS.log.write('ADS.addLoadEvent(...) invoked');
});

// The alternate addLoadMethod which uses the original addEvent method
ADS.addLoadEvent(function(W3CEvent) {
    ADS.log.write('ADS.addLoadEvent(...,true) invoked');
},true);
```

When the page loads, the middle ADS.addLoadEvent() will invoke before the image finishes loading. The first and last load events won't occur until afterward, as shown in Figure 4-17 where the image is still in the process of loading.

If you reload the page and have the image cached, you'll notice that the second set of load events occurs almost instantly as the image is loaded quickly from the cache.

The only caveat is that if your DOM script needs to access image-specific properties such as the size, the images may not be loaded when the script runs—which is the whole point.

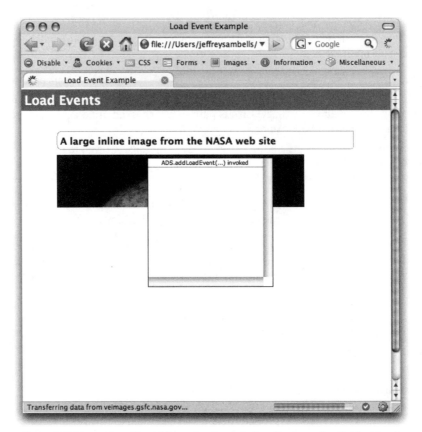

Figure 4-17. The addLoadEvent() log entry shown before the image has finished loading

Accessing the event object from the event listener

So far, you've seen how the event flow works and how to assign event listeners to objects, but we haven't discussed the event listener itself. The event listener is just a regular JavaScript function, but it has a few special requirements.

You'll notice here that I haven't defined any arguments in the function definition:

```
function eventListener() {
    // Your code
}
```

In previous examples, you've been using this, or some variable in the scope chain, to manipulate and affect the document. It's not possible to specify custom arguments in event listeners because there's no way for the browser to know what unique arguments are defined for each listener, so it treats them all the same. This, however, is not always true, but again, it depends on the browser.

In the W3C model, the event listener will receive an argument representing the event itself:

```
function eventListener(W3CEvent) {
    // Your code
}
```

But in Internet Explorer, the listener doesn't receive any arguments, and the event object is located in window.event, so you'll need to do a simple check to switch between the two:

```
function eventListener(W3CEvent) {
    var eventObject = W3CEvent || window.event;
    // Your code
}
```

Syntactical shortcuts

Events are going to have a lot of issues with cross-browser support and will, therefore, require a number of quick checks to select among different methods. Rather than writing out long if/else statements, I'll be saving space and keystrokes by using a number of syntax shortcuts, so you may see something like this:

```
var example = (a != 2) ? 'no' : 'yes';
```

This syntax is called a ternary operator and is a quick and dirty way of writing an if statement. It's the equivalent of writing this:

```
if (a != 2) {
    var example = 'no';
} else {
    var example = 'yes';
}
```

You'll probably run into the ternary operator syntax at some point, so you may as well learn it now.

Additionally, you may see something like this:

```
var example = a || b;
```

In this instance, example should receive the value of a or b. The value of a is assigned to example, except if a is null, undefined, or false. In those cases, the value of b is assigned instead. This is useful for setting defaults that may or may not be specified. Here, b could contain the default value, and if a has a value set, a would override the default value in b.

The ADS.getEventObject() method

Remembering to retrieve the appropriate event will be annoying, so take a moment to add the following ADS.getEventObject() function to your ADS library:

```
(function(){
if(!window.ADS) { window['ADS'] = {} }

... Above here is your existing library ...
```

```
function getEventObject(W3CEvent) {
    return W3CEvent || window.event;
}
window['ADS']['getEventObject'] = getEventObject;

... Below here is your existing library ...

})();
```

Now you'll be able to use the ADS.getEventObject() function to easily access the event object without manually coding the check each time.

```
function eventListener(W3CEvent) {
    var eventObject = ADS.getEventObject(W3CEvent);
    //your code referring to this, the scope chain or the eventObject
}
```

The auxiliary function gives you another layer of future-proofing where you can modify this behavior should another browser with a different method be required. Also, the earlier ADS.preventDefault() and ADS.stopPropagation() methods incorporate this method, so you don't have to remember to include it.

> If you define event listeners outside of the ADS library, you'll need to include the ADS object prefix, as the scope chain of the listener will be outside the library. If you're defining your listeners from within the library, you can leave it off, as the scope chain will include the ADS namespace. For more on scope chains, see Chapters 1 and 2.

But again, the W3C and Microsoft define the event object a little differently, so further checking will be required for a complete cross-browser solution.

Cross-browser event properties and methods

You may want to keep your hands away from your head while reading this section so you won't be pulling your hair out trying to write cross-browser event listeners. We'll start with the W3C DOM2 Events specification and then look at various browser inconsistencies.

In Chapter 3, you saw how each node in the DOM document is actually extended from several other DOM objects. The same applies to events. The event passed into the event listener in the W3C model isn't always identical, but they do have common properties. When your browser invokes the load event, the object passed into the listener is an instance of the DOM2 Events Event object, whereas when the click event is invoked, the object passed into the listener is a MouseEvent object. Just like the DOM document objects, each event extends and maintains the methods and properties of other event objects, as illustrated in Figure 4-18.

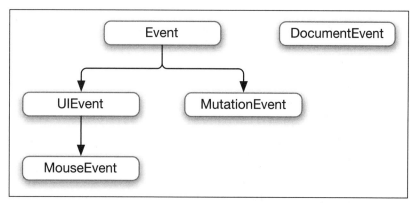

Figure 4-18. The DOM2 Events object inheritance diagram

Let's take a closer look at the properties of the Event and MouseEvent objects to see what they offer.

The DOM2 Events object

The event object contains the methods and properties you'll need to control event flow and target objects. The W3C DOM2 Events model defines the following properties for the Event object:

- bubbles is a Boolean property that indicates if the event is a bubbling event. If it's a bubbling event, bubbles will be true; otherwise, it will be false.

- cancelable is a Boolean property that indicates if an event can have its default action cancelled. If the default action can be cancelled, cancelable will be true; otherwise, it will be false.

- currentTarget is the DOM element in the event flow on which the event listeners are currently being processed. The currentTarget will be different from the target property for event listeners that are not registered on the target but are ancestors of the target in the capturing or bubbling phases of the event flow.

- target is the EventTarget in the DOM document that originally invoked the event sequence.

- timestamp is a DOMTimeStamp object that you can use to determine the number of milliseconds since the epoch at which the event was created, but it may not be available on all systems. Epoch can refer to the time the system was started or to 0:0:0 UTC January 1, 1970.

- type is a string containing the name of the event, such as click.

- eventPhase indicates what phase of the event flow the current listener is in. It's specified using an integer of 1 through 3, but you can use the Event constants CAPTURING_PHASE, AT_TARGET and BUBBLING_PHASE in your comparisons using something like this:

```
function eventListener(W3CEvent) {
    switch(W3CEvent.eventPhase) {
        case Event.CAPTURING_PHASE:
            //code to run if in the capturing phase
            break;
        case Event.AT_TARGET:
            //code to run if this is the target
            break;
```

```
        case Event.BUBBLING_PHASE:
            //code to run if in the bubbling phase
            break;
    }
```

These event properties allow you to ensure that you're accessing the correct object in the correct manner. For instance, rather than relying on the this keyword, you can use the target or currentTarget property depending on the phase of the event:

```
function eventListener(W3CEvent) {
    window.open(W3CEvent.currentTarget.href);
    W3CEvent.preventDefault();
}
var anchor = document.getElementById('example');
anchor.addEventListener('click',eventListener,false);
```

The W3C DOM2 Events model also defines the following methods of the Event object, as we discussed earlier:

- initEvent(eventType,canBubble,cancelable): Use this to initialize an event created through the document.createEvent('Event') method.

- preventDefalt(): Use this to cancel the default action of the object if it is cancelable, such as redirecting the browser to the href attribute of an anchor element.

- stopPropagation(): Use this to stop further execution of the event flow including the capturing, target, and bubbling phases. When called, all listeners will still be executed at the current level, but the flow will not continue beyond the currentTarget.

The DOM2 MouseEvent object

For all W3C DOM mouse events, the event object passed into the event listener will be a MouseEvent. The mouse event includes properties about the position of the mouse pointer as well as information regarding additional keys that may have been pressed at the same time as the mouse event. The MouseEvent properties follow.

altKey, ctrlKey, and shiftKey altKey, ctrlKey, and shiftKey are Boolean properties that indicate if the Alt, Ctrl, or Shift keys were pressed along with the mouse event.

button button will contain an integer representing which button was clicked. The buttons on the mouse are represented as follows:

- 0 indicates the left mouse button.

- 1 indicates the center mouse button (if it exists).

- 2 indicates the right mouse button (or Command-click on a single-button Apple mouse).

Ideally, the W3C should have included constants representing each of the possibilities, so that rather than doing this:

```
if(W3CEvent.button==0) {
        // left click code
}
```

you could have done something a little more meaningful, such as this:

```
if(W3CEvent.button==MouseEvent.BUTTON_LEFT) {
        // left click code
}
```

clientX and clientY clientX and clientY, according to the W3C specifications, refer to "The [horizontal and vertical] coordinates at which the event occurred relative to the DOM implementation's client area." That's OK but not really crystal clear. Do they mean the viewport of the browser or the entire browser window? If you try adding the following click event on the document in a W3C-compliant browser:

```
document.addEventListener('click',function(W3CEvent) {
    alert('client: (' + W3CEvent.clientX + ',' + W3CEvent.clientY + ')');
},false);
```

you'll see that the clientX and clientY positions represent the location relative to the viewport of the browser but not the document, as shown in Figure 4-19. If you scroll the page and click in the same location in the viewport, you'll get the same coordinates.

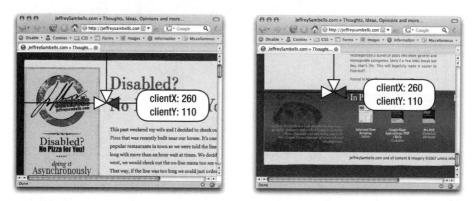

Figure 4-19. The clientX and clientY position on a web page before and after scrolling

screenX and screenY screenX and screenY are similar to the client properties, but they represent the location relative to the client's screen, as shown in Figure 4-20.

MouseEvent The MouseEvent object has a relatedTarget property, which is a secondary target related to the event. In most cases, this will be null, but in a mouseover event, it will reference the previous object that was exited. Likewise, in a mouseout event, it will reference the object that was entered.

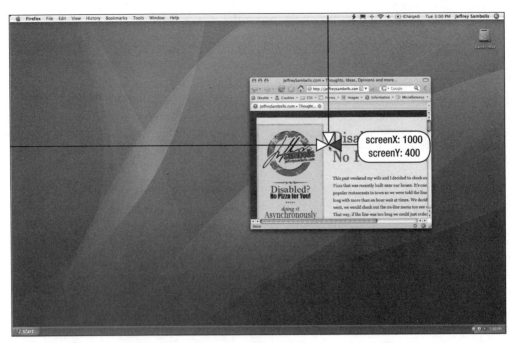

Figure 4-20. The screenX and screenY position on a web page

Browser incompatibilities galore

Sticking to the W3C methods is the ideal solution, but it's not going to be possible if you want a browser-agnostic solution. Here are a few ways to deal with some of the inconsistencies.

Accessing the event's target element This is probably the first troublesome thing you'll run into. Internet Explorer doesn't provide a target or currentTarget property, but alternatively provides a srcElement property. Likewise, Apple's Safari browser also introduces a bit of confusion if the DOM element contains a text node. With Safari, the text node becomes the target rather than the containing element. To deal with this, add the following ADS.getTarget() method to your ADS library to provide a browser-agnostic solution:

```
(function(){
if(!window.ADS) { window['ADS'] = {} }
```

... Above here is your existing library ...

```
function getTarget(eventObject) {
    eventObject = eventObject || getEventObject(eventObject);

    // Check if the target is W3C or MSIE
    var target = eventObject.target || eventObject.scrElement;

    // Reassign the target to the parent
    // if it is a text node like in Safari
```

```
        if(target.nodeType == ADS.node.TEXT_NODE) {
            target = node.parentNode;
        }

        return target;

    }
    window['ADS']['getTarget'] = getTarget;

    ... Below here is your existing library ...

})();
```

This method will allow you to retrieve the target for the given event:

```
ADS.addEvent(window, 'load', function() {

    function eventListener(W3CEvent) {

        //retrieve the target
        var target = ADS.getTarget(W3CEvent);

        //target now refers to the appropriate element.
        window.open(target.href);
    }
    var anchor = document.getElementById('example');
    addEvent(anchor, 'click', eventListener);

});
```

Determining which mouse button was clicked This also creates problems. Recall from the previous section that the W3C deems that

- 0 indicates that the left button was pressed.
- 1 indicates that the middle button was pressed.
- 2 indicates that the right button was pressed.

If you're familiar with arrays, specifically that they are zero-indexed, you can understand that the first button, reading left to right, is at index 0, so left button = 0 does make sense. Also, there are three buttons, so using 0, 1, and 2 makes sense. Microsoft, however, took a different approach by including combinations of buttons as well as a "no buttons" index. Microsoft says that

- 0 indicates that no buttons were pressed.
- 1 indicates that the left button was pressed.
- 2 indicates that the right button was pressed.
- 3 indicates that both the left and right buttons were pressed.
- 4 indicates that the middle button was pressed.
- 5 indicates that both the left and middle buttons were pressed.

- 6 indicates that both the right and middle buttons were pressed.

- 7 indicates that all three buttons were pressed.

This introduces more headaches. For example, with W3C 1 refers to the middle button, but in Internet Explorer, 1 indicates the left button. Also, the W3C and Microsoft use the same button property to hold this information, so it doesn't allow for a nice capability detection solution around the button property.

To create a generic method without using browser detection, you have to be a little creative and use the toString() value of the event object. First, check if the toString() method exists and if its result is a MouseEvent object. If the toString() method is available and it's a MouseEvent, you're in luck, and you can use the W3C methods regardless of the browser. Otherwise, if the button property still exists, you can assume that it's Internet Explorer. Add the following ADS.getMouseButton() method to your ADS library:

```
(function(){
if(!window.ADS) { window['ADS'] = {} }

... Above here is your existing library ...

function getMouseButton(eventObject) {
    eventObject = eventObject || getEventObject(eventObject);

    // Initialize an object with the appropriate properties
    var buttons = {
        'left':false,
        'middle':false,
        'right':false
    };

    // Check the toString value of the eventObject
    // W3C DOM objects have a toString method and in this case it
    // should be MouseEvent
    if(eventObject.toString && eventObject.toString().➥
indexOf('MouseEvent') != -1) {
        // W3C Method
        switch(eventObject.button) {
            case 0: buttons.left = true; break;
            case 1: buttons.middle = true; break;
            case 2: buttons.right = true; break;
            default: break;
        }
    } else if(eventObject.button) {
        // MSIE method
        switch(eventObject.button) {
            case 1: buttons.left = true; break;
            case 2: buttons.right = true; break;
            case 3:
                buttons.left = true;
```

```
                            buttons.right = true;
                        break;
                        case 4: buttons.middle = true; break;
                        case 5:
                            buttons.left = true;
                            buttons.middle = true;
                        break;
                        case 6:
                            buttons.middle = true;
                            buttons.right = true;
                        break;
                        case 7:
                            buttons.left = true;
                            buttons.middle = true;
                            buttons.right = true;
                        break;
                        default: break;
                    }
                } else {
                    return false;
                }

                return buttons;

            }
            window['ADS']['getMouseButton'] = getMouseButton;

            ... Below here is your existing library ...

        })();
```

Your ADS.getMouseButton() method will return an object with left, middle, and right properties indicating true if the button was pressed and false otherwise.

> *Alternatively, you could check for some other method related to the events, such as* addEventListener, *but it's possible that another script could add a custom* addEventListener() *method by adding to the* Object *prototype. Avoiding browser detection, your method will use the correct compliant functions if they're available— regardless of the browser.*

Dealing with the mouse position The majority of the time you're going to want to find the location of the cursor relative to the document's origin, not the screen or the browser's viewport.

To accomplish this, you again need to use a bit of capability detection and adjust which properties you use depending on which browser is accessing the page. Both the W3C and Internet Explorer define the clientX and clientY properties but differ in how they specify the browser-specific scroll offset properties. W3C uses document.documentElement.scrollTop, whereas Internet Explorer uses document.body.scrollTop. In this case, Safari also acts a little differently; it puts the location in the event's pageX and pageY properties. The following ADS.getPointerPositionInDocument() method handles these cases:

```
(function(){
if(!window.ADS) { window['ADS'] = {} }

... Above here is your existing library ...
function getPointerPositionInDocument(eventObject) {
    eventObject = eventObject || getEventObject(eventObject);

    var x = eventObject.pageX || (eventObject.clientX +
        (document.documentElement.scrollLeft
            || document.body.scrollLeft));

    var y= eventObject.pageY || (eventObject.clientY +
        (document.documentElement.scrollTop
            || document.body.scrollTop));

    // x and y now contain the coordinates of the mouse
    // realtive to the document origin
    return {'x':x,'y':y};
}
window['ADS']['getPointerPositionInDocument'] = ➥
getPointerPositionInDocument;

... Below here is your existing library ...

})();
```

With the ADS.getPointerPositionInDocument() method, you can make an element follow the pointer with a mousemove event such as the one in the chapter4/follow/follow.js source:

```
ADS.addEvent(window, 'load', function() {

    // Define an object to move
    var object = document.getElementById('follow');

    // Set it to use absolute positioning
    object.style.position = 'absolute';

    // Create an event listener for the document's mousemove event
    function eventListener(W3CEvent) {
        var pointer = ADS.getPointerPositionInDocument(W3CEvent);

        // Position the object relative to the pointer
        object.style.left = pointer.x + 'px';
        object.style.top = pointer.y + 'px';
```

```
    }

    // Attach the event listener to the document
    // object's mousemove event
    ADS.addEvent(document,'mousemove',eventListener);

});
```

Take a look at chpater4/follow/follow.html, where this mouse move event has been registered. The Follow Pointer element easily follows the pointer around the page, as shown in Figure 4-21.

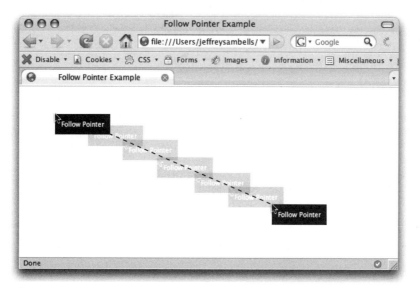

Figure 4-21. An element following the pointer

This is the beginning of the drag portion of a drag-and-drop interface that you'll explore more in Chapter 6.

Accessing keyboard commands

The DOM2 Events specification doesn't provide any access to the keyboard beyond the few key combinations included in the MouseEvent properties. Keyboard commands have been incorporated into the DOM3 Events specification, but as of this writing, the specification is still in draft state and has yet to be finalized. For now, you'll have to rely on the proprietary browser methods (some of which are actually early adoptions of the W3C standard).

Fortunately, modern browsers have all decided to use the same property (hooray!), so you can retrieve the Unicode value of the key press from the event object's keyCode property. It's still a good idea to make an auxiliary function as you did before, so once the W3C methods are implemented, you can easily switch to them. Here's a simple ADS.getKeyPressed() method for your ADS library that you can use to retrieve the key code and related ASCII value:

```
(function(){
if(!window.ADS) { window['ADS'] = {} }

... Above here is your existing library ...

function getKeyPressed(eventObject) {
    eventObject = eventObject || getEventObject(eventObject);

    var code = eventObject.keyCode;
    var value = String.fromCharCode(code);
    return {'code':code,'value':value};
}
window['ADS']['getKeyPressed'] = getKeyPressed;

... Below here is your existing library ...

})();
```

With this simple little function, you can determine which keys are pressed for key events. For example, if you use it in the keydown event of the document, each key press will reveal the key value and the key code as shown in Table 4-2:

```
ADS.addEvent(document, 'keydown', function(W3CEvent) {
    var key = ADS.getKeyPressed(W3CEvent);
    ADS.log.write(key.code + ':' + key.value);
});
```

Table 4-2. ADS.getKeyPressed() key codes

Key	Code
A	65
B	66
C	67
D	68
E	69
F	70
G	71
H	72
I	73
J	74

Key	Code
K	75
L	76
M	77
N	78
O	79
P	80
Q	81
R	82
S	83
T	84
U	85
V	85
W	87
X	88
Y	89
Z	90
0	48
1	49
2	50
3	51
4	52
5	53
6	54
7	55
8	56

Continued

Table 4-2. ADS.getKeyPressed() key codes
(Continued)

Key	Code
9	57
Backspace	8
Tab	9
Enter	13
Shift	16
Ctrl	17
Alt/Command (Option on Apple keyboard)	18
Pause/Break	19
Esc	27
Page Up	33
Page Down	34
End	35
Home	36
Left arrow	37
Up arrow	38
Right arrow	39
Down arrow	40
Insert	45
Delete	46
Left window key	91
Right window key	92
Select key	93
Multiplication symbol (*)	106
Addition symbol (+)	107

Key	Code
Subtraction symbol (-)	109
Decimal point (.)	110
Division symbol (\)	111
Num Lock	144
Scroll Lock	145
Semicolon (;)	59
Equal sign (=)	61
Comma (,)	188
Period (.)	190
Forward slash (/)	191
Opening bracket ([)	219
Closing bracket ([)	221
Single quotation mark (')	222

Summary

This chapter has given you a lot to remember, so I hope you still have room for more. Dealing with events is currently one of the most complicated parts of web development, and we didn't even touch on using your own custom events. The reason it's so complicated is because of the differences among the various browsers and how they do or don't implement the DOM2 Events specification.

This chapter has given you an excellent start on dealing with events in the different browsers and how to deal with things like event registration, event access, event flow, and event listeners. You've also added a number of new browser-agnostic event methods to your ADS library, which will save you a lot of time and effort. This chapter also reiterated the importance of capability detection when dealing with the different event registration and access methods.

In the next chapter, you'll investigate the different ways of manipulating the style of your document including fixing things like PNG transparency in Microsoft Internet Explorer and dynamically accessing and editing the style sheets in your browser. In Chapter 6, we'll put everything together with some progressive behavioral enhancement to build an unobtrusive image cropping and resizing tool.

DYNAMICALLY MODIFYING STYLE AND CASCADING STYLE SHEETS

In Chapter 1, I stressed the importance of separating your markup, behavior, and presentation. The problem with separating everything is that many aspects of the three layers overlap or even collide in an explosion messed-up code. You've already seen how to manipulate the DOM document structure in Chapter 3 and the behavioral event listeners in Chapter 4. Now it's time to discuss the presentation layer and how you can write scripts to modify your presentation. We'll explore ways to modify the presentation without embedding it in the script itself, though sometimes doing so will be unavoidable.

In this chapter, we'll briefly look at the key parts of the W3C DOM Level 2 Style specification along with a variety of methods you can use to keep your presentation separated from your DOM scripts. We'll also discuss one of the biggest misconceptions about the style property as well as a little fix for PNG transparency in some versions of Microsoft Internet Explorer. The last part of the chapter will also deal with creating transitions and effects, which will be further expanded on in Chapter 10.

The W3C DOM2 Style specification

The W3C DOM2 Style specification (http://w3.org/TR/DOM-Level-2-Style/) can appear very scary at first, but if you understand the basics of CSS, you already know the majority of it. Without discussing CSS at length, I'm going to focus on a few of the more compli-cated, and more useful, aspects of the specification, focusing on things you'll encounter in your day-to-day DOM scripts.

CSSStyleSheet objects

The CSSStyleSheet objects represent all of your CSS. These include external and inline style sheets specified using `<style type="text/css"></style>` tags. CSSStyleSheet is constructed from various other DOM2 CSS objects, such as a list of CSSStyleRule objects representing each of the rules in the style sheet.

You'll find a list of your document's CSSStyleSheet objects in the `document.styleSheets` property. Each of the CSSStyleSheet objects has several properties:

- `type` will always be text/css, as you're dealing with Cascading Style Sheets in your HTML documents.

- `disabled` is a Boolean property indicating that the style sheet is applied (false) to the current document or disabled (true).

- `href` is the URL where the style sheet is located relative to the current document, or it's the URL of the current document for inline style sheets.

- `title` is a label that can be used to group style sheets, as you'll see later in this chapter.

- `media` indicates the type of target devices the style applies to, such as screen or print.

- `ownerRule` is a read-only CSSRule object representing the parent rule if the style sheet was imported using @import or something similar.

- `cssRules` is a read-only CSSRuleList list of all the CSSRule objects in the style sheet.

Each CSSStyleSheet object also has methods, including the following:

- `insertRule(rule,index)`: For adding new style declarations

- `deleteRule(index)`: For removing rules from the style sheet

We'll look at these properties and methods in more detail throughout this chapter as you modify and edit the presentation of your documents.

CSSStyleRule objects

Within each CSSStyleSheet is a list of CSSStyleRule objects. These objects each represent a single rule such as

```
body {
    font: 62.5%/1.2em "Lucida Grande", Lucida, Verdana, sans-serif;
    background: #c7f28e;
    color: #1a3800;
}
```

The CSSStyleRule objects have properties that define the rule:

- type is a property inherited from the CSSRule object and is a number between 0 and 6 representing the type of rule. For CSSStyleRule rules this will always be 1, but other rule objects, such as CSSImportRule, which represents @import rules, take other values. The list of type values follows:

  - **0**: CSSRule.UNKNOWN_RULE
  - **1**: CSSRule.STYLE_RULE (indicates a CSSStyleRule object)
  - **2**: CSSRule.CHARSET_RULE (indicates a CSSCharsetRule object)
  - **3**: CSSRule.IMPORT_RULE (indicates a CSSImportRuleobject)
  - **4**: CSSRule.MEDIA_RULE (indicates a CSSMediaRule object)
  - **5**: CSSRule.FONT_FACE_RULE (indicates a CSSFontFaceRule object)
  - **6**: CSSRule.PAGE_RULE (indicates a CSSPageRule object)

- cssText contains the string representation of the entire rule in its current state. If the rule has been modified using other DOM methods, this string will represent the changes as well.

- parentStyleSheet references the parent CSSStyleSheet object.

- parentRule will reference another CSSRule if the rule is within another rule. For example, rules within a specific @media rule will have the @media rule as their parent rule.

Also, the CSSStyleRule objects have CSS-specific properties, such as the following:

- selectorText contains the selector used for the rule.
- style, like HTMLElement.style, is an instance of CSSStyleDeclaration.

You'll also see these properties and methods in more detail throughout this chapter.

CSSStyleDeclaration

The last object we'll look at, and probably the one you'll run into most, is the CSSStyleDeclaration object, which is the object that represents an element's style property. Like the CSSStyleRule object, the CSSStyleDeclaration object has properties such as the following:

- cssText contains the string representation of the entire rule.
- parentRule will reference the CSSStyleRule.

Also, the CSSStyleDeclaration object has several methods, including these:

- getPropertyValue(propertyName) returns the value of a CSS style property as a string.
- removeProperty(propertyName) removes the given property from the declaration.
- setProperty(propertyName,value,priority) allows you to set the value of a given CSS property.

Instances of the CSSStyleDeclaration object, such as the HTMLElement.style property, also have a shortcut access method through CSS2Properties, but we'll discuss that in more detail when we look at the style property later in this chapter.

> *As you'll see later in this chapter, the* style *property doesn't reference the* computed style from the cascade.

A lack of support

Unfortunately, some browsers don't support all the features of the Style specification. Those browsers have similar objects that represent similar features, but they're accessed differently than the DOM2 Style methods. Throughout the rest of this chapter, I'll focus on the W3C methods, but all of the style-related access and manipulation methods you'll be adding to your ADS library will be browser agnostic and include any necessary browser-specific access methods. I'll point out the cases where access differs from the W3C, but I won't go into a lot of detail regarding the proprietary methods. The only exception will be the Microsoft Internet Explorer CSS filter property in the context of translucent PNGs, which I'll cover near the end of this chapter.

When DOM scripting and style collide

The presentation layer in your web application consists primarily of the CSS styles. I'm going to assume that you're at least somewhat familiar with CSS and that you already know the basics, but if you're not, or haven't yet embraced CSS, I highly recommend these additional books:

- *Web Standards Solutions: The Markup and Style Handbook* by Dan Cederholm (friends of ED; ISBN-13: 978-1-59059-381-3)

- *CSS Mastery: Advanced Web Standards Solutions* by Andy Budd with Simon Collison and Cameron Moll (friends of ED; ISBN-13: 978-1-59059-614-2)

- *Transcending CSS: The Fine Art of Web Design* by Andy Clark and Molly Holzschlag (New Riders Press; ISBN-13: 978-0-32141-097-9)

CSS, like DOM scripting, is not a magic fix for your web site. To take advantage of its power and flexibility, you need to implement it properly with all your CSS styles defined in an external style sheet. This will separate the style from the markup, but it poses two problems:

- As I said, CSS is not a magic solution. It often requires additional tags in the semantic markup so that the CSS can manipulate extra elements for stylistic purposes.

- CSS also poses a problem for your behavioral layer. In many, if not most, cases, your behavioral enhancements will involve manipulating the presentation of your elements—but your presentation shouldn't be mixed into your DOM scripts either.

With a bit of forethought and planning, the presentation of your document can be separated from your behavioral elements while maintaining flexibility for both the CSS and DOM script.

Modifying markup for style

Semantic purists will discourage the use of any markup that doesn't directly relate to the semantics of the document, but sometimes it can't be avoided. As you work with CSS, you'll soon realize that its limitations will sometimes require a little extra markup to nudge things around and make them look the way you want—for presentation purposes only—but that's not a bad thing. Personally, I believe a little bit of extra markup isn't going to hurt anyone as long as it's done with forethought and you're not just layering on new markup without considering alternative solutions.

CSS image replacement is a common situation where additional markup is often required. The image could be replacing something as simple as the text in a header or something more complicated, such as a bulleted list or table. Either way, the goal is to provide a visually pleasing alternative to the text, but it should also maintain accessibility to the information.

The resulting markup should still

- be accessible to screen readers
- be understandable when images are off and CSS is on (a problem for many solutions)
- maintain accessibility features such as alt tags and titles
- avoid unnecessary markup—if at all possible

The classic technique is known as Fahrner Image Replacement (FIR). This technique involves adding an extraneous <span> tag around the content within an element such as a header:

```
<h1 id="advancedHeader"><span>Advanced DOM Scripting</span></h1>
```

and then applying CSS to insert a background image on the header and hide the <span>:

```
/* Add a background image to the parent element */
#advancedHeader {
    height:60px;
    background: transparent url(http://advanceddomscripting.com/➥
images/advancED-replace.png) no-repeat;
}
/* Hide the text */
#advancedHeader span {
    display:none;
}
```

The result, with the CSS applied, is a custom styled graphic that replaces the plain browser text, as shown in the chapter5/image-replacement/fir.html file in Figure 5-1; the plain text AdvancED DOM Scripting header has been replaced with an image.

Figure 5-1. The header replaced with an image

Without CSS, the header will gracefully degrade into the plain text alternative shown in Figure 5-2.

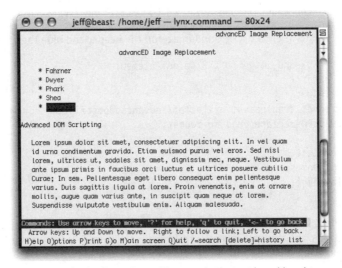

Figure 5-2. The header as it would appear in the text-based lynx browser

There are two problems with the classic FIR method. First, nothing shows if images are disabled, because the span is still hidden. The second problem is that display:none may also hide the content from screen readers that support CSS, effectively destroying the whole point of accessible image replacement.

Other methods have since been devised, such as the following three:

The Dwyer method by Leon Dwyer uses a 0 size for the extra <span>, but like FIR, it doesn't work with CSS turned on and images off, as in the chapter5/image-replacement/dwyer.html example:

```
/* Add a background image to the parent element */
#advancedHeader {
    height:60px;
    background: transparent url(http://advanceddomscripting.com/➥
images/advancED-replace.png) no-repeat;
}
/* Hide the text using a 0-sized box*/
#advancedHeader span {
    display:block;
    width:0;
    height:0;
    overflow:hidden;
}
```

The Phark method by Mike Rundle doesn't require any additional markup and uses a negative text indent to hide the content, but again, it doesn't work with CSS on and images off, as in the chapter5/image-replacement/phark.html example:

```
/* Use a background image along with a negative
text indent to hide the text */
#advancedHeader {
    text-indent: -100em;
    overflow:hidden;
    height:60px;
    background: transparent url(http://advanceddomscripting.com/➥
images/advancED-replace.png) no-repeat;
}
```

Another option is the Shea method by Dave Shea, which still uses an extra empty <span> element:

```
<h1 id="advancedHeader" title="AdvancED DOM Scripting">
    <span></span>Advanced DOM Scripting
</h1>
```

but rather than hiding the text, the span is positioned above the text with a solid opacity to hide the underlying words, as in the chapter5/image-replacement/shea.html example:

```
/* Use relative positioning for the parent
   so children can use absolute */
#advancedHeader {
    height:60px;
    position:relative;
}
/* Hide the text using an opaque background image
   on the absolute positioned span */
#advancedHeader span {
```

```
    background: transparent url(http://advanceddomscripting.com/➡
images/advancED-replace.png) no-repeat;
    position:absolute;
    display:block;
    width:100%;
    height:100%;
}
```

When images are off, the Shea method allows the text to remain visible. Also, the `title` attribute of the header can still act as the equivalent `alt` attribute on the image when hovering the pointer over the header.

Removing the extra markup

The extra `<span>` tag in the preceding image-replacement solutions provides no additional semantic meaning and is really an extra tag. It's not all that bad, but you could use a DOM script to achieve the same goal. If you're happy letting JavaScript-disabled browsers receive the degraded text-only version, you can easily add this extra markup by using a load event listener. To do so, start with a clean header that contains only the necessary identifying markup, as found in the chapter5/image-replacement/advancED.html source:

```
<!DOCTYPE html PUBLIC "-//W3C//DTD XHTML 1.0 Strict//EN"
        "http://www.w3.org/TR/xhtml1/DTD/xhtml1-strict.dtd">
<html xmlns="http://www.w3.org/1999/xhtml">
<head>
    <title>advancED Image Replacement</title>
    <link rel="stylesheet" type="text/css"
        href="../../shared/source.css" />
    <link rel="stylesheet" type="text/css" href="../chapter.css" />

    <!-- ADS Library (full version from source linked here) -->
    <script type="text/javascript"
        src="../../ADS-final-verbose.js"></script>

    <!-- Image replacement -->
    <link rel="stylesheet" type="text/css"
        href="advancED.css" media="screen">

    <!-- The load script -->
    <script type="text/javascript" src="advancED.js"></script>

</head>
<body>
    <h1>advancED Image Replacement</h1>
    <h2 id="advancedHeader">Advanced DOM Scripting</h2>
</body>
</html>
```

Next, include the appropriate CSS rules in the linked advancED.css file. Here, I've chosen to use the Shea method as the base CSS method, but I've added an additional .advancED class to the selectors:

```
/* The styling for the text if images are disabled */
#advancedHeader {
    color: #1A5B9D;
}

/* Sizing the header for the image */
#advancedHeader.advancED {
    height:60px;
    position:relative;
    overflow:hidden;
}
/* Hide the text with the opaque image*/
#advancedHeader.advancED span {
    background: white url(http://advanceddomscripting.com/➥
images/advancED-replace.png) no-repeat;
    display:block;
    width:100%;
    height:100%;
    position:absolute;

}
```

The extra .advancED class is the tricky part, as it doesn't yet appear anywhere in the chapter5/
image-replacement/advancED.html source markup.

With these CSS rules in place as is, a device running without JavaScript will see the header with the
limited CSS (or no CSS if that's not available either), as shown in Figure 5-3.

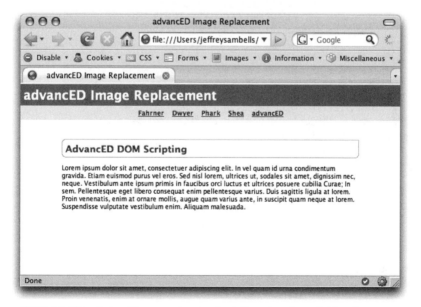

Figure 5-3. The advanced image replacement solution when the script hasn't run

To make everything really snazzy, the load event in the chapter5/image-replacement/advancED.js file is used to inject the extra <span> into the header and add the extra .advancED class name, which completes the transformation:

```
ADS.addEvent(window, 'load', function() {
    // Retrieve the header
    var header = ADS.$('advancedHeader');
    // Create an image element
    var image = document.createElement('IMG');

    // Only add the span and class if the image loads
    ADS.addEvent(image, 'load', function() {

        var s = document.createElement('SPAN');
        // Prepend the span to the header's children
        ADS.prependChild(header,s);

        // Create the title attribute as necessary
        if(!header.getAttribute('title')) {
            var i, child;
            var title = '';
            // Loop through the children and assemble the title
            for(i=0 ; child = header.childNodes[i] ; i++ ) {
                if(child.nodeValue) title += child.nodeValue;
            }
            header.setAttribute('title',title);
        }
        // Modify the class name to indicate the
        // change and apply the CSS
        header.className = 'advancED';
    });

    // Load the image
    // This hardcoded path isn't ideal.
    // You'll revisit this later in the chapter
    image.src = 'http://advanceddomscripting.com/➥
images/advancED-replace.png';

});
```

This example isn't very portable. You must change the script if you want to change the image. We'll solve this problem later in this chapter.

If the image loads successfully, the image's load event will generate the proper markup and trigger the CSS to do its thing:

```
<h1 id="advancedHeader" title="Advanced DOM Scripting" class="advancED">
    <span></span>
Advanced DOM Scripting</h1>
```

The addition of the class is important for degradation and cleanliness. By appending the class with your DOM script, you indicate to the CSS presentation layer that the change to the markup was successful and that the header should be modified. This allows you to keep the actual presentation separate from the DOM script while allowing the DOM script to control the process. At the same time, if either CSS or images are unavailable, the gracefully degraded version will still contain the header text as it appears in the markup.

> *If you try this example as is, you may run into problems when you override an existing class on the header elements. You'll be creating class name manipulation methods for your ADS library to solve that problem later in this chapter.*

The only caveat with this method is that the replacement relies on your DOM script. Depending on the speed of the computer and the Internet connection, there may be a brief flicker when the browser renders the text and the load modification runs (while the image is loading). You'll have to weigh the pro of a clean, accessible, and degradable solution against the con of requiring JavaScript and decide which is right for you.

Keeping style out of your DOM script

Separating your style from your markup is easily done with the appropriate class and ID attributes along with an external CSS style sheet. But, the same concepts are often overlooked in your DOM scripts where it's equally important to separate stylistic changes from behavioral changes. To work properly, your DOM scripts will influence the appearance of your document—but they shouldn't do so in a way that forces you to edit the DOM script when tweaking the design.

In the previous section, you saw how image replacement could be achieved using a combination of CSS and DOM scripting to manipulate the markup. In this section, you'll see that there are a number of ways to influence appearance without directly changing stylistic properties. We'll also start off by taking a look at one of the most misunderstood things in DOM scripting: the DOM style property.

The style property

When applying presentation changes on a small scale, for maybe only one or two elements at a time, you've probably come across a number of examples online—and even in this book—that use the style property of the HTMLElement to modify its presentation. There are two big problems with modifying the style property:

- Using the style property embeds stylistic design into your behavioral DOM script, which isn't any better than using the style attribute in the semantic markup. Sometimes, however, using the style property does make sense for behavior-related properties, such as positioning, or stylistic changes that aren't related to the overall design of the site.

- The style property isn't what you think it is. Let me explain. The style property itself is a CSSStyleDeclaration object representing all the various CSS properties for the given element. What you may not realize, however, is that the style property only provides access to CSS properties declared inline in the element's style attribute. That's it. Nothing else. It *doesn't* contain any CSS properties from the cascades of additional style sheets or properties inherited from parent elements. This means you can't use it to retrieve the overall computed style of the element. For that, you'll have to use a few different objects that we'll discuss later in this chapter.

> *If you thought that the* style *property contained the computed style of the element, you're not alone. This is a common assumption that most people get wrong. Some people assume that the style sheet hasn't loaded yet or that some other browser-loading quirk is interfering with the* style *property, which simply isn't true. By design, the* style *property will never give you that information. It's a good example of why it's smart to spend a little time reading up on specifications so that you can avoid the frustration of spending hours fighting a "bug" that's really a feature.*

Keeping these two things in mind, let's look at the style property and some of its other quirks.

As you've already seen, you can set simple properties, such as the foreground color of the element, using the CSS color property:

```
element.style.color = 'red';
```

And you can set the element's background-color using

```
element.style.backgroundColor = 'red';
```

All the CSS properties follow this same pattern, but you'll notice that the background-color example uses a camel case syntax rather than the more familiar hyphenated CSS syntax. Converting background-color to the camel case backgroundColor syntax—by removing the hyphen and upper-casing the first letter of the following word—is necessary, because you're actually using a shortcut. To properly access style properties, the DOM2 Style CSSStyleDeclaration object has methods such as setProperty(), which use the proper, hyphenated CSS property name and value:

```
element.style.setProperty('background-color','red');
```

Again, the problem is that nonstandard browsers such as Microsoft Internet Explorer don't support the setProperty() method, so you'll have to rely on the shortcut method for cross-browser compatibility.

To keep things agnostic, add the following setStyleById() method to your ADS library along with the setStylesByClassName() and setStylesByTagName() methods. I've set up these methods to use a JavaScript object in the second parameter, so you can use JavaScript object notation to define multiple styles with proper CSS property names, though it will also work with the camel cased version as well:

```
ADS.setStyleById('example'{
    'background-color': 'red',
    'border': '1px solid black',
    'padding': '1em',
    'margin':'1em'
});
```

Within these setStyle methods, the hyphenated version of the CSS properties will be converted to camel case as necessary using the ADS.camelize() method you added when writing the HTML to DOM conversion tool in Chapter 3:

```
(function(){

window['ADS'] = {};

... above here is your existing library ...

/* changes the style of a single element by id */
function setStyleById(element, styles) {
    // Retrieve an object reference
    if(!(element = $(element))) return false;
    // Loop through  the styles object and apply each property
    for (property in styles) {
        if(!styles.hasOwnProperty(property)) continue;

        if(element.style.setProperty) {
            // DOM2 Style method
            element.style.setProperty(
            uncamelize(property,'-'),styles[property],null);
        } else {
            // Alternative method
            element.style[camelize(property)] = styles[property];
        }
    }
    return true;
}
window['ADS']['setStyle'] = setStyleById;
window['ADS']['setStyleById'] = setStyleById;

/* changes the style of multiple elements by class name */
function setStylesByClassName(parent, tag, className, styles) {
    if(!(parent = $(parent))) return false;
    var elements = getElementsByClassName(className, tag, parent);
    for (var e = 0 ; e < elements.length ; e++) {
        setStyleById(elements[e], styles);
    }
    return true;
}
window['ADS']['setStylesByClassName'] = setStylesByClassName;
```

```
/* changes the style of multiple elements by tag name */
function setStylesByTagName(tagname, styles, parent) {
    parent = $(parent) || document;
    var elements = parent.getElementsByTagName(tagname);
    for (var e = 0 ; e < elements.length ; e++) {
        setStyleById(elements[e], styles);
    }
}
window['ADS']['setStylesByTagName'] = setStylesByTagName;

... below here is your existing library ...

})();
```

These methods also provide a nice browser-agnostic way of modifying the style properties of related elements by class name:

```
ADS.setStylesByClassName(
    findClass',
    '*',
    document,
    {'background-color':'red'}
);
```

or by tag name

```
ADS.setStylesByTagName('a',{'text-decoration':'underline'});
```

But again, changing things like the background-color in your script embeds the style in your code. Even if you have no intention of sharing and your code is for you and you alone, it's still a good idea to refrain from mixing CSS style with your DOM scripts. When you're ready to move on from your current design and the time comes to edit your CSS, you'll be much happier messing with a few CSS files rather than sifting through all your scripts line by line, looking for every instance of background-color=red.

The only time mixing style and scripting is really acceptable is in the case of positioning, where the point of things like drag-and-drop interaction is to move the elements around the page. Setting absolute positioning along with the position, as follows, makes sense in the script, because the positioning and location are not part of the visual design, they're directly based on a reaction to the mouse movement on the page:

```
ADS.setStyleById('example',{
    'position':'absolute',
    'top':'10px',
    'left':'20px'
});
```

Font manipulation and color changes, on the other hand, don't belong in your scripts—at least not directly.

Switching styles based on a className

For small- to medium-scale presentation changes, such as colors, borders, backgrounds, and font styles that affect a few elements, you can avoid trudging through the code to look for style properties by implementing className switching. Simply use your DOM script to modify the className property of the desired elements, thus allowing you to alter the appearance based on predefined rules in your style sheets.

From an implementation point of view, this will require the manual or dynamic addition of a style sheet along with your script, increasing the usability and friendliness for designers. In addition, it also allows for reuse of the same DOM script across multiple designs, because your site's design isn't part of the DOM script. For example, instead of modifying the element's background-color directly through the style property, you could define two classes in your CSS file:

```
.normal {
    background-color: black;
}
.normal.modified {
    background-color: red;
}
```

And modify the className property of the element to apply the modified style:

```
var element = ADS.$('example');
element.className += ' modified';
```

Using common classes with className switching

When implementing className switching, it's a good idea to come up with a set of common classes that are only used to indicate changes in the document. These classes can act as pseudo-selectors and should only be used in combination with other selectors to trigger changes based on DOM scripts. For example, you may decide that hover is a reserved word. If a hover class was declared directly, as follows

```
.hover {
    position:absolute:
    top:100px;
    left:200px;
}
```

it would destroy the effectiveness of the DOM script. But if used only in combination with other selectors, like this

```
#cart.hover {
    background-color:yellow;
}
#sidebar.hover a {
    text-decoration:underline;
}
```

the hover class will act as a pseudo-class, in the same way as a CSS a:hover pseudo-class.

Using the className switching approach now maintains the proper separation and opens the presentation to CSS designers using the site's style sheets.

To make this a little easier, add these className manipulation methods to your ADS library:

```
(function(){

window['ADS'] = {};

... above here is your existing library ...

/* retrieve the classes as an array */
function getClassNames(element) {
    if(!(element = $(element))) return false;
    // Replace multiple spaces with one space and then
    // split the classname on spaces
    return element.className.replace(/\s+/,' ').split(' ');
};
window['ADS']['getClassNames'] = getClassNames;

/* check if a class exists on an element */
function hasClassName(element, className) {
    if(!(element = $(element))) return false;
    var classes = getClassNames(element);
    for (var i = 0; i < classes.length; i++) {
        // Check if the className matches and return true if it does
        if (classes[i] === className) { return true; }
    }
    return false;
};
window['ADS']['hasClassName'] = hasClassName;

/* Add a class to an element */
function addClassName(element, className) {
    if(!(element = $(element))) return false;
    // Append the classname to the end of the current className
    // If there is no className, don't include the space
    element.className += (element.className ? ' ' : '') + className;
    return true;
};
window['ADS']['addClassName'] = addClassName;

/* Remove a class from an element */
function removeClassName(element, className) {
    if(!(element = $(element))) return false;
    var classes = getClassNames(element);
    var length = classes.length
```

```
            // Loop through the array deleting matching items
            // You loop in reverse as you're deleting items from
            // the array which will shorten it.
            for (var i = length-1; i >= 0; i--) {
                if (classes[i] === className) { delete(classes[i]); }
            }
            element.className = classes.join(' ');
            return (length == classes.length ? false : true);
        };
        window['ADS']['removeClassName'] = removeClassName;
```

... below here is your existing library ...

```
    })();
```

Looking at the methods, they simply manipulate the className as appropriate:

- ADS.getClassNames(element) returns an array of the class names associated with the element.
- ADS.hasClassName(element, class) checks to see if the class is defined in the elements class name.
- ADS.addClassName(element, class) appends a class to className.
- ADS.removeClassName(element, class) removes the given class from the elements class name.

You can use these methods to easily retrieve all the classes associated with an element:

```
    var element = document.getElementById('example');
    var classes = ADS.getClassNames(element);
    var class;
    for (var i=0; class=classes[i]; i++) {
        //do something with the class
    }
```

or to check if a class is assigned to the element before adding it, to produce a toggle effect:

```
    function toggleClassName(element,className) {
        if(!ADS.hasClassName(element,className)) {
            ADS.addClassName(element,className);
        } else {
            ADS.removeClassName(element,className);
        }
    }
    ADS.addEvent('toggleButton','click',function() {
        toggleClassName(this,'active');
    });
```

You can even reproduce a rollover effect with the appropriate event listeners and a hover class:

```
var element = document.getElementById('example');
ADS.addEvent(element,'mouseover',function() {
    ADS.addClassName(this,'hover');
});
ADS.addEvent(element,'mouseout',function() {
    ADS.removeClassName(this,'hover');
});
```

Drawbacks of using className switching

Using dynamic class names to indicate style changes is great, but it does have some drawbacks.

The first drawback is that the style of an element can influence the interaction in your scripts. Styles declared with different padding and margins can change the size and position of the elements, so your fancy draggable objects may no longer line up properly. Creating a common markup scheme for interactive elements can solve this problem. For example, you might create a policy where all draggable elements have a secondary inner container with a common class that CSS designers are free to manipulate, leaving the outer container to be positioned as expected.

The second drawback is shown in the earlier example when you appended modified to the className without checking to see what was already there. In most cases, you'll be using a more meaningful class name based on the desired action, but you'll also be adding and removing multiple class names for different actions. This will involve some checking to first determine what's already in the className so that you don't clutter it unnecessarily. Likewise, when you want to remove the modified class name, some string manipulation will be required to make sure you're removing the correct portion of the className string. Using the class name methods you added to your ADS library will help solve that problem.

Why not use setAttribute for class names?

At this point, you may be wondering why the examples have all been modifying the className property directly rather than using the setAttribute() method. The className refers to the class attribute of the HTMLElement, so there are actually three different ways you could possibly define the class, but they each work differently depending on the browser:

- element.setAttribute('class','newClassName') works in all W3C-compliant browsers.
- element.setAttribute('className','newClassName') works in Internet Explorer but isn't a W3C-compliant way of setting the value.
- element.className = 'newClassName' works in all browsers.

The third method works in all browsers and is a completely valid way of altering an HTMLElements className read/write property, so we'll stick to it for ease of use.

Switching the style sheet

For changes on a much grander scale, such as changing the layout of the entire page, it doesn't make sense to iterate over the DOM tree and manually modify the style of each individual element. The easiest thing to do would be to simply switch the active style sheet for a completely different one. This can be done several ways depending on how you've set up your CSS style sheets and rules:

- You can use the `rel` property of the `<link>` element to define alternative style sheets and switch among them accordingly.
- You can apply a class to the body tag and modify your CSS selectors depending on the body class—effectively `className` switching using the body tag as the root.
- You can dynamically add and remove style sheets.

Regardless of which method you choose, the desired effect is to drastically change the layout and presentation of most, if not all, of the elements in the document.

Using alternative style sheets

Switching among alternative style sheets was originally proposed by Paul Sowden in his article "Alternative Style: Working with Alternate Style Sheets" (http://alistapart.com/stories/alternate/). This method takes advantage of some of the features of the DOM2 HTML `<link>` element.

If you've been following the separation of presentation and markup methodologies, you'll already be familiar with the `<link>` element. It's used in the head of your document to include your style sheet:

```
<link type="text/css" href="/path/to/style.css" media="screen" />
```

In a `<link>` element

- type is used to indicate the MIME type of the style file, in this case text/css.
- href is used to specify the location of the style sheet.
- media limits the types of devices that should implement the style sheet. However, it's up to the device and software to check the media types. Some devices will ignore the media or use the incorrect one.

These attributes are the most common ones you've dealt with, but there are others. Link elements also include the following attributes (among others):

- rel indicates the relationship between the style sheet and the document.
- disabled indicates if the style sheet is active.
- title is a title associated with the style sheet.

> You'll notice that these attributes are similar to the CSSStyleSheet *properties form the beginning of this chapter.*

You can use the rel="stylesheet" attribute to specify if a style sheet should be applied to a document immediately:

```
<link rel="stylesheet" type="text/css" ➥
href="/path/to/style.css" media="screen">
```

221

or if it should be considered an alternate style sheet and disabled by default using rel="alternate stylesheet":

```
<link rel="alternate stylesheet" type="text/css" ➥
href="/path/to/style.css" media="screen">
```

When the relationship is alternate stylesheet the browser will load the style sheet, but it will also set the disabled flag to true, so it won't be applied to the document immediately.

The title attribute has no effect on the style sheet itself but you can take advantage of it in your script. You can use it as an identifier to dynamically create the list of available styles, allowing the user to switch among them at will. If you take a look at the example in the chapter5/switcher/example.html source, I've included a few example CSS layouts, so you can see the alternate style sheets in action:

```
<!DOCTYPE html PUBLIC "-//W3C//DTD XHTML 1.0 Strict//EN"
        "http://www.w3.org/TR/xhtml1/DTD/xhtml1-strict.dtd">
<html xmlns="http://www.w3.org/1999/xhtml">
<head>
        <title>Style Switcher</title>
    <!--
        The common styles that won't change.
        Leave the title off so they won't be included in the list
    -->
    <link rel="stylesheet" type="text/css"
        href="../../shared/source.css" />
    <link rel="stylesheet" type="text/css" href="../chapter.css" />
    <link rel="stylesheet" type="text/css"
        href="common.css" media="screen">

    <!-- AdvancED DOM Scripting Simple Style (the default) -->
    <link rel="stylesheet" title="AdvancED DOM Scripting"
        type="text/css" href="ads.css" media="screen">
    <!--[if true]>
    <link rel="alternate stylesheet" title="AdvancED DOM Scripting"
        type="text/css" href="adsIE.css" media="screen">
    <![endif]-->

    <!-- A friends of ED style -->
    <link rel="alternate stylesheet" title="friends of ED"
        type="text/css" href="foed.css" media="screen">

    <!-- An Apress style -->
    <link rel="alternate stylesheet" title="Apress"
        type="text/css" href="apress.css" media="screen">


    <!-- ADS Library (full version from source linked here) -->
    <script type="text/javascript"
        src="../../ADS-final-verbose.js"></script>
```

```
<!-- The load script -->
<script type="text/javascript" src="styleSwitcher.js"></script>


</head>
<body>
<h1>Style Switcher</h1>
    <div id="content">
        <h2>It's Easy!</h2>
        <ul id="styleSwitcher"></ul>
        <p>Lorem ipsum dolor sit amet, consectetuer adipiscing elit.
        Quisque iaculis elit in mauris. Mauris euismod tempor tortor.
        Integer fringilla, orci at venenatis consequat, lorem ipsum.
        Morbi ornare sollicitudin justo. Nulla est. Cras lorem.</p>
    </div>
</body>
</html>
```

In this case, the common CSS files have no title, while the friends of ED and Apress styles each have one style sheet, and the AdvancED DOM Scripting style contains two (one just for Internet Explorer). The following empty list in the markup

```
<ul id="styleSwitcher"></ul>
```

is populated by the load event in chapter5/switch/styleSwitcher.js based on the available style sheets and their titles:

```
ADS.addEvent(window,'load',function() {
    // Retrieve all the link elements
    var list = ADS.$('styleSwitcher');
    var links = document.getElementsByTagName('link');
    var titles = [];

    for (var i=0 ; i<links.length ; i++) {

        // Skip <link> element that aren't styles with titles.
        if(links[i].getAttribute("rel").indexOf("style") != -1
            && links[i].getAttribute("title")) {

            // Append a new item to the list if the title hasn't
            // already been added
            var title = links[i].getAttribute("title");
            if(!titles[title]) {

                var a = document.createElement('A');
                a.appendChild(document.createTextNode(title));
                a.setAttribute('href','#');
                a.setAttribute('title','Activate ' + title);
                a.setAttribute('rel',title);
                ADS.addEvent(a,'click',function(W3CEvent) {
```

```
                        // When clicked activate the style sheet indicated
                        // by the title in the anchor's rel property
                        setActiveStyleSheet(this.getAttribute('rel'));
                        ADS.preventDefault(W3CEvent);
                    });

                    var li = document.createElement('LI');
                    li.appendChild(a);

                    list.appendChild(li);

                    // Set the titles array to true for this title
                    // so that it will be skipped if multiple sheets use
                    // the same title
                    titles[title] = true;
                }
            }
        }
    });
```

styleSwitcher.js creates a regular list that you can style as needed, as shown in Figure 5-4.

Figure 5-4. The style switcher list populated from the link title attributes

The resulting list allows you to select among the alternative style sheet sets using the anchor's click event listener and the setActiveStyleSheet() function from Paul Sowden's original article, which follows:

```
function setActiveStyleSheet(title) {
    var i, a, main;
    for(i=0; (a = document.getElementsByTagName("link")[i]); i++) {
        if(a.getAttribute("rel").indexOf("style") != -1
            && a.getAttribute("title")) {
            a.disabled = true;
            if(a.getAttribute("title") == title) a.disabled = false;
        }
    }
}
```

The result is illustrated in Figure 5-5.

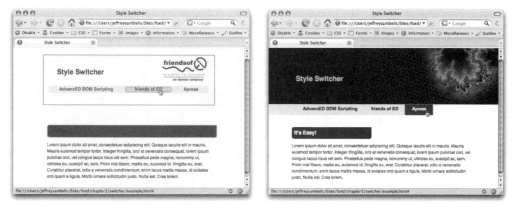

Figure 5-5. The styles as shown when clicking each link

This example is incomplete, as it doesn't maintain the style across multiple pages in your site, but it does illustrate the ability to enable and disable multiple style sheets.

Switching the body className

This idea follows the same principles of className switching that you saw earlier, but in this case, you're switching the className on the body tag. Andy Clarke and James Edwards describe the full body class switching technique in more detail in their article "Invasion of the Body Switchers" (http://alistapart.com/articles/bodyswitchers), but the definition of the CSS rules is the only real difference from the earlier className switching technique applied to elements. To apply styles based on the body tag, you simply include one style sheet that has the body's class selector in all the declarations:

```
/* common Style*/
body {
    font: 62.5%/1.2em sans-serif;
    color: #1a3800;
```

```
        text-align:center;
}

#container {
    text-align:left;
}

/* AdvancED DOM Scripting style */

body.ads {
    background-image: url(images/ads-bg.jpg);
}

body.ads h1 {
    height: 12px;
    margin: 1em 3em 0 30px;
    padding: 2em 0 0 20px;
    padding-bottom: 0em ;
    background: #f06;
    width: 300px;
    overflow: hidden;
    white-space: nowrap;
    -moz-border-radius: 0.5em;
    -moz-border-radius-bottomleft: 0em
}
body.ads h2 {
    border: 0;
    font-size: 3em;
    color: #1A5B9D;
    font-weight: normal;
}

/*  etc */

/* friends of ED style */

body.foed {
    font-family: sans-serif;
    background-color: #fffbf2;
    line-height: 1.8em;
}

body.foed h1 {
    height: 100px;
    color: #f06;
    padding: 40px 0 0 40px;
    background: transparent url(images/foed.png) no-repeat top right;
    border: 2px solid #999;
    width: 460px;
```

```css
    margin: 1em auto 1em auto;
}

body.foed h2 {
    border-width: 2px;
    background: #f06;
    padding: 0.5em;
    width: 100%;
}

/*  etc */

/* Apress style */
body.apress {
    font-family: sans-serif;
    background-color: white;
    line-height: 1.8em;
}

body.apress h1 {
    height: 80px;
    background: black url(images/fractal.jpg) no-repeat top right;
    color: #ffCC00;
    padding: 80px 0 0 80px;
}

body.apress h2 {
    border: 0;
    background: #900;
    padding: 0.5em;
    color: white;
    width: 40%;
}
/*  etc */
```

Next, using the class name methods in your ADS library from earlier in this chapter, or some other function you create yourself, you can switch the body's class dynamically, and the CSS rules will alter the page accordingly:

```javascript
ADS.addEvent('ads-anchor','click',function() {
    ADS.addClassName(document.body,'asd');
});
ADS.addEvent('foed-anchor','click',function() {
    ADS.addClassName(document.body,'foed');
});
ADS.addEvent('apress-anchor','click',function() {
    ADS.addClassName(document.body,'apress');
});
```

Automatically populating a list of styles using this method is a little tricky, as there's no easy way to associate a title with the different sets.

This class name and CSS cascade technique can be applied to any level of the document, not just individual elements and the body.

Dynamically loading and removing style sheets

The third technique involves dynamically loading and unloading the style sheets in your document and is pretty straightforward. All you have to do is create a new <link> through the document.createElement() method with the appropriate properties. Add these two methods to your ADS library, and they will do just that:

```
(function(){

window['ADS'] = {};

... above here is your existing library ...

/* Add a new stylesheet */
function addStyleSheet(url,media) {
    media = media || 'screen';
    var link = document.createElement('LINK');
    link.setAttribute('rel','stylesheet');
    link.setAttribute('type','text/css');
    link.setAttribute('href',url);
    link.setAttribute('media',media);
    document.getElementsByTagName('head')[0].appendChild(link);
}
window['ADS']['addStyleSheet'] = addStyleSheet;

/* Remove a stylesheet */
function removeStyleSheet(url,media) {
    var styles = getStyleSheets(url,media);
    for(var i = 0 ; i < styles.length ; i++) {
        var node = styles[i].ownerNode || styles[i].owningElement;
        // Disable the stylesheet
        styles[i].disabled = true;
        // Remove the node
        node.parentNode.removeChild(node);
    }
}
window['ADS']['removeStyleSheet'] = removeStyleSheet;

... below here is your existing library ...

})();
```

The ADS.addStyleSheet() method will add the style sheet at the given URL and media:

```
ADS.addStyleSheet('/path/to/style.css','screen');
```

Likewise, `ADS.removeStyleSheet()` will remove the style sheet for the given URL and media:

```
ADS.removeStyleSheet('/path/to/style.css','screen');
```

> The `ADS.removeStyleSheet()` *method relies on the* `ADS.getStyleSheets()`
> *method that you'll be adding next.*

By loading and unloading various style sheets, you can switch among as many style sheets as you like.

Modifying CSS rules

When your scripts need to modify the appearance of several related elements on a page, it may be easier to modify the actual CSS rule in the style sheet itself rather than locating all the elements and modifying their individual style properties. This is exceptionally useful if you want a few specific properties to change but, at the same time, you still want the cascade of declarations to apply for things such as an anchor's :hover pseudo-class.

Take these simple anchor CSS declarations:

```css
/* anchor styles */
a {
    font-weight:normal;
}
a:link {
    text-decoration:none;
    color: black;
}
a:visited {
    text-decoration:none;
}
a:hover {
    color: #248030;
    text-decoration: none;
}
```

If you have a few CSS rules applied to a simple paragraph of text with a few links, such as this

```
<p><a href="http://lipsum.com" title="Go to lipsum.com">Lorem ➥
ipsum</a> dolor sit amet, consectetuer adipiscing elit. <a ➥
href="http://lipsum.com" title="Go to lipsum.com">Aliquam ➥
tempor</a> risus ac elit. Nullam consectetuer. Sed feugiat ➥
pharetra enim. Mauris et velit in felis ultricies suscipit. ➥
Proin quam arcu, <a href="http://lipsum.com" title="Go to ➥
lipsum.com">mattis vitae</a>, consectetuer non, cursus non, ➥
mauris. Fusce tristique magna id diam. Mauris sit amet lacus a ➥
elit <a href="http://lipsum.com" title="Go to lipsum.com">auctor ➥
dapibus</a>. Aliquam eros sem, nonummy vitae, mollis et, tempus ➥
vel, neque.</p>
```

you would get something similar to the page in Figure 5-6.

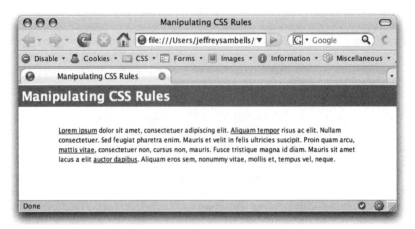

Figure 5-6. A page of text with various links

If you then want your DOM script to reveal the URL behind every anchor on the page, you could take several approaches.

First, you could loop through all the links on the page and modify each element as appropriate using DOM methods to read the href property and append the appropriate content into the anchor. That would work, but it will require the script to search the DOM tree for all the appropriate anchor tags and modify the markup directly. If the browser supports a few CSS2 properties and selectors, such as content and the :after pseudo-class, it can be easily done with a simple CSS rule:

```
a[href]:after {
    content: " (" attr(href) ") ";
    font-size: 40%;
    color: #16009b;
}
```

As an alternative to altering the markup of your DOM document, you can use your DOM script to add or edit the CSS rules in your style sheet—but it gets a little tricky. Your document can contain several style sheets in the document.styleSheets property. Unless you know which style sheet you want to manipulate, you'll have to loop through them all looking for the appropriate selectors. Even if you do know the URL of the style sheet you want, you'll still have to loop through them all to figure out which one it is, as the document.styleSheets list is indexed numerically. Here's a method you can add to your ADS library to help sort out the document.styleSheets list by looking for the appropriate href and media properties:

```
(function(){

window['ADS'] = {};

... above here is your existing library ...
```

```
    /* Retrieve an array of all the stylesheets by URL */
    function getStyleSheets(url,media) {
        var sheets = [];
        for(var i = 0 ; i < document.styleSheets.length ; i++) {
            if (url && document.styleSheets[i].href.indexOf(url) == -1) {
                continue;
            }
            if(media) {
                // Normalize the media strings
                media = media.replace(/,\s*/,',');
                var sheetMedia;

                if(document.styleSheets[i].media.mediaText) {
                    // DOM mehtod
                    sheetMedia = document.styleSheets[i].media.➥
mediaText.replace(/,\s*/,',');
                    // Safari adds an extra comma and space
                    sheetMedia = sheetMedia.replace(/,\s*$/,'');
                } else {
                    // MSIE
                    sheetMedia = document.styleSheets[i].media.➥
replace(/,\s*/,',');
                }
                // Skip it if the media don't match
                if (media != sheetMedia) { continue; }
            }
            sheets.push(document.styleSheets[i]);
        }
        return sheets;
    }
    window['ADS']['getStyleSheets'] = getStyleSheets;

    ... below here is your existing library ...

})();
```

This getStyleSheets() method returns an array of style sheets that match the given href and optional media properties of the CSSStyleSheet objects. In the case of an inline <style> block in the head or body of your document—which you shouldn't be doing—the href will be that of the current page.

Now you can find the style sheets you need and modify them by adding these ADS.editCSSRule() and ADS.addCSSRule() methods to your ADS library:

```
(function(){

window['ADS'] = {};

... above here is your existing library ...
```

```
/* Edit a CSS rule */
function editCSSRule(selector,styles,url,media) {
    var styleSheets = (typeof url == 'array' ? url : ➥
getStyleSheets(url,media));

    for ( i = 0; i < styleSheets.length; i++ ) {

        // Retrieve the list of rules
        // The DOM2 Style method is styleSheets[i].cssRules
        // The MSIE method is styleSheets[i].rules
        var rules = styleSheets[i].cssRules || styleSheets[i].rules;
        if (!rules) { continue; }

        // Convert to uppercase as MSIE defaults to UPPERCASE tags.
        // this could cause conflicts if you're using case
        // sensitive ids
        selector = selector.toUpperCase();

        for(var j = 0; j < rules.length; j++) {
            // Check if it matches
            if(rules[j].selectorText.toUpperCase() == selector) {
                for (property in styles) {
                    if(!styles.hasOwnProperty(property)) { continue; }
                    // Set the new style property
                    rules[j].style[camelize(property)] = ➥
styles[property];
                }
            }
        }
    }
}
window['ADS']['editCSSRule'] = editCSSRule;

/* Add a CSS rule */
function addCSSRule(selector, styles, index, url, media) {
    var declaration = '';

    // Build the declaration string from the style object
    for (property in styles) {
        if(!styles.hasOwnProperty(property)) { continue; }
        declaration += property + ':' + styles[property] + '; ';
    }

    var styleSheets = (typeof url == 'array' ? url :➥
getStyleSheets(url,media));
    var newIndex;
    for(var i = 0 ; i < styleSheets.length ; i++) {
        // Add the rule
        if(styleSheets[i].insertRule) {
```

```
                    // The DOM2 Style method
                    // index = length is the end of the list
                    newIndex = (index >= 0 ? index :➡
        styleSheets[i].cssRules.length);
                    styleSheets[i].insertRule(
                        selector + ' { ' + declaration + ' } ',
                        newIndex
                    );
                } else if(styleSheets[i].addRule) {
                    // The Microsoft method
                    // index = -1 is the end of the list
                    newIndex = (index >= 0 ? index : -1);
                    styleSheets[i].addRule(selector, declaration, newIndex);
                }
            }
        }
    }
    window['ADS']['addCSSRule'] = addCSSRule;

    ... below here is your existing library ...

})();
```

> Remember, when editing rules you can only edit a rule that has been explicitly declared in the style sheet. Also, the ADS.addCSSRule() method doesn't work properly in Safari, but it does work in the latest WebKit release from Webkit.org, so you can expect it to work in a future version of Safari.

Applying these methods to the previous page of text and links, you can make simple modifications, such as highlighting all the anchors with a background color:

```
ADS.editCSSRule('a',{'background-color':'yellow'});
```

> When editing the anchor background color, all the anchors will receive this new color unless another style in the cascade overrides the color. If, for example, a:hover was declared with a different background color, the hover state would still work as expected. Modifying the style property of the element itself can't implement changes such as this.

You can also add a new selector to the style sheet to reveal the URL, as shown in Figure 5-7, but this will only work in CSS 2.1–compatible browsers such as Firefox, Safari, and Opera:

```
ADS.addCSSRule('a[href]:after',{
    'content':'" (" attr(href) ") "',
    'font-size': '40%',
    'color': '#16009b'
});
```

233

In the case of the `ADS.addCSSRule()` method, the third index parameter specifies where in the CSS file the rule should be added, with `null` representing the end of the file.

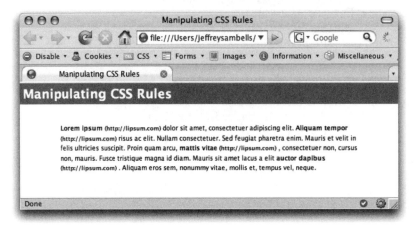

Figure 5-7. Anchors altered to show the href attribute

The page of example text only contains a single style sheet, so the optional `url` and `media` parameters for the edit and add methods aren't necessary. If you have multiple style sheets, you can retrieve just those matching `url` by including an additional parameter:

```
ADS.editCSSRule(
    'a:hover',
    {'text-decoration':'underline'},
    '/path/to/style.css'
);
ADS.addCSSRule(
    'a',
    {'font-weight':'bold'},
    null,
    '/path/to/style.css'
);
```

Modifying each individual style property, switching the body class, and editing the CSS rules each have their advantages, so you'll have to decide which solution is best for your application.

AdvancED image replacement revisited

Earlier in this chapter you created an image replacement script in `chapter5/image-replacement/advancED.html` example that required you to hard-code the URL of the image into the load event:

```
ADS.addEvent(window, 'load', function() {

    ... cut ...

    // Load the image
    // This hardcoded path isn't ideal.
```

```
image.src = 'http://advanceddomscripting.com/images/➥
advancED-replace.png';
});
```

Rather than hard-code the URL into the DOM script, you can specify a style sheet for the image replacement, for example advancED.css, and then search its rules for the required background URL.

To do so, you create a CSS file that follows the same logic of the earlier CSS file, as shown in the chapter5/image-replacement/advancED.css source:

```
/* The styling for the text if images are disabled */
#advancedHeader {
    color: #1A5B9D;
}

/* Sizing the header for the image */
#advancedHeader.advancED {
    height:60px;
    position:relative;
    overflow:hidden;
}
/* Hide the text with the opaque image*/
#advancedHeader.advancED span {
    background: white url(http://advanceddomscripting.com/➥
images/advancED-replace.png) no-repeat;
    display:block;
    width:100%;
    height:100%;
    position:absolute;
}
```

Next, to retrieve the URL of the image, you'll need to examine the selectorText attribute of each rule in the style sheet by locating the ID number and advancED class combination along with the <span> tag:

```
#advancedHeader.advancED span
```

Again, it's a little tricky. This rule could also be defined as

```
.advancED#advancedHeader span
```

or with the a tag, such as a <h2>

```
h2.advancED#advancedHeader span
```

Also, in Internet Explorer, the rule's selectorText property will be converted to .class#id and the tags converted to uppercase, regardless of how it's written in the CSS file:

```
.advancED#advancedHeader SPAN
```

You can repurpose the earlier image-replacement load event into an auxiliary method and simply pass in the ID of the element, as shown in the chapter5/image-replacement-revisited/advancED.js source:

```
function replaceImage(element) {
    // Retrieve the element
    var element = ADS.$(element);
    // Create an image element
    var image = document.createElement('IMG');

    // Only add the span and class if the image loads
    ADS.addEvent(image, 'load', function() {

        var s = document.createElement('SPAN');
        // Prepend the span to the element's children
        ADS.prependChild(element,s);

        // Create the title attribute as necessary
        if(!element.getAttribute('title')) {
            var i, child;
            var title = '';
            // Loop through the children and assemble the title
            for(i=0 ; child = element.childNodes[i] ; i++ ) {
                if(child.nodeValue) title += child.nodeValue;
            }
            element.setAttribute('title',title);
        }
        // Modify the class name to indicate the change
        // and apply the CSS
        ADS.addClassName(element,'advancED');
    });


    // Load the image
    var styleSheet = ADS.getStyleSheets('advancED.css')[0];
    if(!styleSheet) return;

    var list = styleSheet.cssRules || styleSheet.rules
    if(!list) return;

    var rule;
    for(var j = 0 ; rule = list[j] ; j++) {

        // Look for the rule:
        // either: #element-id.advancED span
        // or .advancED#element-id span
        // or as in MSIE: .advancED#element-id SPAN
        // where element-id is the one passed into this method
```

```
        if(
            rule.selectorText.indexOf('#' + ➥
element.getAttribute('id')) !== -1
                && rule.selectorText.indexOf('.advancED') !== -1
                && rule.selectorText.toUpperCase().indexOf(' SPAN') !== -1
        ) {
            // look for a url() in the css using
            // the regex: /url\((([^\)]+)\)/
            var matches = rule.style.cssText.match(/url\((([^\)]+)\)/);
            // matches[1] will contain the value in the
            // capturing parenthesis of the regex
            if(matches[1]) {
                image.src = matches[1];
                break;
            }
        }
    }
}

ADS.addEvent(window, 'load', function() {
    replaceImage('advancedHeader');
});
```

With this load event and replaceImage() method, you achieve the same result by retrieving the advancED.css file and using a regular expression to extract the URL from the appropriate rule. The style of the object is now completely separated from the DOM script, and the CSS is free to change as necessary.

To take it one step further, you can make the DOM script even more unobtrusive by adding an additional class to images your markup:

```
<h2 id="advancedHeader" class="replaceMe">Advanced DOM Scripting</h2>
```

and use the load event to look for any element that match that class and replace them as required:

```
ADS.addEvent(window, 'load', function() {
    var replacements = ADS.getElementsByClassName('replaceMe');
    for(var i=0 ; i< replacements.length ; i++) {
        replaceImage(replacements[i]);
    }
});
```

This last addition makes the script maintenance free, as all you need to do is include the script and mark up your document and CSS accordingly. No additional DOM script editing is necessary.

Accessing the computed style

Before you modify the presentation of an element, you'll want to first determine its current style properties. As you saw, an element's style property only applies to styles defined inline, so you can't use it to retrieve the *computed* style. You could retrieve additional style information from the CSS rules themselves, but it would be a long and complicated process better left to the browser. If you want to access all the computed stylistic properties of an element, as determined by the cascade, you'll need to look at alternative properties.

DOM2 Style includes a method in the document.defaultView called getComputedStyle() for just this purpose. This method returns a read-only CSSStyleDeclaration object with all the computed style properties for the given element, not just those defined inline.

After retrieving the computed style for a given element, you can retrieve the style information the same way you did from the element's style property:

```
var element = ADS.$('example');
var styles = document.defaultView.getComputedStyle(element);
```

Retrieving the background-color is as simple as this:

```
var color = styles.getProperty('background-color');
```

The problem with this is, again, that Microsoft has its own version using the element's currentStyle property, so you'll have to access the proprietary methods as well using the following ADS.getStyle() method in your ADS library:

```
(function(){

window['ADS'] = {};

... above here is your existing library ...

/* retrieve the computed style of an element */
function getStyle(element,property) {
    if(!(element = $(element)) || !property) return false;
    // Check for the value in the element's style property
    var value = element.style[camelize(property)];
    if (!value) {
        // Retrieve the computed style value
        if (document.defaultView && document.defaultView.➥
getComputedStyle) {
            // The DOM method
            var css = document.defaultView.getComputedStyle(
                element, null
            );
            value = css ? css.getPropertyValue(property) : null;
        } else if (element.currentStyle) {
            // The MSIE method
            value = element.currentStyle[camelize(property)];
        }
    }
    // Return an empty string rather than auto so that you don't
    // have to check for auto values
    return value == 'auto' ? '' : value;
```

```
}
window['ADS']['getStyle'] = getStyle;
window['ADS']['getStyleById'] = getStyle;

... below here is your existing library ...

})();
```

The Microsoft filter property

I'm not one to promote proprietary features that aren't standard across browsers—except when you're using them to fix the inconsistencies in the browser they're in. In this case, I'm referring to the Internet Explorer filter property and the ability to "fix" transparent PNG files in Microsoft Internet Explorer version 6 or less.

The object I'm about to present doesn't follow any standards and is only expected to run in Internet Explorer version 6 or less, so the majority of the code is Microsoft-specific. If the code encounters anything greater than Internet Explorer 6 or another browser, it won't run, as it has no need to.

The problem in Internet Explorer 6 is that the translucent areas of a PNG file don't render properly; instead, they appear as a light blue box, as shown in Figure 5-8.

Figure 5-8. Translucent PNG files as they appear in Internet Explorer

This problem can crop up in places such as these:

- An <img> element with a PNG as its source
- Style sheets imported using the <link> element or @import rules that use translucent PNGs in the background of the elements
- Inline style attributes that define translucent PNGs as the background of the element

To work around this problem, you can use the Microsoft.AlphaImageLoader filter, which allows you to use a translucent PNG file as the background of your HTML elements. This can be applied directly in your CSS file by using conditional comments to include a Microsoft-only CSS file:

```
<!--[if lte IE 6]>
    <link rel="stylesheet" href="style-lte-IE-6.css" type="text/css"/>
<![endif]-->
```

and including the appropriate rules for the specific element:

```
#example {
    /* Internet Explorer translucent PNG hack */
    background-color: transparent;
    background-image: url(blank.gif);
    width: 100px;
    height: 100px;
    /* filter requires the full path */
    filter: progid:DXImageTransform.Microsoft.AlphaImageLoader(➡
src="translucent-image.png", sizingMethod="scale");
}
```

The example chapter5/fixMSIEPng/test.html source file includes this fixMSIEPng() method in chapter5/fixMSIEPng/fixMSIEPng.js that runs when the page is loaded and walks through the document and CSS files looking for PNG related files to fix:

```
function fixMSIEPng() {
    if(!document.body.filters) {
        // Not MSIE
        return;
    }
    if(7 <= parseFloat(navigator.appVersion.split("MSIE")[1])) {
        // 7+ supports PNG
        return;
    }
    // Fix the inline images
    if(document.images) {
        var images = document.images;
        var img = null;

        for(var i=images.length-1; img=images[i]; i--) {

            // Check if it's PNG image
            if(img.src
```

```
            && img.src.substring(
                img.src.length-3,
                img.src.length
            ).toLowerCase() !== 'png'
        ) {
            // Skip it
            continue;
        }

        // Build the style property for the outer element
        var inlineStyle = '';
        if (img.align == 'left' || img.align == 'right') {
            inlineStyle += 'float:' + img.align + ';';
        }

        if (img.parentElement.nodeName == 'A') {
            // This image is inside an anchor so show a hand
            inlineStyle += 'cursor:hand;';
        }

        // Make the display inline-block so that it can have a
        // width and height yet still be positioned properly
        inlineStyle += 'display:inline-block;';

        // Grab any other CSS style applied to the element
        if(img.style && img.style.cssText) {
            inlineStyle += img.style.cssText;
        }

        // Wrap a <span> around the image with the appropriate
        // style and information such as className and ID
        img.outerHTML = '<span '
        + (img.id ? ' id="' + img.id + '"' : '' )
        + (img.className ? 'class="' + img.className + '" ' : '')
        + ' style="width:' + img.width + 'px; height:'
        + img.height + 'px;'
        + inlineStyle
        + ';filter:progid:DXImageTransform.Microsoft'
        + '.AlphaImageLoader(src=\''
        + img.src
        + '\', sizingMethod=\'scale\');"></span>';

    }
}

// Create a private method to apply in the next set of loops
// This sets the appropriate styles for the elements
function addFilters(e) {
    // Check if the element has style, a background and verify
```

```
                    // it doesn't already have a filter applied
                    if(
                        e.style
                        && e.style.background
                        && !e.style.filter
                    ) {
                        // Check if it's a PNG
                        var src=null;
                        if(src = e.style.backgroundImage.➥
match(/^url\((.*\.png)\)$/i)) {
                            e.style.backgroundColor = 'transparent';
                            e.style.backgroundImage = 'url()';
                            e.style.filter = 'progid:DXImageTransform.Microsoft.'
                                + 'AlphaImageLoader(src=\''
                                + src[1]
                                + '\',sizingMethod=\''
                                + (( e.style.width && e.style.height ) ? ➥
'scale' : 'crop' )
                                + '\')';
                        }
                    }
                }

                // Create a private recursive processing method to apply the
                // addFilters() method to the style sheets
                function processRules(styleSheet) {
                    for (var i in styleSheet.rules) {
                        addFilters(styleSheet.rules[i]);
                    }

                    //recurse for @import stylesheets...
                    if(styleSheet.imports) {
                        for (var j in styleSheet.imports) {
                            processRules(styleSheet.imports[j]);
                        }
                    }
                }

                // Process each style sheet
                var styleSheets = document.styleSheets;
                for(var i=0; i < styleSheets.length; i++) {
                    processRules(styleSheets[i]);
                }

                // Fix the inline style properties
                if(document.all) {
                    var all = document.all;
```

```
        for(var i=0; i < all.length; i++) {
            addFilters(all[i]);
        }
    }

}
if(window.attachEvent) window.attachEvent("onload", fixMSIEPng);
```

The function will only run in Internet Explorer, as it uses the Internet Explorer–only attachEvent method, and it will transform all the PNGs as shown in Figure 5-9.

Figure 5-9. The PNGs with translucent backgrounds after the fix has run

Please note that the filter property introduces a bug: in some cases, anchors and other clickable elements become inoperative within an element with a filter applied. In the following example, the nested anchor may not work if #background has a filter style applied:

```
<div id="background">
    <div id="content">
        <p>The content with <a href="http://example.com">anchors</a></p>
    </div>
</div>
```

To avoid this, I suggest modifying the markup to something similar to the following, and using CSS to layer the #content above the translucent #background with the filter applied:

```
<div id="background"></div>
<div id="content">
  <p>The content with <a href="http://example.com">anchors</a></p>
</div>
```

Practical example: a simple transition effect

Before I go further, this next example comes with a caution: transition effects should be used unobtrusively to enhance your user's experience, not just because you can. JavaScript got a really bad reputation for introducing obtrusive animation effects that some people considered fun and cool but most people considered very annoying. With standard DOM scripting methods, you can still make the same mistakes, so use things like animation and transitions with a bit of apprehension.

Transition effects are a nice touch when you need to subtly highlight a portion of the page to indicate a change. For example, after you've completed an action in the interface, you may want to indicate if the change was a success or if it failed. Likewise, if one action has an influence on another seemingly unrelated element of the page, you may want to indicate the change there as well.

In order for a transition to work, your script needs to run a periodical method that alters the desired elements over time. For this, you'll need to use the setTimeout() JavaScript function, which invokes a method after a given number of milliseconds. By creating a number of sequential setTimeout() calls that modify the same elements with increasing time, as follows, you can create the desired transitions:

```
setTimeout(modifyElement,10);
setTimeout(modifyElement,20);
setTimeout(modifyElement,30);
setTimeout(modifyElement,40);
setTimeout(modifyElement,50);
//etc...
```

Transition effects are highly customized, so in many cases, you'll have to roll your own solutions, but in Chapter 10, we'll look at a number of JavaScript libraries, many of which have a variety of built-in transition methods to make things a little easier. Until then, let's get your creative juices flowing with a quick example of a fade between two colors:

Using the following fadeColor() method from the chapter5/fadeColor/test.html example, you can specify the two colors as well as the callback method:

```
function fadeColor( from, to, callback, duration, framesPerSecond) {

    // A function wrapper around setTimeout that calculates the
    // time to wait based on the frame number
    function doTimeout(color,frame) {
        setTimeout(function() {
            try {
                callback(color);
            } catch(e) {
```

```
                    // Uncomment this to debug exceptions
                    // ADS.log.write(e);
            }
        }, (duration*1000/framesPerSecond)*frame);
    }

    // The duration of the transition in seconds
    var duration = duration || 1;
    // The number of animated frames in the given duration
    var framesPerSecond = framesPerSecond || duration*15;

    var r,g,b;
    var frame = 1;

    // Set the initial start color at frame 0
    doTimeout('rgb(' + from.r + ',' + from.g + ',' + from.b + ')',0);

    // Calculate the change between the RGB values for each interval
    while (frame < framesPerSecond+1) {
        r = Math.ceil(from.r
            * ((framesPerSecond-frame)/framesPerSecond)
            + to.r * (frame/framesPerSecond));
        g = Math.ceil(from.g
            * ((framesPerSecond-frame)/framesPerSecond)
            + to.g * (frame/framesPerSecond));
        b = Math.ceil(from.b
            * ((framesPerSecond-frame)/framesPerSecond)
            + to.b * (frame/framesPerSecond));

        // Call the timeout function for this frame
        doTimeout('rgb(' + r + ',' + g + ',' + b + ')',frame);

        frame++;
    }
}
```

To invoke the transition, define two JavaScript objects with r, g, and b properties for the starting and ending colors and provide a callback method to apply the new transition color to whichever elements you like. The callback function will receive one argument containing the color in the format rgb(#,#,#):

```
fadeColor(
    {r:0,g:255,b:0}, // Star color
    {r:255,g:255,b:255}, // End color
    function(color) {
        // Apply the color to your elements
        ADS.setStyle('element',{'background-color':color});
    }

);
```

Let's revisit the address postal code example from Chapter 4, where entering a postal code prepopulated the rest of the address fields. It would be beneficial to indicate the successful prepopulation by highlighting the change. Using this fadeColor() method would provide a subtle yet informational touch to the user interface, and it would only involve adding a few lines to the postal code's XMLHttpRequest onreadystatechange method:

```
req.onreadystatechange = function() {
    if (req.readyState == 4) {
        eval(req.responseText);

        if(ADS.$('street').value == '') {
            ADS.$('street').value = street;
            fadeColor(
                {r:0,g:255,b:0},{r:255,g:255,b:255},
                function(color) {
                    ADS.setStyle('street',
                        {'background-color':color}
                    );
                }
            );
        }

        if(ADS.$('city').value == '') {
            ADS.$('city').value = city;
            fadeColor(
                {r:0,g:255,b:0},{r:255,g:255,b:255},
                function(color) {
                    ADS.setStyle('city',
                        {'background-color':color}
                    );
                }
            );
        }

        if(ADS.$('province').value == '') {
            ADS.$('province').value = province;
            fadeColor(
                {r:0,g:255,b:0},{r:255,g:255,b:255},
                function(color) {
                    ADS.setStyle('province',
                        {'background-color':color}
                    );
                }
            );
        }
    }
}
```

When populated, the fields will fade from green to white, indicating a successful prepopulation of the information.

Summary

Dynamically modifying the presentation of elements is a relatively simple task, but doing it right can be a challenge. In this chapter, you looked at a few of the common DOM2 Style objects that you'll be using, and you added a number of methods to your ADS library that provide browser-agnostic access to those objects.

The importance of separating CSS presentation from your DOM script was also stressed throughout the chapter. Some of the methods and techniques included modifying the `style` property and `className` switching for smaller changes, as well as style sheet switching and CSS rule modification for more global changes.

These concepts will be important to keep in mind, not only for large projects with multiple designers and developers but also for small projects that are just yours and yours alone. Separating your presentation from both the document structure and behavioral enhancements helps to future-proof your web application and will inevitably save you time, effort, and money down the road when you decide things are getting a little out of date and you need a redesign.

Now, let's look at a case study in Chapter 6; we'll take everything we've learned so far and use it to create an unobtrusive image resizing and cropping tool.

CHAPTER 6

CASE STUDY: A PHOTO CROPPING AND RESIZING TOOL

Now that you have several new methods in your ADS library, let's create the beginnings of a nice WYSIWYG tool that will allow you to crop and resize photos. Before you get too excited, I should mention that it's not actually possible to crop and resize a photo with your DOM script. The complete tool will require you to write a server-side portion capable of resizing the actual image file. Here, you'll simulate the cropping and resizing actions in the browser so that once it looks the way you want, you can submit the new information to the server and do the actual modifications. This chapter will set up the tool with the basic functionality you'll need and will resemble Figure 6-1.

Figure 6-1. The image editing tool in use on an example image

The test files

To begin, open the chapter6/imageEditor-start folder included with the source for this book. This folder contains the test page along with CSS, script, and image files listed here:

- test.html
- style.css
- imageEditor.js
- images/
- interface/handles.gif

> *Remember, if you would like the code for the starting point, you can download it from* http://advanceddomscripting.com.

The `test.html` file includes two test images and some form markup for general resizing information:

```html
<!DOCTYPE html PUBLIC "-//W3C//DTD XHTML 1.0 Strict//EN"
    "http://www.w3.org/TR/xhtml1/DTD/xhtml1-strict.dtd">
<html xmlns="http://www.w3.org/1999/xhtml">
<head>
<title>Image Editor Test Page</title>
    <!-- Include some CSS style sheet to make
    everything look a little nicer -->
    <link rel="stylesheet" type="text/css"
        href="../../shared/source.css" />
    <link rel="stylesheet" type="text/css"
        href="../chapter.css" />
    <link rel="stylesheet" type="text/css"
        href="style.css" />

    <!-- Your ADS library with the common JavaScript objects -->
    <script type="text/javascript"
        src="../../ADS-final-verbose.js"></script>
    <!-- Log object from Chapter 2 -->
    <script type="text/javascript"
        src="../../chapter2/myLogger-final/myLogger.js"></script>

    <!-- The imageEditor object -->
    <script type="text/javascript" src="imageEditor.js"></script>
</head>
<body>
<h1>Edit Your Images</h1>
<ul>
    <li>
        <form action="/path/to/server/script" method="post">
            <img id="mintImage" src="images/mint.jpg"/>
            <fieldset>
                <legend>New Size</legend>
                <div>
                    <label>Width</label>
                    <input type="text" name="newWidth">
                </div>
                <div>
                    <label>Height</label>
                    <input type="text" name="newHeight">
                    <p>The width and height applies to the
                    original uncropped image</p>
                </div>
            </fieldset>
            <fieldset>
                <legend>Trim Edges</legend>
                <div>
                    <label>Top</label>
```

```
                    <input type="text" name="cropTop">
                </div>
                <div>
                    <label>Rigt</label>
                    <input type="text" name="cropRight">
                </div>
                <div>
                    <label>Bottom</label>
                    <input type="text" name="cropBottom">
                </div>
                <div>
                    <label>Left</label>
                    <input type="text" name="cropLeft">
                </div>
            </fieldset>
            <div class="buttons">
                <input type="submit" value="Apply">
                <input type="reset" value="Reset">
            </div>
        </form>
    </li>
    <li>
        <form action="/path/to/server/script" method="post">
            <img id="babyImage" src="images/baby.jpg"/>
            <fieldset>
                <legend>New Size</legend>
                <div>
                    <label>Width</label>
                    <input type="text" name="newWidth">
                </div>
                <div>
                    <label>Height</label>
                    <input type="text" name="newHeight">
                    <p>The width and height applies to the
                    original uncropped image</p>
                </div>
            </fieldset>
            <fieldset>
                <legend>Trim Edges</legend>
                <div>
                    <label>Top</label>
                    <input type="text" name="cropTop">
                </div>
                <div>
                    <label>Rigt</label>
                    <input type="text" name="cropRight">
                </div>
                <div>
                    <label>Bottom</label>
                    <input type="text" name="cropBottom">
```

```
                    </div>
                    <div>
                        <label>Left</label>
                        <input type="text" name="cropLeft">
                    </div>
                </fieldset>
                <div class="buttons">
                    <input type="submit" value="Apply">
                    <input type="reset" value="Reset">
                </div>
            </form>
        </li>
    </ul>
    </body>
    </html>
```

A CSS file is also included to make the tool look nice, as shown in Figure 6-2.

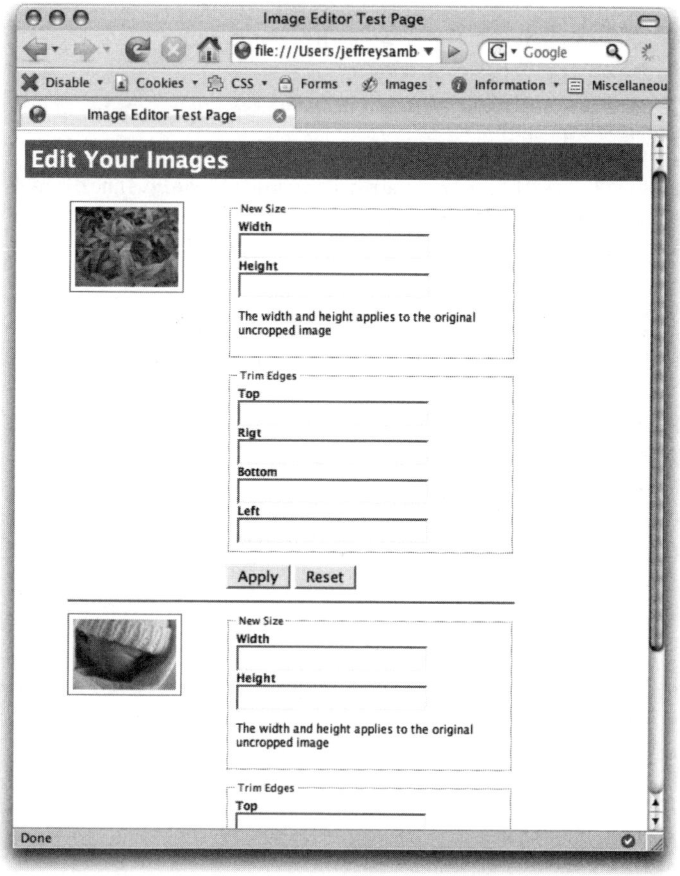

Figure 6-2. The original image editor test file with two images before the tool has been run

I've also referenced the final version of the ADS library in the head of the test.html file, which includes all the appropriate code bits up to this point in the book. If you've already started to customize your library, feel free to use your own instead of the one I included.

This page doesn't actually do anything with the form results, as that's up to you. The page includes form markup so that you can provide a solution for browsers that can't access the fancy drag and drop interface.

For the remainder of this chapter, you'll be working in the imageEditor.js file.

The editor objects

With the appropriate test files in place, take a look at the starting structure for the image editor tool in chapter6/imageEditor-start/imageEditor.js. The empty methods will be filled in as you work through creating the tool in the rest of the chapter:

```
(function(){

// Returns an array with 0 index as width and 1 index
// as height for the browser window
function getWindowSize(){
    if (self.innerHeight) {
        // Most common
        return { 'width':self.innerWidth,'height':self.innerHeight };
    } else if (document.documentElement
        && document.documentElement.clientHeight) {
        // MSIE strict
        return {
            'width':document.documentElement.clientWidth,
            'height':document.documentElement.clientHeight
        };
    } else if (document.body) {
        // MSIE quirks
        return {
            'width':document.body.clientWidth,
            'height':document.body.clientHeight
        };
    }
};

// Returns an object with the width, height, top and left properties
// of the supplied element
function getDimensions(e) {
    return {
        top:e.offsetTop,
        left:e.offsetLeft,
        width: e.offsetWidth,
        height: e.offsetHeight
```

```
        };
    };

    // Sets the top, left, right, bottom, width and height properties
    // of the supplied element
    function setNumericStyle(e,dim,updateMessage) {

        // Check for a message
        updateMessage = updateMessage || false;

        // Assign to a new object so that
        // the original object remains as is.
        var style = {};
        for(var i in dim) {
            if(!dim.hasOwnProperty(i)) continue;
            style[i] = (dim[i]||'0') + 'px';
        }
        ADS.setStyle(e,style);

        // Update the message if there is one
        if(updateMessage) {
            imageEditor.elements.cropSizeDisplay.firstChild.nodeValue =
                dim.width
                + 'x' + dim.height;
        }
    };

    function imageEditor() { };

    // A property to store information while editing
    imageEditor.info = {
        resizeCropArea:false,
        pointerStart:null,
        resizeeStart:null,
        cropAreaStart:null,
        imgSrc:null
    };

    // A property to store the instances of the DOM objects in the editor
    imageEditor.elements = {
        'backdrop': null,
        'editor': null,
        'resizeHandle': null,
        'cropSizeDisplay': null,
        'resizee': null,
        'resizeeCover': null,
        'cropArea': null,
        'resizeeClone': null,
        'cropResizeHandle': null,
```

```
        'saveHandle':null,
        'cancelHandle':null
};

// The method to register the events and modifies the DOM as necessary
// This will automatically run on window load.
imageEditor.load = function(W3CEvent) {

    // Get all the form elements on the page that have the
    // appropriate ADSImageEditor class name

        // Locate the image in the form

        // add the imageEditor.imageClick event to the image

        // Modify the class so that the CSS can modify
        // the style as necessary

        // The CSS file includes additional rules to modify the
        // style of the page if the form is modified.


    }
};

imageEditor.unload = function(W3CEvent) {
    // Remove the editor and backdrop
};

imageEditor.imageClick = function(W3CEvent) {

    // Create a new JavaScript Image object so that
    // you can determine the width and height of the image.

    // This references the clicked image element.

    // Retrieve the page size for the backdrop and centering the editor.

    // Create the backdrop div and
    // make it the size of the entire page.

    // Create the editor div to contain the editing GUI.

    // Create the resize handle.

    // Create the resizable image.

    // Create the translucent cover.

    // Create the crop size display.
```

```
    // Create the crop area container.

    // Create the clone of the image in the crop area.

    // Create the crop resize handle.

    // Create the save handle.

    // Create the cancel resize handle.

    // Add the events to the DOM elements.

    // Resize handle rollovers.

    // Crop handle rollovers.

    // Save handle rollovers.

    // Cancel handle rollovers.

    // Start the image resizing event flow.

    // Start the crop area drag event flow.

    // Start the crop area resize event flow.

    // Prevent the save handle from starting the crop drag flow.

    // Save the image on click of the save handle or
    // dblckick of the crop area.

    // Prevent the cancel handle from starting the crop drag flow.

    // Cancel the changes on click.

    // Resize the backdrop if the window size changes.

};

imageEditor.resizeMouseDown = function(W3CEvent) {

    // Save the current positions and dimensions.

    // Add the rest of the event to enable dragging.

    // Stop the event flow.

};
```

```
imageEditor.resizeMouseMove = function (W3CEvent) {

    // Retrieve the current pointer position.

    // Calculate the new width and height for the image
    // based on the pointer.

    // Minimum size is 42 square pixels.

    // Calculation the percentage from original.

    // If the shift key is pressed, resize proportionally.

    // Calculate the new size for the crop area.

    // Resize the objects.

    // Stop the event flow.
};
imageEditor.resizeMouseUp = function (W3CEvent) {
    // Remove the event listeners to stop the dragging
    // Stop the event flow
};
// The event listener for the mousedown on the crop area
imageEditor.cropMouseDown = function(W3CEvent) {
    // Include the resizee to limit the movement of the crop area
    // Stop the event flow
};
// The event listener for the mousemove on the crop area
imageEditor.cropMouseMove = function(W3CEvent) {
    var pointer = ADS.getPointerPositionInDocument(W3CEvent);
    if(imageEditor.info.resizeCropArea) {
        // Resize the crop area


        // If the shift key is pressed, resize proportionally.
        // Calculate the percentage from original.

        // Check if the new position would be out of bounds.
    } else {
        // Move the crop area

        // Check if the new position would be out of
        // bounds and limit if necessary.
    }
    // Stop the event flow.
};
imageEditor.cropMouseUp = function(W3CEvent) {
    // Remove all the events.
```

```
        // Stop the event flow.
    };
    imageEditor.saveClick = function(W3CEvent) {
        // For now we'll just alert
        // If successful unload the editor
    };
    imageEditor.cancelClick = function(W3CEvent) {

    };
    window['ADS']['imageEditor'] = imageEditor;
})();

// Add the load event to the window object using the ADS.addLoadEvent()
// method because this page may contain a lot of images.
ADS.addLoadEvent(ADS.imageEditor.load);
```

You'll notice this includes a few new utility methods:

- getWindowSize() will return the size of the window as an object with width and height properties.

- getDimensions(element) retrieves the top, left, width, and height properties of the given element (as an object with top, left, width, and height properties).

- setNumericStyle(element,dimensions,message) will set the given style property. This method works the same as the ADS.setStyle() method, but it should only be used with numeric properties as a px postfix. It will be added to the numeric number when assigned to the given property. Also, if the third argument is true, the image editor message will be updated with the given dimensions (we'll get to that shortly).

> The imageEditor tool will be a single instance of an instantiated object, not a constructor. For more on JavaScript objects, see Chapter 2.

Invoking the imageEditor tool

Looking at your test.html file in your web browser, as shown in Figure 6-2, you'll notice it has all the essential inputs required to specify the new size and crop position of each image. Without any enhancement, this page could easily be functional, although it's not very user friendly, as calculating sizes and crop areas would require a bit of math. To make it a little more user friendly, we'll hide the manual input form elements and enable a draggable interface to both resize and crop the image.

Your DOM script should be developer friendly as well. If integrating it requires hours of extra work on the part of developers, it's less likely they'll use it. To provide seamless integration, you need to set up some simple way to invoke the tool with minimal effort. The easiest way for you to accomplish this is to enable the tool by scanning the DOM document for a specific class name and modifying those elements as needed. By defining a specific class name, developers can indicate that the element is in the appropriate format and should be modified to include the cropping tool. Without the class name or JavaScript, the form will continue to work as shown in Figure 6-2, but once enabled through a load event, the user interface will be transformed into Figure 6-3 (as shown in the next section).

For this example, the requirement will be an ADSImageEditor class associated with a <form> tag. To work properly, the form markup will require a single <img> element as a child of the <form>, as shown here:

```
<form action="/path/to/server/script"
    method="post" class="ADSImageEditor">
    <img id="imageID" src="images/image.jpg"/>
    ... cut ...
</form>
```

With the exception of the <img> element, developers can mark up the rest of the form element as they see fit, provided they include the required input elements somewhere in the form.

> *A current limitation of this image editing enhancement is that it will only work for one image per form. Once it's complete, you can modify the events as necessary to work for more than one image.*

Take a moment to edit your chapter6/imageEditor-start/test.html file to include class="ADSImageEditor" on each form tag. This is the only change you or any other developers will need to make to the test file to invoke the tool—nothing more.

The imageEditor load event

When the page loads with JavaScript enabled, you want to automatically scan for the appropriate class name and modify the markup as required. Once modified, the page will look like Figure 6-3; all the elements are hidden away and just the images remain with the appropriate events attached.

Figure 6-3. The test.html file after imageEditor.load() has run

To accomplish this, your load event listener will need to

1. Search the DOM document for form tags.
2. Check if the form className contains the ADSImageEditor class.
3. Hide all the form input elements and markup using CSS style attributes.
4. Add a click event to the <img> that invokes the ADS.imageEditor.imageClick() method.

Take a moment to fill in the imageEditor.load() method with the following code:

```
(function(){
... cut ...
imageEditor.load = function(W3CEvent) {

    // Get all the form elements on the page that have the
    // appropriate ADSImageEditor class name.
    var forms = ADS.getElementsByClassName('ADSImageEditor', 'FORM');

    for( var i=0 ; i < forms.length ; i++ ) {
        // Locate the image in the form.
        var images = forms[i].getElementsByTagName('img');
        if(!images[0]) {
            // This form doesn't have an image so skip it
            continue;
        }

        // Add the imageEditor.imageClick event to the image.
        ADS.addEvent(images[0],'click',imageEditor.imageClick);

        // Modify the class so that the CSS can modify
        // the style as necessary.
        forms[i].className += ' ADSImageEditorModified';

        // The CSS file includes additional rules to modify the
        // style of the page if the form is modified.

    }
};
... cut ...
})();
```

As you can see by reading through the comments, this load() method retrieves all the forms on the page using the ADS.getElementsByClassName('ADSImageEditor','FORM') method and checks to see if it has an image as a child. If it finds an image, the imageClick() event is assigned to the image, and the form class is modified to indicate that the form has been modified.

When modified, the form gains an extra `ADSImageEditorModified` class name that is used in the CSS rules to hide the existing form elements from view:

```
form.ADSImageEditorModified * {
    position: absolute;
    left: -2000px;
}

form.ADSImageEditorModified img {
    position: inherit;
    left: auto;
}
```

As the last line in the file, the image editor's load event is then registered with the window's load event:

```
// Add the load event to the window object.
ADS.addLoadEvent(imageEditor.load);
```

Here, we're using the `ADS.addLoadEvent()` from Chapter 4, because the page will most likely contain a number of images, and you don't want to wait for them all to download before invoking the load event listeners. Once reloaded after your `imageEditor.load()` event has run, your page will resemble Figure 6-3, where the form elements have all been hidden away. You can now click each of the images, invoking the `imageEditor.imageClick()` method on that particular image, but at the moment, invoking the method won't do anything, since you still have a bit of work to do.

Creating the editor markup and objects

The user interface for the tool itself will be a combination of several absolute positioned objects layered on top of the current page with the following unstyled markup; I've included comments indicating what each element is for:

```
<div><!-- backdrop --></div>
<div>
    <!-- editor -->
    <div><!-- resize handle --></div>
    <img src="/path/to/image.jpg">
    <div><!-- translucent cover --></div>
    <div>
        <!-- crop area -->
        <img src="/path/to/image.jpg">
        <div><!-- crop size display --></div>
        <div><!-- crop handle --></div>
        <div><!-- save handle --></div>
        <div><!-- cancel handle --></div>
    </div>
</div>
```

When interacting with the tool, you'll drag the resize handle to resize the image and the crop handle to resize the cropped area. Additionally, you'll want to make the crop area itself draggable, so it can be repositioned around the image. To save and cancel changes, you'll also need a few clickable elements. Figure 6-4 shows an exploded view of the rendered markup of the various elements.

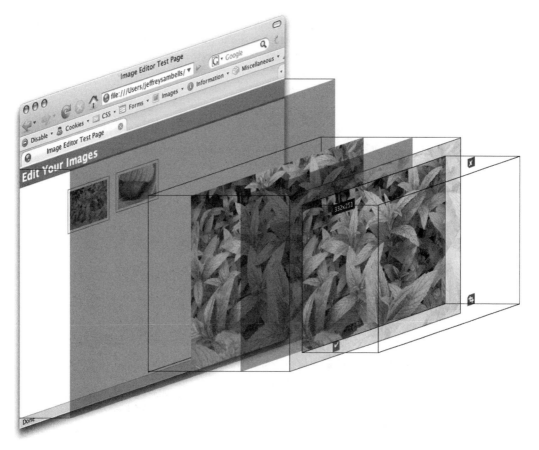

Figure 6-4. An exploded view of the rendered markup for the image editor tool

> *Figure 6-4 represents the visual layering of the pieces, not the nested parent-child relationships in the markup. In the document, the majority of the "layers" are actually elements nested within one another.*

As you can see in Figure 6-4, the bottom layer is a translucent box that covers the entire window area. This will provide visual separation for the editor from the rest of the page. It will also act as a safeguard by catching any clicks outside the image area, so you can't accidentally initiate mouse events on elements of the page under the translucent area while editing the image.

The next few of layers are required for the resizing features of your image editor tool. Resizing the image is easy, as you can modify the width and height properties and let the browser take care of the rest. But it's not quite that simple. All the cropping-related elements also need to be resized along with the image. When resizing, almost every element will be altered in some way.

The complicated part of the editor is simulating the crop. To make it more visually pleasing—and even harder to code—we're going to display the full image grayed out below the cropped one. To accomplish this, you'll need to place a translucent object—with the same dimensions—above the full image, so that it appears "grayed out." On top of that, you'll need another element to simulate the crop, as outlined in Figure 6-5.

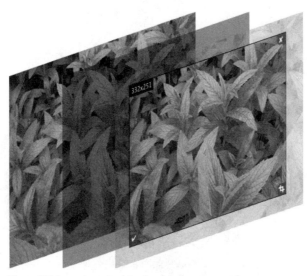

Figure 6-5. Layers required to simulate image cropping

There's no way to actually crop an image in the browser—but you can place the image within another element that's styled with relative or absolute positioning and overflow:hidden. When the image is positioned with a negative top or left value, the element—in this case a <div>—will make the image look cropped, but in reality, portions of it are just hidden by the overflow. The tricky part comes when you drag the crop <div> around the image. When the crop <div> moves one way, you need to adjust the position of its internal image in the opposite direction to make the image appear stationary as the crop area moves, as shown in Figure 6-6.

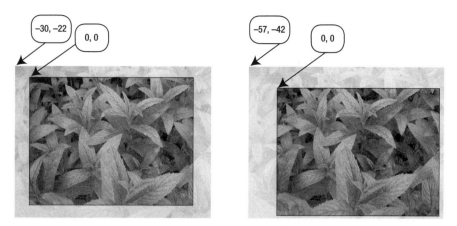

Figure 6-6. Moving the child image in the negative direction to maintian position

Lastly, the various image editor handles will consist of the single image shown in Figure 6-7. The single image will be placed in the background of the various handle <div> tags by shifting the position of the background image around, rather than loading new files to create the rollover effect.

Figure 6-7. The entire handles.png image

Phew—after all that explanation, we can actually code it. The DOM code required to re-create the image editor markup is relatively simple and only involves creating a few <div> and <img> elements. These elements will be added to the DOM document structure when you click the image and invoke the imageEditor.imageClick() method. I won't go into detail about positioning all the elements, as you can easily see in the code how it's done. The original image size is used as the starting size for the editor area and the rest of the layers are positioned accordingly.

Take a moment to fill in your imageEditor.imageClick() method. You'll be revisiting the end of this method in a moment when you register some event listeners:

```
(function(){
... cut ...
imageEditor.imageClick = function(W3CEvent) {

    // Create a new JavaScript Image object so that
    // you can determine the width and height of the image.
    var image = new Image();

    // This references the clicked image element.
    image.src = imageEditor.info.imgSrc = this.src;

    // Retrieve the page size for the backdrop and centering the editor.
    var windowSize = getWindowSize();

    // Create the backdrop div and
    // make it the size of the entire page.
    var backdrop = document.createElement('div');
```

```
        imageEditor.elements.backdrop = backdrop;
        ADS.setStyle(backdrop,{
            'position':'absolute',
            'background-color':'black',
            'opacity':'0.8',
            'width':'100%',
            'height':'100%',
            'z-index':10000,
            // For MSIE we need to use a filter.
            'filter':'alpha(opacity=80)'

        });
        setNumericStyle(backdrop,{
            'left':0,
            'top':0,
            'width':windowSize.width,
            'height':windowSize.height
        });

        document.body.appendChild(backdrop);

        // Create the editor div to contain the editing GUI.
        var editor = document.createElement('div');
        imageEditor.elements.editor = editor;
        ADS.setStyle(editor,{
            'position':'absolute',
            'z-index':10001
        });
        setNumericStyle(editor,{
            'left': Math.ceil((windowSize.width-image.width)/2),
            'top': Math.ceil((windowSize.height-image.height)/2),
            'width':image.width,
            'height':image.height
        });
        // Append the editor to the document.
        document.body.appendChild(editor);

        // Create the resize handle.
        var resizeHandle = document.createElement('div');
        imageEditor.elements.resizeHandle = resizeHandle;
        ADS.setStyle(resizeHandle,{
            'position':'absolute',
            'background':'transparent url(interface/handles.gif) ➡
no-repeat 0 0'
        });
        setNumericStyle(resizeHandle,{
            'left':(image.width - 18),
            'top':(image.height - 18),
            'width':28,
```

```
        'height':28
});
// Append the handle to the editor.
editor.appendChild(resizeHandle);

// Create the resizable image
var resizee = document.createElement('img');
imageEditor.elements.resizee = resizee;
resizee.src = imageEditor.info.imgSrc;

// Get rid of any CSS applied to an img element.
ADS.setStyle(resizee,{
    'position':'absolute',
    'margin':0,
    'padding':0,
    'border':0
});
setNumericStyle(resizee,{
    'left':0,
    'top':0,
    'width':image.width,
    'height':image.height
});


editor.appendChild(resizee);

// Create the translucent cover.
var resizeeCover = document.createElement('div');
imageEditor.elements.resizeeCover = resizeeCover;
ADS.setStyle(resizeeCover,{
    'position':'absolute',
    'background-color':'black',
    'opacity':0.5,
    // For MSIE we need to use a filter.
    'filter':'alpha(opacity=50)'
});
setNumericStyle(resizeeCover,{
    'left':0,
    'top':0,
    'width':image.width,
    'height':image.height
});

editor.appendChild(resizeeCover);
```

```
// Create the crop size display.
var cropSizeDisplay = document.createElement('div');
imageEditor.elements.cropSizeDisplay = cropSizeDisplay;
ADS.setStyle(cropSizeDisplay,{
    'position':'absolute',
    'background-color':'black',
    'color':'white'
});

setNumericStyle(cropSizeDisplay,{
    'left':0,
    'top':0,
    'font-size':10,
    'line-height':10,
    'padding':4,
    'padding-right':4
});

cropSizeDisplay.appendChild(document.createTextNode('size'));

// Create the crop area container.
var cropArea = document.createElement('div');
imageEditor.elements.cropArea = cropArea;
ADS.setStyle(cropArea,{
    'position':'absolute',
    'overflow':'hidden',
    'background-color':'transparent'
});

// Set the dinemsions and update the size display box.
setNumericStyle(cropArea,{
    'left':0,
    'top':0,
    'width':image.width,
    'height':image.height
},true);

editor.appendChild(cropArea);

// Create the clone of the image in the crop area.
var resizeeClone = resizee.cloneNode(false);
imageEditor.elements.resizeeClone = resizeeClone;

cropArea.appendChild(resizeeClone);
cropArea.appendChild(cropSizeDisplay);

// Create the crop resize handle.
var cropResizeHandle = document.createElement('div');
imageEditor.elements.cropResizeHandle = cropResizeHandle;
ADS.setStyle(cropResizeHandle,{
```

```
            'position':'absolute',
            'background':'transparent url(interface/handles.gif) ➥
no-repeat 0 0'
        });
        setNumericStyle(cropResizeHandle,{
            'right':0,
            'bottom':0,
            'width':18,
            'height':18
        });

        cropArea.appendChild(cropResizeHandle);

        // Create the save handle.
        var saveHandle = document.createElement('div');
        imageEditor.elements.saveHandle = saveHandle;
        ADS.setStyle(saveHandle,{
            'position':'absolute',
            'background':'transparent url(interface/handles.gif) ➥
no-repeat -40px 0'
        });
        setNumericStyle(saveHandle,{
            'left':0,
            'bottom':0,
            'width':16,
            'height':18
        });

        cropArea.appendChild(saveHandle);

        // Create the cancel resize handle.
        var cancelHandle = document.createElement('div');
        imageEditor.elements.cancelHandle = cancelHandle;
        ADS.setStyle(cancelHandle,{
            'position':'absolute',
            'background':'transparent url(interface/handles.gif) ➥
no-repeat -29px -11px'
        });
        setNumericStyle(cancelHandle,{
            'right':0,
            'top':0,
            'width':18,
            'height':16
        });

        cropArea.appendChild(cancelHandle);
        ... cut ...
};
... cut ...
})();
```

When you reload your page and click an image, the image editor markup will now appear as desired with everything positioned correctly, but it's far from complete. You still need to add all the dragging and clicking interaction using the appropriate event listeners.

Adding the event listeners to the editor objects

When you use the editor, you'll be invoking several different events as you drag and click the various elements:

- When you roll over the various handles, you need to reposition the background images of each to show the appropriate mouse over and mouse out states. This will help users react correctly when interacting with the various handles.

- When you grab and drag the resize handle, all the elements related to the image will need to maintain relative proportions. The static imageEditor.resizeMouseDown(), imageEditor.resizeMousseMove(), and imageEditor.resizeMouseUp() methods will take care of this.

- When you grab and drag the crop handle, only the crop <div> should be affected, and the crop handle should follow the cursor. Additionally, when you drag the crop area by clicking and dragging inside it, you'll need to adjust the position of the crop area and the internal image. The static imageEditor.cropMouseDown(), imageEditor.cropMouseMove(), and imageEditor.cropMouseUp() methods will take care of these actions.

- When you click the close handle, you'll need to remove the image editor object from the document and reset the appropriate values.

- When you click the save handle, an Ajax request will be made using the original <form> action to commit the changes. For this, we'll just add in a method stub that you can come back to later after reading Chapter 7, which explains adding Ajax.

To finish up the imageEditor.imageClick() method, add all the following event listeners at the bottom of the method after all the DOM elements you just created. Many of the listeners you're about to add won't do anything yet, as the assigned methods aren't complete, but that's OK:

```
(function(){
... cut ...
imageEditor.imageClick = function(W3CEvent) {
    ... cut ...
    // Add the events to the DOM elements.

    // Resize handle rollovers.
    ADS.addEvent(resizeHandle,'mouseover',function(W3CEvent) {
        ADS.setStyle(this,{'background-position':'0px -29px'});
    });
    ADS.addEvent(resizeHandle,'mouseout',function(W3CEvent) {
        ADS.setStyle(this,{'background-position':'0px 0px'});
    });

    // Crop handle rollovers.
    ADS.addEvent(cropResizeHandle,'mouseover',function(W3CEvent) {
        ADS.setStyle(this,{'background-position':'0px -29px'});
    });
```

```
ADS.addEvent(cropResizeHandle,'mouseout',function(W3CEvent) {
    ADS.setStyle(this,{'background-position':'0px 0px'});
});

// Save handle rollovers.
ADS.addEvent(saveHandle,'mouseover',function(W3CEvent) {
    ADS.setStyle(this,{'background-position':'-40px -29px'});
});
ADS.addEvent(saveHandle,'mouseout',function(W3CEvent) {
    ADS.setStyle(this,{'background-position':'-40px 0px'});
});

// Cancel handle rollovers.
ADS.addEvent(cancelHandle,'mouseover',function(W3CEvent) {
    ADS.setStyle(this,{'background-position':'-29px -40px'});
});
ADS.addEvent(cancelHandle,'mouseout',function(W3CEvent) {
    ADS.setStyle(this,{'background-position':'-29px -11px'});
});

// Start the image resizing event flow.
ADS.addEvent(resizeHandle,'mousedown',imageEditor.resizeMouseDown);

// Start the crop area drag event flow.
ADS.addEvent(cropArea,'mousedown',imageEditor.cropMouseDown);

// Start the crop area resize event flow.
ADS.addEvent(cropResizeHandle,'mousedown',function(W3CEvent) {
    imageEditor.info.resizeCropArea = true;
});

// Prevent the save handle from starting the crop drag flow.
ADS.addEvent(saveHandle,'mousedown',function(W3CEvent) {
        ADS.stopPropagation(W3CEvent);
});
// Save the image on click of the save handle or
// dblckick of the crop area.
ADS.addEvent(saveHandle,'click',imageEditor.saveClick);
ADS.addEvent(cropArea,'dblclick',imageEditor.saveClick);

// Prevent the cancel handle from starting the crop drag flow.
ADS.addEvent(cancelHandle,'mousedown',function(W3CEvent) {
        ADS.stopPropagation(W3CEvent);
});
// Cancel the changes on click.
ADS.addEvent(cancelHandle,'click',imageEditor.cancelClick);

// Resize the backdrop if the window size changes.
ADS.addEvent(window,'resize',function(W3CEvent) {
```

271

```
        var windowSize = getWindowSize();
        setNumericStyle(backdrop,{
            'left':0,
            'top':0,
            'width':windowSize.width,
            'height':windowSize.height
        });
    });
};
... cut ...
})();
```

The first set of rollover event listeners is fairly straightforward. The mouseover and mouseout listeners simply reposition the background image shown earlier in Figure 6-7 to create the desired rollover effect.

> *You may wonder why you can't use JavaScript to modify the class name and use a CSS style sheet to create the rollovers or position the various elements. Well, you can, but the sizes of the various elements are closely tied to the interactive elements of the script. You can dynamically load a style sheet using the method from Chapter 5, or you could include the styles in the main style sheet, so feel free to alter this example to use a style sheet if you like.*

Resizing the image

The next set of event listeners is a little trickier and involves a bit of drag logic, as outlined in Figure 6-8.

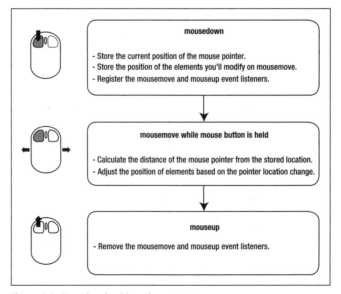

Figure 6-8. Steps involved in a drag event

First, in your imageEditor.resizeMouseDown() event, you need to store the current position of the mouse pointer along with the current size of all the elements you want to modify later. This includes the image, its translucent cover, the crop area, and all the related handles. Also, your imageEditor.resizeMouseDown() event listener will register the imageEditor.resizeMouseMove() and imageEditor.resizeMouseUp() event listeners on the document object:

```
(function(){
... cut ...
imageEditor.resizeMouseDown = function(W3CEvent) {

    // Save the current positions and dimensions.
    imageEditor.info.pointerStart = ADS.getPointerPositionInDocument(
        W3CEvent
    );
    imageEditor.info.resizeeStart = getDimensions(
        imageEditor.elements.resizee
    );
    imageEditor.info.cropAreaStart = getDimensions(
        imageEditor.elements.cropArea
    );

    // Register the rest of the events to enable dragging.
    ADS.addEvent(document,'mousemove',imageEditor.resizeMouseMove);
    ADS.addEvent(document,'mouseup',imageEditor.resizeMouseUp);

    // Stop the event flow.
    ADS.stopPropagation(W3CEvent);
    ADS.preventDefault(W3CEvent);

};
... cut ...
})();
```

Your mousemove and mouseup event listeners are registered on the document, because it's the only way to ensure the event will always occur. If they were registered to the image or the handle, the event would only occur if you're moving the mouse or releasing it over the image or handle. It's possible to move the mouse faster than the object, so if the mouse pointer were to get ahead of the handle, the mousemove event would no longer fire, and everything would stop.

> *If you had elements on the web page with mousemove events prior to invoking the editor tool, they won't be affected by these mouse events. The translucent backdrop behind the tool acts as a catchall. When moving or clicking the pointer over the backdrop, the events are bubbled up to the document. As you saw earlier in Chapter 4, you can't click or affect more than one element at a time. If for some reason you added a mousemove event to the backdrop that prevented the propagation of the mousemove event, the draggable interface would no longer work, because the mousemove event would stop at the backdrop and not bubble up to the document object.*

As you move the mouse pointer around, your imageEditor.resizeMouseMove() event listener will resize the elements based on the current position of the pointer. You'll need to resize or reposition just about every element except the editor box and the backdrop by filling in the listeners as follows:

```
(function(){
... cut ...
imageEditor.resizeMouseMove = function (W3CEvent) {
    var info = imageEditor.info;

    // Retrieve the current pointer position.
    var pointer = ADS.getPointerPositionInDocument(W3CEvent);

    // Calculate the new width and height for the image
    // based on the pointer.
    var width = (info.resizeeStart.width
        + pointer.x - info.pointerStart.x);
    var height = (info.resizeeStart.height
        + pointer.y - info.pointerStart.y);

    // Minimum size is 42 square.
    if(width < 42) { width = 42; }
    if(height < 42) { height = 42; }

    // Calculate the percentage from original.
    var widthPercent = (width / info.resizeeStart.width);
    var heightPercent = (height / info.resizeeStart.height);

    // If the shift key is pressed, resize proportionally.
    if(ADS.getEventObject(W3CEvent).shiftKey) {
        if(widthPercent > heightPercent) {
            heightPercent = widthPercent;
            height = Math.ceil(info.resizeeStart.height
                * heightPercent);
        } else {
            widthPercent = heightPercent;
            width = Math.ceil(info.resizeeStart.width * widthPercent);
        }
    }

    // Calculate the new size for the crop area.
    var cropWidth = Math.ceil(info.cropAreaStart.width
        * widthPercent);
    var cropHeight = Math.ceil(info.cropAreaStart.height
        * heightPercent);
    var cropLeft = Math.ceil(info.cropAreaStart.left
        * widthPercent);
    var cropTop  = Math.ceil(info.cropAreaStart.top
        * heightPercent);
```

```
    // Resize the objects.
    setNumericStyle(
        imageEditor.elements.resizee,
        {'width':width,'height':height}
    );
    setNumericStyle(
        imageEditor.elements.resizeeCover,
        {'width':width,'height':height}
    );
    setNumericStyle(
        imageEditor.elements.resizeHandle,
        {'left':(width - 18),'top':((height - 18))}
    );
    setNumericStyle(
        imageEditor.elements.cropArea,
        {'left':cropLeft,'top':cropTop,
        'width':cropWidth,'height':cropHeight},
        true
    );
    setNumericStyle(
        imageEditor.elements.resizeeClone,
        {'left':(cropLeft * -1),'top':(cropTop * -1),
        'width':width,'height':height}
    );

    // Stop the event flow.
    ADS.stopPropagation(W3CEvent);
    ADS.preventDefault(W3CEvent);

};
... cut ...
})();
```

You'll notice that we also added a few other features along with the resizing one. If the box size shrinks below 42 pixels by 42 pixels, it's deemed too small and stays at 42 pixels. Also, we've checked the event to see if the Shift key was pressed, and if so, we resize the image proportionally based on the size of the image before the resize started:

```
    // If the shift key is pressed, resize proportionally.
    if(ADS.getEventObject(W3CEvent).shiftKey) {
        if(widthPercent > heightPercent) {
            heightPercent = widthPercent;
            height = Math.ceil(info.resizeeStart.height * heightPercent);
        } else {
            widthPercent = heightPercent;
            width = Math.ceil(info.resizeeStart.width * widthPercent);
        }
    }
```

So far, you've started the drag, and you're resizing as you move the mouse, so the last step is ending the drag with the imageEditor.resizeMouseUp() event listener. Here, you just need to remove the imageEditor.resizeMouseMove() event listener, so the elements will remain in their modified state. You'll also need to remove the imageEditor.resizeMouseUp event listener itself, so the mouseup event isn't cluttered with a number of unused events:

```
(function(){
... cut ...
imageEditor.resizeMouseUp = function (W3CEvent) {

    // Remove the event listeners to stop the dragging.
    ADS.removeEvent(document,'mousemove',imageEditor.resizeMouseMove);
    ADS.removeEvent(document,'mouseup',imageEditor.resizeMouseUp);

    // Stop the event flow.
    ADS.stopPropagation(W3CEvent);
    ADS.preventDefault(W3CEvent);
};
... cut ...
})();
```

Testing out your image editing tool, you should be able to grab the resize handle and drag it to resize the image. The crop area, which is currently the same size as the image, should resize along with the image.

Cropping the Image

The crop-related mouse event listeners operate the same as the resize event listeners with one distinct difference: the three handles you appended to the crop area in the imageEditor.imageClick() method (cropResizeHandle, saveHandle, and cancelHandle) are children of the cropArea element. When clicking the handles, the bubbling phase of the event flow will start with the handle and move out to the cropArea. The cropArea element will have the event listeners necessary to enable it to be moved around the image, but you don't want to invoke these movement-related events when you click the handle to resize the crop area, save changes, or cancel it.

In the case of the cropResizeHandle, you'll use the mousedown event to set a special resize flag to true:

```
imageEditor.opts.resizeCropArea = true;
```

which will then be used by the imageEditor.cropMouseMove event listener to determine if you intended to drag the crop area around (when false), or if you want to resize the crop area instead (when true).

If you think back to the discussion of event flow and the ADS.addEvent() method in Chapter 4, you'll remember that ADS.addEvent() only registers event listeners in the bubbling phase. When you click the mouse on the resize handle, the mousedown event listeners bubble, starting with the crop resize handle event listener:

```
ADS.addEvent(cropResizeHandle,'mousedown',function(W3CEvent) {
    imageEditor.opts.resizeCropArea = true;
});
```

The event then propagates through the ancestors to the crop area itself. This is allowed, because your anonymous event listener registered on the cropResizeHandle doesn't do anything to prevent the propagation of the event flow. After the event listener runs, it bubbles to the imageEditor. cropMouseDown event listener registered on the crop area and continues from there.

Fill in the code for your imageEditor crop-related event listeners as follows; these are used to resize the area and move it around:

```
(function(){
... cut ...
imageEditor.cropMouseDown = function(W3CEvent) {

    imageEditor.info.pointerStart = ADS.getPointerPositionInDocument(
        W3CEvent
    );
    imageEditor.info.cropAreaStart = getDimensions(
        imageEditor.elements.cropArea
    );

    // Include the resize to limit the movement of the crop area.
    var resizeeStart = getDimensions(imageEditor.elements.resizee);
    imageEditor.info.maxX = resizeeStart.left + resizeeStart.width;
    imageEditor.info.maxY = resizeeStart.top + resizeeStart.height;

    ADS.addEvent(document,'mousemove', imageEditor.cropMouseMove);
    ADS.addEvent(document,'mouseup', imageEditor.cropMouseUp);

    // Stop the event flow.
    ADS.stopPropagation(W3CEvent);
    ADS.preventDefault(W3CEvent);
};

imageEditor.cropMouseMove = function(W3CEvent) {

    var pointer = ADS.getPointerPositionInDocument(W3CEvent);

    if(imageEditor.info.resizeCropArea) {

        // Resize the crop area.
        var width = (
            imageEditor.info.cropAreaStart.width
            + pointer.x
            - imageEditor.info.pointerStart.x
        );
```

```
var height = (
    imageEditor.info.cropAreaStart.height
    + pointer.y
    - imageEditor.info.pointerStart.y
);

// If the shift key is pressed, resize proportionally.
// Calculate the percentage from original.
var widthPercent = (width
    / imageEditor.info.cropAreaStart.width);
var heightPercent = (height
    / imageEditor.info.cropAreaStart.height);
if(ADS.getEventObject(W3CEvent).shiftKey) {
    if(widthPercent > heightPercent) {
        heightPercent = widthPercent;
        height = Math.ceil(
            imageEditor.info.cropAreaStart.height
            * heightPercent
        );
    } else {
        widthPercent = heightPercent;
        width = Math.ceil(imageEditor.info.cropAreaStart.width
            * widthPercent);
    }
}


// Check if the new position would be out of bounds.
if(imageEditor.info.cropAreaStart.left
    + width > imageEditor.info.maxX
) {
    width = imageEditor.info.maxX
        - imageEditor.info.cropAreaStart.left;
} else if(width < 36) {
    width = 36;
}
if(imageEditor.info.cropAreaStart.top
    + height > imageEditor.info.maxY
) {
    height = imageEditor.info.maxY
        - imageEditor.info.cropAreaStart.top;
} else if(height < 36) {
    height = 36;
}

setNumericStyle(
    imageEditor.elements.cropArea,
    {'width':width,'height':height},
    true
);
```

```
        } else {

            // Move the crop area.
            var left = (
                imageEditor.info.cropAreaStart.left
                + pointer.x
                - imageEditor.info.pointerStart.x
            );

            var top = (
                imageEditor.info.cropAreaStart.top
                + pointer.y
                - imageEditor.info.pointerStart.y
            );

            // Check if the new position would be out of
            // bounds and limit if necessary.
            var maxLeft = imageEditor.info.maxX
                - imageEditor.info.cropAreaStart.width;

            if(left < 0) { left = 0; }
            else if (left > maxLeft) { left = maxLeft;  }

            var maxTop = imageEditor.info.maxY
                - imageEditor.info.cropAreaStart.height;

            if(top < 0) { top = 0; }
            else if (top > maxTop) { top = maxTop;  }

            setNumericStyle(
                imageEditor.elements.cropArea,
                {'left':left,'top':top}
            );
            setNumericStyle(
                imageEditor.elements.resizeeClone,
                {'left':(left * -1),'top':(top * -1)}
            );
        }

    // Stop the event flow.
    ADS.stopPropagation(W3CEvent);
    ADS.preventDefault(W3CEvent);
};

imageEditor.cropMouseUp = function(W3CEvent) {
    // Remove all the events.
    var eventObject = ADS.getEventObject(W3CEvent);
    imageEditor.info.resizeCropArea = false;
```

```
        ADS.removeEvent(document,'mousemove', imageEditor.cropMouseMove);
        ADS.removeEvent(document,'mouseup', imageEditor.cropMouseUp);

        // Stop the event flow.
        ADS.stopPropagation(W3CEvent);
        ADS.preventDefault(W3CEvent);
    };
    ... cut ...
})();
```

Like before, we limit the size and position to remain within the outer image (it doesn't make much sense to drag the crop area outside the image), and again, we've used the Shift key as a signal to maintain proportions while resizing.

The last few mousedown event listeners registered on saveHandle and cancelHandle prevent propagation so that the cropArea event listeners are ignored. The saveHandle and cancelHandle elements also have click event listeners. In this case, the imageEditor.cancelClick event listener simply calls imageEditor.unload to remove all the image editor DOM elements. For the moment, the imageEditor.saveClick event listener won't do anything, as you still need to create the appropriate server-side interaction:

```
(function(){
... cut ...
imageEditor.saveClick = function(W3CEvent) {
    // For now we'll just alert.
    alert('This should save the information back to the server.');

    // If successful unload the editor.
    imageEditor.unload();
};

imageEditor.cancelClick = function(W3CEvent) {
    if(confirm('Are you sure you want to cancel your changes?')) {
        // Unload the editor.
        imageEditor.unload();
    }
};
... cut ...
})();
```

The incomplete image editor

This is where we'll stop with the image editor for now. You have a really nice structure to continue playing with and adding features to. You could make the imageEditor.saveClick() method alter the existing form and then submit the page, or once you've read later chapters, you can come back and make further improvements, such as saving the changes to the server interactively using Ajax.

> You can also download server-side scripts for resizing images from this book's website at http://advanceddomscripting.com.

Summary

In this chapter, you didn't add anything new to your ADS library, but you put it to good use while building the start of an image editor tool. The concept of the image editor in itself is pretty neat, but the point of the chapter was to show you how you can start from an accessible and DOM-script-free document and then put all the library and DOM scripting pieces together to enhance your document. These same ideas can be applied to almost any aspect of your web application; you just have to use your imagination to come up with some creative ideas.

Up next, in Part 2 of this book, you'll explore Ajax and browser to server communications, after which you can return to this example and finish the image editor's saveClick() method so that it can communicate the information back to the server.

Part Two

COMMUNICATING OUTSIDE THE BROWSER

CHAPTER 7

ADDING AJAX TO THE MIX

It's almost impossible to utter a sentence about web technologies without talking about Ajax, JavaScript, Web 2.0, standards, degradability, or progressive enhancement. The latter two ideas—degradability and progressive enhancement—I threw in there because I want them to be more common, but they're often forgotten. That aside, this constant chatter regarding the mixing and matching of technologies in what we now refer to as Asynchronous JavaScript and XML (Ajax) isn't necessarily a bad thing, as it represents the kind of collaborative ideas that we need to keep advancing, but at the same time, we shouldn't forget what we've learned.

The problem with merging technologies such as JavaScript and XML into a new methodology such as Ajax is that we often forget that it is just that, a merging of *existing* technologies. Ajax wasn't a new thing when Jesse James Garrett gave it a catchy name—companies like Google had been doing it for a while, but the name, along with some fancy examples like Google Suggest (http://www.google.com/webhp?complete=1&hl=en) and Google Maps (http://maps.google.com), gave it popularity, and with good reason—you can achieve some amazing advancements to the user experience with Ajax.

Ajax did, however, become something new even though it was something that already existed. As a result, it retains the same inherent cross-browser and technological incompatibilities it always had. In fact, the asynchronous ideas behind Ajax and the way it's implemented open up a whole new area of problems, as you'll see in this chapter.

Now, don't get me wrong; the acceptance of and ideas behind Ajax are wonderful, and I fully support the efforts of the people making fantastic Ajax-enabled web applications, but when implemented incorrectly or without thought, even a wonderful thing can go horribly wrong.

In this chapter, you'll get a quick reintroduction to the XMLHttpRequest object and learn some things you may not yet know about it. Also, you'll look at some of the most common problems you'll encounter when implementing Ajaxy interfaces, as well as how to overcome them, even if it means sticking to a more traditional communication flow.

Merging technology

Proper Ajax is the merging of existing technologies and the following ideas:

- Semantic (X)HTML markup
- The Document Object Model (DOM)
- JavaScript
- XML

I say "proper Ajax," because almost any of the four components can be replaced with an alternative to produce better or poorer results.

Semantic XHTML and the DOM

Using valid semantically correct (X)HTML markup in your document isn't required for Ajax. Any old HTML that renders in a browser will work just fine. Semantic markup will just make DOM scripting a lot easier. In most cases, you'll be using the DOM methods you explored in Chapter 3 to manipulate your markup and document structure based on the results of your Ajax request. If your markup is semantic with the appropriate tags, classes, and IDs assigned to the various elements, you'll find identifying and manipulating the appropriate parts much easier. In addition, a properly marked up document is usually much leaner and less complicated than its nonsemantic counterpart, so your script will require less intense processing as you navigate through your document structure.

JavaScript and the XMLHttpRequest object

The core of every Ajax request is the JavaScript XMLHttpRequest object. Though there is a W3C working draft for the XMLHttpRequest object (http://www.w3.org/TR/XMLHttpRequest), it isn't currently part of any standard or specification. Microsoft Internet Explorer 5 originally introduced the idea as an ActiveX plug-in. Yes, that's right; you could have been doing Ajax in Microsoft Internet Explorer since version 5. As an ActiveX plug-in, you instantiate the object using Internet Explorer's Microsoft.XMLHTTP AcitveX component:

```
var request = new ActiveXObject("Microsoft.XMLHTTP");
```

Since then, other browser manufacturers (and Microsoft, as of Internet Explorer 7) have implemented the same features in an XMLHttpRequest object (but you can still use the ActiveX object in Internet Explorer 7):

```
var req = new XMLHttpRequest();
```

Among the different browsers, the common XMLHttpRequest methods include the following:

- open(method, URL[, asynchronous[, userName[, password]]]) assigns the request URL, method, and additional optional attributes of the request.
- setRequestHeader(label, value) applies a header with the given label and a value to the request. This must be called after the request's open() method has been called but before the send() method is called.
- send(content) transmits the request, including optional content such as the information for a POST request.
- abort() stops the current request.
- getAllResponseHeaders() returns the complete set of headers as a string.
- getResponseHeader(label) returns the string value of a single, given header.

Among libraries such as Prototype and jQuery, the Ajax object usually includes a variety of other methods as well, but they're all wrappers for these methods or the result of a request. In Chapter 9, you'll see a few of these libraries in action, and later in this chapter, you'll be creating your own Ajax object to add to your ADS library.

Making a new request

To make a request, you instantiate a new object using browser capability detection and open() and send() the request:

```
function stateChangeListener() {
    //some code
}

var request = false;
if(window.XMLHttpRequest) {
    var request = new window.XMLHttpRequest();
} else if (window.ActiveXObject) {
    var request = new window.ActiveXObject('Microsoft.XMLHTTP');
}
if(request) {
    request.onreadystatechange = stateChangeListener;
    request.open('GET', '/your/script/?var=value&var2=value', true);
    request.send(null);
}
```

Microsoft Internet Explorer 7 introduced a native XMLHttpRequest object. This is an example where proper capability detection, as discussed in Chapter 1, shows its usefulness. If you had used browser detection to check for Internet Explorer and assumed the ActiveX version, the newer native object will be ignored. Checking first for XMLHttpRequest allows any browser, including Internet Explorer 7, to use the proper object.

This example sends a GET request with any required variables appended to the URL:

```
request.open('GET', '/your/script/?var=value&var2=value', true);
```

In the case of a GET request, the input for the send() method should be null. If you want to perform a POST request, you would specify POST as the method and include the variables in the body of the request by using the send() method rather than variables in the URL:

```
request.open('POST', '/your/script/', true);
request.send('var=value&var2=value');
```

> *Unfortunately, or fortunately from a security standpoint, JavaScript can't access files on the user's system because of the limitations imposed by the browser. This means there's no way to perform a multipart encrypted POST request that includes files selected using a* file *input. In Chapter 8, you'll look at some ways around this.*

Acting on the response

You'll notice in the previous examples that a stateChangeListener() method has been assigned to the request's onreadystatechange property. Whatever method you assign to this property will be invoked several times throughout the various stages of the request. This method allows your DOM script to interact with the request by accessing the XMLHttpRequest object's properties:

- readyState is a status integer representing the following states:
    - 0: Uninitialized
    - 1: Loading
    - 2: Loaded
    - 3: Interactive
    - 4: Complete
- responseText is a string representation of the data returned in the response.
- responseXML will be a DOM Core–compatible document object if the response is a valid XML document with the appropriate headers.
- status is a numeric code representing the status of the request. These will be the HTTP Protocol Status Codes (http://www.w3.org/Protocols/rfc2616/rfc2616-sec10.html) in the response generated by the server, such as 404 for "Not Found" or 200 for "OK."
- statusText is a message related to the status code.
- onreadystatechange should contain the method that will be invoked at the various readyState stages of the request.

Using the method assigned to the onreadystatechange property, along with the other request properties, you can determine attributes such as the state of the request, whether or not it succeeded, and what type of response was returned from the server. A typical onreadystatechange method would look something like this:

```
function stateChangeListener() {
    // Switch functionality depending on the state of the request
    switch (request.readyState) {
        case 1:
            // Loading
            break;
        case 2:
            // Loaded
            break;
        case 3:
            // Interactive
            break;
        case 4:
            // Complete
            if (request.status == 200) {
                // Do something with request.responseText
                // or request.responseXML
            } else {
                // There was a possible error code in request.status
                // with a message as reported in request.statusText
            }
            break;
    }
}
```

The method assigned to the onreadystatechange *property doesn't receive any arguments. In order to access the request and retrieve the* readyState *and* status *values, you need to reference the request from the scope chain. In this example's* stateChangeListener() *method, the request variable references the instance of the* XMLHttpRequest *object and must be defined in the same scope as the* stateChangeListener() *method.*

In all instances, if your request transaction completes successfully, the responseText property will be populated with a string representation of whatever was in the response, but if the Content-Type header of the response is application/xml and the response is a valid XML document, the responseXML property will be populated with a DOM XML document. The DOM representation can be very useful, as you can use all of the DOM2 Core methods from Chapter 3 to navigate and read the responseXML document.

If you want to use the XML format, you have to be sure the Content-Type *header of the response is set to* application/xml; *otherwise, the* XMLHttpRequest *object may assume a text-only response even if it is valid XML. Also, remember that the* responseXML *will be interpreted as an XML document, not an HTML document, so none of the methods in the DOM2 HTML specification will work, even if the document's HTML is valid.*

The key thing to remember when making requests with the XMLHttpRequest object is that the *action* you want to take *as a result of the request* must be invoked through the onreadystatechange listener. If you've played with Ajax before, you may have tried doing something such as the following:

```
...cut...
request.open('GET', '/yourscript/?var=value', true);
request.send(null);
alert(request.responseText);
```

But that won't work as planned, because request was opened in asynchronous mode (the third argument is true). When the XMLHttpRequest object is in asynchronous mode, the request will be sent asynchronously, and the alert will probably execute (with a null value) before the response is returned.

> *Despite what some examples may show, I highly recommend you always set the third argument to* true *and deal with the responses properly. A value of* true *specifies that the request should be in asynchronous mode rather than blocking mode. In asynchronous mode, the script continues to process past the* send() *command before the response is returned from the server, but in blocking mode, the script will stop and wait until the response is returned before continuing. Using asynchronous mode avoids the possibility of accidentally hanging the script and disabling the browser if there's latency in the connection, but it also introduces a number of other problems, which can be dealt with, as you'll see later in this chapter when we look at asynchronous requests in more detail.*

If you want the remainder of the actions in your script to wait until the request is complete, they should be executed with the onreadystatechange method when the response is returned:

```
// Create the request object.
...cut...

// Create the method you want to run.
function alertAndDoWhatever(r) {
    // r is the request object passed in
    // through the onreadystatechange listener
    alert(r.responseText);
    // Continue with whatever you need to do...
}
request.onreadystatechange = function() {
    // Run the method when the request is complete.
    if(request.readyState == 4 && request.status == '200') {
        // The request completed successfully so call your method.
        alertAndDoWhatever(request);
    }
}
// Open the request.
request.open('GET', '/yourscript/?var=value', true);
// Send it.
request.send(null);
```

When using the this keyword from within the method assigned to the onreadystatechange property, this will refer to the method itself, not the XMLHttpRequest object. In the previous example, the request referenced in the anonymous onreadystatechange method is evaluated to the request reference in the scope chain, as discussed in Chapters 1 and 2. The alertAndDoWhatever() method could also reference request in the same way, as it's defined at the same point in the scope chain. Instead, we've passed request into the method as an argument. Later in the chapter, when creating the ADS.ajaxRequest object, you'll be applying the method in a way that the this keyword will refer to the request rather than the method.

Identifying Ajax requests on the server

There's nothing special about an Ajax request. On the server side, your Ajax requests will appear exactly the same as any other request. To make things a little easier, you can send a special header using your XMLHttpRequest objects that will identify the requests on the server.

In a typical XMLHttpRequest transaction, the browser sends a request with a variety of headers, such as:

Host=advanceddomscripting.com
User-Agent=Mozilla/5.0 (Macintosh; U; PPC Mac OS X Mach-O; ➡
en-US; rv:1.8.1.1)
Gecko/20061204 Firefox/2.0.0.1
Accept=text/xml,application/xml,application/xhtml+xml,text/html;q=0.9,➡
text/plain;q=0.8,image/png,*/*;q=0.5
Accept-Language=en-us,en;q=0.5
Accept-Encoding=gzip,deflate
Accept-Charset=ISO-8859-1,utf-8;q=0.7,*;q=0.7
Keep-Alive=300
Connection=keep-alive
Referer=http://advanceddomscripting.com/example/example.html

To identify the request from an XMLHttpRequest object, you can also send along your own headers using the request object's setRequestHeader() method. You can include any headers you want, but you can only call the method after you've opened the request transaction and before you call the send() method:

request.open('GET', '/yourscript/?var=value', true);
request.**setRequestHeader('My-Special-Header','AjaxRequest')**;
request.**setRequestHeader('Sent-By','Jeff')**;
request.send();

With your special addition, the transaction's request will include the extra headers:

Host=advanceddomscripting.com
User-Agent=Mozilla/5.0 (Macintosh; U; PPC Mac OS X Mach-O; ➡
en-US; rv:1.8.1.1) Gecko/20061204 Firefox/2.0.0.1
Accept=text/xml,application/xml,application/xhtml+xml,text/html;➡
q=0.9,text/plain;q=0.8,image/png,*/*;q=0.5
Accept-Language=en-us,en;q=0.5
Accept-Encoding=gzip,deflate

```
Accept-Charset=ISO-8859-1,utf-8;q=0.7,*;q=0.7
Keep-Alive=300
Connection=keep-alive
My-Special-Header=AjaxRequest
Sent-By=Jeff
Referer=http://advanceddomscripting.com/example/example.html
```

You can then check for a special header on server side and act accordingly. In PHP, this would be as easy as reading the header information from the global $_SERVER array:

```php
<?php
if (isset($_SERVER['HTTP_MY_SPECIAL_HEADER'])) {
    // Respond to the XMLHttpRequest
} else {
    // Respond to the traditional request
}
?>
```

> In PHP, the headers are stored in the associative $_SERVER global array with the header names as the keys of the array. The format of the key is slightly altered with text converted to uppercase and all hyphens (-) converted to underscores (_), as shown in the previous example. Also, HTTP is prefixed to the header key to indicate that the information came from the HTTP request.

Likewise, the request object's getResponseHeader() method allows you to retrieve a specific header from the response, so you can alter the script based on information such as the Content-Type in the response:

```
switch(request.getResponseHeader('Content-Type')) {
    case 'text/javascript':
        // use request.responseText as JavaScript;
        break;
    case 'text/xml':
    case 'application/xml':
        // use request.responseXML or read request.responseText as XML
        break;
    case 'text/html':
        // use request.responseText as HTML;
        break;
}
```

Which Content-Type you look for depends on the response your server is using. If your server is returning XHTML rather than HTML, Content-Type could be application/xhtml+xml. The Content-Type header can also include a character encoding:

Content-Type: text/html; **charset=ISO-8859-4**

which would cause the preceding switch to fail, because it would only look for text/html.

You can also use this methodology to verify if the server has returned a proper response. Send a custom header along with the request as follows:

```
request.onreadystatechage = processSpecialRequest;
request.open('GET', '/yourscript/?var=value', true);
request.setRequestHeader('My-Ajax-Request','SpecialValue');
request.send();
```

And then use the same value in another custom header in the response:

```
<?php
if (isset($_SERVER['HTTP_MY_AJAX_REQUEST'])) {
    header('My-Ajax-Response: '.$_SERVER['HTTP_MY_AJAX_REQUEST']);
    echo 'Hello';
}
?>
```

The request's onreadystatechange listener can check if the request has the valid header before proceeding:

```
function processSpecialRequest(request) {
    if(this.readyState == 4) {
        var header = request.getResponseHeader('My-Ajax-Response');
        if(header == 'SpecialValue') {
            // The server responded as expected with the value you sent
            alert(request.responseText);
        } else {
            // The server did something else
        }
    }
}
```

If you want to see the outgoing and incoming headers attached to your requests, I suggest you try Firefox (http://getfirefox.com) with the Firebug (http://getfirebug.com) plug-in. As Figure 7-1 shows, you can see the outgoing and incoming headers on all the XMLHttpRequest requests your browser makes.

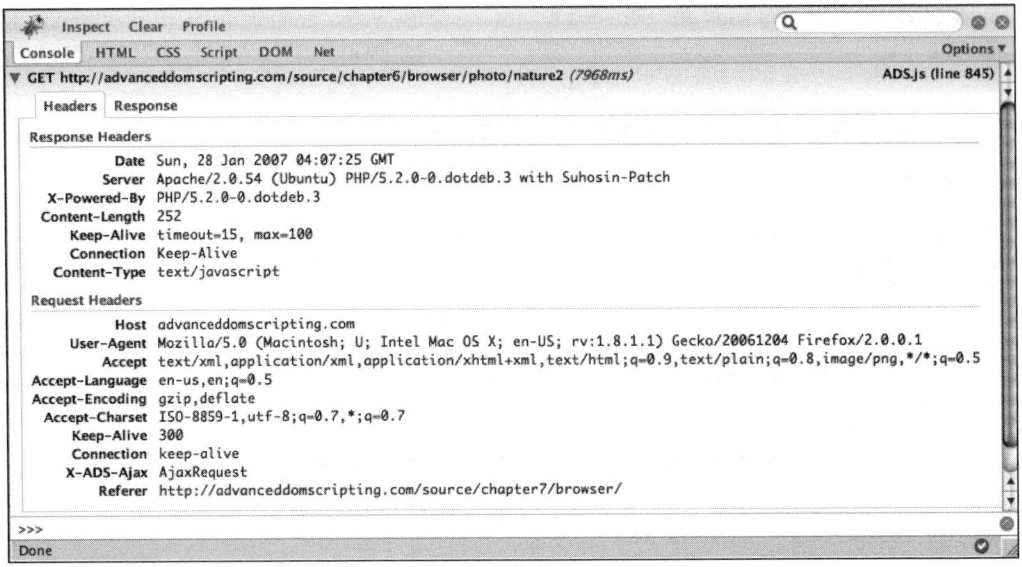

Figure 7-1. Incoming and outgoing request headers for XMLHttpRequest in Firebug while looking at an Ajax photo browser

Beyond GET and POST

One last and often overlooked feature of the XMLHttpRequest object is the ability to send requests other than GET and POST. The open() method can accept a number of methods including:

- GET: For requests that retrieve headers and other information from the server
- POST: For requests that alter the information on the server
- HEAD: For the same requests as GET but HEAD only includes the headers associated with the request, not the body of the request
- PUT: For requests that wish to store information at a specific location on the server
- DELETE: For requests that wish to remove a file or resource for the server
- OPTIONS: Used to list the options request available on the server

Which types of requests are supported will depend on the server you're requesting information from. Most servers support GET, POST, and HEAD, while PUT, DELETE, and OPTIONS are often treated the same as a GET request.

You can use these alternative methods when you don't need all the information from a typical GET or POST request. For example, if you only wanted to check the status of a file on the server and not actually retrieve it, you could use the HEAD method:

```
request.onreadystatechange = function() {
    if(this.readyState == 4) {
        alert(this.status);
    }
}
```

```
request.open("HEAD", '/some/file.pdf');
request.send(null);
```

This, however, could result in an ambiguous response; an error could be because of the network, not a missing file.

XML

The last part of the Ajax mix is the XML response. As a data transport mechanism, XML is great in that it allows you to have DOM-level access to traverse, read, and manipulate your response. Also, if you incorporate an extensible style sheet language transformation (XSLT) parsing mechanism into the processing, the server and client can share XSLT files to ensure you generate the same markup on both the server and in the browser:

```
var xsltProcessor = new XSLTProcessor();
var xslStylesheet;
var xmlDoc;

// Retrieve an XSL file asynchronously.
var requestXsl = new XMLHttpRequest();
requestXsl.onreadystatechange = function(request) {
    xslStylesheet = request.responseXML;
}
requestXsl.open("GET", "example1.xsl", true);
requestXsl.send(null);

// Retrieve an XML file asynchronously.
var requestXml = new XMLHttpRequest();
requestXml.onreadystatechange = function(request) {
    xmlDoc = request.responseXML;
}
requestXml.open("GET", "example1.xsl", true);
requestXml.send(null);


var processor = function() {
    if(xslStylesheet && xmlDoc) {
        clearInterval(this);
        // Transform the XML using the XSLT.
        xsltProcessor.importStylesheet(xslStylesheet);
        var fragment = xsltProcessor.transformToFragment(
            xmlDoc, document
        );
        ADS.$('example').appendChild(fragment);

    }
}
// Check every 200 milliseconds to see if the files are loaded.
setInterval(processor,200);
```

As I said earlier, XML also allows you to use the DOM2 Core methods on the XML response:

```
var messages = request.responseXML.getElementsByTagName('messages');
for(var i=0 ; i < messages.length ; i++) {
    ADS.$('example').appendChild(messages[i]);
}
```

XML does, however, have a few disadvantages. Often, the markup around the data is the bulk of the response, so in high-traffic situations it may be better to use a less bulky method. Also, handling XSLT can become problematic in cross-browser environments. If you're having problems using XML or if it doesn't offer you an advantage, you can consider a few alternatives—but choose wisely, as the incorrect solution can degrade the quality of your application.

Plain text

For really quick and simple requests, you could just return a plain text string without formatting or anything else special. The problem with sending a plain text response is the lack of metadata. If you return a message in a sentence, there isn't any way of indicating if the message informs of success or of an error. However, if you only need to retrieve a yes/no response, you can respond with true or false, or even just t and f, and act accordingly:

```
request.onreadystatechange = function() {
    if(this.readyState == 4 && request.status == 200) {
        if(request.responseText == 't') {
            // The server processing worked
        } else {
            // The server processing failed
        }
    }
}
```

HTML

Another common option is responding with regular old HTML:

```
<p class="success">The response was successful</p>
```

This provides the ability to add metadata through the element attributes, and you can insert the responseText in the document using an innerHTML property:

```
request.onreadystatechange = function() {
    if(request.readyState == 4 && request.status == 200) {
        ADS.$('example').innerHTML = request.responseText;
    }
}
```

In practice, this isn't a good idea for several reasons, including the following:

- Like XML, the response can be unnecessarily bloated with markup that could otherwise be extracted and put into reusable JavaScript objects.

- As a string, the HTML doesn't provide your scripts with any direct hooks to the elements within. You'll have to use document.getElementById() or similar methods to create hooks after the HTML has been inserted through the innerHTML property.

- Responding with HTML doesn't allow for a very good separation of layers within your application. You won't be able to reuse the server or scripting functionality for multiple instances, unless they all use identical markup and methods. It's a much better idea to keep the markup localized as much as possible and only send the necessary information in the response, which can then be manipulated into the appropriate structure using DOM methods.

- The innerHTML property has issues with tables and select lists in Internet Explorer. That's OK if you're not using those as the target container, but that means you're limiting the functionality of your DOM script.

In some situations, HTML may be the easiest and quickest way to achieve the result you're looking for, but the requests will become bloated and less user friendly as a result. Your XMLHttpRequest objects should be as lean as possible so that they can respond as fast as possible.

> *If your response is XHTML and it has the appropriate* Content-Type *property, the* responseXML *property will be populated with a DOM document representation of the HTML. Remember, however, that the DOM document is DOM2 Core (not DOM2 HTML), so many of the attributes you may expect on HTML elements won't be available in the* responseXML *DOM document.*

JavaScript code

As another option, your response could be whatever JavaScript code you want. I'm not referring to JSON here; as you'll see next, I'm referring to full scripts and methods such as a simple alert:

```
alert('The response was successful.');
```

You could then use eval() on the responseText property to execute the code:

```
request.onreadystatechange = function() {
    if(request.readyState == 4 && request.status == 200) {
        eval(request.responseText);
    }
}
```

Using JavaScript poses a few problems. First, using eval() is considered bad practice, because it can create security concerns if you're not very careful. A malicious user could take advantage of your Ajax interface and enter information that, when evaluated, would execute malicious code. As well, using JavaScript is a bad idea for the same reasons that using HTML is: your JavaScript will end up spread across several files in different parts of the application. JavaScript should be in one place and only one place—the .js files included in the head of the document.

JSON

The last alternative is using only JavaScript Object Notation (JSON). Conveniently, JSON is a subset of the JavaScript object literal notation, so you're already familiar with it. For detailed information about the JSON syntax, see http://json.org, but in general, using JSON involves returning a simple JavaScript object in the response such as this:

```
{
    message : 'The response was successful',
    type : 'success'
}
```

You can then use eval() to parse the JSON into a native JavaScript object, from which you can retrieve any information you want:

```
request.onreadystatechange = function() {
    if(this.readyState == 4 && request.status == 200) {

        // Evaluate the JSON to populate the response object.
        var response = eval('(' + this.responseText + ')');

        // Do something with response.

        // With innerHTML
        ADS.$('example').innerHTML = '<p class="'
            + response.type
            + '">'
            + response.message
            + </p>;

        // or alert
        alert(response.message);

        // or DOM using methods...
        var p = document.createElement('P')
        p.className = response.type;
        p.appendChild(document.createTextNode(response.message));
        ADS.$('example').appendchild(p);

    }
}
```

Using eval() to parse the JSON is fast and simple, but it, too, has security vulnerabilities, which make it no better than using regular JavaScript and eval(). A malformed JSON object could easily be exploited to include malicious code that could be evaluated along with the JSON. To overcome this, your best bet is to use a parser that only recognizes valid JSON syntax—combining the cleanliness and simplicity of JSON with a more secure retrieval method. If the parser locates a malformed object, it will simply fail and not execute the malicious code.

If you think writing a JSON parser is a scary thought, don't worry. You can download a freely available public domain parser from http://www.json.org/json.js (this links to the JavaScript version). In the reusable Ajax object you're going to create next, I've included a modified version of the parseJSON() method from json.org for you. If you find you use JSON a lot, you may want to include some of the other methods as well.

> *It's up to you if you want to use eval() instead of the JSON parser. If the information in the response is controlled completely by you—and can't be altered by your users—then you might be fine with using eval(). Using the parser may be a little slower than using the eval() method, but the security gains outweigh the slight performance hit.*

Using a JSON object in the response is a great choice, because it includes the relevant information for the response, along with any additional metadata you want to include with minimal additional markup. The response listener can then transform the data in whatever way is appropriate. This leaves the server-side responses as information only, while the interpretation of the response is left up to your DOM script.

A reusable object

To make the XMLHttpRequest object a little easier to deal with, create the following ADS.getRequestObject() and ADS.ajaxRequest() objects in your ADS library. The getRequestObject() method is just a helper method to set up the XMLHttpRequest object and the onreadystatechange listener:

```
(function(){

window['ADS'] = {};

... above here is your existing library ...

/*
parseJSON(string,filter)
A slightly modified version of the public domain method
at http://www.json.org/json.js This method parses a JSON text
to produce an object or array. It can throw a
SyntaxError exception.
*/
function parseJSON(s,filter) {
    var j;

    function walk(k, v) {
        var i;
        if (v && typeof v === 'object') {
            for (i in v) {
                if (v.hasOwnProperty(i)) {
                    v[i] = walk(i, v[i]);
                }
            }
        }
```

```
        return filter(k, v);
    }


// Parsing happens in three stages. In the first stage, we run the
// text against a regular expression which looks for non-JSON
// characters. We are especially concerned with '()' and 'new'
// because they can cause invocation, and '=' because it can cause
// mutation. But just to be safe, we will reject all unexpected
// characters.

if (/^("(\\.|[^"\\\n\r])*?"|[,:{}\[\]0-9.\-+Eaeflnr-u \n\r\t])+?$/.
        test(s)) {

// In the second stage we use the eval function to compile the text
// into a JavaScript structure. The '{' operator is subject to a
// syntactic ambiguity in JavaScript: it can begin a block or an
// object literal. We wrap the text in parens to eliminate
// the ambiguity.

        try {
            j = eval('(' + s + ')');
        } catch (e) {
            throw new SyntaxError("parseJSON");
        }
    } else {
        throw new SyntaxError("parseJSON");
    }

// In the optional third stage, we recursively walk the new structure,
// passing each name/value pair to a filter function for possible
// transformation.

    if (typeof filter === 'function') {
        j = walk('', j);
    }
    return j;
};

/* Set up the various parts of an XMLHttpRequest Object */
function getRequestObject(url,options) {

    // Initialize the request object.
    var req = false;
    if(window.XMLHttpRequest) {
        var req = new window.XMLHttpRequest();
    } else if (window.ActiveXObject) {
        var req = new window.ActiveXObject('Microsoft.XMLHTTP');
    }
```

```
    if(!req) return false;

    // Define the default options.
    options = options || {};
    options.method = options.method || 'GET';
    options.send = options.send || null;

    // Define the various listeners for each state of the request.
    req.onreadystatechange = function() {
        switch (req.readyState) {
            case 1:
                // Loading
                if(options.loadListener) {
                    options.loadListener.apply(req,arguments);
                }
                break;
            case 2:
                // Loaded
                if(options.loadedListener) {
                    options.loadedListener.apply(req,arguments);
                }
                break;
            case 3:
                // Interactive
                if(options.ineractiveListener) {
                    options.ineractiveListener.apply(req,arguments);
                }
                break;
            case 4:
                // Complete
                // if aborted FF throws errors
                try {
                if (req.status && req.status == 200) {



                    // Specific listeners for content-type
                    // The Content-Type header can include the charset:
                    // Content-Type: text/html; charset=ISO-8859-4
                    // So we'll use a match to extract the part we need.
                    var contentType = req.getResponseHeader(➡
'Content-Type');
                    var mimeType = contentType.match(➡
/\s*([^;]+)\s*(;|$)/i)[1];

                    switch(mimeType) {
                        case 'text/javascript':
                        case 'application/javascript':
                            // The response is JavaScript so use the
```

301

```
            // req.responseText as the argument
            // to the callback.
            if(options.jsResponseListener) {
                options.jsResponseListener.call(
                    req,
                    req.responseText
                );
            }
            break;
        case 'application/json':
            // The response is json so parse the
            // req.responseText using the anonymous
            // functions which simply returns the JSON
            // object for the argument to the callback.
            if(options.jsonResponseListener) {
                try {
                    var json = parseJSON(
                        req.responseText
                    );
                } catch(e) {
                    var json = false;
                }
                options.jsonResponseListener.call(
                    req,
                    json
                );
            }
            break;
        case 'text/xml':
        case 'application/xml':
        case 'application/xhtml+xml':
            // The response is XML so use the
            // req.responseXML as the argument
            // to the callback.
            // This will be a Document object.
            if(options.xmlResponseListener) {
                options.xmlResponseListener.call(
                    req,
                    req.responseXML
                );
            }
            break;
        case 'text/html':
            // The response is HTML so use the
            // req.responseText as the argument
            // to the callback.
            if(options.htmlResponseListener) {
                options.htmlResponseListener.call(
                    req,
```

```
                            req.responseText
                        );
                    }
                    break;
                }

                // A complete listener
                if(options.completeListener) {
                    options.completeListener.apply(req,arguments);
                }
            } else {
                // Response completed but there was an error
                if(options.errorListener) {
                    options.errorListener.apply(req,arguments);
                }
            }
            } catch(e) {
                //Ignore errors.
            }
            break;
        }
    };
    // Open the request.
    req.open(options.method, url, true);
    // Add a special header to identify the requests.
    req.setRequestHeader('X-ADS-Ajax-Request','AjaxRequest');
    return req;
}
window['ADS']['getRequestObject'] = getRequestObject;

/* Send an XMLHttpRequest using a quick wrapper around the
getRequestObject and the send method. */
function ajaxRequest(url,options) {
    var req = getRequestObject(url,options);
    return req.send(options.send);
}
window['ADS']['ajaxRequest'] = ajaxRequest;

... below here is your existing library ...

})();
```

This object takes care of all the necessary response handling by allowing you to specify a number of different methods in the options argument:

- method is the method to use for the request, defaulting to GET.

- send is an optional string to include in the XMLHttpRequest.send() method, defaulting to null.

- loadListener is the onreadystatechange listener invoked when readyState is 1.

- loadedListener is the onreadystatechange listener invoked when readyState is 2.

- interactiveListener is the onreadystatechange listener invoked when readyState is 3.

- jsResponseListener is invoked on a successful request if the response Content-Type is text/javascript or application/javascript, and it will receive the JavaScript string as the first argument. You'll have to use eval() if you want to execute the result.

- jsonResponseListener is invoked on a successful request if the response Content-Type is application/json. The listener will receive the JSON object as its first argument.

- xmlResponseListener is invoked on a successful request if the response Content-Type is application/xml or application/xhtml+html. The listener will receive the XML DOM document as its first argument.

- htmlResponseListener is invoked on a successful request if the response Content-Type is text/html. The listener will receive the HTML string as its first argument.

- completeListener is invoked after the appropriate Content-Type response listener. This method will always be invoked last in a successful response, so if the appropriate Content-Type header wasn't found, you can use this method as a catchall.

- errorListener is invoked if the response status is not 200 but also not 0. If you are running XMLHttpRequests on a system that doesn't provide the appropriate response codes, such as the local file system on your hard drive, the status will always be 0. In that instance, only the completeListener will be invoked.

Along with the request, the ADS.ajaxRequest method also includes an X-ADS-Ajax-Request header, so you can use this header in your server-side scripts to identify the requests.

Using the ADS.ajaxRequest() method in your scripts is as simple as defining the URL and the appropriate listeners:

```
ADS.ajaxRequest('/path/to/script/',{
    method:'GET',
    completeListener:function() {
        alert(this.responseText);
    }
});
```

However, also notice that the request object is referenced using the this keyword from within the listener. Unlike the regular onreadystatechange method, the listeners for your ADS.ajaxRequest object have been called so that this refers to the request object itself rather than the onreadystatechange method. You can access any of the other properties of the XMLHttpRequest using this, such as this.responseXML or this.status.

You'll see more of this object in use later in this chapter, when you look at a simple Ajax-enhanced photo browser. However, before you start using it everywhere, you should ask yourself if Ajax is the right choice, and you should understand what other things you may need to worry about.

Is Ajax right for you?

If you can work with the required technologies such as semantic markup, JavaScript, DOM scripting, and XML, you're off to a good start, but remember, just because you can use Ajax doesn't mean you should. Implemented properly, Ajax methodologies can provide a more desktop-like experience and allow your web application to get things done more efficiently—but I place a lot of emphasis on "implemented properly." Ajax can easily destroy a site's usability and accessibility if not used properly.

As you'll see, there are several instances where Ajax will break everything you know about your web application, and in many ways, it makes things more complicated. Before proceeding with an Ajax implementation, ask yourself a few questions:

- Will Ajax hinder the end user in any way by limiting access, breaking desired features, or requiring additional training and technologies?
- Will Ajax break the consistency of the interface throughout your site?
- Will Ajax increase the development time and cost associated with the application beyond the value of the potential benefits for the end user?
- Will Ajax increase the complexity of either the user's experience or the development requirements?
- Are you going to use Ajax just because you want to "look cool"?

If you answered "Yes" to any of these questions, it may be time to reevaluate why you want to use Ajax. If you answered "No" to all these questions, Ajax may be the right choice, but you're still in for a challenge considering some of the problems we'll discuss in the following section.

Why Ajax may break your site and how to fix it

Many developers, myself included, initially jumped into Ajax without regard for the inherent problems it includes. Beyond inaccessibility, the requirements of asynchronous Ajax interfaces come with problems such as race conditions (more than one request "racing" to do the same thing) and cross-site security restrictions, most of which aren't present in traditional models. Also, Ajax often breaks browser product features, such as back buttons and bookmarks—features that users have come to rely on and that they expect to work a certain way. You'll have to overcome these problems if you want to provide a seamless, problem-free, Ajax experience that improves—rather than degrades—the quality of your web application. In this section, we'll look at how to do that.

JavaScript required for content

One of the biggest mistakes you can make is relying on Ajax to display the primary content of your page, without providing an alternative Ajax-free method. The first rule of writing Ajax applications should be to develop your site without Ajax and enhance the interface with Ajax after the fact. Load events combined with capability detection can gracefully degrade to a less fancy, but still accessible, version when specific technologies are missing.

Some may argue that in the case of a web application where users are forced to log in first, this isn't a big concern. Search engine spiders, the biggest target of technological inaccessibility, won't be visiting the administration area of your web application, so providing a degraded interface may seem unimportant—but in that case, you're discounting the web users with disabilities. Some people accessing your site will be using alternative browsers designed to meet the needs of their specific disabilities. A number of alternative browsers can be found on the W3C Web Accessibility Initiative's Alternate Web Browsing page at http://www.w3.org/WAI/References/Browsing. Most of these browsers won't be able to navigate your fancy Ajax and mouse-based interfaces, so offering a degraded, semantically marked up version that relies on the traditional non-JavaScript, click-reload methodology is the only way they'll be able to easily access and navigate your site.

> *There was a time where it was common to make multiple versions of the same site for a variety of different browsers. If you used a special browser, you could access the alternative version for your specific technology. While duplicating the site in a degraded format is an option, it's also twice the work. There's little point in doubling or tripling your work if one method can take care of all situations. As you've seen, progressively enhancing your web application with degradable solutions isn't difficult; it requires only a slight shift in the way you think about assembling your application and offers benefits beyond simple accessibility, such as increased usability, developer friendliness, and better search engine optimization.*

Bypassing cross-site restrictions with <script> tags

One big limitation you may run into in the XMLHttpRequest object is the inability to request information from sources outside your host domain. All web browsers implement a same-origin security policy that restricts JavaScript communications to the host serving the web page. Typically, all your requests will be between the client's browser and the server from which your application is served. But sometimes, you may want to retrieve information from a different domain that you control, possibly an administration server or a dedicated information server. If you try to pass in a full URL to another domain, the request will display an error and deny you access, as in the Firebug JavaScript console shown in Figure 7-2.

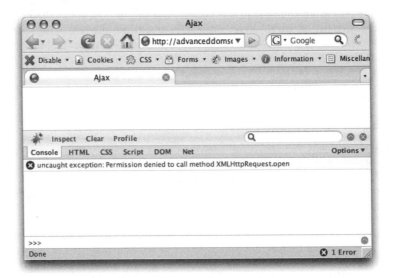

Figure 7-2. A security exception when trying to access a URL outside the current domain

Some people have been crafty and attempted to use an embedded <iframe> to retrieve data from another server. This can be somewhat successful, as you can load an external domain using the iframe and pass in any parameters you like, but you can only submit data, not retrieve it, in this way. Once the iframe is loaded from another domain, the JavaScript can't communicate across the boundary of the iframe, again because of the same-origin policy.

One method of bypassing the barrier is to forget about the fancy XMLHttpRequest object and simply use dynamically generated <script> elements. Script elements can be loaded with a source from any domain and the resulting script will execute just like any other JavaScript you include. As you can imagine, the caveat with this method is that you can only load JavaScript, not any content, as you can with the XmlHttpRequest object. A quick comparison of the XMLHttpRequest method versus script element method is shown in Table 7-1.

Table 7-1. A comparison of XMLHttpRequests versus dynamic script tags

Feature	XMLHttpRequest	Dynamic Script Elements
Cross-browser compatibility	Yes, for class A browsers	Yes, with a few minor bugs
Can be asynchronous	Yes	Yes
Can be synchronous	Yes	No
Restricted to "same origin" policy	Yes	No
Supports multiple HTTP methods	Yes	No, only GET
Access to HTTP status codes	Yes	No
Send custom headers	Yes	No
Supports custom headers	Yes	No
Supports XML as DOM object	Yes	No*
Supports JavaScript/JSON	Yes, must use eval()	Yes
Supports HTML	Yes	No*
Supports plain text	Yes	No*

* However, this feature could be embedded in and extracted from the JavaScript response.

Though not a perfect solution, the <script> method is a start and could lead to building useful third-party tools; Google used it in the Google Maps API (http://google.com/apis/maps). We'll look at more examples of APIs you can use in Chapter 11.

I won't go into too much detail, but to get you started, here's a set of JavaScript objects that use dynamic script elements to load information. For ease of use, I've designed the API of the objects so they resemble the XMLHttpRequest object and the earlier ADS.ajaxRequest() object. This way you can use them the same way—with a few differences:

```
(function(){

window['ADS'] = {};

... above here is your existing library ...


// A counter for the XssHttpRequest objects
var XssHttpRequestCount=0;

// A cross-site <script> tag implementation
// of the XMLHttpRequest object */
var XssHttpRequest = function(){
    this.requestID = 'XSS_HTTP_REQUEST_' + (++XssHttpRequestCount);
}
XssHttpRequest.prototype = {
    url:null,
    scriptObject:null,
    responseJSON:null,
    status:0,
    readyState:0,
    timeout:30000,
    onreadystatechange:function() { },

    setReadyState: function(newReadyState) {
        // Only update the ready state if it's
        // newer than the current state.
        if(this.readyState < newReadyState || newReadyState==0) {
            this.readyState = newReadyState;
            this.onreadystatechange();
        }
    },

    open: function(url,timeout){
        this.timeout = timeout || 30000;
        // Append a special variable to the URL called
        // XSS_HTTP_REQUEST_CALLBACK that contains the name of the
        // callback function for this request.
        this.url = url
            + ((url.indexOf('?')!=-1) ? '&' : '?' )
            + 'XSS_HTTP_REQUEST_CALLBACK='
            + this.requestID
            + '_CALLBACK';
        this.setReadyState(0);
    },

    send: function(){
        var requestObject = this;
```

```
        // Create a new script object to load the external data.
        this.scriptObject = document.createElement('script');
        this.scriptObject.setAttribute('id',this.requestID);
        this.scriptObject.setAttribute('type','text/javascript');
        // Don't set the src or append to the document yet...


        // Create a setTimeout() method that will trigger after a given
        // number of milliseconds. If the script hasn't loaded by
        // the given time it will be cancelled.
        var timeoutWatcher = setTimeout(function() {
            // Repopulate the window method with an empty method
            // in case the script loads later on after we've assumed
            // it stalled.
            window[requestObject.requestID + '_CALLBACK'] = ➥
function() { };

            // Remove the script to prevent it from loading further.
            requestObject.scriptObject.parentNode.removeChild(
                requestObject.scriptObject
            );

            // Set the status to error.
            requestObject.status = 2;
            requestObject.statusText = 'Timeout after '
                + requestObject.timeout
                + ' milliseconds.'

            // Update the state.
            requestObject.setReadyState(2);
            requestObject.setReadyState(3);
            requestObject.setReadyState(4);

        },this.timeout);


        // Create a method in the window object that matches the
        // callback in the request. When called it will process
        // the rest of the request.
        window[this.requestID + '_CALLBACK'] = function(JSON) {
            // When the script loads this method will execute, passing
            // in the desired JSON object.

            // Clear the timeoutWatcher method as the request
            // loaded successfully.
            clearTimeout(timeoutWatcher);

            // Update the state.
            requestObject.setReadyState(2);
            requestObject.setReadyState(3);
```

309

```
            // Set the status to success.
            requestObject.responseJSON = JSON;
            requestObject.status=1;
            requestObject.statusText = 'Loaded.'

            // Update the state.
            requestObject.setReadyState(4);
        }

        // Set the initial state.
        this.setReadyState(1);

        // Now set the src property and append to the document's
        // head. This will load the script.
        this.scriptObject.setAttribute('src',this.url);
        var head = document.getElementsByTagName('head')[0];
        head.appendChild(this.scriptObject);

    }
}
window['ADS']['XssHttpRequest'] = XssHttpRequest;

/* Set up the various parts of the new XssHttpRequest Object */
function getXssRequestObject(url,options) {
    var req = new  XssHttpRequest();

    options = options || {};
    // Default timeout of 30 sec
    options.timeout = options.timeout || 30000;

    req.onreadystatechange = function() {
        switch (req.readyState) {
            case 1:
                // Loading
                if(options.loadListener) {
                    options.loadListener.apply(req,arguments);
                }
                break;
            case 2:
                // Loaded
                if(options.loadedListener) {
                    options.loadedListener.apply(req,arguments);
                }
                break;
            case 3:
                // Interactive
                if(options.interactiveListener) {
                    options.interactiveListener.apply(req,arguments);
                }
```

```
                        break;
                case 4:
                    // Complete
                    if (req.status == 1) {
                        if(options.completeListener) {
                            options.completeListener.apply(req,arguments);
                        }
                    } else {
                        if(options.errorListener) {
                            options.errorListener.apply(req,arguments);
                        }
                    }
                    break;
            }
        };
        req.open(url,options.timeout);

        return req;
    }
    window['ADS']['getXssRequestObject'] = getXssRequestObject;

    /* send an XssHttpRequest */
    function xssRequest(url,options) {
        var req = getXssRequestObject(url,options);
        return req.send(null);
    }
    window['ADS']['xssRequest'] = xssRequest;


    ... below here is your existing library ...

})();
```

These objects and methods will allow you to load scripts from outside the host domain with one requirement: the server responding to the request must return a JSON object wrapped in a function call as defined in the value of the XSS-HTTP-REQUEST-CALLBACK variable in the GET request. As an example, here's a quick PHP implementation of the server-side responder at http:// advanceddomscripting.com/source/chapter7/xssRequest/responder.php:

```
<?php
header('Content-type: text/javascript');

// Only allow number and letters and underscores in the callback.
$callback = preg_replace(
    '/[^A-Z0-9_]/i',
    '',
    $_GET['XSS_HTTP_REQUEST_CALLBACK']
);
```

```
echo "/* XSS request for callback: $callback */\n";

if($callback) {
    $date = date('r');
    echo
<<<JSON
{$callback}({
    message:'response on {$date}'
});
JSON;

}
?>
```

When you make a request using the ADS.xssRequest() object:

```
ADS.xssRequest(
    'http://advanceddomscripting.com/source/chapter7/➥
xssRequest/responder.php',{
        completeListener:function() {
            alert(this.responseJSON.message);
        },
        errorListener:function() {
            alert(this.statusText);
        }
    }
);
```

the response will be loaded as a script, and the function will be executed:

```
XSS_HTTP_REQUEST_1({
    message:'It Worked!'
})
```

The function called in the response matches the one created earlier in the XssHttpRequest object. When the script loads, the function executes and finishes the request by populating the special responseJSON property for the request listener.

You can interact with the response the same way you do with the XMLHttpRequest object, but not all the properties are available. The XssHttpRequest object simulates some of the XMLHttpRequest properties and adds some new ones:

- responseJSON will contain the result of the response. This property is already a JavaScript object, so there's no need to use eval().
- status, in this case, can take the following two values:
  - 1 if successful
  - 2 if there was an error
- statusText will contain the reason for the error.

You can access these properties by using the this keyword from within the following available listeners:

- loadedListener will be invoked when the object is in a loaded state.
- waitListener will be invoked when the object is waiting for a response.
- completeListener will be invoked when the object receives a successful response.
- errorListener will be invoked if the script fails to load the external script or the loaded script isn't in the correct format.

> *For this object to work, the response must call the correct JavaScript function as referenced in the GET variable. In general, your best bet is to pass a JSON object into the function, but if you want to pass an XML file or other information, you could easily include it in the JSON object and parse it as necessary using the response listener.*

Back buttons and bookmarks

Even if you've properly implemented behavioral enhancements that degrade gracefully, there are still a few fundamental issues that Ajax carries with it. These problems apply to any JavaScript behavioral enhancements, not just those using Ajax requests. The most common one is the issue of the back button and bookmarks.

When you click the back button while navigating through a traditional click-reload site, you expect to return to the previous page within that site, as shown in Figure 7-3.

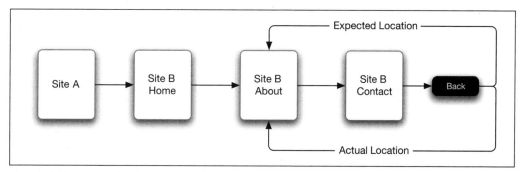

Figure 7-3. The expected and actual return location when clicking the back button in a traditional click-reload workflow

The workflow shown in Figure 7-3 makes sense, and it's also what the average web user expects to happen. Alternatively, when you navigate through an Ajax-enabled site with no traditional request-reload methodology, you're only visiting that one page, but the back button expectation still exists. Clicking the back button when using Ajax results in the wrong behavior and will return you to whatever page you were visiting before the page you're looking at, not the previous Ajax request, as illustrated in Figure 7-4.

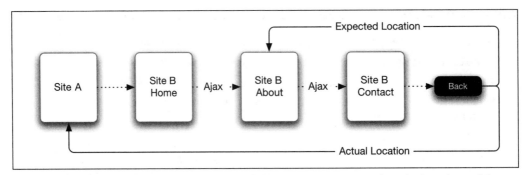

Figure 7-4. The expected and actual return location when clicking the back button in an broken Ajax workflow

If you're using Ajax to simply modify the state of objects in your web application, such as activating and deactivating items in a list, the back button isn't as much of an issue. When you press the back button in that instance, the back action isn't considered an "undo" feature, so even in the traditional request-reload workflow, there wouldn't be an expectation that the action would revert the state of the item, as illustrated in Figure 7-5.

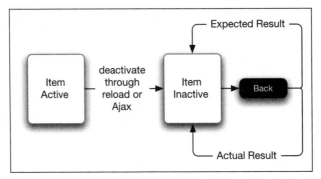

Figure 7-5. The expected and actual result when clicking the back button after a state modification

The problem, as shown earlier in Figure 7-4, is exposed when you decided to use Ajax to navigate what would be considered pages in the traditional method. Clicking navigation tabs to reveal new content pages, or even simply browsing through a list of photos, could be considered multiple page requests by users and will come with the expectation that the back button—or the less commonly used forward button—will take you to the proper page.

Bookmarks are affected in a similar manner. Bookmarking any page built using Ajax requests will always bookmark the initial page, not the content that's currently active under the Ajax navigation.

Using a little DOM scripting and taking advantage of URL hashes can remedy both the back button and bookmark problems. For example, open the photo browser at the following URL in your web browser:

```
http://advanceddomscripting/source/chapter7/browser/
```

Many of the links use a hash (also called an anchor), such as this:

`http://advanceddomscripting/source/chapter7/browser/#photo/1`

> *You'll be re-creating this photo browser later in the chapter so that you can see how some of the various fixes apply to a basic web application.*

The hash indicates to the browser that it should remain in the current page but reposition the view port so that the named anchor matching the hash—or element with the matching ID—is visible. If there is no matching item in the document, the browser only changes the URL in the location bar. The hash can be bookmarked along with the URL, and with a little DOM scripting and hacking, it can be used to update the page when using the back button.

A not so simple fix

Fixing the back button and bookmarks involves watching for and identifying the change of the hash in the URL and using that change to invoke your Ajax requests. To accomplish this, you need to create an object that detects changes in the location hash and reacts with appropriate preassigned methods. Your object will need to do several things:

- Enhance the document using unobtrusive DOM scripting to track page changes
- Allow you to register different methods to react to different hashes
- Watch the location bar for changes and invoke the appropriate registered methods
- Accommodate the various product-related browser quirks when dealing with the back button and bookmarks

To makes things more difficult, each browser deals with the location bar a little differently, so each will need special treatment. A product feature, such as the back button behavior, isn't standard across browsers and isn't governed by any specification:

- In Internet Explorer, the back and forward buttons ignore hashes and navigate based only on the rest of the URL. To over come this, you'll need to use a hidden `<iframe>` to pretend to navigate to different pages by appending the hash to a GET string.
- In Safari, while navigating forward and backward with hashed URLs, the browser's `history` and `history.length` change accordingly. However, the value of `window.location.href` keeps the last location you were in before navigating with the back and forward buttons. For security reasons, you can't access the history URLs, so you need to keep track of the hashes you've visited relative to the length of Safari's `history` and retrieve the appropriate hash from your stored list.
- Firefox and Opera both act in a more expected way, updating the window's location while navigating through the hashes with the back and forward buttons.

Accessing and modifying the URL in the location bar differs among browsers as well. For these reasons, the solution I'm about to present isn't going to be pretty, and it's going to involve doing a bad thing I told you to avoid—browser sniffing.

Browser sniffing for product features

When dealing with browser-specific product features, browser sniffing is an acceptable solution, because it is the only possible solution. Product differences are not specific to the capabilities or objects in JavaScript. Each browser has the same window.location object to access the URL in the address bar, but each browser is influenced differently or reacts differently when navigating URLs with hashes. For browser inconsistencies such as these, object detection doesn't make sense. For example, you could use something like this:

```
if (window.attachEvent) {
    // Then it's Microsoft Internet Explorer
}
```

but the window.attachEvent method doesn't have any direct relevance to the problem you're solving, so it's not an appropriate object. Browser detection is the proper solution.

Tracking location changes

Add the following ADS.actionPager object to your ADS library, and we'll look at how it solves the back button and bookmark problem next:

```
(function(){

window['ADS'] = {};

... above here is your existing library ...

/* a helper method to make callbacks */
function makeCallback(method, target) {
    return function() { method.apply(target,arguments); }
}

/* A URL hash listener used to trigger
registered methods based on hashes */
var actionPager = {
    // The previous hash
    lastHash : '',
    // A list of the methods registered for the hash patterns
    callbacks: [],
    // The safari history list
    safariHistory : false,
    // A reference to the iframe for Internet Explorer
    msieHistory: false,
    // The class name of the links that should be converted
    ajaxifyClassName: '',
    // The root of the application. This will be stripped off the URL
    // when creating the hashes
    ajaxifyRoot: '',
```

```
init: function(ajaxifyClass,ajaxifyRoot,startingHash) {

    this.ajaxifyClassName = ajaxifyClass || 'ADSActionLink';
    this.ajaxifyRoot = ajaxifyRoot || '';

    if (/Safari/i.test(navigator.userAgent)) {
        this.safariHistory = [];
    } else if (/MSIE/i.test(navigator.userAgent)) {
        // In the case of MSIE, add a iframe to track override
        // the back button.
        this.msieHistory = document.createElement('iframe');
        this.msieHistory.setAttribute('id', 'msieHistory');
        this.msieHistory.setAttribute('name', 'msieHistory');
        setStyleById(this.msieHistory,{
            'width':'100px',
            'height':'100px',
            'border':'1px solid black',
            'visibility':'visible',
            'zIndex':'-1'
        });
        document.body.appendChild(this.msieHistory);
        this.msieHistory = frames['msieHistory'];

    }

    // Convert the links to AJAX links.
    this.ajaxifyLinks();

    // Get the current location.
    var location = this.getLocation();

    // Check if the location has a hash (from a bookmark)
    // or if a hash has been provided.
    if(!location.hash && !startingHash) { startingHash = 'start'; }

    // Store the hash as necessary.
    ajaxHash = this.getHashFromURL(location.hash) || startingHash;
    this.addBackButtonHash(ajaxHash);

    // Add a watching event to look for changes in the location bar
    var watcherCallback = makeCallback(
        this.watchLocationForChange,
        this
    );
    window.setInterval(watcherCallback,200);
},
ajaxifyLinks: function() {
```

```
        // Convert the links to anchors for Ajax handling.
        links = getElementsByClassName(
            this.ajaxifyClassName,
            'a',
            document
        );
        for(var i=0 ; i < links.length ; i++) {
            if(hasClassName(links[i],'ADSActionPagerModified')) {
                continue;
            }

            // Convert the herf attribute to #value.
            links[i].setAttribute(
                'href',
                this.convertURLToHash(links[i].getAttribute('href'))
            );
            addClassName(links[i],'ADSActionPagerModified');

            // Attach a click event to add history as necessary.
            addEvent(links[i],'click',function() {
                if (this.href && this.href.indexOf('#') > -1) {
                    actionPager.addBackButtonHash(
                        actionPager.getHashFromURL(this.href)
                    );
                }
            });
        }
    },
    addBackButtonHash: function(ajaxHash) {
        // Store the hash.
        if (!ajaxHash) return false;
        if (this.safariHistory !== false) {
            // Using a special array for Safari
            if (this.safariHistory.length == 0) {
                this.safariHistory[window.history.length] = ajaxHash;
            } else {
                this.safariHistory[window.history.length+1] = ajaxHash;
            }
            return true;
        } else if (this.msieHistory !== false) {
            // By navigating the iframe in MSIE
            this.msieHistory.document.execCommand('Stop');
            this.msieHistory.location.href = '/fakepage?hash='
                + ajaxHash
                + '&title='+document.title;
            return true;
        } else {
```

```
            // By changing the location value
            // The function is wrapped using makeCallback so that this
            // will refer to the actionPager from within the
            // timeout method.
            var timeoutCallback = makeCallback(function() {
                if (this.getHashFromURL(window.location.href) != ➥
ajaxHash) {
                    window.location.replace(location.href + '#'
                        + ajaxHash);
                }
            },this);
            setTimeout(timeoutCallback, 200);
            return true;
        }
        return false;
    },
    watchLocationForChange: function() {

        var newHash;
        // Retrieve the value for the new hash.
        if (this.safariHistory !== false) {
            // From the history array for safari
            if (this.safariHistory[history.length]) {
                newHash = this.safariHistory[history.length];
            }
        } else if (this.msieHistory !== false) {
            // From the location of the iframe in MSIE
            newHash = this.msieHistory.location.href.➥
split('&')[0].split('=')[1];
        } else if (location.hash != '') {
            // From the window.location otherwise
            newHash = this.getHashFromURL(window.location.href);

        }


        // Update the page if the new hash doesn't equal the last hash.
        if (newHash && this.lastHash != newHash) {
            if (this.msieHistory !== false
            && this.getHashFromURL(window.location.href) != newHash) {
                // Fix the location bar in MSIE so it
                // bookmarks properly.
                location.hash = newHash;
            }

            // Try executing any registered listeners
            // using try/catch in case of an exception.
            try {
```

```
                    this.executeListeners(newHash);
                    // Update the links again in case any new
                    // ones were added with the handler.
                    this.ajaxifyLinks();
                } catch(e) {
                    // This will catch any bad JS in the callbacks.
                    alert(e);
                }

                // Save this as the last hash.
                this.lastHash = newHash;
            }
        },
        register: function(regex,method,context){
            var obj = {'regex':regex};
            if(context) {
                // A context has been specified.
                obj.callback = function(matches) {
                    method.apply(context,matches);
                };
            } else {
                // Use the window as the context.
                obj.callback = function(matches) {
                    method.apply(window,matches);
                };
            }

            // Add listeners to the callback array.
            this.callbacks.push(obj)
        },
        convertURLToHash: function(url) {
            if (!url) {
                // No url so return a pound
                return '#';
            } else if(url.indexOf("#") != -1) {
                // Has a hash so return it
                return url.split("#")[1];
            } else {
                // If the URL includes the domain name (MSIE) strip it off.
                if(url.indexOf("://") != -1) {
                    url = url.match(/:\/\/[^\/]+(.*)/)[1];
                }
                // Strip off the root as specified in init().
                return '#' + url.substr(this.ajaxifyRoot.length)
            }
        },
        getHashFromURL: function(url) {
```

```
            if (!url || url.indexOf("#") == -1) { return ''; }
            return url.split("#")[1];
        },
        getLocation: function() {
            // Check for a hash.
            if(!window.location.hash) {
                // Not one so make it
                var url = {host:null,hash:null}
                if (window.location.href.indexOf("#") > -1) {
                    parts = window.location.href.split("#")[1];
                    url.domain = parts[0];
                    url.hash = parts[1];
                } else {
                    url.domain = window.location;
                }
                return url;
            }
            return window.location;
        },
        executeListeners: function(hash){
            // Execute any listeners that match the hash.
            for(var i in this.callbacks) {
                if((matches = hash.match(this.callbacks[i].regex))) {
                    this.callbacks[i].callback(matches);
                }
            }
        }
    }
}
window['ADS']['actionPager'] = actionPager;

... below here is your existing library ...

})();
```

If you read through the comments in the ADS.actionPager object, you'll see that each browser is handled slightly differently.

For Internet Explorer, ADS.actionPager() appends an <iframe> to the document. Internet Explorer ignores hashed URLs in the back button, but at the same time, if you navigate to another page in an embedded iframe, the back button applies first to the embedded iframe and then to the parent page. Once the iframe can't navigate back any further, the parent will change. By updating the iframe with every hash change, the ADS.actionPager() object tricks the browser into remaining on the right page.

The only problem with the hidden iframe is that it needs to reference a real page on your site. The page doesn't have to do anything special; you only need it so that Internet Explorer doesn't try to search for the missing page. You can use whatever page you like, but I suggest linking to a simple empty HTML page:

```
<!DOCTYPE html PUBLIC "-//W3C//DTD XHTML 1.1//EN"
"http://www.w3.org/TR/xhtml11/DTD/xhtml11.dtd">
<html xmlns="http://www.w3.org/1999/xhtml">
<head>
<title>iframe target page</title>
</head>
<body>Nothing to see here</body>
</html>
```

In the preceding ADS.actionPager() source, I've linked to a fakepage script in the root of the advanceddomscripting.com site.

Dealing with Safari is a little tricky as well, because it requires the use of an array and the browser's history.length to figure out what hash to use for the current URL.

Implementing the object is relatively easy. There are only three methods in the ADS.actionPager object that you'll be interacting with:

- ADS.actionPager.init(ajaxifyClass,startingHash) initializes the pager functionality.
- ADS.actionPager.register(hash,listener,context) allows you to register listeners on specific hashes.
- ADS.actionPager.ajaxifyLinks() will automatically convert any identified anchor tags into pager-aware links.

> *The rest of the methods have been left as public methods so that you can integrate additional scripts with the pager to provide more advanced functionality.*

First, write your application as you would without the Ajax features. Also, if possible, make the page-related links in a "pretty URL" format so that they're easier to deal with later. If, for example, each page resides in pages.php?page=1, use URL redirection or some other mechanism so that you can use a URL such as pages/1 or pages_1. This isn't necessary, but it will make the next steps easier.

> *When you look at the photo browser later in this chapter, you'll see URL redirection in more detail.*

Next, identify all the anchor tags that you want converted to Ajax requests with a unique class, such as ADSActionLink:

```
<a href="pages/1" class="ADSActionLink">...</a>
<a href="pages/2" class="ADSActionLink">...</a>
<a href="pages/3" class="ADSActionLink">...</a>
```

You can use whatever class name you like, ADSActionLink is just the default class that will be used if you don't specify a different one. When the init() method runs, it will automatically invoke the

ADS.actionPager.ajaxifyLinks() method, which will convert the href attributes into hashes and append an ADSActionPagerModified class to indicate that the anchor has already been converted:

```
<a href="#pages/1" class="ADSActionLink ADSActionPagerModified">...</a>
<a href="#pages/2" class="ADSActionLink ADSActionPagerModified">...</a>
<a href="#pages/3" class="ADSActionLink ADSActionPagerModified">...</a>
```

The actionPager.ajaxifyLinks() method will also add a click event listener that refers to the ADS.actionPager object to track the clicks as needed:

```
... snippet from ADS.ActionPager.ajaxifyLinks() ...
addEvent(links[i],'click',function() {
    if (this.href && this.href.indexOf('#') > -1) {
        actionPager.addBackButtonHash(
            actionPager.getHashFromURL(this.href)
        );
    }
});
... snippet from ADS.ActionPager.ajaxifyLinks() ...
```

If you wish, you can manually run ADS.actionPager.ajaxifyLinks() any time after you've run ADS.actionPager.init(), which may be useful if other parts of your application are adding additional links that aren't in the correct format. If you call ADS.actionPager.ajaxifyLinks() multiple times, it will ignore any links that have already been converted. Also, the method is automatically called after each registered event so that any added links are also converted.

Once the links have all been converted, clicking them will cause your browser to remain on the same page and simply show a new hash on the URL in the location bar. The back and forward buttons will work along with bookmarks, but the main functionality is still missing.

For each different hash, you need to register a method that will be invoked when the matching hash is detected. This is where the ADS.actionPager.register() method comes into play. For the page/# URLs we discussed earlier, you might register something like the following:

```
ADS.actionPager.register('pages/1',function(hash) {
    ADS.ajaxRequest('pageBits.php?page=1',{
        completeListener = function() {
            // Add this.responseText to the dom tree
        }
    });
});
```

This registered method would only match a URL hash containing page/1.

> The ADS.actionPager *object is set up so that the match only applies to the hash and doesn't include the pound sign (#) as part of the match.*

To make the match more useful, you can register regular expression matches as well. This will allow you to use the same listener for multiple hashes:

```
ADS.actionPager.register(/^pages\/([0-9])$/,function(hash,page) {
    ADS.ajaxRequest('pageBits.php?page=' + page ,{
        completeListener = function() {
            //add this.responseText to the dom tree
        }
    });
});
```

In this case, the regular expression would match hashes page/0 through page/9, and because it also includes capturing parentheses, the listener function will receive additional arguments (page here) matching the regular expression parentheses.

When you use the this keyword from within the registered listener, it will refer to the window object. If you'd like this to refer to a different object, you can change the context using the optional third parameter to ADS.actionPager.register(). By specifying document.body in the following registered hash listener, any hash matching the regular expression (a hash containing page) would make the background-color of the document's body blue:

```
ADS.actionPager.register(/page/i,function(hash,page) {
    ADS.setStyle(this,{
        'background-color':'blue'
    });
},document.body);
```

When the URL hash changes, every registered listener will be evaluated, so you can register multiple listeners for the same hash. The listeners will be processed in the order they're registered, so if you like, you could make one depend on the other.

This solution solves both the bookmark and back/forward button problems with Ajax navigation, but if you incorporate Ajax into the listeners, it could lead to synchronicity problems, as we'll discuss next.

A race to finish the request

Regardless of what you've heard about Web 2.0 and Ajax, one thing is certain: it's asynchronous. What you may not know is that it's also a race, and you may be losing.

Traditionally, your web application followed a regular pattern, as shown in Figure 7-6.

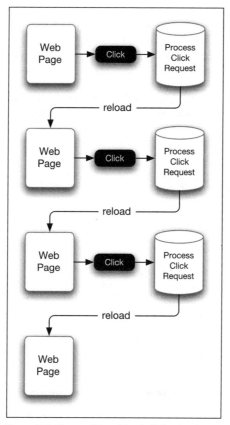

Figure 7-6. The traditional load-click-reload
request workflow

But now, using the XMLHttpRequest object, there's only one page load and a bunch of asynchronous requests, as shown in Figure 7-7.

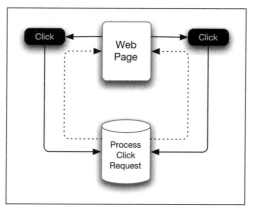

Figure 7-7. The Ajax request workflow

All these asynchronous communications change the very nature of your application's flow. You can't rely on that load-click-repeat cycle, because the page will only load once. So where's the problem? Well, it's not really a problem—if you understand what asynchronous implies. You have to remember that you're doing many things all at once now. Requests are going out every time you send a new XMLHttpRequest request, but they don't necessarily come back in the same order you send them.

As a quick demonstration, try the example at http://advanceddomscripting.com/source/chapter7/latency/. If you click the submit button several times, you'll notice the problem (see Figure 7-8).

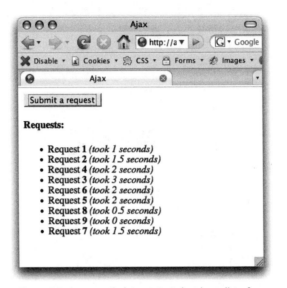

Figure 7-8. An example latency test showing a list of requests returned from the server in the wrong order

The requests in Figure 7-8 were sent in the order indicated by the Request number, but the responses were returned out of order, as indicated by the position in the list. Each time the submit button was clicked, a request was sent to the server, and in this example, some server traffic was simulated by sleeping a PHP script for a random time between 0 and 3 seconds:

```php
<?php
header("Cache-Control: no-cache, must-revalidate");
sleep( $time = (rand(0,6)/2) );
echo "$time";
die();
?>
```

If you had waited at least 3 seconds between each submit, the requests *may* have responded in the same order they were sent, because the process shouldn't take more than about 3 seconds. But, if you quickly make multiple requests several times in succession, there's a good possibility you may have a request of 2 seconds followed by a request of 0.5 seconds. When that occurs, the second request will respond out of order, as it will finish and complete before the earlier request. This demonstrates *asynchronous* requests in action—it's all happening at the same time, out of sync and out of order.

Latency picks the winner

In this race, you can't force the request to go faster by improving your server or scripts. Latency in the request is introduced at several stages, and many of the stages are beyond your control. We're all familiar with the basic communication workflow in our web applications, illustrated in Figure 7-9.

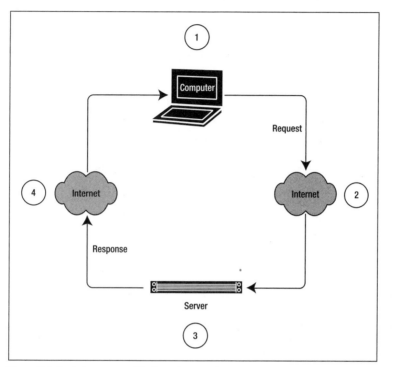

Figure 7-9. Basic Internet traffic flow showing the request/response loop

All your traffic follows the same pattern:

1. Your computer initiates a request to a server to retrieve or modify information.

2. The request is sent through a network of machines to that server.

3. The request is processed on the server.

4. A response to the request is sent from the server back to your computer through another network of machines.

Within the request/response loop, each stage has external influences, so at any time, one stage could slow down and delay the loop, introducing latency into your web application. Lots of Internet traffic can slow both the request and response, as both travel through the network. Also, another process on the server or the requirements of the request itself can delay the response from the server.

To see how a request gets from your computer to the server, you can do a simple traceroute between you and your server. For example, here's a quick traceroute between my MacBook while at home and this book's web site:

```
macbook:~ jeffreysambells$ traceroute advanceddomscripting.com
traceroute to advanceddomscripting.com (216.16.243.44), 64 hops➥
max, 40 byte packets
  1  192.168.1.1 (192.168.1.1)  7.318 ms  0.908 ms  1.025 ms
  2  192.168.2.1 (192.168.2.1)  1.523 ms  1.553 ms  1.589 ms
  3  64.230.197.224 (64.230.197.224)  10.074 ms  9.635 ms  10.294 ms
  4  dis26-toronto63_vlan101.net.bell.ca (64.230.229.81)  ➥
7.740 ms  7.470 ms  7.835 ms
  5  core3-toronto63-gigabite4-0.in.bellnexxia.net (206.108.107.169)  ➥
7.700 ms  7.751 ms  7.870 ms
  6  core1-toronto63_pos0-1.net.bell.ca (64.230.242.94)  ➥
8.853 ms  8.314 ms  8.530 ms
  7  dis1-torontoxn_pos1-0.net.bell.ca (64.230.229.46)  ➥
8.182 ms  8.355 ms  8.078 ms
  8  69.156.254.94 (69.156.254.94)  8.112 ms  8.686 ms  7.986 ms
  9  142.46.128.6 (142.46.128.6)  8.967 ms  8.764 ms  8.728 ms
 10  142.46.128.82 (142.46.128.82)  12.384 ms  13.074 ms  12.263 ms
 11  142.46.130.2 (142.46.130.2)  13.644 ms  12.571 ms  12.729 ms
 12  216.16.255.90 (216.16.255.90)  12.745 ms  12.564 ms  12.943 ms
 13  216.16.255.210 (216.16.255.210)  12.529 ms  12.542 ms  12.552 ms
 14  * * *
```

Line 14 isn't responding because of the firewall on the host where I have my site, but this shows the general path.

This route has 14 or so places where something could go wrong. Also, if I run traceroute advanced-domscripting.com several times, I'll usually get the same route, because each switch or server will generally deem that path to be the best. If, for some reason, traffic is heavy at one of the points along the path or one of the points refuses a connection, each packet could be diverted to another path without warning, at any time. The same applies to the reverse route for the response between the site and my MacBook, which will follow its own distinct path.

With all these points of possible latency, it's no wonder multiple requests can get a little out of sync. If you implement something as simple as a search suggestion box using an Ajax request to fetch suggestions as you type, the results may begin to appear out of order. If you were searching for books I've written and typed in my last name, Sambells, you would expect the suggestions to follow this pattern:

1. Books by S: A list of suggestions for books by "S".

2. Books by Sa: A list of suggestions for books by "Sa".

3. Books by Sam: A list of suggestions for books by "Sam".

4. Books by Samb: A list of suggestions for books by "Samb".

In reality, the preceding request/response loop wreaks havoc at every stage. Results for Books by S may return after results for Books by Samb, so the suggestions would no longer match what's typed in the search box.

This search example may not seem like that big of a deal—so what? A few suggestions may be wrong and you could live with that—but if the requests were also modifying a database at the same time, it would be a big problem. If you want to create a drag-and-drop storable list that saves each modification as items are rearranged, each request will assume the preceding request has already been applied to the data on the server. If the requests are processed in the wrong order, the order of the list will become a chaotic mess, and the server won't match what you're looking at on the screen. There are however a few solutions.

Dealing with asynchronous requests

There are a number of different ways to deal with latency issues in the request/response loop. Here are a few ideas, but this is by no means a complete list.

Ignoring the problem Ignoring the issue is the easiest solution and the one most often "implemented." It's easy to simply leave the problem and assume it will work the majority of the time, but this isn't a good solution for obvious reasons. I, for one, wouldn't want the brakes on my car to only work most of the time.

Turning off asynchronous behavior Setting asynchronous=false on the Ajax object is another option, but you can strike this off your list. If you think you can solve everything by setting the asynchronous flag in the XMLHttpRequest request's open() method to false—running everything in blocking mode—you're wrong. As I mentioned earlier, if you set the synchronous mode on the XMLHttpRequest object, it will process requests in order, but it does so by switching the requests in to a more aggressive blocking mode. This forces your script to stop all execution and wait until your request is complete, possibly causing the script and browser to hang if the response is too slow.

If you were to use the synchronous blocking mode to send ten requests to a server whose processing time varied between 1 and 5 seconds, the sum of the requests could take anywhere from 10 to 50 seconds, and all the while, your browser would be at a standstill until all the requests finished. This also doesn't allow you to provide the necessary loading feedback and other interaction while waiting for the request, so you may as well use the traditional workflow and just reload the entire page.

Queuing the requests client side Queuing is another possible solution. Rather than sending multiple XMLHttpRequest requests all at once, you could choose to send the first request and wait until it responds before sending the next one. Like synchronous requests, if you send ten requests to a server whose processing time varies between 1 and 5 seconds, the sum of the requests could take anywhere from 10 to 50 seconds, but the difference here is that in asynchronous mode, you're free to continue using the page while the additional requests load.

Here's a simple ADS.ajaxRequestQueue() object you can add to your ADS library as wrapper to your ADS.ajaxRequest() method. It will prevent the requests in the same queue from being sent until the previous one is received:

```
(function(){

window['ADS'] = {};

... above here is your existing library ...

/* a helper method to clone a JavaScript object */
function clone(myObj) {
    if(typeof(myObj) != 'object') return myObj;
    if(myObj == null) return myObj;
```

```
        var myNewObj = new Object();
        for(var i in myObj) {
            myNewObj[i] = clone(myObj[i]);
        }
        return myNewObj;
}

/* An array to hold the queues */
var requestQueue = [];

/* Wrapper for the ADS.ajaxRequest method that enables a queue */
function ajaxRequestQueue(url,options,queue) {
    queue = queue || 'default';

    // This object will wrap the option listeners in another function
    // so the option object needs to be unique. If a shared options
    // object is used when the method is called it will get into a
    // recursive mess.
    options = clone(options) || {};
    if(!requestQueue[queue]) requestQueue[queue] = [];

    // The queue needs to invoke the next request using the
    // completeListener when the previous request is complete. If
    // the complete listener is already defined then you need to
    // invoke it first.

    // Grab the old listener.
    var userCompleteListener = options.completeListener;

    // Add a new listener.
    options.completeListener = function() {

        // If there was an old one invoke it first.
        if(userCompleteListener) {
            // this will refer to the request object.
            userCompleteListener.apply(this,arguments);
        };

        // Remove this request from the queue.
        requestQueue[queue].shift();

        // Invoke the next item in the queue.
        if(requestQueue[queue][0]) {
            // The request is in the req property but you also need
            // to include the send option in case it's a POST request.
            var q = requestQueue[queue][0].req.send(
                requestQueue[queue][0].send
            );
        }
    }
```

```
// If there's an error the rest of the queue should be cancelled
// by calling their error methods

// Grab the old listener.
var userErrorListener = options.errorListener;

// Add a new listener.
options.errorListener = function() {

    if(userErrorListener) {
        userErrorListener.apply(this,arguments);
    };

    // Remove this request from the queue as the error
    // was already invoked.
    requestQueue[queue].shift();

    // Kill the rest of the queue as there was an error but call
    // the errorListener on each first. By invoking the error
    // listener on the next item in the queue it will clear all
    // queued requests as each will invoke the next in a chain.

    // Check if there is still anything in the queue.
    if(requestQueue[queue].length) {

        // Grab the next one
        var q = requestQueue[queue].shift();

        // Abort the request.
        q.req.abort();

        // Fake a request object so that the errorListener thinks
        // it completed and runs accordingly.

        var fakeRequest = new Object();

        // Set the status to 0 and readyState to 4 as if
        // the request completed but failed.
        fakeRequest.status = 0;
        fakeRequest.readyState = 4

        fakeRequest.responseText = null;
        fakeRequest.responseXML = null;

        // Set an error so you can show a message if you wish.
        fakeRequest.statusText = 'A request in the queue ➥
received an error';
```

```
                        // Invoke the state change. If readyState is 4 and
                        // status is not 200 then errorListener will be invoked.
                        q.error.apply(fakeRequest);
                    }

                }

                // Add this request to the queue.
                requestQueue[queue].push({
                    req:getRequestObject(url,options),
                    send:options.send,
                    error:options.errorListener
                });


                // If the length of the queue is only one
                // item (the first) invoke the request.
                if(requestQueue[queue].length == 1) {
                    ajaxRequest(url,options);
                }
            }
        window['ADS']['ajaxRequestQueue'] = ajaxRequestQueue;

        ... below here is your existing library ...

        })();
```

This object has the same first two arguments as the ADS.ajaxRequest() method except that ADS.ajaxRequestQueue() has a third optional argument to specify the name of the queue. You can have multiple queues running at one time, and in the event a request reports an error, the remainder of queued requests will trigger the errorListener() method. Implementing queued requests is the same as using your ADS.ajaxRequest() method:

```
// Request 1 in queue 1
ADS.ajaxRequestQueue('/your/script/',{
    completeListener: funcion() {
        alert(this.responseText);
    }
},'Queue1');

// Request 2 in queue 2
ADS.ajaxRequestQueue('/your/script/',{
    completeListener: funcion() {
        alert(this.responseText);
    }
},'Queue2');

// Request 3 in queue 1 will wait until
// request 1 is done.
```

```
ADS.ajaxRequestQueue('/your/script/',{
    completeListener: funcion() {
        alert(this.responseText);
    }
}, 'Queue1');
```

In this case, the first and second requests—in different queues—will run asynchronously at the same time. However, request 3 will wait until request 1 is complete, as they're both in the same queue. The queued requests will be triggered following the successful execution of the complete listener. To test it out, try the chapter7/ajaxRequestQueue example in the source for this book.

Making the request asynchronous but disabling conflicting features Disabling features is probably the most common way to avoid out-of-sync problems. When performing any sort of asynchronous request, it's always important to let the user know that something is going on behind the scenes. This is usually accomplished using some sort of Loading message or animation while the request is waiting for a response. While waiting, your users are free to continue using the application as they see fit, but, it could be potentially disastrous if they impatiently click the same action before it finishes loading (maybe because they're expecting it to go faster).

Beyond a simple Loading message, you can easily disable parts of the application, which would prevent impatient clicking. The only trick is that you will need to reenable each part for either a successful response or an error. If, for example, your web application's interface includes a submit button such as

```
<input type="submit" id="buttonID">
```

you can disable the form submission using something as simple as this:

```
ADS.ajaxRequest('/your/script/',{
    loadListener:function() {
        // Disable the button while loading
        ADS.$('buttonID').disabled = 'disabled';
    },
    completeListener: funcion() {
        // Enabled the button when successful
        ADS.$('buttonID').disabled = '';
        alert(this.responseText);
    },
    errorListener: function() {
        // Enabled the button after an error as well
        ADS.$('buttonID').disabled = '';
        alert('Oops, please try again: ' + this.statusText);
    }
});
```

The request itself is still asynchronous, so you can keep working in the application while the request is processing. But there's no way to initiate a conflicting request, because you've disabled the button, so it can't be clicked again until the response is complete.

The only problem with this approach is that, in some cases, such as the drag and drop sorting, it's just as annoying as the traditional page-reloading workflow. You don't want to disable dragging while the script is waiting for a response, as the point of drag-and-drop user interfaces is to provide an experience that's easy to use and fluid like a desktop application, not one where your user is forced to wait a few seconds between each action.

Rolling your own solution Your own creative solution is very viable as well. This list of options in this section is certainly not complete, and there are several other solutions beyond these. I also haven't mentioned how to deal with keeping requests in sync on the server side, as that's beyond the scope of this book.

> *If you come up with another creative solution, feel free to let me know through this book's web site at* http://advanceddomscripting.com, *and if you like, I'll post your solution there as well.*

Increased resources

Don't be fooled into thinking that adding Ajax interfaces will in any way decrease the use of resources on the server side of your application. If anything, they will probably increase. Increased resources aren't necessarily a problem if you have some to spare, but it may be an issue that you're not expecting.

When your traditional web application requires a lot of overhead, it may not be noticed while you're waiting for the browser to download and render the page. When you interact with the page in a way that's similar to a desktop application, you are expecting immediate results, not wait times. If each asynchronous request also requires the same overhead, the slowness becomes apparent as you sit and wait for a small element of the page to change. Also, multiple requests could be made at the same time from within one page, so your one request has now turned into half a dozen simultaneous requests, all requiring the same overhead and multiplying the resources required to run your application.

Problems solved?

If you carefully consider how you go about implementing your Ajax interfaces, you'll avoid most of the problems I've mentioned, but remember that it will take time and effort to do it properly. Ajax doesn't automatically make your development time faster or easier. The advantages and usefulness, however, can be greater than any additional costs, so let's look at a quick example that utilizes a number of the methods you learned about in this chapter.

Practical example: an Ajax-enhanced photo album

To demonstrate the `ADS.ajaxRequest()`, `ADS.ajaxRequestQueue()`, and `ADS.actionPager()` objects, let's look at a very simple degradable photo album that allows you to navigate both with and without JavaScript enabled. Because of the cross-site restrictions of Ajax and the dynamic nature of web applications, I'll simply point you to the working example at `http:/advanceddomscripting.com/source/chapter7/browser/`, as shown in Figure 7-10.

Figure 7-10. An Ajax-enhanced photo album

It won't be beneficial to walk you through constructing the internals of the application, as it requires access to a server-side scripting language to generate the appropriate pages and responses, which are beyond the scope of this book. The implementations of the request and pager objects are relatively small additions by design, so we'll focus on what's required by the server script and how the JavaScript objects interact with it to create the end product. Also, this browser is obviously incomplete, as it needs loading indicators and such for a polished application. The full PHP source of the server-side script is available in chapter7/browser/index.php, *so you can play with it yourself, but it will require that you have access to PHP 5.*

If you view the following HTML source of any page in the photo browser and try browsing it with JavaScript disabled, you'll notice a few things:

```
<!DOCTYPE html PUBLIC "-//W3C//DTD XHTML 1.0 Strict//EN"
"http://www.w3.org/TR/xhtml1/DTD/xhtml1-strict.dtd">
<html xmlns="http://www.w3.org/1999/xhtml">
<head>
    <title>A Photo Gallery</title>

    <link rel="stylesheet" title="Photo Gallery"
        type="text/css" href="/source/chapter7/browser/browser.css"
        media="screen">

    <script type="text/javascript"
        src="/source/ADS-final-verbose.js"></script>
    <script type="text/javascript"
        src="/source/chapter7/browser/browser.js"></script>

</head>
<body>
    <h1>Photo Browser</h1>
    <div id="content">
        <ul id="pages">
            <li><a href="/source/chapter7/browser/page/1/"
                    class="ajaxify">1</a></li>
            <li><a href="/source/chapter7/browser/page/2/"
                    class="ajaxify">2</a></li>
            <li><a href="/source/chapter7/browser/page/3/"
                    class="ajaxify">3</a></li>
            <li><a href="/source/chapter7/browser/page/4/"
                    class="ajaxify">4</a></li>
            <li><a href="/source/chapter7/browser/page/5/"
                    class="ajaxify">5</a></li>
        </ul>
        <div id="gallery">
            <ul id="list">
                <li id="photo1">
                    <a href="/source/chapter7/browser/photo/nature2"
                        class="ajaxify">
                        <img id="photo1Thumb"
                            src="/source/chapter7/browser/thumbs/➡
nature2.jpg"
                            alt="Photo: nature2.jpg"/>
                    </a>
                </li>
                <li id="photo2">
                    <a href="/source/chapter7/browser/photo/nature3"
                        class="ajaxify">
                        <img id="photo2Thumb"
```

```
                             src="/source/chapter7/browser/thumbs/➥
nature3.jpg"
                             alt="Photo: nature3.jpg"/>
                    </a>
                </li>
                <li id="photo3">
                    <a href="/source/chapter7/browser/photo/natureb1"
                        class="ajaxify">
                        <img id="photo3Thumb"
                            src="/source/chapter7/browser/thumbs/➥
natureb1.jpg"
                            alt="Photo: natureb1.jpg"/>
                    </a>
                </li>
            </ul>
            <div id="preview">
                <div id="previewPhotoFrame">
                    <img id="previewPhoto"
                        src="/source/chapter7/browser/photos/➥
nature2.jpg"
                        alt="Photo: nature2.jpg">
                </div>
                <div id="photoInfo">
                    <dl>
                        <dt>File Name</dt>
                        <dd id="photoFile">nature2.jpg</dd>
                        <dt>Exposure Time</dt>
                        <dd id="photoExposure"></dd>
                        <dt>F-Stop</dt>
                        <dd id="photoFStop"></dd>
                        <dt>ISO Speed Ratings</dt>
                        <dd id="photoISO"></dd> </dl>
                </div>
            </div>
        </div>
    </div>
</body>
</html>
```

First, you'll see in the HTML source that all the anchors use absolute URLs pointing from the root of the site to the desired file:

```
<a href="/source/chapter7/browser/page/1/" class="ajaxify">1</a>
```

I've chosen to format my URLs this way, known as "pretty URLs," for various reasons including search engine optimization, browser friendliness, and the requirements of the application itself. All the URLs for the photo browser that don't point to a real existing file are redirected to a central point by using an Apache RewriteRule:

```
RewriteEngine On
# if it's not an existing file
RewriteCond %{REQUEST_FILENAME} !-f
# or an existing directory
RewriteCond %{REQUEST_FILENAME} !-d
# Redirect to index.php
RewriteRule . index.php [L]
```

> To activate the Apache RewriteRule, place it in a file called .htaccess in the same folder as the browser's index.php file (there's already one in the supplied source code). If this doesn't work, it may be because the server administrator doesn't allow you to override the server's rewrite settings. In that case, contact your server administrator for specific instructions on setting up rewrite rules.

If you like, you can choose to use the traditional GET method in your application:

```
<a href="index.php?page=1" class="ajaxify">1</a>
```

But pretty URLs make it easier to parse the relevant information out of the URL when registering the actionPager() listeners later on. You'll also notice that several anchors in the HTML source have an ajaxify class associated with them:

```
<a href="/source/chapter7/browser/page/1/" class="ajaxify">1</a>
```

These are the anchors that will be identified in the page's load event and are converted to use the ADS.actionPager methods.

Next, you'll notice the entire example works as expected without any JavaScript enabled. The only difference is the page will be forced to reload between each request. This is important not only for search engines and accessibility but because the actionPager will build on these existing URLs to unobtrusively enable the Ajax aspects of the application.

Finally, you'll notice there are two types of URLs—pages and photos:

```
/source/chapter7/browser/page/1
/source/chapter7/browser/photo/nature2
```

Each URL will invoke a different kind of response: one to fetch a new page and the other to fetch a specific photo.

Ajaxify the photo browser

To enhance the behavioral aspects of the photo browser and prevent it from jumping to the top of the page each time you look at a new image, it would be nice to load the pages, images, and associated information using an Ajax request. This is done using the ADS library methods from within the photo browser's custom browser.js DOM script at

```
http://advanceddomscripting.com/source/chapter7/browser/browser.js
```

Adding the Ajax enhancements requires only two things:

- The appropriate JavaScript load events to manipulate the page as required:

```
function updatePhoto(info) {
    ADS.$('previewPhoto').src = info.webHref;
    ADS.removeChildren('photoFile').appendChild(
        document.createTextNode(info.file));
    ADS.removeChildren('photoExposure').appendChild(
        document.createTextNode(info.exposure));
    ADS.removeChildren('photoFStop').appendChild(
        document.createTextNode(info.fStop));
    ADS.removeChildren('photoISO').appendChild(
        document.createTextNode(info.iso));
}

function updateGalleryList(files) {
    // Alter the page as necessary.
    var thumb;
    for(var i=0 ; i<files.length ; i++) {
        if((thumb = ADS.$('photo'+(i+1)+'Thumb'))) {
            var li = ADS.$('photo'+(i+1));

            if (files[i]) {
                // Update the thumbnail with the new image.
                thumb.src = '/source/chapter7/browser/thumbs/'
                    + files[i];
                thumb.title = 'Photo: ' + files[i];
                thumb.alt = 'Photo: ' + files[i];
                ADS.removeClassName(li,'noFile');
                li.getElementsByTagName('A')[0].href = '#photo/'
                    + files[i].split('.')[0];
            } else {
                // There's no thumbnail file so hide this one.
                thumb.src = '';
                thumb.title = '';
                thumb.alt = '';
                ADS.addClassName(li,'noFile');
                li.getElementsByTagName('A')[0].href = '';
            }
        }
    }
}

ADS.addLoadEvent(function() {

    ADS.actionPager.register('start',function(hash) {
        // Any starting event you want to add
        // This will be invoked when the page loads
```

```
                    // without any hash.
        });

        // Photo change listener
        ADS.actionPager.register(
            /photo\/([0-9a-z-]+)\/{0,1}$/i,
            function(hash,photo) {

                // Send a queued ajaxRequest to fetch the photo.
                ADS.ajaxRequestQueue(hash,{
                    // The server is returning an application/json response.
                    jsonResponseListener:function(response) {
                        // Update the thumbnail navigation with the
                        // new list (if any).
                        updateGalleryList(response.currentPageFiles);
                        // Update the preview.
                        updatePhoto(response.currentPhoto);

                        // Update the document title.
                        document.title = 'Photo Album Photo '
                            + response.currentPhoto.file;
                    }
                },'photoBrowserQueue');
            }
        );

        // Page change listener
        ADS.actionPager.register(
            /page\/([0-9]+)\/{0,1}$/i,
            function(hash,page) {

                // Send a request to fetch the new page info
                // Follows the same idea as the photo listener
                ADS.ajaxRequestQueue(hash,{
                    jsonResponseListener:function(response) {
                        updateGalleryList(response.currentPageFiles);
                        updatePhoto(response.currentPhoto);
                        document.title = 'Photo Album Page '
                            + response.currentPage;
                    }
                },'photoBrowserQueue');

        });

        // Start the actionPager by scanning for ajaxify links and
        // make the root of the hashes start after the browser folder.
        ADS.actionPager.init('ajaxify','/source/chapter7/browser/');
});
```

- An addition to the server-side script that will check if the request is coming from the ADS.ajaxRequest() method and return a JSON object with the appropriate information:

```php
<?php

...cut...

if($_SERVER['HTTP_X_ADS_AJAX_REQUEST'] == 'AjaxRequest') {
        header('Content-type: application/json');
        //$currentPageFiles =  "'".join("','",$currentPageFiles)."'";

        echo json_encode(array(
                'numPages' => $numPages,
                'currentPage' => $currentPage,
                'currentPageFiles' => $currentPageFiles,
                'currentPhoto' => array(
                        'webHref' => $currentPhoto['webHref'],
                        'file' => $currentPhoto['FileName'],
                        'exposure' => $currentPhoto['ExposureTime'],
                        'fStop' => $currentPhoto['FNumber'],
                        'iso' => $currentPhoto['ISOSpeedRatings']
                )
        ));

        die();
}

...cut...

?>
```

The JavaScript load event simply registers two ADS.actionPager listeners, as discussed earlier in the chapter. One matches the pages using the regular expression:

```
/photo\/([0-9a-z-]+)\/{0,1}$/i
```

This will locate any hashes ending with photo/ followed by an alphanumeric string and an optional ending slash. The second listener matches photos using

```
/page\/([0-9]+)\/{0,1}$/
```

and does the same, but it looks for page/ followed by a number only.

> If you're not familiar with regular expressions, I suggest you check them out. They can be a very powerful addition to any string manipulation and matching, and they're available in most scripting languages. For more information, see http://www.regular-expressions.info/.

Both these regular expressions use capturing parentheses, so the resulting page number and photo name are passed into the listeners as the second argument.

Next, the ADS.actionPager is initialized, and it converts the anchors with the ajaxify class:

```
ADS.actionPager.init('ajaxify','/source/chapter7/browser/');
```

The root of the browser application has also been specified so that the hashed URLs can be shortened to include only the part after the root. This isn't necessary, as it will work with the full URL, but the following line

```
http://advanceddomscripting.com/source/chapter7/browser/#photos/page/2/
```

looks better than this:

```
http://advanceddomscripting.com/source/chapter7/browser/➥
#/source/chapter7/browser/photos/page/2/
```

The functionality in each of the registered listeners is relatively straightforward; they simply make a ADS.ajaxRequest()—through the ADS.ajaxRequestQueue()—to retrieve the information for the specified hash:

```
// Photo change listener
ADS.actionPager.register(
    /photo\/([0-9a-z-]+)\/{0,1}$/i,
    function(hash,photo) {
        // Send a queued ajaxRequest to fetch the photo
        // and associated information.
        ADS.ajaxRequestQueue(hash,{
            // The server is returning an application/json response.
            jsonResponseListener:function(response) {
                // Update the thumbnail navigation with the
                // new list (if any).
                updateGalleryList(response.currentPageFiles);
                // Update the preview.
                updatePhoto(response.currentPhoto);

                // Update the document title.
                document.title = 'Photo Album Photo '
                    + response.currentPhoto.file;
            }
        },'photoBrowserQueue');
    }
);
```

This results in the appropriate JavaScript response from the server:

```
{
    "numPages":5,
    "currentPage":3,
    "currentPageFiles":["nature6.jpg","natureb4.jpg","nature7.jpg"],
```

```
"currentPhoto":{
        "webHref":"\/source\/chapter7\/browser\/photos\/nature7.jpg",
        "file":"nature7.jpg",
        "exposure":1\/30",
        "fStop":"21\/5",
        "iso":"400"
    }
}
```

And the document structure is altered through the auxiliary updateGalleryList() and updatePhoto() methods. That's it!

Summary

Ajax is a good thing—it's a wonderful merging of existing technologies and has allowed the developers to provide much slicker and sexier solutions to otherwise boring applications. These solutions are becoming more and more like desktop applications, but along with the improvements come more problems.

In this chapter, you learned a lot about the XMLHttpRequest object and the common ways it's used in Ajax-enhanced applications. The ADS.ajaxRequest() method, along with the ADS.ajaxRequestQueue() methods, will go a long way to helping you build your Ajax applications, but they won't solve every problem. You also learned that synchronicity issues with overlapping requests and browser quirks, such as the back button and bookmarks, go beyond simple bugs or inconsistencies, and they required a preorganized plan to ensure your application can avoid them.

Using Ajax isn't difficult, provided you have a solid idea and a plan; just be sure you're not using new ideas and methodologies simply because you can or because you think it will make you look cool.

In the next chapter, you'll look at one feature of your web application that you just can't do with proper Ajax: uploading files through your web site.

CHAPTER 8

CASE STUDY: ENABLING ASYNCHRONOUS FILE UPLOADS WITH PROGRESS INDICATORS

You're probably wondering how you can upload files through your fancy `ADS.ajaxRequest()` method from Chapter 7. Well, you can't—or, I should say, you can't do exactly that. The title of this chapter is a little misleading, as you may have thought that I was implying that you'd be uploading files through the XMLHttpRequest object.

While there are no technical limitations on the XMLHttpRequest object that prevent you from using it to upload files, for very good security reasons, your web browser doesn't allow JavaScript to access local files beyond the cookie. When using form file input elements, such as this:

```
<input type="file" id="newFile1" name="newFile1" ➥
accept="image/jpeg,image/png" />
```

the only bit of information you can glean about the selected file is the path on the local drive—and that's only if the file has been selected after the page has loaded; you can't prepopulate the value.

The real limitation in uploading files through the XMLHttpRequest object isn't with the XMLHttpRequest object itself, but rather the inability to read the file that you want to include in the request. You're free to send whatever headers and data you like using the XMLHttpRequest object, and you can include everything from full multipart/form-data POST requests to PUT requests—you just can't get access to the raw data to send along.

If you could access the binary file information, you could upload the file by doing something similar to the following, where the request is formatted as a `multipart/form-data` request:

```
var request = false;
if(XMLHttpRequest) {
    var request = new XMLHttpRequest();
} else if (ActiveXObject) {
    var request = new ActiveXObject('Microsoft.XMLHTTP');
}

if(request) {
    var boundary = '--ExampleBoundaryString';
    var requestBody =
        boundary + '\n'
        + 'Content-Disposition: form-data; name="exampleText"\n\n'
        + exampleText + '\n\n'
        + boundary + '\n'
        + 'Content-Disposition: form-data; name="myfile"; filename=➡
"example.zip"\n'
        + 'Content-Type: application/octet-stream\n\n'
        + escape(BinaryContent) + '\n'
        + boundary;
    request.open('POST', url, true);
    request.setRequestHeader('Content-Type',
        'multipart/form-data; boundary="'
        + boundaryString
        + '"');
    request.setRequestHeader('Connection', 'close');
    request.setRequestHeader('Content-Length', requestBody.length);
    request.send(requestBody);
}
```

The tricky part is getting the file information into the BinaryContent variable to include in the request. You could do this by manually converting your file into a binary format and then copying and pasting it into a text box, but that's going to require a lot of extra work and technical expertise on your part. Also, in some browsers such as Firefox, it *is possible* to access local files from the browser, but it requires that your edit special security settings in about:config to grant access. This would offer a pure XMLHttpRequest solution, but it would only work in a few browsers. Also, the added complexity or initial apprehension of editing security settings would create additional barriers in the upload process.

An easy (and the only) browser-agnostic way to submit a form with files is through a regular old POST. If you want to refrain from reloading the page, you need to target the form's POST request at another frame, such as an embedded iframe:

```
<!DOCTYPE html PUBLIC "-//W3C//DTD XHTML 1.0 Transitional//EN"
        "http://www.w3.org/TR/xhtml1/DTD/xhtml1-transitional.dtd">
<html xmlns="http://www.w3.org/1999/xhtml">
<head>
```

```
    <link rel="stylesheet" href="style.css"
        type="text/css" media="screen" />
    <title>Form with an iframe as the target</title>
</head>
<body>
<h1>Form with an iframe as the target</h1>
<form action="script/" target="formTarget">
    <div>
        <label for="example">Some text</label>
        <input type="text" name="example" id="example" value="" />
    </div>
    <div>
        <input type="submit" value="Send it to the iframe" />
    </div>
</form>
<iframe name="formTarget" id="formTarget"></iframe>
</body>
</html>
```

> You'll notice in this example that the DOCTYPE is set to XHTML 1.0 Transitional. The iframe element is part of the HTML 4.01 specification (http://www.w3.org/TR/html401/present/frames.html#h-16.5) but only in the transitional (or loose) DOCTYPE (http://www.w3.org/TR/html401/loose.dtd). If you try to use a strict DOCTYPE (http://www.w3.org/TR/html401/strict.dtd) the iframe will be considered invalid along with the target attribute on the form.
>
> The DOCTYPE will also influence the rendering of the CSS and markup, so be aware when switching between the two.

The parent page is then free to continue running scripts while the iframe receives the POST request. This will enable you to upload files while, at the same time, using Ajax and the XMLHttpRequest object to asynchronously track the progress of the upload, which will be the focus of the rest of this chapter.

In this chapter, you're not going to be adding anything else to your ADS library; in fact, you've already added everything necessary for the rest of this book. Instead, you'll use everything you've learned up until now about best practices, JavaScript, the DOM, events, style and Ajax to add real progress indicators to your web application.

A little life in the loading message

It seems real progress indicators, ones that actually indicate what's happening, have always been beyond reach in web development. Most are really just animated GIFs cycling over and over indefinitely with no real end in sight, leaving you wondering if anything is really happening at all. As an example, Figure 8-1 shows the stages of the loading icon from the Tango Icon Library (http://tango.freedesktop.org/), which will spiral forever until it's told to stop.

This isn't to say animated loading images are bad; sometimes there's just no way to tell how long something is going to take so Loading . . . is the best you can do. Other times, if you know the process is only going to take a fraction of a second, showing a progress bar may be unnecessary. But, in the case of longer requests, such as file uploads, or really any process on your web server that will take time, you can take advantage of the asynchronous aspects of the XMLHttpRequest object to display some real live progress indicators.

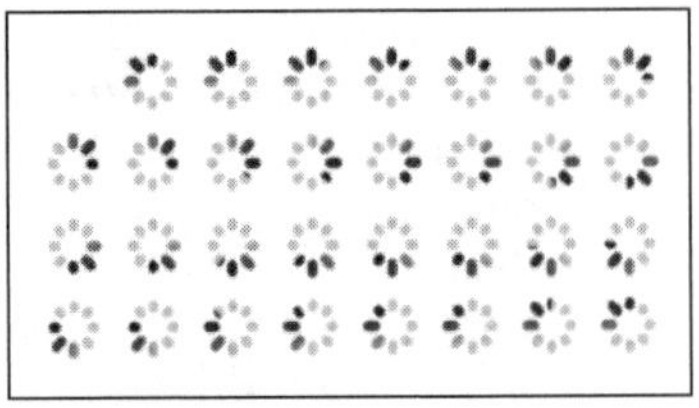

Figure 8-1. The stages of the progress icon from the open source Tango Icon Library

The concept of a progress bar is fairly simple. You really only need two key things to make it work:

- An end goal
- The ability to monitor the process as it moves toward that goal

In most cases, it's the ability to monitor the process that causes the problem. Before the XMLHttpRequest object came about, there wasn't really a good way to query the server to find out how things were progressing. You could use the <script> tag hack from Chapter 7, but that wasn't very developer friendly. If you knew something was going to take a while, the best you could really do was display This is going to take a few minutes. and remind people not to reload or click anything until it was finished. On top of that, estimating things like file uploads required some mental calculation based on the estimated speed of your Internet connection and the size of the file you intended to upload—creating even more confusion.

Technical hurdles in the browser aside, recording progress on the server is also relatively straightforward. You just need some shared storage space, such as a file, to store the end goal at the beginning of the process and your progress toward that goal throughout the process. For example, if you had a for loop on your server that took an excessively long time, you could store your progress toward reaching the end of the loop by counting each iteration, as shown here in pseudo-code:

```
count = 200;
storeProgress('End goal is 200');
for( i = 0 ; i < count ; i++) {
    storeProgress ('I am working with number i. ➥
Only count-i left to go!');
    // Do something really intensive
}
storeProgress('I have reached 200 and I'm done');
```

This isn't real working code, but it illustrates the concept. As long as an additional process on the server, such as an XMLHttpRequest request, can access the shared progress information, it's just a simple matter of calculating the percentage of completion and displaying it appropriately.

In your DOM script, checking the status can be done by periodically querying the server using setInterval() and your ADS.ajaxRequest() method:

```
                // Check once every second
                var watcher = function() {
                    ADS.ajaxRequestQueue('/getProgressScript/',{
                        jsonResponseListener(response) {
                        if(response.done) {
                                // Your code
                            } else {
                                // Update the progress bar
                                ADS.setStyle('progressBar',{
                                    'width' : (response.current/response.total) + '%';
                                });
                                // Wait one second and send another request
                                setInterval(watcher,1000);
                            }
                        }
                    }
                }

                // Initiate the first request
                watcher();
```

This example needs a lot more work before it could be considered complete, but the basics are all there:

1. Retrieve the response once every few seconds.

2. Check if the process is finished.

3. If it's finished, continue with your code.

4. Otherwise, update the progress bar, and make another request.

This technique could be applied to anything from slow scripts to monitoring credit card authorizations to uploading files—which is what you'll focus on in this chapter.

Processing uploads on the server

The biggest technological hurdle with file uploads is accessing the progress of the POST request as it arrives on the server. This part of the process has nothing to do with DOM scripting and isn't the focus of this book. However, progressively enhancing a boring form by adding Ajax-based progress bars definitely is part of DOM scripting, and you need both halves to make it work.

I won't go into a lot of detail regarding the server-side portion, as the necessary files have been included in the source for this book and are available as a download from http://advanceddomscripting.com. Here, we'll just discuss the required input and output that the server-side scripts are expecting, and you can use one of the supplied versions or write your own.

Most server scripting languages begin execution after they've already received the entire request, so there's no way for you to periodically store the progress of the request. The exceptions to this are Perl and a combination of PHP 5.2 (http://php.net) with the most recent APC extension (http://pecl.php.net/apc).

If you can't get the file upload portions working, you can use the simulation script in the chapter8/start/simulation/ *source—written in PHP—which will allow you to work through the chapter. The simulation fakes the progress over 20 requests, so the duration will always be the same, and the files won't actually be stored on your server. The simulation still requires PHP, but it will work in PHP 4 or 5 and doesn't require the APC extension.*

When querying a Perl script, Perl begins executing at the beginning of a request before the request has finished transmission. This allows you to manually process the request yourself and extract the necessary files—giving you an opportunity to do all the progress storage you want. With PHP 5.2, the APC cache extension begins execution at the beginning of the request and will automatically track incoming file uploads if a special hidden field is included in the POST request.

The PHP5.2/APC solution will require APC version 3.53 or greater, as you will need to enable the apc.rfc1867 php.ini option. See http://viewcvs.php.net/viewvc.cgi/pecl/apc/INSTALL?revision=3.53&view=markup *for more information.*

These server-side scripts each have an identical purpose: to store files from a POST request and report on the progress. They've been written to directly receive a POST request that contains only file inputs and a few hidden fields. When you POST a traditional request to the script, it will process the files and tell the browser to redirect back to the originating page. This allows the process to maintain its functionality if JavaScript is disabled, though it won't be as elegant. At the same time, if the appropriate header is identified in the request, the scripts will instead return a progress report in the form of a JSON object as follows:

```
{
    "total":845,                          // Size of the request in bytes
    "current":845,                        // Number of bytes processed
    "currentFileName":"file.jpg",         // The file name in progress
    "currentFieldName":"newFile3",        // The field in progress
    "filesProcessed":[],                  // An array of all processed files
    "error":'',                           // An error message (if any)
    "done":1                              // 0 not done, 1 done
    "debug":"message"                     // Debug message for development
};
```

If you want your forms to include additional information, which you probably will, you'll need to modify these scripts as necessary to accept and store the additional information along with the files. Alternatively, you could move the uploading portion of the tool to a separate form on the page and build an integrated Ajax file browser by combining this chapter with the methods you learned in Chapter 6.

> *For security reasons, I've restricted the scripts so that they will only accept* `.jpg` *or* `.png` *files and the image sizes can't be more than 200KB each. This isn't a limitation of the uploader and is only in place to protect you from accidentally allowing malicious files into your system. Never allow users to upload potentially malicious files that could be executed on the server, and always be sure to properly sanitize and verify any files that are uploaded.*

The magic word

The PHP server-side solution relies on the APC extension and its ability to provide shared memory across multiple server processes. APC 3.5 introduced a special option that automatically tracks the progress of uploads in POST requests only if the special APC_UPLOAD_PROGRESS key is located in the POST request before the file inputs:

```
<form action="script/" target="formTarget">
    <input type="hidden" name="APC_UPLOAD_PROGRESS"
        value="This_Should_Be_Unique"/>
    ... cut ...
</form>
```

The same unique value can be used in additional requests to consistently identify the process. In the case of Perl, the server-side script uses this same APC_UPLOAD_PROGRESS variable for convenience, so your DOM script can be agnostic to the server.

The starting point

For the remainder of this chapter, you'll be focusing on building your unobtrusive DOM script. To get started, choose one of the starting points from the source for this book:

- chapter8/start/php5-APC/
- chapter8/start/perl/
- chapter8/start/simulation/

> *You'll need a server running the appropriate server-side language to work on this example, as the server-side portions can't run on a regular desktop machine—unless you also have the appropriate web server software installed.*

Each folder contains several files. For example, the php5-APC folder resembles this:

```
start/php5-APC
    /actions
        /index.php
    /index.php
    /load.js
```

```
/style.css
/uploader.js
/uploads
```

Each starting point is identical with the exception of the server-side language required to run them. The index file in the actions/ subfolder contains the appropriate server-side script we discussed earlier. I've set up the directory structure this way so that the uploader.js file—where you'll be writing your code—can reference the server script with the same URL for each version:

```
actions/?var=value
```

The only additional requirement for the php5-APC and Perl versions is modifying the permissions on the upload folder. These two versions will store your uploaded files in the uploads/ folder, so it must be writeable by the user running the web server. In an Apache/Linux setup, this might be accomplished by running the following command from within the starting point folder where username and groupname are replaced with the ones you're using to run the web server:

```
chown username.groupname uploads
```

If you're having trouble with the server-side files, please check the website at http:// advanceddomscripting/help/ for more help.

With your appropriate starting point set up, you're already showing some progress—pun intended.

Putting it all together: an upload progress indicator

If you take a look at the index file in the starting point you chose, you'll see it simply retrieves the file listing for the uploads directory and outputs a relatively simple XHTML 1.0 transitional page, as shown in the following php5-APC version:

```php
<?php

// Iterate through the upload directory to retrieve
// the files that have already been uploaded.
$uploads = new DirectoryIterator('./uploads');
$files = array();
foreach($uploads as $file) {

    // Skip . and ..
    if(!$file->isDot() && $file->isFile()) {

        // Append to the array. This will be concatenated together
        // later in the HTML.
        $files[] = sprintf(
            '<li><a href="uploads/%s">%s</a> <em>%skb</em></li>',
            $file->getFilename(),
            $file->getFilename(),
            round($file->getSize()/1024)
        );
```

```
            }
        }

        // Output the page.
        ?>
        <!DOCTYPE html PUBLIC "-//W3C//DTD XHTML 1.0 Transitional//EN"
                "http://www.w3.org/TR/xhtml1/DTD/xhtml1-transitional.dtd">
        <html xmlns="http://www.w3.org/1999/xhtml">
        <head>
            <title>Image Uploader with Progress (php5-APC)</title>

            <!-- Inclue some CSS style sheet to make
            everything look a little nicer -->
            <link rel="stylesheet" type="text/css"
                href="../../../shared/source.css" />
            <link rel="stylesheet" type="text/css"
                href="../../chapter.css" />
            <link rel="stylesheet" type="text/css" href="style.css" />

            <!-- Your ADS library with the common JavaScript objects -->
            <script type="text/javascript"
                src="../../../ADS-final-verbose.js"></script>

            <!-- Progress bar script -->
            <script type="text/javascript" src="uploader.js"></script>

            <!-- load script -->
            <script type="text/javascript" src="load.js"></script>

        </head>
        <body>
            <h1>Image Uploader with Progress (php5-APC)</h1>
            <div id="content">
                <form action="actions/" enctype="multipart/form-data"
                    method="post" id="uploadForm">

                    <fieldset>
                        <legend>Upload a new image</legend>
                        <p>Only jpg/gif/png files less than 100kb allowed.</p>
                        <div class="fileSelector">
                            <label for="newFile1">File 1</label>
                            <input type="file" id="newFile1" name="newFile1"
                                accept="image/jpeg,image/gif,image/png"/>
                        </div>
                        <div class="fileSelector">
                            <label for="newFile2">File 2</label>
                            <input type="file" id="newFile2" name="newFile2"
                                accept="image/jpeg,image/gif,image/png"/>
                        </div>
```

353

```
                        <div class="fileSelector">
                            <label for="newFile3">File 3</label>
                            <input type="file" id="newFile3" name="newFile3"
                                accept="image/jpeg,image/gif,image/png"/>
                        </div>
                        <input id="submitUpload" name="submitUpload"
                            type="submit" value="Upload Files" />
                    </fieldset>

                </form>

                <div id="browserPane">
                    <h2>
                        <span id="fileCount">
                            <?php echo count($files); ?>
                        </span>
                        Existing Files in <em>uploads/</em>
                    </h2>
                    <ul id="fileList">
                        <?php echo join($files,"\n\t\t\t\t\t"); ?>
                    </ul>
                </div>
            </div>
        </body>
    </html>
```

It doesn't really matter to the DOM script how the HTML is marked up. The script you're about to create will appropriately modify any form, as long as it has file inputs. Notice that the index.html file doesn't contain any extraneous markup beyond what would be required to display the page. There's no iframe or other special markup for the progress bar—just the bare-bones requirements.

At the moment, the uploader.js file contains no modifying code, so if you visit the page in your web browser and try uploading a few JPEG or PNG images, it will upload them as expected by reloading the browser page without any progress indication other than what's built into the browser—which is rather limited. This is the same thing that will happen if you disable JavaScript in the completed version. As well, if you try to upload a bad file, you'll see that it does so without complaint until the request is fully processed, as shown in Figure 8-2.

Ideally, with your DOM script available, you would not only provide an upload progress but help avoid these errors by including form verification as well.

There's no need for you to edit anything in the main index file, as all your work will be done in the uploader.js file, so let's take a look at that now.

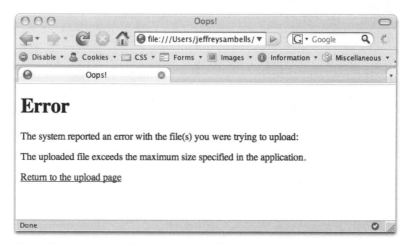

Figure 8-2. An error page indicating that the file type was incorrect

The addProgressBar() framework

If you glance through the following script, you'll see I've included some initial framework as well as requirements of each unfinished method, commented at each stage:

```
function verifyFileType(fileInput) {
    if(!fileInput.value || !fileInput.accept) return true;
    var extension = fileInput.value.split('.').pop().toLowerCase();
    var mimetypes = fileInput.accept.toLowerCase().split(',');
    var type;
    for(var i in mimetypes) {
        type = mimetypes[i].split('/')[1];
        if(type == extension || (type=='jpeg' && extension=='jpg')) {
            return true;
        }
    }
    return false;
}

var addProgressBar = function(form,modificationHandler) {

    // Check if the form exists.

    // Find all the file input elements.

    // If there are no file input then stop.

    // Add a change event to verify the extension based
    // on the mime types.
```

```
            // Append the target iframe for the upload.
            // In IE the name attribute doesn't set properly using DOM
            // such as:
            // var uploadTargetFrame = document.createElement('iframe');
            // uploadTargetFrame.setAttribute('id','uploadTargetFrame');
            // uploadTargetFrame.setAttribute('name','uploadTargetFrame');
            // To work around this create a div and use the innerHTML
            // property which will render the name correctly in IE and
            // other browsers.


            // Modify the target of the form to be the new iframe.
            // This will prevent the page from reloading.

            // Create a unique ID to track uploading.

            // Add the unique ID as the APC_UPLOAD_PROGRESS key.
            // It must be added before the file inputs so that the server
            // will receive it first and trigger the progress information.

            // Create the different pieces for the progress indicator.

            // The bar

            // The inner background container

            // Check for an existing anchor point.
            // It must be a span with the progressContainer class.

            // If it doesn't exist create one and append it to the form.

            // Set the container to a block style.

            // Append the rest of the progress bar.

            // Add a progress message area as well.

            // Create a private method that will be used below by the
            // progress watcher to update the progress bar and message.

            // Initiate the bar at 0% and waiting.

            // Add a the submit event to the form that will verify the form
            // information and update the progress bar.

        }
```

We'll look at each piece as you work your way through the various parts of the process.

The load event

To get things loading, your index.html page also includes a load.js script. If you take a peek at the load.js script, you'll see the unobtrusive load event is very simple, as all the magic occurs in uploader.js:

```
ADS.addEvent(window,'load',function(W3CEvent) {
var fileList = ADS.$('fileList');
    // Modify the uploadForm as necessary.
    addProgressBar('uploadForm',function(response) {
        var files = response.filesProcessed;
        for(var i in files) {
            // Skip empty files
            if(files[i] == null) continue;

            // Create a new element for the file list.
            var li = document.createElement('li');
            var a = document.createElement('a');
            a.setAttribute('href','uploads/' + files[i]);
            a.appendChild(document.createTextNode(files[i]));
            li.appendChild(a);
            fileList.appendChild(li);
        }
        // Update the file count number.
        var countContainer = ADS.$('fileCount');
        ADS.removeChildren(countContainer);
        var numFiles = fileList.getElementsByTagName('LI').length;
        countContainer.appendChild(document.createTextNode(numFiles));
    });
});
```

The window's load event listener simply calls one method to initiate the progress bar modifications:

```
addProgressBar('uploadForm',function(response) { ... });
```

The anonymous function supplied in the second argument is responsible for manipulating the DOM document after the successful upload; in this case, it appends the resulting files to the appropriate file list in the index markup and updates the number in the numFiles element.

> To use the uploader.js *script in a different document, you'll only need to repurpose a load event to alter the markup as necessary. If you find this happens a lot, you could standardize the markup you use for the file list and include these alterations directly within the* addProgressBar() *object.*

The addProgressBar() object

For the rest of the file, you're going to work with the addProgressBar() object in the uploader.js file.

Keeping future reusability and developer friendliness in mind, your addUploadProgress() will require the two arguments as you just saw:

- A reference to the form that should be modified
- A handler method that will be responsible for manipulating the document structure after the submission is successful

In the example index file, the HTML page is set up with a file list at the bottom. You always want to think ahead and set up your scripts to be as reusable as possible, so by extracting this portion, the same method could now be used in another document with completely different markup.

When you glance through the comments in the addProgressBar() object framework, you'll see that you need to do a number of things including:

1. Locate all the file inputs in the given form.
2. Add the event listeners to each file input to verify that the selected files are the right type.
3. Create an <iframe>, and append it to the document so that the form can target the <iframe>.
4. Add a hidden element to enable and track the progress.
5. Create the progress bar elements in a developer-friendly way.
6. Add a submit event listener to the form that will verify the information before submitting.
7. Initiate the required progress tracking.
8. Alter the page as necessary upon success or failure of the requests.

To be friendly to developers, let's start off by checking the input. In this case, addProgressBar() only expects one piece of information—the ID of the form to manipulate—so you can simply pass it into your ADS.$() method from Chapter 1 to retrieve the object reference. If there is no object, just fail silently:

```
// Check if the form exists
if(!(form = ADS.$(form))) { return false; }
```

If you want, you could alert a warning message indicating that the form doesn't exist, but failing silently allows the load event to exist on a dynamically generated page that may not necessarily have the form. This way the page is enhanced if there is a form but ignored otherwise.

Modifying the file inputs

The exact location of your file input elements in the DOM tree isn't important, as you'll only be adding a few event listeners to them. Since you don't need the position, you can quickly retrieve all the <input> elements within the form and iterate over them looking for the specific file types using the getElementsByTagName() method:

```
// Find all the file input elements
var allInputs = form.getElementsByTagName('INPUT');
var input;
var fileInputs = [];
for(var i=0 ; (input = allInputs[i]) ; i++) {
    if(input.getAttribute('type') == 'file') {
        fileInputs.push(input);
    }
}

// If there are no file inputs then stop
if(fileInputs.length == 0) { return false; }
```

With your list of the inputs in fileInputs, you can now do a little bit of error checking to make the form more user-friendly.

File input elements allow you to specify an accept attribute that contains a comma-separated list of allowable MIME types. Most browsers ignore this information, so even if you specify image/jpeg, you can still select and upload any other file types, and the browser won't complain. This is one reason why it's also important to check the file type on the server side and reject anything you're not expecting. You can, however, at least verify that the extensions on the selected files in the file inputs match the desired MIME types, and if not, indicate to the user that what they're about to try isn't going to succeed.

At the top of the uploader.js file, I've included a verifyFileType() method:

```
function verifyFileType(fileInput) {
    if(!fileInput.value || !fileInput.accept) return true;
    var extension = fileInput.value.split('.').pop().toLowerCase();
    var mimetypes = fileInput.accept.toLowerCase().split(',');
    var type;
    for(var i in mimetypes) {
        type = mimetypes[i].split('/')[1];
        if(type == extension || (type=='jpeg' && extension=='jpg')) {
            return true;
        }
    }
    return false;
}
```

This method takes a file input element and verifies if the extension of the selected file matches the MIME types in the accept attribute. This method will only work for MIME types where the second part of the MIME type matches the extension, for example:

image/**png**

and

Filename.**png**

In the case of JPEG files, the MIME type is image/jpeg, but the extension is often simply .jpg, so I've added an additional check. If you want to add additional file types, you'll have to modify this method to match.

Next, In the addProgressBar() method, add the following loop to create a change event listener for each of the file inputs in your fileInputs array:

```
// Add a change event to verify the extension based on the mime types.
for(var i=0 ; (fileInput = fileInputs[i]) ; i++) {
    // Add file type check using a change event listener
    ADS.addEvent(fileInput,'change',function(W3CEvent) {
        var ok = verifyFileType(this);
        if(!ok) {
            if(!ADS.hasClassName(this,'error')) {
                ADS.addClassName(this,'error');
            }
            alert('Sorry, that file type is not allowed. Please ➥
select one of: ' + this.accept.toLowerCase());
        } else {
            ADS.removeClassName(this,'error');
        }
    });
}
```

When the file path is changed in the file input element, your change event listener will invoke to verify the extension against the MIME type and, if necessary, modify the class name to indicate an error. As you saw in Chapter 5, modifying the class name allows you to easily separate the visual appearance from the DOM script.

If you take a quick look at the style.css file, you'll see the error rules associated with the class name changes in the progress bar:

```
input.error {
    background-color: red;
}
p.error {
    color: red;
}
```

If there's a validation error with the file name, the file input's class will be modified to include a class name of error and the page will be modified as shown in Figure 8-3:

```
<input class="error" type="file" id="newFile1" name="newFile1" ➥
accept="image/jpeg,image/gif,image/png"/>
```

If you try out your page with the modifications you've made so far, you'll see that even these simple enhancements improve the overall elegance and functionality—all unobtrusively. The form will still submit and reload the page, but at least you have a little feedback when selecting the wrong files.

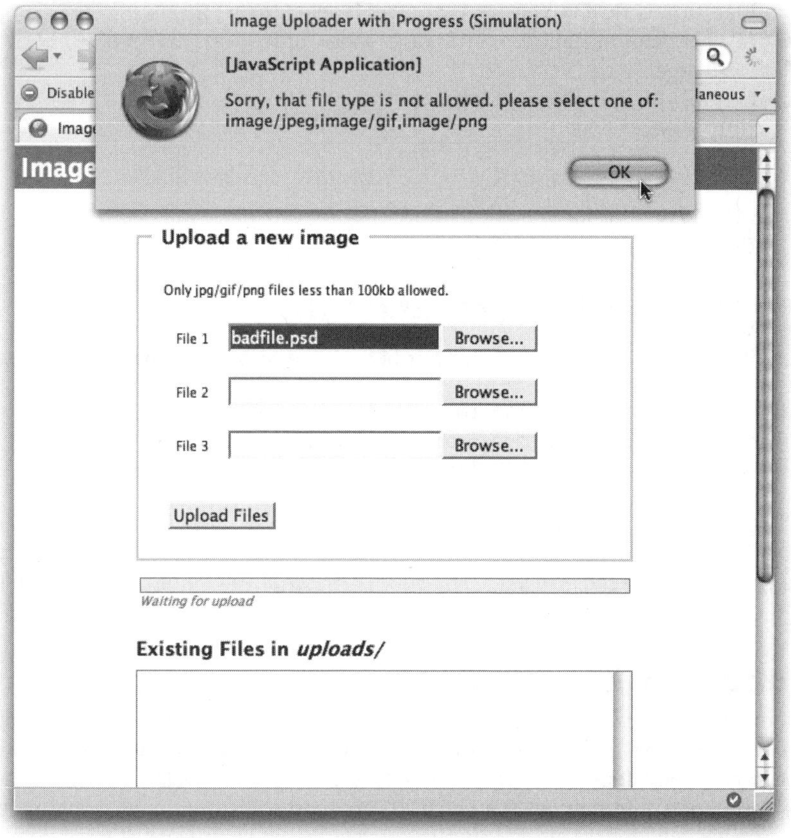

Figure 8-3. A file upload in an error state indicating a wrong file type

Redirecting the form

The next challenge will be to redirect the form to that inline iframe we discussed earlier so that the page doesn't reload when you upload the files. Ideally, you could just use document.createElement() to make a new iframe element, but it's not quite so easy. Internet Explorer doesn't like it when you try to alter the name attribute of an iframe created this way, so you can't target your form at it. As a work around, you'll have to use innerHTML, which will create the object as expected. This also means you need a container to put it in, so you'll have to create a <div> as well:

```
// Append the target iframe for the upload.
// In IE the name attribute doesn't set properly using DOM
// such as:
// var uploadTargetFrame = document.createElement('iframe');
// uploadTargetFrame.setAttribute('id','uploadTargetFrame');
// uploadTargetFrame.setAttribute('name','uploadTargetFrame');
// To work around this create a div and use the innerHTML
// property which will render the name correctly in IE and
// other browsers.
```

361

```
var uploadTargetFrame = document.createElement('div');
uploadTargetFrame.innerHTML = '<iframe name="uploadTargetFrame"↦
id="uploadTargetFrame"></frame>';
ADS.setStyleById(uploadTargetFrame,{
    'width':'0',
    'height':'0',
    'border':'0',
    'visibility':'hidden',
    'zIndex':'-1'
});
document.body.appendChild(uploadTargetFrame);
```

With the new iframe in place, set the target attribute of the form to the name of the new iframe:

```
// Modify the target of the form to be the new iframe.
// This will prevent the page from reloading.
form.setAttribute('target','uploadTargetFrame');
```

This doesn't require you to modify the form action in any way. You still want the page to submit exactly as it did, you just want to prevent the page from reloading. Instead of reloading the page, your new iframe will reload with the new page, and your DOM script will be responsible for modifying the current page to reflect the appropriate changes.

And the magic word is . . .

To track the progress of the POST request, you'll need to create the unique and random APC_UPLOAD_PROGRESS key that you can then pass along with each request. When you submit a request, the server-side scripts will use the key to group together related requests to store and retrieve the appropriate information. The initial POST request will store the goal and update progress along the way, while additional asynchronous requests with the same key will be able to retrieve the progress from the stored information.

> As I mentioned earlier, in the case of the PHP and APC plug-in, this special key must be part of the original POST request and must be called APC_UPLOAD_PROGRESS. For convenience, the Perl version of the script and the simulation script have been written to use the same field name so that the server-side scripts can be interchangeable.

Next, in the addProgressBar() method, you'll need to *prepend* a new hidden input field to the form. It's important that the hidden field comes before the file inputs so that the server can retrieve the special key before processing the files. The hidden filed must be named APC_UPLOAD_PROGRESS, and its value must be a very unique string such as a large random number that would be difficult to predict:

```
// Create a unique ID to track uploading.
var uniqueID = 'A' + Math.floor(Math.random() * 1000000000000000);

// Add the unique ID as the APC_UPLOAD_PROGRESS key.
// It must be added before the file inputs so that the server
// will receive it first and trigger the progress information.
```

```
var uniqueIDField = document.createElement('input');
uniqueIDField.setAttribute('type','hidden');
uniqueIDField.setAttribute('value',uniqueID);
uniqueIDField.setAttribute('name','APC_UPLOAD_PROGRESS');
form.insertBefore(uniqueIDField,form.firstChild);
```

If you reload the page in your web browser, you'll see that the form will now submit—without reloading the page—but it will seem as though nothing is happening, because you still need to create the progress indicator and retrieve the progress information from the server to modify the page as necessary.

The progress bar

The progress bar itself consists of only three nested DOM elements: a container, an outer box, and the progressing bar itself as represented by this HTML fragment:

```
<span class="progressContainer" style="display: block;">
    <span class="progressBackground">
        <span class="progressBar"/></span>
        <span class="progressMessage"></span>
    </span>
</span>
```

The progress of the request will be indicated by adjusting the width of the .progressBar element to the percentage of completion. The reason for the two additional boxes is to allow the stylistic design to place padding and margin styles, if desired, on the .progressContainer and .progressBackground.

If you try to apply a stylistic margin to the .progressBar element, the 100 percent width would cause it to protrude from the side, as the bar will be 100 percent of the parent element—ignoring the margin—as illustrated in the chapter8/progressbar/problems.html file shown in Figure 8-4.

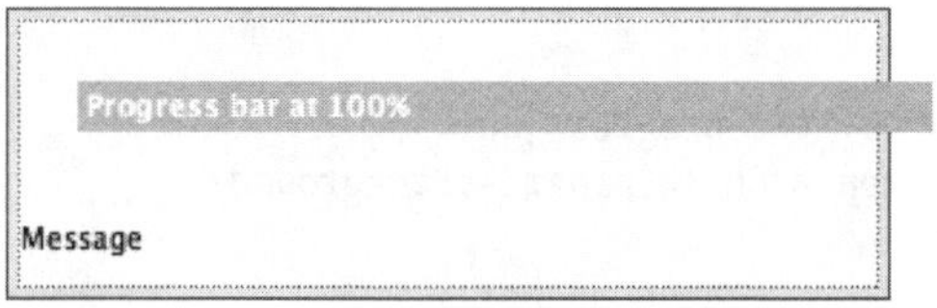

Figure 8-4. The progress bar protrudes from the side of the parent element if you try to apply a stylistic margin to it.

How and where you add the progress bar is up to you, but to be *really* friendly to other developers, you may want to allow them to optionally indicate where the progress bar should be placed in the markup. To do this, add the following to the addProgressBar() method, which includes a check for an existing DOM element with a progressContainer class name:

```
// Create the different pieces for the progress indicator.

// The bar
var progressBar = document.createElement('span')
progressBar.className = 'progressBar';
```

363

```
ADS.setStyle(progressBar,{
    'display':'block'
});

// The inner background container
var progressBackground = document.createElement('span')
progressBackground.className = 'progressBackground';
ADS.setStyle(progressBackground,{
    'display':'block',
    'height':'10px'
});
progressBackground.appendChild(progressBar);

// Check for an existing anchor point.
// It must be a span with the progressContainer class.
var progressContainer = ADS.getElementsByClassName(
    'progressContainer',
    'span'
)[0];

// If it doesn't exist create one and append it to the form.
if(!progressContainer) {
    progressContainer = document.createElement('span')
    progressContainer.className = 'progressContainer';
    form.appendChild(progressContainer);
}

// Set the container to a block style.
ADS.setStyle(progressContainer,{
    'display':'block'
});

// Append the rest of the progress bar.
progressContainer.appendChild(progressBackground);

// Add a progress message area as well.
var progressMessage = document.createElement('span')
progressMessage.className = 'progressMessage';
progressContainer.appendChild(progressMessage);
```

By doing this, you first check for a specific object in the DOM tree marked with the progressContainer class to use as the container such as:

```
<span class="progressContainer"></span>
```

If an element with the appropriate class doesn't exist, you append the progress bar in the default location at the bottom of the form.

Next, to make things a little less redundant, add this private updateProgressBar() method within the addProgressBar() method:

```
// Create a private method that will be used below by the
// progress watcher to update the progress bar and message.
function updateProgressBar(percent,message,satus) {
    progressMessage.innerHTML = message;
    ADS.removeClassName(progressMessage,'error');
    ADS.removeClassName(progressMessage,'complete');
    ADS.removeClassName(progressMessage,'waiting');
    ADS.removeClassName(progressMessage,'uploading');
    ADS.addClassName(progressMessage,satus);

    // The CSS and className will take
    // care of the status indications
    ADS.setStyle(progressBar,{
        'width':percent
    });
}
// Initiate the bar at 0% and waiting.
updateProgressBar('0%','Waiting for upload','waiting');
```

This private method is within the scope of the outer addProgressBar() method, so you can use it to consistently update the progress bar from any point inside addProgressBar(). This will make the rest of the code in the next step a little cleaner.

Tracking progress

The last step in your addProgressBar() method will be to create the form's submit event listener. This will involve a few tricky elements, so first finish the addProgressBar() method by adding the following submit event listener and then we'll look at what it does:

```
// Add a submit event to the form that will verify the form
// information and update the progress bar.
ADS.addEvent(form,'submit',function(W3CEvent){

    // Check the inputs again to make sure they have
    // the right extensions.
    var ok = true;
    var hasFiles = false;
    for(var i=0 ; (fileInput = fileInputs[i]) ; i++) {
        if(fileInput.value.length>0) {
            hasFiles = true;
        }
        if(!verifyFileType(fileInput)) {
            // highlight the file input as an error
            if(!ADS.hasClassName(fileInput,'error')) {
                ADS.addClassName(fileInput,'error');
            }
            ok = false;
        }
    }
```

```
            if(!ok || !hasFiles) {
                // If they don't alert the user to fix the problem.
                ADS.preventDefault(W3CEvent);
                alert('Please select some valid files.');
                return false;
            }


            // Disable the form elements by alerting a warning message.
            function warning(W3CEvent) {
                ADS.preventDefault(W3CEvent);
                alert('There is an upload in progress. Please wait.');
            }
            for(var i=0 ; (input = allInputs[i]) ; i++) {
                // input.setAttribute('disabled','disabled');
                ADS.addEvent(input,'mousedown',warning);
            }

            // Create a function to reenable the form after the upload
            // is complete. This will be called from within the Ajax
            // event listeners.
            function clearWarnings() {
                // Remove the warning from the form elements.
                for(var i=0 ; (input = allInputs[i]) ; i++) {
                    ADS.removeEvent(input,'mousedown',warning);
                }

                // Update the ID and form with a new ID number
                // so that the next upload will not conflict with
                // this one.
                uniqueID = Math.floor(Math.random() * 1000000000000000);
                uniqueIDField.setAttribute('value',uniqueID);
            }

            // Update the progress bar.
            updateProgressBar('0%','Beginning','waiting');

            // set a counter for the simulation
            var counter = 0;

            // Create an new method to trigger a new progress request.
            var progressWatcher = function() {

                // Request the progress using the unique key.
                ADS.ajaxRequest(form.action
                    + (form.action.indexOf('?') == -1 ? '?' : '&')
                    + 'key=' + uniqueID + '&sim=' + (++counter) , {
```

```
// The server side script will be returning the
// the appropriate headers so we'll use the
// json listener.
jsonResponseListener:function(response) {
    // Check the response to see if there was an
    // error in the server side script

    if(!response) {
        // There was an invalid response.
        updateProgressBar(
            '0%',
            'Invalid response from progress watcher',
            'error'
        );
        // The request is finished so clear warnings
        clearWarnings();
    } else if(response.error) {
        // An error was reported by the server.
        updateProgressBar('0%',response.error,'error');
        // The request is finished so clear warnings
        clearWarnings();
    } else if(response.done == 1) {
        // The post has completed.
        updateProgressBar(
            '100%',
            'Upload Complete',
            'complete'
        );
        // The request is finished so clear warnings
        clearWarnings();
        // Pass the new information to the user
        // supplied modification handler.
        if(modificationHandler.constructor == Function) {
            modificationHandler(response);
        }
    } else {
        // Update the progress bar and return the
        // result. The result will be null so the
        // return will simply stop execution of the
        // rest of the method.
        updateProgressBar(
            Math.round(response.current/➡
response.total*100)+'%',
            response.current
                + ' of '
                + response.total
                + '. '
                + 'Uploading file: ' +
                response.currentFileName,
```

```
                    'uploading'
                );

                // Execute the progress watcher again.
                setTimeout(progressWatcher,1000);

            }

        },
        errorListener:function() {
            // There was an error with the ajax request so
            // then the user know
            updateProgressBar('0%',this.status,'error');

            // and clear the warnings
            clearWarnings();

        }
    });
};

// Start watching...
setTimeout(progressWatcher,1000);

});
```

> *You've probably noticed throughout the chapter that the* addProgressBar() *method relies heavily on the closure and scope chain features of JavaScript. At the beginning of the method, you've defined variables such as the list of file input in the* fileInputs *variable, but throughout the rest of the method, that same variable can be referenced in the listener. The listeners execute attached to the various objects, such as the form and file elements, but the scope chain still applies to where the code originated in the written script.*

The form's submit listener starts off by again verifying that the file input paths contain the appropriate extensions. You need to do this again simply because the original change listener warning could have been ignored, and there's no point in submitting the form if it contains invalid files.

Next, you prevent multiple submissions or alterations during upload by adding a warning method as a mousedown event listener on all input elements in the form:

```
// Disable the form elements by alerting a warning message.
function warning(W3CEvent) {
    ADS.preventDefault(W3CEvent);
    alert('There is an upload in progress. Please wait.');
}
for(var i=0 ; (input = allInputs[i]) ; i++) {
    ADS.addEvent(input,'mousedown',warning);
}
```

This will also let your users know that they have to wait until the process is finished and the elements are reenabled, before they can try again.

The progress itself will be monitored using the ADS.ajaxRequest() method from Chapter 7, passing along the unique key with each request:

```
ADS.ajaxRequest ('actions/?key=' + uniqueID,{ ... });
```

To avoid a wildly changing progress bar and conflicts that would behave erratically and reverse direction at times, the completion of a request itself invokes the next request—using setTimeout() to pause for a second:

```
// Execute the progress watcher again.
setTimeout(progressWatcher,1000);
```

> *If you're expecting an excessive amount of traffic you may want to increase the delay between requests. A longer delay will mean a jerkier progress bar but also less traffic and load on the server.*

This also helps avoid a situation where the final "finished" response could arrive before earlier requests, creating a lot of confusion in the script and leaving the progress bar in an unfinished state.

> *The request also includes a counter,* 'actions/?key=' + uniqueID + '&sim=' + *(++counter), which is only used in the simulation script to keep track of how many requests have been sent.*

Each progress response from the server will contain the total and current bytes processed as well as additional information about the current state of the POST request, as you saw earlier in the chapter. The response uses a Content-Type of application/json, so you can use the jsonResponseListener in the ADS.ajaxRequest() request to check the response and update the elements of the page as required.

> *If you alter the server-side script or want to use a different* Content-Type *for your response, you may need to adjust which listener method you're using to process the request in the* ADS.ajaxRequest()*. See Chapter 7 for a list of all the listener methods you added.*

When you encounter an invalid response or an error in the response, you can display appropriate messages and changes using the updateProgressBar() method. Likewise, if successful, you'll pass the list of successfully processed files to the supplied modificationHandler method so that the page can be updated as necessary:

```
    if(!response) {
        // There was an invalid response.
        updateProgressBar(
            '0%',
            'Invalid response from progress watcher',
            'error'
        );
        // The request is finished so clear warnings
        clearWarnings();
    } else if(response.error) {
        // An error was reported by the server.
        updateProgressBar('0%',response.error,'error');
        // The request is finished so clear warnings
        clearWarnings();
    } else if(response.done == 1) {
        // The post has completed.
        updateProgressBar('100%','Upload Complete','complete');
        // The request is finished so clear warnings
        clearWarnings();
        // Pass the new information to the user
        // supplied modification handler.
        if(modificationHandler.constructor == Function) {
            modificationHandler(response);
        }
    } else {
        // Update the progress bar and return the
        // result. The result will be null so the
        // return will simply stop execution of the
        // rest of the method.
        updateProgressBar(
            Math.round(response.current/response.total*100)+'%',
            response.current
                + ' of '
                + response.total
                + '. '
                + 'Uploading file: ' +
                response.currentFileName,
            'uploading'
        );

        // Execute the progress watcher again.
        setTimeout(progressWatcher,1000);
    }

}
```

You also revert the form elements to a usable state by calling the clearWarnings() method after an error or a "finished" response. At the same time, you update the unique ID key associated with the form so that the next upload will have a different ID:

```
// Create a function to reenable the form after the upload
// is complete. This will be called from within the Ajax
// event listeners.
function clearWarnings() {
    // Remove the warning from the form elements.
    for(var i=0 ; (input = allInputs[i]) ; i++) {
        ADS.removeEvent(input,'mousedown',warning);
    }

    // Update the ID and form with a new ID number
    // so that the next upload will not conflict with
    // this one.
    uniqueID = Math.floor(Math.random() * 1000000000000000);
    uniqueIDField.setAttribute('value',uniqueID);
}
```

If you use the same ID over and over, you could run into a situation where two different, unrelated requests begin to conflict with one another. Updating the ID ensures that each form submission will have its own unique ID.

With all this in place, though you can still upload files without JavaScript, with the behavioral enhancements, you'll get a nice indication of progress as you wait for the request to finish, as shown in Figure 8-5.

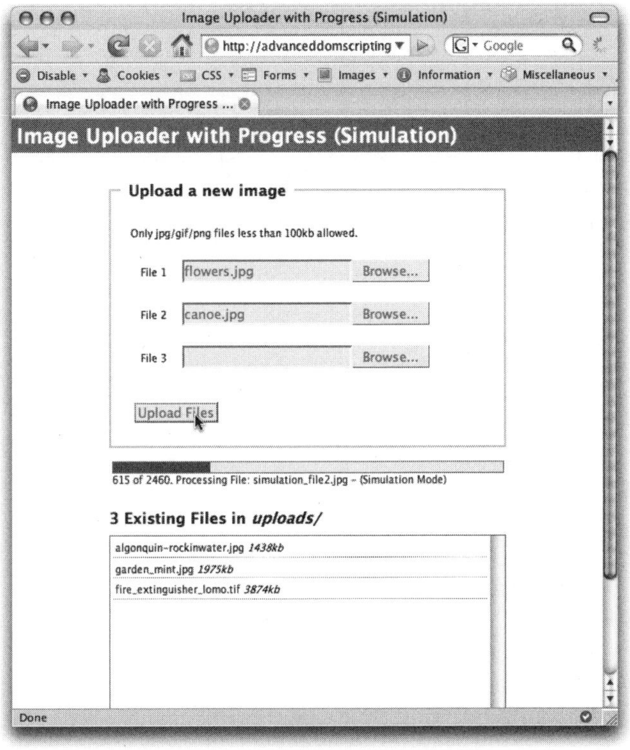

Figure 8-5. The final progress bar in action

Summary

Progress bars are tricky things, especially when trying to track file uploads, but the methods you learned in this chapter can apply to any lengthy process on the server, not just file uploads. You just need to set up a system where progress can be stored and later retrieved. Take a good look at the accompanying server-side script, and you can see how to track progress for the necessary feedback. Providing proper feedback will reduce the frustration users may experience in waiting for an undetermined amount of time.

This chapter concludes Part 2 of the book, and you'll no longer be adding anything to the ADS library. Your personal library is filled with a lot of useful methods that you'll probably use every day. In Part 3, you'll be looking more at third-party libraries, such as Prototype and Script.aculo.us, and you'll see a number of ways to improve your productivity and subtly enhance your web applications with minimal additional work.

Part Three

SOME GREAT SOURCE

Chapter 9

USING LIBRARIES TO INCREASE PRODUCTIVITY

The current state of JavaScript development, as I've alluded to before, is very different from its state four or five years ago. One major change is that we don't need to write all our code ourselves anymore—several means exist to make coding quicker and easier than ever before. In Part 3, we'll be covering libraries, effects, and third-party application programming interfaces (APIs), but the focus of this chapter is libraries.

Libraries are great sources of ready-made code that you can quickly plug into your existing development framework. They provide quick solutions for most of your mundane day-to-day DOM scripting tasks as well as providing a number of unique tools. They are wonderful, but using libraries is not the bandage for every problem.

Before diving into any library, be sure to take the time to actually learn both JavaScript and the DOM. Since Chapter 1 of this book, I've emphasized the necessity of learning *how* things work and not simply what they do. There are many wonderful libraries out there, some of which I'll talk about in this chapter, but having no understanding of what's going on behind the scenes will be detrimental to both you and your web application. Without that deeper understanding, you'll be lost in the small details that a library often assumes you already know.

In this chapter, I'm going to focus on increasing your productivity by using the features of the following libraries:

- **DOMAssistant**: http://www.robertnyman.com/domass/
- **jQuery**: http://jquery.com
- **MochiKit**: http://mochikit.com
- **Prototype**: http://prototypejs.org
- **Yahoo User Interface (YUI)**: http://developer.yahoo.com/yui/

In Chapter 10, we'll look at all the eye candy effects you can add using some of these same libraries along with a few others. Just to be clear, I'm not personally affiliated with any of these libraries, so I have no personal bias toward one or the other, but I have made a few small contributions—sometimes just filling in some missing pieces in the documentation or suggesting improvements. I'm also not saying these libraries are ultimately the best for every situation nor that they are the only ones available. These simply nicely met the criteria for inclusion in this chapter (which I'll discuss next) and provide some of the cleanest solutions for each area I'll discuss.

To focus on productivity, we're going to revisit some of the topics you've already seen in this book including:

- Enhancing the DOM
- Handling events
- Accessing and manipulating style
- Communicating with Ajax

And you'll see how each library handles these tasks. Also, each library can accomplish pretty much every task in one way or another, so I'll point out the two or three methods that I feel are the best or most useful for each area—I won't be covering every aspect of each library, so be sure to check the documentation for each to find out what else is available.

> *All the examples in this chapter can be found in the source code in* chapter9/, *where I've divided up the code by library rather than function.*

After reading this chapter, you'll have a better understanding of what these libraries have to offer and how they differ, so choosing the library that's right for you will be a little easier.

Choosing the library that's right for you

When you decide it's time to investigate a library, the biggest problem is choosing among the hundreds that are available. When deciding, there are several criteria you should consider:

- **Does it have all the features you're looking for?** Mixing and matching libraries can be problematic if they're not set up with proper namespaces and such. Common methods such as $() or get() often use the same syntax but handle things differently. Additionally, if you use more than one library at the same time, you'll usually end up with a lot of duplicated features and redundant code.

- **Does it have more features than you need?** Having too few features is one problem, but a bulky library with too many is also a problem. When a library has more features than you need, you may want to consider a lighter version that won't take as long to download. Many, such as Prototype, also have "lite" counterparts that have been stripped of some features. You can also use a JavaScript compressor to reduce the size of the code. A compressor will rewrite the code so that it uses fewer characters and creates a smaller file—but don't even bother trying to read the code in a compressed version, as it won't be human friendly.

- **Is it modular?** Libraries with abundant features often work around file size problems by modularizing features into different files. This lets you minimize file size by loading only the files and features you need. Most of the time, you'll have to be sure to include all the necessary files, but a few libraries may offer a dynamic loading mechanism where you only need to include one file and that file will fetch others as necessary.

- **Is it well supported?** Lack of an active developer community equals no bug fixes or feature improvements. Also, many eyes looking at and sharing the same library means fewer bugs and more reliable results. A good community behind the library not only brings fixes and features but also a lot of support when you run into a problem and need more help.

- **Does it have documentation?** Without documentation, you'll be lost. Sure, you might come across some example that others have hacked together, but a lack of documentation usually indicates a lack of enthusiasm by developers and thus a project that may be going nowhere.

- **Does it have the right license?** Just because you can view the source online doesn't mean it's free for the taking. Before using a library, verify that its license covers what you intended to do with it. Also, don't forget to check the requirements of the license itself. Many licenses allow you to do whatever you like without consequence, but others require that you release your code under an identical license, making it unsuitable for a closed source proprietary environment.

> *Once you've chosen an appropriate library and you're producing great things, don't forget to try to contribute back to the community! These libraries are all built by dedicated developers who are often working with what little spare time they have to improve the tools you use daily. If you can't help with development efforts or bug testing, you could always provide examples and tutorials or simply help build the documentation—any effort is helpful and will make the library even better.*

The libraries

For this chapter, I've selected a few libraries based on the preceding criteria as well as general popularity and a bit of personal preference. Each has its own pros and cons as outlined in the following sections.

DOMAssistant

DOMAssistant (http://robertnyman.com/domass) "provides a simpler and more consistent way to script against the Document Object Model (DOM) in web browsers." DOMAssistant is lightweight and modular, which is great for keeping your file size down. The lack of Ajax communication methods means you'll need another library—or your own—for those bits, but that's not necessarily a bad thing considering the problems you saw in Chapter 7. Selecting elements is a little limited—including only "by id" and "by class name"—where other libraries have more advanced CSS selector expressions, as you'll see later in the chapter.

- **License**: DOMAssistant uses the Creative Commons Attribution ShareAlike 2.5 license (http://creativecommons.org/licenses/by-sa/2.5/deed.en).

- **Namespace**: If the individual DOMAssistant methods don't already exist in the window scope, the library will register many of them. If you've first loaded another library with conflicting methods, DOMAssistant won't overwrite the existing methods, so you'll need to reference all the DOMAssistant methods by including the appropriate namespace, such as DOMAssistant.$().

jQuery

jQuery (http://jquery.com) "is a fast, concise, JavaScript Library that simplifies how you traverse HTML documents, handle events, perform animations, and add Ajax interactions to your web pages." jQuery's extremely powerful selection method allows you to retrieve DOM elements using a combination of IDs, CSS, and XPath selectors. Simplified Ajax and event methods combined with the chaining syntax will make your code compact and easy to follow. There is also a very large community behind jQuery with a number of different plug-in developers who've added features beyond the library basics.

- **License**: jQuery uses the MIT license (http://www.opensource.org/licenses/mit-license. php) and the General Public License, or GPL (http://opensource.org/licenses/ gpl-license.php).

- **Namespace**: If you're using jQuery by itself, you can use the shorthand $() method as an alternative to the jQuery() method. If you want to use jQuery along with another library, that has already defined the $() function in the window scope, such as Prototype, you need to include a call to the noConflict() method at the start of your script to prevent jQuery from overriding the $() function:

  jQuery.noConflict();

  For more about using jQuery with other libraries, see http://docs.jquery.com/Using_ jQuery_with_Other_Libraries.

Mochikit

According to its web site, MochiKit (http://mochikit.com) "makes JavaScript suck less." Being well tested and documented (but it could use a few more examples), Mochikit offers much of the same DOM manipulation methods as the other libraries. It incorporates color and visual effects, as well as its own logging pane for debugging—making other libraries unnecessary. Custom events and built-in drag-and-drop support also make writing your web applications easier.

- **License**: This library uses the MIT license (http://www.opensource.org/licenses/mit-license.php) and the Academic Free License, v2.1 (http://www.opensource.org/licenses/afl-2.1.php).

- **Namepace**: The MochiKit library is separated into several subobjects within the MochiKit namespace. For example, the ifilter method can be accessed using

```
ifilter(...)
```

or

```
MochiKit.Iter.ifilter(...)
```

When loaded, the methods are all registered to the window namespace. If you want to prevent this, you need to include some inline JavaScript in the head of your HTML file *before* you include the library:

```
<script type="text/javascript">
    // Prevent collisions
    MochiKit = {__export__: false};
</script>
<script src="/path/to/MochiKit.js" type="text/javascript"></script>
```

Prototype

Prototype (http://prototypejs.org) "is a JavaScript Framework that aims to ease development of dynamic web applications." You'll recall that I've already mentioned Prototype a few times throughout the book. It has a number of great DOM manipulation functions as well as one of the more popular Ajax objects and that infamous $() function. My only complaint with Prototype is the lack of a namespace, meaning it doesn't play very well with other libraries.

- **License**: Prototype uses the MIT license (http://www.opensource.org/licenses/mit-license.php).

- **Namespace**: Prototype isn't contained in any sort of namespace, so all methods are registered in the window scope.

Yahoo User Interface library

The Yahoo! User Interface (YUI) library (http://developer.yahoo.com/yui) "is a set of utilities and controls, written in JavaScript, for building richly interactive web applications using techniques such as DOM scripting, DHTML and AJAX. The YUI library also includes several core CSS resources." The YUI has a great developer community and tons of documentation. The libraries are filled with every feature you can think of from simple DOM manipulation to advanced effect and fully featured widgets. As a whole, the library is nicely divided into small files and namespaces, but it sometimes becomes overwhelming trying to determine what you need and where to find it—you know it's big when just the cheat sheet is 20 pages.

- **License**: YUI uses the BSD license (http://developer.yahoo.com/yui/license.txt).

- **Namespace**: The Yahoo library is separated into various subobjects within the YAHOO namespace. The library itself is also divided into several files, so you'll have to be sure to include the appropriate ones for each object. For the specific namespace for each object, check the developer documentation at http://developer.yahoo.com/yui.

> *Not all libraries follow the nice namespace conventions you set for yourself at the beginning of this book. Libraries such as Prototype, jQuery, and DOMAssistant all share the same $() function you added to your ADS library, but fortunately, all the libraries discussed in this section—with the exception of Prototype—have alternative namespace versions, so all of the examples throughout this chapter will use the full namespaces. If you decide to use one of these libraries in your production environment and you only use that one, you could use the short form versions instead. See the documentation for the specific libraries to see what shorthand versions they offer.*

Enhancing the DOM

When it comes to DOM scripting, the DOM enhancements offered by each library are often their biggest selling points. Adding features and dealing with browsers' incompatibilities of existing features is where libraries shine. Let's take a look at a few of the DOM-enhancing features in the libraries I mentioned and see how they can help you get to the elements you need a lot quicker.

Chaining syntax

You're already familiar with simple access methods, such as your ADS.$() function:

```
// Your ADS $() method
var elementReference = ADS.$('browserList');
```

Additionally, you've seen how you can combine different functions, such as using the $() function when retrieving the element object before passing it into the ADS.getElementsByClassName() method:

```
// Your ADS method
var browserAnchors = ADS.getElementsByClassName(
    'browser',
    'a',
    ADS.$('browserList')
);
```

This same idea of single use methods applies to other libraries as well. MochiKit and YUI both follow this same pattern by providing methods to locate elements in a similar way:

```
// MochiKit library
// Locate all the a.browser anchors within the #browserList id.
var browserAnchors = MochiKit.DOM.getElementsByTagAndClassName(
    'a',
    'browser',
    MochiKit.DOM.$('browserList')
);
```

```
// YUI library
// Locate all the a.browser anchors within the #browserList id.
```

```
var browserAnchors = YAHOO.util.Dom.getElementsByClassName(
    'browser',
    'a',
    YAHOO.util.Dom.get('browserList')
);
```

> In both the preceding examples, you don't need to retrieve the DOM reference to browserList and could simply pass in browserList as a string and achieve the same result. I've only shown it this way to illustrate the point of the different methods working together.

This idea of single use methods is common among libraries, and it's the same idea I chose to pre-sent in the ADS library you've been building throughout the book. An alternative, and a methodology that follows the JavaScript syntax more closely, is chaining.

When using your ADS.$() method, you can use it in a chain with other DOM-specific methods, such as getElementsByTagName():

```
var list = ADS.$('example').getElementsByTagName('a');
```

This is great, but you're limited to the DOM-specific methods—you can't use your other custom methods in the same way. Some libraries, such as DOMAssistant, jQuery, and Prototype (along with portions of the others), use their retrieval methods to add additional static methods directly to the returned element(s). Once modified, the additional methods allow you to chain the library-specific methods along with the standard methods in the same call:

```
// DOMAssistant library (using method chaining)
// Locate all the a.browser anchors within the #browserList id
var browserAnchors = DOMAssistant.$(
    'browserList'
).getElementsByClassName(
    'browser',
    'a'
);

// jQuery library (using method chaining)
// Locate all the a.browser anchors within the #browserList id
var browserAnchors = jQuery('#browserList').find('a.browser');

// Prototype library (using method chaining)
// Locate all the a.browser anchors within the #browserList id
var browserAnchors = $('browserList').getElementsByClassName(
    'browser'
).findAll(
    function(e) {
        return e.nodeName == 'A';
    }
);
```

381

This allows you to condense your code into semantic methods without degrading the readability. In most cases, they can also be combined with existing DOM methods:

```
// jQuery library (using method chaining)
// Locate all the a.browser anchors within the #browserList id
// and retrieve the nodeValue of the first node
var value = jQuery('#browserList').find('a')[0].firstChild.nodeValue;
```

Of course, you can still separate out the pieces if need be by assigning the results to variables:

```
var browserList = jQuery('#browserList');
var browserAnchors = browserList.find('a.browser');
var value = browserAnchors[0].firstNode.nodeValue;
```

When using chaining, be careful that you don't assume too much when you combine the regular methods with library methods. If you try the previous example when the #browserList element isn't available on the page, the jQuery methods will deal with the missing element by trying to access the [0] index in the expected array, and you will be notified of the error shown in Figure 9-1.

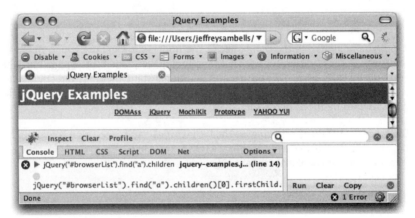

Figure 9-1. An error indicating the chaining syntax failed when accessing the nonexistent array

Advanced selection with expressions

Selecting elements by id is great, but selecting elements using CSS selectors is even better. Many libraries incorporate advanced selector methods:

- The Prototype $$() method:

```
// Prototype library advanced selectors
// Locate all the a.browser anchors within the #browserList id
var browserAnchors = $$('#browserList a.browser');
```

- The MochiKit.Selector.$$() method:

```
// MochiKit library advanced selectors
// Locate all the a.browser anchors within the #browserList id
var browserAnchors = MochiKit.Selector.$$('#browserList a.browser');
```

- The base jQuery() method:

```
// jQuery library advanced selectors
// Locate all the a.browser anchors within the #browserList id
var browserAnchors = jQuery('#browserList a.browser');
```

These three methods provide awesome flexibility when searching for and retrieving elements. You can use a variety of CSS selectors (http://www.w3.org/TR/css3-selectors/#selectors) to select specific elements, and if the browser supports DOM Level 3 XPath (http://www.w3.org/TR/xpath), these queries can be extremely fast (depending on support in the library).

> *The MochiKit $$() selector method is only available in version 1.4 or higher as a member of the* MochiKit.Selector *object. As of this writing, version 1.4 is still in development, so you'll have to download the latest development release to use the advanced selectors.*

Each of the methods supports a number of different CSS selectors:

- * selects all elements.
- tag selects all tag elements for each of the available HTML tags.
- tagA tagB selects all tagB elements that are descendents of tagA elements.
- tagA,tagB,tagC selects all tagA elements, tagB elements, and tagC elements.
- #id and tag#id are ID selectors for any ID or a specific tag-ID combination.
- .className and tag.className are selectors that can be used for any class or tag class combination.
- You can also combine selectors such as #myList li or ul li a.selectMe to select any mix of descendent selectors separated by a space.

Also, you can include CSS 2.1 attribute selectors as follows:

- tag[attr] selects all tag elements that have attribute attr.
- tag[attr=value] selects all tag elements where value is exactly equal to the attr attribute value.
- tag[attr~=value] selects all tag elements where the value is contained in the attr attribute value.
- tag[attr^=value] selects all tag elements where value matches the beginning of the attr attribute value.
- tag[attr$=value] selects all tag elements were value matches the end of the attr attribute value.
- tag[attr|=value] selects all tag elements were value matches the first part of a hyphenated attr attribute value.
- tag[attr!=value] selects all tag elements where value is not equal to the attribute's.

For all attribute selectors, if the value contains a space, it must be enclosed in quotation marks, for example:

    $$('a[title="Hello World!"]');

You can also use a number of different child and sibling selectors as follows:

- tagA > tagB selects all tagB elements that are direct child descendents of tagA elements.
- tagA + tagB selects all tagB sibling elements that immediately follow tagA elements.
- tagA ~ tagB selects tagA elements with a preceding sibling tagB element.

You can also use several pseudoclass and pseudoelement selectors, including these:

- tag:root selects the tag element that is the root of the document.
- tag:nth-child(n) selects all tag elements that are the nth children of their parents, counting from the first one.
- tag:nth-last-child(n) selects all tag elements that are the nth child of their parents, counting from the last one.
- tag:nth-of-type(n) selects all tag elements that are the nth sibling of their type, counting from the first one.
- tag:nth-last-of-type(n) selects all tag elements that are the nth sibling of their type, counting from the last one.
- tag:first-child selects any tag element that is the first child of its parents.
- tag:last-child selects any tag element that is the last child of its parent.
- tag:first-of-type selects any tag elements that is the first sibling of its type.
- tag:last-of-type selects any tag element that is the last sibling of its type.
- tag:only-child selects any tag element that is an only child of its parent.
- tag:only-of-type selects any tag element that is the only sibling of its type.
- tag:empty selects all tag elements that have no children.
- tag:enabled selects all user interface tag elements that are disabled.
- tag:disabled selects all user interface tag elements that are enabled.
- tag:checked selects all user interface tag elements that are checked, such as check boxes and radio buttons.
- tag:not(s) selects all tag elements that don't match the selector s.

> *Prototype version 1.5 does have limitations when it comes to selectors, such as child selectors (>) and adjacent sibling selectors (+). However, version 1.5.1 adds support for virtually all CSS3 selectors and will probably be released by the time this book is published.*

jQuery with XPath

With jQuery, things are a little different, but only because jQuery adds another powerful expressions method: XPath. The jQuery expression engine includes the preceding selectors—with a few exceptions as noted later in this section—along with additional XPath expressions and custom selectors. Attribute selectors in jQuery are also available, but they're formatted a little differently than the regular CSS attribute selectors. To be compatible with the XPath syntax, all attributes must begin with an @ symbol:

- jQuery('tag[@attr]') selects all tag elements with the attribute attr.
- jQuery('tag[@attr=value]') selects all tag elements whose attr value matches the string value.
- jQuery('tag[@attr^=value]') selects all tag elements whose attr value begins with the string value.
- jQuery('tag[@attr$=value]') selects all tag elements whose attr value ends exactly with the string value.
- jQuery('tag[@attr*=value]') selects all tag elements whose attr value contains the string value.

> *Like Prototype's $$() function, jQuery doesn't support some pseudoelements and pseudoselectors including* :link, :visited, :active, :hover, :focus, :target, ::first-line, ::first-letter, ::selection, ::before, *and* ::after. *Also, jQuery doesn't support some selectors because of their lack of real-world usefulness; these selectors include* :nth-last-child(), :nth-of-type(), :nth-last-of-type(), :first-of-type, :last-of-type, :only-of-type, *and* :lang(fr). *However, other expressions or combinations thereof provide similar functionality.*

Beyond simple CSS selectors, jQuery also allows you to use basic XPath expressions. For detailed information about the XPath expression syntax, check out the W3C site: http://www.w3.org/TR/xpath. XPath is a powerful way of querying XML documents, as shown in these jQuery examples:

- Select all the paragraphs that are descended from the body of the document using absolute paths:

```
jQuery("/html/body//p")
jQuery("/*/body//p")
```

- Select using relative paths, relative to the node referenced by this:

```
// Relative Paths
jQuery("a",this)
jQuery("p/a",this)
```

- Select using different axis:

```
// descendent element DIV has a descendent element P
jQuery("//div//p")
// Child element DIV has a child element P
jQuery("//div/p")
```

- Select based on attributes (predicates):

```
// All inputs that are checked
jQuery("//input[@checked]")
// All anchors with a ref of nofollow
jQuery("//a[@ref='nofollow']")
```

- Select using other predicates with a slightly altered syntax:

```
// [last()] or [position()=last()] becomes :last
jQuery("p:last")
// [0] or [position()=0] becomes :eq(0) or :first
jQuery("p:eq(0)")
// [position() < 5] becomes :lt(5)
jQuery("p:lt(5)")
// [position() > 2] becomes :gt(2)
jQuery("p:gt(2)")
```

jQuery allows you to mix and match CSS selectors with XPath selectors, giving you much greater flexibility and quick, direct access to the elements you need.

You can select elements based on lineage, such as all the children of an unordered list, using this:

```
jQuery('ul/li')
```

or you can do the same with a CSS selector:

```
jQuery('ul > li')
```

What's especially nice is the ability to quickly select elements and retrieve values based on element attributes, such as the input field with the name of street:

```
jQuery('input[@name=street]').val();
```

or you can retrieve values for all checked radio buttons:

```
jQuery('input[@type=radio][@checked]')
```

In addition to CSS and XPath selectors, jQuery includes a few custom expressions that you may find useful:

- :even selects every other even-numbered element from the matched element set—great for highlighting table rows!
- :odd selects every other odd-numbered element from the matched element set.
- :eq(0) and :nth(0) select the nth element from the matched element set, such as the first paragraph on the page.
- :gt(n) selects all matched elements whose index is greater than n.
- :lt(n) selects all matched elements whose index is less than n.
- :first is equivalent to :eq(0).
- :last selects the last matched element.

- :parent selects all elements that have child elements (including text).
- :contains('test') selects all elements that contain the specified text.
- :visible selects all visible elements (this includes items that have a display property using block or inline, a visibility property using visible, and aren't form elements of type hidden).
- :hidden selects all hidden elements (this includes items that have a display property using none, or a visibility property using hidden, or are form elements of type hidden).

These allow you to quickly modify elements, such as the font weight of the first paragraph on the page:

```
jQuery("p:first").css("fontWeight","bold");
```

or quickly show all hidden <div> elements:

```
jQuery("div:hidden").show();
```

You could even hide all the div elements that contain the word "scared":

```
jQuery("div:contains('scared')").hide();
```

Lastly, jQuery also includes a number of form-specific expressions you can use to access form elements:

- :input selects all form elements (input, select, text area, button).
- :text selects all text fields (type="text").
- :password selects all password fields (type="password").
- :radio selects all radio fields (type="radio").
- :checkbox selects all check box fields (type="checkbox").
- :submit selects all submit buttons (type="submit").
- :image selects all form images (type="image").
- :reset selects all reset buttons (type="reset").
- :button selects all other buttons (type="button").

Filtering with a callback

When advanced expressions can't provide what you need, you can always walk the DOM with a callback function and run whatever code you like against each element. In all the following examples, returning true from the callback will include the element, and returning false will exclude the element from the resulting list.

Callbacks can be especially useful when you want to create a reverse selector. All CSS 3 selectors identify the rightmost element in the selector, so there's no way to select "All anchor tags that have a single image as a child." You can, however, accomplish this fairly easily with a callback. Let's start with the following list:

```
<ul>
    <li>
        <a name="example1"><img src="example.gif" alt="example"/></a>
    </li>
    <li>
        <a name="example2">No Images Here</a>
    </li>
    <li>
        <a name="example3">
            Two here!
            <img src="example2.gif" alt="example"/>
            <img src="example3.gif" alt="example"/>
        </a>
    </li>
</ul>
```

Using the YAHOO.util.Dom.getElementBy() method, you can simply use existing DOM element properties to filter your list:

```
// YUI library callback filter
var singleImageAnchors = YAHOO.util.Dom.getElementsBy(function(e) {
    // Look for A node with one child image
    return (e.nodeName == 'A' && ➡
e.getElementsByTagName('img').length == 1);
});
```

And the singleImageAnchors variable will only contain a reference to <a name="example1">, as it's the only anchor with one image as a child.

Likewise, MochiKit provides the MochiKit.Iter.ifilter() method that works in a similar way:

```
// MochiKit library callback filter
var singleImageAnchors = MochiKit.Iter.ifilter(
    function(e) {
        // Make sure there is only one child image
        return (e.getElementsByTag('img').length === 1);
    },
    document.getElementsByTagName('a')
);
```

Prototype and jQuery also provide findAll() and filter() methods, respectively. You use these last two in the chaining context to filter out elements returned from the expression:

```
// Prototype library callback filter
var singleImageAnchors = $$('a').findAll(function(e) {
    return (e.descendants().findAll(function(e) {
        // Locate all image elements
        return (e.nodeName == 'IMG');
    }).length == 1);
});
```

```
// jQuery library callback filter
var singleImageAnchors = jQuery('a').filter(function() {
    // Make sure there is only one child image
    return (jQuery('img',this).length == 1)
});
```

In most cases, the Prototype and jQuery expression selectors would be enough to filter the list of elements, but in cases where you need more in-depth analysis of the elements, callbacks can be very powerful.

Manipulating the DOM document

Each library is chock-full of different DOM manipulation methods, so I'll just point out a few and let you explore the documentation for each library to find the rest:

- **DOMAssistant**: http://www.robertnyman.com/domass/modules-domass-content.htm
- **jQuery**: http://docs.jquery.com/DOM/Manipulation
- **MochiKit**: http://www.mochikit.com/doc/html/MochiKit/DOM.html
- **Prototype**: http://www.prototypejs.org/api/element
- **YUI**: http://developer.yahoo.com/yui/dom/

Many DOM-related methods in these libraries are similar to those already in your ADS library, but there are many more as well, such as the few I'll mention in the following sections.

Using DOMAssistant to create elements

DOMAssistant.$(id).create(name, attr, append, content) allows you to create a new DOM element as a child of the element in the chain:

```
// Create a child <div> element in #content with an id of
// myDiv and a className of justAdded and set its content
// to the text "I'm a brand new div!":
$("content").create("div", {
    id : "myDiv",
    className : "justAdded"
}, true, "I'm a brand new div!");
```

Using jQuery to move nodes

The jQuery(expression).appendTo(expression) method lets you locate large sets of elements and move them all to children of another element:

```
// Find all the <li> elements in ul#list1 and
// relocate them to children of the ul#list2
$('ul#list1 li').appendTo("ul#list2");
```

Using MochiKit to create elements

The MochiKit.DOM.createDOM(name[, attrs[, node[, . . .]]]) method allows you to create new DOM elements with given attributes:

```
var newDiv = MochiKit.DOM.createDOM(
    'DIV',
    {'class': 'justAdded'},
    'I\'m a brand new div!'
);
MochiKit.DOM.$('content').appendChild(newDiv);
```

This would create a new div:

```
<div class='"justAdded">I'm a brand new div!</div>
```

You could also pass in additional createDOM() results as the third argument to create a tree.

Using Prototype to clean up your document

The $(id).cleanWhitespace() method allows you to easily remove the white space child nodes from the given element. This is very handy to create a browser-agnostic script. As you saw in Chapter 3, browsers handle white space differently, so stripping out all of it first will give you more consistent results. If you have the following list

```
<ul id="example">
    <li>Item 1</li>
    <li>Item 2</li>
</ul>
```

querying the first child, as follows, will, in some cases, retrieve the white space text node:

```
var node = $('example').firstChild
```

Instead, using cleanWhitespace()

```
var node = $('example').cleanWhitespace().firstChild
```

will convert your HTML representation to

```
<ul id="example"><li>Item 1</li><li>Item 2</li></ul>
```

so the firstChild property will always refer to the first <li> node.

Using YUI to check for intersecting elements

The YAHOO.util.Dom.getRegion(String | HTMLElement | Array) method returns the top, left, bottom, right position of the element on the page as a YAHOO.util.Region object. You can use this resulting object along with another region's intersect() method to test if two regions intersect based on the positioning and styling on the page:

```
var region1 = YAHOO.util.Dom.getRegion('region1');
var region2 = YAHOO.util.Dom.getRegion('region2');
if(region1.intersect(region2)) {
    alert('The regions intersect!');
}
```

Iterating over results

One additional thing I will mention is iteration. Though it's not directly related to manipulation of the DOM, the Prototype and jQuery chaining syntax both provide a very clean way of iterating over a list of elements. In Prototype, if you want to locate all the anchors on a page and subsequently modify them, you can use the each() method whose callback receives the element and its index:

```
// Prototype library iteration using each()
// Iterate over the list of singleImageAnchors
// from earlier in the chapter and add a hasOneImage class.
singleImageAnchors.each(function(e,i){
    e.addClassName('hasOneImage');
});
```

In jQuery, the same can be accomplished using a similar each() method whose callback receives only the index and the method executes in the context of the node, so this refers to the node itself:

```
// jQuery library iteration using each()
// Iterate over the list of singleImageAnchors
// from earlier in the chapter and add a hasOneImage class.
singleImageAnchors.each(function(i){
    jQuery(this).addClass('hasOneImage');
});
```

Other libraries such as MochiKit also provide stand-alone methods such as forEach() for iterating over lists of elements:

```
// MochiKit library iteration using forEach()
// Iterate over the list of singleImageAnchors
// from earlier in the chapter and add a hasOneImage class.
MochiKit.Iter.forEach(singleImageAnchors,function(e){
    MochiKit.DOM.addElementClass(e,'hasOneImage');
});
```

> MochiKit also includes a framework for creating your own advanced iteration objects. For more information see http://www.mochikit.com/doc/html/MochiKit/Iter.html.

Handling events

As you saw in Chapter 4, events are the lifeblood of user interaction. Without events, there wouldn't be much you could do to the page.

391

You already have some basic event methods in your ADS library, but if you chose to use one of these libraries, many have their own event management built in. Also, they offer the ability to register and invoke custom events that aren't part of the built-in browser events or the W3C events.

Registering events

In your ADS library, you have a simple `ADS.addEvent()` method to attach events to elements:

```
// Your ADS library event registration
// Use a window load event to add a click event listener
// to open the #source link in a new window.
ADS.addEvent(window,'load',function() {

    ADS.addEvent(ADS.$('source'),'click',function(W3CEvent) {
        // Open the new window using the existing href value.
        window.open(this.href);
        // Prevent default action of the link
        var event = ADS.getEventObject(W3CEvent);
        ADS.eventPreventDefault(event);
    });

});
```

Each library also has similar methods.

The DOMAssistant way

With the DOMAssistant library, window load events require you to manually edit the DOMAssistantLoad.js file to include the load events you want to run:

```
DOMAssistant.functionsToCall = [
    initPage
];
```

Element-specific event listeners are registered using the `DOMAssistant.$( id ).addEvent()` method on the selected element, which follows the same pattern as your `ADS.addEvent()` method:

```
// DOMAssistant library event registration
// Use a window load event to add a click event listener
// to open the #source link in a new window.
DOMAssistant.$('source').addEvent('click', function(event) {
    // Open the new window using the existing href value.
    window.open(this.getAttribute('href'));
    DOMAssistant.$(this).addClass('popup');
    // Prevent default action of the link
    DOMAssistant.preventDefault(event);
});
```

Unfortunately, like your ADS library, there are no methods in the DOMAssistant library that allow you to manually invoke events.

The jQuery way

jQuery approaches the task a little differently. You can use jQuery's bind() method in the same way as the DOMAssistant addEvent() method, but jQuery elements also inherit the following event-related methods:

- blur(callback)
- change(callback)
- click(callback)
- dblclick(callback)
- error(callback)
- focus(callback)
- hover(mouseover-callback, mouseout-callback)
- keydown(callback)
- keypress(callback)
- keyup(callback)
- load(callback)
- mousedown(callback)
- mousemove(callback)
- mouseout(callback)
- mouseover(callback)
- mouseup(callback)
- ready(callback)
- resize(callback)
- scroll(callback)
- select(callback)
- submit(callback)
- unload(callback)

Using these methods, you can register event listener callback functions for entire groups of DOM elements, such as a click event for every link on the page:

```
// jQuery event registration
// Add a click event listener on every anchor
// that opens the anchor in a new window.
$('a').click( function(event) {
    // Open the new window using the existing href value;
    window.open(this.getAttribute('href'));
    jQuery(this).addClass('popup');
    // Prevent default action of the link
    return false;
});
```

These methods will also invoke the event listener if called without any input:

```
// jQuery invoke an event
// invoke the click event on the first anchor on the page
$('a:first').click();
```

I especially like the hover() method. The JavaScript rollover redux example from the end of Chapter 1 could be simplified even further to one method:

```
// Rollover redux from Chapter 1 using jQuery
jQuery(document).ready( function() {
    jQuery('a.multiStateAnchor').each(function() {
        // Keep anchorImage in this scope
        var anchorImage;
        if(!(anchorImage = jQuery('img:first',this))) return;

        // Parse the extension.
        var src = anchorImage.attr('src');
        var extensionIndex = src.lastIndexOf('.');
        var path = src.substr(0,extensionIndex);
        var extension = src.substring(
            extensionIndex,
            src.length
        );

        // Preload the images.
        var imageMouseOver = new Image()
        imageMouseOver.src = path + '-over' + extension;
        var imageMouseDown = new Image()
        imageMouseDown.src = path + '-down' + extension;

        // Register the event listeners.
        jQuery(this).hover(
            function() {
                anchorImage.attr('src',imageMouseOver.src);
            },
            function() {
                anchorImage.attr('src',path + extension);
            }
        );
        jQuery(this).mousedown(function() {
                anchorImage.attr('src',imageMouseDown.src);
        });
        jQuery(this).mouseup(function() {
                anchorImage.attr('src',path + extension);
        });
    });
});
```

Custom events

The built-in events and event listeners are great for dealing with interaction between the browser and your document. As you interact with various document elements, the browser continually invokes events depending on your actions. From within the DOM document, you have no control over the mouse pointer, so event listeners are the only way to interact with it. This same idea, however, can apply to interaction among multiple scripts. As an example, let's revisit the image editor case study from Chapter 8.

When completing the resizing and cropping process, the image editor code itself was responsible for communicating the changes back to the server using the saveClick() method you stubbed in:

```
// Save the modifications back to the server.
imageEditor.saveClick = function(W3CEvent) {
    alert('This should save the information back to the server.');
    imageEditor.unload();
}
```

The problem here is that the image editor script will require customization upon each install, because the server processes may differ. Also, it would be necessary to alter the appropriate form inputs and update the inline image to match the newly edited image. To create a much nicer, self-contained object that didn't require any interactions with the server itself, your saveClick() method could simply invoke a custom event on the original image. It would then be up to the developer of the page to register the appropriate listener to deal with actually resizing the image file.

You can register and invoke custom events with many of the regular event registration methods such as MochiKit's MochiKit.Signal.connect() method. The registered event listener can then be invoked using the MochiKit.Signal.signal() method. If you put this in context of the imageEditor. saveClick() method, you might invoke an event called editComplete and pass along the appropriate image size and cropping information as an object:

```
imageEditor.saveClick = function(W3CEvent) {
    MochiKit.Signal.signal(
        imageEditor.DOMObjects.originalImage,
        'editComplete',
        {
            imageWidth:imageEditor.DOMObjects.resizee.style.width,
            imageHeight:imageEditor.DOMObjects.resizee.style.height,
            cropTop:imageEditor.DOMObjects.cropArea.style.top,
            cropLeft:imageEditor.DOMObjects.cropArea.style.left,
            cropWidth:imageEditor.DOMObjects.cropArea.style.width,
            cropHeight:imageEditor.DOMObjects.cropArea.style.height
        }
    )
    imageEditor.unload();
}
```

This way, the image editor's only responsibility is to "signal" the original image to indicate a change. For the server-side portion to work, the original image must have an event registered with the MochiKit.Signal.connect() method that deals with the custom editComplete event:

```
MochiKit.Signal.connect(
    MochiKit.DOM.get('the-image'),
    'editComplete',
    function(event) {
        var properties = event.event();
        // Do something with properties.imageWidth etc.
    }
);
```

Here's the same idea using the jQuery library:

```
// jQuery library custom event registration
// Register an event listener for the editComplete method.
$('the-image').bind(
    'editComplete',
    function(event,imageWidth,imageHeight,cropTop,➥
cropLeft,cropWidth,cropHeight) {
        // Do something with imageWidth etc.
    }
);
```

```
// jQuery library invoke a custom event with arguments
// Invoke editComplete with the appropriate properties.
imageEditor.saveClick = function(W3CEvent) {
    $(imageEditor.DOMObjects.originalImage).trigger(
        'editComplete',
        [
            imageEditor.DOMObjects.resizee.style.width,
            imageEditor.DOMObjects.resizee.style.height,
            imageEditor.DOMObjects.cropArea.style.top,
            imageEditor.DOMObjects.cropArea.style.left,
            imageEditor.DOMObjects.cropArea.style.width,
            imageEditor.DOMObjects.cropArea.style.height
        ]
    )
    imageEditor.unload();
}
```

Using custom events such as these allows you to increase the reuse of your scripts by separating out customized logic. This modified image editor script could now be used in any web applications provided they are also using the same library.

Accessing and manipulating style

None of these libraries offer much beyond your current ADS CSS style methods. Some, however, also include positioning methods. Prototype, for example, has methods such as these:

- `Element.cumulativeOffset()` returns the top-left corner of an element relative to the document's top-left position.

- `Element.relativize()` converts an element into a relatively positioned element without altering its current position on the page. This method can be especially useful if you want to use absolute positioning for child elements.

You'll see these methods in action in Chapter 12, when you examine how to beautify your <select> lists.

Communication

The last area I'll discuss in this chapter is browser communication. Since the explosion of Ajax, JavaScript libraries have become more and more popular. The first object in many libraries was the Ajax object, or at least, it was the object that made the library popular.

Of the libraries I've chosen to discuss, DOMAssistant is the only one without a built-in Ajax object. This may seem like a negative mark against DOMAssistant as a production-ready library, but it's not. Ajax workflows are tricky things that shouldn't be taken lightly. Considering all the additional issues you were introduced to in Part 2 of this book, leaving an Ajax object out of a library is actually a plus in most cases. However, now that you've already read Chapters 7 and 8 and you're familiar with all the Ajax quirks, using a library object isn't so unacceptable.

Prototype Ajax object

Probably the most popular Ajax object is the one in the Prototype library, which was popularized by the Ruby on Rails framework. Prototype offers a few different flavors of Ajax methods:

- `Ajax.Request(url[, options])` performs a basic XMLHttpRequest request.

- `Ajax.Updater(element, url[, options])` is a wrapper for a request that automatically appends the content of the request to a given DOM node.

- `Ajax.PeriodicalUpdater(element, url[, options])` automatically appends the content of the request to a given DOM node on a regular interval. This is not a wrapper for `Ajax.Updater()`, so some methods, such as evalJSON, are not available. Also, the onComplete callback is overridden internally to perform the update on the DOM element, so you'll have to use onSuccess to run additional code (but onSuccess will occur before the onComplete update has occurred).

The options for each method are similar to the `ADS.ajaxRequest` method options you created in Chapter 7 and include several properties:

- asynchronous switches the object between asynchronous and synchronous (blocking) mode, but as we discussed in Chapter 7, you should always leave this set to true. The default value is true.

- contentType is the Content Type header for your request. The default value is application/x-www-form-urlencoded.

- encoding is the encoding for the content of the request. Generally, you won't have to change this. The default value is UTF-8.

- method is the HTTP method for your request. Prototype treats many other request types, such as put and delete, by overriding them with post and including the original request method in a _method parameter in the request. The default value is post.

- parameters are the parameters to send along with the request. You can define this using a URL-encoded string like you'd include on a get request, or you can use any hash-compatible object, such as an array or object with property names representing the parameter names.

- postBody, which defaults to null, is the content you'd like to include in the body of a POST request. If empty, the body will include the contents of the parameters option.

- requestHeaders is an object or array representing the additional headers you'd like to include in the request. In object form, the property name and value will represent the request header name and value, respectively. Arrays are a little tricky, as the even indexed items—starting with 0—represent the header names while odd indexes—starting at 1—represent the previous header's value. By default, Prototype will include a few headers if not overridden in this property:

  - X-Requested-With, by default, is set to XMLHttpRequest.

  - X-Prototype-Version is set to Prototype's current version number.

  - Accept, by default, is set to text/javascript, text/html, application/xml, text/xml, */*.

- Content-type is built based on the contentType value and encoding options.

Along with these properties, there are also a number of callback methods you can use to run code at various stages of the request or based on the response from the server. Each of the following callback methods will be invoked with two arguments including the XMLHttpRequest object (or Internet Explorer ActiveX equivalent) and the JavaScript object in the response if and only if the response contains an X-JSON header. If the X-JSON header is missing, the second argument will be null. The only exception to this is the onException callback, which will receive the Ajax.Request instance as the first argument and the exception object as the second. The callbacks are listed here in the order they will be invoked in the request:

- onException(ajax.request,exception) will be invoked when an error arises in the request/response and can occur mixed in at any point with the callbacks below.

- onUninitialized(XHRrequest,json) may be invoked when the request object is created, but it may not always be invoked, so avoid using it.

- onLoading(XHRrequest,json) may be invoked when the request object is set up and its connection is opened, but again, it may not always be invoked, so avoid using it,

- onLoaded(XHRrequest,json) may be invoked when the request object has finished setting up and the connection is open and ready to send the request—but again, it may not always be invoked, so avoid using it.

- onInteractive(XHRrequest,json) may be invoked when the request object has received part of the response and is waiting for the remainder of the request. As you can guess, it may not always be invoked, so avoid using it.

- on###(XHRrequest,json) will be invoked provided the appropriate response code is set. ### represents the HTTP status code for the response. The callback will be invoked once the request is complete but before the onComplete callback. It will also prevent the execution of onSuccess and onFailure callbacks.

- onFailure(XHRrequest,json) will be invoked in the event a request completes but its status code is defined and not between 200 and 300.

- onSuccess(XHRrequest,json) will be invoked when the request completes and its status code is undefined or is between 200 and 300.

- onComplete(XHRrequest,json) will invoke at the end of the request as the last possible callback in the chain.

Prototype also includes a global Ajax.responders method for controlling and accessing all the Ajax requests coming in to and out of the various Ajax.request methods. For more on the Ajax.responders method, see the Prototype online documentation at http://www.prototypejs.org/api/ajax/responders.

Putting all this into action, you can see a number of different requests in the chapter9/Prototype/prototype.html example file:

```
// Prototype Ajax.Request
// Create a new one time request and log its success.
new Ajax.Request(
    '../ajax-test-files/request.json',
    {
        method:'get',
        onSuccess: function (transport) {
            var response = transport.responseText || Â
"no response text";
            ADS.log.write('Ajax.Request was successful: ' + response);
        },
        onFailure: function (){
            ADS.log.write('Ajax.Request failed');
        }
    }
);


// Prototype Ajax.Updater
// Create a one time request that populates the #ajax-updater-target
// element with the content of the responseText.
new Ajax.Updater(
    $('ajax-updater-target'),
    '../ajax-test-files/request.json',
    {
        method: 'get',
        // Append it to the top of the target element
        insertion: Insertion.Top
    }
);


// Prototype Ajax.periodicalUpdater
// Create a periodic request that will automatically populate
// the #ajax-target-element every 10 seconds.
new Ajax.PeriodicalUpdater(
```

```
        $('ajax-periodic-target'),
        '../ajax-test-files/periodic.json',
        {
            method: 'GET',
            // Append it to the top of the existing content.
            insertion: Insertion.Top,
            // Run every 10 seconds
            frequency: 10
        }
    );
```

Another very simple, yet very good, use of the Ajax.Request object is for intermittently saving the information in a form. This is especially useful in a blogging situation, where you may be sitting on the page for some time without any means of really saving what you're doing. The Ajax.Request() object, along with Prototype's Form serialization methods, could retrieve the current information in the form and save it to the server every few minutes, ensuring you don't lose all your hard work:

```
    // autosave using Prototype
    // Save the content of the #autosave-form every 30 seconds
    // and update the #autosave-status to indicate the save.
    setTimeout(function() {
        new Ajax.Updater(
            $('autosave-status'),
            '../ajax-test-files/autosave.json',
            {
                method:'post',
                parameters : $('autosave-form').serialize(true)
            }
        );
    },30000);
```

jQuery keeps Ajax simple

jQuery also includes a low-level jQuery.ajax method that you can use to specify all sorts of properties, but I prefer the quick and easy methods that let you get at the information you need with minimal work:

- jQuery.post(url, params, callback) retrieves data through a POST request.
- jQuery.get(url, params, callback) retrieves data through a GET request.
- jQuery.getJSON(url, params, callback) retrieves a JSON object.
- jQuery.getScript(url, callback) retrieves and executes a JavaScript file.

These methods are all wrappers for the jQuery.ajax() method and their callback methods, in all cases, are invoked as the jQuery.ajax() success callback. Each receives two arguments that define the request's responseText and the status of the request respectively:

```
    jQuery.get('../ajax-test-files/request.json',
        { key: 'value' },
        function(responseText, status){
```

```
            // Your Code
        }
    );
```

The status will be one of these:

- success
- error
- notmodified

In the cases of both the getJSON() and getScript() methods, the response will be evaluated, so the argument for getJSON() will be a JavaScript object.

Again, you can see some of these methods in action in chapter9/jQuery/jquery.html:

```
// jQuery.get() for quick ajax calls
// Create a one time request and log its success.
jQuery.get('../ajax-test-files/request.json',
    { key: 'value' },
    function(responseText,status){
        ADS.log.header('jQuery.get()');
        ADS.log.write('status: ' + status);
        ADS.log.write('successful: ' + responseText);
    }
);

// jQuery.getJSON() to load a JSON object
// Create a one time request to load a JSON file and log its success.
jQuery.getJSON('../ajax-test-files/request.json', function(json){
    ADS.log.header('jQuery.getJSON()');
    ADS.log.write('successful: ' + json.type);
});
```

jQuery also includes an additional load() method:

- jQuery(expression).load(url, params, callback) loads the result of the URL into the DOM element.

This method acts the same way as the Prototype Ajax.updater() method and will automatically populate the element or elements with the result:

```
// jQuery(...).load() to automatically populate an element
// Create a one time request that populates the #ajax-updater-target
// element with the content of the responseText.
jQuery("#ajax-updater-target").load(
    '../ajax-test-files/updater.json',
    { key: 'value' },
    function(responseText,status) {
        ADS.log.header('jQuery(...).load()');
        ADS.log.write('status: ' + status);
```

```
                ADS.log.write('successful: ' + responseText);
                ADS.log.write('jQuery(\'#ajax-updater-target\').load successful');
            }
        );
```

The jquery() method can be used equally well for the periodic saving mechanism:

```
    // Autosave using jQuery
    // Save the content of the #autosave-form every 10 seconds
    // and update the #autosave-status to indicate the save.
    setTimeout(function() {
        jQuery('autosave-status').load(
            '../ajax-test-files/autosave.json',
            jQuery.param({
                title:jQuery('#autosave-form input[@name=title]').val(),
                story:jQuery('#autosave-form textarea[@name=story]').val()
            })
        );
    },10000);
```

jQuery also has a number of plug-ins available, such as Mike Alsup's Ajax Form plug-in (http://docs. jquery.com/Plugins), which make dealing with forms and Ajax even easier. Need to submit a comment form via Ajax? It's as simple as this:

```
    $('#commentForm').ajaxForm(function() {
        alert("Thank you for your comment!");
    });
```

This method serializes the contents of the form and sends it to whatever script is referenced in the form's action attribute.

Summary

In this chapter, I have touched on a few of the features of the DOMAssistant, JQuery, MochiKit, Prototype, and YUI libraries that can help you accomplish your daily scripting tasks. This was by no means a complete description of every library, so I highly suggest that you browse the documentation for each library to see what else each of them has.

When evaluating which library is right for you, be sure to take a good look at each one you're considering. Check for things like the proper namespace, too little or too many features, a strong community, and good support. Once you've chosen one, make sure to take advantage of all it has to offer, but at the same time, take the time to learn how and why the library works the way it does. Relying on a library is fine as long as you're not taking it for granted.

In Chapter 10, we'll take another look at a few of these libraries along with a few others that offer a number of simple visual enhancements that can, if used properly, add a little extra flare to your web applications.

Chapter 10

ADDING EFFECTS TO ENHANCE USER EXPERIENCE

HTML is boring. Regardless of what you might think, every web surfer, including you, wants to be dazzled by your site, but finding the right balance of eye candy and interactivity is the trick. When discussing effects and their usefulness, I'm often reminded of the Shakespearean line, "All that glitters is not gold." It's true; just because you can add an effect doesn't mean you should. Remember the <blink> tag anyone? The most important thing to ask is this: "Are my effects enhancing the user experience?" Many times the answer is actually, "Yes."

Used properly, subtle effects can provide visual cues to changes that would otherwise go unnoticed. They can call attention to certain aspects of the interface and guide interaction in the right direction, or they can simply impress and delight the viewer—adding a little bit of life to your otherwise boring old HTML.

In this chapter, you'll look at a few assorted techniques and situations where effects can be beneficial. You'll also get an introduction to the Script.aculo.us and Moo.fx libraries, each of which can take a lot of hassle out of creating effects, and you'll be using parts of them to create better error feedback in an order form as well as a drag-and-drop shopping cart.

Do it yourself

All effects in JavaScript are based on one thing—time. Other animation plug-ins, such as Adobe Flash, are based on individual visual frames with a number of frames per second, but regular DOM scripting provides no such feature, because the speed is dependent on a number of different variables including browser, the user's computer, and more. To achieve motion, animation, or any sort of change over time, every effect relies on either the setTimeout() or setInterval() core JavaScript method.

You've already come across the setTimeout() and setInterval() methods in several places where you needed to process an event on a regular interval. The only difference between the two methods is in the number of times the callback function is invoked:

- setTimeout(callback, milliseconds) will invoke the callback function *once* after the given number of milliseconds.

- setInterval(callback, milliseconds) will invoke the callback function *indefinitely* after each interval of the given number of milliseconds—until you remove the interval function using clearInterval().

These methods provide the "frames per second" in your effects by executing the callback function on a regular interval—provided the browser and computer can keep up. If you want to achieve any animation, transition, or effect, you only need to write the appropriate function to incrementally manipulate the desired elements and then run it using setInterval() as shown in the chapter10/dom-animation/animation.html example here:

```
ADS.addEvent(window,'load',function() {
    // Move an element from its current
    // position +300px to the right and down.
    var moveMe = document.getElementById('element-id');
    ADS.setStyle(moveMe,{
        position:'absolute',
        border:'1px solid black',
        width:'100px',
        height:'20px'
    });

    var startLeft = moveMe.offsetLeft;
    var startTop = moveMe.offsetTop;

    // Create the interval.
    var mover = setInterval(function() {
        var remove = false;
        var currentLeft = moveMe.offsetLeft;
        var currentTop = moveMe.offsetTop;

        // Move in 2 pixel increments.
        var newLeft = currentLeft + 2;
        var newTop = currentTop + 2;
        if (newLeft > startLeft + 300 || newTop > startTop + 300) {
            // If the new position is greater than the desired
            // target, reset the values to the desired target
```

```
            newLeft = startLeft;
            newTop = startTop;
        }

        // Reposition the element.
        moveMe.style.left = newLeft + 'px';
        moveMe.style.top = newTop + 'px';
    },10);
});
```

As you can see by running the preceding example, achieving change over time isn't that difficult. The hard part is writing the callback methods used by setInterval() that manipulate all the elements in your document. Providing these manipulation methods is where libraries come in very handy. Libraries also provide wrappers for the interval methods, so you don't need to manually set them up as you did here.

Show me the content!

Remember accessibility. When you start adding bling to your web application, be sure to do so in a way that won't degrade the accessibility of the application itself. Consider a very simple fade effect where the element starts off completely translucent with an opacity of 0 percent and ends opaque with an opacity of 100 percent, as illustrated in Figure 10-1.

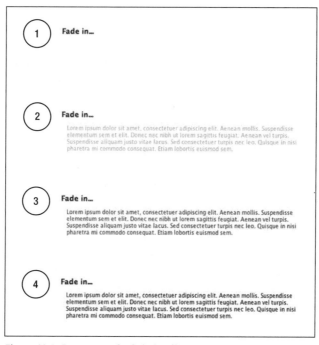

Figure 10-1. Four steps of a fade-in effect on a paragraph of text starting at 0 percent and ending at 100 percent

You may not realize it, but there's a big problem. You may have set up the initial state in your CSS style sheets by setting the element's visibility to hidden or display to none. But what if the browser supports CSS but not JavaScript? In that case, the object will never appear, because there's no script to make it visible.

A quick solution is to initially hide the element using a load event as follows; that way, when your DOM script can't run, the element will remain visible:

```
ADS.addEvent(window, 'load', function() {
    ADS.setStyle('element-id', { 'visibility' : hidden });
});
```

This will work in many cases, but it may also present unwanted results. If the page load event is invoked too late, as we discussed in Chapter 4, the element will still be visible while the page loads.

As an alternative solution, you can use the <noscript> element. The <noscript> element is usually used to show alternate content for inline JavaScript. For all the DOM scripts in this book, you've been using external files—so <noscript> wasn't necessary—but you can still take advantage of it. The content of a <noscript> element will be rendered as part of the DOM tree when JavaScript isn't available, but at the same time, it will be hidden when JavaScript is enabled. The only caveat is that the content of <noscript> is simply a text node within the <noscript> node and isn't a parsed DOM fragment.

To take advantage of the hidden content in the <noscript> element, you'll need to retrieve it when the page loads and append it to your document. Given the following bits of HTML, which are found in the chapter10/noscript/noscript.html source test file:

```
<h4>Fade in starting with <code>visibility:hidden;</code></h4>
<div id="start-css">
    <p>Lorem ipsum dolor sit amet, consectetuer adipiscing elit.
    Aenean mollis. Suspendisse elementum sem et elit. Donec nec nibh
    ut lorem sagittis feugiat. Aenean vel turpis. Suspendisse aliquam
    justo vitae lacus. Sed consectetuer turpis nec leo. Quisque in
    nisi pharetra mi commodo consequat. Etiam lobortis
    euismod sem.</p>
</div>

<h4>Fade in starting with <code>&lt;noscript&gt;
&lt;/noscript&gt;</code></h4>
<noscript id="start-noscript-wrapper">
    <div id="start-noscript">
        <p>Lorem ipsum dolor sit amet, consectetuer adipiscing elit.
        Aenean mollis. Suspendisse elementum sem et elit. Donec nec
        nibh ut lorem sagittis feugiat. Aenean vel turpis.
        Suspendisse aliquam justo vitae lacus. Sed consectetuer
        turpis nec leo. Quisque in nisi pharetra mi commodo
        consequat. Etiam lobortis euismod sem.</p>
    </div>
</noscript>
```

and the appropriate CSS styles for testing:

```
#start-css {
    visibility: hidden;
}
```

you can use regular old DOM methods and innerHTML or specialized library methods, such as the jQuery ones shown here, to retrieve the <noscript> content and append it as a sibling to the original <noscript> DOM element:

```
jQuery.noConflict();

ADS.addEvent(window,'load',function() {

    // Display a transition on the #start-css element
    // from transparent to opaque using moo.fx
    var myFx = new Fx.Style(
        'start-css',
        'opacity',
        {duration:2000}
    ).start(0,1);

    // First retrieve the content of the <noscript> and append
    // it as a sibling to the noscript element. You could remove the
    // <noscript> element but it's not necessary.
    var wrapper = jQuery('#start-noscript-wrapper');

    var content = wrapper.text() || wrapper.html();
    if(content) {
        jQuery('#start-noscript-wrapper').after(content);

        // Display a transition on the #start-noscript element
        // from transparent to opaque using moo.fx
        var myFx = new Fx.Style(
            'start-noscript',
            'opacity',
            {duration:2000}
        ).start(0,1);
    }

});
```

This example currently doesn't work properly in Safari, as Safari doesn't offer DOM access to the content of the <noscript> element.

In either case, you'll achieve the appropriate effect, and both paragraphs will be visible in JavaScript-enabled browsers, as shown in Figure 10-2.

Figure 10-2. The example HTML in a JavaScript-enabled browser

But only the second case will be accessible in a browser with CSS but without JavaScript, as shown in Figure 10-3.

Figure 10-3. The example HTML without JavaScript enabled

Providing feedback

Subtle effects are great for saying, "Hey! Look over here! Something just happened!" And they're especially useful when using Ajax workflows. As you saw in Part 2, it's vitally important to update your user interface along with your communication pattern. In a traditional workflow, the action and change are revealed with the page reload. With Ajax however, only a small portion—if any—is modified, thus there's no inherent indication of change, so you need to indicate it yourself.

The Yellow Fade Technique

One of the more popular methods is the Yellow Fade Technique (YFT) popularized by the 37signals Basecamp application. The technique uses a subtle background fade from yellow to white on any affected portions of the page. This subtle yet obvious fade provides the necessary feedback when you dynamically modify the page.

It's nothing fancy or complicated, but it's effective. You can apply the same logic to the autosave mechanism from Chapter 9, as shown in chapter10/fade-technique/fade.html, using a combination of the jQuery library for the Ajax call and the Moo.fx library for the effects:

```
setInterval(function() {
    jQuery.getJSON(
        '../../chapter9/ajax-test-files/autosave.json',
        jQuery.param({
            title:jQuery('#autosave-form input[@name=title]').val(),
            story:jQuery('#autosave-form textarea[@name=story]').val()
        }),
        function(response, status) {
            if(status == 'success') {
                var color = '#00ff00';
            } else {
                var color = '#ff0000';
            }
            jQuery('#autosave-status').html(response.message)
            var myFx = new Fx.Styles(
                'autosave-status',
                {duration:2000}
            ).start({
                'background-color':[color,'#ffffff'],
                'opacity':[1,0]
            });
        }
    );
},5000);
```

When the save occurs, the message will update as it did in Chapter 9, and the form background will fade from a color to white as well, as shown in Figure 10-4. This example takes the yellow fade a step further by using green to indicate a successful save and red to indicate a failure.

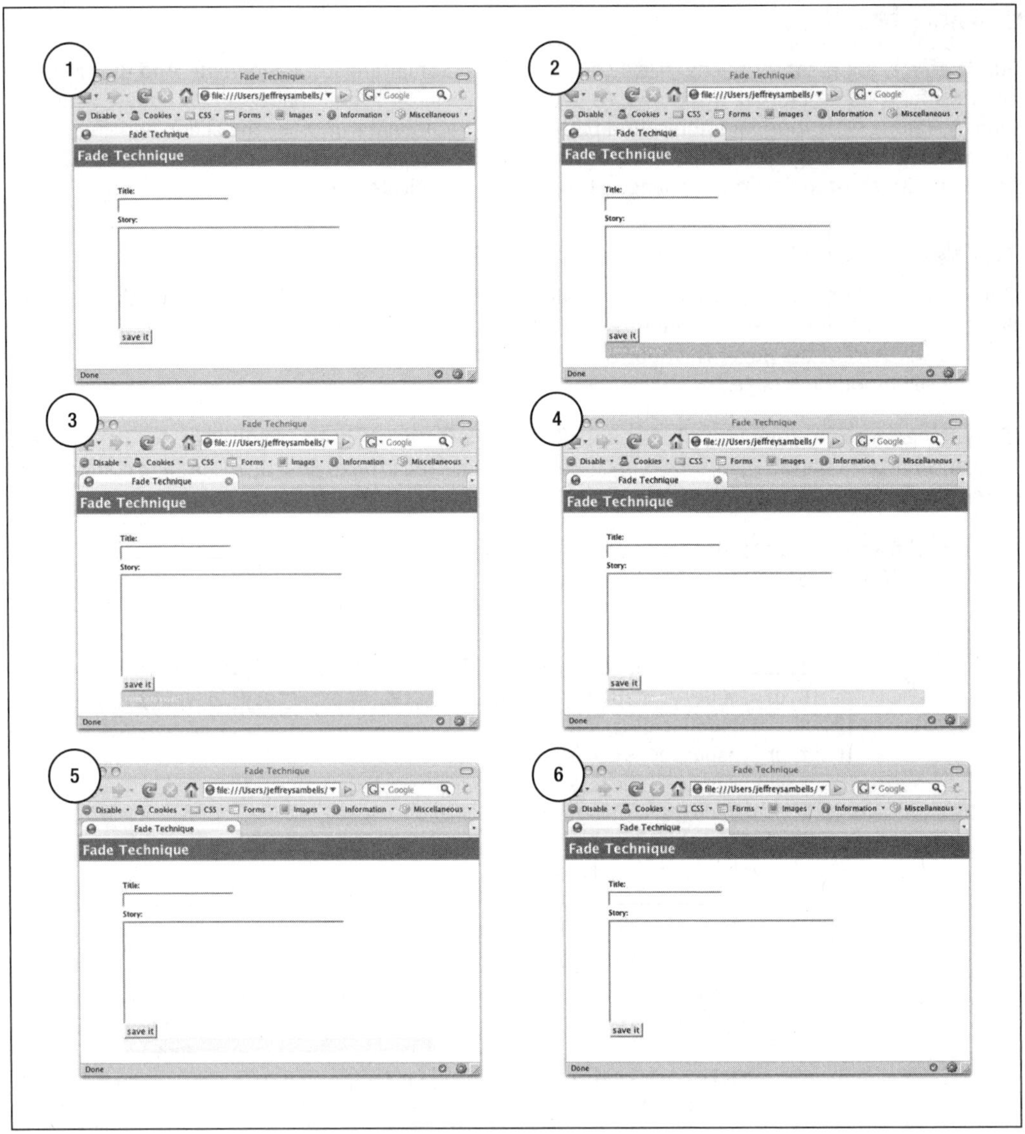

Figure 10-4. The Chapter 9 autosave with subtle enhancements

Avoiding shifting content

Another common problem you'll run into with effects is shifting content. When things start appearing in your document, they occupy space. If that space isn't accounted for in the initial layout, the rest of the content on the page will shift around to accommodate the new element. In some cases, that may be desired, but often, the shift creates a visual distraction that pulls your eyes away from the initial focus of the effect. Figure 10-5 shows a page in chapter10/no-shift/no-shift.html before and after a message was added. Notice how the content below the message has now shifted down the page.

Figure 10-5. Viewing the page before and after inserting the message box shows the shift in content.

You can avoid "the shift" by accounting for the message box area in your design and using visibility: hidden rather than display:none. The visibility property maintains the relative size and position of the element but, at the same time, makes it invisible. When creating the message, you then need to append it to only the appropriate elements and make it visible. As long as the newly added content doesn't alter the size of the box, the result is a visible message box but no shifting content, as shown in Figure 10-6.

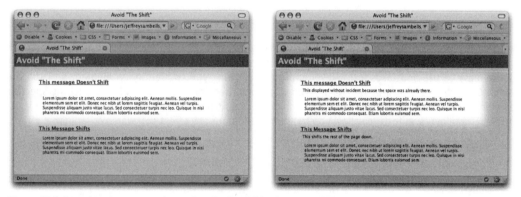

Figure 10-6. Inserting the message box using display:visible shows no shift in content.

When you initially mark up the elements in your document, they may be empty. In the preceding example, the message area contained no message. To avoid using a fixed height, I simply prepopulated the message area with a nonbreaking space ( ), which will allow the area to expand with a larger text size. If the message contains more than one line, the page will still shift in this case, as I've assumed the new messages will fit on one line.

413

A few visual effects libraries

In the last chapter, we focused on productivity and faster DOM scripting. In this chapter, we're focusing on visual aesthetics and interactivity, so we'll be looking at two more libraries:

- Moo.fx
- Script.aculo.us

Both of these libraries are built on top of Prototype, but in the case of Moo.fx, it's also available as part of the Mootools JavaScript library (http://mootools.net). For this chapter, I'm going to use the Mootools version of the Moo.fx library, as it contains a few extras not available in the Prototype version.

> *Moo.fx relies on the $() and $$() methods to retrieve elements. In the example source files and code of this chapter, the $() and $$() methods refer to the ones in the Mootools library. For the purposes of this chapter, assume they operate the same as the equivalent methods in the Prototype library you saw in Chapter 9. If you are going to rely heavily on the Moo.fx library for Mootools, you may want to consider Mootools as an alternative for the libraries I presented in Chapter 9 and investigate its documentation further at* http://docs.mootools.net/.

Moo.fx

Moof.fx (http://moofx.mad4milk.net/) describes itself as "a superlightweight, ultratiny, megasmall JavaScript effects library, to be used with prototype.js or the Mootools framework." Overall, Moo.fx is very easy to use and takes a low-level approach, allowing you to identify an element and specify which CSS properties to modify over a given duration. These modifications will apply to the specific element only, not to its children (unless the children inherit the CSS property through the cascade as usual). These low-level features allow you to create just about any effect you want with minimal effort.

Namespace: Fx (depending on which version)

License: MIT-style license (http://moofx.mad4milk.net/License.txt)

Dependencies: Mootools as a built-in component (http://mootools.net) or Prototype (http://prototypejs.org) with the stand-alone version

Script.aculo.us

Script.aculo.us (http://script.aculo.us) "provides you with easy-to-use, cross-browser user interface JavaScript libraries to make your web sites and web applications fly." Script.aculo.us takes a high-level approach and specifies five core effects and combinations thereof. With these high-level effects, all children of the given element may also be affected. When invoking an effect such as Effect.Scale on a paragraph, the font size will be scaled along with the physical width and height of the bounding element and any child elements within the paragraph. These high-level groupings make applying large, complicated effects simple, as it's all done for you.

Namespace: Varies depending on the desired effect object

License: MIT-style license (http://wiki.script.aculo.us/Script.aculo.us/show/License)

Dependencies: Prototype (http://prototypejs.org)

Some visual bling

Visual effects, when used appropriately, give your web applications that little extra edge, and effects can add a bit more life to a somewhat mundane web experience. To get a better understanding of each library, we'll look at a few of their key methods.

Mootastic CSS property modification

As I said, Moo.fx allows you to modify an element's CSS properties. This is accomplished primarily through two objects in the Fx namespace:

- Fx.Style(element, property, options) can be used to modify any numeric CSS property including hex colors.
- Fx.Styles(element, options) allows you to apply effects to multiple properties of the same element all in one effect.

To create a new effect, you simply instantiate a new instance of the appropriate Fx method:

```
var myFx = new Fx.Style($('element-id'),'opacity');
```

At this point, however, the effect is just an object and hasn't actually done anything. To get everything going, you need to call an additional method such as set() or start(), which you'll see shortly.

You can further modify each of the Fx style methods using several option properties, including the following:

- duration defines the length of the effect in milliseconds.
- fps defines the number of frames per second the animation should attempt—defaulting to 30.
- transition is a mathematical calculation that will alter the linear intervals in the animation.
- unit defines the units associated with the numerical value. The default is px, but you may wish to use others such as em or %.
- wait is used to indicate if the transition should wait for other transitions on the element to end before it begins. The default is true.

> *You'll see the transition property in more detail shortly when we discuss making effects look more realistic.*

415

Along with the preceding properties, there are also three callback options you can specify using a function:

- onStart is invoked when the effect starts.
- onComplete is invoked when the effect ends.
- onCancel is invoked when the effect is cancelled or interrupted.

These callback methods can be useful to make additional changes in the document after an effect has completed or before it starts.

You specify each option in the Fx.Style()'s third argument using the familiar object syntax as follows:

```
var myFx = new Fx.Style($('element-id'),'opacity' {
    duration: 1000,
    onComplete: function() {
        alert('Hello!');
    }
});
```

For your opacity effects to work in Internet Explorer, you have to give elements a layout. To apply a layout to an element, you must use one of the following settings:

- Set a width or a height property (which will only work on inline elements if you're using a nonstandard doctype).
- Set the display property to inline-block.
- Set the position property to absolute.
- Set the writingMode property to tb-rl.
- Set the contentEditable property to true.

> For more on layout in Internet Explorer and its various quirks, see http://www.satzansatz.de/cssd/onhavinglayout.html.

One property at a time

Once you have an effect instantiated, you need to invoke it.

When using the Fx.Style method, you can, if you want, immediately set the value of the effect's CSS property using the set() method, such as:

```
// Set the opacity to 50%.
var myFx = new Fx.Style($('element-id'),'opacity').set(0.5);
```

In most cases. however, you want the value of the property to transition between two values using the start() method, which takes the initial starting value and the desired ending value as follows:

```
// Fade the opacity from transparent to solid.
var myFx = new Fx.Style($('element-id'),'opacity' {
    duration: 1000
}).start(0,1);
```

The starting value of the start() method is optional. If you only specify a single value, the current value of the property will be used as the starting point, for example:

```
// Fade to 50% opacity from either solid
// or transparent depending on the current state.
var myFx = new Fx.Style($('element-id'),'opacity',{
    duration: 1000
}).start(0.5);
```

A mix of properties all at once

To change multiple properties at the same time with the Fx.Styles() object, you use the same start() method, but it works a little differently. The Fx.Styles() method takes only the element and the options for its input, as follows:

```
var myFx = new Fx.Styles($('element-id') { duration: 1000 });
```

while the specific properties and start/end values are specified directly in the start() method using object notation with key/value pairs representing the properties and values respectively:

```
// Alter the opacity, border-width and
// font-size all at the same time
var myFx = new Fx.Styles($('element-id'),{ duration: 1000 }).start({
    'opacity':[0,1],
    'border-width'[4],
    'font-size':[24]
});
```

In this case, the opacity will fade from transparent (0) to opaque (1), and at the same time, the border-width will change from the current value to 4 and the font-size from the current value to 24.

Reusing the effect

The nice thing about Moo.fx objects is that you can reuse them multiple times. When you instantiate the Fx style objects, you can call the set() or start() methods multiple times with different values. To make the opacity of an element throb, you can simply reuse an opacity effect with multiple values in sequence like this:

```
// Create an opacity Fx object.
var myFxOpacity = new Fx.Style(
    $('element-id'),
    'opacity',
    {wait, true}
);
// Fade in from 0 to 0.9
myFxOpacity.start(0, 0.9);
```

417

```
// Fade back to 0.5
myFxOpacity.start(0.5);
// Fade back to 0.9
myFxOpacity.start(0.9);
// Fade back to 0
myFxOpacity.start(0);
```

In the preceding example, it's important to set the wait option to true so that each effect will wait its turn. By default, wait is true, but I've included it here as a reminder.

Multiple effects on multiple objects

Moo.fx includes a third method, Fx.Elements(elements,options), which takes an array of elements to modify. The only difference here is that the start() method uses another syntax to specify each element in the array as indicated here:

```
// Apply an effect to list elements.
var myFx = new Fx.Elements($$('li'),{
    duration: 1000
}).start({
    // Fade first element to solid.
    '0': { 'opacity':[0,1] },
    // Fade second element and move in from the right.
    '1': {
            'opacity':[0,1],
            'left':[-500,300]
        }
    // Fade third element background from current to green.
    '2': { 'background-color':['#00FF00'] }
});
```

Each property of the start() input object relates to the index of the elements in the array and is defined using the same object as you used for the Fx.Styles(. . .).start(. . .) method.

Sliding with Moo.fx

The only specialized built-in effect is Fx.Slide(element[, options]), which is the slider effect shown in Figure 10-7.

> This method is available only as part of the Mootools version of the Moo.fx package, not the Prototype version.

The slider will work on any block elements, but the element can't have any positioning such as absolute or margins. If you need to position it in your document, you'll need to position its parent element.

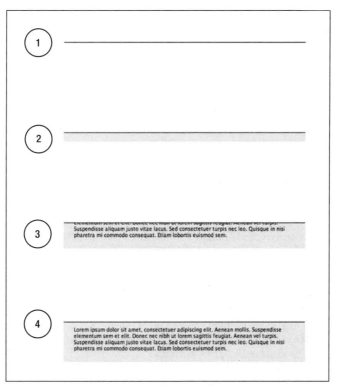

Figure 10-7. The Moo.fx slider

To create a new slider, you instantiate the object using the same options as the Fx style methods—with the exception of the mode option:

```
var myFxSlider = new Fx.Slide($('slide-me'), {
    duration: 500,
    mode:'horizantal'
});
```

The Fx.Slider has one additional option—mode, which defines the slide direction:

- vertical makes the slider a vertical slider (the default).
- horizontal makes the slider a horizontal slider, as it is here.

Like the Fx style instances, the slider instance is invoked using one of five methods depending on the action you want to take:

- slideIn() slides the element in, making it appear.
- slideOut() slides the element out, making it disappear.

- toggle() toggles between slideIn() and slideOut() and executes whichever is the opposite of the current state.

- hide() simply hides the element without any transition.

- show() shows the element without any transition.

Unfortunately, the content of the slider is always fixed to either the top or left edge. If you try to slide up from the bottom or out from the right, the content will move along with the slide.

Form feedback made pretty

To get a better idea of how these effects all work together, take a look at the simple customer information form I included in the chapter10/form/form.html source, which includes the following very basic HTML page:

```
<!DOCTYPE html PUBLIC "-//W3C//DTD XHTML 1.0 Strict//EN"
    "http://www.w3.org/TR/xhtml1/DTD/xhtml1-strict.dtd">
<html xmlns="http://www.w3.org/1999/xhtml">
<head>
    <title>Moo.fx Customer Information Form</title>
    <link rel="stylesheet" href="../../shared/source.css"
        type="text/css" media="screen" />
    <link rel="stylesheet" href="../chapter.css"
        type="text/css" media="screen" />
    <link rel="stylesheet" href="form.css"
        type="text/css" media="screen" />
    <script src="../../ADS-final-verbose.js"
        type="text/javascript"></script>
    <script src="../../libraries/moo.fx-mootools.js"
        type="text/javascript"></script>
    <script src="../../libraries/jquery.js"
        type="text/javascript"></script>
    <script type="text/javascript" src="interactive.js"></script>
</head>
<body>
<h1>Customer Information</h1>
<div id="content">
    <h2>Moo.fx Effects Example</h2>
    <div id="customer-info">
        <form id="customer-form" action="POST">
            <fieldset>
                <legend>
                    <span class="sign"> Personal Information</span>
                </legend>
                <div class="required">
                    <label for="name" accesskey="1">Name</label>
                    <input title="your name" name="name" id="name"
                        tabindex="1" type="text"/>
                    <span id="name-error" class="error"></span>
                </div>
```

```
                <div class="required">
                    <label for="street" accesskey="2">Street</label>
                    <input title="your street" name="street"
                        id="street" tabindex="2" value="" type="text"/>
                    <span id="street-error" class="error"></span>
                </div>
                <div class="required">
                    <label for="city" accesskey="3">City</label>
                    <input title="your city" name="city" id="city"
                        tabindex="3" value="" type="text"/>
                    <span id="city-error" class="error"></span>
                </div>
                <div class="required">
                    <label for="region" accesskey="4">Province</label>
                    <input title="your state / province" name="region"
                        id="region" tabindex="4" value="" type="text"/>
                    <span id="region-error" class="error"></span>
                </div>
                <div class="required">
                    <label for="postal">Postal Code</label>
                    <input title="zip or postal code" name="postal"
                        id="postal" tabindex="5" value="" type="text"/>
                    <span id="postal-error" class="error"></span>
                </div>
                <div>
                    <label for="website" accesskey="6">Website</label>
                    <input title="your website" name="website"
                        id="website" tabindex="6" type="text"/>
                    <span id="website-error" class="error"></span>
                </div>
                <div class="required">
                    <label for="email" accesskey="7">Email
                        (for Verification)</label>
                    <input title="your email" name="email"
                        id="email" tabindex="7" type="text"/>
                    <span id="email-error" class="error"></span>
                </div>
                <div class="buttons">
                    <input type="submit" value="Save Information"
                        tabindex="7"/>
                </div>
            </fieldset>
        </form>
    </div>
    </div>
</div>
</body>
</html>
```

It also includes this style sheet:

```
/*
The rest of the layout is located in source
source/shared/chapter.css
source/chapter10/chapter.css
*/

/* Give the error messages a height to prevent shift */
span.error {
    display:block;
    color:red;
    height:1em;
}

/* Position the slider attached to the bottom of the form */
#slider-wrapper {
    margin: 0;
    padding: 0;
    position:absolute;
    left: 20px;
    display:none;
    width: 436px;
}
#slider-wrapper div {
    margin: 0;
    padding: 0;
}
#slider-wrapper span {
    padding: 1em;
    display: block;
}
#error-slider {
    margin: 0;
    background:red url(images/arrow.png) no-repeat left center;
    color:white;
}
```

Without any load events or JavaScript, my form looks half decent and would submit normally for server-side processing. However, to make things a little nicer, I've also included a load event in the interactive.js file—using the jQuery library from Chapter 9—that does a bit of simple verification when you submit the form:

```
// Prevent conflicts
jQuery.noConflict();

// The load event
jQuery(document).ready( function() {
```

```
// Add a nonbreaking space to the error
// message elements to ensure they have a height.
jQuery('.error').html(' ');

var form = jQuery('#customer-form');

// Add some simple error checking to the inputs that are
// in .required
var inputs = jQuery('.required input',form);

// On focus, clear the error message.
inputs.focus(function() {
    jQuery('#' + jQuery(this).attr('id') + '-error').html('');
});

// On blur, check if the field was filled in.
inputs.blur(function() {
    var input = jQuery(this);
    if(!input.val()) {
        jQuery('#' + input.attr('id') + '-error').html(
            'Please fill in '
            + input.attr('title')
            + '.');
    }
});

// Add a submit event that will also check for errors.
form.submit(function() {

    var error = false;

    inputs.each(function(e) {
        var input = jQuery(this);
        if(!input.val()) {
            error = true;
            jQuery('#' + input.attr('id') + '-error').html(
            'Please fill in '
            + input.attr('title')
            + '.');
        }
    });

    if(error) {

        // Return false to prevent the default action in jQuery.
        return false;
    }
```

```
        return true;

    });

});
```

With the addition of this jQuery load event, the form will indicate errors by including a message under the field, as shown in Figure 10-8.

Figure 10-8. A simple customer information form indicating a field was not completed

But it could still be improved. If you're focused on the bottom of the form, you may not notice the appearance of the error messages at the top of the form. You could also add an alert() method to indicate there were errors, but to give it more life and make it a little more appealing, you can use the Moo.fx methods to apply the error styling and message. For example, use an Fx.Slide() effect to slide in an indicator over the top of the Save Information button to indicate that there was an error. Covering the continue button momentarily will ensure that the user realizes there was an error in the form. Here's the same file modified to add the effects:

```
jQuery.noConflict();
jQuery(document).ready( function() {

    jQuery('.error').html(' ');

    var form = jQuery('#customer-form');

    // Append an error slider to cover the submit button if
    // there's an error.
    jQuery('#customer-form .buttons').append('<div➥
id="slider-wrapper"><div id="error-slider">➥
Oops! It seems you forgot something.</div></div>');
```

```
// Instantiate the slider effect.
var mySlider = new Fx.Slide('error-slider', {
    duration: 600,
    wait:true
});

// Hide the slider to start.
mySlider.hide();

// Instantiate a fade effect on the slider element.
var mySliderFade = new Fx.Style('error-slider', 'opacity', {
    duration: 500,
    wait:true,
    onComplete: function() {
        // When the fade completes, hide the slider and
        // reset the opacity back to 100%
        mySlider.hide();
        mySliderFade.set(1);
    }
});

var inputs = jQuery('.required input',form);

inputs.focus(function() {
    jQuery('#' + jQuery(this).attr('id') + '-error').html('');

    // Fade out the warning slider if there is one.
    mySliderFade.start(0);
});

inputs.blur(function() {
    var input = jQuery(this);
    if(!input.val()) {
        jQuery('#' + input.attr('id') + '-error').html(
            'Please fill in '
            + input.attr('title')
            + '.'
        );
    }
});

form.submit(function() {

    var error = false;

    inputs.each(function(e) {
        var input = jQuery(this);
```

```
            if(!input.val()) {
                error = true;
                jQuery('#' + input.attr('id') + '-error').html(
                    'Please fill in '
                    + input.attr('title')
                    + '.'
                );
            }
        });

        if(error) {
            // If there is an error, slide up the
            // box to make it obvious.
            jQuery('#slider-wrapper').css('display','block');
            mySlider.slideIn();
            setTimeout(function() {
                // Fade out the box automatically after 3.5 seconds
                mySliderFade.start(0);
            },3500);

            return false;
        }

        return true;

    });

});
```

Now, when an error occurs, it will be much more obvious, as shown in Figure 10-9, and the slide is more visually pleasing than alert().

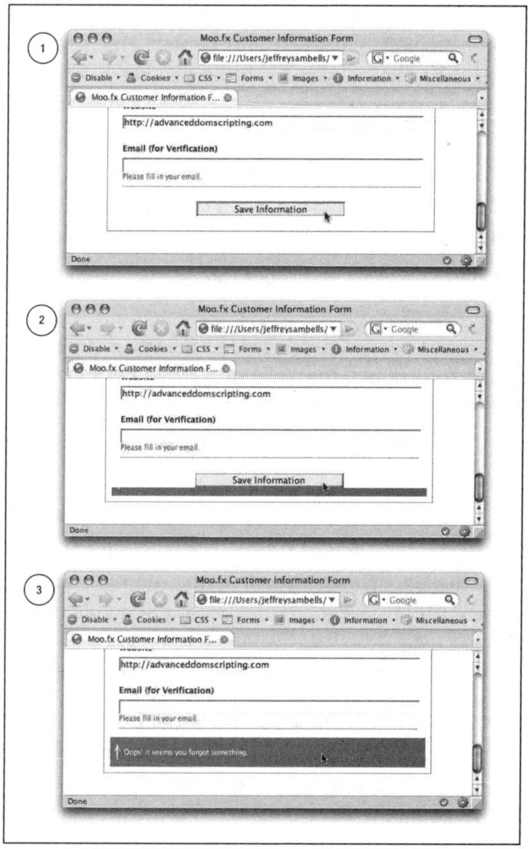

Figure 10-9. Improved error indication on the sample customer information form

Visual effects with Script.aculo.us

The second visual effects library we'll look at is Script.aculo.us. As I mentioned, Script.aculo.us takes a higher-level approach and provides four core effects:

- `Effect.Opacity('element-id' [, options])` changes the element's opacity.

- `Effect.Scale('element-id', percent [, options])` changes an element's width and height dimensions as well as the base for em unit calculations. This can also affect the child elements within the given element. This effect has additional custom options:

  - `scaleX` tells the effect to scale horizontally. The default is `true`.

  - `scaleY` tells the effect to scale vertically. The default is `true`.

  - `scaleContent` allows you to scale the content of the element, not just the outer element itself. The default is `true`.

  - `scaleFromCenter`, if true, tells the element to scale with the center of the element remaining in the same position on the screen. The default is `false`.

- scaleMode is either "box," which scales the visible area of the element, or "contents," which scales the complete element. You can also control the size the element will become by assigning the originalHeight and originalWidth variables to scaleMode using an object such as:

  scaleMode: { originalHeight: 100, originalWidth: 150 }

  The default for the scaleMode is box.

  - scaleFrom sets the starting percentage for scaling, defaults to 100.0.

- Effect.MoveBy('element-id', y, x [, options]) moves an element by a given X/Y pair of pixels.

- Effect.Highlight('element-id' [, options]) flashes a color as the background of an element. This can be used to produce the YFT you saw earlier in the chapter. This effect also has additional custom options:

  - startcolor sets the color of first frame of the highlight. The default is conveniently #ffff99 (light yellow).

  - endcolor sets the color of the last frame of the highlight. Generally, this would be set to the background color of the highlighted element. The default is #ffffff (white).

  - restorecolor sets the background color of the element after the highlight has finished. This defaults to the current background color of the highlighted element.

Each of the core effects supports a number of common options, including the following:

- duration defines the duration of the effect in seconds and should be given as a float. The defaults value is 1.0.

- fps is the desired frames per second rate; it defaults to 25 and can't be higher than 100. This is used to adjust the internal timer, and the actual frame rate will depend on other factors, such as the speed of the computer and browser.

- transition is a function that alters the motion in the effects animation. You can specify a number of built-in transitions including:

  - Effect.Transitions.sinoidal (the default)

  - Effect.Transitions.linear

  - Effect.Transitions.reverse

  - Effect.Transitions.wobble

  - Effect.Transitions.flicker

- from is the starting point of the transition defined as a float between 0.0 and 1.0. The default value is 0.0.

- to is the end point of the transition defined as a float between 0.0 and 1.0. The default value is 1.0.

- sync, when true, indicates that the effect will be manually rendered by calling the render() method. The effect is used in the Effect.Parallel effect you'll see later.

- queue determines the position in the queue. You can define it using one of front or end, and the effect will be queued in the global effects queue. You can also use an object in the form {position:'front/end', scope:'scope', limit:1} to indicate a different queue. For more on the queuing object, see the documentation at http://script.aculo.us.

- direction sets the direction of the transition for grow and shrink effects. The value can be one of top-left, top-right, bottom-left, bottom-right, or center (which is the default).

Like Moo.fx, there are also several callback methods you can specify to invoke code throughout the effect:

- beforeStart is invoked before the effect begins.

- beforeUpdate is invoked on each "frame" of the effect before the frame is drawn.

- afterUpdate is invoked on each "frame" of the effect after the frame is drawn.

- afterFinish is invoked when the effect ends.

To invoke the core effects in the Scripaculous library, you instantiate the desired Effect object, such as the Effect.Opacity effect shown here:

```
// Fade the #element-id from transparent to solid
new Effect.Opacity($('element-id'),{
    duration: 1.0,
    from: 0,
    to: 1
});
```

Unlike Moo.fx, the effect is invoked immediately on instantiation, and no additional method call is required.

Parallel effects

When you instantiate the effect in Script.aculo.us, it's automatically invoked at that instant. If you want to combine multiple effects and have them all run at the same time, you need to use the fifth core method Effect.Parallel(effects[, options]). Unlike the rest of the effects, Effect.Parallel is an effect in itself and doesn't take an element as a parameter but rather an array of subeffects that should be combined:

```
// Move an object and fade it in from 0% to 100% opacity.
new Effect.Parallel([
    new Effect.MoveBy(
        $('element-id),
        400,
        400,
        { sync: true }
    ),
    new Effect.Opacity(
        $('element-id'),
        { sync: true, to: 0.0, from: 1.0 }
    )],
    {
```

429

```
            duration: 0.5
        }
    );
```

The resulting effect will combine the MoveBy and Opacity effect into one. The sync property prevents the individual effect from automatically rendering their own frames—the frames will be rendered by the Parallel() method.

For convenience, Script.aculo.us provides a number of built-in combination effects that invoke one or more of the Core effects. These combination effects such as Effect.Appear follow the same ideas:

```
    new Effect.Appear('element-id', { duration: 3.0 });
```

I won't discuss the details of all the combined effects, so check out the Script.aculo.us online documentation at http://wiki.script.aculo.us/scriptaculous/ for the specific details on each of the effects listed here:

- Effect.Appear('element-id')
- Effect.Fade('element-id')
- Effect.Puff('element-id')
- Effect.BlindDown('element-id')
- Effect.BlindUp('element-id')
- Effect.SwitchOff('element-id')
- Effect.SlideDown('element-id')
- Effect.SlideUp('element-id')
- Effect.DropOut('element-id')
- Effect.Shake('element-id')
- Effect.Pulsate('element-id')
- Effect.Squish('element-id')
- Effect.Fold('element-id')
- Effect.Grow('element-id')
- Effect.Shrink('element-id')
- Effect.Highlight('element-id')
- Effect.toggle('element-id','name of effect')

Realistic motion using Moo.fx

Have you ever seen an effect that basically looks and behaves the same as another effect, but for some reason, one just looks and feels a little more real? Well, that's probably because of subtle differences in the motion of the effects.

In the real world, where mechanical processes do not control us, things move organically. When you move your hand, it doesn't go from point A to point B with equal speed throughout the motion. Your arm, depending on how you move it, may do something similar to this:

1. Start off stationary at one side.
2. Accelerate toward the other side.
3. Reach an average speed.
4. Decelerate as it nears the end.
5. End stationary at the other side.

On top of this, when you start and stop moving your arm, it may not be perfectly stationary. You may slightly overshoot the end and wiggle back or maybe stop short and accelerate again. It's all these inconsistent motions that make things look real. If you recorded your arm movement and captured a frame every few milliseconds, it may look something like Figure 10-10.

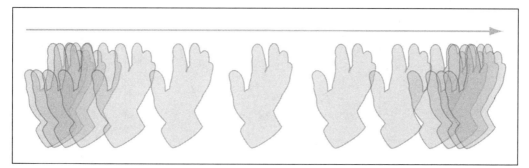

Figure 10-10. An illustration of nonlinear movement through a one-second duration while moving from point A to point B

A typical unsophisticated web animation using the `setTimeout()` method—like the one you did at the beginning of the chapter—is rather different. If you move an element from point A to point B with a `setInterval()` method like one at the beginning of the chapter, the result is a linear motion with consistent intervals, as shown in Figure 10-11.

Figure 10-11. An illustration of linear movement through a one-second duration while moving from point A to point B

If you compare Figures 10-10 and 10-11, you can see the difference. Both move from A to B in the same time frame and achieve the same goal, but the locations of the objects between start and finish are very different. To achieve a more realistic feel in your effects, you need to make them look more like Figure 10-10 or, more correctly, less like Figure 10-11.

Happily, the Moo.fx library includes a large number of `Fx.Transitions` that do exactly this. The transitions in this case are mathematical calculations that alter the actual position of the object relative to the regular interval straight line shown in Figure 10-10. For example, the motion of your arm I described earlier could be calculated using this sinusoidal mathematical formula from the source of the Moo.fx `Fx.Transitions.sineInOut` method:

431

```
... cut ...
/* Property: sineInOut */
sineInOut: function(t, b, c, d){
    return -c/2 * (Math.cos(Math.PI*t/d) - 1) + b;
}
... cut ...
```

If you were to apply this function and plot the object's position relative to time on a graph, it would look something like Figure 10-12.

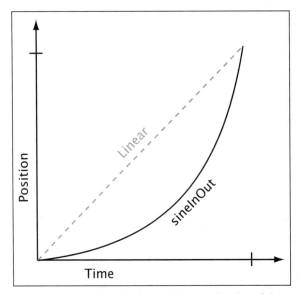

Figure 10-12. A graph indicating position as a function of time using the Fx.Transition.sineInOut method

I'm not going to get into the math behind this, but the important thing to understand is how the position of the element now varies differently over time—it no longer moves in equal increments. Depending on the type of motion you want to achieve, different calculations are required. If you want the element to bounce at the end of the motion, you might use an equation such as the one in `Fx.Transitions.bounceOut`:

```
/* Property: bounceOut */
bounceOut: function(t, b, c, d){
    if ((t/=d) < (1/2.75)){
        return c*(7.5625*t*t) + b;
    } else if (t < (2/2.75)){
        return c*(7.5625*(t-=(1.5/2.75))*t + .75) + b;
    } else if (t < (2.5/2.75)){
        return c*(7.5625*(t-=(2.25/2.75))*t + .9375) + b;
    } else {
        return c*(7.5625*(t-=(2.625/2.75))*t + .984375) + b;
    }
}
```

If you're cringing at the sight of all this math, don't be scared. You don't actually have to remember any of these equations. Applying an Fx.Transition equation to one of your effects in the Moo.fx library is as easy as this:

```
var myFx = new Fx.Style($('element-id'),'left' {
    duration: 1000,
    transition : Fx.Transitions.sineInOut
}).start(10,400);
```

That's it. With this transition, the animation of the element will take the same amount of time, but the position of the element will follow the alternate nonlinear movement.

The Moo.fx Fx.Transitions object includes the following transition methods, which are based on a number of different calculations:

- Fx.Transitions.linear
- Fx.Transitions.quadIn
- Fx.Transitions.quadOut
- Fx.Transitions.quadInOut
- Fx.Transitions.cubicIn
- Fx.Transitions.cubicOut
- Fx.Transitions.cubicInOut
- Fx.Transitions.quartIn
- Fx.Transitions.quartOut
- Fx.Transitions.quartInOut
- Fx.Transitions.quintIn
- Fx.Transitions.quintOut
- Fx.Transitions.quintInOut
- Fx.Transitions.sineIn
- Fx.Transitions.sineOut
- Fx.Transitions.sineInOut
- Fx.Transitions.expoIn
- Fx.Transitions.expoOut
- Fx.Transitions.expoInOut
- Fx.Transitions.circIn
- Fx.Transitions.circOut
- Fx.Transitions.circInOut
- Fx.Transitions.elasticIn
- Fx.Transitions.elasticOut
- Fx.Transitions.elasticInOut
- Fx.Transitions.backIn

433

- Fx.Transitions.backOut

- Fx.Transitions.backInOut

- Fx.Transitions.bounceIn

- Fx.Transitions.bounceOut

- Fx.Transitions.bounceInOut

When considering transitions, don't forget that these don't apply just to moving things around. Any change, such as in color or opacity, can benefit from seeming less linear as well:

```
var myFx = new Fx.Style($('element-id'),'opacity' {
    duration: 1000,
    transition : Fx.Transitions.sineOut
}).start(0,1);
```

> The majority of the Moo.fx transition calculations are based on the work of Robert Penner. If you're interested in these types of organic equations, or you'd like more information, take a look at his explanations of tweening and easing at http://www.robertpenner.com/easing/.

Customer form revisited

Revisiting the customer information form from earlier in the chapter, you can make a few revisions to the effects to include transitions:

```
// Instantiate the slider effect.
var mySlider = new Fx.Slide('error-slider', {
    duration: 600,
    wait:true,
    transition:Fx.Transitions.elasticOut
});

// Hide the slider to start.
mySlider.hide();

// Instantiate a fade effect on the slider element.
var mySliderFade = new Fx.Style('error-slider', 'opacity', {
    duration: 500,
    wait:true,
    transition:Fx.Transitions.sineIn,
    onComplete: function() {
        // When the fade completes, hide the slider and
        // reset the opacity back to 100%.
        mySlider.hide();
        mySliderFade.set(1);
    }
});
```

The result will be the same, but you can change the user experience by changing the type of transition. A bounce or elastic slide will give your application a more playful and fun feeling, while a simple linear transition would give it a more mechanical feel.

Try experimenting with different effects to see how each influences your interaction. You may be surprised that some effects invoke different feelings, even though they're all displaying the same information.

Rounding corners

The last visual effect I'll mention is rounded corners—a staple of Web 2.0 goodness. Until widespread CSS3 support comes to fruition and we can all use the built in border-radius property:

```
.rounded {
    border-radius: 1.6em;
}
```

or multiple background images:

```
.fancyRounded {
    background-image: url(top-left.gif), url(top-right.gif),➥
url(bottom-left.gif), url(bottom-right.gif);
    background-repeat: no-repeat, no-repeat, no-repeat, no-repeat;
    background-position: top left, top right, bottom left,➥
bottom right;
}
```

easy rounded corners seem to be a thing of myth. If you don't want to clutter your markup with unnecessary elements, and you don't mind if your corners are square when JavaScript isn't available, you can always use a DOM script to apply the corner rounding markup for you.

The MochiKit library you saw in Chapter 9 also offers a corner rounding solution. MochiKit's MochiKit.Visual.roundElement(element [, options]) method takes the given element and the following options:

- corners: Specifies which corner to round and is defined as either all or a space-separated string including one or more of these: tl, tr, bl, br for top-left, top-right, bottom-left, and bottom-right, respectively. The default value is all.
- color: The color for the fill of the element. The default value is the evaluated current fill color.
- bgColor: The color for the fill color of the background. The default value is the color of the parent.
- blend: A Boolean that, when true, makes the colors blend together. The default value is true.
- border: A Boolean that indicates if a border should be included. The default value is false.
- compact: A Boolean that indicates if compact (smaller) rounded corners should be used. The default value is false.

Implementing rounded corners on an element is as simple as calling the `roundElement()` method:

```
MochiKit.Visual.roundElement('element-id',{
    corners: 'bl tr',
});
```

This results in something similar to the box shown in Figure 10-13 with rounded top-right and bottom-left corners.

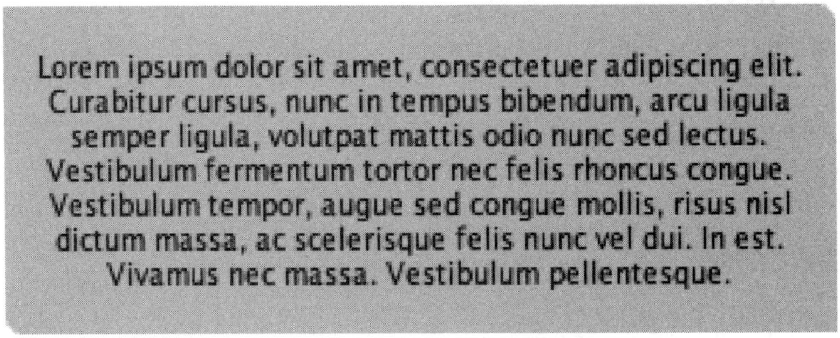

Figure 10-13. An element with rounding applied to the bottom-left and top-right corners

The `roundElement()` method applies the appropriate formatting to the element. If the element was a simple div such as this:

```
<div id="round-me">
    <p>Lorem ipsum dolor sit amet, consectetuer adipiscing elit.</p>
</div>
```

the rounded corners are achieved by appending several 1X1 pixel elements, positioned to form the rounded corners:

```
<div id="round-me">
<div>
    <span style="border-style:solid; border-color:rgb(230, 230, 230);
    border-width: 0px 2px 0px 0px; overflow: hidden;
    background-color: rgb(204, 204, 204); display: block; height: 1px;
    font-size: 1px; margin-right: 3px; margin-left: 0px;">
    </span>
    <span style="border-style:solid; border-color:rgb(230, 230, 230);
    border-width: 0px 1px 0px 0px; overflow: hidden;
    background-color: rgb(204, 204, 204); display: block; height: 1px;
    font-size: 1px; margin-right: 2px; margin-left: 0px;">
    </span>
    <span style="border-style:solid; border-color:rgb(230, 230, 230);
    border-width: 0px 1px 0px 0px; overflow: hidden;
    background-color: rgb(204, 204, 204); display: block; height: 1px;
    font-size: 1px; margin-right: 1px; margin-left: 0px;">
```

```
    </span>
    <span style="border-style:solid; border-color:rgb(230, 230, 230);
    border-width: 0px 1px 0px 0px; overflow: hidden;
    background-color: rgb(204, 204, 204); display: block; height: 2px;
    font-size: 1px; margin-right: 0px; margin-left: 0px;">
    </span>
</div>
<p>Lorem ipsum dolor sit amet, consectetuer adipiscing elit.</p>
<div style="background-color: rgb(255, 255, 255);">
    <span style="border-style:solid; border-color:rgb(230, 230, 230);
    border-width: 0px 0px 0px 1px; overflow: hidden;
    background-color: rgb(204, 204, 204); display: block; height: 2px;
    font-size: 1px; margin-left: 0px; margin-right: 0px;">
    </span>
    <span style="border-style:solid; border-color:rgb(230, 230, 230);
    border-width: 0px 0px 0px 1px; overflow: hidden;
    background-color: rgb(204, 204, 204); display: block; height: 1px;
    font-size: 1px; margin-left: 1px; margin-right: 0px;">
    </span>
    <span style="border-style:solid; border-color:rgb(230, 230, 230);
    border-width: 0px 0px 0px 1px; overflow: hidden;
    background-color: rgb(204, 204, 204); display: block; height: 1px;
    font-size: 1px; margin-left: 2px; margin-right: 0px;">
    </span>
    <span style="border-style:solid; border-color:rgb(230, 230, 230);
    border-width: 0px 0px 0px 2px; overflow: hidden;
    background-color: rgb(204, 204, 204); display: block; height: 1px;
    font-size: 1px; margin-left: 3px; margin-right: 0px;">
    </span>
</div>
</div>
```

The rest of the libraries

So far, I've only touched on Moo.fx and Script.aculo.us, but many of the other libraries such as MochiKit, jQuery, and YUI also include a number of effects and animation methods that I suggest you explore. For the remainder of this chapter, we'll be looking at some overall user interface enhancements, such as drag and drop, that incorporate many of the effects discussed previously in this chapter. This time, we'll use them in a way that interacts with the user rather than just making things look attractive.

Behavioral enhancements

When visual effects combine with user interaction, you get some great behavioral enhancements such as drag and drop.

437

Drag and drop with Script.aculo.us

In Chapter 6, you were introduced to the concepts of dragging by using the appropriate mouse events. Drag-and-drop objects are a staple in many libraries. Libraries such as MochiKit and Mootools have built-in drag-and-drop functionality that works in a similar way, but in this case, I'm only going to discuss Script.aculo.us. The general features allow you to drag items anywhere, restrict them to a region or direction, and drop them on other targets.

Drag anywhere

Creating draggable objects using Script.aculo.us is an extremely simple task and generally involves one line of code, such as this:

```
// Make the element draggable.
var draggable = new Draggable('element-id');
```

Once instantiated, the element associated with the new Draggable(element[, options]) object will be draggable to any location on the page. You can restrict the movement and influence the element through various options including:

- handle defines the element that will be used to invoke the drag. The default value is the entire base element, but you can use this property to specify a child element, such as a title bar on a window. If a handle is defined using an object reference or a class selector dragging, that child element will invoke the drag on the entire element.

  ```
  Draggable('element-id',{ handle: 'title-bar' });
  ```

- revert can be either a Boolean value that, when true, returns the element to its original position:

  ```
  Draggable('element-id',{ revert: true });
  ```

  or it can be defined using a callback function that will be invoked when the element is released:

  ```
  Draggable('element-id',{ revert: function() {
      alert('Drag over');
  }});
  ```

  The default value is false.

- snap alters the position of the element and snaps it to a grid and can be specified three ways:

  - If you define it using a value, the value will be used as a modulo for each coordinate such that if snap is 15, the element will snap to a coordinate (x, y) where x modulo 15 is 0 and y modulo 15 is 0:

    ```
    Draggable('element-id',{ snap: 15 });
    ```

  - If you define it using an array, the values will be used as a modulo for each coordinate (x, y):

    ```
    Draggable('element-id',{ snap: [10,30] });
    ```

- If you define it using a callback function, the function will receive the current x and y coordinates, and it should return a two-element array representing where the element should actually be placed:

```
Draggable('element-id',{ snap: function(x,y) {
    // code
    return [newX,newY];
}});
```

- zindex is the CSS z-index of the draggable item. The default value is 1000.

- constraint can be horizontal or vertical and allows you to constrain the element to dragging only horizontally or vertically.

- ghosting creates and drags a translucent clone of the element rather than the original. The clone will be destroyed when it's released.

- starteffect specifies the effect to apply to the elements when the drag starts. The default is an Effect.Opacity effect.

- reverteffect specifies the effect to apply when the revert option is true and the element reverts back to its original position. The default is a move effect.

- endeffect specifies the effect to apply to the elements when the drag ends. The default is an opacity effect.

Additionally, the change option allows you to specify a callback to invoke as the element is repositioned throughout the drag. This is similar to the mousemove event.

Specifying these options allows you to control the dragged element by constraining it to an area, snapping it back into place, or simply dragging a clone, which you'll see shortly when you create a simple drag-and-drop shopping cart.

Dropping on a target: the droppable

Dragging elements around the screen to reposition them is only half the process. The majority of the time, you'll be dragging with a purpose, or at least with a destination in mind. The destination object on which you drop your element is known as a droppable. When you release a draggable on top of a droppable, the droppable will react in whatever way you specify.

In the case of Script.aculo.us, you don't need to instantiate the droppable object. Instead, you use the add() method of the Droppables (plural) object to create a new droppable:

```
Droppables.add('element-id', {
    hoverclass:'drop-it'
});
```

The Script.aculo.us droppable includes several options that allow you to specify additional properties:

- accept: A string representing the allowable draggable's CSS class selector. Any draggable dropped on this droppable must have this class. If you want to specify more than one class, use an array of class selectors.

- containment: Restricts the accepted droppables to those that are children of the specified element(s). This can be a single string representing one element or an array of multiple elements.

- hoverclass: The class name that will be applied to the droppable when an acceptable draggable is positioned over the top of it. Use this for indicating that the element can now be dropped.

- overlap: If set to horizontal or vertical, the droppable reacts to a draggable only if it's overlapping by more than 50 percent in the given direction. This is mainly used by sorting objects.

- greedy: When true, prevents additional droppables positioned under this droppable from reacting to the draggable. The default value is true.

Additionally, the droppable also includes the following callback options:

- onHover: Invoked whenever an acceptable draggable is moved over the droppable; it receives three arguments:
  - The draggable element
  - The droppable element
  - The percentage of overlap as defined by the overlap option

- onDrop: Invoked whenever an acceptable draggable is released over the droppable; it receives three arguments:
  - The draggable element
  - The droppable element
  - The event

When reacting to draggable elements, you'll be using the onDrop callback to further manipulate the page, as you'll see next when building a shopping cart.

Building a drag-and-drop shopping cart with Script.aculo.us

Shopping carts are almost a staple application in most product websites. Take a look at the very simple shopping cart page in the chapter10/cart/cart.html starting point:

```
<!DOCTYPE html PUBLIC "-//W3C//DTD XHTML 1.0 Strict//EN"
        "http://www.w3.org/TR/xhtml1/DTD/xhtml1-strict.dtd">
<html xmlns="http://www.w3.org/1999/xhtml">
<head>
    <title>Scriptaculous Shopping Cart Example</title>
    <link rel="stylesheet" href="../../shared/source.css"
        type="text/css" media="screen" />
    <link rel="stylesheet" href="../chapter.css"
        type="text/css" media="screen" />
    <link rel="stylesheet" href="cart.css"
        type="text/css" media="screen" />

    <!-- Include the prototype and script.aculo.us libraries -->
    <script src="../../libraries/prototype.js"
        type="text/javascript"></script>

    <script src="../../libraries/scriptaculous/src/scriptaculous.js"
        type="text/javascript"></script>
```

```
        <script type="text/javascript" src="interactive.js"></script>
</head>
<body>
    <h1>A Simple Shopping Cart</h1>
    <div id="content">
        <h2>Buy Some Books!</h2>
        <div id="product-wrapper">
            <ul id="products">
                <li class="product-item" id="pid-1">
                    <img src="books/1590593812.jpg" alt="Web➡
Standards Solutions: The Markup and Style Handbook"/>
                    <a href="server.json?id=pid-1"
                        title="Add to cart">Add</a>
                </li>
                <li class="product-item" id="pid-2">
                    <img src="books/1590595335.jpg" alt="DOM➡
Scripting: Web Design with JavaScript and the Document Object Model"/>
                    <a href="server.json?id=pid-1"
                        title="Add to cart">Add</a>
                </li>
                <li class="product-item" id="pid-3">
                    <img src="books/1590596145.jpg" alt="CSS➡
Mastery: Advanced Web Standards Solutions"/>
                    <a href="server.json?id=pid-1"
                        title="Add to cart">Add</a>
                </li>
                <li class="product-item" id="pid-4">
                    <img src="books/1590596382.jpg" alt="Web➡
Accessibility: Web Standards and Regulatory Compliance"/>
                    <a href="server.json?id=pid-1"
                        title="Add to cart">Add</a>
                </li>
                <li class="product-item" id="pid-5">
                    <img src="books/1590597656.jpg" alt="HTML➡
Mastery: Semantics, Standards, and Styling"/>
                    <a href="server.json?id=pid-1"
                        title="Add to cart">Add</a>
                </li>
                <li class="product-item" id="pid-5">
                    <img src="books/1590598032.jpg" alt="Web➡
Standards Creativity: Innovations in Web Design with XHTML, CSS,➡
and DOM Scripting"/>
                    <a href="server.json?id=pid-1"
                        title="Add to cart">Add</a>
                </li>
                <li class="product-item" id="pid-5">
                    <img src="books/1590594304.jpg" alt="Web➡
Designer's Reference"/>
                    <a href="server.json?id=pid-1"
```

441

```
                            title="Add to cart">Add</a>
                    </li>
                </ul>
                <div class="clear"></div>
            </div>
            <h3>In Your Cart...</h3>
            <p id="message"> </p>
            <div id="cart-wrapper">
                <ul id="cart">
                    <li class="cart-item">
                        <img src="books/1590598032.jpg" alt="Web➥
Standards Creativity: Innovations in Web Design with XHTML, CSS,➥
and DOM Scripting"/>
                        <a href="server.json?id=pid-5"
                            title="Remove from cart">Remove</a>
                    </li>
                    <li class="cart-item">
                        <img src="books/1590596145.jpg" alt="CSS➥
Mastery: Advanced Web Standards Solutions"/>
                        <a href="server.json?id=pid-3"
                            title="Remove from cart">Remove</a>
                    </li>
                </ul>
                <div class="clear"></div>
            </div>
        </div>
    </body>
</html>
```

Like the earlier customer information form, this cart is set up to work without JavaScript, listing each product with its own add button along with a bit of CSS:

```
/* cart and product specific styles */
#products, #cart {
    list-style: none;
    clear: both;
    margin: 0;
    padding: 0;
}
#products li, #cart li {
    display: block;
    height: 40px;
    width: 33px;
    float: left;
}
#products li img, #cart li img {
    height: 40px;
    width: 33px;
}
#products li a, #cart li a {
```

```
}
#product-wrapper {
    background: #efefef;
    padding: 15px;
    margin: 1em;
    width: 430px;
}
#cart-wrapper {
    background: #fff9ea;
    padding: 15px;
    margin: 1em;
    width: 430px;
}
#cart-wrapper.drop-it {
    background: #eaffea;
}
#message {
    font-size:1em;
    height: 1em;
}
.product-item *, .cart-item * {
    display: block;
    clear: none;
}
```

The shopping cart's page will resemble the one shown in Figure 10-14.

Figure 10-14. A typical shopping cart

Again, keeping things accessible, you're starting with a working web application (assuming you've written the rest of the required server-side code) that doesn't rely on any JavaScript, but let's make it a little fancier with some drag-and-drop interaction.

Start off by opening the chapter10/cart/interactive.js file and reading through the comments:

```
// A load event using Prototype
Event.observe(window, 'load', function(event) {

    // Hide all the add and remove buttons.

    // Make all the products draggable in a special queue
    // so you can apply additional effects later.

    // Make all the existing cart items draggable in a special queue
    // so you can remove them from the cart later by applying
    // additional effects.

    // Create a Boolean that will be used to indicate
    // if an item should be removed.

    // Make the cart droppable.

    // Create an observer that will remove items dragged
    // out of the cart.

});
```

Because you started with a working web application without a drag-and-drop interface, the markup has a few extras such as add and remove links, so you'll need to hide them first:

```
// A load event using Prototype
Event.observe(window, 'load', function(event) {

...cut...

    // Hide all the add and remove buttons.
    $$('li.product-item a','li.cart-item a').each(function(e) {
        e.setStyle({
            position:'absolute',
            top:0,
            left:'-10000px'
        });
    });

...cut...

});
```

> *How you add an element and maintain accessibility is up to you. The intention of this example is only to demonstrate the drag-and-drop capabilities of Script.aculo.us. In a real shopping cart application, you would also apply the appropriate tab indexes and access key shortcuts and treat the links in various ways to maintain accessibility.*

I've already included some CSS styles for these alterations, so the page should now resemble Figure 10-15.

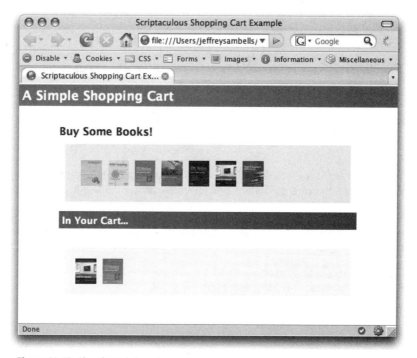

Figure 10-15. The altered shopping cart page

Next, all you have to do is convert all the products and existing cart items to draggables and set a keepMe variable to false:

```
// A load event using Prototype
Event.observe(window, 'load', function(event) {

...cut...

    // Make all the products draggable in a special queue
    // so you can apply additional effects later.
    $$('li.product-item').each(function(e) {
        new Draggable(e,{
            revert:true,
            queue:'cart_draggables'
```

```
            });
        });

        // Make all the existing cart items draggable in a special queue
        // so you can remove them from the cart later by applying
        // additional effects.
        $$('li.cart-item').each(function(e) {
            new Draggable(e,{
                revert:true,
                queue:'cart_draggables'
            });
        });

        // Create a Boolean that will be used to indicate
        // if an item should be removed.
        var keepMe = false;

    ...cut...

    });
```

The keepMe variable, in the scope of the load event, will be used later on to keep track of which items should be removed from the cart. By default, you'll remove an item unless it's been dropped on the cart.

Next, make #cart-wrapper a droppable that accepts only the appropriate .product-item and .cart-item draggables:

```
    // A load event using Prototype
    Event.observe(window, 'load', function(event) {

    ...cut...

    // Make the cart droppable.
    Droppables.add($('cart'),{

        // Accept on products and cart items
        accept:['product-item','cart-item'],

        // Change the class of the cart to indicate when
        // it's the target.
        hoverclass:'drop-it',

        // Add items to the cart as necessary.
        onDrop:function(draggable, droppable, event) {

            // Items dropped on the cart won't be deleted
            // this will prevent removal of the cart items if
            // they're dropped within the cart.
            keepMe = true;
```

```
                // Only add .product-item classes
              if(draggable.className == 'product-item') {

                   $('message').innerHTML = 'Contacting server...';

                   //Save the addition to the server.
                   new Ajax.Request(
                       draggable.getElementsByTagName('A')[0].➡
getAttribute('href'),
                       {
                           method:'get',
                           onSuccess: function(response) {
                               $('message').innerHTML = ➡
response.responseText;

                               // Create a new DOM node for the list with
                               var newItem = document.createElement('LI');
                               newItem.className = 'cart-item';
                               var newThumb = ➡
document.createElement('IMG');
                               var oldImage = ➡
draggable.getElementsByTagName('IMG')[0];
                               newThumb.src = oldImage.src;
                               newThumb.alt = oldImage.alt;
                               newItem.appendChild(newThumb);
                               var newAnchor = document.createElement('A');
                               newAnchor.setAttribute(
                                   'href',
                                   'server.json?id=' + draggable.id
                               );
                               newAnchor.setAttribute(
                                   'title',
                                   'Remove from cart'
                               );
                               newAnchor.style.display = 'none';
                               newItem.appendChild(newAnchor);

                               // Make the new items dragable as well.
                               new Draggable(newItem,{
                                   revert:true,
                                   queue:'cart_draggables'
                               });

                               // Make the new items fade in.
                               new Effect.Opacity(newItem,{from:0,to:1});

                               $('cart').appendChild(newItem);
                           },
                           onFailure: function() {
```

```
                              $('message').innerHTML = 'Could not add';
                          }
                      }
                  );
              }
          }
      });

      ...cut...

      });
```

In your Droppable options, the onDrop callback does the bulk of the work for the cart. The addition of the item to the cart is communicated back to the server using the same URL in the Add button. Second, if the addition was successful—which it always will be in this case, because there is no real server side—a copy of the product image is added to the cart along with a remove anchor. These two steps complete the process of adding to the cart, but don't forget that people may also want to remove things from the cart.

> *This example doesn't incorporate any keyboard navigation or other nonmouse navigation. You should also attach various key-related events or additional attributes to the new cart items to allow better access.*

To remove things from the cart, you could simply set up another object as a droppable trash can and allow the items in the cart to be dragged onto it. That would follow the identical process you used here to add items to the cart, with the exception that the onDrop event would remove the items from the server and the cart. Alternatively, we'll just allow people to drag items out of the cart area and drop them anywhere they like. This required making the new cart items draggable as you already did previously:

```
// Make the new items dragable as well.
new Draggable(newItem,{
    revert:true,
    queue:'cart_draggables'
});
```

It also requires accessing properties and methods of the Draggables object itself to create an observer that will interact with all draggable elements.

Interacting with draggables through an observer

Moving draggables and dropping them onto droppables is probably sufficient for most cases, but the Script.aculo.us library also allows you to access the global list of draggable and droppable objects through the Droppables object. I won't go into detail about each of the methods with the exception of the observer: the Droppables object allows you to add additional elements that will act as observers of the drag process.

The observer is an object with an element property and one or more of the following callback methods:

- onStart is invoked when you start to move any Draggable on the page.
- onDrag is invoked on each mousemove during the drag.
- onEnd is invoked when dragging is done.

Each of the callback methods will be invoked with two arguments: the eventName and the instance of the draggable element that is associated with the current drag action.

In the case of your shopping cart, objects dragged out of the cart have no droppable target, so you use an observer to watch for those instances and remove them as appropriate:

```
// A load event using Prototype
Event.observe(window, 'load', function(event) {

...cut...

// Create an observer that will remove items dragged out of the cart.
Draggables.addObserver({
element: null,
onEnd:function(eventName, draggable) {

    // Get the current position of the draggable so that you
    // can move it back if the server request fails.
    var delta = draggable.currentDelta();

    if(!keepMe && draggable.element.className == 'cart-item') {
        // This item should be removed.

        // Calculate the offset position from the original
        // starting point.
        var topOffset = delta[1]-draggable.delta[1];
        var leftOffset = delta[0]-draggable.delta[0];

        // Prevent the draggable from reverting while
        // you check with the server.
        draggable.options.revert = false;

        new Ajax.Request(
            draggable.element.getElementsByTagName('A')➡
[0].getAttribute('href'),
            {
                method:'get',
                onSuccess: function(response) {

                    // Removal on the server was successful so
                    // destroy the draggable and fade it out.
                    $('message').innerHTML = 'Remove: '
```

```
                            + response.responseText;
                        draggable.destroy();

                        // Add the fade to the end of the draggable queue.
                        new Effect.Fade(draggable.element, {
                            duration:0.2,
                            queue: {
                                scope:'cart_draggables',
                                position:'end'
                            },
                            afterFinish: function(){
                                // Remove the draggable element
                                // once it's finished.
                                draggable.element.remove();
                            }
                        });

                    },
                    onFailure:function() {
                        // Removal failed so revert the draggable back to
                        // its original position in the cart.
                        $('message').innerHTML = 'Could not be removed';

                        var dur = Math.sqrt(Math.abs(topOffset ^2)
                            + Math.abs(leftOffset ^2)) * 0.02;
                        new Effect.Move(draggable.element, {
                            x: -leftOffset,
                            y: -topOffset,
                            duration: dur,
                            queue: {
                                scope:'cart_draggables',
                                position:'end'
                            },
                            afterFinish: function() {
                                // Reset the current delta to the new
                                // position and enable revert.
                                draggable.delta = draggable.currentDelta()
                                draggable.options.revert = true;
                            }
                        });
                    }
                }
            );
        }

        // Reset keepMe the flag to false.
        keepMe = false;
    }
});
```

```
...cut...

});
```

This observer will trigger at the end of *every* drag action, regardless of the class, and in this case, it will check to see if the dragged element should be removed.

The `cart-items` in your cart are associated with a different class name to distinguish them from the regular product items. The observer checks the class name to ensure it matches the `.cart-item` elements, and it checks to see if the keepMe Boolean is `false`. Your #cart droppable's onDrop callback sets the keepMe Boolean to `true` when the items are dropped on it, so the only time it will be false is if the dropped object is outside the cart. If both conditions are met, the element will be removed from the cart; otherwise, it will revert to its original location.

> *This example cart is far from complete and production ready, but it provides the necessary examples for a typical drag-and-drop application. For more on the* Draggables *object and other properties, see the* http://wiki.script.aculo.us/Script.aculo.us/show/Draggables *documentation site.*

More drag and drop fun

Drag-and-drop interfaces open up a whole new possibility for interactive web applications, but always remember accessibility. If you expect devices without a mouse to access your site, be sure to provide alternate methods or at least indicate that disabling JavaScript altogether will provide a consistent mouse-free experience.

To whet your appetite a little more, I'll leave you with this. In the Script.aculo.us library, another handy effect is the ability to incorporate sortable lists. With minimal effort you can take a list, such as this:

```
<ul id="categories">
    <li>Markup</li>
    <li>Style</li>
    <li>Behavior</li>
    <li>Server Scripts</li>
    <li>Browsers</li>
</ul>
```

and with only one line of code, such as this:

```
Sortable.create('categories');
```

your list is now drag-and-drop sortable. Now that's pretty cool. There are a number of options for sortables, including sorting between lists, using nested lists, and dragging and dropping among multiple lists. You can see all the options by checking out the documentation at http://wiki.script.aculo.us/scriptaculous/show/Sortable.create. Combined with an Ajax request after each change, you could provide a much nicer alternative to entering numbers in text boxes when resorting list items.

Summary

In this chapter, you were introduced to basics of creating your own effects using the JavaScript setTimeout() method as well as a couple libraries that can make your everyday web applications a little flashier. You saw a few simple effects, such as the Yellow Fade Technique, and you learned how adding the proper effects to your web application can influence interaction as well as the overall feeling and tone users will experience.

When implementing effects, keep accessibility in mind. Your site may look great when things are flashy and fun, but if the effect limits the ability to access the desired information, you have a problem.

In the next chapter, you'll look at a few of the available application programming interfaces (APIs) that you can use to add lots of great features, such as mapping and searching, with minimal effort.

Chapter 11

MASHUPS GALORE! USING APIS TO ADD MAPS, SEARCHING, AND MUCH MORE

A mashup is just as it sounds—the mashing of two or more applications into one. The most common mashup examples usually involve plotting some information onto a map using Google Maps, which we'll look at later in this chapter. Map mashups include everything from the "Top 10 beaches with WiFi access" (http://www.geekabout.com/2007-01-18-78/top-10-beaches-with-wifi-internet-access.html) to real-time train locations (http://www.mackers.com/projects/dartmaps/) to indications of global incidents (http://www.globalincidentmap.com/).

Regardless of the type of mashup you're using, in most cases, your mashup will involve taking data you've collected yourself, or data you've retrieved from a public data source, and mashing it with a public service using an application programming interface (API). The results will be displayed or consumed on your own site, providing a powerful service with minimal work.

The service providing the API is what makes the mashing possible. Its API is a collection of predefined and open communication interfaces that allow you to programmatically query and interact with the service. It will have a specific set of documented methods and requirements just like the APIs for the DOM scripting libraries you played with in Chapters 9 and 10. These web service APIs come in several flavors and can be implemented using server-side protocols or sometimes directly in the browser using JavaScript or other plug-ins, such as Adobe Flash.

The most common APIs use a server-side language, such as PHP, to retrieve and submit information. For example, you can create a list of the most recent photos posted to http://flickr.com with only a few lines of PHP code:

```
<!DOCTYPE HTML PUBLIC "-//W3C//DTD HTML 4.01//EN"
    "http://www.w3.org/TR/html4/strict.dtd">
<html>
<head>
    <title>Recent Flickr Photos!</title>
</head>
<body>
<?php
    $url = 'http://www.flickr.com/services/feeds/photos_public.gne';
    foreach(simplexml_load_file($url)->entry as $item) {
        echo $item->content;
    }
?>
</html>
```

Likewise, APIs can be as simple as adding a few HTML elements to your markup. To include an inline video in your site, you could upload it to http://youtube.com and simply embed the appropriate link in your website:

```
<!DOCTYPE HTML PUBLIC "-//W3C//DTD HTML 4.01//EN"
        "http://www.w3.org/TR/html4/strict.dtd">
<html>
<head>
    <title>My YouTube Video!</title>
</head>
<body>
<object width="425" height="350">
    <param name="movie" value=➥
"http://www.youtube.com/v/hFFH8DaOHQg"></param>
    <param name="wmode" value="transparent"></param>
    <embed src="http://www.youtube.com/v/your_video_id"
        type="application/x-shockwave-flash"
        wmode="transparent" width="425" height="350"></embed>
</object>
</body>
</html>
```

Unlike the APIs for your DOM scripting libraries, service APIs such as these are hosted by the service itself. You can't download the Flickr API or serve a video for YouTube from your own machine. This allows the server to provide updates and new features on a whim, and it allows you to always access the most recent version without upgrading local software. The only requirement of the service API is that you follow the API documentation to make the appropriate requests and, in turn, receive the appropriate response.

The Flickr and YouTube examples are rather simplistic. The Flickr API allows you to do a lot more than just retrieve recent photos—as you'll see later in this chapter—and embedding a Flash file from YouTube isn't much different from any other Flash file.

Interacting with server-side API's may also involve implementing communication protocols such as these:

- Simple Object Access Protocol (SOAP)
- Representational State Transfer (REST)
- XML remote procedure calls (XML-RPC)

These protocols can be very powerful, but their specifics are beyond the scope of a DOM scripting book, so I won't be discussing any of them in detail.

In this chapter, I'll go through the basics of mashups with APIs. I'll start with a few powerful client-side JavaScript APIs that allow you to interact with maps and search results. In the second part of the chapter, I'll touch on integrating your DOM scripts with server-side APIs using proxy scripts.

API keys

Throughout the chapter, you'll be required to sign up for several different API keys in order to interact with many of the services. API keys are unique identifiers that allow the service to know who's accessing and requesting information. Each service will handle their keys a little differently or require different types of authentication methods so I'll point each out as we go, but be sure to use your own key as indicated in the examples. Without your special key registered to you, many of these examples will not work.

> *When signing up for your API keys and accounts, also be sure to read the terms of services for each API. In many cases, the API may have requirements or limitations that you have to abide by to maintain access to the API.*

Client-side APIs: some JavaScript required

Client-side JavaScript APIs can offer a host of awesome features but there's one potential downfall—JavaScript is required. Providing a site that relies exclusively on JavaScript can cause some accessibility issues, as you've seen throughout the book, so be sure to provide the appropriate alternatives as necessary. In this section, I'll demonstrate two JavaScript APIs—the Google Maps API and the Google Ajax Search API—along with a mashup that combines the two. The examples I provide in this chapter will continue to keep accessibility in mind where possible by providing alternative methods and using progressive enhancement.

Maps put mashups on the map

The term mashup, along with Ajax, became popular when Google introduced their public Google Maps API. The Google Maps API allows you to embed a fully functioning map, similar to the one at http://local.google.com, directly in your own website. You can then add whatever markers and data you want, opening up a whole world of possibilities (pun intended) and allowing all kinds of location-based data to be displayed graphically using an interactive map—working entirely in JavaScript.

Integrating a Google Map into your website is exceptionally easy. You only need to register for an API key at http://www.google.com/apis/maps/signup.html. Be sure to read the highlights from the terms of service to see what you can and can't do, as there are some limitations; then, enter the URL of your website, and click Generate API Key, as shown in Figure 11-1.

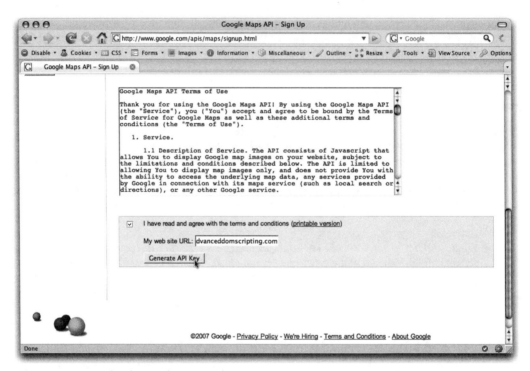

Figure 11-1. Generating the Google Maps API key

On the resulting page, you'll be presented with your API key, which will resemble a random string of characters such as this:

```
ABQIAAAAFOOBBfcVGVmeJR5FXDm_1BR2mdOh-K__WeD915i1OJagt9QYmBRA7MOsv8c➥
dXJDNdSN1EozosIssBA
```

And you'll be presented with a simple "Hello World" example:

```
<!DOCTYPE html PUBLIC "-//W3C//DTD XHTML 1.0 Strict//EN"
  "http://www.w3.org/TR/xhtml1/DTD/xhtml1-strict.dtd">
<html xmlns="http://www.w3.org/1999/xhtml">
  <head>
    <meta http-equiv="content-type" content="text/html;
        charset=utf-8"/>
    <title>Google Maps JavaScript API Example</title>
    <script src="http://maps.google.com/maps?file=api&amp;v=2➥
&amp;key=ABQIAAAAFOOBBfcVGVmeJR5FXDm_1BR2mdOh-K__WeD915i10Jag➥
t9QYmBRA7MOsv8cdXJDNdSN1EozosIssBA"
        type="text/javascript"></script>
    <script type="text/javascript">

    //<![CDATA[

    function load() {
      if (GBrowserIsCompatible()) {
        var map = new GMap2(document.getElementById("map"));
        map.setCenter(new GLatLng(37.4419, -122.1419), 13);
      }
    }

    //]]>
    </script>
  </head>
  <body onload="load()" onunload="GUnload()">
    <div id="map" style="width: 500px; height: 300px"></div>
  </body>
</html>
```

If you copy and paste the example into an HTML file—and change the API key to the one you registered for—you'll see a page centered on Palo Alto, California, as shown in Figure 11-2.

The Google Maps API key is linked to your domain name, so if you have the wrong key, you'll receive an alert message indicating that you should go sign up for a key. The only special case is when you open the examples for a file located directly on your hard drive. If the URL in your browser begins with file://, the API key isn't restricted to a specific domain, as Google considers the request a developer request. The examples in the source for this book don't have a proper API key, so they won't work on a website until you add your own key. However, they will work if you open them in a browser from the source files directly on your hard drive.

Figure 11-2. The "Hello World" Google map centered on Palo Alto

Google's example doesn't separate the JavaScript from the markup as you've done throughout the rest of the book, so I suggest you take a moment to separate the two. I've provided a separated version in the chapter11/map/google.html source file that also contains a few CSS files:

```
<!DOCTYPE html PUBLIC "-//W3C//DTD XHTML 1.0 Strict//EN"
  "http://www.w3.org/TR/xhtml1/DTD/xhtml1-strict.dtd">
<html xmlns="http://www.w3.org/1999/xhtml">
  <head>
    <meta http-equiv="content-type"
        content="text/html; charset=utf-8"/>
    <title>Google Maps JavaScript API Example</title>
    <link rel="stylesheet" href="../../shared/source.css"
        type="text/css" media="screen" />
    <link rel="stylesheet" href="../chapter.css"
        type="text/css" media="screen" />
    <link rel="stylesheet" href="map.css"
        type="text/css" media="screen" />
    <script src="../../ADS-final-verbose.js"
        type="text/javascript"></script>

    <script src="http://maps.google.com/maps?file=api&amp;v=2&amp;➥
key=YOUR_API_KEY" type="text/javascript"></script>
    <script src="map.js" type="text/javascript"></script>
  </head>
  <body>
```

```
    <div id="map"></div>
  </body>
</html>
```

I've included the following ADS load event listener along with the chapter11/map/map.js source file:

```
ADS.addEvent(window,'load',function() {

    if (GBrowserIsCompatible()) {

        // Instantiate the map API (version 2).
        var map = new GMap2(document.getElementById("map"));

        // Instantiate a new latitude and longitude coordinate.
        var location = new GLatLng(37.4419, -122.1419);
        // Set the center of the map to location
        // with a zoom level of 13
        map.setCenter(location, 13);

        // Instantiate a new marker using the location.
        var marker = new GMarker(location);

        // Add the marker to the map.
        map.addOverlay(marker);

        // Add a zoom/pan and type control.
        map.addControl(new GLargeMapControl());
        map.addControl(new GMapTypeControl());

    }
});

ADS.addEvent(window,'unload',GUnload);
```

If you take a look at the earlier example or the map.js file, you'll notice that the Maps API code is wrapped in a GBrowserIsCompatible() statement. This acts like the ADS.isCompatible() method explained in Chapter 1 and ensures that the browser is compatible with all aspects of the Google Maps API. You'll also notice that only three lines of code invoke all the markup and interaction required for the fancy map. The first creates the map instance in the #map div:

```
// Instantiate the map API (version 2).
var map = new GMap2(document.getElementById("map"));
```

and the next two set the center location of the map based on a geographic latitude and longitude:

```
// Instantiate a new latitude and longitude coordinate.
var location = new GLatLng(37.4419, -122.1419);
// Set the center of the map to location with a zoom level of 13.
map.setCenter(location, 13);
```

The GLatLng object is a representation of a latitude and longitude intersection on the surface of the earth and is used to locate all the objects you place on the map. The latitude of a point is the number of degrees north (+) or south (–) of the equator and can range from +90 degrees, which is the north pole, to –90 degrees, which is the south pole. Longitude represents the number of degrees east (+) or west (–) of the prime meridian and can range from +180 degrees to –180 degrees, covering the full 360 degrees of the earth. Latitude and longitude are shown in Figure 11-3.

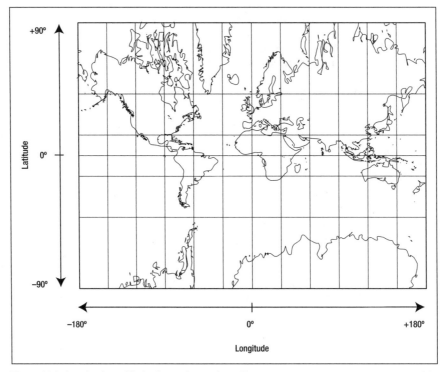

Figure 11-3. Longitude and latitude on the earth surface

If you don't know the latitude and longitude of the locations you want to show, don't worry. We'll discuss geocoding—programmatically turning an address into a latitude and longitude—a little later.

I've separated the latitude and longitude location in this example, so you can use it to create a marker overlay on your map using a new instance of the GMarker() object. The GMarker object creates the upside-down teardrop markers common to Google Maps and requires a GLatLng object to specify its location:

```
// Instantiate a new marker using the location.
var marker = new GMarker(location);
```

Once instantiated, you still need to add the marker to the map using the map's addOverlay() method:

```
// Add the marker to the map.
map.addOverlay(marker);
```

The result is a map with a nice marker at the location and some controls, as shown in Figure 11-4.

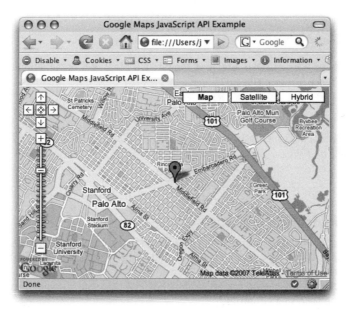

Figure 11-4. The Google map with a marker

To provide more interactivity such as zooming and panning, as shown in Figure 11-4, you can also enable a number of different controls on the map. The Google Maps API includes five controls:

- GLargeMapControl is a large pan and zoom control similar to the one found on http://maps.google.com.
- GSmallMapControl is a smaller version of the map control.
- GScaleControl is a metric and imperial scale indicator.
- GSmallZoomControl is a smaller zoom control.
- GMapTypeControl creates a list of the available map types, such as a road map or a satellite map.

These controls can be enabled through the map's addControl() method by specifying a new instance of one of the controls in the preceding list. For example, you can add a GLargeMapControl and a GMapTypeControl as follows:

```
// Add a zoom/pan and type control.
map.addControl(new GLargeMapControl());
map.addControl(new GMapTypeControl());
```

You can see how easy it is to create a fully functional interactive map with a few lines of code using the Google Maps API. There's a lot more you could do too. For example, you can

- Add informational window bubbles to each of your markers
- Change the icon of the markers
- Create custom objects and image overlays
- Integrate your own map types and tiles
- Include driving directions from one location to another.

For all the features of the API, take a look at the Google Maps API documentation at http://www.google.com/apis/maps/documentation/.

> If you're interested in creating Google Maps with more powerful features, check out my other books on beginning Google Maps Applications with PHP and Ajax and with Rails and Ajax (Apress, ISBN-13: 978-1-59059-707-1 and 978-1-59059-787-3) at http://googlemapsbook.com.

Retrieving latitude and longitude

Placing markers on your map requires that you know the latitude and longitude of the points you want to plot. Luckily, the Google Maps API also includes a geocoder in the GClientGeocoder object that allows you to retrieve the latitude and longitude for popular locations, cities, and postal addresses. The accuracy of the information depends on the data available, but in general, the geocoder covers the following countries:

- The United States
- Canada
- France
- Germany
- Japan
- Italy
- Spain
- Australia
- New Zealand

Using the GClientGeocoder is very similar to an Ajax call, except you give it the address and a callback function to execute when loaded:

```
var geocoder = new GClientGeocoder();
var address = '1600 Amphitheatre Parkway Mountain View, CA';
geocoder.getLatLng(
    address,
    function(point) {
        if (!point) {
```

```
            alert(address + " not found");
        } else {
            // Recenter the map on the address and create a marker.
            map.setCenter(point, 12);
            var marker = new GMarker(point);
            map.addOverlay(marker);
        }
    }
);
```

If successful, the callback argument will be passed a GLatLng object representation of the latitude and longitude that you can use to position a new marker. If you simply want to retrieve the latitude and longitude for some other purpose, you can use the point.lat() method to retrieve the latitude value and the point.lng() method to retrieve the longitude value.

Like an Ajax request, the geocoder request is also an asynchronous request, so refer to Chapter 8 for information regarding the complications with asynchronous requests.

> *The geocoder can also be accessed on the server side to retrieve the same information. It's highly recommended that you not use the JavaScript geocoder to continually request the same locations every time you reload the page. Instead, create a server-side script that will fetch the latitude and longitude information for each point you plan to show and store the results in a database. This will make your map much faster, and it will avoid the possibility of hitting your geocoding limit for the day when your site becomes really popular.*

Maintaining accessibility using microformats

A fun little interactive map of all your data points is great, but what happens when the map can't be accessed? As an alternative to the map, offer a DOM-script-free version that can also act as the initial database of points by incorporating microformats.

A microformat (http://microformat.org) is a way of marking up data so that both humans and machines can easily and consistently interpret it. There are a number of different microformats, but the one we're interested in here is the geo format (http://microformats.org/wiki/geo), which is a subset of the hcard format (http://microformats.org/wiki/hcard) and is used to indicate geographic latitude and longitude information as follows:

```
<div class="geo">
    <abbr class="latitude" title="45.27">
        45&#176; 16&#39; 12&#34; N
    </abbr>
    <abbr class="longitude" title="-75.42">
        75&#176; 25&#39; 12&#34; E
    </abbr>
</div>
```

To see the microformat in action, take a look at the truncated chapter11/map-accessible/ cities.html source as follows:

```
<!DOCTYPE html PUBLIC "-//W3C//DTD XHTML 1.0 Strict//EN"
  "http://www.w3.org/TR/xhtml1/DTD/xhtml1-strict.dtd">
<html xmlns="http://www.w3.org/1999/xhtml">
  <head>
    <title>An Accessible Google Map</title>
    <link rel="stylesheet" href="../../shared/source.css"
        type="text/css" media="screen" />
    <link rel="stylesheet" href="../chapter.css"
        type="text/css" media="screen" />
    <link rel="stylesheet" href="map.css"
        type="text/css" media="screen" />
    <script src="../../ADS-final-verbose.js"
        type="text/javascript"></script>

    <script src="http://maps.google.com/maps?file=api&amp;v=2&amp; ➡
    key=YOUR_API_KEY" type="text/javascript"></script>
    <script src="map.js" type="text/javascript"></script>
  </head>
  <body>
    <h1>An Accessible Google Map</h1>
    <div id="content">
      <h2>Capital Cities of the World</h2>
      <div id="map"></div>
        <ul id="cities">
          <li class="vcard">
            <div class="adr">
              <div class="country-name">
                Heard Island and McDonald Islands
              </div>
            </div>
            <div class="geo">
              <abbr class="latitude" title="-53">53&#176; ➡
00&#39; 0&#34; S</abbr>
              <abbr class="longitude" title="74">74&#176; ➡
00&#39; 0&#34; E</abbr>
            </div>
          </li>

          ... cut ...

          <li class="vcard">
            <div class="adr">
              <span class="locality">Reykjavik</span>,
              <div class="country-name">
                Iceland
```

```
                    </div>
                </div>
                <div class="geo">
                    <abbr class="latitude" title="64.1"> ➥
64&#176; 05&#39; 60&#34; N</abbr>
                    <abbr class="longitude" title="-21.57"> ➥
21&#176; 34&#39; 12&#34; W</abbr>
                </div>
            </li>
        </ul>
    </div>
  </body>
</html>
```

This page, shown in Figure11-5, contains a simple unordered list of all the capital cities of the world, but each listing has a few special features:

- The geo microformat to specify the latitude and longitude of the city
- The addr microformat to specify the city and country, which will be used to populate the marker's info window

Figure 11-5. An unordered list of cities incorporating the geo microformat to indicate their locations

To create a map from the list, you can use the various DOM methods you've used throughout the book to parse and obtain the necessary information before invoking the Google Map API. For example, you could use a load event such as this:

```
ADS.addEvent(window,'load',function() {

    if (GBrowserIsCompatible()) {

        // Modify the style to show the map.
        ADS.setStyle('map',{
            width:'300px',
            height:'300px',
            float:'left'
        });

        ADS.setStyle('cities',{
            width:'180px',
            height:'300px',
            overflow:'auto',
            float:'right',
            "list-style":'none',
            margin:0,
            padding:0
        });

        // Instantiate the map API.
        var map = new GMap2(document.getElementById("map"));

        // Instantiate a new latitude and longitude coordinate.
        var location = new GLatLng(0, 0);

        // Set the center of the map to location with
        // a zoom level of 13.
        map.setCenter(location, 2);

        // Add a zoom/pan and type control.
        map.addControl(new GLargeMapControl());
        map.addControl(new GMapTypeControl());

        // Retrieve all city <li> vcard elements.
        var cities = ADS.$('cities').getElementsByTagName('li');

        // Use a function to maintain the proper variable
        // scope for the info window information.
        function makeInfoWindow(marker,city) {
            var node = ADS.getElementsByClassName(
                'adr',
                'div',
                city
```

```
            )[0].cloneNode(true);
            GEvent.addListener(marker,'click',function() {
                marker.openInfoWindow(node);
            });
            ADS.addEvent(city,'click',function() {
                GEvent.trigger(marker,'click');
            });
            ADS.addEvent(city,'mouseover',function() {
                ADS.addClassName(city,'hover');
            });
            ADS.addEvent(city,'mouseout',function() {
                ADS.removeClassName(city,'hover');
            });

        }


        // Loop through each city and retrieve the
        // latitude and longitude from the microformat.
        for(i=0 ; (city = cities[i]) ; i++ ) {

            // This assumes all the elements exist and doesn't do any
            // error checking.
            var latitude = ADS.getElementsByClassName(
                'latitude',
                'abbr',
                city
            )[0].getAttribute('title');
            var longitude = ADS.getElementsByClassName(
                'longitude',
                'abbr',
                city
            )[0].getAttribute('title');

            // Create and add the marker to the map.
            var marker = new GMarker(
                new GLatLng(latitude, longitude)
            );
            makeInfoWindow(marker,city);
            map.addOverlay(marker);
        }
    }
});

    ADS.addEvent(window,'unload',GUnload);
```

With the list available as an alternate data source, the information that would regularly be shown in the map in Figure 11-6 is still accessible when the visual map can't be seen or used. You could use the same idea with a list of postal addresses by incorporating the GClientGeocoder to encode the addresses as necessary for the map.

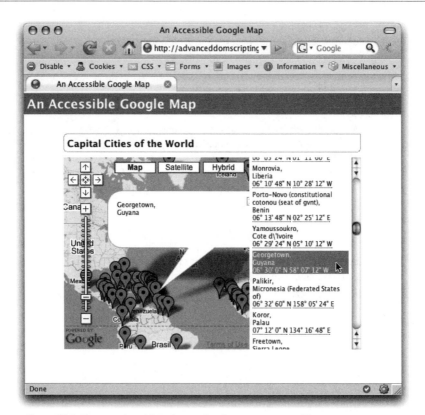

Figure 11-6. The unordered list of geo microformats converted into a map

Ajax search requests

The Google Ajax Search API (http://code.google.com/apis/ajaxsearch/) is another nifty JavaScript API that offers you a way to provide integrated and customized Google search results directly in your site.

Like the Google Maps API, you'll need to sign up for an API key at http://code.google.com/apis/ajaxsearch/signup.html to gain access to the API. After you've retrieved your key, it will also provide you with a quick example to get you started:

```
<!DOCTYPE html PUBLIC "-//W3C//DTD XHTML 1.0 Strict//EN"
    "http://www.w3.org/TR/xhtml1/DTD/xhtml1-strict.dtd">
<html xmlns="http://www.w3.org/1999/xhtml">
  <head>
    <meta http-equiv="content-type" content="text/html;➥
charset=utf-8"/>
    <title>My Google AJAX Search API Application</title>
    <link href="http://www.google.com/uds/css/gsearch.css"
        type="text/css" rel="stylesheet"/>
```

```
        <script src="http://www.google.com/uds/api?file=uds.js➥
&amp;v=1.0&amp;key=YOUR_API_KEY" type="text/javascript"></script>
        <script language="Javascript" type="text/javascript">
        //<![CDATA[

        function OnLoad() {
          // Create a search control.
          var searchControl = new GSearchControl();

          // Add in a full set of searchers.
          var localSearch = new GlocalSearch();
          searchControl.addSearcher(localSearch);
          searchControl.addSearcher(new GwebSearch());
          searchControl.addSearcher(new GvideoSearch());
          searchControl.addSearcher(new GblogSearch());

          // Set the Local Search center point.
          localSearch.setCenterPoint("New York, NY");

          // Tell the searcher to draw itself and tell it where to attach.
          searchControl.draw(document.getElementById("searchcontrol"));

          // Execute an initial search.
          searchControl.execute("Google");
        }
        GSearch.setOnLoadCallback(OnLoad);

        //]]>
        </script>
    </head>
    <body>
      <div id="searchcontrol"/>
    </body>
</html>
```

The example shows off the basics of the following API objects:

- GlocalSearch
- GwebSearch
- GvideoSearch
- GblogSearch

The following objects are not included in the example:

- GnewsSearch
- GbookSearch

You can check the documentation of each object at http://code.google.com/apis/ajaxsearch/ documentation/ to see specific features.

Depending on the options you choose to implement, the generated results will include expandable results, filters, and other options, as shown in Figure 11-7.

Figure 11-7. Search results from the example page

By default, the results don't include any inline styling. But the example and Figure 11-7 resemble the typical Google results color scheme, because the Google gsearch.css style sheet has also been included in the <head> of the document:

```
<link href="http://www.google.com/uds/css/gsearch.css"
    type="text/css" rel="stylesheet"/>
```

Without the CSS file, the page would resemble Figure 11-8.

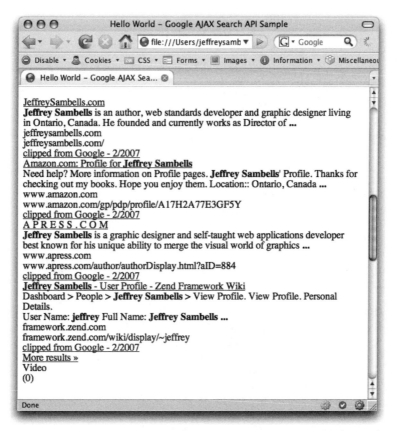

Figure 11-8. The example page results without any CSS styles applied

The generated markup includes a number of classes that identify the various parts of the result, as shown in the following markup that was generated by a GwebSearch search request. I've added the comments in this markup to indicate what each area is; the comments are not part of the generated markup:

```
<div id="search-related" class="gsc-resultsRoot gsc-tabData ➥
gsc-tabdActive gsc-resultsbox-visible">
    <!-- A table for the expanding controls and result count -->
    <table cellspacing="0" cellpadding="0" class="gsc-resultsHeader">
        <tbody>
            <tr>
                <td class="gsc-twiddleRegionCell gsc-twiddle-opened">
                    <div class="gsc-twiddle">
                        <div class="gsc-title">
                            This Site
                        </div>
                    </div>
                    <div class="gsc-stats">
                        (4)
```

```
                            </div>
                            <div class="gsc-results-selector ➥
gsc-more-results-active">
                                <div class="gsc-result-selector ➥
gsc-one-result" title="show one result">
                                     
                                </div>
                                <div class="gsc-result-selector ➥
gsc-more-results" title="show more results">
                                     
                                </div>
                                <div class="gsc-result-selector ➥
gsc-all-results" title="show all results">
                                     
                                </div>
                            </div>
                        </td>
                        <td class="gsc-configLabelCell">
                    </tr>
                </tbody>
            </table>
            <div class="gsc-results gsc-webResult" style="display: block;">
                <div class="gsc-webResult gsc-result">
                <!-- The first result is contained in this element -->
                    <div class="gs-webResult gs-result">
                        <div class="gs-title">
                            <!-- The title of the result -->
                            <a href="http://playground.jeffreysambells.com ➥
/category/lipsum/" class="gs-title" target="_blank"></a>
                            <div class="gs-title">
                                <!-- Matched words are wrapped in a <b> -->
                                <strong>Lipsum</strong> archive at ➥
JeffreySambells.com - Play
                            </div>
                        </div>
                        <div class="gs-snippet">
                            <!-- The snippet from the site surrounding
                            the match(s) -->
                            Published September 8th, 2006 in another,
                            testing and <strong>Lipsum</strong>. 0
                            Comments.<br>
                            Lorem ipsum dolor sit amet, consectetuer
                            adipiscing elit. Donec viverra mauris nec
                            <strong>...</strong>
                        </div>
                        <div class="gs-visibleUrl gs-visibleUrl-short">
                            <!-- The domain where the result was found -->
                            <a href="#" class="gs-visibleUrl"></a>
                            <div class="gs-visibleUrl">
```

```
                            playground.jeffreysambells.com
                        </div>
                    </div>
                    <div class="gs-visibleUrl gs-visibleUrl-long">
                        <!-- The full URL where the result was found -->
                         <a href="#" class="gs-visibleUrl"></a>
                        <div class="gs-visibleUrl">
                            playground.jeffreysambells.com/category/lipsum/
                        </div>
                    </div>
                    <div class="gs-watermark">
                        <!-- A reference as to when the result
                        was returned -->
                        <a href="http://code.google.com/apis/ajaxsearch ➥
/faq.html" class="gs-watermark" target="_blank"></a>
                        <div class="gs-watermark">
                            clipped from Google - 2/2007
                        </div>
                    </div>
                </div>
            </div>
        </div>
        <div class="gsc-expansionArea">
            <!--
                Everything but the first result is contained in
                the expansion area element but each result follows
                the same pattern as the first result.
                -->
            <div class="gsc-webResult gsc-result">
                <div class="gs-webResult gs-result">
                    <div class="gs-title">
                        <a href="http://playground.jeffreysambells ➥
.com/archives/" class="gs-title" target="_blank"></a>
                        <div class="gs-title">
                            Archives at JeffreySambells.com - Play
                        </div>
                    </div>
                    <div class="gs-snippet">
                        Browse by Category. Uncategorized; another;
                        testing; <strong>Lipsum</strong>
                    </div>
                    <div class="gs-visibleUrl gs-visibleUrl-short">
                        <a href="#" class="gs-visibleUrl"></a>
                        <div class="gs-visibleUrl">
                            playground.jeffreysambells.com
                        </div>
                    </div>
                    <div class="gs-visibleUrl gs-visibleUrl-long">
                        <a href="#" class="gs-visibleUrl"></a>
                        <div class="gs-visibleUrl">
```

```
                            playground.jeffreysambells.com/archives/
                        </div>
                    </div>
                    <div class="gs-watermark">
                        <a href="http://code.google.com/apis/ ➥
ajaxsearch/faq.html" class="gs-watermark" target="_blank"></a>
                        <div class="gs-watermark">
                            clipped from Google - 2/2007
                        </div>
                    </div>
                </div>
            </div>
        </div>
        <div class="gsc-trailing-more-results">
            <a href="http://www.google.com/search?hl=en ➥
&amp;source=uds&amp;q=Lipsum%20site%3Ajeffreysambells.com" ➥
class="gsc-trailing-more-results" target="_blank"></a>
            <div class="gsc-trailing-more-results">
                More results »
            </div>
        </div>
    </div>
</div>
```

The various search objects will generate additional classes depending on their results, so you'll have to explore those results to locate the specific classes you need. If you plan on editing the look of the results, be sure to read the Terms of Service, as Google stipulates that you must maintain some elements of the branding in order to use the service.

Search results for your site only

To integrate search results for only your site using the Google Search engine, you can use the GwebSearch object. GwebSearch allows you to specify restrictions on the search, such as which site to search or a customized search engine to use (http://google.com/coop/cse/). To search only the http://advanceddomscripting.com site, you can use the GwebSearch's setSiteRestrictions() method:

```
// Create a search control.
var searchControl = new GSearchControl();

// Create a new web search object.
var siteSearch = new GwebSearch();
// Restrict the search to advanceddomscripting.com
siteSearch.setSiteRestriction("advanceddomscripting.com");

// Add the web search to the control.
searchControl.addSearcher(siteSearch);

// Tell the searcher to draw itself and tell it where to attach.
searchControl.draw(document.getElementById("searchcontrol"));
```

Now searches will be restricted to only the advanceddomscripting.com domain, but the results will be integrated directly into your site.

By default, the results are appended to the element you pass into the search control's draw() method. To place the results elsewhere in your document, you can specify an alternative results container using the search control's setRoot() method:

```
searchControl.setRoot(document.getElementById('search-results'));
```

We'll look at customizing the results in the next section.

The only two caveats with the Google Ajax Search are that it relies on JavaScript and, of course, you'll have to wait for Google to index your site before you get any results. If you're launching a brand-new site you may want to wait a little while to ensure the index is up to date before adding this feature.

> For quicker indexing in the Google Search results, I suggest signing up for the Google Webmaster tools at http://www.google.com/webmasters/. As well, you can also create a sitemap.xml file (http://www.sitemaps.org/) to tell Google and other search engines how to index your site.

Related links

Frequent bloggers may find it useful to include search results for related topics along with their blog posts. If you only want to include related materials from within your own site, you can use the previous example to restrict results, but otherwise, you can include links to anywhere on the Web. In either case, the only addition is to automatically invoke the search when it loads by using the search control's execute() method along with a search string:

```
var searchControl = new GSearchControl();
var siteSearch = new GwebSearch();
searchControl.addSearcher(siteSearch);
searchControl.draw(document.getElementById("searchcontrol"));

// Automatically retrieve results related to the string in keywords.
searchControl.execute(keywords);
```

The keywords in this case could be anything from the title of your post to a list of words associated with the post itself.

To take this idea a step further, look at the HTML source for chapter11/related/post.html:

```
<!DOCTYPE html PUBLIC "-//W3C//DTD XHTML 1.0 Strict//EN"
  "http://www.w3.org/TR/xhtml1/DTD/xhtml1-strict.dtd">
<html xmlns="http://www.w3.org/1999/xhtml">
  <head>
    <meta http-equiv="content-type" content="text/html;
        charset=utf-8"/>
    <title>Related Blog Posts</title>
```

```
        <link rel="stylesheet" href="../../shared/source.css"
            type="text/css" media="screen" />
        <link rel="stylesheet" href="../chapter.css"
            type="text/css" media="screen" />
        <link rel="stylesheet" href="related.css"
            type="text/css" media="screen" />
        <script src="../../ADS-final-verbose.js"
            type="text/javascript"></script>

        <script src="http://www.google.com/uds/api?file=uds.js&➥
v=1.0&key=YOUR_API_KEY" type="text/javascript"></script>
        <script src="related.js" type="text/javascript"></script>
    </head>
    <body>
        <div id="content">
            <div id="post">
                <p>Lorem ipsum dolor sit amet, consectetuer adipiscing
                elit. Cras leo. Vestibulum fermentum nisl vel lectus.
                Nam at quam. Nulla vulputate lacus eu enim. Sed a sapien
                at arcu tristique tempus.
                <p id="keywords">Lorem ipsum dolor sit amet</p>
            </div>
            <div id="related">
                <h4>Related Links</h4>
                <div id="search-controls"></div>
                <div id="search-related"></div>
                <div id="branding"></div>
            </div>
        </div>
    </body>
</html>
```

With the following load event, your page will retrieve the keywords from the post keywords list and dynamically create a related links list from other blog posts using the GblogSearch object:

```
ADS.addEvent(window,'load',function() {

    GSearch.getBranding(ADS.$("branding"));

    var siteSearch = new GwebSearch();
    siteSearch.setUserDefinedLabel("This Site");

    var blogSearch = new GblogSearch();
    blogSearch.setUserDefinedLabel("blogosphere");

    searchOptions = new GsearcherOptions();
    searchOptions.setExpandMode(GSearchControl.EXPAND_MODE_OPEN);
    searchOptions.setRoot(ADS.$("search-related"));
```

```
searchControl = new GSearchControl();
searchControl.addSearcher(siteSearch,searchOptions);

var options = new GdrawOptions();
options.setDrawMode(GSearchControl.DRAW_MODE_TABBED);
searchControl.draw(ADS.$("search-controls"), options);

searchControl.setResultSetSize(GSearch.SMALL_RESULTSET);
searchControl.execute(ADS.$('keywords').innerHTML);

});
```

This load event creates the related links output, as shown in Figure11-9.

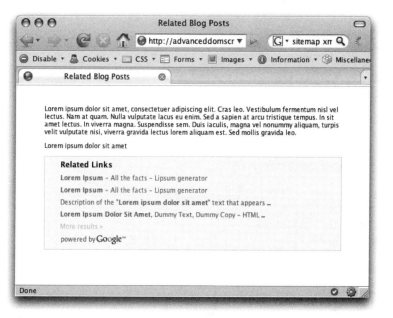

Figure 11-9. The customized related links list

Figure 11-9 also incorporates a custom results area, reformatted style, and relocated branding using a few CSS rules to hide elements that aren't necessary and format the results to fit the style of the blog:

```
#search-controls {
    display:none;
}
#related {
    background: #fefde0;
    border: 1px solid #e0e0e0;
    padding: 0.5em;
}
#related h4 {
```

```css
    padding-left: 20px;
    margin: 0;
    font-size: 1.2em;
}

#search-related a {
    padding-left: 20px;
}

#search-related a:link {
    text-decoration: none;
    color: #6b6b5f;
}
#search-related a:visited {
}
#search-related a:hover {
    text-decoration: underline;
}
#search-related a:active {
    color: red;
}
#search-related table,
#search-related .gs-snippet,
#search-related .gs-visibleUrl,
#search-related .gs-watermark
{
    display:none;
}
#search-related .gs-result {
    margin: 0.7em 0;
}
#search-related a.gsc-trailing-more-results {
    color: #d1d2ba;
}
#search-related a.gsc-trailing-more-results:hover {
    color: #6b6b5f;
}
.gsc-branding {
    text-align: right;
    margin-top: 4px;
    width: 120px;
    padding-left: 8px;
```

```
}
.gsc-branding table {
    margin-left: auto;
    width: 100%;
}
.gsc-branding-text {
    display: block;
    font-size: 1em;
    color: #676767;
    padding-right: 0.3em;
    margin-left: auto;
    text-align: right;
    width: 100%;
}
```

You'll notice that the actual search control is hidden from view by the CSS rule:

```
#search-controls {
    display:none;
}
```

As a stipulation of the Google Ajax Search API, you must maintain the "Powered by Google" branding text, so that text was reassigned to another <div> element at the bottom of the search results by using the GSearch.getBranding() method:

```
GSearch.getBranding(document.getElementById("branding"));
```

There dozens of ways you can customize the results. For more ideas, take a look at the examples Google provides with the Google Ajax Search documentation (http://code.google.com/apis/ajaxsearch/).

Mashing Search with Maps

The last client-side mashup we'll look at incorporates both the Google Maps API and Google Search API to create the GSmapSearchControl, which is part of the Google Ajax Search API. With very little effort, you can create a search tool that shows search results centered on a geographic area. Want to find the particular location of a brick and mortar franchise near you? Try the example in chapter11/map-search/google.html, and enter whatever you're looking for in Toronto, Ontario, Canada, as shown in Figure 11-10.

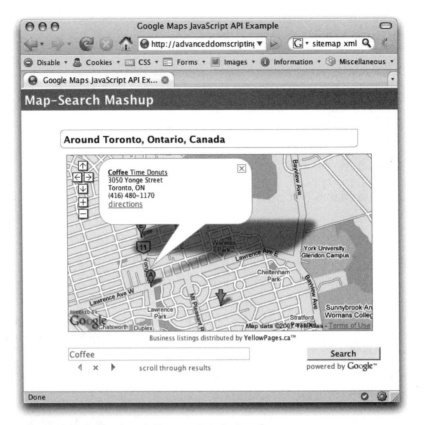

Figure 11-10. Coffee shops in Toronto, Ontario, Canada

The example returns geocentric search results plotted on a map around Toronto. All you need to do is create a simple HTML file linking the Google Maps API, the Google Ajax Search API, and the mapsearch mashup script along with the appropriate keys:

```
<!DOCTYPE html PUBLIC "-//W3C//DTD XHTML 1.0 Strict//EN"
    "http://www.w3.org/TR/xhtml1/DTD/xhtml1-strict.dtd">
<html xmlns="http://www.w3.org/1999/xhtml">
<head>
    <meta http-equiv="content-type" content="text/html;
        charset=utf-8"/>
    <title>Google Maps JavaScript API Example</title>
    <link rel="stylesheet" href="../../shared/source.css"
        type="text/css" media="screen" />
    <link rel="stylesheet" href="../chapter.css"
        type="text/css" media="screen" />
    <link rel="stylesheet" href="mapsearch.css"
        type="text/css" media="screen" />
```

```
        <script src="../../ADS-final-verbose.js"
            type="text/javascript"></script>

        <script src="http://maps.google.com/maps?file=api&v=2➥
&key=YOUR_API_KEY" type="text/javascript"></script>
        <script src="http://www.google.com/uds/api?file=uds.js➥
&v=1.0&source=uds-msw&key=YOUR_API_KEY"
            type="text/javascript"></script>
        <style type="text/css">
        @import url("http://www.google.com/uds/css/gsearch.css");
        </style>

        <!-- Map Search Control and Stylesheet -->
        <script type="text/javascript">
        window._uds_msw_donotrepair = true;
        </script>
        <script src="http://www.google.com/uds/solutions/mapsearch➥
/gsmapsearch.js?mode=new" type="text/javascript"></script>
        <style type="text/css">
        @import url("http://www.google.com/uds/solutions/mapsearch➥
/gsmapsearch.css");
        </style>
        <script src="mapsearch.js" type="text/javascript"></script>
    </head>
    <body>
        <h1>Map-Search Mashup</h1>
        <h2>Around Toronto, Ontario, Canada</h2>
        <div id="mapsearch"></div>
    </body>
</html>
```

Then, all you need is a little bit of CSS, such as this:

```
#mapsearch {
    width : 365px;
    height : 350px;
    margin: 10px;
    padding: 4px;
}
.gsmsc-mapDiv {
    height : 275px;
}

.gsmsc-idleMapDiv {
    height : 275px;
}
```

and the necessary load event:

```
ADS.addEvent(window,'load',function() {

    new GSmapSearchControl(
        document.getElementById("mapsearch"),
        "Toronto, Ontario, Canada",
        {
            zoomControl : GSmapSearchControl.ZOOM_CONTROL_ENABLE_ALL,
            idleMapZoom : GSmapSearchControl.ACTIVE_MAP_ZOOM,
            activeMapZoom : GSmapSearchControl.ACTIVE_MAP_ZOOM
        }
    );

});

ADS.addEvent(window,'unload',GUnload);
```

As you can see, the load event is very trivial and simply specifies the center location for the map based on an address along with a few options for the map, such as the controls and zoom levels.

Server-side APIs: some proxy required

The client-side JavaScript APIs are great, but there are hundreds of other APIs available that require server-side interaction, including services such as the following ones, just to name a few:

- Amazon product information and management (http://aws.amazon.com)
- Basecamp project management (http://www.basecamphq.com/api/)
- eBay auction services (http://developer.ebay.com/common/api)
- FedEx shipping services (http://www.fedex.com/us/solutions/wis/)
- Flickr photo sharing (http://www.flickr.com/services/api/)
- Google services for everything from Calendar to AdWords (http://code.google.com/apis/)
- YouTube video sharing (http://www.youtube.com/dev)

The majority of these are server-side-only APIs for several reasons:

- Access and interaction requires more advanced technologies such as SOAP, REST, or some proprietary methods.
- Large amounts of data are transferred; this would be inefficient and too repetitive through client-side methods.
- Access restrictions, such as the browser's same-origin security policy, block access to the service or would make it too complicated to implement.
- The service incorporates a more secure access method, such as a private key or username/password authentication, that can't be done through a client-side browser API.

So the problem becomes how to use your DOM scripts to access all these great and wonderful APIs. The solution is to create a server-side proxy script.

To access the server-side-only APIs directly from the DOM scripts in your browser, you need to create a server proxy component in your application that allows Ajax calls to retrieve the necessary information from your server, which, in turn, retrieves it from the desired API, as illustrated in Figure 11-1.

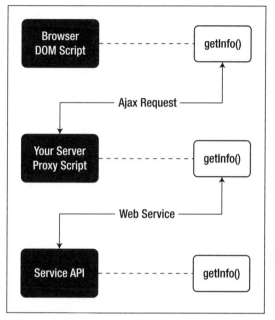

Figure 11-11. A server-side proxy example

The server-side proxy can be as simple as a one-line PHP file that fetches any XML document from the given URL:

```php
<?php
echo @simplexml_load_file($_GET['url'])->asXML();
?>
```

or much more complicated proxies using custom methods as specified by the API. You could combine the preceding PHP proxy with any of the common Ajax request objects and use it to fetch an RSS feed:

```
ADS.ajaxRequest(
    '/path/to/proxy.php?url=http://advanceddomscripting.com/rss',
    onComplete : function() {
        //parse the feed and add it to the document
    }
);
```

However, these simple proxies do have problems. Simply passing a URL allows anyone to pass in *any* URL they want, which allows anyone to request files while masquerading as your server. Someone with bad intentions could start requesting random URLs for random files, and your server may become unresponsive as a result. If you were going to use a solution such as the preceding one, I suggest adding additional security, such as checking the referrer and specifying the URLs using keywords, as shown here:

```php
<?php
if(strpos(
    strtolower($_SERVER['HTTP_REFERER']),
    'http://advanceddomscripting.com'
) !== 0 ) {
    die('Not Allowed');
}
switch($_GET['do']) {
    case 'advanceddomscripting';
        $url = 'http://advanceddomscripting.com/rss';
        break;
    case 'jeffreysambells';
        $url = 'http://jeffreysambells.com/rss';
        break;
    default:
        die();
}

header('Content-type:application/xml');
echo simplexml_load_file($url)->asXML();
?>
```

For this example, only requests referred from http://advanceddomscripting.com will be accepted and rather than pass the URL, the proxy will only accept one of the following URLs:

```
/path/to/proxy.php?do=advanceddomscripting
/path/to/proxy.php?do=jeffreysambells
```

> *Checking the referring URL doesn't really add any additional security. A malicious user could easily spoof the referrer and send the one your proxy script is expecting, but checking it prevents other websites from casually linking to your proxy scripts when they shouldn't.*

In the case of an RSS feed, you'll probably want to include some sort of server-side caching mechanism so that you aren't requesting the feed on every page load and your application will respond a little faster.

With the proxy prepared to accept requests, your client-side DOM scripts are now free to make the appropriate calls to the proxy and retrieve whatever information you've specified. To include the recent RSS items from http://advanceddomscripting.com inline in your personal site, you can use the preceding proxy to retrieve the RSS XML file—after modifying the referring URL—and parse it as necessary into your DOM document:

```
ADS.addEvent(window,'load',function() {
    // Create an Ajax request for the RSS feed.
    ADS.ajaxRequest('proxy.php?do=advanceddomscripting',{
        completeListener:function() {
            // only DOM2 Core methods will work - not DOM2 HTML
            // Parse the RSS feed.
            var doc = this.responseXML;
            var posts = doc.getElementsByTagName('item');
            // Loop through each post.
            for(i=0; (post = posts[i]) ; i++) {
                var title = post.getElementsByTagName('title')[0];
                var description = post.getElementsByTagName(➥
'description')[0];
                var link = post.getElementsByTagName('link')[0];
                // Create a new list item.
                var li = document.createElement('li');

                // Check for a title and add it.
                if(title && title.firstChild) {
                    var h4 = document.createElement('h4');
                    if(link && link.firstChild) {
                        var a = document.createElement('a');
                        a.setAttribute('href',➥
link.firstChild.nodeValue);
                        a.setAttribute('title','Read more about: '
                            + title.firstChild.nodeValue + '');
                        a.appendChild(title.firstChild)
                        h4.appendChild(a);
                    } else {
                        h4.appendChild(title.firstChild);
                    }
                    li.appendChild(h4)
                }
                // Check for a description and add it.
                if(description && description.firstChild) {
                    var p = document.createElement('p');
                    p.appendChild(description.firstChild);
                    li.appendChild(p)
                }
                // Append the item to the list.
                document.getElementById('rss-feed').appendChild(li);
            }
        }
    });
});
```

By incorporating proxies into your web applications, you can access any web service you like.

Next, we'll look at two examples that require a little more than a simple request for an XML file. The first will interact with the Basecamp project management API and allow you to retrieve and add items to your Basecamp to-do lists (great for working on web development projects!), and the second example will retrieve a Flickr buddy icon from an e-mail address supplied in a user signup form.

> *The following examples will all use PHP for their server-side proxy component. Similar techniques and methods can be applied using most server-side languages. All you require is a method to send the appropriate requests specified by the API.*

An integrated to-do list with Basecamp

Basecamp (http://basecamphq.com) is a wonderful little web-based project management application by 37Signals. Along with all the great project management features, it offers an API that allows you to manage your Basecamp account via regular HTTP POST requests with special headers. In this example, we'll use the API to interact with your Basecamp account (you can sign up for free) and create an online to-do list for your website, as shown in Figure 11-12.

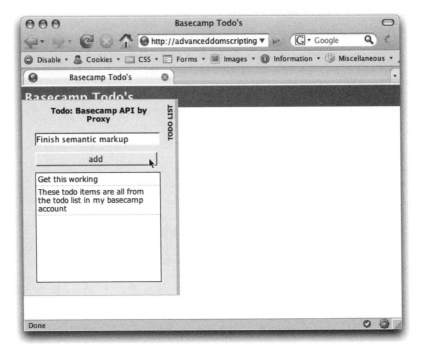

Figure 11-12. An integrated to-do list using the Basecamp API

Your Basecamp account information

To begin, you'll need a Basecamp account, so if you don't already have one, go to http://basecamphq.com and sign up. To let you try it out, they offer a free, one-project account that will suit the purposes of this example just fine. Next, follow these steps:

1. Create your new project, and call it whatever you like.

2. Create a to-do list in your project, called whatever you like.

 While on the To-do lists page, hover over the header of the list, and copy down the URL of the list; see Figure 11-13.

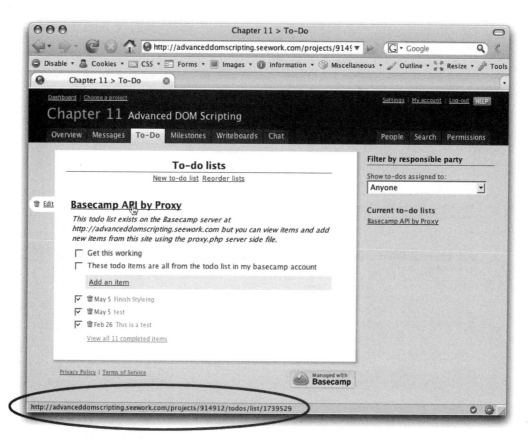

Figure 11-13. Your to-do list URL

 This URL will resemble this:

```
http://advanceddomscripting.seework.com/projects/914912/➥
todos/list/1739529
```

and contains several pieces of information, including

- **The URL of your Basecamp account**: http://advanceddomscripting.seework.com
- **The project ID**: 914912
- **The to-do list ID**: 1739529

You'll need these three pieces of information when interacting with the API, along with the username and password for authentication.

3. The last thing you'll have to do before playing with the API is enable API access for your Basecamp account. Go to the Dashboard, and select the Account tab, as shown in Figure 11-14.

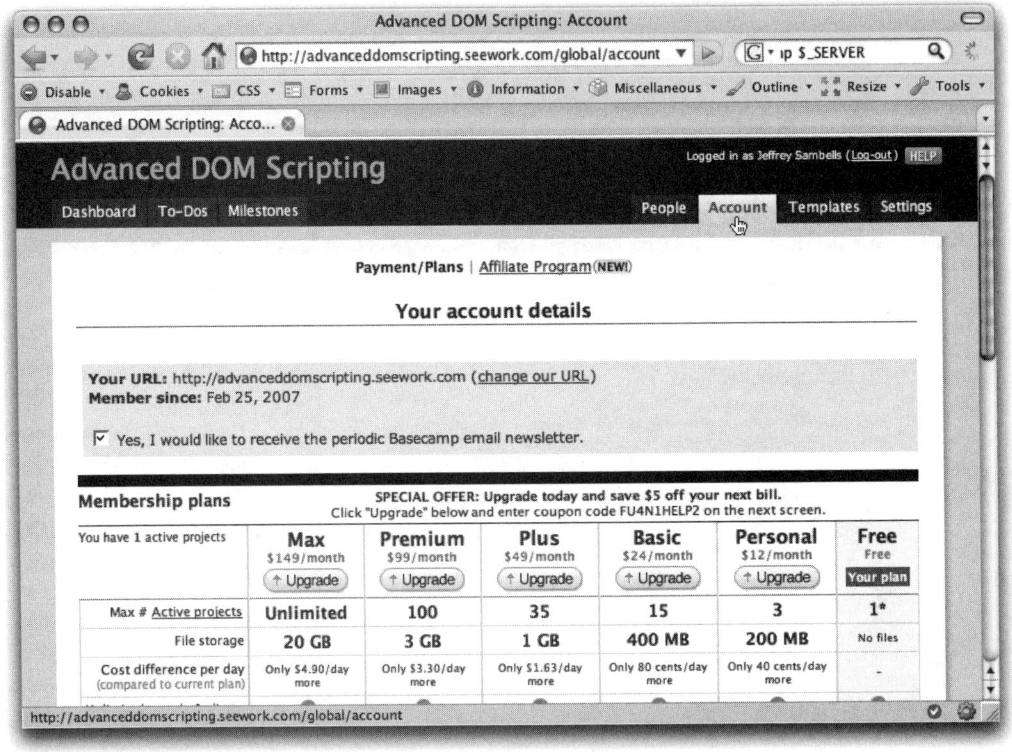

Figure 11-14. The Basecamp Account tab

4. Enable the Basecamp API after you've read the terms of service, as shown in Figure 11-5.

This will allow you to use the features of the Basecamp API to manage your account.

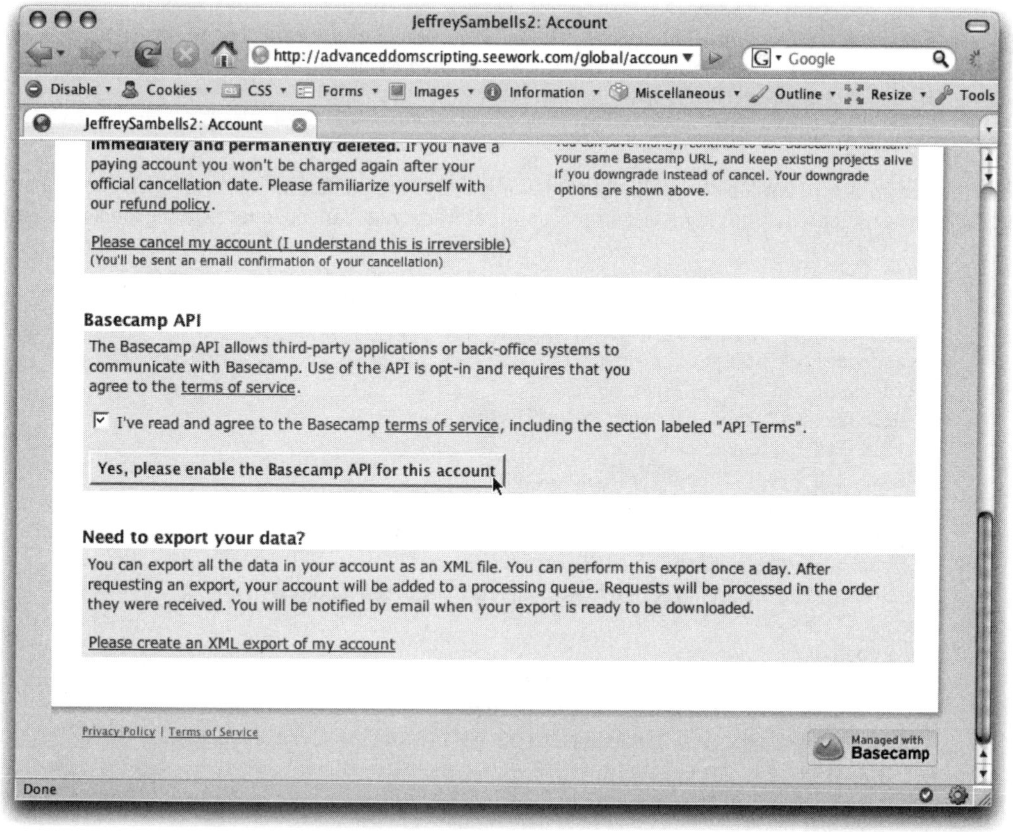

Figure 11-15. Enabling Basecamp API access for your account

Building the Basecamp proxy

Your Basecamp proxy script will do two things:

- Retrieve the list of items from the to-do list you just created
- Allow you to add new items to that same to-do list

If you glance at the Basecamp API documentation (http://www.basecamphq.com/api/), you'll see that these two items will require accessing two different URLs. The first URL retrieves a list of all the items in your to-do list by specifying a URL for the list where *id* is the ID of the to-do list that you wrote down earlier:

```
http://your-basecamp-domain/todos/list/id
```

> If you try to access this URL in your browser, you won't get the expected result. That's OK, as the server-side proxy you'll create in a moment will automatically log into the service and send special headers to retrieve the expected XML output.

The result of this query will be an XML file containing all the metadata and items for the specified list, such as this example list from my Basecamp account at http://advanceddomscripting.seework.com:

```
<todo-list>
  <completed-count type="integer">0</completed-count>
  <description>This list will be editable via proxy from ➡
advanceddomscripting.com</description>
  <id type="integer">1739529</id>
  <milestone-id type="integer"></milestone-id>
  <name>Proxy Updater</name>
  <position type="integer">1</position>
  <private type="boolean">false</private>
  <project-id type="integer">914912</project-id>
  <tracked type="boolean">false</tracked>
  <uncompleted-count type="integer">2</uncompleted-count>
  <todo-items>
    <todo-item>
      <completed type="boolean">false</completed>
      <content>Get this working</content>
      <created-on type="datetime">2007-02-25T20:11:35Z</created-on>
      <creator-id type="integer">1259600</creator-id>
      <id type="integer">9219994</id>
      <position type="integer">1</position>
      <complete>false</complete>
    </todo-item>
    <todo-item>
      <completed type="boolean">false</completed>
      <content>#{My Todo item}</content>
      <created-on type="datetime">2007-02-25T21:08:21Z</created-on>
      <creator-id type="integer">1259600</creator-id>
      <id type="integer">9220511</id>
      <position type="integer">2</position>
      <complete>false</complete>
    </todo-item>
  </todo-items>
  <complete>false</complete>
</todo-list>
```

The second URL you'll need to query follows:

```
http://your-basecamp-domain/todos/create_item/id
```

It creates new to-do items by specifying the same to-do list ID, but in this case, the API also expects your request to contain XML in the POST body that specifies the new to-do item:

```
<request>
  <content>The new todo item</content>
<request>
```

> The create_item request also allows you to specify additional properties of the to-do item, such as the individual assigned to the task. For the purposes of this example, we'll just be adding items to the list without any additional properties. Later, you can edit these items in Basecamp and assign them to specific people. You can also add additional features to the proxy that allow you to select the person when creating new tasks.

Along with the appropriate URLs and request formats, the Basecamp API also requires that you send two specific headers in your request:

- A Content-Type header of application/xml
- An Accept header of application/xml

These two headers allow the Basecamp system to recognize the request as an API request rather than a regular browser request. Without the additional headers, you won't receive the appropriate response for your requests.

Assembling all these items together, your PHP proxy might resemble the following script that uses the CURL program to send and receive requests along with the special headers:

```php
<?php

// The target URL:
// http://advanceddomscripting.seework.com/projects/➡
914912/todos/list/1739529

// A function to actually make the requests using
// CURL through the command line.
function makeRequest($url,$data=null) {
    $url = 'http://advanceddomscripting.seework.com'.$url;
    $authent = 'username:password';
    if($data) {
        $data = ' -d '.escapeshellarg($data);
    }
    $command = "curl -H 'Accept: application/xml' -H ➡
'Content-Type: application/xml' -u {$authent} $data $url";
    $output = null;

    exec(
        $command,
        $output
    );
```

```
        if($output) {
            $xml = new SimpleXMLElement(join($output));
            return $xml;
        }

        return false;
    }

    // Switch actions based on the do=var in the request GET string.
    switch ($_GET['do']) {
        case 'create' :
            // Create a new todo item
            if(!$_GET['todo']) die('');
            $request = <<<REQUEST
<request>
  <content>{$_GET['todo']}</content>
<request>
REQUEST;


            if(($xml = makeRequest(
                '/todos/create_item/1739529',
                $request
            ))!==false) {
                echo json_encode($xml);
            } else {
                echo 'false';
            }

            break;
        case 'list':
            // Get a list of the todo items.
            if(($xml = makeRequest('/todos/list/1739529'))!==false) {
                echo json_encode($xml);
            } else {
                echo 'false';
            }
            break;

    }
    ?>
```

This proxy script expects two types of URLs, one specifying do=list for retrieving the list of items:

/path/to/proxy.php?**do=list**

and another specifying do=create along with a URL encoded todo argument for creating the new to-do item:

/path/to/proxy.php?**do=create&todo=A%20New%20Item**

In both cases, the proxy script will return a JSON object that you can then use in your DOM script to create the list.

> *This script doesn't have any additional security built into it. Anyone could view items in the list and add new items, so you may want to add additional authentication appropriate to your development environment.*

The Basecamp DOM script

The final piece is the DOM script that interacts with the server proxy. In this case, your DOM script will create all markup for the to-do list, so it will work in any HTML file. The load event creates an absolute positioned element that pops in from the side of the screen when you mouseover the viewable portion. A `<form>` for creating new to-do items is also included:

```
var todoContainer;
var todoList;

function createTodoBar(data) {
    // Create a container to hold the todo list elements.
    todoContainer = document.createElement('DIV');

    // Style the container.
    ADS.setStyle(todoContainer,{
        'width': '250px',
        'overflow': 'hidden',
        'border': '1px solid #ccc',
        'border-right-width' : '5px',
        'background': '#fed url(images/todo.gif) no-repeat right top',
        'color': '#000',
        'font':' 12px/13px verdana,tahoma,sans',
        'text-align':'left'
    });

    // Set the starting position so that only a small
    // bar is left in the window.
    var basePosition= {
        'position' : 'absolute',
        'opacity' : '.55',
        'z-index' : '2000',
        'top' : '20px',
        'left' : '-235px'
    }
    ADS.setStyle(todoContainer,basePosition);

    // On mouseout set the style to the base position.
    ADS.addEvent(todoContainer,'mouseout',function() {
        ADS.setStyle(todoContainer,basePosition);
    });
```

```
// Set the hover position so that the window
// pops out of the side.
var hoverPosition= {
    'opacity' : '1',
    'left' : '0px'
}
// On mouseover set the hover position.
ADS.addEvent(todoContainer,'mouseover',function() {
    ADS.setStyle(todoContainer,hoverPosition);
});

// Add a header.
var h4 = document.createElement('h4');
ADS.setStyle(h4,{
    'color': '#000',
    'padding': '5px 20px',
    'margin': '5px',
    'font':'bold 12px/13px verdana,tahoma,sans',
    'text-align':'center'
});
h4.appendChild(document.createTextNode('Todo: ' + data.name));
todoContainer.appendChild(h4);

// Add a form so that you can add new items to the list.
var form = document.createElement('form');
ADS.setStyle(form,{
    'display': 'inline',
    'border': '0',
    'padding': '0'
});

var text = document.createElement('input');
text.setAttribute('type','text');
ADS.setStyle(text,{
    'width':'200px',
    'margin':'5px 20px',
    'margin-right': '25px'
});

var submit = document.createElement('input');
submit.setAttribute('type','submit');
submit.setAttribute('value','add');
ADS.setStyle(submit,{
    'width':'200px',
    'margin':'5px 20px',
    'margin-right': '25px'
});
```

```
form.appendChild(text);
form.appendChild(submit);
todoContainer.appendChild(form);

// Create a list for the todo items.
todoList = document.createElement('UL');
ADS.setStyle(todoList,{
    'height':'170px',
    'border':'1px solid black',
    'padding': '0',
    'margin': '5px 25px 20px 20px',
    'list-style':'none',
    'overflow': 'auto',
    'background':'white'
});

todoContainer.appendChild(todoList);
document.body.appendChild(todoContainer);


// On submit, contact the server proxy to add the new item.
ADS.addEvent(form,'submit',function(W3CEvent) {

    if(text.value) {
    // Only run the request if there is a value.
    ADS.ajaxRequest('proxy.php?do=create&todo='
        + escape(text.value),{
        completeListener:function() {

            // When the request is done refetch all the items
            // that should be in the list.
            ADS.ajaxRequest('proxy.php?do=list',{
                completeListener:function() {
                    text.value='';
                    eval('addTodoItems('
                        + this.responseText + ')');
                }
            });
        }
    });

    }

    var event = ADS.getEventObject(W3CEvent);
    ADS.preventDefault(event);

});
```

```
    }

    function addTodoItems(data) {
        // Repopulate the list with the new items.
        ADS.removeChildren(todoList);
        for (var i in data['todo-items']['todo-item']) {
            var item = data['todo-items']['todo-item'][i];
            if(item.completed == 'false') {
                var li = document.createElement('li');
                li.appendChild(document.createTextNode(item.content));
                ADS.setStyle(li,{
                    'border': '0',
                    'padding': '0.25em',
                    'margin': '0',
                    'border-bottom': '1px dotted #ccc'
                });
                todoList.appendChild(li);
            }
        }
    }

    // when the page loads create the todo list box and populate it
    ADS.addEvent(window,'load',function() {
        ADS.ajaxRequest('proxy.php?do=list',{
            completeListener:function() {
                eval('createTodoBar(' + this.responseText + ')');
                eval('addTodoItems(' + this.responseText + ')');
            }
        });
    });
```

The result is the integrated to-do list you saw earlier in Figure 11-12. When implemented in your site, this will be a great tool for the review process—your clients could add the necessary to-do items as they find bugs. Basecamp provides a host of additional features that could improve this idea even more by integrating messaging and other project management features.

> *In this case, the to-do items aren't accessible without JavaScript. The example here is intended as a development tool where you have control over the devices and types of browsers accessing the system. If accessibility is an issue for you, there's no reason the list couldn't be populated automatically when the page initially loads, allowing the list to be available as part of the original markup.*

Buddy icons with Flickr

When creating user accounts for your sites, you may include an option that allows the registrant to specify a URL for an icon that would represent them (an avatar). If you also require an e-mail address in your form, you can ask for the e-mail address first and check with a service such as Flickr to automatically retrieve the static image that's the buddy icon for that user, as shown in Figure 11-16.

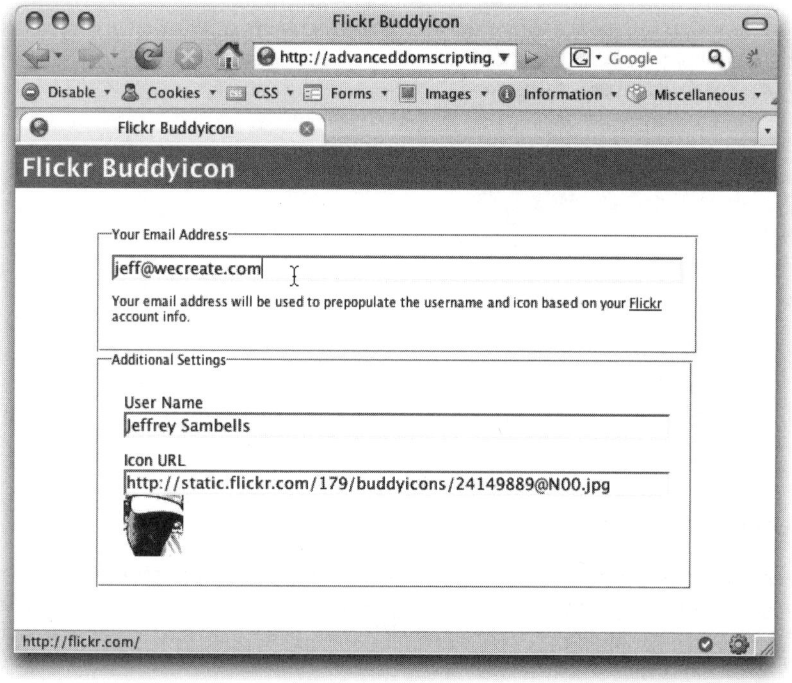

Figure 11-16. Retrieving the Flickr buddy icon and user name based on an e-mail address

The Flickr API key

To access the Flickr API, you'll need to sign up for an API key (http://www.flickr.com/services/api/keys). The key will be a random string of numbers and letters similar to the Google API key you created earlier in the chapter. I'm not going to include an example here, as giving away my key would allow you to access the API and pretend you are me. Once you have your own key, you can access any of the features of the Flickr API (http://www.flickr.com/services/api).

Building the Flickr proxy

To retrieve a customized buddy icon associated with a Flickr account—if one exists—you need a few pieces of information about the user's account. The buddy icon URLs reference a custom JPG file on a specific Flickr icon server in the following format:

```
http://static.flickr.com/icon-server/buddyicons/nsid.jpg
```

where nsid is the user's flicker ID and icon-server specifies on which server the icon is stored. These are the two pieces of information you'll need to retrieve from the API.

499

To retrieve the ID, Flickr provides a `flickr.people.findByEmail` method that returns the nsid as well as the username associated with a given e-mail address. For example, if you want to retrieve my Flickr nsid, you can call the following REST service URL after including your own Flickr API key:

```
http://api.flickr.com/services/rest/?method=flickr.people.➥
findByEmail&api_key=YOUR_FLICKR_API_KEY&find_email=➥
jeff%40advanceddomscripting.com
```

> Note the e-mail address is escaped, so the @ symbol in the e-mail address has been converted to %40.

If successful, you should see the following XML result:

```
<rsp stat="ok">
    <user id="24149889@N00" nsid="24149889@N00">
        <username>Jeffrey Sambells</username>
    </user>
</rsp>
```

You now know my nsid, which is 24149889@N00, as well as my current username.

After retrieving my nsid, you can use a number of other API methods to retrieve even more information about my account. To find my buddy icon, you need to look up the icon server associated with my account. This information can be found using the `flicker.people.getInfo` method, again using the following REST service URL after including your own Flickr API key:

```
http://api.flickr.com/services/rest/?method=flickr.people.➥
getInfo&api_key=YOUR_FLICKR_API_KEY&user_id=24149889%40N00
```

The result will reveal several pieces of information about my account, including the iconserver and the number of photos I have in my account:

```
<rsp stat="ok">
    <person id="24149889@N00" nsid="24149889@N00" isadmin="0" ➥
ispro="0" iconserver="179" iconfarm="1">
        <username>Jeffrey Sambells</username>
        <realname/>
        <mbox_sha1sum>48185cbcf809b112eb63690fb552ea5716b865b2➥
</mbox_sha1sum>
        <location/>
        <photosurl>http://www.flickr.com/photos/jeffreysambells/➥
</photosurl>
        <profileurl>http://www.flickr.com/people/jeffreysambells/➥
</profileurl>
        <mobileurl>
            http://www.flickr.com/mob/photostream.gne?id=7084143
        </mobileurl>
        <photos>
```

```
            <firstdatetaken>2006-09-08 22:25:14</firstdatetaken>
            <firstdate>1172458623</firstdate>
            <count>9</count>
        </photos>
    </person>
</rsp>
```

> *If the* iconserver *in the result is* 0, *the user associated with the* nsid *hasn't chosen to customize their default buddy icon. In those cases, the default icon at* http://www.flickr.com/images/buddyicon.jpg *is used instead.*

You now have all the information required to construct the URL for my buddy icon, which is shown in Figure 11-17:

```
http://static.flickr.com/179/buddyicons/24149889@N00.jpg
```

Figure 11-17.
My Flickr buddy icon

You can assemble all this into a server-side proxy script the same way you did with the Basecamp API; only, here, you can use the PHP5 simplexml_load_file() method to retrieve the API responses:

```php
<?php
$apiKey = 'your api key';

switch ($_GET['do']) {

    case 'getFlickrInfo' :
        if(!$_GET['email']) die('');
        $email = urlencode($_GET['email']);
        if(!$xml1 = simplexml_load_file("http://api.flickr.com/➥
services/rest/?method=flickr.people.findByEmail&api_key={$apiKey}&➥
find_email={$email}")) die('false');

$nsid = $xml1->user[0]['nsid'];

        if(!$xml2 = simplexml_load_file("http://api.flickr.com/➥
services/rest/?method=flickr.people.getInfo&api_key={$apiKey}&➥
user_id={$nsid}")) die('false');

        if( $xml2->person['iconserver'] > 0) {
            $icon = "http://static.flickr.com/{$xml2->➥
person['iconserver']}/buddyicons/{$nsid}.jpg";
        } else {
            $icon='';
        }

        echo <<<JSON
{
```

```
            'username':'{$xml1->user->username}',
            'icon':'{$icon}'
        }
JSON;


        break;
    }


    ?>
```

Your proxy script expects only one specific URL specifying the action to take and the e-mail address to look up:

```
proxy.php?do=getFlickrInfo&email=jeff%40advanceddomscripting.com
```

and it will respond with a JSON object populated with the information (or null if no result was found):

```
{
    'username':'Jeffrey Sambells',
    'icon':'http://static.flickr.com/179/buddyicons/24149889@N00.jpg'
}
```

The DOM script

Your DOM script, in this case, will only retrieve the information and prepopulate both the username and icon URL, if they haven't already been specified in the registration form:

```
<!DOCTYPE html PUBLIC "-//W3C//DTD XHTML 1.0 Strict//EN"
    "http://www.w3.org/TR/xhtml1/DTD/xhtml1-strict.dtd">
<html xmlns="http://www.w3.org/1999/xhtml">
<head>
<title>Flickr Buddyicon</title>
    <link rel="stylesheet" type="text/css"
        href="../../shared/source.css" />
    <link rel="stylesheet" type="text/css"
        href="../chapter.css" />
    <script type="text/javascript"
        src="../../ADS-final-verbose.js"></script>
    <script type="text/javascript" src="flickr.js"></script>
</head>
<body>
<h1>Test Page</h1>
<div id="content">
<form>
    <fieldset>
        <legend>Your Email Address</legend>
        <input type="text" id="email" name="email">
        <p>Your email address will be used to prepopulate the
```

```
                username and icon based on your <a href="http://flickr.com">
                Flickr</a> account info.</p>
        </fieldset>
        <fieldset>
            <legend>Additional Settings</legend>
            <div>
                <label for="username">User Name</label>
                <input type="text" id="username" name="username">
            </div>
            <div>
                <label for="icon">Icon URL</label>
                <input type="text" id="icon" name="icon">
            </div>
        </fieldset>
    </form>
    </div>
    </body>
    </html>
```

The script itself needs to fetch only the proxy information by passing in the supplied e-mail address after a change event listener has been invoked on your e-mail field:

```
ADS.addEvent(window,'load',function() {

    var iconInput = ADS.$('icon');
    var preview = document.createElement('img');
    preview.alt = 'Icon preview';
    preview.src = iconInput.value;
    ADS.setStyle(preview,{
        width:'48px',
        height:'48px'
    });
    ADS.insertAfter(preview,iconInput);

    function updateInfo(data) {
        var username = ADS.$('username');
        if(data.username && !username.value) {
            username.value = data.username;
        }
        var icon = ADS.$('icon');
        if(data.icon && !iconInput.value) {
            iconInput.value = data.icon;
        }
        preview.src = iconInput.value;
    }

    ADS.addEvent(ADS.$('email'),'change',function(W3CEvent) {
        if(this.value) {
            ADS.ajaxRequest('proxy.php?do=getFlickrInfo&email='
```

503

```
                         + escape(this.value),{
                         completeListener:function() {
                             eval('updateInfo(' + this.responseText + ')');

                         }
                     });
                 }
             });

             ADS.addEvent(iconInput,'change',function() {
                 preview.src = this.value;
             });

         });
```

The result is a seemingly regular form that's a little smarter than most, as you saw earlier in Figure 11-16. If you combine this with the postal code lookup examples from Chapter 4, you could possibly pre-populate much of the form with only the postal code and e-mail address.

Summary

APIs offer a wide variety of services that you can use to enhance your site with minimal effort. Many offer powerful tools that can help you display, retrieve, and manipulate information, while others offer management solutions. When APIs are server-side only, there's no reason you can't incorporate a server-side proxy script, as you saw in this chapter, to allow you to access the server-only API via your DOM scripts, opening up many more possibilities.

When using APIs, remember to keep accessibility in mind by using the same progressive enhancement methodologies you've seen in the rest of this book and incorporating standard markup, such as micro-formats, where possible.

Now, take your newfound knowledge of best practices, JavaScript, events, style, libraries, and every-thing in between and create a site that's not only attractive to look at but works beautifully in every situation.

In the next chapter, you'll look at a case study by Aaron Gustafson, in which you'll take a typical form selection element and stylize it using a combination of CSS, DOM scripting, and the Prototype Framework.

Chapter 12

CASE STUDY: STYLE YOUR SELECT WITH THE DOM

by Aaron Gustafson

For the last few years, I've had somewhat of an unhealthy obsession with the select element. Perhaps "unhealthy" is a bit too strong (or gives you the wrong idea), but let's just say that I've done a lot of thinking about select elements and what I would do differently if I were in charge.

I'm not sure when it all started. Perhaps it was when I first discovered the truly elegant way Internet Explorer 5 on Mac (IE5/Mac) handles select elements containing organizational optgroup elements (see Figure 12-1, left). Or maybe it was when I really started to dive into CSS and realized that I couldn't so much as change the border-style from the ugly default (it's inset in most browsers as shown in Figure 12-1, center) or escape from the OS X native user interface (UI) controls (no matter how attractive) in Safari and Camino (see Figure 12-1, right).

Figure 12-1. From left to right: an open optgroup-organized select in Internet Explorer 5.2 on OS X Panther, the quintessential select in Internet Explorer 6 on Windows XP (classic theme), and the native UI control-based select in Safari 1.3 on OS X Panther

However my obsession may have begun, I've spent the last few years searching for better ways to work with select elements and bend them to my will (and yours). The script presented in this case study represents the latest of efforts and offers a way for you to style the classic select pretty much any way you want.

That classic feeling

As you saw in Figure 12-1 the classic select is really quite boring. In addition, its form is inconsistent across browsers, with the greatest number of variations being seen among browsers on the Mac. Figure 12-2 summarizes the look of the standard select element (both open and closed) across much of the browser spectrum.

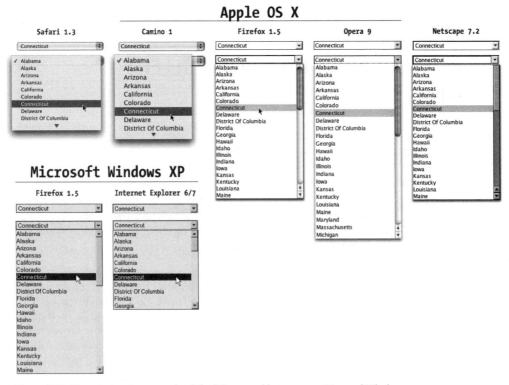

Figure 12-2. The select as it appears by default in several browsers on Mac and Windows

I'm sure I don't need to tell you the number of times I've heard, "The page you built doesn't match the design." Or how about the times I've heard that the blue used in the OS X UI control clashes with the design? My personal favorite is, "The design looks different on my Mac at home than it does on my PC at work."

Some folks that swear by system UI controls for forms because of users' familiarity with them. On one level, I agree, but I have to admit the thought of having a unified, styleable select control gives me a warm tingly feeling. And the thought of being able to avoid the aforementioned conversations will help keep me sane.

Building a better select

So how do we do it? Well, we need to create a surrogate select that acts just like a select element while remaining styleable. What we need is a *faux* select.

I'd like to say that building one is simple, but what worthwhile endeavor ever is? Truth be told, it's a rather complex undertaking, but dividing the work into manageable chunks makes the task easier. First, let's look at the markup of a classic select, in this case, a state selector control for a U.S. address:

```
<select name="state">
  <option value="AL">Alabama</option>
  <option value="AK">Alaska</option>
  <option value="AZ">Arizona</option>
  <option value="AR">Arkansas</option>
  <option value="CA">California</option>
  <option value="CO">Colorado</option>
  <option value="CT" selected="selected">Connecticut</option>
  ...
</select>
```

That's simple enough. Now, what are the essential characteristics of such a select?

- It contains several option elements.
- When closed
  - It displays the selected option or the default option.
  - Clicking the displayed option opens it.
- When open
  - All (or if the list is long, a portion) of the options are displayed.
  - The options have a hover state.
  - The currently selected option is designated in some way.
  - Clicking an option will set it as the value and close the select.
  - Clicking outside of the drop-down list will cause it to close.
  - Clicking the displayed option (the one clicked to open it) will cause it to close.

OK, so that's not too terrible. Let's see what we can do to re-create some of these characteristics, starting with creating the first one.

Containing several option elements? Hmm, that sounds a lot like a list to me. Alright, so our first task in creating our faux select will be to build a list. Some might argue that an ordered list is more appropriate, but it's going to be an unordered list—this allows us a bit more freedom, and I never was much for numbers:

```
<ul class="faux-select">
    <li>Alabama</li>
    <li>Alaska</li>
    <li>Arizona</li>
```

509

```
    <li>Arkansas</li>
    <li>California</li>
    <li>Colorado</li>
    <li>Connecticut</li>
    ... cut ...
  </ul>
```

Okay, pretty simple so far. Now what?

When closed, it displays the selected option or the default option? We need to show one option. We could do that by classifying one of the <li> elements as "selected":

```
<li class="selected">Connecticut</li>
```

But that is limiting if we also want it to appear in the drop-down list when we click to open our faux select (as of now, we don't have a reliable way to make one element appear in two places at once). A better idea would be to place the selected option (let's just refer to it as the *value*) in its own element (for instance a p) and place both it and our ul inside a container element, say a div:

```
<div class="faux-container">
  <p class="faux-value">Connecticut</p>
  <ul class="faux-select">
    <li>Alabama</li>
    <li>Alaska</li>
    <li>Arizona</li>
    <li>Arkansas</li>
    <li>California</li>
    <li>Colorado</li>
    <li>Connecticut</li>
    ...
  </ul>
</div>
```

Now, we have a semantically appropriate markup plan for our faux select, so let's jump in and start writing some JavaScript to build it for us.

Strategy? We don't need no stinkin' strategy . . .

OK, maybe we do.

To make this script flexible (and impress our friends), we're going build it using object-oriented programming (OOP) methods that were discussed in Chapter 2 and leverage some of the JavaScript libraries you looked at in Chapter 9. But first things first: we need to figure out how we want this script to work.

Here's the basic outline of what needs to happen:

1. Determine if the script should run.
2. Collect all of the select elements on the page.

3. Iterate through them, building a faux select for each:

   a. Collect all of the options.

   b. Assign each option to a list item.

   c. Assign the selected option (by default, the first one) to the value.

The files

To get things going, I've created a starting point for you in the in the chapter12/faux-select-start source folder, which includes several files:

- /test.html
- /main.css
- /faux-select.css
- /faux-select.js
- /prototype.js
- /mod-moo.fx.js

The test file (test.html) is the HTML file we will be manipulating. As our script will alter select elements, I've included a U.S. state selector along with some additional form markup in that file.

Opening the file, you'll notice we will be working with two libraries:

```
<script type="text/javascript" src="prototype.js"></script>
<script type="text/javascript" src="mod-moo.fx.js"></script>
```

We are going to use the Prototype library (http://prototypejs.org) to make class creation, property manipulation, and event management a bit easier. We'll also add some effects using a slightly modified version of the Moo.fx library (http://moofx.mad4milk.net) for Prototype.

> For more on the Prototype and Moo.fx libraries, see Chapters 9 and 10.

The main.css file contains some basic styles for laying out the page (typography, backgrounds, and so on). Its sole purpose is to provide a little context within which to style our select. We will add a few styles to this file to customize the look and feel of the faux select shortly, but we will also be working with faux-select.css to manage the styles that drive our faux select.

If you open test.html in your browser, you should see something like Figure 12-3.

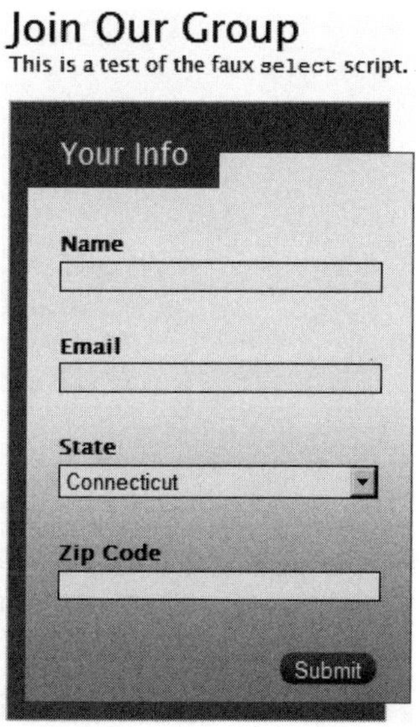

We will be focusing most of our development in two files: faux-select.js and faux-select.css.

Figure 12-3. The test.html file viewed in Firefox

The FauxSelect objects

To maintain some order (and obtain economies of scale), let's create two objects in faux-select.js. The first object is going to be our conductor; I call it that because it will orchestrate the select replacement. It will maintain a list (an array) of the faux selects on the page and trigger them to be built with its initialize() method. FauxSelectConductor will also be the keeper of several properties we will need for all of our faux selects, and it will hold some DOM nodes for us to clone as we need them (after all, cloning is much less expensive than creating a new node each time). So that you can easily follow along, I've included the structure of the object in the faux-select.js file along with comments about what we'll be doing with it:

```
var FauxSelectConductor = {
  // A list of all the faux SELECTs
  list:      [],
  // The faux-SELECT-specific CSS styles
  cssFile:   'faux-select.css',
  // The layer for the faux SELECT
  zindex:    10000,
  // The default maximum size of the drop-down
  maxHeight: 300,
  // The height of the BODY
  bodyHeight: 0,
  // "model" elements for cloning
  elements:  { li:  document.createElement( 'li' ),
               div: document.createElement( 'div' ),
               p:   document.createElement( 'p' ),
               ul:  document.createElement( 'ul' ) },
  initialize: function( params ){
    // collect any params

    // set the body height

    // attach the standard CSS file

    // collect the SELECTs
      // loop through the collection
      // give the SELECT an ID if it doesn't have one
      // make it into a FauxSelect
  }
};
```

The second object we will be working with will be the one associated with each faux select on the page (to maintain its events and so forth). We'll call it (shockingly) FauxSelect, and use the Prototype library's Class object to do the object creation. Here is the basic the object structure from faux-select.js:

```
var FauxSelect = Class.create();
FauxSelect.prototype = {
  // the ID of the SELECT
  id:        false,
```

```
// the original SELECT element
select:     false,
// the DIV containing the faux SELECT
container:  false,
// the faux SELECT UL
faux:       false,
// the faux SELECT P (seen as the selected value)
value:      false,
// The closer DIV for this faux SELECT
closer:     false,
// type of SELECT (standard, multiple, or optgrouped)
type:       'standard',
// keep the faux SELECT from closing? fixes a blur bug
preventClose: false,

initialize: function( id ){
  // builds our faux SELECT and sets up the event handlers
},

// --- DOM Building Methods
makeFake:   function( node ){
  // we will use this to make OPTIONS, but eventually for more
},

// --- faux SELECT Actions
open:          function(){
  // opens the faux SELECT
},
close:         function(){
  // closes the faux SELECT
},
flip: function(){
  // flips CLASSes and performs other housekeeping
},

// --- Faux SELECT Events
clickValue: function(){
  // value click event handler
},
clickUL: function() {
  /* what happens when you click inside the UL;
     used for managing a browser bug */
},
clickLI:       function(){
  // faux OPTION click event handler
},
mouseoverLI: function(){
  // faux OPTION mouseover event handler
},
```

```
      mouseoutLI:  function(){
        // faux OPTION mouseout event handler
      },

      // --- Faux SELECT Housekeeping
      selectLI:    function(){
        // updates the real SELECT and selects a faux OPTION
      },
      deselectLI:  function(){
        // deselect a faux OPTION
      },

      // --- Real SELECT Events
      focus:       function(){
        // SELECT focus event handler
      },
      blur:        function(){
        // SELECT blur event handler
      },
      updateFaux: function(){
        /* updates the faux SELECT from the real one
           (used for keyboard events) */
      }
    };
```

As you can see, our FauxSelect will have a bit more to keep track of, such as the id of the select it is replacing (stored as FauxSelect.id), a DOM reference to the select itself (FauxSelect.select), and a DOM reference to the actual faux select we'll be creating (FauxSelect.faux). It also has a lot of methods that handle all of the interactions within the faux select. We'll cover each of those in turn, but first, let's revisit the FauxSelectConductor.

Getting the faux select going

Now that we have established the framework of our two objects, we can dive in and start making some magic happen. First, we need to make it initialize upon page load. For this object, we'll use Prototype's Event.observe() method. In the faux-select.js file, add the following:

```
    // if Prototype, selects and required DOM methods are available
    if( typeof( Prototype ) != 'undefined' &&
        typeof( Fx ) != 'undefined' &&
        document.getElementById &&
        document.getElementsByTagName &&
        document.createElement &&
        document.getElementsByTagName( 'select' ) ){
      Event.observe( window, 'load', function(){
        FauxSelectConductor.initialize();
      }, false );
    }
```

Instead of pushing all of our method detection into the initialize() method of FauxSelectConductor, we're wrapping it around the Event.observe() method call. The reason for this is that we don't even want to bother running initialize() if the methods we want aren't available. You'll also notice that part of the detection syntax includes object detection for both Prototype (typeof(Prototype) != 'undefined') and Moo.fx (typeof(Fx) != 'undefined'). If either of these libraries are not available, we're going to run into problems, so it's best to fail early (and silently) if they aren't.

Event.observe() works very similarly to ADS.addEvent from Chapter 1, and in this case, it sets FauxSelectConductor.initialize() to run when the page is loaded.

You'll notice that we've used an anonymous function around the initialization of the FauxSelectConductor object. The reason for that has to do with JavaScript's handling of this. I'll explain. If we assigned the FauxSelectConductor.initialize method to the window's load event like this:

```
Event.observe( window, 'load', FauxSelectConductor.initialize, false );
```

The this keyword within FauxSelectConductor.initialize() would refer to the window object and not the FauxSelectConductor.

To make this refer to the correct object, we assign the anonymous function as the method of the window, keeping the initialize() method within the FauxSelectConductor object. From within FauxSelectConductor.initialize() we can now use this as often as we want to refer to the FauxSelectConductor object itself—with a few restrictions, as you'll see.

> *As it is a somewhat intense script, you may want to consider triggering* FauxSelectConductor.initalize() *to run once the DOM is available but before supplementary items (such as images) have finished loading into the browser. Firefox and Opera support the nonstandard* DOMContentLoaded *right out of the box, but others, like Internet Explorer, do not. They can, however, be tricked into implementing it. jQuery (*http://jquery.com*) and several other libraries support this functionality, but as of this writing, Prototype does not have it in a released version. Dan Webb's LowPro (*http://svn.danwebb.net/external/lowpro/tags/rel-0.4/dist/*) will fill the gap if you're interested in staying in the Prototype family.*

So, now we have a simple object literal called FauxSelectConductor and its initialize() method is set to run when the content of the page finishes loading.

Locating the select elements

According to our earlier to-do list, we need to collect all of the select elements on the page. That's easy enough using document.getElementsByTagName():

```
var FauxSelectConductor = {
    ... cut ...
    initialize: function(){
        ... cut ...
        // collect the SELECTs
```

```
      var selects = $A( document.getElementsByTagName( 'select' ) );
      ... cut ...
   }
};
```

If you only wanted to apply the script to a few predefined select elements, you could change the line to read

```
var selects = $$( 'select.faux-me' );
```

and use Prototype's $$() method, which finds elements by CSS selector. Then any select with a class of faux-me will be chosen.

> *Prototype's $$() is a bit of overkill for something simple, such as replacing a* docu-ment.getElementsByTagName() *call; native JavaScript methods will always be faster, because they are just that . . . native. It does, however, make sense to use $$() in sit-uations where a native method is not available, such as selecting by CSS selector or by* class *name, neither of which are native to JavaScript.*

Now, we need to iterate through the list of selects (in this case, just one) and build a faux select for each. We will instantiate a new FauxSelect for each of the selects we've collected, passing in the id of that select. Then, we can construct the faux select markup with the initialize() method of the FauxSelect object (recall that initialize() is automatically called by Prototype whenever the class is instantiated). It may sound a bit confusing, but let's add the following code in the FauxSelectConductor.initialize() method; then, all will be clear:

```
var FauxSelectConductor = {
  ... cut ...
  initialize: function(){
    ... cut ...
    // collect the SELECTs
    var selects = $A( document.getElementsByTagName( 'select' ) );
    // loop through the collection
    selects.each( function( item, i ){
      // get the id
      var id = item.getAttribute( 'id' );
      // give the SELECT an ID if it doesn't have one
      if( id === false ){
        id = 'auto-ided-select-' + i;
        item.setAttribute( 'id', id );
      }
      // make it into a FauxSelect
      this.list[id] = new FauxSelect( id );
    }.bind( this ) );
    ... cut ...
  }
};
```

> *In programming, there's more than one way to do just about anything. We are using Prototype's enumerable method* each() *to stand in for a simple* for *loop. This is just one more example of Prototype making your code a little easier to read, but if you are more comfortable with the traditional methods, by all means, use them.*

We are using each() to iterate through the collection of select elements and do something with *each* of them (how novel). We are also checking to see if the select has an id (which it should if you are using explicit association with your labels), and if it doesn't, we're assigning one that shouldn't conflict with anything else on the page (auto-ided-select-*i*, where *i* is the counter value for the select in our loop).

> *In order to keep the scope of* this *correct (so we can reference* this.list *inside our* each() *loop), we are using Prototype's* bind() *method.*

A little housekeeping

Before we move on to the FauxSelect object, I just want to touch really quickly on a few other pieces we'll need to add into the FauxSelectConductor. First of all, notice the comment about params:

```
var FauxSelectConductor = {
  ... cut ...
  initialize: function(){
    // collect the params
    ... cut ...
  }
};
```

Since we want to keep this script flexible, we will provide the means for users to configure FauxSelectConductor as they wish. You may want to provide more configuration options, but I'll show you a simple example—add the bolded code shown here:

```
var FauxSelectConductor = {
  ... cut ...
  initialize: function( params ){
    // collect the params
    params = params || {};
    if( typeof( params.maxHeight ) != 'undefined' )
      this.maxHeight = params.maxHeight;
    ... cut ...
  }
};
```

Now, when we call initialize(), we have the ability to pass it one or more arguments in an object. We've just set it up to allow you to adjust the height of a faux select when it is open. Calling initialize() like this

```
FauxSelectConductor.initialize( { maxHeight: 200 } );
```

517

would cause FauxSelectConductor.maxHeight to be 200 pixels instead of the default of 300 pixels. You can feel free to update this to allow configuration of many of the default properties of FauxSelectConductor, such as zindex or cssFile (which we'll use later).

The final housekeeping note I'll make is with regard to the bodyHeight property. This will be used a little later, but for now, we'll just set it to the height of the body element—do this now:

```
var FauxSelectConductor = {
  ... cut ...
  initialize: function( params ){
    ... cut ...
    // set the BODY height
    this.bodyHeight = $(
      document.getElementsByTagName( 'body' )[0]
    ).getHeight() + 'px';
    ... cut ...
  }
};
```

We are using Prototype's $() function to turn the body element into a Prototype object and then we are getting its height using the getHeight() method Prototype adds to Element objects.

Building the DOM elements

You may recall from the skeleton of the FauxSelectConductor that we created a property called elements whose value was an object containing four reusable DOM nodes: a list item (li), a division (div), a paragraph (p), and an unordered list (ul). These will be used time and time again by each of the FauxSelects we initialize to build our markup. Add the following:

```
var FauxSelectConductor = {
  ... cut ...
  // "model" elements
  elements:   { li:  document.createElement( 'li' ),
                div: document.createElement( 'div' ),
                p:   document.createElement( 'p' ),
                ul:  document.createElement( 'ul' ) },
  ... cut ...
};
```

If we used document.createElement() each time we initialize() the FauxSelect object, we'd generate more overhead and cause our script to take longer to run. Using cloneNode() on a representative (or model) of the element we plan to use reduces that overhead.

Now that we've covered that, we can jump over to the FauxSelect object and show it some love. We'll start by storing some properties and then it's time to build our faux select elements. Add the following:

```
FauxSelect.prototype = {
  ... cut ...
  initialize: function( id ){
```

```
        // store the ID
        this.id = id;

        // store the SELECT node
        this.select = $( id );

        // -- BUILD THE FAUX SELECT -- //
        //--- create the faux SELECT UL
        this.faux = $( FauxSelectConductor.elements.ul.cloneNode( true ) );
        this.faux.addClassName('faux-select');

        //--- Create a container DIV
        this.container = $( FauxSelectConductor.elements.div.➥
          cloneNode( true ) );
        this.container.addClassName( 'faux-container' );
        this.container.setAttribute( 'id', 'replaces_'+id );

        //--- create the value P
        this.value = $( FauxSelectConductor.elements.p.cloneNode( true ) );
        this.value.addClassName( 'faux-value' );

        // append it all to the document
        this.container.appendChild( this.value );
        this.container.appendChild( this.faux );
        this.select.parentNode.appendChild( this.container );
    }
};
```

To speed up access to the key elements in each faux select, we've assigned them to properties of the FauxSelect object: container (for the container div), value (for the paragraph), and faux (for the ul). These references will allow us to access the same element from other methods within the FauxSelect using syntax like this.faux instead of requiring us to look them up again and again. We've also made each element a Prototype object, using $() when we cloned the element from the FauxSelectConductor, so keeping the reference will allow us to use the Prototype methods as well.

We've also assigned a unique id to the container, which relates it back to the original select:

```
        this.fauxcontainer.setAttribute( 'id', 'replaces_' + id );
```

In the case of our test page, it is given an id of replaces_join-state. Using a naming structure like this will isolate the faux select elements in the DOM and keep them from conflicting with other identified elements. You can then use the ids in CSS rules or other scripts where you don't already have a reference to the object. It also helps to identify the element when debugging the rendered source.

As you saw in Chapter 9, the Prototype $() function is an alias for document.getElementById(), a very common method call in DOM scripting. As of version 1.5, the $() function also adds a number of methods to the element's prototype property to enable chaining methods together. The addClassName() method used previously is one a handful of methods that allow for easy access to add elements (with addClassName()), remove elements (with removeClassName()), and test for the existence of classes of an element (with hasClassName()). These are similar to the style methods you added to your ADS library in Chapter 5, except here they're applied directly to the element as a method, so you only need to specify the class in the arguments.

Creating a faux value

If you refresh your page now, you won't see anything different, since we've only added a few empty tags. As it stands, we have an empty paragraph (which will eventually contain our faux select's value) and an empty unordered list (which will contain all of the available values) inside a div. To fill those elements, we need to do a little more DOM work.

We'll start with the easy one—getting the text for the value. I say this is "easy," because select elements have a nice property called selectedIndex that tells us which option (if any) is selected. We can add a few (relatively) simple lines to FauxSelect.initialize() method and it's finished:

```
FauxSelect.prototype = {
  ... cut ...
  initialize: function( id ){
    ... cut ...
    //--- create the value P
    this.value = $( FauxSelectConductor.elements.p.cloneNode( true ) );
    this.value.addClassName( 'faux-value' );
    // set the default selected to be the value
    this.value.appendChild( document.createTextNode(
      this.select.getElementsByTagName(
        'option'
      )[this.select.selectedIndex].firstChild.nodeValue
    ) );
    ... cut ...
  },
  ... cut ...
};
```

I realize this looks anything but simple, so let's break it down:

- this.value.appendChild() is appending the child to the value (a p).
- document.createTextNode() is doing just as it says—creating a text node out of what we supply.
- this.select.getElementsByTagName('option') gets all of the option elements in the select but is further modified by supplying the selectedIndex inside the square brackets, thereby getting just the selected option.
- firstChild.nodeValue is what we are collecting from that option (i.e., the text inside the option) and is what is supplied to document.createTextNode().

There, that wasn't so bad. Refreshing the page now reveals a value right below the existing select element, as shown in Figure 12-4.

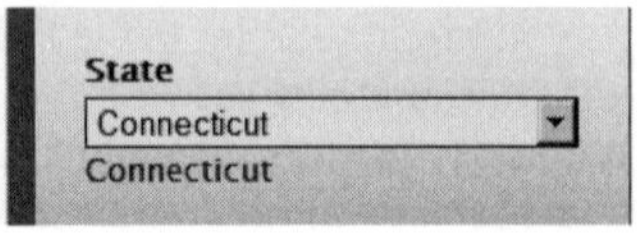

Figure 12-4. The select value populated into our new faux select value

Creating faux options

Now, we need to collect all of the options from the original select to create a faux option for each. We do that as follows:

```
FauxSelect.prototype = {
  ... cut ....
  initialize: function( id ){
    ... cut ...
    // collect the children & make them enumerable
    var children = $A( this.select.childNodes );
    children.each( function( item, i ){
      if( item.nodeName.toUpperCase() == 'OPTION' ){
        // build the faux OPTION
        var el = this.makeFake( item );
        // append it to the faux SELECT
        this.faux.appendChild( el );
      }
    }.bind( this ) );
    ... cut ...
  },
  ... cut ...
};
```

> You'll notice that bind() *is back again, ensuring that the* this *keyword refers to the correct instance of the* FauxSelect *object.*

To keep the code a little more legible, we're using FauxSelect's makeFake() method, passing it the option we want to replicate as a faux option:

```
FauxSelect.prototype = {
  ... cut ...
  makeFake:   function( node ){
    // clone the model LI
    var el = $( FauxSelectConductor.elements.li.cloneNode( true ) );
    // store the faux OPTION's value
    el.val = node.getAttribute( 'value' );
    // set the faux OPTION's text value
    el.appendChild( document.createTextNode( node.firstChild.➥
      nodeValue ) );
    // check for selected
    if( el.val == this.select.value ) el.addClassName( 'selected' );
  },
  ... cut ...
};
```

> You may be wondering why the method is named makeFake *instead of something more descriptive like* createOption. *The answer is simple: in an even more advanced version of this script (which I will provide a link to at the end of the case study), this method does double duty, creating both faux* options *and faux* optgroups. *For that reason, it needs a more general name, and* makeFake *has a nice ring to it.*

What we've done here is

1. Clone the model list item (li) from the FauxSelectConductor.
2. Create a property on that list item called val, and set it equal to the value attribute of the option.
3. Append some text to list item equal to the text in the option.
4. Test to see if we should classify this faux option as selected.
5. Return the newly created list item, so it can be appended to the faux select.

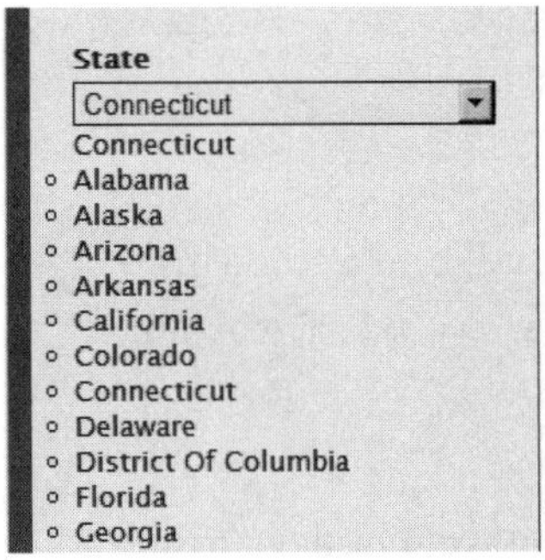

Figure 12-5. The list of states now appears along with the value.

When you run the script in your browser, you should see the actual select, followed by the default value in its own paragraph and then an unnumbered list containing all the states, as shown in Figure 12-5.

Each faux option li has a property called val, which is equal to the value of the option it's simulating. We will use this later to update the value of the real select (to make sure the values are submitted along with the form).

Generating life and other memorable events

Now that we have generated the elements for our faux select and appended them to the document, it's time to make it do something.

Opening, closing, and clicking the select

There are three basic events we need to simulate from a select—opening it, closing it, and selecting a value—but their interaction is a little tricky:

- When you click the displayed value of a standard select element, it opens, and if you click that same value again, it will close.
- Clicking one of the options when the select is open will trigger two events:
  - The value of the select will be updated.
  - The select will close.
- If you click anywhere that is not inside the select while it is open, the select will also close.

Sounds like fun, so let's get to it! Note that this is going to take a few steps before you really see anything happening.

To start, we need to invoke our FauxSelect open() and close() methods. These methods will be called from within the FauxSelect's clickValue() method, but first, we have to register clickValue as an observer for our value element in the initialize() method:

```
FauxSelect.prototype = {
  ... cut ...
  initialize: function( id ){
    ... cut ...
    // this will be the trigger to open the faux SELECT
    Event.observe( this.value, 'click',
                   this.clickValue.bind( this ), false );
    ... cut ...
  }
  ... cut ...
};
```

The clickValue() method will handle opening the faux select when you click the value. To do so, you need to check to see if it's open, and then close or open it as necessary by doing the following:

```
FauxSelect.prototype = {
  ... cut ...
  clickValue: function(){
    // Open/close the faux select
    if( this.faux.hasClassName( this.type + '-open' ) ){
      // The faux SELECT is open
      this.close();
    } else {
      // The faux SELECT is closed
      this.open();
    }
  },
  ... cut ...
};
```

Whoa, what's going on there? First, we adjust the behavior of the faux select's value, based on whether or not the faux select is open, so it opens it if it is closed and closes it if it is open. That means we need to track the state of the faux select. The open and closed states are directly tied to the visual appearance of the faux select, so, to keep track of how it looks, we give it a close class name when it's closed and an open class name when it's open.

> *Actually, it's not an open class name but rather a type-open class name. The default value of the type property is standard (for standard select types), so for the moment, this will always be standard-open. Later in the chapter, we'll be altering the type to indicate scrolling in the faux select, which will be tracked in the class name. Also, in the more advanced version, the class will track optgroup selects and multiple selects, all using the class name as an indicator, which makes styling a cinch.*

523

Next, edit the FauxSelect's open() and close() methods, and include the following class name changes:

```
FauxSelect.prototype = {
    ... cut ...
    open: function(){
        /* Indicate the state of the faux SELECT by removing the
           closed CLASS and adding opening */
        this.faux.removeClassName( 'closed' );
        this.faux.addClassName( 'opening' );
    },
    close: function(){
        /* Indicate the state of the faux SELECT by removing the
           open CLASS and adding closing */
        this.faux.removeClassName( this.type + '-open' );
        this.faux.addClassName( 'closing' );
    },
    ... cut ...
};
```

These class changes work along with the FauxSelect.clickValue() method (among others), which will call FauxSelect.open() or FauxSelect.close() based on the class name.

Looking at what you've done so far, you'll realize there's still something missing. We've added opening and closing classes in the open() and close() methods, but we haven't added the actual open and close classes yet. This is the last piece of the puzzle, and there's a clue in the opening and closing class names.

To make our faux select even fancier, we're going to open and close it with a sliding effect made simple by the Moo.fx library. When the effect ends, we'll call FauxSelect's flip() method, which will complete the state change and set up the rest of the class names. The problem, however, is that we haven't done anything to make our faux select look good, so adding an effect right now isn't going to work out that well. We'll be getting to style shortly, but for now, let's fill in the flip() method and call it directly from the open() and close() methods as follows:

```
FauxSelect.prototype = {
    ... cut ...
    open: function(){
        /* Indicate the state of the faux SELECT by removing the
           closed CLASS and adding opening */
        this.faux.removeClassName( 'closed' );
        this.faux.addClassName( 'opening' );
        this.flip( this.faux );
    },
    close: function(){
        /* Indicate the state of the faux SELECT by removing the
           open CLASS and adding closing */
        this.faux.removeClassName( this.type + '-open' );
```

```
      this.faux.addClassName( 'closing' );
      this.flip( this.faux );
    },
    ... cut ...
    flip: function(){
      // If it's opening close it otherwise open it
      if( this.faux.hasClassName( 'opening' ) ){
        // Mark it open
        this.faux.removeClassName( 'opening' );
        this.faux.addClassName( this.type + '-open' );
      } else {
        // Mark it closed
        this.faux.removeClassName(  'closing' );
        this.faux.addClassName( 'closed' );
      }
    },
    ... cut ...
};
```

We'll relocate the calls to this.flip() when we add the effect, but now, let's add some event handlers to our faux options.

Selecting a faux option

We need to handle the click event for a faux option (for which we created the FauxSelect. clickLI() method), but most implementations of select also give visual feedback in the form of a hover effect when you move your mouse over an option. You might think that doing this with CSS is the way to go, but Internet Explorer 6 does not support the :hover pseudoclass selector on anything other than the anchor element (a), so we will add some event handlers for the mouseover and mouse- out events as well. Jump back to the FauxSelect.makeFake() method, and add the following three events:

```
FauxSelect.prototype = {
    ... cut ...
    makeFake:   function( node ){
       ... cut ...
       // set the event handlers
       Event.observe( el, 'click', this.clickLI.bind( this ), false );
       // click
       Event.observe( el, 'mouseover', this.mouseoverLI, false );
       // mouseover
       Event.observe( el, 'mouseout',  this.mouseoutLI,  false );
       // mouseout
       return el;
    },
    ... cut ...
};
```

Next, we'll populate the hover effects in the mouseoverLI() and mouseoutLI() methods, since that's super easy:

```
FauxSelect.prototype = {
    ... cut ...
    mouseoverLI: function( e ){
      Event.element(e).addClassName( 'hover' );
    },
    mouseoutLI:  function( e ){
      Event.element(e).removeClassName( 'hover' );
    },
    ... cut ...
};
```

All we're doing here is using Prototype's class manipulation methods to add the hover class to and remove it from the element in question, which is retrieved using Prototype's Event.element() method—short and sweet. Now, let's move on to FauxSelect.clickLI(), which, coincidentally, also uses Event.element().

We know that when clickLI() is called, we need it to deselect whatever faux option is currently selected, select the faux option that was clicked, and then trigger the faux select to close. We will accomplish this by calling three different methods—deselectLI(), selectLI(), and close()—as follows:

```
FauxSelect.prototype = {
    ... cut ...
    clickLI:    function( e ){
      var el = Event.element( e );
      // normal SELECT behavior
      var fOpts = $$( '#replaces_' + this.id + ' li' );
          this.deselectLI( fOpts[this.select.selectedIndex] );
      this.selectLI( el );
      this.close();
    },
    ... cut ...
};
```

Everything in that method is pretty straightforward, with the possible exception of the bit concerning fOpts. Starting on line three of the method, we are using $$() to collect all of the list items within an element identified as replaces_*something* (where *something* is our real select's id). That collection is named fOpts, because it is a collection of our faux options. The method then deselects the faux option corresponding to the selectedIndex of the real select. It looks a little daunting at first but is really quite simple when you break it down.

Now, we just need to fill in some logic for selectLI() and deselectLI():

```
FauxSelect.prototype = {
    ... cut ...
    selectLI:    function( el ){
      // "select" the faux OPTION
```

```
      $( el ).addClassName( 'selected' );
      // set the real SELECT's value
      this.select.value = el.val;
      // set the faux SELECT's "value"
      this.value.firstChild.nodeValue = el.firstChild.nodeValue;
    },
    deselectLI:  function( el ){
      el.removeClassName( 'selected' );
    },
    ... cut ...
  };
```

selectLI() classifies the clicked li as selected, updates the displayed text in the value (this.value.firstChild.nodeValue) to be equal to the clicked li's text (el.firstChild.nodeValue), and sets the value of the real select equal to the clicked li's val property. deselectLI() is even simpler; it just removes the selected class.

Now that we've wired up the click events for our faux options, we can actually see some interactivity on the screen. After refreshing your browser, click the list items in the faux select, and watch in utter amazement as the text of the faux select's value changes *and* the value of the real select changes (ooh . . . aah . . .).

Before you start getting all chuffed with yourself, we really should do something about the look of that faux select. After all, isn't that the whole point of this chapter?

Bling-bling for da form t'ing

Let's start styling this thing up. To keep it flexible, we're going use one style sheet (faux-select.css) to hold the core styles needed to make this whole faux select thing work. Next, we're going to add some styles to our main style sheet (cleverly named main.css) to make the faux select look the way we want it to in the context and style of our page.

First things first, we need to determine how this whole thing fits together. We have essentially three elements to work with: div.faux-container, p.faux-value, and ul.faux-select. To replicate the look of a real select, we need the paragraph to float on top of the unordered list, and we need the unordered list to be able to expand and contract without pushing other elements on the page around. For that, we need to work with absolute positioning, and to do *that*, we need to establish a containing block. Before we get into actually writing the style, take a look at Figure 12-6 to see how a faux select should be laid out.

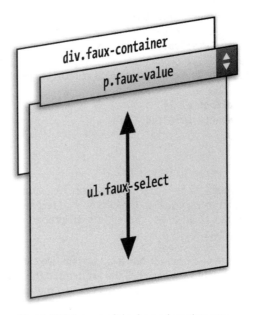

Figure 12-6. Layout of the faux select elements

So, we need to establish a containing block to keep the components of our faux select from flying all over the page. In the faux-select.css file, add a rule for the container:

```
/* Position the container */
.faux-container {
  position: relative;
}
```

Once that's done, we can also absolutely position both the paragraph and the unordered list within it:

```
/* Position the elements within it */
.faux-select {
    position: absolute;
}
.faux-value {
    cursor: pointer;
    position: absolute;
    top: 0;
}
```

Notice that we aren't setting a left or right side-offset property for either of these elements and for ul.faux-select, we aren't even setting a top or bottom side-offset. This is key to making the layout work.

> *Sharp eyes will also have noticed the* cursor: pointer *rule, which gives us the nice little hand cursor when we mouse over the faux value.*

Setting an element to position:absolute takes it completely out of the normal flow of the document (i.e., it takes up no space), but if you refrain from setting any side-offset properties on that element, they all default to what they would be if it were not positioned at all; this keeps the element in the same position when absolutely positioned as if it were statically positioned. This is one trick that is often overlooked in CSS layouts, but it's exactly what we need in this situation.

Let's adjust a few more CSS properties to give it some default styling. We'll override these in a moment with our own custom styles in main.css, but it is always good to set some foundational styles for any component like this, so others have a place to begin when making their own. Add the following changes to the faux-select.css file:

```css
/* Give the select a general style */
.faux-select {
  background: #fff;
  border: 1px solid;
  list-style: none;
  margin: 0;
  padding: 0;
  position: absolute;
}
.faux-select li {
  cursor: pointer;
  line-height: 1.25;
  margin: 0;
  padding: 0 .25em;
  white-space: nowrap;
}
.faux-value {
  background: #fff;
  border: 1px solid;
  cursor: pointer;
  position: absolute;
  top: 0;
}
```

We now have a nice baseline style for the faux select, but we can't see the results, because we haven't linked to it from our page yet. Rather than having to remember to link faux-select.css on every page where we use the script, we can just have the FauxSelectConductor add it to the page when it initializes. To do this, we simply create a link element and supply it with the proper details before appending it to the head of the page. To keep things a little more organized (and easy to update), we'll use the path in the cssFile property from the FauxSelectConductor:

```javascript
var FauxSelectConductor = {
    ... cut ...
    // The faux SELECT specific CSS styles
    cssFile:    'faux-select.css',
    ... cut ...
    initialize: function( params ){
       ... cut ...
       // attach the standard CSS file
```

```
      var css = document.createElement('link');
          css.setAttribute('rel', 'stylesheet');
          css.setAttribute('type', 'text/css');
          css.setAttribute('href', this.cssFile);
      document.getElementsByTagName( 'head' )[0].appendChild( css );
      ... cut ...
    },
    ... cut ...
};
```

> Be careful when defining the URL to the CSS file. If you're using a dynamic web site where pages are at various depths in the URL, you'll need to specify an absolute URL for the file beginning with a backslash (/), such as /path/to/faux-select.css, or you'll need a server-side rewrite rule to catch the file request and redirect it appropriately.

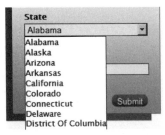

Figure 12-7. The somewhat gussied-up form layout in Firefox 2 on Windows XP

Once you've got the CSS file loading bit squared away, you should see something like Figure 12-7 when you refresh your browser.

The next thing we want to tackle is the width of the drop-down, because that variable-width list just won't do. But how wide should it be? Well, it seems to make sense that it should be as wide as the select it is replacing. Let's make that happen. We can set the script to automatically make the faux select just as wide as the original one, based on dimensions we can obtain from the Prototype getWidth() method (which relies partially on the element's offsetWidth property)—but there's a problem with this:

```
this.faux.style.width = this.select.getWidth() + 'px';
```

> When working with the DOM, make sure you append an element to the document before attempting to access its dimensions via its inherent properties (such as offsetWidth) or methods such as Prototype's getWidth(). Until an element is rendered on the page, it has no dimension. In this case, we're retrieving the values from the select that is already rendered on the page, so they are already available.

This width retrieved from getWidth() also includes the padding and border widths of the element. If we want to define our own padding and border for the faux select, we have to get rid of those values in the width by updating our FauxSelect object, as follows:

```
FauxSelect.prototype = {
  ... cut ...
  initialize: function( id ){
    ... cut ...
    // create the faux SELECT UL
    this.faux = $( FauxSelectConductor.elements.ul.cloneNode( true ) );
```

```
      this.faux.addClassName('faux-select');
      /* set the width, based on the existing SELECT
         (subtracting any border or padding) */
      this.faux.style.width = (
        parseInt( this.select.getWidth() )
        // Subtract borders
        - parseInt( this.select.getStyle( 'border-left-width' ) )
        - parseInt( this.select.getStyle( 'border-right-width' ) )
        // Subtract padding
        - parseInt( this.select.getStyle( 'padding-left' ) )
        - parseInt( this.select.getStyle( 'padding-right' ) )
      ) + 'px';
      ... cut ...
    },
    ... cut ...
};
```

> The Prototype getStyle() method returns the computed style of the element, not just the inline style, as discussed in Chapter 5. The values will contain the units, such as px, so you need to use JavaScript's parseInt() method to retrieve the numeric value. The only caution with this is that you may get unexpected results if you mix and match different units, such as em for padding and px for borders.

Now, let's work a bit in main.css, and start adding some additional styles to bring our faux select components better in line with the look of our page. We'll start by adding basic styles for the p.faux-value, ul.faux-select and the faux options classified as .selected or set to .hover (see Figure 12-8):

```
/* =faux SELECT STYLES */
p.faux-value {
  background: #eee;
  border: 1px solid;
  line-height: 18px;
  width: 175px;
  padding: 0 20px 0 3px;
}
ul.faux-select {
  background: #c4c4c0;
}
ul.faux-select .hover,
ul.faux-select .selected {
  background: #006;
  color: #fff;
}
```

Looking at Figure 12-8, you can see we're getting close, but you'll also notice that the value is hidden by the faux select list. This is because both elements have been positioned absolutely, and because the list comes later in the markup, it has a higher position in the stacking order. We can overcome this by setting `margin-top` on `ul.faux-select` equal to `line-height` of `p.faux-value` in our `main.css` file and then bringing our value forward:

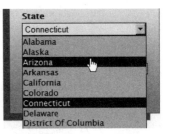

Figure 12-8. Our faux select gets a little CSS love, but we've got an overlap issue.

```css
ul.faux-select {
    background: #c4c4c0;
    margin-top: 18px;
}
.faux-value {
    background: #fff;
    border: 1px solid;
    cursor: pointer;
    white-space: nowrap;
    position: absolute;
    top: 0;
    z-index: 100;
}
```

> As `faux-select.css` is added to the document at runtime by our script, it is appended further down in the head of the document than the style rules we are applying in `main.css`, giving it greater weight in the cascade. To make sure our `main.css` rules take precedence, we need to increase the specificity of the selectors we're using. By adding an element selector (`ul`) to the class selector (`.faux-select`), we get just enough specificity to come out ahead, making our `margin-top: 18px;` rule trump the `margin: 0;` rule we set in `faux-select.css`—got to love specificity.

As you can see in Figure 12-9, what we've essentially done here is style the open state of our faux select (at least the basics).

Next, it's time to go back and make the `ul.faux-select` expand and collapse.

Figure 12-9. Now we can see the value above the faux select.

> True, we could write our own effect script, but we're going to simply leverage the beautiful work already done by Valerio Proietti in the Moo.fx library (`moofx.mad4milk.net`).

We'll eventually sprinkle at bit of the code throughout the FauxSelect object, but we'll start in `initialize()` with the basic setup. First, we employ Moo.fx's `fx.Style()` method as a property of the faux select (`heightFX`), so we can tap into it later (`fx.Style()` allows easy transitions of style values from one to another and doesn't require us to include anything apart from the base Moo.fx file). To keep it nice and smooth, we'll set the duration of the animation to be 350 milliseconds. Add the following now:

```
FauxSelect.prototype = {
  ... cut ...
  initialize: function( id ){
    ... cut ...
    // set up the height FX for the faux SELECT so it can open
    this.faux.heightFX = new fx.Style(
      this.faux, 'height',
      { duration: 350 }
    );
    ... cut ...
  },
  ... cut ...
};
```

Then, we'll collect the full original height of ul.faux-select. Once we have that, we'll make it a property of the faux select to reference it later (to be thorough, we'll store the collapsed size (0 pixels) as a property of the faux select as well):

```
FauxSelect.prototype = {
  ... cut ...
  initialize: function( id ){
    ... cut ...
    // get the original height of the UL for when it's open
    this.faux.openHeight = this.faux.getHeight();
    this.faux.closedHeight = 0;
    ... cut ...
  },
  ... cut ...
};
```

Finally, we can drop the height of the faux select to zero by using the set() method from Moo.fx, thereby collapsing (or closing) the element. While we're at it, let's add a class to the faux select to indicate its initial state—closed:

```
FauxSelect.prototype = {
  ... cut ...
  initialize: function( id ){
    ... cut ...
    // add the "closed" CLASS to the faux SELECT
    this.faux.addClassName( 'closed' );
    // close the faux SELECT
    this.faux.heightFX.set( this.faux.closedHeight );
    ... cut ...
  },
  ... cut ...
};
```

533

Now, that's all well and good, but depending on where in your code you made the previous two modifications, this.faux may not have been added into the document yet and won't have a height to get. To avoid this issue, keep it invisible for now by adding the following:

```
FauxSelect.prototype = {
  ... cut ...
  initialize: function( id ){
    ... cut ...
    // -- BUILD THE FAUX SELECT -- //
    // create the faux SELECT UL
    this.faux = $( FauxSelectConductor.elements.ul.cloneNode( true ) );
    this.faux.addClassName('faux-select');
    ... cut ...

    // collect the children & make them enumerable
    var children = $A( this.select.childNodes );
    children.each( function( item, i ){
      ... cut ...
    }.bind( this ) );

    /* append the faux SELECT to the SELECT's parent, but keep it
       invisible because we don't want it to appear quite yet.
       We do need to append it though because we can't get its
       height (which we'll need in a moment) without doing so */
    this.faux.style.visibility = 'hidden';
    this.select.parentNode.appendChild( this.faux );

    ... cut ...

    // add the "closed" CLASS to the faux SELECT
    this.faux.addClassName( 'closed' );
    // set up the height FX for the faux SELECT so it can open
    this.faux.heightFX = new fx.Style(
      ... cut ...
    );

    // get the original height of the UL for when it's open
    this.faux.openHeight = this.faux.getHeight();
    this.faux.closedHeight = 0;
    // close the faux SELECT
    this.faux.heightFX.set( this.faux.closedHeight );

    // remove the faux SELECT and re-append to our container
    //this.faux.parentNode.removeChild( this.faux );
    this.container.appendChild( this.faux );
    this.select.parentNode.appendChild( this.container );

    // show the ul
    this.faux.style.visibility = null;
```

```
  ... cut ...
},
... cut ...
};
```

By appending the list to the document after setting its `visibility` to hidden, we have the ability to obtain dimensional information from it without it being seen by the user. We just need to remove it from the document and append it to the container once it's available. After that, we reset the visibility, and we're back in business. There's a nice side effect to doing it this way as well—you don't see the list flash before it is collapsed.

Ah, but we're not completely out of the woods yet. A quick refresh of the browser will show that the list is collapsed, but all of the faux options will still be visible (albeit with no background). To fix that, we'll need to add some additional rules to `faux-select.css`:

```css
.faux-select {
  background: #fff;
  border: 1px solid;
  list-style: none;
  margin: 0;
  padding: 0;
  overflow: hidden;
  position: absolute;
}
```

And with that taken care of, we get what you see in Figure 12-10.

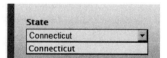

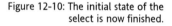

Figure 12-10: The initial state of the select is now finished.

Refreshing your browser now will show a collapsed faux select, but we don't have any way to open it back up. To do that, we need to make an addition to our `open()` method. First, remove the earlier reference to `this.flip()`, and then add the following:

```
FauxSelect.prototype = {
  ... cut ...
  open: function(){
    ... cut ...
    this.flip( this.faux );

    // Stop the effect if we're halfway through.
    this.faux.heightFX.stop();

    // Open the fauxSelect by invoking the effect
    this.faux.heightFX.custom(
      this.faux.getHeight(),
      this.faux.openHeight
    );
  },
  ... cut ...
};
```

First, we stop the effect if it's already in motion—which might happen if you close the faux select but change your mind before it finishes—and then we tell the effect to expand from the current height to the original height.

> The stop() method is not part of the core Moo.fx library (at least not as of this writing), and this is why the file is named mod-moo.fx.js. The addition, by this book's author, can be seen by viewing the source of mod-moo.fx.js.

We also need to update close() to collapse the faux select again. Essentially, we are doing the same thing, just in reverse:

```
FauxSelect.prototype = {
  ... cut ...
  close: function(){
    ... cut ...
    this.flip( this.faux );

    // Stop the effect if we're halfway through.
    this.faux.heightFX.stop();

    // Open the fauxSelect by invoking the effect
    this.faux.heightFX.custom(
      this.faux.getHeight(),
      this.faux.closedHeight
    );
  },
  ... cut ...
};
```

Now, all that's left is to call the flip() method. We need the method call when the effect ends and the faux select reaches its fully closed or fully open point. Conveniently, Moo.fx has an onComplete property in its effects just for this purpose. All we have to do is add it to the effect in the FauxSelect.initialize() method, like so:

```
FauxSelect.prototype = {
  ... cut ...
  initialize: function( id ){
    ... cut ...
    // set up the height FX for the faux SELECT so it can open
    this.faux.heightFX = new fx.Style(
      this.faux, 'height',
      { duration: 350,
        onComplete: this.flip.bind( this ) }
    );
    ... cut ...
  },
  ... cut ...
};
```

> *Don't forget the comma after the duration property!*

Now, when you refresh your browser and click the value, the list will expand. Clicking it again will cause it to collapse. Similarly, since we already wired up the faux options to trigger close() when clicked (in clickLI()), opening the faux select with the value and then clicking a faux option not only changes the value of the faux select and the real select, it also closes faux select (snazzy).

Of course the faux select is opening up to full height, which is a bit much. If you recall, the FauxSelectConductor has a property called maxHeight. We can use that to establish a maximum height for our faux select to reach when it opens, which will keep it from getting excessively long:

```
FauxSelect.prototype = {
  ... cut ...
  initialize: function( id ){
    ... cut ...
    // get the original height of the UL for when it's open
    this.faux.openHeight = this.faux.getHeight();
    /* if this faux SELECT has a lot of OPTIONs, it could
       end up being overly tall, we need to trim it down
       to a reasonable height, based on whatever we set in
       the FauxSelectConductor */
    if( this.faux.openHeight > FauxSelectConductor.maxHeight ){
      // mark this as an overflowing faux SELECT
      this.type = 'overflowing';
      // reset the height
      this.faux.openHeight = FauxSelectConductor.maxHeight;
    }
    this.faux.closedHeight = 0;
  },
  ... cut ...
};
```

Notice that we've introduced a new type to the mix—overflowing. Now we can add styles specific to that type of faux select in our faux-select.css file:

```
ul.faux-select.overflowing-open {
  overflow: auto;
  overflow-x: hidden;
}
```

By setting the overflow property to auto, we ensure the scrollbars will appear for all users. Setting the CSS3 property, overflow-x, puts an additional restriction on modern browsers, forcing them to only allow scrolling vertically (i.e., *not* along the x axis).

537

> *The* overflow-x *and* overflow-y *properties are well supported in Internet Explorer on the PC (version 6 and above), Firefox, and Camino. At the time of this writing, Dave Hyatt of the Safari team had just committed a patch to the nightly builds of that browser to support these two CSS properties, meaning (fingers crossed) they should be supported in the next official upgrade to the browser. Opera 9 does not appear to support these properties, yet.*

Since we're doing a little CSS work, let's jump back over to our `main.css` file, and make our faux select a little fancier:

```
p.faux-value {
    background: #eee;
    background: url(value.png) top left no-repeat;
    ... cut ...
}
```

And while we're at it, let's add a focused style for the faux value, so we can make it look like it's actually focused (like a real select–see Figure 12-11); we'll wire it up in a moment:

```
p.faux-value.focused {
    background-image: url(value-focused.png);
}
```

> *You'll find the images we're using in this example included in the project folder.*

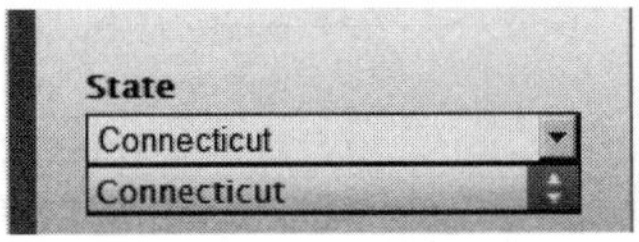

Figure 12-11. Our faux select is all grown up.

With a few final tweaks, we'll be able to wrap up this puppy.

Behavioral modifications

We have a functional faux select, but we need to add some polish to really make it shine and get it acting like a real select.

Closing the faux select

Our first challenge is to mimic the select element's behavior of closing when you click outside of the list. When clicking outside a regular select list, the list closes, but if you click another clickable element (e.g., a link), the click doesn't activate any other events. It is considered a close action, and you need to click again to initiate the click event on the element under the cursor.

To trigger a FauxSelect's close() method when you click outside it, we need to assign an event handler to whatever is going to be clicked. However, it doesn't really make sense to assign such an event to everything on the page, because it will become an event management nightmare.

> *If Internet Explorer supported the capturing phase of the event flow, this whole problem would be easily solved, as we could just register the listener in the capturing phase on the document and cancel any other events. But, alas, that isn't going to work, so we have to be tricky.*

The easiest way to both capture all mouse events and prevent any other actions is to put up a great big wall between the mouse pointer and the document. Essentially, this means making one element cover the entire page, on which we'll register a click event to close the faux select. We can create it when the object initializes but keep it in our pocket until the moment is right—when the FauxSelect.open() method is invoked. At that point, we can append the element to the document so it sits atop everything else. We'll call this element the closer.

We've already got a property on the FauxSelect waiting for it (FauxSelect.closer), so all we need to do is make it and wire it up to be added to the document when the FauxSelect opens and removed when it closes again:

```
FauxSelect.prototype = {
  ... cut ...
  initialize: function( id ){
    ... cut ...
    // -- BUILD THE CLOSER -- //
    this.closer = $( FauxSelectConductor.elements.div.➥
      cloneNode( true ) );
    this.closer.addClassName( 'closer' );
    /* we will use this hidden DIV to close the faux SELECT
       when you click outside of it */
    Event.observe( this.closer, 'click', this.close.➥
      bind( this ), false );
    ... cut ...
  },
  ... cut ...
  open: function(){
    ... cut ...
    // append the closer to the document
    document.getElementsByTagName( 'body' )[0].appendChild( this.➥
      closer );
  },
  close:    function(){
    ... cut ...
    // remove the closer
    this.closer.parentNode.removeChild(this.closer);
  },
  ... cut ...
};
```

Next, we add a few style rules to `faux-select.css` so that the closer will cover the entire body of the document:

```
.closer {
  position: absolute;
  top: 0;
  right: 0;
  left: 0;
}
```

Ideally, I would like to use fixed positioning and set the top, right, bottom, and left values all to zero, but, sadly, the use of fixed positioning introduces some odd behavior in Firefox and Camino on Mac (it makes the scrollbars disappear). Plus, there's the fact that Internet Explorer 6 doesn't support it. In order to get around those two issues, we're going to stick with absolute positioning.

Getting Internet Explorer 6 to behave is a breeze, as it supports CSS expressions. They aren't standards compliant, but if delivered to Internet Explorer 6 only (in our case, by employing the Tan hack), I think their use is justifiable. CSS expressions work pretty much like JavaScript, so in order to set the width and height of the closer to the full size of the page, we can do this:

```
* html .closer {
  width: expression( document.body.scrollWidth );
  height: expression( document.body.scrollHeight );
}
```

Those CSS expressions assign the width and height of the closer div to be the scrollWidth and scrollHeight, respectively, of the body element. Now, we need to take care of every other browser. If you recall, the FauxSelectConductor has a property called bodyHeight, which we can set when that object is initialized:

```
var FauxSelectConductor = {
  ... cut ...
  initialize: function(){
    // collect the params
    params = params || {};
    if( typeof( params.maxHeight ) != 'undefined' ) this.maxHeight =➥
      params.maxHeight;
    // set the BODY height
    this.bodyHeight = $( document.getElementsByTagName( 'body' )[0] ).➥
      getHeight() + 'px';
    ... cut ...
  }
};
```

Then, we can use that value in our FauxSelect object to set the height of the closer:

```
FauxSelect.prototype = {
  ... cut ...
  initialize: function( id ){
    ... cut ...
```

```
// -- BUILD THE CLOSER -- //
this.closer = $( FauxSelectConductor.elements.div.➥
  cloneNode( true ) );
this.closer.addClassName( 'closer' );
this.closer.style.height = FauxSelectConductor.bodyHeight;
... cut ...
},
... cut ...
};
```

But we're not quite finished. If you add a translucent background color, say pink, to the closer CSS

```
/* for testing */
.closer {
    background: pink;
    opacity: 0.6;
    filter: alpha(opacity=60);
}
```

and test your page, you'll see that it doesn't do exactly what we want. It covers everything—including the faux select (see Figure 12-12).

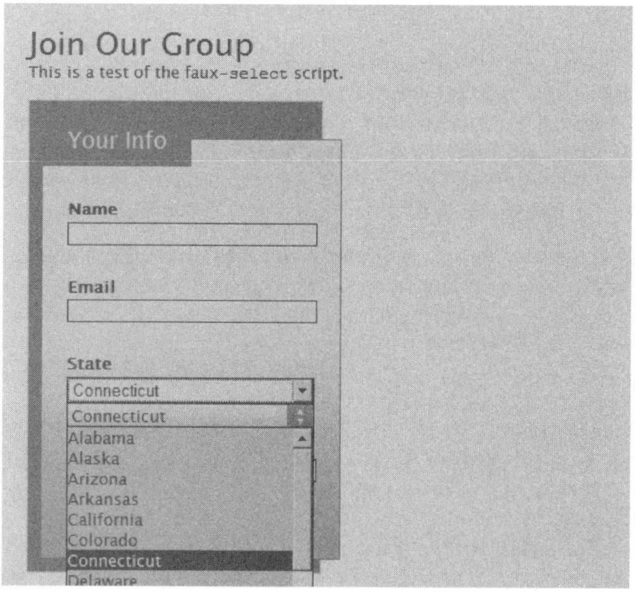

Figure 12-12. Covering everything isn't much good.

The real trick of dealing with the closer has to do with making sure it always sits on top of every element on the page yet remains below the faux select. Sounds like we're going need to get familiar with z index.

Z index to the rescue!

Coincidentally, in dealing with this layering issue, we can also solve another dilemma—stacking order: when using several faux selects in a single page, their drop-downs may overlap other faux selects. And, as we discussed, default stacking order places positioned elements that come later in the markup *above* positioned elements that are earlier in the markup, meaning that, without adjustment, we could have a page that looks like Figure 12-13.

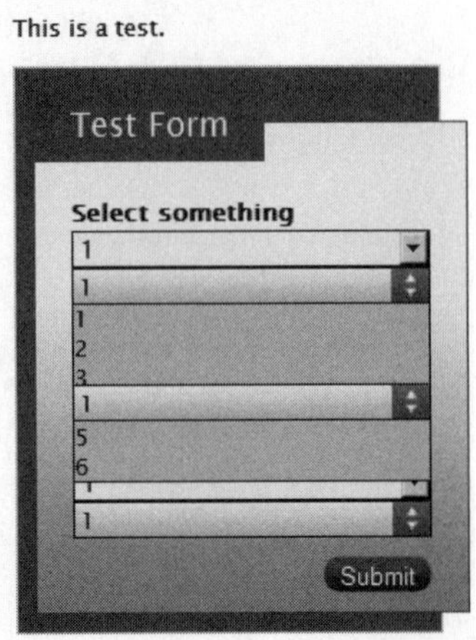

Luckily, we can overcome this by dynamically adjusting the z index of the elements (moving them along the page's z axis). Fully explaining the intricacies of the z index is outside the scope of this chapter (which is long enough already), but if you're keenly interested in the topic, I highly recommend checking out Aleksandar Vacic's exhaustive article on the topic (http://www.aplus.co.yu/css/z-pos/).

For those of you who couldn't care less and just want to see it work, here's what were going to do: First, we'll set a very high default z index (which we, coincidentally, already have waiting for us in the FauxSelectConductor) so that whatever element receives it will be above anything else on the page. Then, when we open the faux select, we'll set its z index to that number and the closer's to one less.

Figure 12-13. These faux selects are victims of default stacking order. Notice how the drop-down of the first faux select is obscured by the value of the second (oh, the injustice).

> *Starting with a z index of 10,000 is an arbitrary decision that will allow the closer to be positioned above other elements that also have a z index set. If we only started at zero, another script may position elements above the closer, which would complicate things a little. Still, another script could be using a larger number, so if you run into that issue, simply make this default value larger. Whoever has the biggest z index wins.*
>
> *If you're very adventurous, you could make this into another manageable property, like* maxHeight, *which can be set when* FauxSelectConductor *is initialized.*

To accomplish this z index juggling, we simply tap into our open() and close() methods like so:

```
FauxSelect.prototype = {
  ... cut ...
  open: function(){
    ... cut ...
    // Set the z-index of the faux SELECT container
    this.container.style.zIndex = FauxSelectConductor.zindex;
    // Set the z-index of the closer to one less than the
    // faux SELECT container
    this.closer.style.zIndex = FauxSelectConductor.zindex - 1;
    // Append the closer to the document
    document.getElementsByTagName( 'body' )[0].appendChild( this.➥
      closer );
  },
```

```
close:     function(){
  ... cut ...
  // remove the closer
  this.closer.parentNode.removeChild(this.closer);
  // reset the z-indexes
  this.container.style.zIndex = this.closer.style.zIndex = null;
},
... cut ...
};
```

Refresh the browser, and you should see something akin to Figure 12-14.

Figure 12-14. The z index values are inverted, and closer is tucked neatly beneath the faux select, so all is right with the world.

Next challenge, please!

Keyboard controls and other niceties

Now that we've got our faux select working nicely with the mouse, it's time to show the keyboard some love. A large number of web users prefer keyboard controls, especially when filling out forms. I, for instance, simply hit the C key three times in a state selector to enter Connecticut, rather than opening the form control and scrolling to it. Furthermore, most browsers support find-by-typing interfaces in select elements, so typing CON would also allow me to select Connecticut. It makes sense to allow users the same options when interacting with our faux select.

Each browser handles the keyboard control of a select a little differently. So, to make coding easy, it's best to simply let the browser work as it normally does without interfering. If we keep the real select available on the page—just hidden from view—we can hook into it, allowing our faux select to not just update the real select but also be *updated by it*. We can listen for keyboard events on the select when it's in focus and then simply update the faux select as the real select element's value is changed—easy peasy.

Selecting options

Hooking onto the select for keyboard interaction will involve using the FauxSelect.updateFaux() method to handle the heavy lifting, and just to be different, we'll assign the listener in initialize() using Prototype's bindAsEventListener() method:

```
FauxSelect.prototype = {
  ... cut ...
  initialize: function( id ){
    ... cut ...
    // -- HANDLE EVENTS ON THE REAL SELECT -- //
    // typing
    this.select.onkeyup = this.updateFaux.bindAsEventListener( this );
  },
  ... cut ...
};
```

Next, we'll use the FauxSelect.last property to keep track of the last selectedIndex of the real select element, so we can easily deselect it as keyboard events are fired. We'll start by picking it up when the script initializes, and we'll update it whenever selectLI() is called:

```
FauxSelect.prototype = {
  ... cut ...
  // the index of the last value selected
  last:       false,
  ... cut ...
  initialize: function( id ){
    ... cut ...
    // store the SELECT node and its selectedIndex
    this.select = $( id );
    this.last = this.select.selectedIndex;
    ... cut ...
  },
  ... cut ...
  selectLI:   function( el ){
    ... cut ...
    // update this.last
    this.last = this.select.selectedIndex;
  },
  ... cut ...
  updateFaux: function( e ){
    var el = Event.element( e );
    var fOpts = $$( '#replaces_' + this.id + ' li' );
    this.deselectLI( fOpts[this.last] );
    this.selectLI( fOpts[el.selectedIndex] );
  }
};
```

Using FauxSelect.last to remember the previous selectedIndex of the real select saves us from having to loop through all of the faux options to figure out which to deselect.

Maintaining focus

While we're at it, we should also hook up that focused class we created way back when. To do that, we'll tap into the focus and blur events on the select and trigger the focus() and blur() methods. These methods will just alter the class name of our value so that the focused style is applied:

```
FauxSelect.prototype = {
  ... cut ...
  initialize: function( id ){
    ... cut ...
    // -- HANDLE EVENTS ON THE REAL SELECT -- //
    // focus
    Event.observe( this.select, 'focus', this.focus.➥
      bind( this ), false );
    // blur
    Event.observe( this.select, 'blur', this.blur.bind➥
      ( this ), false );
    // typing
    this.select.onkeyup = this.updateFaux.bindAsEventListener( this );
  },
  ... cut ...
  focus: function(){
    this.value.addClassName( 'focused' );
  },
  blur: function(){
    this.value.removeClassName( 'focused' );
  },
  ... cut ...
};
```

Figure 12-15 shows our focused class applied.

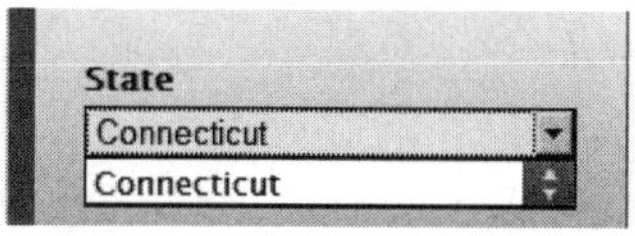

Figure 12-15. Our faux select now reacts to focus being placed on the real select. The value has been styled with a different background image (white) to indicate this visually.

By adding the following to the open() method, we can also shift focus to the real select when the value of our faux select is clicked, so keyboard events will still be tracked in mixed keyboard and mouse usage:

```
FauxSelect.prototype = {
  ... cut ...
  open: function(){
    ... cut ...
    // Trigger the focus event on the SELECT
    this.select.focus();
  },
  ... cut ...
};
```

Closing the faux select

A select also has a few additional key combinations that do special things. To trigger the drop-down to close, you can press Enter or Esc, so we'll need to add a tiny check for their key codes (lucky 13 and 27, respectively) to the updateFaux() method, as follows:

```
FauxSelect.prototype = {
    ... cut ...
    updateFaux: function( e ){
        ... cut ...
        // special case for Enter and Esc to close the faux select
        if( this.faux.hasClassName( this.type + '-open' ) &&
            ( e.keyCode == '13' ||
              e.keyCode == '27' ) ){
          this.close();
        }
        ... cut ...
    }
    ... cut ...
};
```

We also need to add keyboard control for the combination of the Alt key with the up or down arrow key (key codes 38 and 40, respectively). In most browsers, this triggers a focused select to open, or if it is already open, to close. To mimic this behavior, we'll need to add a little more logic to the updateFaux() method, having it trigger our already existing clickValue() method (which does the exact same thing), whenever it encounters an up or down arrow in the company of the Alt key:

```
FauxSelect.prototype = {
    ... cut ...
    updateFaux: function( e ){
        ... cut ...
        /* special case for Alt+up & Alt+Down allows opening of
           the faux SELECT without updating the value with each
           keypress. To confirm a value change, Enter must be
           pressed */
        if( e.altKey &&
            ( e.keyCode == '38' ||
              e.keyCode == '40' ) ){
          this.clickValue();
          return;
        }
        ... cut ...
    }
};
```

It seems we've done a lot for keyboard users, but this is no time to rest on our laurels; there are still a few more interactions left to manage. The first of these is what happens when keyboard controls for directional movement are used when the faux select is open. You see, when the select is open, using the directional keys does not trigger a change of the selectedIndex, so to keep up with the keyboard, we need to be able to update our faux select while this sort of interaction is occurring. To do that, we add the following to updateFaux():

```
FauxSelect.prototype = {
  ... cut ...
  updateFaux: function( e ){
    ... cut ...
    if( this.faux.hasClassName( this.type + '-open' ) ){
      var fOpt = false;
      // back
      if( e.keyCode == '37' ||
          e.keyCode == '38' ){
        if( this.select.selectedIndex > 0 )
          fOpt = fOpts[this.select.selectedIndex - 1];
      }
      // forward
      if( e.keyCode == '39' ||
          e.keyCode == '40' ){
        if( this.select.selectedIndex < fOpts.length )
          fOpt = fOpts[this.select.selectedIndex + 1];
      }
      // top
      if( e.keyCode == '33' ||
          e.keyCode == '36' ){
        fOpt = fOpts[0];
      }
      // bottom
      if( e.keyCode == '34' ||
          e.keyCode == '35' ){
        fOpt = fOpts[fOpts.length-1];
      }
      if( fOpt ){
        this.deselectLI( fOpts[this.select.selectedIndex] );
        this.selectLI( fOpt );
      }
    } else {
      this.deselectLI( fOpts[this.last] );
      this.selectLI( fOpts[el.selectedIndex] );
    }
    ... cut ...
  }
};
```

You'll notice that we've also moved the nonopen behavior inside the conditional, so it isn't triggered if the faux select is open. Now we've handled almost all of the keyboard events. The final one is to manage what happens when a user tabs away from the select, triggering the blur event. If the faux select is open, we need to close it:

```
FauxSelect.prototype = {
  ... cut ...
  blur: function(){
    this.value.removeClassName( 'focused' );
```

```
      if( this.faux.hasClassName( this.type + '-open' ) ) this.close();
    }
};
```

Of course, this means we could end up with multiple calls to close(): As you click a value to open the faux select, it passes focus to the real select. When you then click a faux option in the open drop-down (triggering clickLI()), focus is taken away from the select in most browsers, meaning both the call to close() in clickLI() and in blur() are executed. To keep this conflict from occurring, we'll add an additional check to our close() method before it runs, to ensure we're not trying to close a faux select that's already closed:

```
FauxSelect.prototype = {
  ... cut ...
  close: function(){
    // Check if the menu is open and if it isn't return
    if(!this.faux.hasClassName(this.type + '-open')) return;
    ... cut ...
  },
  ... cut ...
};
```

One other problem introduced by this is that Internet Explorer will remove focus from the select when you scroll an overflowing faux select, causing it to collapse prematurely. To counteract this, we can use another property on our FauxSelect object—preventClose. We will need to tap into a few places in our FauxSelect object to get it wired in:

```
FauxSelect.prototype = {
  // keep the faux SELECT from closing? fixes a blur bug
  preventClose: false,
  initialize: function( id ){
    ... cut ...
    /* Bind a mousedown event to the faux select to indicate when
       we click the menu. The blur event in some browsers will trigger
       when we try to scroll so we need to prevent the menu from
       closing. */
    Event.observe( this.faux, 'mousedown', this.➥
      clickUL.bind(this), false );
  },
  ... cut ...
  clickUL: function() {
    // Prevent closing after a click in the scroll bar
    this.preventClose = true;
  },
  ... cut ...
  blur:        function(){
    ... cut ...
    if( this.faux.hasClassName( this.type + '-open' ) &&
        !this.preventClose ) this.close();
    /* If preventClose was true, the call to blur wasn't the
       one we wanted. The next one will be, so set preventClose
```

```
            back to false */
        this.preventClose = false;
    },
    ... cut ...
};
```

The most important change to pay attention to is in the blur() method. We've adjusted the conditional to make sure this.preventClose is false before we actually close it. This way, if someone clicks the value to open the faux select, focus is passed to the real select. When that person clicks the ul to scroll it (the ul, mind you, not the list items or faux options), the clickUL() method is called and preventClose is set to true before blur() has a chance to close the faux select. The blur() method does, however, reset preventClose, so next time, the faux select will close as it should.

Is select too big for its britches?

Earlier, we briefly covered what to do to keep the faux select from being excessively tall, but simply setting the maxHeight isn't really giving our users the best overall experience. We still need the scrollbar to keep pace with the user if they are using a keyboard to enter the value (say, CON for Connecticut) or if they are simply pressing the arrow keys. To do this, we apply a little mathematical formula to see if the highlighted faux option falls within the bounds of those currently visible. If it doesn't, we update the position of the scroll to make sure it does:

```
FauxSelect.prototype = {
    ... cut ...
    updateFaux: function( e ){
        ... cut ...
        // adjust the scroll if there is one
        if( this.faux.className.indexOf( 'overflowing' ) != -1 &&
            this.faux.hasClassName( this.type + '-open' ) ){
                var ulHeight = this.faux.getHeight();
            var liHeight = $( this.faux.firstChild ).getHeight();
            if( // going down
                ( ( el.selectedIndex+1 ) * liHeight >
                  this.faux.scrollTop + ulHeight ) ||
                // going up
                ( ( el.selectedIndex * liHeight ) < this.faux.scrollTop ) ){
                this.faux.scrollTop = el.selectedIndex * liHeight;
            }
        }
    },
    ... cut ...
};
```

Here's the *Cliff's Notes* version of what this little bit of code does: First, it tests to see if the FauxSelect overflows and if it is open. It then proceeds to do a little reconnaissance, gathering information about the height of the faux select, as well as the height of one faux option. Next, it compares the scrollTop property of the faux select (i.e., the position of the scrollbar) to the vertical position of the currently selected faux option and determines if that faux option falls outside the viewable range (above or below). If it does, the scrollTop property of the faux select is updated.

549

To cover all the bases, we can also add a slightly scaled back version of this checker to the `flip()` method, so that the currently selected faux option is always within the displayed range:

```
FauxSelect.prototype = {
  ... cut ...
  flip: function(){
    // If it's opening close it otherwise open it
    if( this.faux.hasClassName( 'opening' ) ){
      ... cut ...
      // If this is an overflow, scroll to the selected LI
      var heightLI = $( this.faux.firstChild ).getHeight();
      var top = heightLI * this.select.selectedIndex;
      if( this.type == 'overflowing' && (
          this.faux.scrollTop > top || this.faux.scrollTop
          + FauxSelectConductor.maxHeight < top + heightLI ) ) {
        this.faux.scrollTop = top;
      }
    } else {
      ... cut ...
    }
  },
  ... cut ...
};
```

While we're in there, we should take care of one other little difficulty—sometimes hover states from faux options do not go away when the faux select closes (i.e., the blur event never runs). To compensate, we can simply add the following to the `flip()` method:

```
FauxSelect.prototype = {
  ... cut ...
  flip: function(){
    // If it's opening close it otherwise open it
    if( this.faux.hasClassName( 'opening' ) ){
      ... cut ...
    } else {
      ... cut ...
      // Ensure all the li elements have their
      // hover class removed. It can stick around
      // because we manually closed the faux select
      $A( this.faux.childNodes ).each( function( child ){
        if( child.hasClassName( 'hover' ) ) child.➥
          removeClassName( 'hover' );
      } );
    }
  },
  ... cut ...
};
```

Knock, knock . . . housekeeping!

Can you sense it? The finish line is just ahead. There's only a little bit more code before we're finished. You're probably asking, "Are we finally going to get rid of the original select?" Why, yes, we are. In perhaps the simplest maneuver in this whole script, we'll wipe that select from the face of the page. To witness the magic, first add the following:

```
FauxSelect.prototype = {
   ... cut ...
   initialize:      function( id ){
      ... cut ...
      // and finally hide the original select
      this.select.addClassName('replaced');
   },
   ... cut ...
};
```

Next, in faux-select.css, add a rule to shift the original select way off to the left, which will leave it available for keyboard navigation, but hide it from view:

```
select.replaced {
   position: relative;
   left: -999em;
}
```

Of course, that does leave us with an empty space where the select used to be, but we can easily fill that by applying a negative top margin to the container:

```
FauxSelect.prototype = {
   ... cut ...
   initialize: function( id ){
      ... cut ...
      // but don't forget to shift the faux selector up a bit
      this.container.style.marginTop =
         '-' + this.select.getHeight() +'px';
      ... cut ...
   },
   ... cut ...
};
```

And, as Figure 12-16 shows, there you have it.

Figure 12-16. Look Ma—no select.

Further adventures in select replacement

If you're truly daring, consider enhancing this script by adding support for multiple selects and optgroup-organized selects. Or if you're feeling lazy, you can just grab it from chapter12/ faux-select-advanced or see if there's a newer version at http://code.google.com/p/ easy-designs/wiki/FauxSelect. Figure 12-17 shows an example of how nice your forms can look. Good luck!

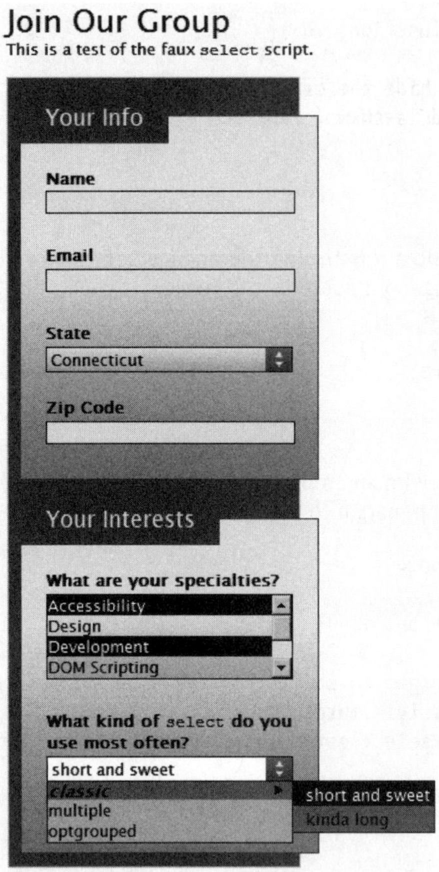

Figure 12-17. Prettier forms with *FauxSelect*

Summary

Apart from providing a very useful script, especially if you're as visually inclined as I am, the case study in this chapter provided a real-world example of how, why, and when to use JavaScipt libraries. It also showed that even a daunting task like rebuilding a select form control is not insurmountable if you break it down into simple steps; small steps can accomplish big things. As Ovid said, *"Gutta cavat lapidem"* (dripping hollows out rock).

Now get out there, and make something amazing!

INDEX

Special Characters

$$( ) method, 414, 516
$_SERVER array, 292

A

<a> tag, 8, 10–11
abort events, 152–153, 177
abort( ) method, 287
absolute property, 416
accept attribute, 359
accept property, 439
accessibility, 16–17, 407, 410
actionPager( ) listeners, 338
actions/ subfolder, 352
add( ) method, 439
addClassName( ) method, 219, 520
addControl( ) method, 463
addCSSRule( ) method, 231, 233–234
addEvent( ) method, 24, 171, 178–179
addEventListener( ) method, 26, 172, 182, 185, 195
addLoadEvent( ) method, 183, 185
addOverlay( ) method, 463
addProgressBar( ) method, 360, 362–364, 368
addProgressBar( ) object, 355–358, 371
    modifying file inputs, 358–360
    overview, 358
    progress bar, 363–365
    redirecting form, 361–362
    tracking progress, 365–371
addStyleSheet( ) method, 228
addUploadProgress( ) object, 358
Adobe Flash, 455
ADS-final-verbose.js file, 20
ADS library
    adding to, 131–133
    overview, 20–21
ADS.$( ) method, 22–24, 358
ADS object, 11, 21
ADS prefix, 23
ADSActionLink class, 322
ADS.actionPager object, 316, 321, 323, 334, 338
ADSActionPagerModified class, 323
ADS.addEvent( ) method, 22, 24–26, 34, 47, 152, 178–179, 276, 515

ADS.addLoadEvent( ) method, 22, 152, 262
ADS.ajaxRequest( ) method, 304, 329, 332, 341–342, 345, 348, 369
ADS.ajaxRequest object, 291, 299, 307, 334
ADS.ajaxRequestQueue( ) method, 342
ADS.camelize( ) method, 133
ADS.eventPreventDefault( ) method, 25
ADS.generateDOM object, 132
ADS.getElementByClassName( ) method, 47
ADS.getElementsByClassName( ) method, 26–28
ADS.getEventObject( ) function, 187–188
ADSImageEditor class, 260–261
ADS.imageEditor.imageClick( ) method, 261
ADSImageEditorModified class, 262
ADS.insertAfter( ) method, 28–30
ADS.isCompatible( ) method, 21–22, 461
ADS.js file, 21
ADS.log object, 96
ADS.node.COMMENT_NODE, 108
ADS.node.ELEMENT_NODE, 138
ADS.node.TEXT_NODE, 138
ADS.prependChild( ) method, 29–30
ADS.removeChildren( ) method, 29–30
ADS.removeEvent( ) method, 24–26
ADS.setStyle( ) method, 259
ADS.toggleDisplay( ) method, 28
ADS.xssRequest( ) object, 312
afterFinish option, 429
afterUpdate option, 429
Ajax, 285–286, 305, 343
    bookmarks, 315
    choosing, 304–305
    Document Object Model (DOM), 286
    example, 334, 343
    JavaScript, 286–295
        acting on responses, 288–291
        identifying Ajax requests, 291–293
        making requests, 287–288
        methods, 294–295
        overview, 286–287
    overview, 285–286
    problems, 305–334
        asynchronous behavior, 324–334
        back buttons, 313–324
        bookmarks, 313–324

bypassing cross-site restrictions with <script> tags, 306–313
increased resources, 334
JavaScript required for content, 305–306
overview, 305
requests, identifying, 291–293
reusable objects, 299–304
search requests, 470–481
overview, 470–476
related links, 477–481
search results, 476–477
semantic XHTML, 286
XML, 295–299
HTML, 296–297
JavaScript code, 297
JavaScript Object Notation (JSON), 298–299
overview, 295–296
plain text, 296
XMLHttpRequest object, 286–295
acting on responses, 288–291
identifying Ajax requests, 291–293
making requests, 287–288
methods, 294–295
overview, 286–287
Ajax object, 397–400
ajaxifiy class, 342
Ajax.PeriodicalUpdater( ) method, 397
Ajax.Request( ) method, 397
Ajax.Request object, 400
Ajax.responders method, 399
Ajax.Updater( ) method, 397
Ajax.updater( ) method, 401
alert( ) function, 36, 424, 426
alertAndDoWhatever( ) method, 291
alertName( ) method, 63
anchor (<a>) object, 102
anchors collection, 126
anonymous functions, 33–34
APC_UPLOAD_PROGRESS key, 351, 362
APIs (application programming interfaces), 51, 375, 455
client-side, 457–484
Ajax search requests, 470–481
example, 481–484
maps, 458–469
keys, 457, 499
server-side, 484–504
Basecamp, 488–498
Flickr buddy icons, 498–504
overview, 484–488
appendChild( ) method, 8, 115, 118
appendToMessage( ) function, 67, 71
applets collection, 126
application programming interfaces. See APIs
application/xhtml+xml file, 293
application/xml file, 289
apply( ) method, 73–74, 76
Array object, 30, 39, 52, 60

asynchronous behavior, 324–334
asynchronous requests, 329–334
latency, 327–329
overview, 324–326
asynchronous file uploads, 345–372
loading message, 347–351
overview, 347–349
processing uploads on server, 349–351
overview, 345–347
starting point, 351–352
upload progress indicator, 352–371
addProgressBar( ) object, 355–371
load event, 357
overview, 352–354
asynchronous property, 397
asynchronous=false option, 329
attachEvent( ) method, 172, 181
ATTRIBUTE_NODE, 143
attributes
manipulating, 119–120
Node object, 111–114
attributes property, 111–114
attributes.getNamedItem( ) method, 113
Attr.nodeName object, 104
Attr.nodeValue object, 105

B

back buttons, 313–324
browser sniffing, 316
fixing, 315
overview, 313–315
tracking location changes, 316–324
Basecamp, 488–498
account information, 489–490
DOM scripts, 495–498
proxy scripts, 491–495
beforeStart option, 429
beforeUpdate option, 429
beginReading event, 150
behavior, separating from markup, 6–14
adding JavaScript, 6–8
javascript: prefix, 8–14
behavioral enhancements
drag and drop, 438–451
dragging anywhere, 438–439
droppables, 439–440
observers, 448–451
shopping carts, 440–448
best practices, 3–49
enhancement, 4–5
example, 40–48
JavaScript, 5–30
accessibility, 16–17
human intervention, 30
namespaces, 17–19
reusable objects, 19–30

separating behavior from markup, 6–14
syntax problems, 30–40
version checking, 14–16
overview, 3
bgColor option, 435
BinaryContent variable, 346
bind( ) method, 393, 517, 521
bindAsEventListener( ) method, 543
bindFunction( ) method, 74
blend option, 435
<blink> tag, 405
blur events, 161–163, 177
blur( ) method, 544, 548
body element, 518
body property, 53, 126
body tags, className switching on, 225–228
bodyHeight property, 518, 540
bookmarks, 313–324
    browser sniffing, 316
    fixing, 315
    overview, 313–315
    tracking location changes, 316–324
Boolean object, 52
border option, 435
border-radius property, 435
border-style element, 507
box element, 154
breaking lines, 31–32
browser sniffing, 14–16, 316
browser.js file, 338
browserList, 381
#browserList element, 382
browsers, choosing, 98
bubbles property, 189
bubbling events, 173–176
<button> element, 128, 387
button property, 194

C

call( ) method, 73–76
calling functions, 40
camelize( ) method, 132, 215
cancelable property, 176, 189
cancelBubble property, 175
cancelHandle event listener, 280
capability detection, 14–16
capturing events, 173–175
#cart droppable, 451
.cart-item draggable, 446
#cart-wrapper droppable, 446
Cascading Style Sheets (CSS), 4
    modifying style, 203–247
        accessing computed style, 237–238
        example, 244–246
        Microsoft filter property, 239–244
        modifying markup for style, 206–213

separating style and markup, 213–237
        W3C DOM2 Style specification, 203–206
    property modification, 415–426
        example, 420–426
        multiple effects on multiple objects, 418
        multiple properties, 417
        reusing effects, 417–418
        single properties, 416–417
        slider effect, 418–420
case sensitivity, 30
catch control structure, 76–77
CDATASection.nodeName object, 104
CDATASection.nodeValue object, 105
change event listener, 360
change events, 163–165, 177
change option, 439
:checkbox element, 387
checkForVariable( ) method, 134, 139
> (child selectors), 384
child selectors (>), 384
childNodes property, 108, 114
class attribute, 26
Class object, 512
.className elements, 383
className property, 144, 163, 217
className switching, 217–220
    on body tags, 225–228
    drawbacks, 220
    setAttribute method, 220
    using common classes, 217–220
cleaning up document, with Prototype library, 390
$(. . .).cleanWhitespace( ) method, 390
cleanWhitespace( ) method, 390
clearMessage( ) method, 64, 71
clearWarnings( ) method, 370
click event, 34, 149, 156, 171, 177, 180, 393
click event listener, 34, 36, 74
clicked( ) function, 34
clickedLink object, 74, 76
clickedLink.sayGoodbye( ) method, 74
clickLI( ) method, 526, 548
clickUL( ) method, 549
clickValue( ) method, 523, 546
client-side APIs, 457–484
    Ajax search requests, 470–481
        overview, 470–476
        related links, 477–481
        search results, 476–477
    maps, 458–469
        example, 481–484
        microformats, 465–469
        overview, 458–464
        retrieving latitude/longitude, 464–465
cloneNode( ) method, 518
close class, 523
close( ) method, 523, 536, 538, 548
closures, 34–38

color option, 435
Comment.nodeName object, 104
Comment.nodeValue object, 105
compact option, 435
completeListener property, 304, 313
computed style, accessing, 237–238
constraint option, 439
constructors, 61–63
containment property, 439
:contains('test') expression, 387
Content-Type header, 289, 293, 398
Content-Type property, 297
contentEditable property, 416
contentType property, 397
converting
    hand-coded HTML to DOM code, 127–146
        adding to ADS library, 131–133
        DOM generation tool HTML file, 128–130
        generateDOM object framework, 133–146
        overview, 127–128
        testing with HTML fragment, 130–131
cookie property, 126
Core module, 94
corners option, 435
createAttribute( ) method, 121
createCDATASection( ) method, 121
createComment( ) method, 121
createDocumentFragment( ) method, 121
createDOM( ) method, 390
createElement( ) method, 8, 81, 121
createEntityReference( ) method, 121
create_item request, 493
createOption method, 522
createProcessingInstruction( ) method, 122
createTextNode( ) method, 84, 122
createWindow( ) method, 79–83
cropping and resizing tool. See photo cropping and
        resizing tool
cropping images, 276, 280
cropResizeHandle event, 276
cross-browser events, 188–201
    accessing keyboard commands, 197–201
    Event object, 189–190
    MouseEvent object, 190–197
    overview, 188
cross-site restrictions, bypassing with <script> tags,
        306–313
CSS. See Cascading Style Sheets (CSS)
`SS2 module, 94
    `le property, 529
        `eDeclaration objects, 205–206
            `ule objects, 204–205
                `t object, 204
                `v, 205
                    `rty, 238
                        `ty, 189–190
                            `–396

D
Date object, 52
dblclick event, 156
default action, canceling, 176
DELETE request, 294
deselectLI( ) method, 526
detachEvent( ) method, 181
DHTML (Dynamic HTML), 90
direction option, 429
disabled property, 221
dispatchEvent( ) method, 182
display property, 28, 416
display:none property, 413
<div> element, 78, 264, 361, 387, 481
div.faux-container element, 527
do=create argument, 494
DOCTYPE specification, 8
document element, 154
Document object, 120–122
    creating nodes with document methods, 121–122
    document.documentElement property, 121
    locating elements with document methods, 122
    overview, 120–121
Document Object Model. See DOM
document trees
    iterating, 122–124
    traversing, 122–124
document.all object, 90
document.body.getElementsByTagName, 15
document.body.toString( ) method, 56
document.createElement( ) method, 228, 361, 518
document.createEvent( ) method, 182, 190
document.createTextNode( ) method, 520
document.documentElement property, 121
documentElement object, 103
DocumentFragment.nodeName object, 104
DocumentFragment.nodeValue object, 105
document.getElementById( ) method, 22, 55, 117–118,
        121, 297, 519
document.getElementsByTagName( ) method, 123, 515
Document.nodeName object, 104
Document.nodeValue object, 105
document.styleSheets property, 204, 230
DocumentType.nodeName object, 104
DocumentType.nodeValue object, 105
document.write( ) method, 7–8
do=list argument, 494
DOM Core, 91
DOM (Document Object Model), 4, 89–147, 286, 378, 391.
        See also DOM scripts; DOM2; DOM3
    chaining syntax, 380–387
        advanced selection with expressions, 382–384
        jQuery with XPath, 385–387
        overview, 380–382
    converting hand-coded HTML to DOM code, 127–146
        adding to ADS library, 131–133
        DOM generation tool HTML file, 128–130

generateDOM object framework, 133–146
overview, 127–128
testing with HTML fragment, 130–131
creating documents, 96–98
description, 90–91
elements, 518–522
filtering with callback, 387–389
levels, 91–93
manipulating DOM document, 389–391
iterating over results, 391
overview, 389
using DOMAssistant to create elements, 389
using jQuery to move nodes, 389
using MochiKit to create elements, 390
using Prototype to cleanup your document, 390
using YUI to check for intersecting elements, 390–391
methods, 468
overview, 89, 380
scripting libraries, 456
DOM HTML, 91
DOM scripts
Basecamp, 495–498
Flickr buddy icons, 502–504
DOM2 Core, 91, 100–124
Document object, 120–122
creating nodes with document methods, 121–122
document.documentElement property, 121
locating elements with document methods, 122
overview, 120–121
Element object, 119–120
locating objects, 120
manipulating attributes, 119–120
overview, 119
inheritance, 102–103
iterating document trees, 122–124
Node object, 103–118
attributes, 111–114
children, 108–114
duplicating nodes, 117–118
manipulating DOM node tree, 115–117
moving nodes, 117–118
names, 103–108
overview, 103
ownerDocument property, 113
parents, 108–111
siblings, 108–111
types, 103–108
values, 103–108
overview, 100–101
traversing document trees, 122, 124
DOM2 Events specification, 151
DOM2 HTML, 125–127
HTMLDocument object, 126–127
HTMLElement object, 127
overview, 125
DOM3, 93

DOMActivate event, 166, 177
domain property, 126
DOMAssistant, 376, 389
DOMAssistant.$(. . .).addEvent( ) method, 392
DOMAssistant library, 378, 389
DOMAssistant way, 392
DOMAssistant.$(id).create(name, attr, append, content) method, 389
DOMAssistantLoad.js file, 392
DOMAttrModified event, 166, 178
DOMCharacterDataModified event, 166, 178
DOMContentLoaded event, 185
DOMFocusIn event, 166, 177
DomFocusOut event, 166, 177
DOMImplementation object, 93
DOMNodeInserted event, 166, 177
DOMNodeInsertedIntoDocument event, 178
DOMNodeRemoved event, 166, 177
DOMNodeRemovedFromDocument event, 166, 178
DOMSubtreeModified event, 166, 177
domTesting.js file, 96, 103, 111
drag and drop, 438–451
dragging anywhere, 438–439
droppables, 439–440
observers, 448–451
shopping carts, 440–448
Draggable(element[, options]) object, 438
Draggables object, 448, 451
draw( ) method, 477
droppables, 439–440
Droppables object, 439, 448
duplicating nodes, 117–118
duration option, 428
duration property, 415
Dwyer method, 209
Dynamic HTML (DHTML), 90

E

each( ) method, 391, 517
editComplete event, 395
editCSSRule( ) method, 231
editor objects, 254–281
adding event listeners to, 270–272
creating editor markup and objects, 262–270
cropping image, 276–280
imageEditor load event, 260–262
incomplete image editor, 280–281
invoking imageEditor tool, 259–260
overview, 254–259
resizing image, 272–276
Effect.Appear effect, 430
Effect.Highlight('element-id' [, options]) method, 428
Effect.MoveBy('element-id', y, x [, options]) method, 428
Effect.Opacity effect, 429
Effect.Opacity('element-id' [, options]) method, 427
Effect.Parallel effect, 429

Effect.Parallel(effects[, options]) method, 429
Effect.Scale effect, 414
Effect.Scale('element-id', percent [, options]) method, 427
element attributes, 386
Element object, 102, 119–120
    locating objects, 120
    manipulating attributes, 119–120
    overview, 119
element property, 449
Element.cumulativeOffset( ) method, 397
element.insertAfter( ) method, 28
ELEMENT_NODE nodes, 139
Element.nodeName object, 104
ELEMENT_NODES node, 141
Element.nodeValue object, 105
Element.relativize( ) method, 397
elements
    creating with DOMAssistant library, 389
    creating with MochiKit library, 390
    intersecting, 390–391
    locating with document methods, 122
<em> element, 27
encode( ) method, 133–134
encoding property, 397
endcolor option, 428
endeffect option, 439
Entity.nodeName object, 104
Entity.nodeValue object, 105
EntityReference.nodeName object, 104
EntityReference.nodeValue object, 105
:eq(0) expression, 386
error events, 152–153, 177
errorListener listener, 304
errorListener( ) method, 332
errorListener property, 313
escape( ) method, 133
eval( ) method, 297
:even expression, 386
event flow, 167–176
    bubbling events, 173–175
    canceling default action, 176
    cancelling bubbling events, 175–176
    capturing events, 173–175
    order of events, 171–172
    overview, 167–171
event listeners
    accessing event objects from, 186–188
        ADS.getEventObject( ) function, 187–188
        syntactical shortcuts, 187
    adding to editor objects, 270–272
event models
    Microsoft-specific, 181
    traditional, 179–180
    W3C DOM2, 181–183
Event object, 189–190
event objects, accessing from event listeners, 186–188
    ADS.getEventObject( ) function, 187–188

syntactical shortcuts, 187
Event.element( ) method, 526
eventListener method, 180
Event.observe( ) method, 514
eventPhase property, 189
eventPreventDefault( ) function, 176
events, 149–166, 173–176
    cross-browser events, 188–201
        accessing keyboard commands, 197–201
        Event object, 189–190
        MouseEvent object, 190–197
        overview, 188
    DOM2 Events specification, 151
    event flow, 167–176
        bubbling events, 173–175
        canceling default action, 176
        cancelling bubbling events, 175–176
        capturing events, 173–175
        order of events, 171–172
        overview, 167–171
    event listeners, 186–188
    handling, 391–396
        custom events, 395–396
        overview, 391–392
        registering events, 392–394
    overview, 149–150
    registering events, 178–185
        ADS.addEvent( ) method, 178–179
        inline registration model, 178
        load events, 183–185
        Microsoft-specific event model, 181
        traditional event model, 179–180
        W3C DOM2 Events model, 181–183
    types, 151–166
        custom events, 166
        form-related events, 159–165
        keyboard events, 159
        mouse click events, 156–159
        mouse movement events, 153–156
        object events, 151–153
        W3C DOM-specific events, 165–166
Events module, 94
example( ) function, 70
example2( ) function, 70
execute( ) method, 477
Extensible HyperText Markup Language (XHTML), 4, 286
external files, 8

F
fadeColor( ) method, 244, 246
fakepage script, 322
faux select element
    closing, 546–549
    initializing, 514–515
    options, 521–522, 525–527
    value, 520

faux-select.css file, 528–529, 532, 537, 540, 551, 553
faux-select.js file, 512
FauxSelect object, 512–514, 516, 521, 530, 538–541
FauxSelect open( ) method, 523
FauxSelect.clickLI( ) method, 526
FauxSelect.clickValue( ) method, 524
FauxSelect.close( ) method, 524
FauxSelectConductor object, 514–515, 529, 537, 540, 542
FauxSelectConductor.initialize( ) method, 515
FauxSelectConductor.maxHeight object, 518
FauxSelect.initialize( ) method, 520, 536
FauxSelect.last property, 544
FauxSelect.makeFake( ) method, 525
FauxSelect.open( ) method, 524, 539
FauxSelect.updateFaux( ) method, 543
feedback, 411–413
    overview, 411
    shifting content, 412–413
    Yellow Fade Technique (YFT), 411
file input, 351
file uploads. See asynchronous file uploads
fileInputs array, 360
fileInputs folder, 359
fileInputs variable, 368
filter( ) method, 388
filter property, 243
findAll( ) method, 388
finishedReading event, 150
Firebug, 98
fireEvent( ) method, 181
firefoxLi variable, 118
:first expression, 386
firstChild property, 109, 390
firstChild.nodeValue method, 520
fixMSIEPng( ) method, 240
Flash, 455
flicker.people.getInfo method, 500
Flickr buddy icons, 498–504
    DOM scripts, 502–504
    Flickr API key, 499
    proxy scripts, 499–502
flickr.people.findByEmail method, 500
flip( ) method, 524, 536, 550
focus events, 161–163, 177
focus( ) method, 544
focused class, 544–545
<font> tags, 6
for loop, 39, 348
forEach( ) method, 391
form-related events, 159–165
    blur events, 161–163
    change events, 163–165
    focus events, 161–163
    form submit events, 159–161
    reset events, 159–161
Form serialization methods, 400
<form> tag, 260, 495

forms collection, 126
fps option, 428
fps property, 415
from option, 428
func argument, 74
$( ) function, 379, 518
function keyword, 61, 65
Function object, 52, 54, 61–63, 69, 74
functions
    anonymous, 33–34
    calling, 40
Fx namespace, 415
Fx style methods, 415, 419
Fx.Elements(elements,options) method, 418
Fx.Slide( ) method, 418, 424
Fx.Style( ) method, 416, 532
Fx.Style(element, property, options) object, 415
Fx.Styles( ) object, 417
Fx.Styles(. . .).start(. . .) method, 418
Fx.Styles(element, options) object, 415
Fx.Transitions library, 431
Fx.Transitions.bounceOut method, 432
Fx.Transitions.sineInOut method, 431

G

GblogSearch object, 478
GBrowserIsCompatible( )statement, 461
GClientGeocoder control, 469
GClientGeocoder object, 464
General Public License (GPL), 378
Generate API Key, 458
generate( ) method, 134–135
generateDOM( ) method, 129, 131
generateDOM object framework, 133–146
    checkForVariable( ) method, 134
    encode( ) method, 133–134
    generate( ) method, 134–135
    overview, 133
    processAttribute( ) method, 136–146
    processNode( ) method, 136–146
generateDOM.js file, 129, 133
GET method, 338
get( ) method, 377
GET request, 288, 294, 311
getAllResponseHeaders( ) method, 287
getAttribute(name) method, 119
getAttributeNode(name) method, 119
getBrowserWindowSize( ) function, 82
getClassNames(element) method, 219
getComputedStyle( ) method, 238
getDimensions(element) method, 259
getElementByClassName( ) method, 122
getElementById( ) method, 26, 54, 105, 122
getElementByTagName( ) function, 39
getElementsByClassName( ) method, 27

getElementsByTagName( ) method, 26, 120, 122–123, 358, 381
getElmentById( ) method, 121
getEventObject( ) method, 176
getHeight( ) method, 518
getJSON( ) method, 401
getKeyPressed( ) method, 197
getMouseButton( ) method, 194–195
getPointerPositionInDocument( ) method, 196
getRequestObject( ) method, 299
getResponseHeader( ) method, 287, 292
getScript( ) method, 401
getStyle( ) method, 238, 531
getStyleSheets( ) method, 231
getTarget( ) method, 192
getWidth( ) method, 530
getWindowSize( ) method, 259
ghosting option, 439
GLargeMapControl control, 463
GLatLng object, 462
GMapTypeControl control, 463
GMarker( ) object, 462
Google Ajax Search API, 457, 470
Google Maps API, 457
GPL (General Public License), 378
graceful degradation, 4
greedy property, 440
groupname file, 352
GScaleControl control, 463
gsearch.css style sheet, 472
GSearch.getBranding( ) method, 481
GSmallMapControl control, 463
GSmallZoomControl control, 463
GSmapSearchControl, 481
:gt(n) expression, 386
GwebSearch search request, 473

H

<h1> element, 27
<h2> element, 27
handle option, 438
handling events, 391–396
    custom events, 395–396
    overview, 391–392
    registering events, 392–394
        DOMAssistant way, 392
        jQuery way, 393–394
        overview, 392
hasAttributes( ) method, 114
hasChildNodes( ) method, 114
hasClassName(element, class) method, 219
hasFeature( ) method, 93
hasOwnProperty( ) method, 39
HEAD request, 294
<head> tag, 7–8, 72, 472
header( ) method, 79, 85

height property, 416
:hidden expression, 387
hide( ) method, 420
history property, 315
history.length object, 322
history.length property, 315
horizontal option, 419
hover( ) method, 394
:hover pseudoclass selector, 525
hoverclass property, 440
href attribute, 6, 8–9, 25, 130, 190, 323
.htaccess file, 338
HTML, 296–297
    converting to DOM code, 127–146
        adding to ADS library, 131–133
        DOM generation tool HTML file, 128–130
        generateDOM object framework, 133–146
        overview, 127–128
        testing with HTML fragment, 130–131
HTML module, 94
HTMLAnchorElement object, 56, 102, 106
HTMLBodyElement object, 55
HTMLDocument object, 126–127
HTMLElement object, 122, 127
HTMLEvents module, 95
HTMLParagraphElement object, 102
htmlResponseListener listener, 304
HyperText Markup Language. *See* HTML

I

icon-server argument, 499
id attributes, 102
#id elements, 383
id object, 23, 491
id variable, 72
id="outer-wrapper" attribute, 122
if control structure, 32
if statement, 21
<iframe> element, 315, 321, 346, 361
:image element, 387
imageClick( ) event, 261
imageEditor load event, 260–262
imageEditor tool, 259–260
imageEditor.cancelClick event listener, 280
imageEditor.cropMouseDown event listener, 277
imageEditor.cropMouseDown( ) method, 270
imageEditor.cropMouseMove event listener, 276
imageEditor.cropMouseMove( ) method, 270
imageEditor.cropMouseUp( ) method, 270
imageEditor.imageClick( ) method, 262, 265, 270, 276
imageEditor.js file, 254
imageEditor.load( ) method, 261
imageEditor.resizeMouseDown( ) method, 270, 273
imageEditor.resizeMouseMove( ) method, 273
imageEditor.resizeMouseUp( ) method, 270, 273
imageEditor.resizeMousseMove( ) method, 270

imageEditor.saveClick( ) method, 280, 395
images collection, 126
<img> element, 47, 152, 240, 260
index file, 338, 352, 354, 357–358
inheritance, 53
init( ) method, 322–323
initAnchors( ) function, 36
initEvent(eventType,canBubble,cancelable) method, 190
initialize( ) method, 512, 515, 523, 532
initMultiStateAnchors function, 47
initPage( ) function, 73
inline-block property, 416
inline event attributes, 11
inline registration model, 178
innerHTML method, 409
innerHTML property, 8, 83, 135, 296–297
<input> element, 358, 368, 387
insertAfter( ) method, 116
interactive.js file, 422
interactiveListener listener, 304
Internet Explorer Developer Toolbar, 98
intersect( ) method, 390
intersecting elements, 390–391
isCompatible( ) check, 22
iterating
    document trees, 122–124
    over objects, 39–40

J

JavaScript, 5, 30, 286–295
    accessibility, 16–17
    acting on responses, 288–291
    code, 297
    human intervention, 30
    identifying Ajax requests, 291–293
    javascript: prefix, 6, 8–14
    making requests, 287–288
    methods, 294–295
    namespaces, 17–19
    overview, 286–287
    required for content, 305–306
    reusable objects, 19–30
        ADS library, 20–21
        ADS.$( ) method, 22–24
        ADS.addEvent( ) method, 24–26
        ADS.getElementsByClassName( ) method, 26–28
        ADS.insertAfter( ) method, 28–29
        ADS.isCompatible( ) method, 21–22
        ADS.prependChild( ) method, 29–30
        ADS.removeChildren( ) method, 29–30
        ADS.removeEvent( ) method, 24–26
        ADS.toggleDisplay( ) method, 28
    separating behavior from markup, 6–14
        adding JavaScript, 6–8
        javascript: prefix, 8–14
        overview, 6

syntax problems, 30–40
    anonymous functions, 33–34
    breaking lines, 31–32
    calling functions, 40
    case sensitivity, 30
    closures, 34–38
    Iterating, 39–40
    overloading, 33
    parentheses, 32–33
    quotes, 31
    referencing, 40
    scope, 34–38
    semicolons, 32–33
    version checking, 14–16
JavaScript Object Notation (JSON), 69, 298–299
jQuery, 393–394
jQuery library, 378
    using to move nodes, 389
    with XPath, 385–387
jQuery( ) method, 378, 383, 389, 402, 409
jQuery.ajax( ) method, 400
jQuery.getJSON(url, params, callback) method, 400
jQuery.getScript(url, callback) method, 400
jQuery.get(url, params, callback) method, 400
jQuery.post(url, params, callback) method, 400
jQuery('tag[@attr]') attribute, 385
jQuery('tag[@attr$=value]') attribute, 38
jQuery('tag[@attr*=value]') attribute, 385
jQuery('tag[@attr=value]') attribute, 385
JSON (JavaScript Object Notation), 69, 298–299
json.org property, 299
jsonResponseListener listener, 304
jsResponseListener listener, 304

K

keepMe variable, 445
keyboard commands, 197–201
keyboard controls, 543–549
    closing faux select element, 546–549
    focused class, 544–545
    selecting options, 543–544
keyboard events, 159
keyCode property, 197
keydown event, 159, 198
keypress event, 159
keyup event, 159
key:value,key:value syntax, 69
keywords, 477

L

:last expression, 386
lastChild property, 109
latency, 327–329
<li> element, 28, 510

libraries, 20, 375–402
    accessing and manipulating style, 396–397
    choosing, 376–377
    communication, 397–402
        jQuery keeps Ajax simple, 400–402
        overview, 397
        Prototype Ajax object, 397–400
    DOMAssistant, 378
    enhancing DOM, 380–391
        chaining syntax, 380–382, 384–387
        filtering with callback, 387–389
        manipulating DOM document, 389–391
        overview, 380
    handling events, 391–396
        custom events, 395–396
        overview, 391–392
        registering events, 392–394
    jQuery, 378
    Mochikit, 378–379
    overview, 375–376
    Prototype, 379
    Yahoo! User Interface (YUI), 379–380
Lightbox, 13
<link> element, 221, 240, 529
link object, 80
links collection, 126
ljQuery, 400–402
load event listeners, 26, 40, 47
load events, 44, 149, 151–152, 154, 177, 183–185,
        357, 408
load( ) method, 261, 401
loadedListener listener, 304
loadedListener property, 313
loading style sheets, 228–229
load.js script, 129, 357
loadPage function, 40
location changes, tracking, 316–324
logWindow object, 82
logWindow property, 79, 81
LS-Async module, 95
LS module, 95
:lt(n) expression, 386

M

main.css file, 511, 529, 531
makeFake( ) method, 521
manipulating
    Element attributes, 119–120
    node trees, 115–117
#map div, 461
map.js file, 461
maps, 458–469
    example, 481–484
    microformats, 465–469
    overview, 458–464
    retrieving latitude/longitude, 464–465

mapsearch mashup script, 482
margin-top, 532
markup
    modifying for style, 206–207, 213
        overview, 207–210
        removing extra markup, 210–213
    separating style from, 213–237
        className switching, 217–220
        modifying CSS rules, 229–237
        style property, 213–216
        switching style sheets, 220–229
mashups, 455–504
    API keys, 457
    client-side APIs, 457–484
        Ajax search requests, 470–481
        maps, 458–484
    overview, 455–457
    server-side APIs, 484–504
        Basecamp, 488–498
        Flickr buddy icons, 498–504
        overview, 484–488
Math object, 52
maxHeight property, 537, 542
media property, 221, 537, 542
message argument, 62
$( ) method, 377, 414
methods
    document, 121–122
    JavaScript, 294–295
    public, 64–65, 67–68
    static, 63–64, 67–68
Microsoft filter property, 239, 244
Microsoft.AlphaImageLoader filter, 240
Microsoft.XMLHTTP object, 286
Mochikit library, 378–379, 390
MochiKit.DOM.createDOM(name[, attrs[, node[, . . .]]])
        method, 390
MochiKit.Iter.ifilter( ) method, 388
MochiKit.Selector.$$( ) method, 382
MochiKit.Selector object, 383
MochiKit.Signal.connect( ) method, 395
MochiKit.Signal.signal( ) method, 395
MochiKit.Visual.roundElement(element [, options])
        method, 435
mod-moo.fx.js file, 536
mode option, 419
modificationHandler method, 369
Moo.fx, 414–435
    CSS property modification, 415–426
        example, 420–426
        multiple effects on multiple objects, 418
        multiple properties, 417
        reusing effects, 417–418
        single properties, 416–417
        slider effect, 418–420
    realistic motion using, 430–435
mouse click events, 156–159

mouse movement events, 153–156
mousedown event, 156–158, 177, 276, 280, 368
mousedown image, 48
MouseEvent object, 182–183, 190–197
MouseEvents module, 95
mousemove event, 177, 273, 439
mouseout event, 177, 525
mouseoutLI( ) method, 526
mouseover event, 177, 495, 525
mouseover image, 48
mouseoverLI( ) method, 526
mouseup event, 156–158, 177
mouseup event listener, 273
MoveBy effect, 430
multipart/form-data POST request, 345
multipart/form-data request, 346
multiStateAnchor class, 47
MutationEvents module, 95
myConstructor function, 61–62, 65
myConstructor( ) object, 67
myConstructor property, 69
myFunction( ) method, 33–34
myLogger constructor, 80
myLogger( ) object, 78–80
myLogger.createWindow( ) method, 80–82
myLogger.header( ) method, 85–86
myLogger.js file, 78, 96–97
myLogger.write( ) method, 85–86
myLogger.writeRaw( ) method, 82–85
myMessage property, 62
myNamespace namespace, 19
myNamespace.showNodeName( ) function, 19
myObject instance, 62
myObject variable, 60
myObject.alertMessage( ) method, 66
myObject.separator function, 66
myOrneryBeast( ) method, 71, 73, 76
myOwner property, 65
myVarialbe scope, 34

N

NamedNodeMap object, 39
namespaces, 17–19
new keyword, 52, 62, 68–69
new operator, 52, 61
nextSibling property, 110–111
noConflict( ) method, 395
node filter, 27
Node object, 103–118
    attributes, 111–114
    children, 108–111, 114
    duplicating nodes, 117–118
    manipulating DOM node trees, 115–117
    moving nodes, 117–118
    names, 103–108
    overview, 103

ownerDocument property, 113
    parents, 108–111
    siblings, 108–111
    types, 103–108
    values, 103–108
NodeInsertedIntoDocument event, 166
NodeList object, 108–109
nodeName property, 17, 103
NodeNameMap object, 113
nodes
    creating with document methods, 121–122
    duplicating, 117–118
    moving, 117–118
    moving with jQuery library, 389
nodeValue property, 104–105, 113, 143
<noscript> element, 408
Notation.nodeName object, 104
Notation.nodeValue object, 105
nsid argument, 499
:nth(0) expression, 386
Number object, 52

O

obj argument, 74
object detection, 14–16
object events, 151–153
    abort events, 152–153
    error events, 152–153
    load events, 151–152
    resize events, 153
    scroll events, 153
    unload events, 151–152
[object HTMLDocument] object, 54
object literal, 68–71
object members, 53–56
Object object, 30, 52, 54, 60
objects, 16
    DOM specification, 90–91
    JavaScript logging, 78
    reusable, 19–30, 299–304
        ADS library, 20–21
        ADS.$( ) method, 22–24
        ADS.addEvent( ) method, 24–26
        ADS.getElementsByClassName( ) method, 26–28
        ADS.insertAfter( ) method, 28–29
        ADS.isCompatible( ) method, 21–22
        ADS.prependChild( ) method, 29–30
        ADS.removeChildren( ) method, 29–30
        ADS.removeEvent( ) method, 24–26
        ADS.toggleDisplay( ) method, 28
    window, 56–60
observers, 448–451
:odd expression, 386
offsetWidth property, 530
onCancel function, 416
onclick attribute, 9, 73, 179

onclick method, 180
onComplete function, 416
onComplete property, 536
onDrag method, 448–449, 451
onEnd method, 449
onException(ajax.request,exception) callback, 398
onFailure(XHRrequest,json) callback, 399
onHover option, 440
onInteractive(XHRrequest,json) callback, 398
onLoaded(XHRrequest,json) callback, 398
onLoading(XHRrequest,json) callback, 398
onreadystatechange listener, 290, 293, 299
onreadystatechange method, 185, 304
onreadystatechange property, 288, 291
onStart method, 416, 449
onSuccess(XHRrequest,json) callback, 399
onUninitialized(XHRrequest,json) callback, 398
onWhenAnEntryIsAdded event, 83
on###(XHRrequest,json) callback, 398
Opacity effect, 430
open class, 523
open( ) method, 287, 294, 535, 545
optgroup element, 507
option element, 509, 521
option properties, 415
options argument, 303
OPTIONS request, 294
overflow property, 537
overflow:hidden element, 264
overlap property, 440
overloading, 33
override( ) function, 57
override.js file, 57
ownerDocument property, 113

P

<p> element, 27
parallel effects, 429–430
Parallel( ) method, 430
parameters property, 398
:parent expression, 387
parentheses, 32–33
parentRule property, 69, 205, 430
parse error, 31
parseInt( ) method, 531
parseJSON( ) method, 299
:password element, 387
/path/to/faux-select.css file, 530
p.faux-value element, 527, 531
Phark method, 209
photo cropping and resizing tool, 249–281
    editor objects, 254–281
        adding event listeners to the editor objects, 270–272
        creating editor markup and objects, 262–270
        cropping image, 276–280
        imageEditor load event, 260–262

incomplete image editor, 280–281
        invoking imageEditor tool, 259–260
        overview, 254–259
        resizing image, 272–276
    overview, 249
    test files, 250–254
php5-APC folder, 351
.png file, 351
point.lat( ) method, 465
point.lng( ) method, 465
popup class, 12
.popup CSS selector, 12
popup( ) function, 10
popupLoadEvent.js script, 11
position property, 416
position:absolute element, 529
POST request, 288, 294, 346, 350, 362, 369, 488
postBody property, 398
preload( ) function, 44
prependChild( ) method, 116
preventDefault( ) method, 176, 188, 190
previousSibling property, 110
private members, 65, 67–68
privileged members, 65, 67–68
processAttribute( ) method, 136–146
ProcessingInstruction.nodeName object, 104
ProcessingInstruction.nodeValue object, 105
processNode( ) method, 136–146
.product-item draggable, 446
.progressBar element, 363
progressContainer class, 363
progressive enhancement, 4
Prototype library, 379, 390
prototype property, 63–64, 70, 520
prototype.js file, 414
proxy scripts
    Basecamp, 491–495
    Flickr buddy icons, 499–502
public methods, 64–65, 67–68, 80
PUT request, 294
px postfix, 259

Q

queue option, 429
quotes, 31

R

:radio element, 387
Range module, 95
reading event, 150
readyState property, 288–289
referencing, 40
referrer property, 126
RegExp object, 52
register( ) method, ADS.actionPager, 322–323

registering events, 178–185, 392–394
  ADS.addEvent( ) method, 178–179
  DOMAssistant way, 392
  inline registration model, 178
  jQuery way, 393–394
  load events, 183–185
  Microsoft-specific event model, 181
  overview, 392
  traditional event model, 179–180
  W3C DOM2 Events model, 181–183
registerListener( ) function, 37
registerMultiStateAnchorListeners( ) function, 48
rel="stylesheet" attribute, 221
removeAttribute(name) method, 119
removeAttributeNode(oldAttr) method, 119
removeChild( ) method, 117, 119
removeClassName(element, class) method, 219
removeEvent( ) method, 24
removerEventListener( ) method, 182
removeStyleSheet( ) method, 229
removing
  extra markup, 210–213
  style sheets, 228–229
repeat( ) method, 132
replaceImage( ) method, 237
replaces_join-state object, 519
replaces_something element, 526
representational state transfer (REST), 457
request property, 290
requestHeaders property, 398
requests
  asynchronous, 329–334
  making, 287–288
:reset element, 387
reset events, 159–161, 177
resize events, 153, 177
resizing images, 272–276
resizing tool. *See* photo cropping and resizing tool
responseJSON property, 312
responses, acting on, 288–291
responseText property, 288–289, 296–297
responseXML property, 288–289, 297
REST (representational state transfer), 457
restorecolor option, 428
returnValue property, 176
reusable objects, 19–30, 51–87
  ADS library, 20–21
  ADS.$( ) method, 22–24
  ADS.addEvent( ) method, 24–26
  ADS.getElementsByClassName( ) method, 26–28
  ADS.insertAfter( ) method, 28–29
  ADS.isCompatible( ) method, 21–22
  ADS.prependChild( ) method, 29–30
  ADS.removeChildren( ) method, 29–30
  ADS.removeEvent( ) method, 24–26
  ADS.toggleDisplay( ) method, 28
  catch control structure, 76–77

creating, 60–71
  constructors, 61–63
  object literal, 68–71
  overview, 60–61
  private members, 65, 67–68
  privileged members, 65, 67–68
  public methods, 64–65, 67–68
  static methods, 63–64, 67–68
definition, 52–60
  closures, 60
  inheritance, 53
  object members, 53–56
  scope, 60
  window objects, 56–60
example, 78–86
  JavaScript logging object, 78
  myLogger( ) object, 78–80
  myLogger.createWindow( ) method, 80–82
  myLogger.header( ) method, 85–86
  myLogger.write( ) method, 85–86
  myLogger.writeRaw( ) method, 82–85
exceptions, 76–77
overview, 51
this keyword, 71–76
  apply( ) method, 73–76
  call( ) method, 73–76
  overview, 71–73
try control structure, 76–77
reusing effects, 417–418
revert option, 438
reverteffect option, 439
RewriteRule object, 337
rounded corners, 435–437
roundElement( ) method, 436

S

saveClick( ) method, 395
saveHandle event listener, 280
sayGoodbye( ) method, 74, 76
scaleContent option, 427
scaleFrom option, 428
scaleFromCenter option, 427
scaleMode option, 428
scaleX option, 427
scaleY option, 427
scope, 34–38, 60
Scripaculous library, 429
<script> element, 6, 11, 72, 306–307, 313, 348
Script.aculo.us, 414–415
  drag and drop, 438–451
    dragging anywhere, 438–439
    droppables, 439–440
    observers, 448–451
    shopping carts, 440–448
  visual effects with, 427–430
scroll events, 153, 177

scrollHeight property, 540
scrollTop property, 549
scrollWidth property, 540
select element, 507–553
    behavioral modifications, 538–550
        adjusting z index, 542–543
        closing FauxSelect, 538–541
        height, 549–550
        keyboard controls, 543–549
    classic, 508
    clicking, 522–527
    closing, 522–527
    eliminating original, 551
    improving, 509–510
    opening, 522–527
    overview, 507–508
    strategy, 510–522
        DOM elements, 518–522
        FauxSelect objects, 512–514
        files, 511
        locating, 515–518
    styling, 527–538
select event, 177
selectLI( ) method, 526, 544
selectorText attribute, 235
selectorText property, 235
semicolons (;), 32–33
; (semicolons), 32–33
send( ) method, 287, 291, 303
separator property, 65–66
server-side APIs, 484–504
    Basecamp, 488–498
        account information, 489–490
        DOM scripts, 495–498
        proxy scripts, 491–495
    Flickr buddy icons, 498–504
        DOM scripts, 502–504
        Flickr API key, 499
        proxy scripts, 499–502
    overview, 484–488
set( ) method, 415–417, 533
setActiveStyleSheet( ) function, 225
setAttribute( ) method, 119, 143
setAttributeNode(newAttr) method, 119
setInterval( ) method, 185, 348, 406, 431
setNumericStyle(element,dimensions,message) method,
    259
setProperty( ) method, 214
setRequestHeader( ) method, 287, 291
setRoot( ) method, 477
setSiteRestrictions( ) method, 476
setStyleById( ) method, 214
setStylesByClassName( ) method, 214
setStylesByTagName( ) method, 214
setTimeout( ) method, 244, 369, 406, 431
shifting content, 412–413
shopping carts, 440–448

showNodeName property, 19
sibling selectors (+), 384
+ (sibling selectors), 384
Simple Object Access Protocol (SOAP), 457
simplexml_load_file( ) method, 501
singleImageAnchors variable, 388
slideIn( ) method, 419
slideOut( ) method, 419
slider effects, 418–420
snap option, 438
SOAP (Simple Object Access Protocol), 457
sound variable, 73
source/chapter6/imageEditor-start folder, 250
<span> tag, 207
src property, 47
srcElement property, 192
standards compliant, 5
start( ) method, 415–418
startcolor option, 428
starteffect option, 439
stateChangeListener( ) method, 288–289
static methods, 63–64, 67–68
status property, 288–289, 312
statusText property, 288, 312
stop( ) method, 536
stopPropagation( ) method, 175–176, 188, 190
+ (string concatenation operator), 32
string concatenation operator (+), 32
String object, 52, 56, 131
style attribute, 6, 144
style, modifying, 203–247
    accessing computed style, 237–238
    example, 244–246
    Microsoft filter property, 239–244
    modifying markup for style, 206–207, 213
    separating style and markup, 213–237
    W3C DOM2 Style specification, 203–206
style property, 76, 213–216
<style type="text/css"></style> tags, 204
style.css file, 360
StyleSheets module, 94
styling, select element, 527–538
:submit element, 387
submit event, 166, 177, 365
switching style sheets, 220–229
    alternative style sheets, 221–225
    className switching on body tags, 225–228
    loading, 228–229
    removing, 228–229
sync option, 428

T

tag elements, 383
tag filter, 27
tagA elements, 383
tagA > tagB elements, 384

tagA + tagB elements, 384
tag[attr] attribute, 383
tag[attr~=value] attribute, 383
tag[attr$=value] attribute, 383
tag[attr=value] attribute, 383
tag[attr|=value] attribute, 383
tag[attr!=value] attribute, 383
tagB elements, 383
tagC elements, 383
tag:checked selector, 384
tag.className elements, 383
tag:disabled selector, 384
tag:empty selector, 384
tag:enabled selector, 384
tag:first-child selector, 384
tag:first-of-type selector, 384
tag#id elements, 383
tag:last-child selector, 384
tag:last-of-type selector, 384
tag:not(s) selector, 384
tag:nth-child(n) selector, 384
tag:nth-last-child(n) selector, 384
tag:nth-last-of-type(n) selector, 384
tag:nth-of-type(n) selector, 384
tag:only-child selector, 384
tag:only-of-type selector, 384
tag:root selector, 384
Tamperdata, 98
Tango Icon Library, 347
target attribute, 8, 362
target property, 189–190
tb-rl property, 416
test.html file, 251, 259, 511
:text element, 387
Text nodes, 101, 116
TEXT_NODE nodes, 139
Text.nodeName object, 104
TEXT_NODES node, 141
Text.nodeValue object, 105
this keyword, 66, 71–76, 180, 190, 324
    apply( ) method, 73–76
    call( ) method, 73–76
    overview, 71–73
this keyword method, 179
this.createWindow( ) method, 83
this.flip( ) method, 535
this.preventClose property, 549
this.select.getElementsByTagName('option') method, 520
this.value.appendChild( ) method, 520
timestamp property, 189
title property, 69, 126, 189, 221
to option, 428
todo argument, 494
toggle( ) method, 420
toString( ) method, 56, 194

traceroute request, 327
tracking location changes, 316–324
transition option, 428
transition property, 415
Traversal module, 95
traversing document trees, 122–124
trim( ) method, 132, 139
true property, 416
try/catch control, 77
try control structure, 76–77
type property, 69, 189, 221

U
UIEvents module, 95
ul.faux-select element, 527–528, 531
unit property, 415
unload events, 151–152, 177
unobtrusive object, 4
unobtrusiveRollovers.js script file, 45
updateFaux( ) method, 546
updateGalleryList( ) method, 343
updatePhoto( ) method, 343
updateProgressBar( ) method, 364, 369
uploader.js file, 352, 354, 357
URL property, 126
username file, 352

V
val property, 522, 527
Validation module, 95
var example2 = function( ). . . syntax, 70
var keyword, 35, 65
verifyFileType( ) method, 359
version checking, 14–16
vertical option, 419
Views module, 94
visibility property, 413
visibility:hidden property, 413
:visible expression, 387
visual effects, 405–452
    accessibility, 407–410
    behavioral enhancements, 437–451
    feedback, 411–413
        overview, 411
        shifting content, 412–413
        Yellow Fade Technique (YFT), 411
    libraries, 414–415, 437
        Moo.fx, 414–415, 430, 434–435
        rounded corners, 435–437
        Script.aculo.us, 414–415, 427, 429–430
    overview, 405–407
visual effects libraries, 414–415

W

W3C DOM-specific events, 165–166
W3C DOM2 Style specification, 203, 206
  browser support, 206
  CSSStyleDeclaration objects, 205–206
  CSSStyleRule objects, 204–205
  CSSStyleSheet objects, 204
wait property, 415
waitListener property, 313
walkElementsLinear( ) method, 123
walkTheDom( ) function, 124
walkTheDOMRecursive( ) method, 124, 135
Web Developer toolbar, 98
"what you see is what you get" (WYSIWYG) editor, 30
width property, 416
window method, 19
window namespace, 379
window objects, 19, 35, 56–60, 73, 76, 151
window.alert( ) function, 59
window.document property, 121
window.location object, 316
window.location.href property, 315
window.onload function, 26
window.open( ) method, 8
write( ) method, 79, 85–86
writeRaw( ) method, 79, 82, 84
writingMode property, 416
WYSIWYG ("what you see is what you get") editor, 30

X

X-ADS-Ajax-Request header, 304
X-JSON header, 398
X-Prototype-Version header, 398
X-Requested-With header, 398
XHTML (Extensible HyperText Markup Language), 4, 286
XML, 295–299
  HTML, 296–297
  JavaScript code, 297
  JavaScript Object Notation (JSON), 298–299
  overview, 295–296
  plain text, 296
XML module, 94
XML-RPC (XML remote procedure calls), 457
XMLHttpRequest object, 286–295, 299, 306, 325, 345, 348, 398
  acting on responses, 288–291
  identifying Ajax requests, 291–293
  making requests, 287–288
  methods, 294–295
  overview, 286–287

XMLHttpRequest onreadystatechange method, 246
XMLHttpRequest requests, 293
xmlResponseListener listener, 304
XPath, jQuery with, 385–387
XSS-HTTP-REQUEST-CALLBACK variable, 311
XssHttpRequest object, 312

Y

Yahoo Libraries, 17
Yahoo! User Interface (YUI) library, 379–380, 390–391
YAHOO.util.Dom.getElementBy( ) method, 388
YAHOO.util.Dom.getRegion(String | HTMLElement | Array) method, 390
YAHOO.util.Region object, 390
Yellow Fade Technique (YFT), 411
YUI (Yahoo! User Interface) library, 379–380, 390–391

Z

z index, 542–543
zindex option, 439